THE MEMOIR
OF A
Schizophrenic

THE MEMOIR

OF A

Schizophrenic

Revised Version

Karl Lorenz Willett

Publishing Push Ltd
The Courtyard
30 Worthing Road
Horsham
West Sussex
RH12 1SF
United Kingdom
www.publishingpush.com

ISBN: (Hardback) 978-1-80227-203-1
ISBN: (Paperback) 978-1-80227-204-8
ISBN: (eBook) 978-1-80227-205-5

Disclaimer

"This book is a work of non-fiction based on the author's experiences and to protect privacy, some names, identifying characteristics, dialogue and details have been changed or reconstructed".

Acknowledgements

My thanks to the editor for the consultation and the partial editorial work in preparing this manuscript.

Huge thanks to my loving mother and dad for their prayers and their unconditional love. Enormous gratitude also to my sisters and brother for their faith and endless support.

My special thanks most of all to my darling wife, Euphemia, for her constant love, enduring friendship and support.

Final thanks to our children, Katrina, Georgina, and Jonathan, for enriching my life and serving the purpose of their creation, having thoughtfulness, kindness and an incredibly caring nature.

Contents

Karl Lorenz Willett

Author's Notes

This book contains my self-portrait in the form of text. It conveys what it is like to live at the edge of human experience and wrestle with spiritual thoughts, darkness and light, reason and chaos. I took a fatal gamble to create the self-images I had of myself of old and still hold today. I desire always to stay stable and keep the devastating mental condition drugged up to control the symptoms. If social or emotional pressures exacerbate it, and the trigger is fired, it will never again become chronic because what I say can hurt and wound deeply. It is shameful; it embarrasses me how my words – even when speaking about the past - appear highly self-centred and oblivious to my spouse's feelings, which I failed to recognise was painful for her in the extreme year on year.

I had very little awareness of where the boundary line is and overshared my unhealthy emotional boundaries, and it may have hurt all involved in the disclosures.

I try so hard not to let the condition rule my life, and my wife is an angel and a saint on earth to have coped with how the illness affects me. Thirty-five years of intimate thoughts and feelings are woven between the stories; some so dark and shameful, my guards were perhaps down a little too low. However, I spilt my guts out to reveal my unique perspective on life, and it reminds us that we are all flawed and complicated. Most of us are doing the best we can; none of us is free from suffering.

I trust that the value I shall leave behind in this book is enlightenment, wisdom, rare beauty and utterly devoid of self-pity. There are passages of love of life and marriage that, for many reasons, aim to reach the sky.

As the author of The Memoir of a Schizophrenic, I took the unusual step of re-reading my work and conducting a critical self-examination of my narratives. I realise it may seem freaky to some that the self should examine itself. I will bust the myth of split-mind by your mere observation of me before, during and after a breakdown, in my relation between thought, emotion and behaviour leading to faulty perception, inappropriate actions and feelings, withdrawal, and losing touch with reality.

My holistic mind observed this split from reality, which resulted in difficulties in determining what existed as 'real' and what did not, instead of an idealistic or notional idea. The vividly detailed account of events and emotions were written as each incident happened. It is also based on an autobiographical memory played out in my mind like a video from the past. It was a highly reconstructive process of self-enhancing biases of feelings, beliefs, self-image, needs, and goals. Re-visiting my writing, I can assure you that the factual aspect of the memories is highly accurate.

The flexible, pliable memory maintained a profound struggle with living, both positive and negative, which brought about psychological fights, the demise of my professional career and almost physical departure from this vast world. In the writings, social themes ultimately reach the truth about life and exhibit human vulnerability under stressors. The passion in the story will touch hearts, and it will hold you, in sympathy and gratitude, as you are mentalising the impairment in my mind, which was my lived experience. The book also illustrates my well-being with my logic intact, reason and rational deliberations, but my thought process is dysfunctional most of the time. I cannot filter the preconscious view properly and gave too much significance to the information that would usually be filtered, overloading my mind. My automatic actions are sometimes faulty, resulting in delusions of my activities created by an outside force.

I asked the sane-self, the God in me, below the neck, which is not fear-based, ego-based, or nagging, nagging from inside the skull, "Why, oh, why does my emotional state have critical differences from other people's in controlling emotions, beliefs, desires, and intentions? Also, it was hard to identify the emotional state of others. So, I opened up my soul and documented stories that expose my dark side – brutally honest, unfaithful, hurtful, horrendous, lustful, and a far cry from the good self of love, kindness, gentleness, and empathy and compassion.

From the beginning, I asked questions revolving around duty, obeying secular ethical authority and having a pattern of existence that is obedient to God and experiences God as a subjective truth. Then I questioned the answers, which are impossible to know and must rely on beliefs. As a knight of faith, I fought the epic inner conflicts that tormented my mind over what's getting taught as fact but were indeed untrue, misleading or damned lies. Ultimately, it shaped my identity from the experiences gained through the search for meaning and purpose. The reader's belief system becomes pressured if they believe differently, and that is one of the 'hooks' that will forever remain unresolved. The Memoir of a Schizophrenic is awash with what seems to be unsolvable dilemmas, with conflict that continues right up to the final page tugging on your heartstrings.

Data from my writings show having schizophrenia comes with a progressive decline in intelligence quotient (IQ). I did observe that having multiple episodes of psychosis deteriorated my intellectual abilities.

I was sure my IQ was average. However, when the psychotic disorder occurs, my brain's frontal lobe and hippocampus, my physician says, are particularly affected, leading to the gradual deterioration whereby average intellectual capacities fall below-average intellectual abilities.

Current symptomatic treatment strategies are ineffective in treating cognitive deficits in me at risk of psychosis and represent a challenge for research.

Karl Lorenz Willett

To my children and their children

Written November 1982

Now that I am twenty-six years old, I have decided to give you, my family, an account of the exciting happenings in my life, a life with some of the most peculiar, unique adventures.

I shall try to describe events that had come to mind and capture them on paper so that, when they revolved in the kaleidoscope of time, they will build an image of the changes through which I have lived and the problems I have had to solve. I hope by reading these recollections, with all their imperfections, that you, my children and your children, may attempt to learn something about the world in which my parents and I were born and grew up.

I believe that yours will be a very different world, where average, moderate people will stop the rise of dangerous extremist groups alongside environmental changes. By the time the youngest of you are adults, even your present-day may have become unrecognisable.

This book will be nothing more than exploring a part of myself, recognising how much I genuinely love about my family and gaining a sense of personal accomplishment by writing down what I feel. I find it helpful to keep a journal of my thoughts because the writing comes from my heart, digging deep into the part of my soul that inspires me and continues to search.

I write accounts of events so that the changes and ideas that have taken place in my life are recorded. Adrenaline is racing through my body, placing energy right up to my fingertips, allowing me to capture quickly in writing some of the incidents of the past years before I forget and channelling through my pen will be what is rooted in my heart. I will try to convey with precision and feeling what I want to say. It appears, from this moment with my pen poised, that I yearn to tell you how charming the cloud that's hanging over me looks as I observe my self-consciousness. The enriching personal satisfaction I shall gain from writing will no doubt change my lifestyle. I will take life less seriously, ease up on competitiveness, relentless self-pressure, and feel free to laugh at myself and the world.

Although this book is primarily for the family, it could be wise to publish it as a teaching tool. It might benefit the general public and students to learn something about me, a spiritual man with mental health illness accusations.

The church rarely taught love, compassion, understanding, joy and happiness; it focused on preaching gloom and doom and the coming of Christ consigning everyone to Hell and the wages of sin. I became depressed because something must be done to stop the souls from being punished in Hell, and I could not see a straightforward way of helping. I had repeated attacks of irrational fear and had muddle-headed ideas.

In this light, non-fictionalised passionate autobiography, the vein of nostalgia is being touched. I reflect in the mirror of memory, and there are some shadowy areas, and I write in such a way as to inform that I am losing my senses/ mind. I hope to tell in crystal clear lines the experiences of having a mental illness and the Love of the Gospel; not for sensationalism, but because I had to untangle creativity from self-destruction and was unable to; I ultimately had breakdowns.

Its ugly effects on my life are not dramatised; it's straightforward and is told. I acquired a survival instinct. I now think whatever I am going through is what it is supposed to be. I wished it were tomorrow, but that is impatience over what may be.

I thank God that we are secure and my family are well, and I work. If I fear anything, it is that any harm should come to my wife and children, accidentally or in any other way. My house's pillars are my children, my wife and me working, but I am far from thinking that my old life is sacred. On the contrary, I believe that their lives are far superior and sacred to mine and more important than anything else. We all have a choice in which way we want to go through life. At the moment, I have good fortune, but it may not last, of course, so now one must be positive, joyful and content in a period when life is good and beneficial to us.

From birth to adulthood

Written in the year 1982

I am Karl Lorenz Willett, born in St. Kitts, West Indies, to Afro-Caribbean parents on Friday 14th September 1956. My father's name is Nelson, and my mother is Catherine. I am the second son, the fourth born of their five children. I have two older sisters, an older brother and a younger sister.

Although my early childhood memories are minimal, those first recollections are taught at the Davis Village Infant School – fairy stories, nursery rhymes, and learning the Lord's Prayer. At recess, I would spend time in the mixed-sex playground, enjoying games of marbles, hopscotch, skipping and acting out some nursery rhymes rather adventurously.

We lived in a small village called Phillips, just a few minutes' walk from Davis Village, with our nanny and her husband, who, although not related through blood, acted as our guardians when our parents left for England. I do not remember my dad or mother getting involved in the first eight years of my childhood. It was when I came to England that I got to know my parents. They were financing our keep by sending money from England and gifts from time to time, but I had only a black-and-white photograph of them in the house, and my nanny, who we called Mum, would remind me that the couple in the picture were our mother and father. I could not remember when I was last physically held by them, and even with the photo, I didn't know them. Still, the presents from England were the most magnificent expression of my parents' love for us, their way of letting us know they were thinking of us and that they were alive.

As a child, I never saw our family as inferior because we were comfortably better off than most, and others were the victims of back-breaking toil. I was an urchin, a happy child playing with toys sent from my mother and dad in England, and I always had clean clothes to change into when I got dirty, had shoes to wear and plenty to eat. We dressed in our immaculate uniforms every school day and had clothes called our 'Sunday best', which we could only wear to church and special occasions.

Our nanny's name was Chalice Thomas, and her husband was Jeremiah. When he died of old age, peacefully in his sleep in the house in the small village, I was curious to see what happened to his body before being laid to rest, whereas my sisters and brother were afraid. So I peeped in as the preparations were done, and I saw Jeremiah lying in his coffin before the lid closed.

The days and weeks passed swiftly after Jeremiah's death, although I had no fundamental concept of time. Then, one day, we moved from the village to a town called Molineux into a large house. The move meant that I started at Molineux school, where children were taught reading, writing, and mathematics from age four to adolescence.

They were the critical lessons for the pupils to learn under the strictest discipline. We grow up to respect elders, humble ourselves, continue the religious practices we were brought up in, and obey the church's teachings. Nanny brought us up as Pentecostals, but we became members of the Congregational Church when we came to England. From as far back as I can remember, I admired truth, moral goodness and religious understanding. I had a deep sense of belonging and develop hope, optimism and a sense of purpose and meaning. I feared to sin but found no power in my childhood to restrain my fears and check my sins and foolishness. We went to church every Sunday, and the only time we would be excused from attendance was if we had a severe illness.

On 1st May 1966, we immigrated to England; my eldest sister had gone before us in the previous year. My nanny, two sisters, brother, and I came ashore when the passenger liner Carubia docked at Southampton. Then we travelled in a minibus from there to Wellingborough in Northamptonshire. My education in England started at All Saints School, where boys and girls played in their separate playgrounds. Then, at the age of eleven, I moved to Westfield Boys' School.

The first awakening of my soul and the consequent doubts, temptations and perplexities came when I was an adolescent. It was not until I was on the threshold of my adult life that I became, in some inexplicable way, detached from the reality of the world in which I lived, and my behaviour became opposed to how my former self had been. My thinking powers were confused, and there was a marked disturbance of my emotional response and conduct. I grew suspicious of people and quickly took offence, and I experienced short-lived delusions and visual hallucinations.

It was not until I had spent a short spell in a mental hospital that my thoughts – divorced from reality as they had been – came back to me without conflict. I believed that religion, social conditions, career and the opposite sex had somehow led to my slow and apathetic descent into insanity in my young adult life. Thank goodness for the support of my family. Without a doubt, they were instrumental in my speedy recovery.

I had mentioned social conditions as partly responsible for becoming mentally ill because of the nature of the recognised social pressures on young blacks to achieve something in a racist society. It drew me to the unconscious racial stereotype image that some white people have of black people. As a result, I gave up the struggle to move into an affluent society because joining the mainstream of British life was hindered by deep-rooted racial myths and prejudices. So, I turned to the black church with its hopes and salvation through negative energy instead of fighting back with resilience and strength to disregard the stereotypical negatives that some white people saw in us.

My life might have been reaffirming all the negative subconscious ideas I was taught to suspect about myself, making it easy to give up. These non-aggressive characteristics, such as passivity, dependency and lack of assertiveness, will take time to reverse. It's a black people's dilemma, not just a personal one, which needs to be unlearned. It should be no surprise that minority groups have a high mental disorder rate because of their factions' stresses.

The most disturbing thing that happened in my life came after peace and happiness were restored in my mind, and I began to strive towards personal growth and goals that would structure my existence with creativity and commitment. As I write, I wonder how my normal developing adolescent difficulty ended and mental illness began. Do you know? It is difficult to understand since the same problems can be in typically developing adolescents to some extent. Can any of you tell when my mind had become disintegrated?

Recovered from the illness, I went around for weeks and months seeing the world as a place of beauty and hope, rather than ugliness and despair. I fell in love with a woman who recognised qualities in me that I thought I had almost lost touch with – creativity and affection – which was terrific. She was compassionate and understanding, not judgemental or critical.

My affectionate lady friend became the catalyst in a period of tremendous change in my life. Of course, one notices more of the sky's beauty by falling in love, but I found it challenging to think of anything except my lover. The feelings were intense, and I felt vulnerable that I might be rejected and hurt by her, but I wanted the security of knowing that she loved me as much as I loved her, making the relationship safe. Previously, I've been in a relationship where I gave more than I received, and as you can gather, it was awful. Worse still would be the fear that one might not fully recover from the damage this time around.

When my first real girlfriend broke up with me, it helped destroy me and put me in a mental hospital. I thought that I never again could love anyone like that because love was such a cruel, irrational emotion that I could not trust it. The feeling of falling in love was a solid initial affection I had for a girl who was my first true love, but now, I think of it as something that must be worked on to achieve understanding, respect, and empathy. I love my compassionate lady friend, and she loves me. I am in love. However, I am not ecstatic, romantic, and slightly unrealistic before I call it love and respect. I have grown through that stage with my new partner.

My 'love' means loving friendship, caring acceptance. Knowing her very closely, trusting her and constantly feeling at ease with her, I experienced a relaxed and comfortable, which made me feel far more secure and prepared to build a steady relationship. To find the existence of another loving person who was dear to me reawakened a buried joy in my life and a feeling that something in the universe clicked into place when I met her. The person I am speaking of is, of course, now my darling wife and your mum.

Unemployed 1981 - 1982

Written in the year 1982

Despite social and economic changes, 1981 saw an unemployment rate that equalled this country's economic depression of the nineteen-thirties. In addition, I faced redundancy that year, and the reality of it was bitter. Although I knew being out of work was less humiliating than it used to be, at first, I was ashamed and, at times, did not care to admit it to our friends.

Every other Thursday, I went to sign on at the Social Security office. Three rows of claimants shuffled slowly forward from the fire door, and beyond that, a single-file queue stretched back as far as the entrance door. I could tell which men had been out of work the longest because some wore bell-bottomed trousers and platform shoes, the fashion from two years ago.

I thought I would get a job before too long, but after visiting local firms and some in the surrounding districts, I still could not find a way back into the industry. After months of pushing to find work that I was qualified to do, I expanded my search and began trying for any jobs and all jobs, no matter what. Anything is better than being idle – and we were getting desperate.

In September 1981, a few days before my birthday, I had a brainwave. I would write letters to local employers who I had not already approached regarding specific vacancies. So, I sent out eight letters and received seven replies, of which six began with the word 'unfortunately'. One letter, however, was inviting me for an interview. I got the job! It was factory work, and the place was in a deplorable condition. Here, I experienced hard work pressure without satisfaction, repairing moulds amid the constant dirt and noise.

After a while, I moved from this to a different position, manually opening and closing pair dies, removing a moulded component between them under a strict production timescale. The work was harsh, an insult to my intelligence and abilities, but I gave my best effort because I needed the money. However, I was not meeting the required quota, which made me nervous about losing the job.

We set the 24th October 1981 for the wedding, and the job came along at the right time. But I felt I was being used as a cog in a machine without a decent break. We went to a new bank in Wellingborough, opened an account and applied for a loan to cover the wedding costs. The bank approved a maximum of £500 to Euphemia, seeing as she'd been employed the longest, while I was only in the probation period of my job.

A few weeks before the wedding day, I was given the devastating news that my services were no longer required. Once again, I found myself thrown on the dole, and it made me realise that the primary aim of industrial work was not to make the job satisfying but to raise productivity and profits. So, label me as undesirable because I am a slow, conscientious worker. I felt I was suffering and in pain – not the same kind of feeling as worthlessness or despair, but the suffering of losing my new livelihood and not seeing any possibility of finding further work in my old occupation. The job was partly lost because I am in the ticked box bracket for 'slowest worker', and it was last in, first out to go back on the dole.

The fact remained, I needed work. No matter what effort I made, I was robbed of my livelihood and, with it, a massive chunk of my consciousness because I couldn't feel useful and earn a living. Being unemployed did not fill up a typical working day satisfactorily, and I needed a job to do this and give me a sense of identity in society.

On Wednesday 11th November 1981, two weeks and four days after our marriage, my nanny died in hospital. About a year earlier, she had been admitted to hospital following a stroke that left her unable to speak and paralysed down the left side of her body. 1981 had come to an end, and we began the New Year desperate for money to pay the bills. The mortgage was in arrears, rates (poll tax) were outstanding, and there were no presents for anyone at Christmas. We were incredibly damned hard up. A high fuel bill remained partly unpaid. On our minds as well at that time were thoughts of when we should start a family. We knew it would be challenging to have a baby under our present circumstances, and we decided to wait until I was confident of employment.

Now in a tremendous rush to get a job, I could not find one that gave full employment rights on a PAYE basis. I answered a job advert in the local paper for a salesman on a self-employed basis with training provided. The company was based in Leicester, and my area would be Leicestershire and Northamptonshire, selling life assurance policies. I did not fully understand the self-employed system and having a wage from an employer and canvassing. Still, I was accepted on the training course to gain product knowledge and learn ways of selling to make the most commission and hit the sales targets, maybe even make Salesman of the Week and earn bonuses.

The sales techniques, as I observed, were crooked, devious, manipulative and pushy. I thought I'd give it a go anyway, but it didn't work out because there was too much dishonesty on all sides of the business – the product, the salesmen and a client, all crooked. It was pricking my conscience because we had to sell the policies with the least protection to the policyholder, giving the salesman the most significant commission.

Meanwhile, my brother had given me £100 to improve my driving. Although I passed my driving test at 17 years old, I had not driven since I commuted on a Honda 250cc motorbike. In my one month of selling insurance, the only policy I sold was to a family friend. After I called at a house in a deprived area of Leicester, I quit the job. The person who answered the door said he was interested in the policy, but he did not live there. He gave me his address so that I could explain more, and then he would sign up. The address turned out to be a road with a row of garages.

Apathy, fatalism and passivity quickly took over my positive feelings and the reservoir of good energy I had not begun to use seemed already consumed. I felt my failure keenly and wondered what kind of a father I should be when I couldn't even find a suitable job. Will it be too much of a strain, being a husband and father, out of work and with substantial commitments? I felt that I must do something to symbolise my hardship and the decay of labour, so I became a one-person activist for a day in London. I made a sandwich board out of cardboard and carried it on my shoulders, delivering my testimony to number 10 Downing Street on 20th February 1982. I handed in the letter addressed to Margaret Thatcher, Prime Minister, then I walked and protested in central London's streets and market places.

As a result of being featured in the local newspaper, I was offered employment with an engineering firm. I had previously had an interview with them, but they had set someone else on. Luckily, they had kept my name on file. I worked there as a centre lathe turner for six months. Still, I lost the job because I didn't have the aptitude to increase productivity, and my engineering skills had diminished to those of an average first-year apprentice.

I had such a strong sense of bruised intelligence, wounded talent and rejected abilities, yet I knew I had only myself to blame for this. Every day living with unemployment appears like a lifetime without dignity that had led me to become an activist. Still, because my lack of ability caused me to lose my last job, I saw an opportunity to improve myself through my studies.

I took up yoga exercises and went to classes to learn relaxation, temporarily putting the job search on hold. I also attended Adult Literacy and Basic Skills classes to help restore my damaged self-image and self-worth. It was there that the tutor advised me to write my autobiography because she considered that I had a special kind of writing ability.

To improve my chances of finding new employment, I kept my mind active by learning new skills or brushing up old ones. No matter how unfortunate and unlucky 1982 had been on the job front, I had the comforting spirit of my wife, who helped restore my shattered confidence.

The month is December 1982, and I am emerging into a new year without job prospects, but I can only hope that the continued spell of being without work will soon cease.

Marriage
Written in the year 1982

Next to falling in love with your mum, Euphemia, the other most compelling reason for me to marry was to make a home, raise children in wedlock, provide security for my family, and always be there for them.

The chief ingredient of my love, in the beginning, was fancy mixed up with various emotions. Then I had an overriding obsession with the future when I discovered that I had been blessed with a partner who loved me and was willing to have an intimate long-term relationship with me in married bliss. It did seem like a dream, but it was within our grasp. Securing our identity and trust in each other, we embarked on married life to share and enjoy together. And as well as being committed to each other in our growth and sharing of self-discovery, we also wanted to experience together whatever crises of life we would face, to end up in our old age a more affectionate and loving couple.

On the eve of our wedding day, I cannot remember if I was feeling pre-wedding nerves, but I asked myself, am I doing the right thing? Am I worthy of the match? In my heart, I knew marriage was proper for me, to help me focus and give love to one exceptional individual, to make a family and extend this love to them. In my head, I was unable to provide appreciation in the broader community because I abandoned sharing universal love by not having a career in the church or working in a job where I would be helping people.

I have been candid with Euphemia about my suffering from mental illness, and she could always be confident that she would come to no harm because of it. I encouraged her to go with me to see my psychiatrist and discuss any anxieties she might have. I needed us to learn if my illness would be passed down to children and if my injected medication could cause any baby deformity.

I am pleased that Euphemia always attended my appointments when the relationship became serious, right through our engagement. And in our marriage, she was fully involved in knowing about my treatment. She must always feel comfortable with me because I know that my delusions when I am unwell are hard to deal with and can be challenging. I asked Euphemia to call the doctors if she ever felt threatened or frightened whenever my behaviour seemed strange. "I will never hurt you, directly or indirectly", I told her before we tied the knot. I understood she was taking on a big challenge, and I admired her courage and bravery because the risks were there. I wished I could have guarantees that nothing wrong would happen, on the basis that I am a man of God, a man of peace and a man of non-violence, which I hoped would get us through safely when the illness would strike. I believe I could not harm her, nor could I self-harm, because I feel I am good through and through, and the cruel parts of the sickness would fade when confronted with the God-given goodness in me.

I did not have a 'stag do' to end my days of being a bachelor. I was home alone in the house we bought in 1980, playing music into the early hours until I went to bed with thoughts like, 'gone are the days now when I just opened tins and never thought of a balanced diet'! I knew I would be thrilled in the sacrament of Christian marriage.

Though we were engaged, Euphemia had not had a sleepover in the three-bedroomed House in Bedale Road, Wellingborough. It was my bachelor pad until she stopped living with her parents on our wedding day.

On Saturday 24th October 1981 at 2:30 pm, the ceremony was at Our Lady of the Sacred Heart Catholic Church, with my brother as my best man. I was behaving extroverted because I loved being the centre of attention with my bride-to-be at my side. All eyes were on us pretty well all the time, and I loved every moment of it until a problem developed that knocked my confidence. I believe I had an anxious neurosis because I lost faith and experienced terrible physical trembling in front of the altar. Fortunately, however, something soothing about the ceremony made my nervous state diminish, and we pledged to be loyal and faithful to each other until death. The words were both beautiful and meaningful. The exchange of vows touched my soul deeply because we had got blessed into a God-ordained institution. I felt proud that God had put us together.

As we walked back down the aisle, my eyes began to tense, as if they were being rolled up, lifted underneath my eyelids. I was consciously trying to stop my eyes from flicking upwards. While this was happening, my new bride guided me, helping me along, and I only lost my footing once during the slow walk out of the church. We had photographs taken outside the church and more later at the reception. We were eventually able to relax after all the photos had been taken. After that, we had nothing to do except my short speech, cutting the cake and appearing amiable during the other addresses!

Relatives and friends on both sides spoke. I noticed that my parents had tears in their eyes, and one or two other relatives were showing a slight flush of emotion. I felt a little nervous and had minor trembles while giving my speech, but it did not stop the inner joy and the happiness I felt from showing. I purposely regarded the adult crowd before me like an ardent multitude dying to hear my words and eager to acclaim when I finished. Happily, it worked.

Our first wedding anniversary
Written in the year 1982

On our first anniversary, 24th October 1982, known traditionally as the paper anniversary, I realised that we had maintained the mixed ingredients of physical, mental and spiritual attraction with affection. We were cherishing each other, and neither of us had made the other a prisoner of our love. We had learnt and were still learning how to make allowances for each other's temperaments and behaviours.

The bulk of our happy memories from the first year of married life differ slightly from reality. I had forgotten the row that had arisen and why that argument brought misery and overshadowed happiness. I am delighted that Euphemia is my spouse because my darling showed skill in caring and thoughtfulness right from the start. Thank God for this good woman for me to love and cherish every night before I fall asleep.

The day was marked with enjoying a meal together and being glad and joyful that we matched as a perfect couple, but I felt a sense of failure because I was unemployed and could not finance even a weekend away. We'd not had our honeymoon yet, and on such a special day as this, it felt like I was not fulfilling my part of the obligation because I was broke. I thought my beautiful wife deserved better than me, but she had not complained; she is wonderfully excellent and lovely.

We had anniversary greetings, and cards were conveying best wishes from relatives. I gave the dearest person in my life a bunch of flowers and a card to remind her that nothing meant more to me than sharing life's experience with her. And it was painful that I had no money to show it with a luxurious worldly possession or going out to celebrate this important day in our lives.

The meaning of love is a bit ambiguous when my emotions are affected by my nervousness. I believe that I did not provide Euphemia with anything except the roof over her head, and now we were expecting our first baby.

However, this nervous aspect became less apparent because the affection and admiration we had for each other, and the support we gave each other buoyed us.

Euphemia and I were becoming more considerate as a couple and developing our skills around caring for one another in making a reality out of the idealisation we may have had of marriage.

We had talked about how the child's upbringing should be. That would involve knowing the Catholic traditions and worship in a Catholic church and other Christian churches. The child should go to a good church or state school to have a good education that is not strict on Catholic Christian doctrines. Euphemia was brought up a Catholic like her parents, and I can only say I am a Christian believer in God, not tied to the church's human-made false doctrines and beliefs.

The Period of Pregnancy
and Birth of our Child
Written in the year 1982

Towards the winter season's close, my wife and I merged into the beautiful union of love's act to start creating our family.

Euphemia told me she had missed her regular period, and I suspected that she was pregnant. She said not to jump to conclusions, that she might just be late and may need a few days to be sure. I was so glad that Euphemia could be pregnant; I urged her to go to the doctor's immediately for tests. She took my advice and saw the doctor that same day – the result was negative. I was astonished to hear that, but the doctor asked her to come back a week later and retake the test, and that one proved decisive. We were thrilled with the confirmation of pregnancy, and within a few days, we told our closest relatives. They were delighted with the happy news and congratulated us heartily.

Beneath this happy excitement of my wife having conceived was my fear that our baby might be imperfect, and my anxiety grew because of my past nervous disorder. Still, my psychiatrist told me it was not necessarily an inherited illness. I always hoped that we would not have to face the tough decision of being martyrs to a genetic accident.

On Monday, 14th June 1982, Euphemia and I attended the hospital for the ultrasound test to trace pictures of the baby's form in the womb, to check if the baby was growing naturally. The images of our baby were thrilling – it was like looking at an astronaut doing a spacewalk, with our baby suspended in the centre of the womb, actively floating while connected to the umbilical cord. It was incredible, looking into the womb and seeing our baby's fingers, toes, tiny face, witnessing the heart beating and hearing the loud sound it made. It was difficult at times to recognise some parts without the nurse pointing them out. And, as she scanned Euphemia's womb, I felt incredible, overwhelming joy at hearing those sounds and seeing our baby moving – with small kicks like an underwater swimmer.

Ultrasound was a new technology becoming more widely used in hospitals to check early-stage babies in the womb. Still, the pictures can look like black-and-white shadows that only resemble a baby when carefully studied for a layperson.

On 28th June at 11:20 pm, Euphemia felt our baby's movement inside her for the first time. Then, I saw and felt our baby moving on 17th July at 10:40 pm, with my hand on her tummy. We went together to parent craft classes at the local hospital and the antenatal clinic, but my dear wife worried and feared the birth. We read leaflets and books on pregnancy and childbirth to ease her fears at home, and I reassured her, but she grew tired of us studying so much about it and told me not to read anymore.

Just past midnight on 1st November 1982 after doing a few yoga exercises on the bedroom floor, I lay in bed, wrestling with thoughts on improving the Missionary Song and adding the fourth verse. (The Missionary Song was an inspired song written to express a deep desire to get chosen to take the Gospel of Jesus Christ to the world as well as an invitation to others who have a firm conviction but can't make up their mind about the calling.) I pondered out my thoughts on the making of the new verse by candlelight. Euphemia woke with tightness and muscle contractions in her lower abdomen and pain across the waist. She desired to empty her bowel at 1:30, just as I was attempting to extinguish the candle. Twenty minutes or so later, dilating-like sensations came on again and lasted twenty to thirty seconds. It came back after an interval of seven to ten minutes with more intensity. I told her that she is in the first stage of labour, and we smiled at each other with a definite feeling of inner joy that the baby was ready to come out of the womb at last. A mixture of excitement and anxiety aroused in us as we realised that this would be the day the baby would be born.

Euphemia did the breathing exercises she learnt at the antenatal classes all the time when the contractions came on and rested during the interval of no pain and said, "I can't stand it anymore - it's too much." She looked very uncomfortable, but the only help I could give was being a supportive talker and lightly rubbed her stomach when the contractions took hold and encouraged her to do the proper breathing. The time was 4:10 am; the contractions became more frequent and with more vigorous intensity, and the desire to empty her bowels came too, but she couldn't, but a slight discharge was noticed. I pondered whether to call the hospital at that stage and decided not to until the waters broke, indicating the second stage of labour. If it looked likely that her contractions were unbearable and the mother and baby's safety was at risk, I will act quickly and call the ambulance.

As Euphemia left the bathroom, a gripping contraction started and brought her to her hands and knees on the floor. She crawled on all fours and attempting to get back to the bedroom; the contractions were coming every five to seven minutes and lasting a minute or so. I helped her back to the bedroom, and she was exhausted. I monitored her pulse rate, and it was normal, and I felt her forehead to find out if she had a high temperature, but it was normal. From about 4:55 am, the contractions came every three to four minutes and lasted seventy to eighty seconds, making Euphemia repeat, "I can't stand it anymore." Finally, she added, "I am tired and sleepy." It was well noticeable that Euphemia was fatigued because at the pause of the contractions, she collapsed beside the bed and her body and limbs were as floppy as an un-pulled string puppet.

I got her back into bed, and we lay there holding hands. As the pain eased, we closed our eyes to get a little sleep, but that was not to be because the contractions were coming with perfect regularity. Euphemia squeezed my hand tightly when the contractions occurred, and my hand felt tightened in a vice for seconds, but it was nothing to what I think she was experiencing in her abdomen. Euphemia was not asking me to call an ambulance, but it was not a home birth we wanted for our first baby; she only told me she was tired and sleepy. At 5:40 am exactly, Euphemia, with a mighty yell, proclaimed that the waters had broken. She was in distress and held onto me saying nervously, "Don't leave me!" And I said, "I have to call the hospital now, darling". I tapped on her hand gently before going downstairs to the telephone.

I telephoned the hospital to let them know that Euphemia was coming in and dialled the number they gave to call the ambulance. I had taken the already-packed suitcase from the bedroom and opened it to put Euphemia's medical card in it, but I had misplaced it after the phone call I made to the hospital. I gave information from the card to the hospital receptionist, but I couldn't find it. Euphemia was shouting from the bedroom so that I could hear through my frantic downstairs search where she thought I might have left it. I ran up and down the stairs without thinking about where really to look because I was panicking. The bathroom suddenly came into my thoughts, but it was not there. I rushed back to the bedroom and paused for a few seconds, and then it occurred to me that I had left it in the telephone area codebook. I swiftly ran down the stairs and was relieved to find it there. I hurriedly dressed to be ready before the arrival of the ambulance. Finally, at 5:47 am, the ambulance arrived, and I pointed them in the bedroom direction and went into the living room to get my keys. Euphemia was able to walk downstairs to the waiting ambulance and said to remember the house key. Within minutes, the ambulance drove off, and

Euphemia was given oxygen through a mask placed over her face as I steadfastly held on to her hand, clenching it into a fist representing strength and bravery.

I explained to one of the ambulance crewmen when the contractions started, and that Euphemia had noticed a mucus discharge. The contractions became more intense and regular now that her fluid had automatically released from around the baby's crown as the water burst. He then said, "You didn't give the hospital and us much time - the baby may be due soon now that the water has broken, but you'll learn!" Those words alarmed me because I began to get irrational worries and anxiety. Is it to get delivered in the back of an ambulance? Will the ambulance make it to the hospital before the baby is born? - Have I put mother and baby in danger or at a higher risk? The ambulance man went on to say that when the discharge was first noticed, that was the correct time to have called the hospital. I began to think I had done wrong to have waited that long. My wife was saying she'd had enough of the pain and wanted to get to sleep.

At 6 am, we arrived at Kettering General Hospital and my Aunt Lorna, a Midwifery Sister, greeted us. Auntie then told me to wait in the corridor, and when they were ready, they would call me. I murmured to myself that I did not think she knew I wanted to be at the actual birth of my child. I wanted to be in the room when it was happening, being with my wife and not just presented with the baby bound in a blanket after birth.

I love and care about Euphemia and wanted to comfort her through the ordeal of giving birth. Being present is reassuring that she is the most precious person in my life who is about to give birth to our baby.

I spent anxious moments sitting crossed-legged on a chair, asking passing hospital staff the time because I thought I had been waiting too long. Every moment seemed to be lengthier than the last time I had asked the time. I had forgotten my watch, and the hospital clock was situated in a restricted zone and I could not see the clock face. I continued to wait but got out of the chair and paced up and down the corridor. I was trying to recall why Euphemia did not tell me to call the hospital during her distress and discomfort at home. Then I remembered her preference to stay at home as long as possible during labour without having a home birth with our first child. My wife is braver than a war hero and more courageous than a moth around a hot light bulb, and the most demanding and possibly dramatic experience of her life was taking place right now. I prayed in my heart for all to go well, and that nature would not dash our hopes and expectations but give us a blessing without disguises, a normal healthy baby.

I was called into the labour ward at 6:33 am, just a few minutes after asking a passing nurse for a time check. A blue hospital gown was put over my cardigan as I briskly walked to the delivery room. When I was there, I did not record any time check or write little notes on the labour progress like I had been doing to capture precisely the live event in my own words. Time passed without my knowledge, and the experience from then until birth would be etched into my memory to write down later.

My aunt said she was off duty soon, and the baby's birth was expected in a short time because Euphemia's cervix had opened widely. Euphemia was having strong muscular contractions and had been given gas and air to ease the discomfort. Euphemia was monitored periodically by a new midwife in charge of delivery with a new staff sister's assistance.

To me, Euphemia seemed to be suffering the degree of pain a torturer would inflict on his prisoner before he goes unconscious because the contractions looked agonising. Euphemia became impatient and asked, "Why is it not out yet?" The midwife replied, "Not long to go now". Relaxation and breathing exercises did not seem to work for her because of her great pain, which did not appear tolerable even though Euphemia used the gas and air machine to help her. They gave her painkilling injections, but somehow, she was overriding them because the birth's climax was prolonged by three and a half hours. At times, it appeared that tears had moistened her eyelashes, and sweat had polished her brow, but Euphemia's back, sides, legs and behind were inflamed with pain and just so very uncomfortable. Euphemia wanted to get up and go to the toilet but began to scream every time the contractions intensified.

Seeing Euphemia in agony made it a startling childbirth event instead of a pleasurable experience. If I could, I would have taken the pain of delivery from her and carried it upon myself so she could have a pain-free birth. The nearest to that was to wish that they would give her an epidural, for to watch Euphemia's face in agony and to hear her cry, "OH GOD HELP ME!" – magnified to me that she was enduring a high degree of pain. The labour highlight came when the first half-inch of the baby's head, lightly covered with black hair, appeared at eleven o'clock, and it was ceremoniously exciting. "It's coming, darling", I said, but the effort it took to push the head down was very exhausting for Euphemia. The baby's head was coming up to the surface and almost disappearing again as Euphemia pushed down, but somehow Euphemia could not breathe long enough before the contractions became intense.

It was an ordeal - I could see Euphemia fighting to capture the deep breath she so desperately needed to push the baby out, but her breathing method was making the baby's head move like waves washing up on a beach. A small area of the baby's crown surfaced to the outside world on the push. However, the baby was not progressing to the surface as Euphemia was too weak to push during the contractions.

The next time, she had it right as I held Euphemia's chin down; Euphemia was throwing it back and unable to keep her head in the correct position during agonising contractions. It was 11:25 that day, Tuesday 2nd November 1982, when the baby's head was finally born. The glorious moment came when the tiny human was wholly released from the birth canal. The moment I saw that the baby was a female, I told its mother, "It's Katrina, darling; it's a girl."

Baby Katrina has disconnected from the placenta soon after, and Euphemia was exhausted. Twenty minutes or so later, the afterbirth was removed from her body. I adored Katrina immediately and touched her shiny, almost unwrinkled skin as baby Katrina was placed on her mother's chest after a few minutes of brief checks by the midwife. – I was overwhelmed by the reflexes in Katrina's hands and feet causing them to close up instantly on feeling the touch of my finger. I touched under and above her chin and around her mouth. Her cheeks tightened and relaxed, showing incredible comical facial expressions. Katrina made her first cry, not when she entered the world and breathed air. When the midwife gave her an injection, five seconds of scream emerged, and her face blushed with the redness of strawberries. If I had not been concentrating, I would have missed it. This first little cry was the most pleasant thrill of sounds, though it was slightly distressing for baby Katrina. I was thrilled on hearing her give a function cry. The tone of her voice was stored in my memory, and as I looked at our little angel, my imagination popped the five-second sound like surround sounds in my head. It played it repetitively in my head like a permanent automatic replay record on a gramophone.

Baby Katrina had only glimpsed the new environment, and she was in a saturated sleepy state during medical checks. Katrina awoke. Her eyes gave a few graceful blinks, and for a few seconds, perceived space outside the womb and then fell back into a deep sleep. I rejoiced in seeing she was responding in a natural, healthy manner.

Euphemia had to have stitches for tears, and later, in the maternity ward, she told me that having sutures was more uncomfortable than childbirth itself. I was taken aback to learn this. She also said that when the nurse took baby Katrina to the nursery to sleep, she cried.

I picked up baby Katrina from out of the cot in the maternity ward and then handed her over for breastfeeding. – The bond Euphemia formed with our baby when she breastfed needed to be observed by the individual to capture the nurturing that words cannot convey fully. It's a mother's love, an emotional, physical, and mental fondness for the child that becomes harmonised.

I am proud to have witnessed the miracle of God's creation coming into the harsh reality of this world and having the blessings of a normal healthy child whose senses and rational thoughts will guide her safely through this life, helped by her influence at home. We trust and pray that those things and others will make Katrina Natasha a happy and loved individual.

Euphemia and I are happy to have a relationship that evolved from friendship with goals to this time of further happiness and another fulfilment. The joint endeavour of Euphemia and me in experiencing our child's birth is hugely fulfilling, and nothing but fading memory shall rob us of this unique ecstasy. It's the experience of our child being born and the nine months leading up to this happy day.

Our baby at home and the second year of marriage

Written in the year 1982 – 1983

After nine months of planning, waiting and dreaming, the startling and overwhelming incident had taken place – our baby was born in Kettering General Hospital on Tuesday, 2nd November 1982. Five days later, the tiny, helpless bundle of blessings came home into the loving care of her parents.

It was an anxious twenty-four hours when baby Katrina and her mum arrived because it was my first day of practical, hands-on childcare. Unfortunately, the cot we had bought for the baby would not get delivered for another week, and we could only think of laying her in the brand-new pram's carry-cot.

She was a very restless baby and could not sleep. Something was irritating her. As we investigated what might be the cause, it dawned on us that the pram interior had a sickening chemical smell that was quite potent.

Euphemia had the idea of using the most significant, big dressing-table drawer as a temporary cot, and I found it would fit perfectly into the pram frame.

We arranged for the Catholic priest to come to the house and bless our child and our home. We both believed that those upon whom God bestowed divine favours and grace could, by supernatural means, protect those consecrated against the kind of corrupt, evil, malevolent entities that possess the mental or moral nature of us humans. The priest performed the ceremony as a symbolic gesture of protection, and with God's grace, our home would be granted happiness and prosperity.

The baby began sleeping very well inside the dressing-table drawer that became her bed. I was astonished at how baby Katrina was breathing almost silently, and the dreadful thought of 'cot death' flashed through my mind at intervals during the night. I wheeled the makeshift cot, in the pram frame, to my bedside so that when the fear arose, I could reassure myself without getting out of bed, seeing her little chest moving, or listening carefully for the faint sound of her breathing.

The cot finally arrived, and the baby started sleeping in it most nights, but when she was challenging to settle, we would place her between us in our double bed. I would try to remain awake and lay on my side very close to the edge of the bed. On rare occasions, baby Katrina slept in the arms of her mother until feeding time, and then after feeding gently, she would lie in the cot and fall asleep.

Our bedroom was transformed into a sensory area to create calmness. The lighting was a blue electric light bulb, giving the appearance of moonlight in the room, and we played classical music as the baby slept. After almost a week in the house, little Katrina developed a snuffling, grunting and other breathing noises, making me fearful, but my fear would subside when I looked at her. It did seem that she could not breathe properly, which was a worry. My anxiety lasted about a week, then she sneezed out some mucus, and I was able to sleep again until her cry would wake me.

Having a baby to take care of is as beautiful and natural, at times, as conception. This wanted child's arrival brought a more prosperous, fulfilled relationship because baby Katrina is unique as her fingerprints. Sometimes, when I felt unsure of myself and so inadequate that the reality of it all would hit me, it felt very different. I found it a terrific adjustment. I think I was a real expert in making mountains out of molehills when it came to baby care because I would become concerned about any slight deviation from what I thought of as usual for our baby. I reasoned there was a world of difference between father's love on the one hand and, on the other, information and experience in caring for the child. I had passed through the baptism of fire in the two months of our little girl's life, and it was a unique experience, different from anything I had ever known before.

The fulfilled relationship we have had since the birth of our first child has influenced my whole life. Having a wife to love, depend on and share things makes me manage and enjoy our relationship and other people.

In 1983, our second year of marital happiness might have looked like magic or things happening in a fairy tale. Conscious effort on both sides enabled continued satisfaction and maintaining this happiness. In our continual change process, which is also within ourselves, the relationship itself and our achievements or lack thereof, building and maintaining satisfaction is a complicated form of skill to learn. We have changed to a certain extent, but we have not stretched ourselves out of shape from our character to cause distortion that makes us false to ourselves and untrue to others. We have been able to be ourselves by maintaining our individuality and separate identity and not a mere reflection and echo of the other.

I sometimes wanted to adapt to my wife's minor criticisms, but I think I'd be losing integrity if I gave in to everything. We both hold high expectations of our loving relationship, but it seems static at times, however blissful it is. A trace of disenchantment is often felt when our struggle to work through difficulties makes love seem not ideal, and we have to acknowledge our differences. In the end, we become softened and share some of our most precious, most rewarding experiences.

I found my wife to be a direct speaker and she never pretends when she admits things and has disagreements. We feel the lasting quality of each other's love when this happens. The growth in spirit is fundamental in our relationship this year, 1983 - I am afraid that I may be unworthy of her love and care because we lack material growth. But this is groundless and irrational. My desire to achieve through hard work is evolving. My success-oriented desires and the stereotypical male image have peeled back or been laid under the intellectual Me's fresh skin.

This writing-up of the second year of our marriage presents a man who loves and looks after his family. But I find it hard to accept that I am doing well because I cannot hold down a steady job. I love my wife, our kid and the comfort of home and share in household responsibilities and child-rearing duties.

Unemployment 1983 – 1984 and Ruminant on 1st Mental Breakdown

Written in March 1983 – 1984

My chances of finding work remain the same as last year, and it is now March 1983. Suppose I take a nostalgic look at the time when employed as a centre lathe turner. In that case, I must have had a lapse of mental health because there were periods when I suffered from headaches and nervous disability. I would need to go to the loo frequently. Although I am a person of reasonable intelligence, whenever stress develops in my everyday life, I become vulnerable, resulting in an inability to concentrate.

Left crippled by the experience of my mental ill health, I fear a relapse. My wife shares my anxiety and helps to cushion it. I am living a reasonably healthy life outside of the hospital. My illness is kept at bay by regular, carefully regulated drug injections to match my personal needs. I dare not fail to take it, or else good mental health will rapidly decline, with dire consequences for me, my wife and our child. I am beginning to lose confidence that I will ever find work again.

The expectation and desire to be an employee diminished because it seemed that only luck would make it possible to get a job rather than skill or merit. To be confident of a job, it appeared that it must be self-generated by possessing enterprising ideas and talent. I thought long and hard about what I could do to create work for myself and considered spending some time developing hobbies that I had enjoyed, like drawing and painting pictures. I also enjoyed writing, and the prospect of writing a novel or short story seemed a real possibility, so I searched my imagination to come up with a story.

I felt I had some potential for idealism and creativity as real as any other abilities, but there was disillusionment. The problem was that I could not easily see how to expand my horizons beyond what I saw at the time in my daily orbit. I knew I must keep stretching my imagination to find a broader background horizon because it would give me more joy, dignity and inspiration to know my sweat provided for my nuclear family. Every day that passed caused me a little more anxiety with the increasing difficulty of getting interviews. Job-hunting was a full-time effort taking all of my concentration, leaving me feeling resentment and bitterness. Either I failed in some way to meet the specifications required for the job, or it was just bad luck, or I could even have had discrimination. Any success seemed delayed, and I needed to review the objectives.

I sought help from my family and analysed what I had to offer an employer. It didn't have to be a detached professional view of my talents and experiences for it to be sensible advice, and I was grateful for their opinions and encouragement. After that, I would eagerly search through job advertisements each day as a self-marketing exercise, and I would look forward to selling my product, which was my labour, to the prospective buyer – the employer.

Continuing to pursue jobs to end my unemployment, I still have faith in others and aspirations for myself. I desperately need to foresee a demand for a particular product or service that will bring about a quick end to my persistent lack of work, but I cannot come up with anything.

Being unemployed for such a long time was quite emotionally disturbing, and it made me feel as though I was talking myself into believing that any job would be the right one. I thought that any work was better than none for some time, so I had lowered my sights, but no such luck. I tried to adopt a realistic and positive approach to job-hunting, but I grew weary at times. I would persist in my efforts to retain my confidence and self-respect. I had a realistic plan for the future and a strategy for achieving the target – with luck playing an important part. To get back into working life, I would need to retrain to improve my engineering skills or join the self-employed ranks by turning an amateur hobby into a profession that would provide an income.

I was confident I could be cured of the mental illness because I returned to a sensible, healthy lifestyle; knowing I had held down jobs in the past gave me confidence, but things looked very different now. The disease was kept at bay with prescribed drugs, so suggesting that I had a cure would be wrong. Although this was a great deal to be thankful for because I was much better, my healing was temporary; I couldn't get healed in the accepted sense of the word. That could be a problem when filling out application forms because mental ill-health had become a case of disability, a handicap, and one with no cures. Employers, I felt, would not employ me when there was a more non-disabled person in the pool of the unemployed – even though I had not registered as disabled.

I did well selling myself when face-to-face with potential employers, leaving the interview with self-positive feedback. The goalposts had moved, and most application forms included health questionnaires. I believe that the interview opportunity virtually dried up because of this. The employers would read the health section and reject my application, even though it's the law not to discriminate in this way due to disability, race, religion, sex, sexuality or ethnic origin. I decided to adopt a different strategy – if I didn't reveal everything and got the job, they would never find out.

Budgeting our income from the fortnightly state benefits is a big task that cannot allow savings or luxuries. As my wife is out of work since having our baby daughter, Katrina, she now receives unemployment benefit, which is added to my unemployment benefit, plus some supplementary benefits. This total amount has to pay for everything, including part of the mortgage. We have to rely on help from our parents to support our essential living costs. Money has become tighter to budget, and it is challenging to meet half-yearly payments: I'll be forced to make dramatic cuts in shopping expenditure. With other secondary necessities, the house security and contents insurance had to go instead of renewing them. It may mean that road tax and car insurance cannot be continued either, with obvious dire consequences to my ability to travel to job prospects.

I no longer hold high ideals about getting a job because interviews have dried up, and travelling for work is now merely wishful thinking. I am waiting for the right incentive programme to come from the government- every so often, new schemes get launched, and I hope there will be one soon that I can benefit from doing.

Recently, there was one; the government launched a retraining and refresher programme, and I eagerly enrolled on the twelve-week course. Now facing the future with long-term optimism and thinking, I would soon be better positioned to impress employers. While I was training, my wife found full-time employment locally, and we arranged for little Katrina to be looked after by my relatives, mainly my mother. The course improved my engineering skills, and I have been stepping up my efforts to find work again.

Following eight various applications for advertised jobs, I had a positive response from one employer about the possibility of work after the summer holiday period.

During the final week of the training, a job advert came into the training centre via TV, known as Teletext. I applied for it, as did others on the course, and I was fortunate. I was offered the job as a miller turner based on monthly reviews. Two weeks into this new work, I heard back from one other application - an offer of a job as a surface grinder machinist. It was a permanent position, but the pay was less than the job I had taken, a more significant downside. The items to be manufactured were machined to minimal tolerances, necessitating the operator maintaining a high level of concentration at all times, which would be very stressful for me. One lapse and items may get rejected, which would only add to the stress. I had no choice; I declined the offer and stayed where I was. At the end of the first month, along came the review. My employer had no problem with my work's accuracy or quality, but the number of items produced was unsatisfactory. I felt entirely drained while working and tended to doze off during the fifteen-minute tea breaks and the half-hour lunch. I had no clear explanation for this apparent weakness, except that getting back into daily work was causing exhaustion in mind and body.

The symptoms persisted, and I had to tell the foreman a somewhat dishonest story to give me the chance to go home and sleep for a few hours. I told him I was going to the dentist, and he asked that I bring the proof. So before returning to work, I went to my dentist's surgery, asked for an appointment card, filled in the appointment date, and showed it to the foreman. He didn't suspect a thing.

My livelihood was on a knife-edge again, and I was almost unbearably frustrated because the tiredness would not go away, even though I would regularly splash plenty of cold water on my face. In the second month, my output had not improved since day one, and therefore I was unsuitable for this work. Once more, I had to depend on government benefits for survival. My wife, however, felt we were still blessed because she was working.

I had already experienced the uniquely painful blow of lost livelihood that was fundamentally self-threatening. I now felt typecast because the vision and values to lead to a better lifestyle had shattered, leaving me trapped in this state of repeated job losses. As a result, I was unable to contribute to the family's financial well-being.

My mental health check-up could not have been better timed. The psychiatrist told me about Workbridge, a charity business supporting people with mental health problems. The conditions were the same as for full-time work, but the maximum weekly pay for turning up to the workshop was £4.00 for what was known as work therapy. Imagine the damage to my self-esteem. It was also a pride killer.

The Workbridge centre was open five days a week from 9:30 am to 4 pm, and we had 20 minutes for a tea break and half an hour for lunch. The work was monotonous, and it didn't matter how long it took to complete the batches of work. The workshop staff taught us how to use a sewing machine, and, once you were confident doing that, you then went on to sewing black bin liners. Packaging is for less able workers. Sorting envelopes and cards into different sizes and looking for rejects in batches of colour photos was done.

I grieved over losing my job, and taking this lowly work left me feeling vulnerable and exploited. Then, when I was ready to face the world of work again, the idea was that the manager at Workbridge would act as an advocate, a voice to influence potential employers, and I was uncomfortable with that, believing I would get viewed stereotypically negative terms.

I gave myself a self-imposed suspension from Workbridge at the Christmas break closure in December 1984, planning to review my decision in the new year.

My wife and I looked toward the new year with optimism because we took strength from our relationship, which we always knew we could use to help us accomplish our goals.

I had wondered if I ought to write an in-depth account of the bizarre things that happened when I was taken mentally ill in 1979. I cannot remember what the psychiatrist had diagnosed, but he may have said it was a form of schizophrenia. I decided to write about it to communicate that I was still a natural person with real feelings and thoughts underneath all the terrible symptoms. As bizarre as I may have been, nothing took over my mind.

People held on to ideas from ancient superstitions and beliefs described in words from the English language, such as possessed, evil or devil. These terms come from the Dark Ages but are still used to breathe fear of the unknown into the masses and control them. I became caught up in accepting the traditional idea that I was mad and possessed by the devil.

Having gone through the sickness of a brain illness, I was able to self-educate myself and know the truth, to learn about something unknown to ordinary people: they cannot experience it unless they, too, have travelled through this particular illness of the brain. My deep-seated mind, the self, was intact, and my soul and everything else that makes up a living person, including feelings and emotions, were not interfered with as the ill brain gave out symptoms that are natural for a diseased mind. I did not get robbed of anything that makes me, me – Karl. The fact is that positive things were added to my experience, especially when compared to people living with Alzheimer's, in which their illness robs them of a part of themselves.

The illness experience was profound when it happened, and it was a great insight and knowledge, now that I can reflect on it. But the onset of the disease was ever so frightening. Thank God it is over, but the hidden feeling of guilt that I was responsible for causing the pressures that made my brain freak out is still there, even though the psychiatrist said it was not my fault. So although I have gained this new knowledge, I secretly and silently blamed myself.

Happy childhood; I was always curious and eager to learn about things and fascinated by nature and heavenly things. I would dismantle toys and then try to rebuild them in my exploration of the material world's artificial and natural processes. I later developed abstract ideas, and in certain subjects I studied at secondary school, I could not grasp the logic. I could not get my head around some mathematical equations, and I had many questions about faith. Biology and sciences left me in awe of nature, and religion gave me a sense of belonging to spiritual life. On the other hand, I was troubled by the existence of suffering and man's inhumanity to man. I did not want to leave school because I was cocooned from what harm adults were causing the planet and people who are different instead of cherishing their diversity.

I expected to find society harsh and knew that people were harming the planet, so I formed no clear idea of what work I should do. When offered a suitable apprenticeship, I chose to train to be an engineer, with practical learning in both college and the workplace, while earning a wage at the same time. College covered the theoretical aspects, and at the end of the course, I could obtain a recognised qualification.

Initially, I knuckled down in college to work through the three-year course in mechanical engineering and tool-making. But then I had cold feet in the first full year at college, and I told the tutors I wanted to quit, but they persuaded me to carry on.

Over the next two years, I attended college one day a week, known as 'day release', and I spent the rest of the week employed in the workplace. As years two and three passed by, I became engrossed in the student union's newly formed Christian movement, and I found that one day a week of studying engineering lacked any real progress.

The Christian cult identified with the things I was searching for, like exploring spirituality and connecting to a higher power, so I joined. That was the driving force that led me to become fanatical. I felt empowered to change the world with Jesus's revolutionary teachings when I first hit the college campus, but I changed my mind, and I was left stuck with a burning desire for something – but what? After only three years of leaving school and working in the community, I realised that the world was moving into an ever-deepening crisis. I was genuinely afraid for people who didn't believe in God. I led a life of prayer carrying the entire burden of others' emotional baggage, and I did not know how to let go. I prayed, worshipped, and ministered to others that the world was doomed and that humankind was moving towards a significant tragedy. The fear may have caused my depression and despair because I had no peace of mind, and that, in turn, may have led to schizophrenia.

I thought there had to be an explanation for why I must continue to study so hard when the world was indeed coming to an end soon. Although I wanted to make good grades to be the best craftsman, deep within myself, I felt not just an eager urge, more an energetic commitment to devote my life to missionary work. This zeal to be a missionary was so strong that I was inspired to write a song that would show my faith's heroic exercise. I also wanted to exert the influence of good in the world through my kindness and tender-heartedness. Through sheer motivation and hard work, I did well in the first two years at college, and then in the final year, I began to suffer mood disorders.

My career in engineering, my studies and the community volunteering work that I did were all affected. I withdrew from every project and only involved myself in church-based activities. I went to all church meetings and conventions and took the gospel onto the streets and parks. In my low mood, tears soaked my pillow as I prayed before falling asleep, and I cried for my great sins to get lifted and the world's affairs to improve. I lost my appetite; sadness and impairment in sleep patterns slowed my ability to think. A feeling of unworthiness and ideas of suicide came into my head.

I spoke to the Samaritans on the phone. I went to an office in Northampton to talk face to face with a volunteer counsellor about my suicidal ideas and why I must pursue my ambition to become a religious leader. I studied the Bible at the church classes and home, I read it like it was a fix of some addictive substance, and I would sing religious songs with the church outreach group. Independently, I talked to young people in the local park about the Bible and the gospels. My young friends and children outside my church community began to call me Jesus, their nickname for me when they saw me in the streets. Week by week in the park, they would say, "Here comes Jesus." I was fully conscious with no memory impairment, for I knew these children were taking the Mickey in the main, but my thinking became confused over time.

At work, I lost concentration and misjudged the surface grinding of a component on a precision grinding machine. The high-speed grinding wheel plunged into the part, and I thought the device surely was controlled by a malicious person in the drawing office. The drawing office was on the first floor, and it overlooked the workshop. Even in the face of hearing an explanation that the machine could not have operated remotely, I persisted in the false belief. At nights, my sleep was interrupted, I would glance around in the darkness and see people floating around the room, and some of them were coming towards me. I quickly closed my eyes, and they disappeared, only to reappear after a few seconds when I opened my eyes again in the gloom. If I put the bedroom light on, it tended to flicker and then glow bright white, and I suspected that friendly ghosts were visiting me.

I must have been nineteen years old when, one night, I became so frightened that I developed twitches in my side and chest that terrified me – it was as though invisible knives were stabbing me. I twisted and turned violently in the bed to fight off my attackers, but the twitchiness intensified. My eyes were firmly closed, but I could see the neatly bearded faces of unknown white men. I screamed and screamed in the middle of the night and called out, "Help me! Help me, please!" My mother came into the room and settled me. I was having a nightmare. Mother slept the rest of the night on the lower bunk bed, which my brother usually occupied, but he had joined the Royal Navy.

Another weird thing happened when I awoke and looked out of the bedroom window in the morning. The landscape appeared alien; it seemed our house had moved during the night, for in my sleep, I sensed the house was shifting through space, and this was confirmed when I saw through the window that the house was on another planet – or perhaps somewhere in the future. I confined myself to the house and did not want to go outdoors. When I would venture outside, people were standing having a conversation on the pavement. Rolling thoughts would come to mind that they were plotting to harm me, and I hurried back indoors or gave a rude hand gesture (the V sign) and walked on. As I lifted my arm in slow motion, it made a creaking sound.

A disturbing phenomenon happened when I felt that my most intimate thoughts, feelings and actions were known to others, and supernatural forces were at work, influencing my thoughts and deeds in ways that were bizarre. I had come to believe the odd delusion that possessed me was the work of devilry-spirited invisible people, and I began to do weird things that I felt I had no control over. I hallucinated hearing voices addressed to me, and everyday objects in the bedroom appeared sinister. I found myself being turned against my will, around and around in a circle in the room, and I cried out, "No! No!" then became dizzy and disorientated. I tried to reverse the direction of the spin in an attempt to stop it, but my conscious action had my neck stiffly tightened and twisted and my head near to being sheared off from my body. I had to go with the force, which was driving me towards the door. I managed to turn the doorknob. As the door opened, I consciously experienced something inside me trying to push me persistently from the top of the stairs. I yelled, "No! No!" and held as tightly as I could onto the handrails... I sat on the top step and then slid on my bottom down each stair until I reached the ground floor. I then went into the living room and blurted out to my family what had happened – I spoke in an almost incomprehensible language because the alien was withdrawing my thoughts inside my head and acting up my body, and I was trembling from shock.

Following a home visit from a psychiatrist, I was admitted to a mental hospital diagnosed with mental illness. The psychiatrist looked like someone out of a Hitchcock horror movie – such a sinister doctor with a pipe and protruding eyes and ashen skin; I felt he was out to do me harm, and as he attempted to touch me, I screamed and screamed. I was terrified of him – and of being murdered.

An ambulance was taking me to St Crispin's hospital in Northampton. As I lay there, strapped to a couch, I was frantically struggling to free myself because, in the image inside my head, the couch was vertical, and I was bound and tied for crucifixion. I persistently yelled that I was not Jesus; "I am not Jesus!" I continued until someone gave me an injection to calm my nerves. More bizarre things happened in the hospital. My body was growing and taking on giant proportions, and a battle was raging with tanks and missiles in this new environment.

As I was starting to get better in the hospital, I realised more and more that my perceptions were abnormal, as the raging battle turned out to be the ancient heating system in the boiler room, making those noises that I misinterpreted. I continued to improve when I discovered more about the hospital's dimly lit corridors—my bed in a dormitory in this Victorian security house set in a deep, dense forest. There was a stench about the place that could upset the stomach. A heavy growling sound ran through the building, and the other patients, lethargic in their illness, would shout and scream their demands, while the hospital staff only served to put fear in me, which seemed illogical. The thing is, I thought my logic was entirely intact, but sometimes the perceptions I had on which to build conclusions were unsound.

I benefited from the affliction because a more vibrant and more robust person in character came out of the ordeal, and I have learned life's lessons well. I could now endure the trials of life patiently when meeting with adverse influences. Hospitalisation created a unique set of problems, and in my state of psychosis, I was notably unable to deal with them. Reassurances in the hospital were exceptionally helpful, and I needed a lot of that because I was susceptible to kooky ideas. Although my illness was unpleasant, I cannot say that I completely regret it happening. The psychosis was an experience in learning, problem-solving and perceptual broadening, opening the visual field wider and expanding thinking. It has undoubtedly made me wary of people who speak of a phenomenon and background religious experiences.

I still believe in a beyond based on the act of creation and the gospel story, which is no longer of delusional proportions that were utterly out of this world. As recorded in history, divinity is present in all humankind; therefore, faith in Jesus is rational because we have this in common. Like Jesus, we are dependent on God.

My family are very supportive. Mother and Dad have been exceptional in their devotion and love to see me better. I thank God for them and my sisters and brother. I could have sensed that something was wrong with me but did not see myself as a person who needed professional psychiatric help. I had found that I could not express my feelings and thoughts clearly, and I was frustrated by my inability to tell my family of the symptoms and experiences. When the family suspected that I was not my usual self, their well-meaning attempts to reason or even argue with me usually developed into a heated dispute when they would tell me to see the doctor. I eventually went and was prescribed pills that I did not take in the illness's prodromal stage. Before I sat down properly or explained how I was feeling, the doctor glanced at me, wrote something on his prescription pad, and handed me the paper slip. My darling wife has been an excellent listener to my repetitive accounts of my unrealistic experiences and fantasies caused by the illness with great understanding and compassion. Still, the uncertainty of the outcome and the disease's insidious course are factors that, if thought about too much, can cause anxiety.

The struggle to keep sane under stresses

Written in the year 1984

The tentacles of unemployment have touched every skill and profession and made the days of the common labourer obsolete. Although the unemployed's social profile is getting bigger, increasing week by week, it's growing at a slower rate. It all seems a tremendous waste of resources that is causing the disappearance of a worthwhile life because having a single, reliably stable job for life has gone.

I am in a different rank in the nation's ugly statistic of 13% of the working population, which is unemployed. I am an invisible category because I am no longer a victim of the trend of reduced human resources, a victim of colour discrimination, or a victim who wants to better themself in the struggle for an opportunity.

The trend in the engineering industry has changed to that of growth and expansion. Still, my pitiful career weakness has marked a profound learning problem, which caused unsatisfactory performance, a removable scratch. I need to refresh my training to get better at it or abandon engineering altogether.

My learning difficulty lessened my marketable skill in the engineering trade. I think I'll force myself to abandon my engineering career because I am generally a slower worker, and I feel like a dunce, probably due to the side effects of the psychiatric medication. Productivity is something I struggle with, and that's not tolerable in the industry. The lack of success in engineering may have sprung from study disturbance in college days when I became a fanatic for Jesus and the unconscious erased engineering studies due to unique burdens from the worrying of how to 'save' unsaved souls.

The major challenge I faced in 1984 is the same challenge I met in 1983 - being unemployed. Some present troubles encountered are the past, the learning difficulties, and the quest to be a religious leader.

And I have remained a victim of the history of my muddleheaded ideas and feelings for others I have no control over. A paradox! – Yes! It might seem so, but to remain in a feeble learnt engineering trade is a black hole in my experience because

I am not getting better at learning; it is suicidal. Nothing is coming out of it, and it appears an insane policy to struggle through something that is ego-bashing, amongst other things. So I concentrate on following a systematic method of doing things and working out how to do my job analytically and rationally, but this self-scientific development is slow.

The rules for playing the game of getting ahead will get delayed when confronted with new and unprecedented opportunities. I couldn't compete because my work speed is slow, and I lack an accurate understanding. With such a challenge, I certainly need my wife's support to healthily survive and be at my side to enhance my success, which will undoubtedly continue to bind our union.

My wife understands my quest for success and is very supportive. She has adopted a patient approach; although she has much to worry about and be disappointed, she remains tranquil. The high-risk adventure of the self-employed has interested me as an alternative to pride-killing unemployment. Since acquiring engineering skills, I marketed these skills, showing that I have the training to display to prospective employers, but this had failed me miserably. Opening the door to self-employment would be a most welcoming challenge.

I have thought, and weighed up the best and the worst that can happen, but the choice seems to be between lives. The constant failings severely restrict me from maintaining a job because of poor performance and feeling able to survive the battle as a self-employed person looks rosier rather than battling to be an employee again.

The task looks the same as a doctor on a battlefield - choose the healthiest to save. It's a risky decision because I seldom accurately anticipate the outcome of my decision; what happens is usually unexpected. I want to be self-employed, but the choice is a journey and not merely a destination. I realised that the years would go by anyway, but the steepness of the way puts me off. A sequence of self-questioning typically made me ask myself again – "What's the worst that can happen?" It will fail, and I will be worse off than before I had started. The facts are clear about looking for employment, but adverse circumstances stand in the way of the right decision. I am liable to drift into any job. If I stick to the most traditional form of earning a living, the alternative turns away from being an employee and rows upstream towards the self-employed. It goes against the flow, yet, with my stress-related illness, it must remain medically controlled to cushion the induced stress. No doubt, difficulties will tend to shrink the closer I get to them. So I shall delay the decision, imagine myself a long way down life's road, and wonder what I would say. Either – "I am sorry I did," or – "I wish I did." I have an exhibition of my artworks that I produced during my lazy, non-productive time developing this hobby in drawing and painting last year, 1983, to kill the boredom of being unemployed. I thought it might become a catalyst to earning a living.

The time is coming to exhibit them at Wellingborough library on 2nd July 1984. I want headlines about my artistic work to be recognised by professional critics and commissioned to paint pictures in oils or watercolours. The important message I desire to put across is that I can think in the abstract. My talents have flexibility, diversify in any medium, and I can create visuals from my imagination.

I can contribute to society through Art – if not engineering – and make a profitable living. My new ambitions to show off my artworks are smartening up, coming on nicely and looking good, almost fully prepared for the day of the show as I go about the relevant changes. Great thought and time go into the works I paint, which give purpose and breath. Through experiments and diversities, I am sure I have created some masterpieces. I enjoy my worthwhile leisure activity, and I am sure it will unlock the door to the fascinating art world, preserve my artistic ideas, and communicate with people. Nothing brings headlines more swiftly than imagination that is distasteful. I have painted a dark, imaginative picture that might cause a stir because of its content. The painting shows our closest genetic species to humans, the chimpanzee, hanging from a symbolic Christian cross. I hope it will be out of the limelight as soon as my other works' excellence in creativity is seen, and the chimpanzee painting is no longer the topic of conversation. I recognised in my other pieces the quality of beauty.

The 'Chimp on the Cross' misused my creative imagination, but there's good use to it too. It makes one see what one feels in the picture, suffering, extinction, conservation, change, rescue and abandonment. Being a low-educated black man, I am plunging headlong into a new adventure rigged with problems to achieve success.

Although the relevant promotional drive to market my art to the media and the general public is enjoyable, I feel the strain because I often experience feelings of anxiety disproportionate to what's happening. Maybe I am losing my marbles, emotional and mental stability because my tiredness has increased to a 'hangover' level, even though I never drank alcohol. The 'eye problem' that first came to light on my wedding day became a significant problem. It worries me that it may characterise a symptom of another mental ill-health issue. It was checked out, and I had an EEG test to check if the 'eye problem' was related to epilepsy or a brain disorder. The EEG result was reasonable, showed no brain abnormality, and my tiredness, including the eye problem, was a functional nervous weakness. I was prescribed a tiny pill to prevent the eyes from functioning irregularly. Unfortunately, concentration became harder after two hours of painting and ideas forming, and the saga of continuing tiredness persisted.

Undoubtedly, what has consistently dominated my mind and body is a nervous disability that affects my mood, intelligence, and emotional drive-in things I enjoy, especially when the 'norm' for others is my extreme.

I have captured the beautiful world in lines and colours in my paintings, unlocked my imagination's powerhouse, and proudly showed diverse ideas at the public exhibition. I was ambitious to succeed in the public eye by having several sales. Still, I was left to enjoy my artistic vision, develop them, and show them proudly to my family, friends, and acquaintances. The general public hadn't bought any of my pictures or commissioned me to produce new works. I had promoted my art pieces in the library strongly through diverse media. Some of my communication and actions fell on deaf ears, and I recorded them as unsuccessful. Those that listened and gave me an opportunity are registered as successful.

Unsuccessful:

1. I wrote to a leading daily newspaper, The Daily Telegraph, inviting them to send an art critic to see my exhibitions. I received a postcard of acknowledgement from the art editor.
2. A letter was sent to a popular tabloid Sunday newspaper, The Sunday People - No reply.
3. I had sent a message well in advance to a leading critic in the Northamptonshire Evening Echo and made numerous telephone calls in the month leading up to the exhibition. Personal visits to the newspaper left written messages, and I eventually spoke to him on the phone. He would view the exhibits if he could get away from the difficult current affairs news, but he could never.
4. I wrote to BBC Television and TV-AM - No reply.
5. I went to Anglia Television regional news collecting centre in Northampton on two occasions. The second time, I was told that there is currently plenty of 'hard news', making it unlikely the film crew would cover my story.
6. I was unsuccessful in studying Art and drawing at Art college because my academic qualifications were too low.

Successful:

1. Galleries will accept my work in the future if I can produce a higher number of exhibits.
2. A leading chain store, Boots, will be willing to view my work to see if they are suitable for sale in their stores.
3. I was on the airwaves on local Radio Northampton discussing some of my pieces from an interview recorded at the library.
4. The leading local evening newspaper, Evening Telegraph, carried my story, and the free weekly publications slotted their report in the entertainments /what's on the spot.
5. I was accepted to the Manpower Services Commission's one-day seminar on planning to set up my own business.
6. I was allowed on the Blackwood Hodge Management centre Bridge programme, although it was designed for unemployed managers.
7. I was accepted to study art at the 'A' level standard at a community college, and I didn't have the entry qualifications. The fee was free, being unemployed. My exhibits were considered to show potential.
8. A local organisation is willing to help me in the method of attaining sponsorship.
9. The local Art Society will permit me to exhibit my work at the town's new street art festival.

It is plain to see that I had scored much success in exhibiting my work to the public. I desire to eradicate weak spots and close the gap in my amateurism by taking up offers to learn artistic mastery techniques. I want to know the essential practical techniques – without theoretical padding. I wish to systematically develop a talent that was given to me in the cradle. It needs nursing, promotion and guidance by others who are successful so that it is a sure way to paint masterfully and create masterpieces. Art college or 'A' level study seems indispensable for attaining my artistic goal because I need to learn drawing principles. The 'A' level is free of theoretical padding and is practical, but I need the full range of equipment from easel to paint pots, and I cannot afford them. The route from amateurism to artistic maturity and making my mark is sketchy. After all, I may need theoretical knowledge, for it will free me from turning into a copyist.

Between April and August 1984, the struggle to sustain my happiness with my family, help others and understand extreme events without threatening my comfort and joy was remarkably damn tricky.

The hammer was cocked when the situation regarding my unemployed brother-in-law, who was staying with us, was inflicting more considerable hardship and to move him forward looked hopeless.

The sensitive lining of my stomach was touched. I was upset to watch or read media's reports on international global events and national news that IRA extremists had representatives in the Stormont democratic parliamentary government.

My reasoning and IQ became a little blunt because of all the bad news. Seeing advertisements and billboards of American evangelist Billy Grahame everywhere, his Britain evangelist mission, made me feel ill. His tour cost thousands and thousands of pounds, and it was highly commercialised and sensationalised. Religion makes me sick, not because it contains God, but because something about it threatens my emotional stability, sanity, and happiness; because I am compassionate, conscientious, and an easily confused soul, religion does my head in. I can live my life very happily without religious faith but not without God and my family. I will lift my pen off the paper at the close of the paragraph because I do not wish to record the fine details of the struggle to keep sane under stress. The memory is too fresh, but one day, when I sit writing with my pension money supplying me with paper, I might vividly remember the drama that nearly ended my happiness. If only I could say it was my imagination running wild, but the incident was as natural as tying my shoelaces.

When I was living alone, and the crying of a distressed cat in the night frightened me because its calls sound like Kul, Kul, Kul, it feels rational (Karl, Karl, Karl, Karl) – my name. The recent few months' incidents threaten my happy existence; was I hearing and seeing things and making the wrong assumptions? I feel I was falling ill, and the nervous energy, thoughts and ideas that I have may tumble out on top of each other, resulting in a jumble. If I am brutally honest, I need to learn to relax, ignore, ease up, and reduce my anxiety levels. My stress level falls, and I return to my norm by not wearing my watch or spectacles unless vital.

The days have slid to today, Sunday 23rd September 1984. I am a happy man because words said in a heated quarrel, i.e., "Things will never be the same between us," were never meant to last in a relationship that is still buoyed up in love and understanding.

The biggest crisis I know for sending a marriage onto the rocks reared its head in our marriage's short history. On the other hand, my wife is such a remarkable lady who wanted me to use the little money I encouraged her to save for herself, to equip myself with the materials I needed to study 'A' – level art.

Regarding employment, I have continued applying for jobs instead of going into the self-employed world. The possibility of getting the one I want is an infinite number to one, but I continue to try, but without any measured amount of hope and expectations. My wife bought a gift and a card to express the happiness I brought into her life on my birthday, and it will be the last words.

More than a few years, my children, shall pass before I write again, but be sure in your hearts that when you turn the new leaf of the book, it will reveal the beginning of a new chapter in my life. God only knows how happy I am that my darling accepted my love and heart right from the start. I shall pump the permanent pen's ink from the ballpoint pen real smoothly on this page of the message in the card so that smudges and misprints may be prevented from blemishing even the quality of the written words my darling wife gave me on my birthday.

The Birthday Card Message:

For all our tomorrows, whatever they hold, and for sharing a love that will never grow old, this brings all my love, passion and a unique wish too, that you'll be as happy as I am with you!

The psychotic breakdowns and the blessing of a second child
Written 31st December 1986 – 3rd March 1987

Two years on, this book's continuation is from ongoing self-examination and studying my family life. The people I give credit for whatever virtues this book may have are in no way accountable for any of its deficiencies. My wife's influence has been invaluable. You might remember I stopped writing because I was becoming stressed following a quarrel, and life's unfairness made me ill. Impulses would have me rushing headlong into the future, but I have to move forward at a leisurely pace, neither anxious to leave the past behind nor reach ahead to make the future happen all the sooner.

I tend to think about Katrina and our second child, Georgina, not just their welfare but also about the broader environment in which they will lead their lives. I do not know how to make their surroundings safe for them. But if I could, it would take away the future's acute anxieties and help combat the feeling of helplessness. I shall endeavour to present my life and its setting attractively to you. My chief intent, still, is to delight and engross you in all the stories. I write with entertainment to myself, and I feel I live my life again, day by day. On each page, I'll convince you that what is to come is still unsure.

1985 was probably the worst year of my entire life. I endured a living hell – twice. And I do not think anyone can imagine what it was like, but it was a terrible, frightening experience for my wife, Euphemia, to witness. That year, I suffered two psychotic episodes with severely distorted perception, and my behaviour posed a threat to the ones I loved, but not intentionally.

The year was not entirely ruinous because, on Thursday 19th September 1985, Georgina was born. Children, it seems a pity that I found myself unable to cope with media stresses about world affairs and life in general, and I failed to see growth in its entirety. As you can all probably gather, I had some negative experiences during my formative years, and I do not intend to write any more about them or recent illnesses.

59

So, you need not become uneasy. However, I have probed deep into my mind and explored regions that healthy people would find weird and fear the consequences of the symptoms. I have damaged my brain and now need medication for the rest of my life.

Children, don't be alarmed. I feel more like my authentic self now than I ever have. Today, 3rd March 1987, I plan to be confident, optimistic, positive, relaxed, and safe when I act. I could go on and on, but I am sure it will reveal itself in my writings. I feel like a new person, not in any bizarre sense, but it is like discovering a more confident and wiser side. I am still Karl, but the 'Karl' whose character is strong, 'Karl' with a personality boost and 'Karl' has grown in wisdom and understanding.

Going back two years, I had a plot of land on the same site as my father-in-law's co-operative allotment. He secured the plot of land when my wife saw I was disgruntled at not having a job. From 1984 to 1986, comfortable life was a long time coming, and digging the land did not take away the thoughts of having to feed and raise my children on a non-existent income. I had monetary help from my mother to buy garden tools to work the allotment and plant seeds. I was only able to afford the seeds for the first harvest. Seasons passed, and I would dig the plots but had nothing to put into the soil except the potato crop's seedlings. I kept hoping that we could add seeds to one of our weekly shopping lists but, no, we couldn't afford them. When my interest waned, weeds took over the potato crop. I was becoming seriously mentally ill again.

Despite changing attitudes, my children, I was still too sensitive to my negativity, inner sensations, and external events. Self-confidence had gone, so my spirit was weak, which meant the fight had gone out of me. Only thoughts of the love I had and the love I know others held for me would keep me going. But the hope that I might win and stay clear of a nervous breakdown faded. It became a struggle for survival and reaffirmed love. Slowly, my broken mind healed. The great affliction was a test of the limits of my human frailty. Its success could have destroyed my life. Its failure has strengthened me.

The world Georgina was born into on that Thursday morning was tranquil. Curtains of cotton clouds hung in an electric blue sky over Isle Brooke Hospital in Wellingborough. I had felt guilty and anxious about Euphemia having another baby because I was apprehensive about the pain she would have to go through. She went into hospital at 3:30 am because I was frightened of the baby being born at home with no medically trained staff, only nervous me. Euphemia wrestled with bewildering contractions during labour, and her mouth was dry, so I moistened her lips with a damp cloth. And as she got thirsty, I gave her a drink of water through a straw. If I could have, I would have gone through all the pain for her, for her contractions made me feel useless. Finally, the ordeal to give birth was coming to an end. The midwife asked for my help when the baby was crowned. This moment had its magic. I truly appreciated what Euphemia had gone through for me, and I felt guilty at the fact that she suffered while I did not. I had a seventy-times-seven type of joy, unimaginable happiness.

My relief at seeing our beautiful baby daughter was overwhelming; ecstasy. And this was the world the baby would inherit, and I was happy to have seen her in it and healthy. Having had a somewhat practical part to play in delivering our baby and emotionally supporting Euphemia throughout rid me of the feeling of uselessness. The midwife congratulated me on my courage in doing what most fathers won't participate in doing. Baby Georgina weighed 7 pounds and 1 ounce, and I suddenly worried about picking her up; she was fragile. I thought I would be cack-handed when holding her, similar to when I had Katrina for the first time. I was concerned that I'd accidentally let the baby's heavy, warm head flop back and that her neck would snap. I was rendered almost speechless at the sight of the pulping soft spot on top of her skull. She was a delight to all and left hospital swaddled in her mother's arms, safely brought home in a taxi.

Many communities widely believe that second babies come into the world more quickly than first-born. Still, to our surprise, Georgina's journey was only two minutes shorter than our firstborn child, Katrina. Euphemia and I had done the most human things; we had made love and created a brand-new human being, a miracle of God. Georgina made the family proud.

Fatherhood is a remarkable experience—one of the most enriching things in my life. Euphemia fell in love with Georgina immediately, the natural maternal love for the baby. Georgina was as eager as Katrina had been to take her place in the world. She was very responsive and performed certain reflexive things, but her behaviour appeared to respond to stimulus. As a result, Georgina thrived, and her development was healthy.

The most noticeable changes occurred in Georgina's life pattern when she became one year old. She walked without support on her first birthday. There was quite a mischievous side to her now, which imposed much strain on her mother. Georgina had mastered specific skills by the time she was 12 months old that appeared to involve understanding. She was so eager to learn about the world that her urge for independence sometimes got the upper hand.

There have been very slight differences in Georgina's and Katrina's stages of development. As an observant parent, so much has unfolded during this past year with Georgina and over the four years of Katrina's life, and I experienced seeing healthy babies growing steadily. There is a particular kind of pleasure in seeing the development of their distinct personalities. That was fascinating. Katrina's intellectual development was a marvellous thing to witness, and I always allowed myself time to savour it as I saw her inscrutable mind working.

I am teaching Katrina how to play chess, and she is taking it in with overwhelming ease. Only adults know about colour prejudice because Katrina goes to nursery school and plays with white and Asian children. To think that, not too long ago, Katrina and Georgina were single-cell organisms, and now they are sociable, developing, loving human beings is fantastically incredible.

Work and struggles from 1986 to 1989
Written 30th December 1987 – 3rd March 1989

The struggle of getting a foothold in the world of work had started again. With some help, luck and effort, I found a job in the year 1986.

In the New Year, I went back to Workbridge to let them know I wouldn't need their work therapy anymore because I felt better. The manager persuaded me to stay on as they were looking to find me a work placement. In the first week of January 1986, Workbridge supported me in finding full-time employment. There was a vacancy in a shoe factory, and I attended for an interview.

In a few days, it will be the second year in the job that is not taxing my brain, no pressure in that way, but I am working damn hard. I was glad to take any job because this has brought an end to my negativity about looking for work.

In the first few months in the post, I was very anxious because I was unsure if I would be accepted since I was the only male on the all-female line of workers who prepared the shoe soles before glueing the upper part. My task was to wear a pair of gloves and use a cloth dipped in an active chemical agent to rub clean the shoe soles, and it made me feel sick the first morning of working with it because there is no ventilation; nothing extracts the fumes. It was a monotonous job I could do blindfolded. Once I was used to the smell, I was pleased when the end of the day came, knowing I had met production targets.

When I first stepped into this shoe factory, nothing mattered about the conditions, earnings, training or any prospects there. I was in, it's work, and that's all that mattered. It was a small weekly wage packet; £73.00 basic pay, not much more than I was getting on the dole from Social Security. It's the sense of worth that work and earning a living gives that mattered most. That was my only concern then.

Today, 30th December 1987, almost two years on, we are still struggling to make ends meet. Taking a low-paid job has made us worse off because we now get nothing free from the state. My wage was topped up with the government Family Income Supplement for the first year because I did not earn over the maximum qualifying amount every week. I cannot reapply for the top-up benefit as my wage now exceeds that amount.

The monotonous rubbing down of shoe soles ended in August 1986 when I moved to work a plastic extrusion shoe moulding machine in a separate section of the factory—using my hands to pull the shoe soles quickly out of the dies. Again, I saw a moderate increase in pay, and plenty of overtime was offered to make up a better wage. But, on the other hand, I became faintly bored with being engaged in a monotonous job where I felt like a tiny cog in a giant machine, again.

The month of October arrived when the air was rich and damp with autumn, and I began agonising about wishing I had been able to remain a press toolmaker at the firm where I served my apprenticeship. You see, children, I had to work seventy hours a week to earn a skilled toolmaker's equivalent wage. That makes me feel sorry for myself. Being of a nervous disposition, I am pleased to find the stability this job provides, but the happiness would fade a little if I kept that thought in my head – If only I could turn back the clock. The shoe factory's hours were from 4 am to 9 pm, and there was plenty of work. In addition, they operated night shifts from 8 pm to 8 am, which I sometimes worked. It was tough.

I have looked at all the things around me and examined what is inside me. I cannot run away from it because it is me, or I will be running away from who I am, what I want and what I do best. There needs to be a change in my employment or something, or I would be forever there grieving.

Back in June 1986, we had re-mortgaged our house to raise capital to modernise it. We put in double-glazed windows and a new front door, a modern bathroom suite, redecorated most rooms, and completely re-wired and wholly rendered the mid-terrace house.

It was then, and still is now in March 1989, the best-looking mid-terrace house in the street with Georgian style windows and front door. It sets a new character to the pre-1920's homes along both sides of the road.

We are delighted with our home, but there is still a lot that needs doing to bring it up to scratch. Oh dear, I realised only too well how urgent it's becoming to bring the kitchen up to a more reasonable standard and put in central heating. The kitchen ceiling was damaged by water soaking in from the upper floor, and all the units need replacing. With God's grace, in time, it will be fixed and refurbished. When I sit comfortable, cosy and warm in our home with your mum and all of you present, I looked back at how I came to get it.

I bought the house on an £11,000 mortgage in joint names, furnished through the years and it had warm-looking coloured wallpaper and carpeted floors. We even had a few luxuries, a colour television, a stereo record player, and a telephone landline. I would suddenly throw my arms over the settee and put my head back and smile joyously, almost childish smiles of triumph. It's ours! All of it! Humming a popular pop song to myself, I'd turn the gas fire down a little from full heat to continue to remain comfortable. It burnt with stunning colours, yellows, bright white with copper flames that changed almost to scarlet.

I am a proud husband and father, and when I fall asleep before the last daylight fades, I am still smiling. By dawn the next day, I am happy to get out of bed and work to earn the pennies to keep my family home, our very castle. It's not without bleary eyes in front of the bathroom mirror, as I try to organise enough of myself to at least get the razor out to shave. I am knackered, so very tired out, fatigued absolutely, but I want to work.

The end of 1986 arrived; I was not thinking about the 'now' at the heart of good living. I was thinking about my dreams and hopes for the future. Though 'now' is the only moment one can ever live, that is all there is, and the future is just another present moment to live when it arrives. We merged into 1987 with new challenges. I knew that God was aware of our trials and 1987 turned out to be very good to us, although we were immobilised for a time. I was eager that year to buy a motorcar, but I had no money to buy one. The thing was, I always felt uncomfortable about driving cars. Although I had passed my test the first time, I did not feel happy driving, so I remained on motorbikes. Only in that year, 1987, I thought that I was able to handle a car again. The only way I can describe how I felt is that I now believed in myself wholeheartedly. No activity was beyond my potential. The entire experience was mine to enjoy, but there were not any guarantees. I looked at myself with fresh eyes and wanted to be open to experiences I had cancelled out of my life. I was rigid before, but my zeal to drive, just for the sake of it, led me boldly to open up to new experiences. I surrendered the notion that I could not drive by totally believing that I had not forgotten how to.

To fund my new desire, I took out a loan secured on the house. I knew the make of car I wanted, so I had a few driving lessons with a driving school and bought a car soon after, a week before our sixth wedding anniversary, October 1987. Euphemia was very keen to learn and took lessons with a driving school. Unfortunately, she failed the driving test and then began to take classes in our car. When she retook the trial, she passed. It was an achievement for her – everyone could see that. Euphemia used to think that there was a lack of accomplishments in her life, which she felt, and is now proud of her achievement.

That same year (1987), I had the persistent thought that we should try for a baby boy to be the last child. Since you were born, Katrina and Georgina, we had Jonathan William for a boy's name. Jonathan because it's a name we liked and William after your great-great-grandfather. It was also your grandfather's second Christian name. My dad did not know his father William because he died when Dad was a child, so your mum and I thought we would have a boy and call him Jonathan William. We had no other boy's names in mind. If God blessed us with a third girl, we believe a proper name would pop into our heads, on which we would agree.

We tried for almost a full year to conceive, still only having the confidence that we would be blessed with a baby boy and no other names came to mind than Jonathan William. I offered up prayers to God, hoping the certainty we felt that my wife would conceive a boy to carry on the family name and gene pool into the next generation would be so. Not only that, but he would be a way in which we expressed our love and fulfilled relationship again. Girls, Katrina and Georgina, your births were also critical to us. You too carry the gene pool into the next generation but, most importantly, you were all wanted children and loved very, very much, and you also expressed the fulfilment of our marriage.

In May 1988, it was confirmed that your mum had conceived a baby boy whose expected birth would be February 1989. I was delighted, but Euphemia seemed worried and said she had mixed feelings and wondered if she'd be able to cope.

At the same time, work at the shoe factory was declining. From May 1988, there was no more Saturday work, and weekday overtime was limited to a few hours a week. The management had also introduced tightened work practices, and I was fed up with reaching the production targets. They demanded more and more from me, and I was getting weary with it all, for we had to work like robots. I became so disgruntled that I somehow allowed myself to under-achieve. I wanted to change my job, so when the opportunity arose to work at the company's other factory where they made the beading for shoes, I jumped at the chance.

I felt I must leave that place and find another job. I was not contented, and I saw no satisfaction in learning that job. Now that my wife was expecting our third child, we needed more money, so I looked through the newspapers each night to find a job that beat boots-and-shoe wages. Eventually, one September evening, I came across an advert for dispatch riders for a new carrier company setting up in the region. I applied, and the interview took place at my house. A few days later, I started to deliver parcels on the company's 750cc Kawasaki motorbike. I sold my motorcycle to a dealer. But, since my youth, I'd enjoyed riding bikes, and this opportunity to ride a big motorbike was like a dream come true. Dispatch riding was an attractive proposition because thoughts of travelling all around the country at speed and meeting new people appealed to me.

However, I had a problem with meeting the delivery schedule. The manager suggested breaking the legal speed limits but told me not to tell anyone he said that. In the fifth week, I was sacked for not delivering most parcels on time.

Three weeks before, on 24th September 1988, my brother married my parent's friend's daughter, and I was his best man. Can you believe this, children? I stood up to say a speech I had written and memorised – but not a 'dicky bird'!! Not a single word could leave my lips, although I was not nervous or anything. All was not lost, though, because I had a copy of the speech on notepaper and read beautifully from it.

Children, I had taken a gamble taking on the dispatch rider job, and I had lost, having neglected for a moment that I am a family man instead of wanting to experience the thrills of riding a big fast motorbike. I did not think that it would be at the expense of throwing my family life into more considerable hardship. I faced the now, with a wife expecting our third child, repaying the loan on the car and having to meet an increasing repayment on the mortgage, plus the council tax and bills.

I went to the Jobcentre, checking what vacancies they had. I was taken aback to see so many engineering vacancies, and I became repeatedly amazed at the number of job interviews I rode my old two-stroke Yamaha motorbike to in a day. I was looking for semi-skilled or unskilled jobs, and by the second day of unemployment, I had a fruitful conversation at an engineering factory called BB Engineering Limited. The vacancy I applied for was factory cleaner, and I filled in the application form, expecting an interview for that position. Instead, the works manager told me that they also had a skilled engineering vacancy. My application form showed that I was a qualified engineer with past work experience but out of practice. I told him I was interested but had other interviews to go to that same day. The works manager asked the foreman to show me the machines I would be operating. The primary tools were vertical and horizontal milling machines. He asked me the sequence of operation in making a component from an engineering drawing he showed me. I managed to tell him slowly most of it, but he interrupted me and explained the final few steps. I had wondered, could I possibly read those big sheets of engineering blueprints? I needed to believe in myself fully again, but I was not quite sure of my confidence. The foreman and manager stepped away to talk and then returned to say I just needed a refresher, and it would all come back to me.

When I got home after the day of interviews, Euphemia asked how I'd got on. I had found the work I'd been looking for in engineering. The other places were dirty, noisy and the factory was cold. But, to my surprise, the cleaner job I went for had turned into an offer of a skilled engineering job, and I thought I would take it if they came back to me with an offer. The following day, I received a telephone call, saying that the job was mine if I wanted it. The proposal was confirmed in a letter advising that I would be on a three-month probation period at the cleaner's start rate of pay.

I have been there for four months, and it feels good to be in a professional, skilled job. In the second month, I was paid the capable man's wage and had minimal work problems. My ego gets boosted now and again when the other workers call me skilled; man – it's fantastic.

Our third child was born in 1989, and the house for sale

Written in December 1989 – 1st January 1991

On Tuesday, 21st February 1989, Jonathan William was born at 7:55 am, weighing 7 pounds 8 ounces. I just missed being at the labour ward of Kettering General Hospital by twenty-five minutes. When I arrived, I felt an enormous surge of love and affection towards my wife and baby. I saw he was a fine-looking baby boy, and every time I picked him up, he appeared to know he was loved. I had natural, easy confidence in myself and realised that my awkwardness when holding a tiny baby had gone and I did not feel Jonathan was too small for me to handle. I learned about managing a baby by making a few minor mistakes with our first two children, doing what comes naturally, rather than worrying about it and going by the book. When Jonathan was four weeks old, he steadily gained weight, which stopped me from wondering about his well-being.

Now, ten months on, Jonathan has been crawling, and it is fantastic and quite hilarious to see him suddenly discovering the joy of scampering around on his hands and knees. He sometimes pulls himself upright, and I am sure by the New Year, he'll be taking a few unaided steps. It is fascinating to watch Jonathan develop increasing mobility.

Those steps will represent a symbolic achievement in his development because they will be the first step towards independence.

I trust that Jonathan will allow me to be a warm and affectionate father as he grows up, as I am with his sisters, and I remain a real masculine influence. My fatherly closeness and friendliness will have a substantial effect on Jonathan and all of you. Your spirit and characters will all be affected for the rest of your lives.

The process which always seems miraculous to me is learning to walk and talk. It happens at such a continuous dynamic pace. As I watch you grow, Jonathan, Georgina and Katrina, I marvel at the miracles that something so beautiful and full of potential has been a creation out of no more than the love between your mother and me. The decision to have children was one that has bound your mum and me more permanently than anything else can. The creation of you all shall always be a link between us.

I sort of bulldozed your mum into pregnancy, but she said it was more pleasant the third time. The third birth was more straightforward and less painful than the first and second, mainly because it was quick. However, your mum feels that each delivery was unique and that being pregnant for the third time seemed more natural to cope with, I suppose, as it was a familiar experience.

Georgina is growing out of toddlerhood and has started afternoon nursery. It is still fascinating to watch all of you learn new skills through your early months and years. Katrina is doing well at school and has a good reading ability. She was given a leading role in the school Christmas performance, playing a mother. I've seen my two daughters learn how to feed themselves. I've also seen them fumbling with buttons and zips then being able to dress and undress completely. The only exception is that Georgina cannot tie her shoelaces at the moment and has an odd problem with complicated clothes, like dungarees, but she manages most of the time. Katrina has no issues at all now. She helps out in the home, such as setting the table and feeding baby Jonathan.

Children, these stories of your development are the continual show of growth towards more and more independence in every area of life until you are adults. The structure of the family is not rigid. It allows you all to develop your full potential as you change, and family life is shaped and determined by the needs and demands of you, all of you.

I see each child as a tiny being that is an eternal, pure, undamaged promise. I can see the innocent new life as a symbol of hope for all human beings in all of you. My mystical dream is the eternal optimum of a world where parents' responsibility is not merely limited to giving a child the practical tools to cope with life on a seemingly confused planet. I have a heartfelt duty to offer you a vision for the future, which includes both a realistic perception and assessment of troubled times and an awareness of the incredible poignancy of life. I want you all to discover the wonder of life, the joy of exploring and learning and the beauty of understanding. As you all grow from babies to childhood through adolescence, it remains essential to feel happy with yourself - fat or thin. You may be criticised or ridiculed at school, then become depressed and grow to dislike yourself and find life does not seem worth living. Your growth and development to reach womanhood and manhood will take a lot of energy. Sometimes you may be upset or lacking confidence, or feeling insecure. Please, please, children, Katrina, Georgina, Jonathan – see Mummy or me. We will comfort you and be a source of advice and encouragement.

Teenage years can seem like an assault course. Your mum and I do not want to nag excessively but to ask about those feelings so that you can spell out any difficulties. It may be that we, the parents, are the problem because we 'automatically jump down your throats' with judgement and criticisms. It may be beneficial, but you may not think it is until you become a parent. Parenthood is itself a problem-ridden experience too. We want to show a united front when dealing with problems and make firm, sensible rules that can be the basis for security and agreement. Children, it's a beautiful, moving, incredible experience that you are born.

We had fixed the kitchen ceiling by claiming on the building insurance, and we wanted to move and start to make our vision a reality, to live in a nearly new house with a garage in an area in the town that is posh. There was always something that needed fixing or doing to the house, and to carry out further refurbishment would not be fully productive. It would require a home improvement loan to upgrade the house further - loft and cavity wall insulation, a new kitchen and a boiler need to get installed for central heating and hot water. We have rising damp in the kitchen, and getting a parking space directly outside our house is always a struggle. There are too many car owners to the ratio of car spaces, and there is frustration with neighbours parking legally on the public road, which the homeowner considers as his patch.

The estate agent sent many prospectors each week to view the house, but nothing materialised. I am earning good money as a skilled miller, and we could carry on living in this terraced house as it is, but it needs a lot of work. So we decided to move upmarket, buying a more contemporary property. Our earnings would cover the type of lifestyle and the housing we want.

The house we liked was link-detached, and the asking price was £58,000, but within weeks it was sold, and we did not have a buyer for ours. Seeing how the property market was going, we decided to withdraw our house from a market with prices tumbling. The media were saying it was an excellent time to buy but a lousy time to sell.

Now, quite often, Euphemia feels depressed. She takes some of my perfectly harmless remarks in ultimately the wrong way and gets upset. The burden of dealing with me and having to look after the children is not at all easy. I try to give a sympathetic ear and be objective about day-to-day problems, but she says I am continually sleeping. I pride myself on being a thoroughly modern father. I am determined to be very involved and thought I was a very liberated husband, but your mother will say I am always sleeping. Your mum is right. It appears that I am still sleepy at many times of the day. I somehow manage to get through the working day, but I am exhausted when I get home.

Some weekends I can't seem to kick off the drowsiness. I can see the problem, and I am hoping to remedy this persistent problem. I am determined to be a father involved in your childhood, but I have not yet managed to do so effectively; I am trying!

After reading newspaper reports of how the property market is going, on 1st April 1990, I decided to put the home back up for sale at £43,995 with a new estate agent. We planned to purchase a house in Steele Road on 1st May for £58,000 and hoped the deal would proceed smoothly. At the same time, we had a buyer for our house who came from outside the area. He had put forward an offer of £41,500, which we accepted. His building society turned down his mortgage application, and it was now the end of June 1990. Our vendor at Steele Road was willing to wait for several months, if need be, for our buyer to obtain a mortgage or until we found another buyer. The date for exchanging contracts was cancelled.

Our buyer eventually obtained a mortgage with his bank. His surveyor found some rising damp and a structural fault that was a severe safety issue. They had to be fixed before the lease would get granted 100%. There was no lintel beam supporting the upper floor. Initially, the living room and the dining room had been separate spaces before being knocked through to make one large room by our previous owner. As a result, the supporting beam was missing, and the upstairs area could collapse at any time. We set another date for exchanging contracts, but on 19th July 1990, the vendors at Steele Road withdrew from their house's sale. Our buyer was not told of this dramatic development but asked if the exchange of contracts date could be moved back by two weeks, making it 24th August 1990.

That left us about four weeks to find our ideal home, making us anxious because our solicitor made it clear that we would have to be out of the house in Bedale Road by noon on the 24th of August.

We viewed various properties in and around the area we wanted to live in, but they were unsuitable or too expensive. A week later, I saw a property advertised by our agent and another agent also. Although it was outside our catchment area, it could be the house or us. On Sunday, after viewing it, I informed our agent that I was almost sure I would like to buy the property. On Monday, I told our agent we would definitely buy the property at Kennet Close at the asking price of £55,000 or less. They appeared to be doing nothing about my request, and I thought someone else might have put in a bid for the property. So, I asked Euphemia to chase it up with the other agent. The other estate agent managed to acquire it for us at £54,000. Lucky for us, the vendor at Kennet Close could be out of the property by the contractual date. Our mortgage for the property came through on 3rd August 1990.

Taking out an endowment policy meant specific health questions the insurance company requested my doctor to answer about me. Since Christmas 1989, I had reduced my medication to twice a day. When I advised my doctor of this, he wasn't alarmed because possibly I looked very well and stable, but he advised me if I intended to reduce it anymore, I must see him first. Children, I know I have the correct dose now because my persistent tiredness is no longer a recurring problem.

Living here in our nearly new modern semi-detached house with a garage in a cul-de-sac is a bit hard on the purse but very rewarding and delightful.

At Kennet Close, we moved to this house on 24th August 1990, ten days before the autumn school term began. We had chosen the school for the children near Steele Road, and Kennet Close was probably about two miles further away. So, we decided not to change schools since the children were already enrolled and had several pre-inductor visits before the summer holidays. The bus service does not run on this fairly new housing estate, and we pre-booked a taxi service to take them to school.

Georgina, you are now old enough to start infant school and Katrina, you will be attending primary school. Georgina attended her school for mornings only until half term in October 1990 and is now going full time. They adapted to school life very well, but I am concerned about Katrina's fear of most imaginary creatures like those on the TV programme Doctor Who. Maybe she muddles dreams and future aspirations. It is an observable fact that we all inhabited a world of fantasy and a world of order experience, and a world of words and concepts. Katrina is discovering human fullness, the fears, the dreams, the aspirations and doubts. Katrina, it's okay to be social with the joys and struggles that this implies. Mum and I have been through similar experiences, and we understand the scariness of horror films.

Children, we humans are parts of the universe and parts of God, who are usually omniscient. You will all learn that God is a pantheistic God, and what God has arranged or arranged and sealed in our nature, education enlightens us in all aspects of this. Culture and your schooling give only a tiny trace of moral teachings. Your God-given gifts and qualities give rise to the essential question of purpose in life, and our human evolution is revealed through consciousness. Providentially, activity comes about in the best way that it can come out because God is good and knows everything.

Through storytelling and television, the world presents to our consciousness what makes fantasy authentic, sometimes more accurate than the given world of sensory impressions and the projected world of words and explained concepts. I had realised imagining may be just seeing pictures in my mind. Some of my learning has been acquired through believing, seeing an image of what is yet to be discovered. Imagine reading what I have written without picturing it or tackling a maths problem without seeing the symbols. Children, do not worry about your fantasising or imagining, but maintain control of these things. Imagery is not only the essential ingredient of all artistic creativity but has also found its place in scientific and mechanical processes. To give you an example, they say that Albert Einstein visualised himself riding through the universe on a beam of light and came up with the relativity theory.

My children, I have taken on another job after full-time work is over at 5:30 pm, packing shelves at a supermarket from 6 pm till 10 pm Monday to Wednesday and Thursday and Friday from 7 pm till 11 pm. It's only temporary until your mum goes back to work. It brings in extra money, and I realise that I hardly see you because I come home late weekdays and work mornings 8 am till noon at weekends at the store since Saturday morning overtime working at the engineering factory has ceased. The twilight shift's latest hours had changed to 9 pm, and the lost hours I made up by working Saturday mornings. Daddy loves you all!

We have enjoyed our first Christmas in our new home, Kennet Close. Today it's the 1st January 1991 - HAPPY NEW YEAR! Children, the media's report for the new year is a gloomy one. Unemployment is rising, international affairs worsen, etc., etc., never again will I get depressed or disillusioned by them. I have no control over those matters, but we do not know what the year has in store for us. My children, do not be troubled about what is insurmountable – you do not deserve to be worried. The older generation has caused it, and in our age, we pray that their attempts to heal the wounds are working. I see hope for the future, a promise of possible things to come; a vibrant extensive vision of how life can be and of what it may become. Children, you must be encouraged to live each new awakening as a creative step in God's unfoldment and a grand opening to the fascinating world in which you find yourself. Learn to respond to the unknowns by being positively cheerful, full of curiosity and excitement.

Dying and Making a Living Will
Written 31st May 1991

One day, it will be my death, and many decisions and arrangements will get made at a time of distress. It has come into my mind at this time because my sister's brother-in-law died on holiday, and, in recent months, friends or people known to me are ill in hospital or have suddenly died.

Since May 1988, I have carried a donor card so that after my death, any part of my body can be used for the treatment of others or my whole body be used for medical research and teaching purposes. I love people, and it's my last ultimate gift of giving. I wish to help someone live a healthier life and prolong their existence on earth by giving my organs. It is my act of love that extends further than family and friends. This donation is for anyone found to be a suitable match. Time on this earth is short, and eternity is eternity, and it's the last thing I can give when my spirit has gone deep into the cosmos, waiting for an encounter with what made creation. If a natural illness caused my death, but the doctors wish to learn more about the cause of death, having a post-mortem examination, the medical school will refuse the body. However, they will accept the body for teaching purposes for up to three years if the only part removed is a cataract in the eye. After that, the medical school advise relatives when the body is available for the funeral.

Cremation is my option of disposing of my remains, and if a cremation certificate was refused because the cause of death was unknown, it should be referred to the coroner. Katrina, Georgina and Jonathan, you may be well into your adult life or young still when I pass this life. It might seem cold and final but take heart.

Let me explain where God fits into dying and how I see the body and brain's death is not the soul and spirit's death. Death is only final in the flesh on this earth. I imagine that when we die, our spirited soul and mind consciousness energies leave our bodies and live on in the fullness of the structure of space. All around, the mortal body perishes as the lively soul leaves. But it can't see or feel the darkness of matter or solar air until it's lit. Then, the light meets with the elements our energy will latch on to guide our waking existence towards the new world.

Bodies are reformed again by the matter in the universe, formed ultimately by a creator. There will be many new worlds; believers in God, repentant souls, and the righteous will find themselves on any of these planetary systems. The unrighteous cannot latch on and will have the final parts of them - the soul and spirit – die when they pass through the element of life, and the whole of their consciousness would be forever dead. Children, it could take millions of years, and during all that time, our spirit will be sleeping or dormant in deep space, and that consciousness may be the underlying reality in the universe.

It experiences a wake-up shake, wobbling the fabric of space when we are formed in the new world. The communication will be so effective that finding all of you on whichever planet, galaxy or universe will be a matter of pure telepathic thought or using ESP technology hardware to reach you. Until one's number is (up) 'called', the existence on this earth we live on now maybe one of suffering or endurance. So far, I may see God as a molecule or something alien, but here on earth, God is a personal God and perceived in the way Jesus Christ portrayed Him.

Children, I love facts and truth, and so far through my life, Jesus Christ remains controversial, and it rests on what one believes about him and his connection with God. Doubts about Jesus and religion are not about the existence of a creator God-

it's more a pessimistic prognostication that something dreadful will happen to humankind in the cosmic plan. I could throw away the Bible or never hear of the life of a man on earth called Jesus Christ. My emotions and thinking mind, my whole being, will let me acknowledge a personal God's existence in the universe, especially here on earth. My mind continues on this journey partly by faith and probability when everything else has been tried so far, and there is no other explanation.

Children, you will come to a point in your life when humanist, realist, moralist, or Darwinist theories will make you wonder, but keep a hold on tested scientific principles and the thoughts of your mind. The world is not built on common-sense bias: do and believe in what makes you happy. Trust in yourself and be confident in yourself. If you decide that you do not believe in God, still, you will live a good life as an intellectual when the developed intellect has given rise to incapacity in the mind that takes one out of the realm of God.

God acknowledges you as you continue to evolve and settle happily without knowing or believing in Him. My faith rests on divine truth, and my imagination conjures eternal bliss.

Children, can you remember what I recorded at the beginning of 1981, about the eye of the media reporting on national and global affairs? Unemployment rising, and international relations worsening! As long as the earth continues to exist in time, it will take almost that number of generations for human greed to be passive and humankind to evolve to eternal bliss. All through my life, unemployment, environmental pollution and the threat of war and wars have existed. These threats put the young in a state of disillusionment with the world. And what adults have done to it. As a result, Young people develop deep fears and unhealthy fantasies. So, children, do not be surprised that the same three things will be the threat of your decade.

The dream of peace on earth and goodwill to all humankind exists in all good people of every generation. You, too, carry that dream into your true selves. The time will come when my death may feel like a sad loss. I'll be going on a journey where the mind will meet with the fresh-minded in the new world on the other side of the universe. Katrina, Georgina and Jonathan, things have a way of working out. It may be in a sad way, but they work out. I am confident that we will meet again in the afterlife amongst all good and God-loving people. The experience you will have because of the death of a loved one may give way to tears. You must endure the extreme grief of bereavement but do not remain in sorrow because we have hope. The promise of a beautiful future is almost scientifically seen and proven by our pure thoughts and imagination. That is because simple ideas, thinking with vision, comes before science can develop proof. We are ahead.

You may draw comfort from the hope of resurrection, that life is not really at an end, and you must continue to live yours to the full on earth first before you too can take part in the afterlife. I shall wait until my relief comes, but it's also sad for me because I have to wait until the law of the universe is ready to act for us to reunite. Children, great sadness is not usually experienced when a dear one goes on a journey, for you expect to see them again. So, the profound grief, the loss of me, whenever that is, may be somewhat lessened if you look upon the death of an ultimate reality truth-searcher Daddy in the same way and write me a letter. Your daddy seeks to find infinite truths, honesty and knowledge through education and faces bias and discrimination. Some of my most profound facts have formed through my experience of trial and error.

Continue in your interests and do not yield to self-pity, but give each other the support you need. The change of circumstances, however bitter, will enable you to draw wisdom and strength from your spirit within. It will supply the power required to ride the grief and come through with tested, strengthened faith. Look after your mother, look after yourselves and look after one another if I die suddenly, and write me a letter so you can say things to me. I do not foresee my life coming to an end or anything like that, as I don't determine when I will leave the earth, so I will continue to write on these pages.

For most of us, death remains a foreign concept. We see a lot of killing on TV, but the actual end, natural death, I saw when I did voluntary work with young people with severe physical disabilities who were not expected to live past their 30th birthday. The body cold, the colour drained from the cheeks, the gaping mouth and the hard, complex waxy texture that comes to the skin remains strangely taboo. When death approaches, we hide it in hospitals and nursing homes. Crematoria landscaped all around to be out of sight, and our funeral parlours are like forbidding places with windows painted out to discourage casual visitors. Death is viewed as a bad thing, but it's not all bad. People generally imagine all ends to be unfortunate, and it's just awful, and there's almost nothing positive to be said about the death of a child. It might sound like a contradiction in terms, but end in later life can be a good thing. Right, in the way that birth, puberty and making love are right. In the sense of natural and inevitable good, right, in the sense that a book can have a good ending – even if it's a tragic one. Death can be appropriate, inspiring and life-affirming, although, as with birth, one needs a bit of luck and a bit of planning to achieve this. I believe in the afterlife and am cheerful about the prospect of my ashes being buried or scattered. I like the idea of re-joining the soil of the earth.

You may not get over the death of your parent but only gradually come to terms with it, and it may take months or years. There is no magical day for a full recovery but resist the temptation to be brave and put on a front. Putting off grieving until later, bottling it up, or false stoicism may cause problems later in life. Each must decide if it will help see my body, and only you can do that: anyone else thinks or does irrelevant. Grief has no normality; anger and relief are reactions when someone you love dies after a long illness, but the shock of sudden death makes people behave strangely. You'll be susceptible to a feeling of rage, helplessness and isolation. Keep family bonds, and do not point the blame for what happened to yourself or anyone else. Hostility towards friends who may step in as parents when Mum and I have gone would be valid in grief, but alcohol and promiscuousness are short-term ways of shutting out pain – and unwise. When anniversaries arrive, loved ones live on in the memory, and by remembering and talking about those you have lost, you are keeping them alive and therefore do not be morbid. Eventually, you will have to let go and get on with life, and as you learn to take responsibility for yourself, it can come as a relief and help you regain control.

I hope to discuss what I have written with you because I do not determine when I will be going to the other side of the universe. I will share in your daily lives and be with your mother, involving myself in your joys and your sorrows. It is doubtless sad that I have gone, died, and you will remember clearly for a while as you are young. Then I will exist only as a memory, already beginning to fade in your mind. It is natural for memories to fade; I hope your recollection of me would never disappear – what I was actually like, how my voice sounded, and how my touch felt would be preserved. I wish to be around for a long, long time, but we cannot always have what we want, and we must prepare for and accept those changes over which we have no control. Some of my most intimate and essential thoughts are in this book which may be as far away as our bookshelf. If I miss anything, ask your mum, who can explain when I have gone.

Don't be angry with me when you need me and I am not there, for I cannot determine my death. I would like nothing more than to be with you all, always. I love you all deeply, and you have given me much happiness. So wherever I am when you take down this book and read it, or when you stumble and fall, know my thoughts are with you, and I'll be smiling and watching on the other side, cheering you on so that you can get up again.

I am making a '**Living Will**', a gift to the family that would spare you all agony at times of acute distress. I direct my physician to withhold or withdraw treatment if I should be in an incurable or irreversible mental or physical illness with no reasonable expectation of recovery. If I am (A) in a terminal condition, (B) permanently unconscious, or (C) if I am minimally conscious but have irreversible brain damage and will never regain the ability to make decisions and express my wishes, I wish to refuse treatments such as cardiac resuscitation (CPR), mechanical respiration, tube feeding, and antibiotics. I do want maximum pain relief, even if it hastens my death. I signed: Karl Lorenz Willett, signature: KL. Willett.

I assure you all that I do not dread death if it seems I want to prolong life when recovery seems slim. I wrote the 'living will' because God will take me by the mind's soul into what lies ahead. Modern theology no longer allows that the soul leaves the body and, after death, flies heavenwards to spend eternity with the Almighty. As you may have noticed, I conceived my theology on these pages that man's (our) consciousness should be called a spiritual soul, entirely separate from the mind's working.

The soul encompasses virtually everything a person values most highly, like the aims and purpose of life, the sense of human solidarity with others, the recognition of the moral dimension of actions and the distinction between good and evil, and an awareness of God. In failing to recognise the spiritual potency in my life, the psychiatrist has committed a grave error believing only drugs will help me. This omission prevented a proper understanding of my behaviour, which reflected a spiritual disturbance in my life. People with a complete absence of guilt, no concern for others' feelings, an inability to form relationships, and a high level of aggression, must, to my mind, have a complete lack of spiritual or moral values. They must be said to have no soul, or the soul is suppressed. The absence of religious values can discern the reality and importance of the human soul that guides and controls our lives. It may not be demonstrable by experiment yet, and it may not float heavenwards at our departing, but it exists.

Since learning quantum information can never be destroyed, some of our essences could live on after death. I think even those of us who rationally reject the idea of an afterlife will have trouble letting go of the opinion that we cease to exist entirely.

Habitually, we can all put ourselves in other people's shoes and imagine their thoughts and feelings, and it can then be hard to believe that those thoughts and feelings can cease to be when ours still feel so real. When our consciousness slips away, the blood has stopped flowing, the muscles cool chilly, and we die. However, the body microbes and organisms rapidly digest flesh, and consciousness leaves a backdoor to an afterlife. I bank on it. We can live on after death. Our physical disappearance happens in burial and instantly at cremation but consciousness and the soul, whatever that is, slip away taking their energy out of the body.

The soul's journey from its bodily home to its union with God can be an unsuccessful spiritual journey due to blame projection and deceit. It is part of the price we pay for educating our consciousness with unfairness, untruthfulness and training the aggression tendency. Therefore, we should all pursue truth even when it seems daunting and complicated. Value honesty and integrity and seek the truth even if the fact exposes us for doing something wrong.

In this earthly life, telling the truth doesn't come naturally; warriors of the truth are fighters to preserve their peace of mind. People need to swallow their pride in their ego, giving an authentic and sincere apology for doing something wrong.

Chance is playing a significant role in keeping the earth fit for life still. The universe is a flowing line of concentrated energy of God, driving the accelerating expansion without end. It flows through space and time regions, and the God particle is a source of matter that exists at a single point without beginning. Waves are living everywhere except at the moments that create them.

My writing is in a virtual national language, English, and the culture I am in has a mythology that the only actual pure language is the Europeans' and all the others are corrupt. The origins of how I speak in my writing are even a little comical if anyone has studied it. English is known as the language of literature, but my comments don't quite follow my thoughts. It can be poetic and brutal to clarify terms to express the truth well because it is not lucid and may be seen as telling fantasies falsehoods.

I have found a different way of speaking English, similar to other prestigious speakers, like bishops and the elite. They had crazy ideas about the English language. They authorised the critical structures in English to be legislated that dictate how we are supposed to speak, breaking human language rules in us. It, therefore, has to be taught over and over again in school. Nobody actually teaches a person's language; the language grows inside our heads. The invented English is artificial and does not match the speaker's very own representations. Decoding the speech we heard must be converted closer to listening to our inner interpretation, where speaking differs. I have avoided writing in black English; it's considered not quite proper English. English has an inevitable dominance and is appealing in every stage of history's language, and attitudes established the British English speaking as pure. Conquering groups or a wealthy group or priestly caste were considered good English-speakers, and others were wrong. Writing has rules that are taught that say lousy grammar and terrible grammar are literary language errors. Still, the academic standard in English is not so radically different from what is learned in the street because it has some principles associated with it.

This month of May 1991, there has been a massive explosion in my head, releasing these thoughts and ideas. From the very beginning of this 'big bang' on hearing of the sudden death of my brother-in-law, aged 29, I yearn to write while inspiration pulses the nerves in my fingers. My mind had become saturated with thoughts about life, death, justice and unknowns. I reached the pinnacle of imagination and at the limits of my understanding which were entirely absorbent and meditative. I had wacky ideas that could lead to progress or be a stumbling block to the world's correct knowledge, space, and time.

The Twilight Shift 1990 and Phenomenon flashback
Written Saturday 8th June 1991 – 20th October 1991

I had accurately calculated that we could manage, just, on my wages and child benefits. There is nothing extra, though – only paying bills, buying shopping, and buying some presents for birthdays and Christmas in 1990.

Things would change when Euphemia started a suitable part-time job. No employer would consider her now, with a child under five, not even ready for nursery.

It was in early October 1990 when I saw an advertisement in a supermarket for twilight shift workers. The job involved stacking shelves and helping load and unload the lifts, from 6 pm till 10 pm, Monday to Wednesday and 7 pm until 11 pm, Thursday and Friday. Nothing but more money in my pocket entered my head. Euphemia asked me, "How can you do this job? When you get home from the engineering factory, you fall asleep on the settee! In the morning, you can't get up early enough to have breakfast. You would not see the children all week". I said it would be alright. The drive for more money to buy luxuries for the new house was enough to make me think I could work at least until February 1991, when Jonathan is two years old, and Mum could go out to work.

Leaving the factory at 5:30 pm, I travelled to the supermarket by bicycle and arrived at 5:50 pm. I was like a powerhouse that seemed to produce limitless energy because even after the twilight shift, I felt so good - my whole being was on a high. I did not feel sleepy or exhausted at night; I lay in bed until my eyelids closed in the early hours, at around 2:30 am most weekdays. By 7 am, I was awake, and my stamina kept me going for another 19-hour working day. It seemed there was to be no let-up. I kept this up until Christmas, and it was then my brain became exhausted. I went on against all the odds because I needed the money, I told myself. Money, money – it was impossible now to do without this extra cash. The foreman at the factory informed me that my work and efficiency standard had fallen, and I used to do better. A lad at the factory, no older than me, had two jobs with even longer hours than mine, and his energy level remained high, mentally and physically, and he copes with the work. When we took our breaks, he relaxed and alert and dealt well with the factory workers. What's wrong with me? I should be able to do the same!

The hours on the twilight shift had changed in the New Year 1991. The latest finishing time was 9 pm, and I made up the reduced hours by working Saturday mornings. What's wrong with me? Have I not learnt anything about myself? The second job resulted in a decline in the day job's performance, but I still stuck to both tasks, even though high efficiency is required. I was dead tired and breaking up in body and mind – why did I continue to stress myself in this way, in denial of my interior signals? It was terrible. Each day at the factory, evidence of brain tiredness and physical fatigue became paramount. I made a big mistake, and I should have left the evening job, but I could not.

One day at the factory, I made blunders on a well-explained and straightforward piece of work. The part had to be scrapped. Foreman Steven said something to me most calmly and sympathetically that caused my blood to rush and my heart to pound like it would burst from my chest. This sudden physical panic made me realise I needed to pack in the second job.

His message came as though God was using this person to bring me to my senses and finally stop me from overdoing things. Steven said, "Karl, after all – it's only money. I am not telling you how to live your life, but it really is only money. You're not being threatened with dismissal, but you must think about your work here. I know you can do better."

Instantly, I was in a casualty emergency mode; every conceivable nerve ending in my brain was tingling, and my heartfelt like it had been brutally punched. The urgency to do something about it was incredible, like a panic attack. I gave in my notice that evening at the supermarket, to finish on 23rd February 1991. The slowest and longest week of my life was working my notice. I felt I could not go on to the end of the week. I was living in a constant state of emergency. I told the store manager I wanted to leave right away and not work the notice. He explained that I'd lose out a lot if I did that because of the PAYE tax system. At my day job, I told foreman Steve, - "I will be taking time off work to rest because for four months I have been going to bed at 2 am since taking on the evening job, and I am exhausted. I need to rest so that I stop making silly mistakes," Steve replied, "There is no one else to do your job. If you go, it will be there when you come back and more. I'll be here to support you through the challenges you may now have with the work". Steve was five years younger than me.

Why do I go to the limits of my human frailty? I am not a fool, but there is no difference by not acting on what I had learned about myself from the great teacher, experience. I am a product of my own life experiences and a victim of the hard way I learn. Today is Saturday 8th June 1991, and I have come through that stressful period, October 1990 to February 1991, when holding down two jobs.

June 8th. It's now four months since packing up the supermarket job, and the standard of my work at the factory is disappointing. I am not motivated, nor do I feel I am skilled enough to continue working as a miller, and I skived on the job, staying in the toilet to write notes and take naps; I had unofficial breaks and would walk around the building.

I found this note among the hand-written journal pages when I came to write in it, and I have it in front of me. I am not sure when it was written, but I suspect it was in May or June 1991. The note says:

I love people and care about the environment, and I work in the engineering industry. The end product of my labour gives satisfaction but without fulfilment. I am looking at my life and my purpose. My innermost desire is challenging me to move into a job that brings rewards to my heart's most eternal quest; to help in caring for others and exercise my love for people. My mind has begun wondering, resulting in needless mistakes and poor performance in a career that supplies me with good money and honest living. I feel I am cheating my employer, but I am trying to do a good job. My doubts and absent-mindedness make me fail miserably sometimes. I have to answer whether to take further training in engineering skills and become brilliant at it or train for social work and satisfy a quest, so I can say I am glad I had a go. The chemistry within me is mighty powerful, and it's streaming through me like an electric current. It's going directly to the source that makes the decisions. I am anxious now to start evening classes at the college in this autumn term (1991) and continue with my engineering career, at which I will always try and do my best.

After failings in my work on 17th June 1991 at 10:30 am, when machining a job went wrong, I tried a new piece of steel again. The iron material I had machined was continually undersized. I kept making silly mistakes; I should not continue scrapping the firm's new components. The foreman has been helpful, but I could not be bothered to tell him I had blundered, yet again. I thought my absent-mindedness would eventually get me the sack. I had to find time to think things out. I wrote a note on a piece of paper; "The job is wrong again, and I have gone home to think about my future with the firm, Karl". I left it on my vertical milling machine, walked out of the workshop and off the premises.

The work manager phoned me at home and called me back to discuss the crisis. I let him know that I found myself unable to do the job I was employed to do effectively, and I considered packing it in and taking up social work. However, I had spoiled so much of the firm's material that I felt I had to go. The manager said my job was safe at the factory, and there was a touch of humour in leaving the note on the machine. If I returned to work immediately after the discussion, I would receive full pay for the day doing a less demanding job. He thought I was taking an extreme view of a matter that was not that important.

I stayed the afternoon on a different job, more straightforward, tapping holes using a hand tool and some work requiring a tapping machine. By coincidence, Euphemia had started work that same day with her former employer. So when we got home that evening, Euphemia and you, the children, were involved in my final decision to stay on at the factory.

In my first job after leaving school, I was told as an apprentice toolmaker going through a crisis that the company was not a charity, and they were in business to make profits and achieve productivity.

I am happy to have found a company that does not come down on me like a ton of bricks when my problems are spoiling my performance.

The two nervous psychotic breakdowns in 1985 convinced me that some phenomenal supernatural force of energy existed within the inner self's framework and not outside oneself. Yes, not outside ourselves. I believe it strongly; I know for sure. The mind invented the phenomenon when the brain is too stressed and used faulty subconscious motor movements that operate automatically below awareness. Pure energy goes to body parts, but 'criticising systems' in my mind and body were in disarray. I also think my frightening unexpected body impulses and terrible dreams may be responsible for my weird feeling when it seemed like paranormal activity changed the environment six years ago. In 1985, I took those paranormal activities to be what my faulty neuron connections translated to my mind as a supernatural intervention. Since then, my mind has been in flux, and when the 'big bang' in May 1991 released some more odd thoughts and ideas, I became puzzled and confused about what was coming out of my head.

I still remember the phenomenon of 1985 vividly and pick up my pen to write them down accurately.

I had stopped sleeping in the marital bed because I was feeling weird. I first stopped cuddling my wife in bed because I had no control over impulses that worked my body, and I was afraid my arms might fold involuntary and cause my wife harm. Katrina was aged about two years and seven months; she was moved out of the second bedroom and put in with Euphemia, so I moved into the spare room. Something seemed to be present in there - I sensed things buzzing through switches and sockets, a hissing continuously all around, and the air felt cold in the room on a warm summer's day. It was the first unexplained weird incident.

On a late summer's evening in July, when it was still light outside, I lay on top of the bedsheets, and it happened. Not an apparition, just a strong feeling that something was affecting me, and there was something calm in the room. Looking out from behind my closed eyelids, I saw pitch blackness with tints of redness, and I quivered in the warmth. I felt I had been lifted slightly off the bed, and after the spirit of what I 'sensed' had returned, I quickly opened my eyes and began to jump all over the bed with my hands in motion, flapping and shouting out, "I am flying! I can fly!" I continued to shout and dance, using the bed as a trampoline until Euphemia came into the room and told me to stop that. "Stop being silly and get down off the bed!" I froze, my body stiff, and it was as if I became fully conscious. I knew what had happened, but it did not make sense that my body worked without conscious effort. That was a shock. It was frightening but yet intrigued me. Euphemia sat on the edge of the bed and talked to me. I stood in the middle of the floor. "The bed is tipping - it's leaning", she said. I thought I understood what she said, but I looked and saw no tilt or lift. My conscious mind did not process the word 'leaning' accurately.

It made me think I might be losing my mind because Euphemia said she would stay no longer in the room because she felt funny. That worried me, Euphemia being about seven months pregnant with our second child.

I hoped to God that nothing would hurt her or our baby. I sat on the bed, and gradually I turned myself toward the window. The top quarter was hinged partially opened. Again, it seemed something tranquil and of peace that I could not see but sensed, left my being and floated straight through the window pane and into the redness of the late evening sky. There were times in the night when I closed my eyes and looked behind my eyelids and again saw creepy crawling creatures. I had also sensed that I was travelling through time and space, seeing stars and clusters of stars as I whizzed through the universe, seeing those creatures that were an apparition under my eyelids as I drifted off to sleep.

I went into the hospital voluntarily and returned feeling normal and a realist. I went back to sleep in the double bed but thought it wasn't right to cuddle my wife when she was asleep. We could fall asleep together, holding hands, or I could turn my back to her for safety reasons.

Euphemia can recall dramatic events that seemed unworldly, but you must believe her, too, because she saw things from a rational perspective. My mental instability was unbelievably terrifying for Euphemia, and I hope she can tell the stories before they fade from her memory.

I had a second hospital admission about seven to eight weeks after the last one, August to early September 1985, when I was sectioned under the Mental Health Act. I had to leave our bed again and stay in the spare bedroom because I felt weird; thoughts were jumping in and out of my head, and everyday things took on a sinister appearance. I could look at still pictures, sequences of changing scenes and evolving faces in family portraits. Looking into mirrors or seeing my reflection anywhere was uncomfortable. I could not tell it was me because the face was distorted and changeable. I believed I could experience remote viewing of places by just closing my eyes. I knew where my wife and child were in town when they went shopping and the people they met. It was extraordinary. I was also predicting who would call at the door – my relatives or Euphemia's. Having this sense of remote viewing allowed me to know what was happening in the community, so I didn't need to leave the house. Over a short time, I neglected my appearance, had poor hygiene, and repeatedly wore the same clothes. I didn't comb my hair or shave, and I developed poor mental images of what was happening around me. A thought jumped into my head to get rid of the full-length standing mirror in the main bedroom. Euphemia was downstairs, and my mother had Katrina at her house.

On that day, I brought terror into the life of my pregnant wife, who believed she had to run for her life when I took the heavy framed mirror from the bedroom and lamely strolled along the landing, calling to Euphemia to tell her I was getting rid of the mirror. Before I could, Euphemia called out at the bottom of the stairs, "Karl, what are you doing with that mirror?" I was at the top step, and the mirror slipped out of my hands and careering down fourteen steps and smashed into pieces. Thank God she was not hurt, but the noise it made was horrendous. I came downstairs and went to the kitchen to get a pan and brush to clean up the mess, and Euphemia carefully stepped through the broken glass and went upstairs.

Meanwhile, I was scratching my head, and voices were saying, "What have you done? You nearly killed her. Put a knife into the electric socket and kill yourself." The voices grew louder in my head, but it seemed my ears were picking up the sound telepathically, out there in the air from somebody. "Take a knife and put it into the electric socket and kill yourself." I took all the knives and cutlery out of the kitchen drawer and hurried to the hallway, shouting, "No! No! No!" I then threw the blades at the front door. I went back into the kitchen, and the voices told me where the large kitchen knives were and that I must put them into the electric socket and kill myself. I carefully held the handles of the cooking knives and went to throw them beside the door.

I met Euphemia as she was opening the front door. She had already stepped over a load of broken glass and the messy obstacle of scattered knives and cutlery. She screamed when she noticed I was carrying the shipment of big knives. I shouted, "No! No, No!" Euphemia ran from the house, leaving the door open. I dropped the knives, closed the door and locked it. Euphemia had run to the doctor's surgery around the corner in the next street. A doctor and a psychiatrist came to the house, trying to persuade me to open the door. I refused and demanded to see my mother and dad. Finally, I opened the door when I heard their voices at the door. I broke down crying profusely and went into the hospital.

After the spell in the hospital, twenty-eight days, I returned home feeling normal. Katrina went back to her room but found it difficult to sleep and cried out that she was falling off the bed and was frightened by it. We separated the bunk beds in the third bedroom, putting one single in the main bedroom. Georgina, now born, her cot was situated at the end of our bed. I went back and slept in the other room to see if I would experience any strange phenomenal forces acting up. As I stood in the place where I had felt as if I was turning, then spinning gradually and experiencing a feeling of sickness in the pit of my stomach, I found that didn't happen, nor did I experience any apparitions. I asked Euphemia to see if she again felt funny in the room. She recalled taking an afternoon nap in there when the bed leaned inwards, and she had to hold on to the side of the bed for balance. We decided to completely redecorate the room and move the bed to the opposite wall.

Since doing so, nothing sinister has happened ever again. I have slept like a log many times since we rearranged the room, and Euphemia finds it is okay. Katrina went back to the second bedroom when Georgina was at the end of her infancy, and they both slept peacefully in that room until we moved house.

Our Son Asthmatic Attack
Written in October 1991

On 29th July 1991, I took the family on a coach trip to the seaside, in the summer holiday. We had a wonderful time. Unfortunately, on the return journey, two-year-old Jonathan became asthmatic. By the time we reached home, his condition had worsened, so I had called the doctor, who decided to hospitalise him. It was sad and moving to see innocent children suffering in that place, and I felt very emotional.

The crimes nature had committed against them, such as brain tumours, epilepsy, and asthma, were treated in a loving, caring environment alongside some medical blunders. Being with our son and the other children on the ward caused me to want to give something to keep the children happy, smiling and responsive. They responded positively to me because I made them laugh.

Two days on, Jonathan was well enough to leave the hospital, and I felt sad for the other children, so courageous, fighting their illnesses. I left a message for their parents to contact me if they wanted me to continue entertaining their children. None did, but I was partly pleased with that because it would have meant a dramatic change in our lives. To travel by transport to and from the hospital when public transport is sketchy would have posed a problem! I continued to hold these children in my thoughts because they had captured the spirit in my heart.

I am helping the children and their parents in the only way I can now by praying occasionally and wishing them the very best for the future.

When I spent those two days with our son in the hospital, my interaction with most children in the ward reminded me of my days of volunteering with young, physically disabled people in a residential home. I met up with one of the residents a year ago, and we have kept in touch ever since. I was volunteering alongside my day job before my marriage and family commitments. I gathered courage and strength from those people with a handicap. When the bottom seems to be falling out of my world or desires were hard to curb, I love the person and hate the disability. They tugged me with love and kindness and challenged me to reform my little prejudices.

I admire them and their sheer fight for ridding fear and preconceived ideas the non-disabled have about them.

The real handicap is in the mind of the non-disabled, whose prejudices and fear prevent them from seeing the whole person.

I know handicap is a part of the world order; it does not imply that they are suffering or have a low quality of life. On the contrary, they radiate the greatest quality one can show to another human being, and they enrich nations with this unselfish love. Therefore, society should learn from this small community not to discriminate and understand how to live a just life, loving each other.

The other cheek
Written in October 1991

Halfway through my working life, I have maintained a spotless ethical conduct record through hard work and honesty. However, it was all shattered in less than a minute of extreme frustration caused by workmates provoking me.

On Friday 13th September 1991, workmates were horsing around, and as I sat on the loo, someone threw a cup of water over me. Later, they rolled adhesive tape in a ball and threw it at me while I operated machinery. I always warned those I suspected of doing it, telling them of the dangers of such foolish behaviour, but they continued to attack me and denied any involvement.

My resistance broke down when a half-rotten apple hit me on the side of my head as I was working a milling machine. In a fit of pent-up anger, I immediately squared up to the person I believed had thrown the apple and slapped him hard across the face. He had an ear stud, and the ear lobe bled a little. I had lashed out, and my actions were reported to the foreman, Steven, and then to the work's manager. I had nearly fifteen years working in the industry with a clean slate, and now I earned a black mark against my character. I had survived hostilities, discrimination, previous provocation, and verbal abuse at various workplaces, but never in a million years was an affray my usual response to a workmate's insensibility. I took disciplinary action very hard. It is because I am a man of peace, discipline and order, a man of honesty, worthy of being trusted. I believe that I'm a man of conscience, and here I was, questioning my values and what made me, me.

Following a hearing at midday on that Friday, the manager sent me home immediately. On Monday morning, I was called to the office where the manager read out and explained the firm's misconduct policy and handed me a final written warning. The person I slapped also received a final written notification. He had admitted throwing the apple, and workers near the incident told the foreman they saw the whole thing. Two other workers also received written warnings.

Some factory workers believed I was victimized, and others thought it was the only action the company could take. I knew I'd be for the high jump, as they say, but this sort of conduct went on in the factory most of the time, alongside mindless vandalism of company property. So I did what I did to bring attention to a problem that was going on unchecked. – "You are here to work; do your work, and that's all that is expected of you. If you have a problem, see Steven or me; I am not a social worker," said the manager.

I would tell him that I had never seen such stupid horseplay in my years of working and that this was going unchecked, including vandalism, but I did not. It seemed like only the so-called 'affray' was punishable, and both culprits had to pay. I had been involved in a confrontation with this same lad before in full view of the foreman. I don't know why he disliked me and wanted me to go outside and settle things, but that time I just said my piece and walked away. To me, the foreman seemed not to know what to do in a situation regarding discipline. He was a brilliant foreman in most ways, but he failed, not knowing what to do without training in managing workplace bullying. The workmates who saw the incident suggested to the lad that his behaviour was uncalled for and that he should apologise to me for what he had done, but he never did.

What is the trouble with us?

Written in October 1991

Love, from all its precious facets, radiated through our home and family. Or so I thought. No one could say that we were not close or that our marriage was unhappy. After an argument over money, I was shocked to realise the relationship seemed to have broken down. Each accused the other of not caring and taking them for granted. Feeling upset, I was looking for reasons to blame, and without thinking, I said I didn't care.

Discussing problems to do with money is taboo. It put a division between us, which I had never known before. Even telling Euphemia to be more thoughtful caused an outburst, with accusations that I found fault with her and was no longer in love with her. I knew all of it to be untrue, but I could see her reasoning as a form of selfishness.

My feelings for Euphemia run more in-depth than any ocean, are as immovable as any mountains, and as vast as the universe.

I had asked her to show a little more practical expression of her love for me, and I said that in what I thought was a loving relationship that could stand criticism after nearly ten years of intimate living together. But, unfortunately, the freedom to spend more money since going back to work seemed to have led Euphemia to slave for riches rather than putting her family's needs first. So on the night of 6th September 1991, it looked like our marriage was over.

In sadness, I walked out of the house after the argument and went to see my eldest sister, Constance, to talk it over with her, and returned home in the early morning. The careless attitude Euphemia was taking on since the argument about our relationship and the home was appalling, and it was scary times. I soon felt the children would sense something was wrong between them and us, unable to see our adult problem was not about them, and they would become troubled. So I contacted Euphemia's eldest brother, and I asked him to talk to her to help restore communication and not let her throw away nearly ten years of happiness and care over money. I began to remember when the powerful feelings welled up in my heart during the days and weeks after our first child's birth. I pondered over the beginning of that new life and our other two children who followed. The children our inheritance can only be brought up successfully with us being happily married, and I feared that the bottom was dropping out of this world. Why can't I say what I like and feel about my partner on any matter that is the talk of the day, without her terrible feeling lasting forever? When she felt hurt, or we couldn't agree, we should make up. I'd say sorry but still recognise our differences. Our marriage's downturn could only be brought back up if deep love still existed between the two of us.

I question what Darling really wants and what she truly holds for me. Does Euphemia like me, our children and our home life, or a new relationship? She does not seem to know when she is better off, lucky or loved. I trust she will come to see where her most enormous riches are.

At the height of the discord, my sleep pattern was in disarray. My insides could not settle. Two to three times in the night, I needed the bathroom. There was a terrible tension in my grumbling stomach. My gut was in mourning, and it felt like I would suffer a loss. I wanted to hold on to my love, but I would have to let go and get over the hurt in time if she did not love me any longer. I was powerless to stop my body and mind from acting up. It was a reaction to my worst nightmare, the worry of my wife leaving me.

I cannot be without her, playing her part in my life and being part of it, for good or indifference. I love her very much. Instead, I would rather never mention the things that play on her nerves than go through the pain of my love walking out on us. Things are not much better a month on; Euphemia is not cooperating, and she is causing living with her to be demanding most of the time. Today, 24th October, is our tenth wedding anniversary, and I wrote on the gift box containing a half eternity ring, "Darling, we've been going through some challenging times in our relationship lately. Please accept this gift as continued devotion to my eternal love for you, and I hope that we'll grow happier. Ever-loving, Karl." I received a stunning gold-plated watch from my love and a card that indicated that Darling is committed to mutual respect and loves me still. The marital road that seemed to have met a crossroads, where we were beginning to travel separate ways, has become straight again with today's little romance. I trust we will be together for the rest of our lives and enjoy each other even more.

Euphemia told me she talked to the Catholic priest in the past week about our marriage and was advised to attend Relate's marriage guidance counselling service. I was glad that she had taken this step, wanting the relationship to work, and had done something about it. What was happening to us? We were committed to making the relationship work and to having excellent communication again. It combined with understanding and support, would, I was sure, build a very successful family life again. Euphemia felt that she had to get to know me all over again. Bless her! But was I too paranoid, reading her intents and feelings out of proportion, and became excessively worried that it may lead to an awful outcome, that she would leave me? But thank God, we were in the 'light' of maintaining a healthy relationship to keep us all happy.

The situation with your mum and me has improved. I am trying hard not to bring up issues or create conditions that may cause quarrels or demands. When she is not pleased with me, I do not comment, or I say very little. I want to keep the peace. Things have happened that prompted me to pray inside my head many a time. I cannot explain why I saw my marriage had come to an end, when in fact, we had made up. I keep going back to the same disagreement, and I cannot believe that she, too, is committed to the relationship. I have been as much to blame for past conflicts as my love, who was tangoing with me.

I had comforted you, children, when you needed it, and whatever you desired, I tried to do or give. At the height of the dispute, we had lived in the house like strangers. We were well distant in the bedroom, and I continued to play the game the way I felt my love was doing to me – but was it a delusion? It was painful. I thought I could no longer act out this sort of unkindness with three small children in our care. It was hurtful when I watched my love stray from what I thought was the norm for a loving couple with children. I believed I was making subtle changes to reconcile, but the problem was I had a faulty perception of how things were, so Euphemia did not recognise my attempts. The way I see this standoff, I cannot be sure I was deluded because it looked like things were going wrong continuously and the making up seemed faulty. I couldn't make any proper sense of the situation. On the night of 14th December 1991, my inner emotions ruptured and burst in the early hours of the morning. Tears fell from my eyes as I looked at our wedding pictures over and over before going to bed. The weeping developed into bawling as I remembered the early years. "Why can't it be like that anymore?" I asked myself. I felt threatened that the marriage was over because we were letting things slide, but I could not go on this freeway and see our relationship smashing up. Each morning at the factory, I wondered if my pretend thick skin would break down and expose my family difficulties, affecting my work performance once again.

I really cannot carry hate or dislike in the same part of me as love, and I cannot be in such a conflict. I take no other vessel than the one I have with my Darling, and it is filled with the goodness I see in her and the richness she has given my life. I have gone back to the beginning of our relationship by living on past happiness to ease the present moment's misery.

On 22nd October 1991, your mum and I spoke to the psychiatrist at the Radcliffe Psychiatric Clinic. They checked how I was getting on and informed us of the progress of the disease. I was to be followed up and seen by a psychiatrist once a year, but it has been four years since I last saw one. For the first time, I was told my illness was paranoid schizophrenia. The doctor sent me leaflets about schizophrenic conditions, and the subject was generally becoming more talked about, probably because one in ten people had the disease. The government's policy of closing mental hospitals has exacerbated mentally ill people's problems before providing adequate alternative care in the community. My psychiatrist said the illness was a battlefield for experts, with muddied, conflicting and unproven ideologies. In my case, he believed the mental illness was due to a biochemical imbalance in my brain. Some considered it a response to deprivation and the demands of modern society. The truth probably lies between the two schools of thought – where genetic vulnerability and emotional and social pressures meet.

Children, information may be a poor substitute for a cure, but I firmly believe that it can go a long way towards reviving the will to win against stigma and secrecy. It provides a voice of comfort and reason in a world where liberal ideas about dealing with mentally ill people have failed, and commonly misconceived myths abound for people to turn to and call one mad. At one time, I did not know schizophrenia was so widespread. It is affecting 55 million people worldwide, between the ages of 19 and 25. It is undoubtedly sad that the illness strikes and makes one lose one's grasp on reality at a stage when one is looking to and striving towards personal goals and commitments.

My first attack of the illness was in that age range, too. Throughout the years of enduring sickness, I have been writing. I have brought to the surface the sadness and what can be a paralysing fear. I wrote so that nothing became buried in my daily existence, living with the schizophrenic condition.

I can successfully fight back to believe that the drug will ease the internal discord and suppress the devastating paranoia until an antidote is found. I am operating conventionally, still taking medicine daily. Yet, at the back of my mind, I am aware that my ideas may be considered as springing from a suffering schizophrenic mind, even when I am healthy and sane. I value my independence, and I don't need monitoring by social workers, psychiatric nurses, or attending out-patient clinics very often. I am free to see my GP, who will give support, and the NHS can take over if it comes to that, to ease my family's worries.

If you have a mental condition, being treated as a normal human being is still not the norm. Society must stop treating all mentally ill as inadequate people and provide them hostels or sheltered housing. I am no longer fighting a daily battle against the disease, as I was in the nineteen-eighties.

I think my stubborn courage ultimately made me triumph over living inside a contemporary artificial realism. The doctors told me that the medication dose I am taking is the minimum required to maintain relative stability. Reduced any further, it could draw back the chemical curtain and expose schizophrenia to reveal another journey through madness, when I would fall prey to the illness again.

Children, the closest and most accurate way to describe how the sickness acted on me is that it was more like a separation from the real world, a fragmentation of thoughts and perceptions. It radically changed the whole of my personality, not a Jekyll and Hyde syndrome. One still retained a common sense so that family, experts and friends talked to me, allowing me to trust them so that I could believe in the sane and remain in it. I was overwhelmed by inner torment, but I retained the insight to search for rational symbols to express the real world I left while being bombarded with irrational thoughts and worries about things I had no control over. At the start of this book, the first intention was to help the family understand the dilemma and then inform the world about the experiences and spread awareness. This book, I feel, could reach through the isolation of sufferers against stigma, secrecy and the onslaught of mental illness. There is a need to persuade the outside world that schizophrenia is an illness imposed on a rational, reasonable person like any other disease. I have made this my quest. I had entered those outposts of my mind that I described in some earlier pages as weird, feared and scary. People reading my universal emotions and anxieties may see the tragedy of schizophrenia.

When I am not in the grip of the illness, I am a rational and intelligent person. In a way, I am a textbook example of care in the community, with a sort of cure. I have achieved my independence but could, if I choose to, see a consultant psychiatrist. I regularly pick up repeat prescriptions from the GP, and he can help while being careful not to intervene, leaving full responsibility with me. This way suits me fine, although it assumes that I would be willing and able to seek help when I need it. Unfortunately, the mental illness's same symptoms – the delusions, the paranoia and the pride – might prevent me from asking for the help I desperately need when I am somehow conscious that I am ill.

How I met your mum
Written 28th December 1991

I came to a crossroads in my life. I was suffering from conflicts. Should I continue to realise that I desire to serve God full-time as a pioneer, with a loving wife to help me maintain my courage and faith to preach the good news of Jesus Christ? Or should I be an ordinary man doing a regular job, carry my faith and not interfere with other people's beliefs, party like everyone else and not think of the consequences? On the other hand, should I live like the majority of the population, happy to go to work, aim to marry and bring up a family? I was unsure of what to do, and I sat on the fence until I was forced to go one way or the other.

I had been enjoying pioneering God's work by taking part in open-air meetings and services with a local black-led church and its sister churches in other counties and cities. I made religious sketches on cardboard and was a one-person activist in Christ's message. I travelled by train to Birmingham, the second biggest city in England, to preach away from home. My aunt and daughter, cousin Lorna, who lives in Birmingham, went shopping and saw me walking around the city, preaching. I stopped outside the Bullring Shopping Centre, displayed the posters near Saint Martin's parish church, and began my work. Any opportunity I had to talk about the work of the Bible, I did.

My baptism took place in the church pool, and my family came to support me in becoming a born-again Christian. At college and in the worldly youth clubs, I strived to convert the young to follow Christ's way. I was a youth myself, aged between 17 and 19 years old, and I took up volunteering work alongside my day job as an apprentice toolmaker. I helped out once a week at a play centre for children with learning difficulties. Each week, I helped inmates come to Christ at the local Youth Custody Centre and worked at a home for physically disabled young adults. Every Sunday afternoon before the evening service, I would go to the parks and talk to the young people and children, discussing Jesus Christ with them.

I rose in the church and was appointed youth leader. Both young and old seemed to admire me. The elders saw me as a fine young man who could go far in promoting the work of God, and most of the young ladies took a shine to me. For a long time, I had no genuine interest in being in love with a girl. I had formed friendships with girls, but that was as far as I wanted it to go. Then, a thought suddenly came out of nowhere – as I struggled with conflicts, it would be better if I had a partner who wanted to do the work of God with me. So I prayed in earnest, asking God to let me meet the lady who would eventually be my bride and become spiritually mature to take the word of Jesus Christ to the world. I prayed in isolation in my bedroom, and at other times I would ride my motorbike in the evenings and stop at deserted places like a lay-by, where I would look up at the evening sky and pray till nightfall.

I was aware of the approaching church convention service to be held in the community centre. I prayed to believe that I would meet the lady who would be blessed to support me in taking the gospel to communities throughout Britain. I went to the service with a confident glow spreading from the pit of my stomach and my mind wondering if it's possible to fall in love at first sight. I sat down among the large congregation and began to look around the hall for my potential mate. Finally, the distinguished speakers took their seats on the platform.

One of them was a young lady, and every time I looked at her, I had a warm feeling that mingled with the vibrant glow in my stomach. Unfortunately, her eyes were never on me, and I was too far away from the platform. I continued having a good look around the room to see if I had missed any potential partner. Then, my eyes focused on the stage again. Delightful feelings and the bright fairies played with my insides, warming my heart, too. I had fallen in love at first sight, and like magic, my eyes opened wide and remained so fixated on her. The service took second place.

At the end of the service, everyone lingered. Finally, it was time for me to meet the lady my gut, heart, head, and eyes had selected. At that time, the youth leader was a girl, and she introduced me to the lady I believed was God's choice for me. Her name was Floretta. She was very friendly and had a pleasant personality. She gave no inclination that she had felt anything for me, and I acted as normal as I could. As I talked to her, I liked her more and more. I tried not to show my feelings, but my hand felt clammy when I shook her hand, and my eyes still seemed wide open. My heart beat faster, and I was flushed, my face blushing so that I was sure people could tell I fancied her as if I were saying aloud, "I'm in love!" That night, I prayed and thanked God, and by day and night, I dreamed of our next meeting. Each day, I counted down to the date of the next convention.

During every conference, we met and talked. Church elders and others in the churches were wondering if there was a romance going on. Floretta told me that she lived in Wolverhampton and had a call to be a missionary and travel to Africa.

I thought, "Bingo!" or something similar, and she told me that she was studying at the Nazarene Bible College. I am no longer sure what part of the country it is in, but I think it was Manchester. Love flourished between us, and even in my tiredness, I would phone her at the college or send her love letters with heart-warming thoughts and passages from the Bible, usually taken from Psalms or Proverbs.

I visited Floretta at the Bible College, and we fell really in love. We talked about the beauty of a loving kiss and our innocence to intimacy and that one day we'd be married. I visited her at her home when she was on a half-term break. Her mother and stepdad went out for the day. Floretta cooked a lovely candlelit dinner, and the evening was romantic, and I presented her with a musical vanity case.

She wrote to me many times and phoned, mentioning her hope to finish college and of us being together. Floretta visited me and met my parents and my sisters. I think my family liked her; she was intelligent, educated, lovely, and good-looking. She carried herself like a fine lady. Everyone was pleased.

I began to get ill at some point. I will record the incident, but I do not remember the exact order of the events. I had become more active in organising events for the children and the young people in the church as a youth leader, but they would not cooperate in the way I expected them to. The pastor seemed to be having a race with me when I declared to the church that my conviction was to go to Bible College. He began preparing his way to go, too. At the same time, the pastor's wife and others who were the elders considered me a threat. I could not believe what they were saying and thought I could make them see I was no such thing, only there to learn and find the truth. My family told me to leave that church, but I had my girlfriend there, who I loved. So I was not prepared to do anything but stay. At the same time, I had to concentrate more on college and at work. It may have been my final year at college, and my job was more technical and challenging. I had to do better than a past grade of the type of engineering I was doing. I needed a credit or distinction pass in the exam, or I would lose the job.

The concentration I needed to produce good quality and accurate work was sliding because all areas of my life had high stressors that retained my motivation, I thought. I attended a seminar held at the Bible College, and the pastor also came along. The first realisation I had was getting educated to have a good English language standard. I enrolled in evening classes at the local technical college to study 'O' level English. As the lecturer spoke, I was feeling angry and furious that there are things that the educators are not telling the people and the ordained ministers are not telling the parishes or congregations. It is part truth they are preaching to the people, only telling them what they want to hear, speaking down to them on a naïve level.

They suppress their black brothers and sisters, not preaching theology and not speaking the gospel truth about Christianity. I felt a substantial challenge at first, a gut reaction to what I heard the lecturer said. I wanted to preach the truth, the whole truth, but I realised having an 'O' level in the English language was essential to gain entry to the college. Then it hit me. It seemed like it must all be common sense. If people are not superstitious and the myths, legends and fairy tales are taken away, believing in God is as natural as having an appetite. People ought to know about theology and make decisions based on the existence of a Creator.

My family told me I was taking on too much and must drop some of what I was doing. I told them I had people depending on me, from my volunteering work to the church. "But Karl, you still have to study for your career and work at the factory", they said. Finally, they pleaded with me, and my mother said, "Karl, you will fall ill if you continue this way, not resting. If you do not make up your mind what you would like to do, you will break down."

As the days passed from morning to night, it appeared as if daytime was too close to the night. I was in bed, and I was out again because the morning was back. I saw nothing other than the sunrise redness and the redness of the sky at night. When I awoke at times, I was uncertain, for a few minutes, if it was morning or late evening.

One evening, I phoned Floretta at the college, but it was the end of the term. I rang her newly installed phone at her house, and I was very anxious. I must ask her about marriage, as I feared losing her because I could not think straight. I became bombarded with irrational fears and ideas that sent me into a panic. Rolling thoughts were making me change my mind frequently. During the rushed conversation, I asked her if she would marry me. She said, "Yes, when the time is right, I love you too."

I became obsessed with talking about marriage and taking my exam, and attending Bible College next year to become a religious leader. Floretta said she would be with me if it were God's will. She was chatting Bible language such as having a calling, a revelation, and by the Grace of God. I became muddled because I was trying to interpret what is meant by those terms. I told her how it came about that I fell in love with her. "It's God's will that we should be together to preach the Word to the world." She said that she held no particular feelings for me when we first met, but her feelings grew and grew, and now she was in love with me. For some reason, because of my muddle-headed thinking, I said, "I'll not marry you", at which she felt hurt and shouted down the phone in a loud voice, "Karl, it's not nice playing with people's emotions!" I then said I would marry her, and I asked again, "Will you marry me?" She answered, "When the time is right – it's not right now because we are still studying." I went to bed that night with her on my mind. Floretta loves me and will marry me! I visited her house and spent a pleasant time with her as our love flourished, but when I left, I said I could easily find my way to the bus stop from her directions, so there was no need to walk with me. I went on the wrong side of the street to catch the bus, and we drove back along her road, so I ducked my head as the bus passed her house again.

I caught the train from Wolverhampton to Birmingham, then got on what I thought was the correct train, knowing I needed to change at Leicester. I fell fast asleep and missed the connection, ending up in a seaside town in Lincolnshire. I could see the seafront from the station platform. The train terminated there and would leave again at 5 am the next day. I managed to find my way to the police station, but they didn't want to know how will I get home. I hitched rides where I could and tried to remember the geography of the county borders. None of the car drivers or lorry drivers who picked me up had ever heard of Wellingborough, but they had heard of Northampton. I walked and hitched a ride, walked and hitched, through the night and early morning. I sang to myself to keep my spirits up and sang aloud when I walked into creepy places where the moonlight twinkled through the branches of the trees. The feeling of standing still, and everything else turning around me, was chilling. The wind rattled branches, animals in the night dashed to the sides of the road, and creatures down the banks rustled foliage by the highway. I made it back home and had a long hitch to Northampton, then my final one to Wellingborough. I went straight to bed.

The last time I remember travelling to see her was at Bible College. We lingered in each other's arms; we craved for each other and did not want to part. We waited until the last minute to say goodbye, and I almost missed the bus to the train station. I fell asleep on the train and ended up in London. I had to come out of Euston Station and take the short walk to King's Cross to get home. I had no money. The guard would typically call the police, but he didn't when I explained what had happened. Forms were filled out, and a demand letter from British Rail arrived at the house two days later. I arrived home at 7 am Monday, and I had to start work at 7:45 am.

There was a revival service in the local church, and East Midlands District churches attended, but the Wolverhampton church is in the West Midlands, so it was not taking part. In the local church, we were to invite people from the town of

Wellingborough to the service. As an active church member, I met almost everybody and met all the latest local people who attended the church service. I met this lady who came with a friend sometimes for the Sunday services. I just saw her and had a warm feeling of fancying this lady. I said hello, and it triggered a tingling shockwave in my insides. I had to say to myself, "Oh God, if I am not to stay in this church with my present girlfriend, Floretta, I would like to meet up again with this lovely local lady, and possibly she will be my girlfriend, the one I'll marry."

That night, I had a conflict that I wanted to resolve. I had never looked at or thought of any woman other than Floretta, and something was moving me, warming my belly, my heart, and changing my thinking to recognise the lady in the local church as a possible soulmate. I could not understand how I could have such a massive tug on my heartstrings when I had only met her once. I felt a powerful emotional reaction to this lovely young lady. She had come from the outside world and pulled more than a few strings inside me. The emotions were running high, and I now began thinking about the two women.

Should I stay in the church with my girlfriend, take the assignment and be a missionary for the Lord? Or leave the church, get to know this local girl, study hard, pass my engineering exam with good grades, and devote myself to life as an ordinary disciple who will get married, have children, and continue to love God? I wrestled with the thoughts but did not make a decision. I left the dilemma in my head and thought I would see how it worked out by doing nothing. I fell asleep, and that night a sound shattered my sleep. I heard a voice, not inside my head but external, and it spoke to me, although nobody was physically in my room. My behaviour was sexual, and I believed that something supernatural was acting on me, controlling my actions and thoughts. I was frightened, and even today, December 1991, I still do not know how I did not die of fright, for I was in severe, unbearable total shock. I had suffered my first psychotic nervous breakdown, and it was the year 1977. I think it was at the end of the Christmas holiday.

The news went around the town swiftly, and a member of the Northampton church was a cleaner at St Crispin's mental hospital. So the church members from near and far got to hear I was in a mental hospital. At that time, 1977-1978, 'mental hospital' to most people meant madness, looney bin, evil... and religious people were of the widespread belief that the place was satanic, nothing to do with treating sickness. So people were saying, "He is mad; evil spirits possess him, and he has been put away!"

In my pain of mental torture, I called out for my girlfriend, Floretta. "I want to see her!" My parents tried to phone her home several times, but Floretta never answered. Her mum denied she lived there or put the phone down when she heard my parents' voices. I could not believe it, and it caused more torment in my mind, but the local church members and the cleaner wanted to visit me in the hospital. It was an awful storm in my head. "No, they must not see me! I don't want to see them – don't let them come! I only want to see Floretta... Floretta."

The realisation that Floretta never wanted to see me didn't come while in chronic sickness, but I asked for writing materials and posted a letter in the internal post box in that state. I tried to spell her address the best I could and bought a stamp, probably not the correct value. My family told me there were plenty more fish in the sea and I would find another girlfriend to love again. "I wanted Floretta – nobody else. She was intelligent and educated – she should know I am not mad or possessed by an evil spirit. I am a good lad but just a little sick. We were lovers, and she must have known I was not my usual self lately and was becoming mentally stressed out". Everything I said in the hospital reflected the need to talk to Floretta.

It was not until I started to use the past tense that I realised I was on the road to recovery. I was convinced, probably wrongly, that Floretta was to take some of the blame for me being freaked out under stressors. Warmth, joy and the feeling of the sun rising on the horizon of my soul, the first feeling of peace of mind and having ridden out the storms. I left the hospital with nothing but beauty, an impression of love all around me, from family, friends and the rest of the world. The fresh air filled my nostrils with the sweetness of dew that perfumed me as I walked in the crisp, white snow of winter. I was happy to be alive in the real world. I then suddenly remembered the lady at the revival service and wanted to meet her again. Then the universe clicked because everything was in order now, and I knew what I wanted out of life. It was to be my passage of devotion, reaching towards real goals, commitments, with a better structure in my life in reality, and I would ride the storms of experience as a family man, married with children.

When I was discharged from the day hospital, I returned to working at the factory where I had served my apprenticeship. I probably only worked there for a few weeks because I was told it was best to attend Leicester's rehabilitation programme. After the period of rehab, I found a press toolmaker job in Bedford. I now felt comfortable in myself and could plan my future.

As for the young lady at the revival service, I wanted her to be part of my future. I looked for this lady with the very unusual pretty name, but I couldn't remember it. I found myself desperately wanting to meet her again because I thought of her as my soul partner. I went to local dances looking for her, looked around the town centre when I went shopping, hoping to bump into her. When I went to buy petrol for my motorbike, I spotted her with the girlfriend who sometimes came to Sunday church services. I was no longer involved with the black-led dark-skinned church worshippers. My worship was at the United Reform church now, where my family attended and where there was an ordained black minister preaching love and forgiveness rather than Hell and the Second Coming.

Since seeing her again, my mind was never really on my work; I thought of nothing else but the lady who might become my lover. After work, I raced along Gold Street each evening and got further and further until I located where she worked. On every occasion, I saw her and the friend, I waved and smiled, and they did the same. I would often ride back, only to see her disappearing between the houses on a council estate.

One summer's day, as the lady of my obsession passed by, a lad I knew was hanging around the area with his rather adventurous friend. The lad was known to be interested in his friend's sister. I asked him who that girl was who just passed by and where she lived. He told me his friend was that girl's brother and gave me the answers to all my questions. I held my breath and gasped, "Wow!" I said to a voice in my head; I knew where the object of my desire worked, where she lived and who her girlfriends were, but did she have a boyfriend? I wondered to myself the question of her having a close relationship with a boy.

This pretty, elegantly dressed young lady must have a boyfriend! If she has, I will not pursue wanting to get to know her better. She must be pure if I go out with her and for something to come of it. I saw her most days in the working week in the usual way, a glance as I rode by on my motorbike, this lady with lovely rosy cheeks and hairstyles that she changed most days. I admired her more and more. Her charming smile through sparkling white teeth captured my heart. If I had any doubt about her purity, even though she may have been out with boys, I could not ask her for a date. I filled my motorbike at the petrol station and waited to see her. When she had gone by, I brushed away my shyness and rode up to her, dismounted and, after mentioning the weather etc., etc., popped the question. She said yes, with the most innocent, warm, sexy look I have ever seen in a lady. This lady was, of course, your mother, Euphemia.

Our first date was at the local cinema to see Star Wars and then down to the pub for a drink. After the pub, we danced late into the night at a disco nightclub.

I have no regrets that your mum is my partner, even in this period of not seeing eye to eye. On the contrary, I continue to hope that things will get better. We are on the last day of the senior year, 31st December 1991, and it has been a year of my outpouring emotions for our romance.

It was looking fruitless, but survive, we must. The tribulation, the anxieties and caring involvement in our relationship and our children are burdens and stresses. We must resist the temptation to fail, do nothing. If we trust ourselves and our partner, we love as we try to provide life's necessities; a loving family, we shall win. The keen edge of my sorrow is poignancy; it is a reminder of life's journey. Despite such headache, I mean to go on and step into 1992 confident that love shall win. What may be dangerous times socially, economically and relationship-wise, Happy New Year, 1992! 1991 must be laid to rest now, as I look forward to 1992 being a fantastic year.

Easter morning in 1992
Written 19th April 1992

I woke this morning and had to find a pen quickly because I felt blessed, and my ideas about Easter needed to be written down.

I draw a line where I believed in Jesus – to the point where I doubt or can no longer accept what seems ridiculous and a kind of superstitious idiocy that is racist. Based on my higher profile thinking, there is neither a beginning nor an end to my thoughts about God. HAPPY EASTER, as I look for the pure truth. Still, the evidence is confusing, and my imagination is taking me on a journey to explain the justification of my belief in God, just like my average intelligence has done on other matters. Much of what I am writing is based not on tested theology but theology, strategic thinking and life experiences.

With my inquisitiveness and analytical mind, I felt compelled to continue to learn. I guess what I came up with, those theological ideas I put into practice, are the same as any college professor or textbooks would say, but I found the answer through my intellect and skipped studying and college. I am not a very good reader, so it would only be a hindrance. My inquiring mind pushes questions about life, and it's a curious sort of pain that comes to an end, satisfied by an understanding of truth and religious belief.

I am neither a Christian nor a Jehovah's Witness. I have no religion, and I do not want to form one. The church has failed to provide rest and food, but the one I attend, United Reform, sometimes leads by a good example and educates. However, some burn with emotionalism and others with classism, but we need rest and food when we become emotionally exhausted and nervous.

I do not believe that Jesus of Nazareth is divine, three in one, but a man, a prophet made by God to live a life based on love and peace and spread God's word on matters of liberation and freedom. To declare any laws that degrade human personality is not law; when justice is dealt with on skin colour or merely injustice diminishes God's creatures. One must walk and talk in the manner of love, for God is love, and true love must be shown to our neighbours. Existent truth for every

107

race, creed and religion does not accept that God offers salvation only through Jesus Christ. Multifaith has a part in it, too. This conflicts with the Christian duty to proclaim the Gospel and deny the uniqueness and finality that Christ is the only saviour. Christ must be seen in the context of first-century Jewish preachers and may have suffered from a mental health problem in his ministry. But it is hush-hush to say that Jesus lost his mind. Some of our most inspirational forebears like John the Baptist, St. Paul and St. Francis and other figures from the Bible may have been mentally ill from time to time.

I can no longer call myself a Christian because Christians fear encountering other faiths, and I think that other religions are vital in God's order, and I have no doubt about what I am saying. They have diversity, but yet one common concern – God. Where are the churches with flexibility built into their faith? There should be tolerance. After all, only Christianity says there is only one God! Multi-racial culture – yes, differences in colour, other religions and social customs bring rich diversity and stamp out bigotry. There is a force field in the universe, and one can see that the God particle is in it, out there, and the existence of our consciousness brings the area of that eternal field directly into our lives.

I do not believe in the presence of a devil or the fallen angel story. I hold some Christian principles and teach the children the Christian way of life. That is good, but there will come a time when they will either accept it all or just parts of it because of paradoxes. Children, you will be taught the whole story and be encouraged to take the sacrament, the bread and wine supper, and see God as Mother and Father God, non-gender God. A God that is not only He the Creator, but She is the Almighty powerful particle, The God.

When the church says "Jesus Christ, son of God", there's overwhelming evidence for Jesus Christ's existence. It comes from the letters of St. Paul and the Gospels themselves, but only since the early Christians, the claim arises that Jesus is the saviour of the world. Those writings are complicated theological documents. They express unanimity on the basic facts that he was born somewhere between 6BC and 8BC, not 1992 years ago. He ministered in Galilee and was crucified around 30AD under the authority of Pontius Pilate. We must raise black consciousness to see God as God. On earth, a man claims "no one comes to the Father but by me" – it is crucial to raise consciousness to confront this claim. In our mind, there is a pure truth that common sense can take us so far with historical evidence that challenges the authority of infinite truth in reality. Christianity has a slave morality mentality that does not allow thinking for ourselves, and we being the master of our perception and values and master of our own lives.

Be proud of your belief. It is foolish to think it's our wisdom and strength we must rely on, but the spirit of God must affect us, and it shakes me to find out what was made up by theorists of the day. My unswerving commitment to truth and philosophical inquiries makes my God-conscious, never-ceasing devotion to 'the will' from my godly mind. What may seem misguided is pouring out of my head like wisdom that only comes about by years of learning the absolute truth.

We black people need to be independent thinkers and understand religious slave-like obedience language. The language was given to us; it's not our own and has a master morality that gives the elite people pride, and us Blacks, in shame. We must understand the period and the Jewish mind, that is Judaism. Black people had no power in the English language history because of the lack of inferencing social and political relations.

We have to confront the big questions in our heads and give ourselves suitable rational answers that do not hurt the brain when the inner conflict of good and evil communicates the idea of war in the mind.

The spiritual dilemmas that drive good people into a deep depression encounter God in the darkness, and He gives us the inner light. We all have a shadow side to our personalities that takes courage to face – our being's dark, negative side. The pressures within us, the need to act out our secret desires, can lead to behaviour unacceptable to society and the church. However, it's already known to God, who accepts us, pimples and all, and only by the grace of God and his disciplines can one contain some temptations.

As we go through life, attractions may get the better of us, and we fail. Go on. Accept the unacceptable self, that dark side. Not reluctantly, but positively. To acknowledge the reality and depth of our darkness and accept others' darkness, too, opens the way to light and truth. That is my belief. It transforms our personalities and eases personal problems because we know the truth and live a fruitful faith. But some churches are suffering truth decay. Theological differences and various denominations within the Christian church have divided the church. Charismatic worship is spreading from the evangelical churches, with their repetitive choruses have a hypnotic quality, not far removed from nightclub pandemonium.

Christians claim that God was made flesh through Jesus Christ, but other faiths claim the contrary. There is only one God, and I would feel happy worshipping in any faith to 'The God' in any church or home and not get tied to a selfish, narrow-minded religion that claims 'I am the only way to the Almighty'. The mother-father God that I envisaged, the Almighty, who created a big bang that produced a unified and ordered universe with some weird ecosystems that clean up debris, has accepted me as I am, on this turning, changing planet. I think He/ She offers salvation through repentance. Human-made catastrophes cause disastrous havoc and tragedy, but The God particles must be super aliens for making neurons and sustaining this vast universe and suspending us in this reality our organic mind comprehends.

The emphatic supreme particle of God exists alone, and by the human systems of spiritual beliefs, we can feel The God who makes the thing that it is.

We are all waiting for the emphatic, absolute ultimate God to face the deep spiritual issues before us. I may have it wrong in my desire to get it right, but seeking God is a temptation. It is extraordinary that God would presumably make Himself known. In the 'stillness' of silence and listening to calm in peacefulness, God's unexpected presence is there. Even in dramatic events – mighty winds, earthquakes, the circumstances of life – the presence of God is known to us. There are forgiveness and encouragement in being obedient to God, and God's blessings change my consciousness. The levels of awareness are profoundly moving in demonstration of the reality and validity of our human spirit.

Drugs do not artificially induce the thoughts I have. My thoughts are wholly the product of an ongoing belief in God, together with reasoning with my godly minds. My conscious mind and the subconscious mind are synchronized and communicate as partners. My brain reacts to this, building up a perception of the world and God, ignoring any information to the contrary.

I rarely read the Bible anymore. I am developing my spiritual life without it, and now and again, I attend church. I know that rightly, the Bible is a handbook that aids the growth of religious life.

Through prayer, meditation and contemplation, a level of spiritual awareness can change and enable me to touch and handle things unseen. I do not usually pray aloud to God; I concentrate it in my mind and pass it through my mind into the universe. I most often say thanks to God and express wishes for others, the blessing and the peace. Whenever I go into prayer, other than when giving thanks, I quickly become drained.

God, the Mother and Father of us all, whose love can be seen in the faithfulness and care of humans, male and female, has guided my unconscious that triggers the source of my creativity.

We need a liberated theology, where women can be ordained, and the churches' injustice can be squeezed out in the temples and mostly, of course, in society. Churches should adopt the non-sexist language and ordain women as priests because they must indeed have the conviction in the way of the 'call' as men do.

Nuns should mate. Surely, conscience will show it's intolerable to leave women out of the top jobs in the church and society. God is an ideal parent; the image's maleness is not essential to its meaning, so priests should not only be men. We are all made in the image of God, and priests should be able to marry if they think it's in their 'calling'. Praying and thinking about God will show that much of traditional God-talk legitimises and perpetuates males' privilege. Where is equality? The Bible writers had inspiration from God, but they unwittingly inserted their ideas of what God is in God's name.

Due to the paradoxes around Christianity, after AD325, there has been no knowledge of Jesus or his world. The whole question of divinity and the entire concept of Jesus – the Messiah, the virgin birth – were made up by theorists of the day to explain a delivery outside of wedlock. A baby born in Galilee grew to be a man who fell afoul of Jerusalem's authorities as he worked as a holy man, healer, exorcist, and preacher. Some of these things have baffled my mind for a long time. I have been aware of them, and it did not come easy to disconnect Jesus from the learnt untruth about him. They had penetrated my inner passion, and all my emotional feelings were tied to him. I had to use intellectual courage to free my heart's attitude and unlock the pressure to feel God in my chest and not have to go through Jesus Christ for forgiveness and my worthiness to talk to my maker.

I shaped my life around the sacraments and the creed and found my heart, in some mystical sense, in touch with traditional Christianity. Still, I cannot honourably and truthfully continue to believe the orthodox Christian teachings about Jesus. I respect the memory of Jesus, but I had to abandon Christianity and retain God's messages in it.

Once I had abandoned the negative feeling of guilt with lots of prayer from the head, a surge of relief followed, where reason and rational thoughts lay. It was overwhelming to overcome feelings – to escape the working of the theological theory with which I had deeply set my life to model Jesus of the trinity in the heart. It took the certainty of my conviction and balanced thinking to overcome the brainwashed fears of the consequences for no longer suggesting Jesus as a personal saviour of my sins or the saviour of the world and a way to have access into the afterlife.

The decision was then accompanied by passionate excitement, no longer committed to defending what seemed ridiculous to the head but was accepted by the heart. It was the reality of God's infinite love that made me feel better and better about this decision to abandon the traditional teaching of Christianity completely.

The sacrament is not part of my worship, for it is awful to think I symbolise drinking holy human blood and eating holy human flesh. So I avoid it discreetly when I can or take it and put a spin on its symbolism, that is, to think of those who have no clean water to drink and people who have no food to eat. I ask that they will be blessed with sustenance.

I feel strengthened when I digest hymns by singing them in my mind without voicing the words. I rarely sing aloud, but my thoughts are on every word, which acts directly on my subconscious through to my soul. Theorists, prophets, priests and preachers are among those who have responded to the call to communicate God's mind accurately to a continually changing world. "How shall they hear without a preacher?" asked St Paul of the Romans. The prophet, old Isaiah, said, "Here I am, send me."

All need to imagine the assurance of forgiveness and the new life, and the great truths of the faith with its endless varieties should reach very different people. The essential fact, one 'God', is described differently in other religions depending on the present background, interest, and history. Believing in God is dynamic because its meaning is a purpose; it is reconciliation and a relationship.

In a world of some inner despair and outward devastation, faith in God continues to give wholeness to a reason for life when depressed by vague feelings of hopelessness and purposelessness. I am struggling with His real purpose for me. Why? When I am happy in this state, married with children! I was confused by theories and cults, but purpose and suffering raise extensive, deep questions. So I turned my back on Christianity and confronted the pain of confession for my unintentional wrongdoings and sins.

I stopped believing absurd stories from the ancient past. The negative guilt or the inappropriate guilt, a sense of responsibility not explicable in terms of my conscious values but heartfelt, reached the chambers of my heart in a way that is difficult to define. I am not a traditional Christian; Paul and the early Christians created myths that create a sense of unworthiness, anxiety, and fear, leading people to 'decision' and 'surrender'. We must use our heads and choose through consciousness, bring the forgiving love of God into our choice, then practice and proclaim the essence of faith. I want to exercise a rational religion.

'Jesus is God' is not on, but Jesus, son of God, that's better; we are all sons and daughters of the creator God. An icon of the invisible God as all of us are, made in God's image, we must welcome.

Many faithful and good people have suffered intolerable treatment, as did Jesus. Man's inhumanity to man is still happening today. They made up the early Christian myth-makers, theorists of the day, the crucifixion and the ascension into heaven. Jesus is all but Divine; he was a far more traditional Jew than his followers allowed, and they found a theory to keep his image alive. My reasons are not incompatible with belief, but the distinctions between making up things that could have happened, and the facts, are boundaries. Changes in my philosophy of life, aims, attitudes, and reactions may not be God's actions but the vocabulary of faith. Through grace, it commands me to contribute that prayers of good people to God's grace and power can completely change the direction of people's lives and the world's workings. I may try to manufacture things by dreams and ideas, but prayer is the process through which we cooperate with God by bringing about change and providing direction. I pray for peace, but it seems like I often require war for the conflict to advance the course of truth. The aspiration of people is unstable, and peace on earth will probably never exist. The order of God, which is a peace in our hearts, is not part of humanity's reasonable condition because our ancestors enjoyed hunting and killing to enable them to survive until the dawn of self-consciousness.

The conflict appears to be due to rational values. By seeking to defend or to advance them in situations, they prompt collision with competing groups. I want to write with a smile and a laugh and reaffirm the goodness in human life, but based upon my experience of human nature, it's a terrible thing that people can do to people in the name of God and extremism. So I smile and laugh, seeing only how ordinary people live their lives. Still, with mass education and political groups wanting to achieve their flawed moral ideology through violent behaviour, it seems that values are advanced by human conflict. The advancement of truth is promoted and reached through controversy, only when more men and women try to understand and make bearable the brief view of themselves, often overly eccentric and extremist. Knowing we are part animals and yet capable of looking down on ourselves for self-reflection is an accomplishment that puts us close to God.

To kill our kind for power or territorial acquisition, other than survival, is mean jealousy and envy. Our evolution, by the grace of God or whatever, has induced guilt and terror. Still, some people exaggerate it and commit violence, crimes, and experience ecstasy from the mutilation of human flesh. It is within our minds that we begin to understand the brain. Still, scientists have to learn how to trigger back the chemistry or whatever, so that people live an ordinary life by remaining within the law, respecting other people's values and recognising the importance of custom, tradition and decent behaviour. If people override the harmfulness in their capacity to be forceful, they can reconcile for love.

It may be that people will never love deeply yet get on well with fellow humans because they are conditioned towards amiability. The desire to meet God makes some people sacrifice human flesh or animals. It seems like animals were liberated in the New Testament when Jesus drove out the money lenders and those dealing with the animal to be sacrificed. God's mercy and love extend to all animals, not just the human species. Still, only we have an inbuilt sense of sadness, full of anguish and remorse when we violate human rights and exploit animals that a loving, compassionate God gave us to raise. Our evolutionary consciousness and self-reflection awaken us to correct the wrongs we do or repent and never again inflict suffering on creatures and humankind.

If redemption is to be meaningful, it's dying, not only for humans but also for animals. We humans domesticated species that we promised to have as pets to love and be with us in paradise, and nature by itself would calmly discipline wildlife to be with us in heaven. By taking an animal's place, Jesus identified with animals and stopped the Christians from offering animal sacrifices altogether. Jesus, what a brave and godly, ethically disciplined man. A great example of the highest level of love in a human being. People, wake up! This is the voice of an ordinary black man teetering on theology. I have no education in this sort of thinking, and I cry out to my fellow black and minority groups who need liberation. Wake up! Face the possibility that some of your teachings may have to be unlearnt when you're thinking triggers your inner wisdom to see preposterousness in the typical traditional views on Christianity.

It creates belief through persuasion rather than through thought. My opinion is truthfully honest as far as my human weakness can lessen my proper observation probing the evidence and giving it thought.

Every waking second, my subjective awareness experiences my mind on my conscious perceptions, emotions, memories, and intention. However, these words you are reading help you guess how the world looks to me based on my behaviour and utterances. As my thought process probe the central dilemma of human life, arguably it's not the inevitability of suffering or death, but is consciousness an ultimate fact, and are humans the only conscious beings in the universe? Our ancestors may have dreamed up the supernatural entity, God, who remains in our minds today and bears witness to our innermost fear and desires.

God see our souls, our most secret selves and loves us anyway. A marvellous invention started with an ancestral dream that works well in our modern time. Hence, no matter how lonesome we feel, how alienated from our fellow humans, God is always there watching over us.

To a Head

Written 27th June 1992

On the 17th of April 1992, Euphemia and I discussed a possible break-up. It was Good Friday.

It was a tough week because I was just being ignored, so I intended to take the children to stay at my mother's if Euphemia would not try and understand what I saw as necessary. It's difficult to cope under those conditions, with us not talking – something that had become the norm. The urge to confide in the person closest to me was almost overwhelming, but I turned away because Euphemia seemed fed up. So instead of burying our faces in each other's comforting shoulders, we adopted the stubborn attitude of 'I will be all right then, too.' instead of burying our faces in each other's comforting shoulders.

The anxiety was apparent. Our relationship was in jeopardy because of the strain of not being able to unwind and confide in someone I love about the day's problems. It created tension within me. The only thing Euphemia considered as important was going to dinner and dance with me at the weekend. I told her that I would not go with her; she could go alone. The way we had been living made me unhappy, yet I was happy to be with her. Euphemia spoke of the tension and stress she was carrying, and I continued to talk about my feelings, too.

I said many hurtful things to her that night, only to test her love for the children and me. Nevertheless, at the eleventh hour, I am pleased that we reached a place of better understanding each other. (My logical processes had broken down, and my thoughts and behaviour were odd, and Euphemia was a gem to have a greater understanding and manage to cope in such difficult times.)

From then on, our relationship blossomed. Things were working out well, and more and more, we shared our daily trials and the intimacy between us. We had started a new life together, understanding each other better. I learned more about my wife in one week than in ten years of marriage, and I think she was likewise with me. We saw this as a new beginning together because something symbolic happened.

As we calmly discussed our future, I had been slowly rubbing my wedding ring, and, just as our conversation ended, the ring split open. Euphemia promised to buy another ring and get it blessed in the church. The next day, we noticed our wedding photograph had fallen off its stand. I looked intently at my wife as I poured out my heart. It appeared things would have ended because I was very stressed and may not have been seeing things for how they were. I sensed I had been foolish.

On the morning of our new covenant, we looked at each other with adoring eyes, and suddenly I was able to see her frailties. She has a beauty that owes nothing to cosmetics and a special glow from being sure of a good husband's love and having a secure family life. I know now Euphemia felt more positive, and her smiles lit up her face, a sure sign of happiness. The creation of our healing was from our Godly minds. Together, we were the cornerstone of the family that brought back normality. Still, I especially thank Euphemia for the generous love and care that she gives. I am such a fool to get bogged down in self-pity as this good woman tries to make me see sense.

Today, it's 27th June 1992. I am pleased with my wife's adjustments regarding money, family life, etc., and my happiness remains. I am trying to make our home a secure and loving environment, and Euphemia is also committed to this.

Day-to-day problems between parents can colour the children's development. We nurture the sense that they belong to two loving, caring parents who know how fragile this existence is, and we give the children a healthy sense of priority. We will continue to bring them up to be good people and value themselves as much as possible. Raising them is a journey, both for the children and for us as well. I thank God for luck and good faith in keeping us travelling life's path together.

It was regrettable when our loving relationship broke down, but I was glad to restore trust and truth. My ability to love and my relationship with my wife is essential to my well-being, inner health, and spiritual wholeness. They are in good order because I commit myself to look upwards to God and work at having a fulfilled marriage, even in uncertain times.

Stars were in our eyes, and we were going into orbit, literally, when we hugged and kissed and cut a rug at the dance that weekend. Since then, the most exciting aspects of life have been seeing the children grow and studying the development and progress of our marriage.

Message to the Children in 1992

Written July 1992

The nurturing that the children need to grow up striving is the ongoing giving and building of their confidence, providing motivation and strengthening their will to survive.

Katrina: You're a lovely, loving, conscientious girl who experiences intense self-doubt. You are physically maturing quickly but developing moderately in your inner self. We try to help, but sometimes your spirit is so weak that you cry and talk gloomily. It is only because of the lack of confidence and being too hard on yourself, attempting to be a perfectionist. Academically, you are doing very well, but you still worry. Your school report reads excellently, and I tell you to stop worrying, to enjoy life. It's all right to fail and to make mistakes. You are less skilled in physical activities like field sports. It is one area that will help you to cope with failure and remain able to go on. Don't be too hard on yourself; we all make mistakes and fail in certain areas in our lives but try not to linger on this and press forward. You must survive the intenseness of life's trials, even while so young. Do not look for perfection in everything.

I am conscious of overprotectiveness with all the children. Although I would like you to have more freedom, it's painful to back off and let you make your own mistakes, but I feel I must. Katrina, you had slept away from home when you were on school trips and at Brownies' camp. On such occasions, you pull and stretch my heartstrings. I want you to go but want you to remain with us. You adapted well to the freedom and found it exciting so that on your return, you found home life boring.

I found it hard – with a daughter away, even when well supervised – for my heartstrings not to be tugged when hopes that you were safe and having a wonderful time ran through my mind.

On your walk to school and when climbing the stairs quickly, Mum noticed you were out of breath, and we thought you had put on too much weight. On the 12th of June 1992, the doctor said you were asthmatic and gave you an inhaler to use daily.

Mum's words, and sometimes mine, or having a little smack for discipline, cause you to feel hurt. It isn't deliberate, and we want you to think about the consequence of your behaviour. It upsets me when this leads to crying or moodiness. You are usually very well behaved and happy, but I sense you need to find your feet, and I apologise to you for the mental and physical hurt. You have a childhood dream to be a bank manageress when you grow up. The reality of this is possibly shaping up because you try hard to learn sums and love counting money.

Katrina, you mix with only a small circle of friends you get on well with, but sometimes a friendship can be lost for a time, making you sad. But, when you have made up, the smiles return to your face.

You are a bit shy and respond when stimulated to give your view or ideas on matters intelligently. You are uncomfortable talking about science, dealing with space and time, and still partly frightened by science-fiction and make-believe.

Georgina: You are a lovely, loving, thoughtful child, but your desire to have some things is so great that tantrums arise. My reasonable request to not do or not have something brings persistent tantrums. Therefore, I want to give you a very light little smack but retreat and seek your mum's advice. It causes me so much pain to lash out to discipline you, and I apologise to you for the physical pain it must have caused you. However, like Katrina, you usually have exemplary behaviour, and you are happy, so when the response is intolerable, I am conscious that I need to be more patient.

Georgina, your childhood career choice is to be a nurse. Hospital and medical programmes on TV hold your attention right up to the end. Your school report provides excellent reading, and you are a trendy girl whose manners, sensible attitude and appropriate answers to questions make you a joy to be around in the classroom and the playground. You openly asked me about human reproduction, although you had seen films, and on previous occasions when I told Katrina the facts of life, you were there.

Jonathan: You are a loving and remarkably obedient child, but I can restrain you and remain very calm when you are obstinate. We rarely use smacking as a means of control because it creates inner pain in me, and I have to ask you about your well-being as soon as you calm down.

Jonathan, you love going to a predominantly Asian playgroup at Stanley Road. In September, you are looking forward to the change I want you to have in a different playgroup to bring a fresh mix of children for you to play and get along with as friends. You are an active, happy boy, but still like a buggy ride and resist giving up the feeding bottle. It is interesting to see you get involved in the girls' play activities. Your cognitive skills and vocabulary are developing well, except the letter 'G' is not pronounced clearly.

Jonathan, you also enjoyed watching hospital and medical programmes and said you want to be a doctor when you grow up.

Children: You are all ordinary children, yet beautiful. You will have a beautiful life by learning to develop the gift given to you from the cradle.

That strong bond that stretches through the years ahead may pass its limit. Still, it will never be allowed to break because, whatever problems or difficulty you face, you are all welcome to come back to home security and gather strength, no matter how old you are. The connection between us remains for all the days of our earthly life and in life after that.

Sometimes, when something we say to you is hurtful, it's uncharacteristic of us, but it has to be, for your good. You are rational children, caring kinds of human beings, and at the time of your birth, I had a sense of fulfilment, knowing I had done something worthwhile. I realised what a triumph it is to have a family. My life is relatively straightforward. I know what my duties are and the rules by which the whole thing is organised. All the work to support the family that I do is getting repaid. By it is more than enough the pleasure of being with you every day. I want you to have a happy life, have the right amount of love and freedom, and radiate that love with your mum and me.

Science and the soul and dark skin People might Disappear

Written July 1992

Science has brought about many great benefits in better health care, food production, and less arduous physical labour. But it is sliding inexplicably to abandoning the true self that needs the vision that humankind is a creation of God.

The thinking which explains life, the universe and everything in terms of religion is restraining the vision of the great prophecy that predicts God is alive - exists. Science has done some spiritual damage in abandoning the true self. It wants to diagnose the 'soul', but it has yet to find it. Without a balanced formula with faith, science has fallen from grace.

It seems humankind is an intelligent animal without considering ourselves made in God's image, which has forfeited the basis of human dignity. Science can describe the universe in terms of an abstract mathematical formula, but for people to lose any sense of what is holy or divine is appalling. Science can make us reject our humanity because attitude is not scientific. The eternal game has an equilibrium with science and Darwin's primitive life forms of creation, and Freud's finding, as I understand it, of the unconscious mind gets filled with craven lust and perverted desires. It strikes at the heart of our morality, and they say the human mind can be explained in terms of behaviour and conditional reflexes; these thoughts need an insurance policy.

Death is certain. We do not know when we are going or for what reason, but we need an insurance policy to survive the changes that thoughts and the environment may throw at us. To me, there is no better policy than what spirituality and science offer as an equilibrium. Our ignorance is not only bliss, but it's our survival and what makes us human beings. There is something about the human mind that, since biblical times, has been changing alarmingly and has brought about catastrophe or apocalypse.

A scare about 1984 and scientific guesswork brought attention to what humans thought had been predicted since the beginning of time. The horror of an irreversibly degrading world remains a possibility, but the European sees its rule as a dominant, exploiting society coming to an end and scaring the nations. The 'white' race believes they are superior and threatens the country that the year 2,000 will see human history bursting into an irreversible decline. So they declared the 1990s as a decade of evangelicalism.

The 'black' race must wake up and put their stories into non-fiction and fiction as they see the world; write novels about black achievements in science fiction and life.

The science-fiction world seems to prefer aliens with two or more heads than the superiority of a dark-skinned human. Science is trying to predict the disappearance of dark-skinned people, which has to do with the problem of aids and deadly bugs in Africa, killing off species. The media are portraying dark-skinned people as villains or baddies. It is, of course, a myth, but it's believed.

Europeans are demanding a third revolution to bring back their superiority over the rest of the world. The European people need to respect humanity better and the environment, which they exploited well before the industrial revolution and are still doing today. The gross disparities between rich and developing nations, wealth, power, priorities, and unfair trading in the rich countries, the debt crisis, are profound on an unpredicted scale. Democratic systems of governance should have built-in sensitivity towards environmental issues.

The earth is the Lord's, proclaimed the psalmist. The creator has committed his world into human hands and sought to glorify by looking after its resources. Instead, the earth has been abused, primarily by industrial nations. Atmospheric pollution, rivers poisoned, etc., and some of his creatures are under threat of extinction. Now the rich nations are compelled to reassess their relationship with the earth. The world is in recession, and it's easy to see, in this country, that it's in a recessionary summer because thousands per week are losing their job. The selfish economic division in troubled places clarifies that reconciliation with our brothers and sisters is needed. Loving our world, our Neighbour and ourselves can grow if the fundamental importance of love, written in the New Testament, 'to love God and your Neighbour' and have a positive new, creative relationship to the earth is to obey.

The AIDS threat and morals

Written July 1992

The AIDS crisis has brought about organised social fear. AIDS is a massive threat to modern society. In the early years, it generated violence, prejudices and bigotry against people with the illness, and people believed that badness and guilt deserved the misfortune of the AIDS disease.

The idea that a significant illness, such as AIDS, is a form of punishment that may have stemmed from childhood, or the thinking that one deserves to be punished, cannot be accurate. Surely, illness could never be a punishment? How can God or humans want anyone to suffer painfully through sickness because of some wrongdoing? Although behaviours have consequences, that cannot possibly be the right outcome. God is not hitting wrongdoers in that way; He is leaving them to come to repentance – or face the ultimate death of the soul.

There is a racial myth or fantasy that the Europeans formed about black people since the AIDS scare. It was suggested that AIDS started in Africa, so black people were seen as diverse and responsible for the problem. Back in the day, sexual ailments in Europe were labelled about another country: in Italy, it was called the French disease; in France, the German disease. The response to AIDS was destructive because it was seen as belonging somewhere else. The society sought scapegoats and posed blame, saying the country of origin was responsible for AIDS but not guilty. They denied it and were not taking responsibility.

AIDS has caused the act of love, for some, to be the agent of death. There is very little doubt that the idea of the sex act causing death is terrifying.

AIDS strikes at the heart of everything and produces a social depression because it hits at pleasure and sources of happiness. It also strikes at the purpose of reproduction and the spirit of human nature. Sexual love, the chief life-enhancing experience, has become related to death and illness, a life-threatening incident. Never before has the threat been so significant that sexual desire is exploitive; love is no longer straightforward. It can destroy a relationship and cause distrust in the pleasure of it.

122

It appears that sex is the vessel in which human indulgence releases tender-heartedness, kindness, tolerance, and generous benefits transmitted from generation to generation. The disease became embedded in the act. AIDS is the ultimate sexual disease, weighed against innocent pleasure. It has become, in some way, part of destiny. The moment of passion has become a potential death sentence for changing partners freely.

The media has used hysterical language to inspire fear which then becomes counterproductive. The deliberate exaggeration, engineered by the media about AIDS, was unreal, and there is a quietness now that makes me wonder where it has gone. People should learn the limits of their fear through their intelligence, and by doing so, morality will help them lead a good life. Being morally lazy is becoming scary, but the primary prevention of AIDS is morality. Sexual union has been cheapened and is, in many cases, no longer treated as the ultimate physical expression of a couple in love. Still, it is an act that brings momentary pleasure, physical relief, and in some cases, if not sufficiently protected with a condom – AIDS.

Children, I have written about a subject that has caused me embarrassment and shyness for many years, but I was motivated to find my emotional integrity. Sex is a motivating factor in us human beings; otherwise, we would not be here. The important thing is that it should not be addressed with prurience or hypocrisy. The drive for sexual union is a life force, but it is promoted, these days, to be about attraction and fascination that can be bought and sold, which is degrading beyond belief.

Sex is a gift from God, and it is an expression of the gift of love in a relationship. It should have enjoyment, not for its own sake only, or self-aggrandisement, but as a loving purposeful and creative thing that one gives to another. God did not only bless sexual union when performed for the possibility of conceiving a child in wedlock.

I became aware of a sort of physical restlessness inside me. It was a pain that seemed like my body, at times, screaming out for satisfaction. I found the commitment to celibacy challenging to cope with, and the desire to preach love and give love leads to marriage. I indulged in the act without wanting my wife to conceive a child. From the brightest lights, it has been said; the darkest shadows are cast. It is accurate, and I never pretended to be a perfect man. God only knows I am motivated to do good to others and represent a catalyst that may link people and show love by living by my beliefs. I never set out to be a moralist, a saint or a hero, but merely an example of life's ordinariness with genuine sensitivity.

I hope to bring the children up correctly to know the facts of life and not lose pride in themselves if they ever lost faith and had an affair. Then, as they mature by developing their morals and being most sensible and wise, they will not only feel good but will reap the reward.

I bought books to educate my sexual curiosity. Unfortunately, the family only had an extensive medical journal that was not sexually explicit and did little to help. The books helped when I embarked on love and my sex life, but they lacked any emotional aspect and simply had medical diagrams of the reproductive system. Reading them enabled me to have sexual confidence, but the thing is, today, sex is no longer just a private activity. It is an intimate part of adult human life, but it is portrayed as a leisure pursuit, almost a hobby, which is terrible. People must be encouraged to think about moral issues and what is right – and the image they are projecting of themselves.

As you grow up and become secure in your personality, you may clash with us, your parents, as young teenagers. Think about the clothes you want to buy to feel and look comfortable wearing. Work out a style that feels relaxed, and when it comes to sex, it's not wrong or evil; it's a very positive force for good. It's a beautiful expression of love between a man and a woman. However, it's such a powerful urge that it is used to exert control over partners and could easily lead to being hurt by suffering jealousy or experiencing rejection. Keeping sex within the bounds of marriage protects you from harm.

Once you have given yourself to another person as thoroughly as you do when making love, you make yourself very vulnerable. Not just to the danger of unwanted pregnancy or disease, but to lose respect for yourself and others if it doesn't lead to living together in a loving relationship. The teenage years may sway you to yield to peers and society, persuading you to be sexually active and boast about your sex life. By saving yourself in the first stage of a relationship, keeping a physical proof of love for later will honourably keep your desire for each other bright and alive so that you can be unique to one another. Don't live with your head in the clouds. It is easy to get carried away by emotions when touching another's body. Still, you must determine how far you want an honest, natural, healthy relationship to go. The desire to make love must adhere to morally taught behaviour standards to prevent AIDS and other sexually transmitted diseases.

Moral teaching, be it from the Bible or from the thoughts that give rise to ethical theories, is a duty of parents or schools, who need to teach children so they can be helped to determine what is right or wrong. To survive, people need to behave honourably, respectfully, and decently to other people for their spiritual essence, that non-material part of them. They should also respect the earth's resources so they can support all the species.

We wish to do good to others and not hurt or harm anyone, but treat people fairly. We owe this to each other, not to bricks and mortar. Teaching discipline in our lives gives a certain degree of accuracy in deciding what is right or wrong. People can tell when something is 100% right or 100% wrong, but there is a probability calculation or estimation of how right or wrong they could be when they are unsure. If people believe in getting a fair, honest, ethical answer, they will use the law rule in nature and their regulations or scientific principles to thrash out the rights and wrongs.

During the years of growing up and probably for countless generations, the rights and wrongs were taught by telling us not to do this or that. Why? It is the way it is, and we should behave needs justification; explaining right and wrong guides the child to reason it out and develop critical thinking. They will better learn the universal laws of how things are and form opinions more easily. Not to teach what's right or wrong, telling a child that's not the way to behave, or it is the wrong answer because I say so, needs better justification. Tell the child your reason or reasons for your decision or let them know it's the law.

There is a powerful sense in our home that the children are absorbing religion through everyday life. My habit before they go to sleep is to say, "Goodnight, sweet dreams, see you in the morning. Nighty, nighty, and God bless". The practice they have of singing church hymns they learnt at the C of E school and in church and at Brownie parades gives them a healthy consciousness about faith. We do our best to discuss the subject honestly when it comes up. Katrina reads the Bible sometimes before going to bed, and they all know the Lord's Prayer, even though they don't say it very often. Instead, they repeat the 'goodnight' sayings and go off to sleep.

Yet, I became constrained by the feeling that there must be a delicate balance between the preposterous promises indoctrinated in a child and learning through play or taught ethical codes with vows that might worry a child.

Religious teaching, or rather, faith, helps form a personal moral and ethical code. Still, expressions of righteous certainty bring feelings that they are brainwashed by teaching solemn promises and are being influenced convincingly. Later on, they will have to unlearn stories with meanings other than literal ones, descriptions of one thing under images of another thing, and the untruths about Jesus.

Some people believe that Adam and Eve were the first humans, and others think we are the fish's progeny. Feebly, we learn what may be the truth, and yet people are willing to teach Santa Claus's existence. With its teaching, the Bible is an excellent book, especially to reflect on. The stories are not literal, and it uses parables to say something about the human condition.

In time, I hope the children will see through the hypocrisy of consumerism that is a form of religion today, the irreverent side of the Old Testament, the informed prophesying of Judaism and the early Christianity in the New Testament.

The children have developed religious views that cannot be dismissed as half-baked but are wise in a dimension seldom given credit.

The inner challenges
Written in September 1992

In all of the states I have created for myself or find myself in, discontentment in me urges me and pushes me, but positively, to be creative and find opportunity within the limitations and hardships of my set of circumstances. My mind is plagued and saturated with God, the science. It wants to think, understand and use the knowledge that God provides.

The relationship between us and the universe is to do with the will and the understanding of our mind. I came to faith to answer questions and accept immaterial or spiritual elements distinct from the purely physical, intellectual, volitional and emotional methods in all of us.

My reasons and 'will' are rooted in a space that is not organic. If there is such a thing as a 'call' from God, I am experiencing it. My understanding, thinking, and the use of the knowledge that I have acquired in doing my engineering job – none of this is working out at all satisfactorily because verities, noble truths and justices are manipulating my mind. Nevertheless, my God-consciousness is nagging me to co-operate with God.

I have not moved confidently to understand how to undertake a task in engineering or think out the necessary way of doing the job using my skills and knowledge adequately and effectively. I have to quit working as an engineer because of the vibes leaving my mind. I am apprehensive that it's an element of schizophrenia that is somehow its orgiastic base and has a physical cause. For non-sufferers, people would readily accept it as an initial call from God, but sufferers must be cautioned. I know I have long had a spiritual quest – is it this that is resurfacing?

A turning point in my life caused a conversion to affirm the faith that has always been there. The need is to know where I stand as a result of it. It's charging me with commitment and concern. The faith journey had long begun; I am standing in a gap that desires a lifetime of involvement in service, in worship and fellowship to an idea. My thoughts' encounter is brain biochemistry, triggering an unnatural essence of a 'call' from the Divine to trust in the unknown and go into the world in service to faith. The thoughts are acting in my mind like a compulsion, a must-do. Is this not what one gets in a call? Is it God's calling to be a nurse, an engineer, doctor, a clerk, or any job or duty that convicts a person to carry it out devotedly? Imagination is an enormously powerful thing, and at times when I try and switch off, I come back quickly, and I think, "Oh gosh (or God), how could I have switched off like that?" But I need to switch off, for my mind is a plague of concentrated thoughts, causing me misery. There is an unfulfilled other inside the person who wants to present itself to the world, but it will take years of study and training to become free.

The drive and the motivation are alive, and some analytic process needs to stop the craziness in my head. I feel like I am caged, but the ending drives me on because my inner self would be pleased, satisfying the whole self.

Love is the centre of life, and I am suppressing the urge, that crawling feeling from my gut, to work in care. Love leaks out into every bit of my body and drives the self to have something practical to plough into barren lives other than our own. It is something that demands my determination and hidden talent, but I am so afraid. I have so much love to give, which should not be restricted to my wife and family. I am living with the benefit of a life that I ought to share before I can go to the other side of the universe when I die. For all of life's bleakness, all its madness and terrors, I feel blessed with a kind of inner singing of hymns and love songs that keep up a murmuring continuity.

I hit rock-bottom sometimes. That's why I write as I do, and it's a struggle to keep intense energy on the boil. By digesting hymns, I grasp back that energy. The chamber of myself that I had entered might never have been ventured into if the aspect had seemed utterly bonkers. The in-depth writing will be portraying the want to control fears and anxieties. So, as one's mind becomes opened, one's heart is opened, too. The opening of the mind springs from the most profound passionate source, the centre of life. Faith will carry me safely – if only I dare to take that walk.

The spiritual quest may have diminished, but the great blessing is really to know that I am travelling in the right direction. The pilgrimage I take is hopeful, but the thing is, I might never arrive because studying is hard and my memory is poor. What my mind is telling me now is what my experience has demonstrated.

I need to fulfil inner happiness in having my family and religious servitude or caring for people and environmental issues. I had asked insistent questions of my mind – why are humans so inhumane to other human beings, and what is the meaning of our creation? The senselessness of undeserved, unnecessary suffering, the wickedness of human ingenuity. Sometimes, seeing my best intention or very best effort, resulting in harm to myself or others, makes it hard not to make sense of this terrible reality. Yet still, I try.

Faith in God meets my human hunger for explanations and goes far beyond the available evidence. It seems to be helpful as a source of inspiration and a means of support. It gives me confidence that everything will work out for the best, and things will be alright in the end. I think great satisfaction comes from a longing to appease the appetite that challenges my existence as it is. Although I dearly love family life, I wonder whether I understood the divine vocation correctly or if it's just my mind under the stresses of creativity having a delusion leading me into another occupation in faith. I may be worshipping an idea that formed the basis of my religion, and it is important to me and seemed to defy definition. My views on existence and the afterlife has coloured everything I do or say. It differs from others because it moves me and twitches my mind. It makes me take courage to reach out towards a goal that may never be within my grasp but not beyond challenge.

To have faith in God and the next world required a leap in imagination. Having seen goodness as a reality that needs no reward brings hope that good will win over evil and badness, given the enormity of human suffering, the obscenity of violence in behaviour and the reality of people's selfishness and corruption. The universe with God inside it offers faith for lost hope to the fearful and the confused, love. But believing in God must be taken up by all people working for a better world. We who see the struggle of our times – the efforts politically, economically, socially, and the moral decay - would boldly proclaim things that are most surely believable. We no longer have models of spiritual excellence. The qualities that were admired in humanity and the pursuit of ultimate truth should go hand in hand. Humanity may become damaged, but it is of infinite value. Through the rehabilitation of behaviour, the ugliness of nature can turn into the beauty of holiness and kindness.

However, essential, material things are transitory, but the 'not seen,' the eternal, invisible dimension that constitutes ultimate reality, should be believed.

The Flirting

Written in October 1992 (adult theme.)

I have an obsessive liking for a thirty-ish-year-old Indian woman in the supermarket where I do our shopping. Unfortunately, I had felt powerless to modify or control the sexual attraction and the concerns I saw myself having for her. As a result, I have grievous fancies for her and have a desire to flirt with her.

It all came about that this ordinary, decently dressed woman was stocking the shelves in the supermarket. Suddenly, as I passed her stocking the low shelves, I was sexually aroused. Oh, my God! I thought to myself. Every week this apparent sexy feeling came over me as I approached the aisle where she was working. I questioned myself; why am I getting these intense arousals? My love and sex life are excellent, and I love my wife, even though there is a little difficulty in my marriage. I am fond of my wife, and we still hold sparks for each other. So, why the sexy feeling for another woman? I am not able to give myself an answer.

The cage that carries the stock for the shelves was in the middle of the shop floor, and I had to ask her to excuse me so that she could move the cage to let me pass. She looked up at me from the bottom shelf where she placed the tins, with penetrative eyes, adoring eyes and opened lips that spread a warm smile along her face, long enough to allow her beautiful white teeth to just begin to shine. From then on, each week, we communicated, and it became pleasant to see another woman liking and having an interest in me, other than my spouse. The depth of our respective looks into each other's eyes, given in observation as we talked about ourselves, gave me the temptation to form a friendship that may extend into an affair. Still, then I thought it would affect the core structure of my life, my marriage, the family, and it may lead to separation and divorce. I love my wife and children and do not wish any of those things to happen, but can one man be in love with two women?

When the moment of the conversation is coming to an end and signals the time to leave, I warmly touch her hands or shoulder because the need to touch her brown flesh relaxes my fluttering feelings.

It was becoming noticeable that I was getting home later than usual, and before my lady wife asked questions, I told her of the acquaintance I had made with a female shelf-packer at the supermarket. The wife said she was pleased that I have women as friends but will only worry if I become secretive and go out at night, leaving excuses to get away for a bit of hanky-panky. I think she knows that this woman has entered the reserve compartment of my heart where my overspill of love for her goes; for now, my wife asks how my girlfriend is.

The next time I saw her, she revealed that she is married and her life faced tragedy in trying to have children. Oh! How I felt the want to comfort her, but only warmly closed my hand over her hands and said, I understood the pain she had suffered. She has accepted that miscarriages cannot be changed so far, but true contentment has arisen through them. The injustice of life struck me and made me feel angry. Here is a young woman eager to have a family, without a doubt, who would love the child yet had miscarried. Yet, men and women out there who produce offspring repeatedly in an unholy manner aborted a child, abandoned the unwanted child, or abused them. Oh God, what has become of your creation?

I asked her about her husband, and she told me his name is Prakash. I was astonished and said to her, "I knew a Prakash who was a good friend of mine, and my wife knew him too. I have not seen him in over ten to fifteen years. Could he be your husband?" She was bewildered and sighed, "Oh, my God!" She began to talk about his looks, age, family, work, parents' home, hobbies, and academic abilities. I, in response, was saying yes to her statements of information about her husband. The profile fitted extraordinary well to the man I knew as Prakash, except the name of the road and the town where she said his parents' house was. I was sure that had been his home over the years, where I knew many years ago, and where he now lives are in a different place. The description of the interior of the house was amazingly accurate, along with everything else. Except for the two exceptions that I wanted to ignore, I wanted to meet the man I knew to be her husband. I disregarded these two pieces of information that did not fit the puzzle and convinced myself that her husband must be the Prakash I knew.

I saw her sometime in the town centre streets, and we talked of nothing else other than if my friend could possibly be her husband. My friends spotted us talking and wanted to know if I was romantically involved with the young woman and began to speculate. I wondered how I spoke to women friends in the street and never had any of my friends or people I knew had asked if I was involved with them, other than this one woman now. It cannot be because she is an Indian woman. After all, I have had a few woman friends in the past who were Asians. I said to her, "It looks like your husband is my old friend. It may have killed our flirting romance." She laughed. I suggested that we, my wife and I and her and her husband, meet over dinner at a restaurant so she can get to know my wife, and Prakash and I could talk and catch up on things. She told her husband about me, but he could not place the name; he had never met me. Due to his work's nature now, she says it will be difficult for us to meet up, but I hope it will be possible one day. The first bumping into her on the street stopped my arousal. I felt awkward, but nothing to do with sexual feelings. As I looked at her as we talked, the sexual desires never arose, but I felt my heart responding like falling in love and it soaking up the energy of friendship without wanting to be sexual partners or lovers.

She promised to show me a photograph of her wedding in India to end the speculation about whether it's her husband I had known. Then, I was finally convinced that it was, but she held an open mind and preferred to wait until I saw the photograph.

The day she was to bring the photograph for me to see, she had forgotten it, and my tenseness and eagerness got prolonged for almost another week. Finally, I called into the store on a day I do not usually, and she happened to have the photograph with her things in the staff room. I got presented with the picture, and my tension was immediately relieved as I stood motionless. My eyes peeked at it as if I had seen a nude. "This is not the Prakash I knew," I said. I studied the photograph even more carefully, and she said, "Even the structure of the face has no resemblance?" "No! But I'd still like to meet him," I replied. I commented that she looked lovely as a bride, and they both looked delighted. The picture portrayed the depth of her culture and the region's poverty, and they seemed pleased. "I love my husband; he is mine, he is mine - I will never leave him, ever; he is my man," she said out of the blue.

I love my wife too, and loyalty is the same as hers to her husband. So I would not leave my wife either. Then we laughed and laughed. I was at a loss to know what brought on that message out of the blue. She met my wife, Euphemia, when the whole family went shopping. The next time I went to the store, she said, "You have a very nice wife who is not a bitch, and you have lovely children". I smiled and said, "Oh, thanks, but she is sometimes discontented". "Your wife is lucky - what more does a woman want but a good man to love and to make love to". I pushed her slightly as the words triggered me into an outburst of laughter that cracked me up and almost left me with a stitch. She laughed also and added, "You must think I am awful and bad".

One day, I wandered around the store, and she spoke freely, being extremely friendly to a male customer. I felt a sense of hurt and jealousy and wanted to ignore her as I passed by, but I said hello with a 'down in the dumps' cold facial expression and, for many weeks, never returned to the store on the days I know she works. When I did come to terms with my behaviour after many weeks and thought that it was just plain silly and childish, I returned to the store, hoping she had never seen the change in me. She was not there, and I went to the other shop where she has part-time hours. She was there; seeing her, I sensed something was up that did not seem to be related to my absence. Her skin's golden-brown colour turned peachy pale, and her personality's charm was without its usual vibrancy. She told me she quit the other job because she may have to go back to India - her uncle had died. The shine had gone out of her. She tried to give a smile, but I could see she was going through the grieving process.

I had just picked up two twenty-four exposure photographs that got developed at a chemist of my child's birthday party and pictures of our home. I showed them to her, and they warmed her heart, and she smiled from the time she viewed them and said - "They are nice and thanks for showing them to me". Sadness returned quickly to her face that had once shown cheerfulness. Her grief got buried, and I wanted to share in her sorrow and be supportive. I put her hands into my palm and closed my other hand sensitively around hers, and conveyed my condolences over the passing of her close uncle. Her father had passed away when she was very young and lived in India, and grieving the loss of a close relative had not become any more comfortable. She thanked me for my kind thoughtfulness, and I could see visible tears getting held back as I showed her my sympathy by listening to the tragedy that had hit her life again.

After the weekend, I handed an inspirational card to her at work, a message from Euphemia and me. It was a non-Christian card because she is a Hindu and told me that she was warmly blessed when she saw me again and thanked me for it. "It was very nice, and it made me felt a little better."

My relationship with Pirja, the young woman, has been transformed and like a sister. Pirja is part of my feelings because she is someone I love and has entered my family, but only my wife is related to me through sexual love. So I have just a brother's love to a sister for Pirja, made up of friendship, care, and belonging. So I hope that Pirja will long remain my adopted surrogate sister.

Finding Pirja in this part of my life, enrolled in my friendship, shall enable us always to remain good companions and a blessing to each other.

The Holiday to Blackpool
Written 30th October 1992 adult theme

In the late summer of 1992, I worked out our finances. I squeezed into the budget a weekend holiday break for two to Blackpool Illuminations with an overnight stay at a hotel on our eleventh wedding anniversary. The following morning, a tour of the Peak District, then home.

We both started our annual autumn holiday from our jobs at the same time, on 23rd October. The planned weekend break would be like a long-awaited honeymoon, spending the weekend away as a couple for the first time. One evening at the dinner table during a conversation, Euphemia sighed heavily, saying she could do with a holiday. That's when I broke the news to her and the children. At first, they couldn't believe I'd booked a holiday – least of all, Euphemia after she'd been hoping for so many years.

The children were first to be convinced when I asked them, "Have you ever known me to tell a lie to the family?" Then Euphemia soon realised that the holiday would be her anniversary present! The children were delighted for us when they learned that Mum and Dad had never been away and stayed overnight together in over ten years of being married. Auntie Joan would look after them while we were out. They loved spending time with her, and they started telling us that the trip was coming soon.

I put together a folder containing all the relevant information about the trip in an unforeseen tragedy. Policy documents relating to the house mortgage, accident insurance, hospital Guild and pension were there. I tried not to overlook anything, and the folder contained those items that made it seem almost like a will.

The week of the trip, it was arranged that cousin Dorrell, who lived close by, would come and stay with the children until Joan arrived mid-morning from Northampton.

The 24th of October arrived, and Dorrell was on her way. We hugged and kissed the children, and I gave them a lift-up, then we left. For the first time since having the children, my thoughts were on us as a couple, and I felt romantic as we smiled at each other – born-again lovers, as we travelled to the coach pick-up stop. The home's departure was remarkable because the children were all pleased, even though Dorrell had not arrived before we left. I was unusually relaxed and anxiety-free, as I knew the children would be in good hands with their cousin and auntie.

We would be enjoying our trip like a long-awaited refreshment that would put some spark back into our marriage. Our romance would have a fresh start, and I found it ironic that we were going to the seaside.

We had a lovely position sitting in the coach, just behind the tour manageress at the front. From the time we started our journey to the time we reached Blackpool, some five and a half hours later (two of which were spent in a traffic jam), my wife looked at me as I remembered she did on our wedding day. The gentle expression in her twinkling dark eyes seemed to radiate from within, and I was happy to see the attraction was still there. I placed a soft, gentle kiss on her glossy lips and hugged her warmly. "Happy anniversary, darling," I said, and my darling responded, "Happy anniversary, Karl", with constant smiles exposing her beautiful white teeth and looking sweet and cute like the blossom of a prized rose. Our feelings were electric. We held hands, and our hands passed the current of love oscillating from one to the other, gently tingling through the warmth of our fingers.

We were travelling in blustery wind and rain, and the sky was very overcast. Now and again, the sunshine's hazy rays peeked through the patch of sky where dark grey clouds were moving along. It was beyond belief that Euphemia did not have her brolly with her because locally, she takes it every time she is out, rain or shine, without fail.

When we reached Blackpool, we had to buy a brolly because it drizzled on and off, and the windy conditions flattened our coats tightly against our bodies. At the precise time of 2:30 pm, marking the moment when we married eleven years ago, I tried to give the wife a kiss and a hug in torrential wind and rain that tossed her hair into mopped strands across her face. She pushed me away, and I was embarrassed and felt hurt by the quick, immediate reaction. I walked a pace ahead to prevent her from holding my hand right away, but I soon stopped and took Euphemia's hand, holding it by my side, for the wind was strong, and it was the right thing to do as we sought shelter. As we ran for cover, Euphemia said, "That was not the right time to do that in the middle of a storm... I am hungry!" I quickly realised my darling was right; even though my heart was in the right place for a symbolic expression of thanks at the precise time we tied the knot eleven years ago, the high wind and pouring rain could not have been romantic for her, as I had thought it would be. At the height of my realisation, I self-talked to my higher consciousness that I was sorry and ashamed of my reaction. It was wrong, but I didn't reveal to Euphemia my desire to say sorry.

We had a meal and then made our way towards the sights of Blackpool. Now the rain had died down. I stopped a passer-by and asked him to take a photo of us on our wedding anniversary. The wind blew as if it wanted to blow off our clothes and unashamedly expose our nudity. I hoped the camera captured the moment beautifully as we posed in the windy conditions.

In the early evening, we went back to the coach and were driven along the promenade. The spectacle of the famous illuminations with so many lights was lovely. Along the route, there was a fascinating variety of features displayed, each telling its own story.

We then travelled to the hotel for an overnight stay. The hotel room was magnificent, with built-in wardrobes, a control for the colour tv, an alarm clock radio, a video by the double bed, telephone and reading lamps. The dressing table had a built-in hairdryer and a trouser press next to it, and the bath included an overhead shower. "Wonderful!" we thought. However, I initially felt that the place may have been bugged and have two-way mirrors in the bathroom. Still, my paranoid state soon diminished as I appreciated the things in the room while looking for 'electronic bugs' and making funny faces in the mirror, laughing and throwing myself on the bed and thinking, how silly!

We freshened up then went to the disco, and as we checked out the atmosphere, we walked to the bar and bought our drinks. As we strolled by the first dance platform, heads gradually turned, making us attracted over the music, for some stopped dancing and looked on for a moment. We never took long to get into the swing of things because the music was 'stinging' and made us move to the beat. I felt sadness, seeing some young girls showing no decency in dressing, smoking and drinking alcohol excessively. It was hard not to feel a sense of shame and pain on their behalf. As my attention focused again on my wife, our dancing electrified us to the spot where we chose to dance, and we never left that area until the disco finished at 2 am.

I was entranced by my wife's face the whole time. The 'sweet eye' she gave me all evening. The sudden sharp winks of her right eye that curled her face into a sexy look and her head at a tilt had me flirting with her all night. We hugged and danced, watched each other intensely and sincerely, felt the marriage 'knot' bond holding us.

The giving and receiving of pleasure just by our mutual looking and touching hands and faces gave me real intimacy that was passionate and fun. Euphemia brought something to my attention, saying, "Look, those couples are copying us – they were sitting for ages, and now they're dancing and doing what we are doing". I thought to myself, look at what love can do to a man and a woman, and the making of love in marriage can say no more than when unmarried. With mutual acceptance, we can become celibate because we can separate love from sex.

I enjoyed my wife's company and friendship immensely, and my heart was melting like warm chocolate as we communicated being genuinely in love. The power of her beautiful looks suggested that we were enjoying each other's charms with pleasure. As we'll share the same bed without having sexual relations, it seemed to bring a sort of uniqueness and particular respect to the relationship. The question of what is 'normal' when the desire is there, and we have forbidden ourselves to eat the sweets – in other words, to have sex – when it comes like an appetite! If this is the step we are taking, the change will come quickly, not gradually, because two human beings can change from loving sexual life to just sleeping together. We can give spice to the marriage by giving and receiving pleasure in other beautiful and marvellous ways, other than making love.

We carried back to our hotel room that seemingly magical feeling that welled up in our hearts and minds, of love and sex. We went on to have our last ultimate lock-in embrace between man and woman before Euphemia fell asleep. I could not fall asleep because our security and safety control was not in my charge but with the hotel staff. I was used to locking up, securing our environment, and making safety provisions, but this was taken out of my control in a hotel. I had to rely on good hotel management, but being in a nice cocooned room was not enough to put my mind at ease. I stayed awake to keep a watchful eye over us.

I needed to rest during the night, but my body and mind had managed to retain stamina, and I remained good-spirited by watching television and later switching to the radio. By morning, I was drowsy, even after a refreshing shower. Finally, I went down for breakfast. Now and again, I nodded at the cereal in the bowl and the English breakfast on the plate.

Soon after breakfast, we left the hotel to travel to the Derbyshire Peak District. Unfortunately, I could not stay awake for the first part of the journey. My neck just kept cracking as my head jerked to and fro from the coach's movement, and this occasionally broke my sleep. However, my full awakening always seemed to come when the tour guide commented on the beautiful unspoilt region and explained why England's valleys were the loveliest.

When we stopped at picturesque villages, my eyes lost all their tiredness, and I could appreciate the splendid views. We got home mid-evening. This trip to Blackpool will always be memorable as long as I have faculty because of so many good things it has created or made me recognise in Euphemia and our living togetherness. Marriage is a great adventure in life, and I am so blessed in my relationship; we are deep lovers. The making of our children has them bound in this force-field, and we are profoundly dedicated to them. I recognised Euphemia as my soul mate, more so since that holiday, and I am having an enriching love affair with her. And she is my life's absolute treasure – better than money and fame because we are happy. I feel we must make our life a gift and live it intensely, not be promiscuous, greedy or foolish, and learn from it if we fall from grace and make loads of mistakes.

No one can ever guarantee to have one more hour in time to live, and the feeling that the rhythm of time is beating its way through my life faster had slowed. So I have a bank of time behind me, years since birth and some memories that put me back into dark areas that revealed sin in my head long before I realised that I had explored my environment and sexuality, causing me to shed my innocence as a boy.

The desire to create goodness was very stressful because frightening psychological strength was acting in opposition. I am thrilled it's finished, and I came out into the twinkling of a sunlit landscape that shines through the blemishes.

Today is the 1st of November 1992. By discovering my deeper inner self that searched out primitive ignorance and superstition, I have reached a state of enlightenment today lost during mental illness.

Marriage may have been designed to socialise man to commit himself to one mate and have offspring. I have been married for eleven years and think longevity in marriage is excellent, and the art of love with one person needs to be cherished and promoted.

Macho men think they are the best kind of male, but to us other males who have moved on from beastly behaviours and show empathy and emotional intelligence, macho man is threatening us to man-up, be as they are – physical, tough guys. Still, they miss the joy of feeling fully humane in the sense that aggressions and fights are taken out of us when we become more emotional creatures.

The love between more than one man and more than one woman could exist if men lived up to their responsibility as human beings, making us different from the animal kingdom. I do not like macho males because they retain everything beastly and see no need for sensitivity and feelings. They need to know that they should change and bring out the characteristic that forms humanity. 'Real' men are said to be healthy, sturdy, and masculine. I am glad I am a human male who has discovered humanity, who uses sensitivity and emotions. I desire a society of love and peace that channels our aggression into sporting friendliness and personal challenges that harm no one. To conform to this means males can show sad emotions, be always ready for growth as a whole humane person, be sensitive to fights, and be brave enough to leave organic beastly behaviours behind.

By expressing sorrow with crying, one is considered a sissy, queer, a poof, and called offensive words that degrade women's body parts, just because men like me have the characteristics associated with women. The macho aggressive man makes it seem impossible to love someone they disagree with, impossible to have an amicable agreement, make peace, and have responsibility for decent behaviour; it is a long time coming. They need to show emotions and feelings for others and stop being full-blooded animalistic males.

I know that society covers vast groups of people, but for people who are different, we see man's humanity, the human being and not the human-animal, does not make them less of a person but more so. Women come out in society as saints because some men may have been born into the world as monsters, and women are a little more self-sacrificing and generous but less decent.

To be afflicted with mental illness as a sensitive man needs policing because it challenges my humanity. I fight with the bully within to be less of a macho, aggressive man. There may be all sorts of psychological reasons why men are more extreme and for violence. Women are not naturally born openly wildly aggressive, but that changes because some consciously act like macho, bold, aggressive men.

Christmas Anguish
Written 25th December 1992

The contemporary world scene causes much anguish. Many parts of the world are breaking out in wars, racial attacks, or experiencing terrorism caused by religious differences. It seems like the people involved are motivated by vengeance, not against individuals who have wronged them in the present time, but against long-dead individuals and people far back in time who mistreated their ancestors. So they are taking revenge, terrorising ordinary people to get even.

Evil people want bad things and understand why they are that way; they require science to break into the selfish evolutionary gene, jealousy, and envy gene and manipulate them. Consciously, bad people choose not to change, not to want to do good. The scientific reasoning has a speculative premise and presumes a universe with God, left to will and repentance to make them change. Still, scientists are very good at achieving things with God's grace, and they will eventually acquire the know-how to make people pleasant.

Religion provides an excellent falsehood for people looking for an escape from wonder and truth. The universe is incomparably more beautiful than anything theology or historical account has ever had to offer. Through this book, my testimony will open the average population's eyes to see that a universe with a God would be very different from one without God. It's because we have something profound embedded inside ourselves that goes far beyond the ego or will. Call it what you may – spirit, soul, etc., it's inescapable in the person, and it can come out of the body. I imagine an actual existence, a real God for it to go to when it leaves the body. In their belief, Christian fundamentalists may believe that God inspired every comma and full stop in the Bible, and other people see the Bible as a superstitious myth. Most people do not want to look silly in their religious belief, so, like me, they look for intellectual respectability in putting their confidence in the foundation that can stand up to criticism.

People who are averagely devout to God can find Anglican and Roman Catholic churches, two authorities that never agree exactly where the middle ground lies. The

Gospel is history, and the imaginative reconstructions of what might have happened were shown like today's drama documentaries on television. Matthew, Mark, Luke and John presented the narrators as having originality, unwittingly making a piece of the story myth. Luke narrated the birth story, and Matthew supplied details that Luke omitted, like Joseph's decision to adopt Jesus after his betrothed, Mary, became pregnant. The Three Wise Men enter the story, and the words collectively accumulate more errors from theological interpretation by overzealous interpreters down the centuries.

Today is Christmas Day, the date adopted from local pagan festivals marking midsummer, as indicated in the Julian calendar. The vision of a bright star was such a noticeable heavenly event, like witnessing a supernova that happened around 6BC, and it is more likely that the Magi were astrologers.

Did the massacre of innocents ordered by Herod really happen? Herod would surely have been remembered in many mothers' grieving hearts, so why was it not mentioned throughout the Gospels? The Christmas story can ring bells; it no longer rings through to my intellect, but it moves my heart. It is fascinating that the birthday of an ancient leader, Jesus, who Christians say is the Father of humanity, was chosen to give us a public holiday. We could have had mathematical Copernicus Day or, in more modern times, Einstein Day, Darwin Day as a way of showing human achievement.

I am pleased that Christmas is a bank holiday because it's Jesus Christ's birth that ties the creator God to humankind's greatest need, the necessity of ordinary people to have religion. For this, He is profoundly different from most achievers in terms of humankind's understanding of self, environment, and divine qualities. Of course, governments may want to cancel out a national holiday, and Christmas might come under the hammer to be abolished or given a name change. However, there is no other historical figure worshipped by westerners whose celebration provides a festival with such generosity and happiness.

Christmas offers an insight into the nature of vocation, too, be it a nurse, doctor, teacher or anyone whose job is more than a career option. I know that one day I will have to take up a vocational task. Conscience, do not take no for an answer; it is a calling from a 'voice' within, which I will have to accept and obey unconditionally. I was willing to be an officer in the kingdom who carries a particular vocation, lighting the darkness of lies, badness, ignorance, disease or poverty, and uplifting people's hearts and minds. The church professionals are servants and should not measure what the people are worth to the church by their wallet size or the kind of property.

To make a fortune and a profitable living and levy from the poor by pressuring the disadvantaged at the end of sermons to give money must be condemned. The church may have a cash shortage. Still, they are not in the business to make money but to proclaim God, and it takes a certain kind of person who is willing to sacrifice a lifetime in a humble profession and be modest and moderate in their standard of living.

I want to get out of manufacturing into the caring profession to care for mortals instead of working at the engineering factory that uses hard steel and aluminium to produce harmful war machinery components. I am concerned about souls, and metals are cold to work with – they have no soul. I have warmth, I have love, and I have an empathy that brings comfort to the needy. It was not a career choice if I stay at the engineering factory for more than ten years or retire after manufacturing metal parts for warfare. I did it because of a weak economy, and I had no vocational choice. The professional option is part of a dream to be happy in work and live in an ethical, trustworthy and rewarding occupation.

The job hits my conscience hard because I know that the end product is for the military, and I am here to do a job and get paid, but I cannot stop my mind from not wanting any part of manufacturing equipment for the Gulf War. I calmed myself by suggesting it is for defending us from the invader or the aggressor. Working to manufacture equipment for the act of war makes me think that humans are lost as a species. We have the technology for good or bad, and we are cruellest because every so often, there is a modification to the weapons that cause massive destruction of human life. Animals kill primarily for food. Harsh as it might seem, in tearing their living prey apart, they can never invent technology. Therefore, we are lost as a species and may not exist as such two thousand years on.

It's happening again, and I am ill.
Written 31st May 1993- Sunday 13th June 1993

Note adult theme

In the space of time from December 1992 to March 1993, I was living in a deluded state, seeing everything that family life stood for had broken down. I believed that I had to do everything domestic, except the ironing, and the vivid dominant message I had been trying to tell my wife began to fall on deaf ears. Euphemia was not listening to what I said about money, our relationship and the children. She saw things completely different from me and said I was spoiling things but couldn't seem to see that. I saw her as complaining and being cynical about us and saying she was unhappy. Of course, it was all a fabrication in my head, but I agonised for days over what I should do. By the time I had decided, I felt myself getting ill.

I made an appointment to see the GP but had three weeks to wait for the doctor of my choice. So I went to see my mother and told her I was getting ill, that I would see the doctor in three weeks, and that I thought I could hold out.

At the same time, working at the factory was becoming more unsatisfactory. Workmates regularly borrowed my tools and left them lying about or managed to break them and did not bother to replace or pay for them. I decided to charge ten pence per day to use my tools, but I would exempt staff and management. I put up notices at the work area with the words: 'Due to the damage and breakage of my tools, I find it necessary to impose a charge of ten pence per day for their use; staff and management exempted.' I find it hard to tell workmates not to use my tools because I may need to borrow some of theirs. One manager had borrowed something of mine, and two weeks later, it still hadn't been returned, but he had asked me to remind him. I thought it was appalling, but I wrote in the admin staff's exception and privilege of management.

Since October 1992, I had developed anxieties based around a painting competition I wanted to enter, for which I tried to paint a scene of Wellingborough or Northamptonshire. While stressing over finishing the painting by the deadline,

I was close to a nervous breakdown. The competition would be judged in February 1993, and the winner would receive a prize of £1,000 with second and third places also winning money.

On a lovely warm autumn day in October 1992, when the pale blue sky hung high in the serene atmosphere, I took my camera and snapped fifteen picturesque scenes in Wellingborough and had the film developed. I asked the family which was their favourite, and the unanimous choice was Gloucester Place.

I enlarged the photo, then set about getting materials to paint and preparing to display my work at Christmas 1992. I asked my wife to cooperate with me because the painting looked very good, and I would run out of time if I continued to do the chores and painting. So I needed to do fewer tasks and get on with the picture. Still, Euphemia said, "You will not be able to finish the painting because you left it too late". I replied, "I could, only if I am left to concentrate on painting after work because I think I am creating a masterpiece which will lead to recognition of my talent in art".

I had used most of our housekeeping money to buy my raw materials and felt I could predict that a financial slump was lurking. I had my heart set on at least winning the amateur prize money to pull us through. There was this particular feeling that gripped my mind and soul. If I finished the painting, there was no way I could not win one of the prizes. I was driven on by this endless sort of 'twitching' and by support from family and friends saying the painting was magnificent, but I had to come to terms that it was now too late to enter this year's competition, and I must think of it for next year.

The painting was only half-finished, and I only had one more weekend to work on it, and it had to be ready by the following Wednesday to be submitted. I had not come to terms with abandoning the rush to get finished by the deadline. I worked on it with a massive hefty head cold over that weekend and took the unusual step of taking Monday off. My cold was so bad it gave me an extra day to work on the painting at home. Over the weekend, I had taken the art to a framing shop to be sized for a frame. Unfortunately, some of the paint had rubbed off during handling and caused restoration work to be carried out when I got home.

On Monday, I had a quarter of the painting left to finish off. I battled at my agonisingly slow pace to finish the picture in the kitchen as the evening meal was getting cooked. Moist air was present in the room, but I forgot the condition would not be ideal for painting and found the finished part of the watercolour painting was melting on the paper and merging into a paste that made the details disappear.

I almost panicked to rush the picture out of the steamy kitchen. Still, I carefully carried it into the lounge, shouting, "Oh, no! oh, no!" furious with myself that it was almost spoiled, but I had not yet thought of giving up my attempt to finish it. After dinner, I returned to finish the painting and repair the damage when the chores were done.

It was 9 pm when it occurred concretely in my mind to stop. However, it would not be finished, so give it up and abandon the struggle. I searched for cosmic meaning and purpose to settle my unhappiness, and all I could think about were aspirations. I wanted to be happy, and not entering the competition hit my stressed nerves and was frustrating.

The factory's work always seemed to be completing rushed orders, and I was getting jumpy and absent-minded. I was unhappy that my unfinished painting was not in the competition. I was miserable, too, that my wife saw that the picture was exquisite but could not accept that having too many domestic chores had put me behind with the painting.

She did not go along with my suggestion to reduce my housework chores to have more time to spend on the art. The wife persistently said I had left it too late to start the picture, and due to having an eye for detail and my speed of filling in those details on the paper, I was slow, which had made it beyond my ability to make the deadline. Her logical reasoning was not getting through to me, and I blamed her, even more when the exhibits went on public display because the winning painting looked so amateurish. An excellent professional picture did not take a prize. I thought mine could have been a winner, and I took it out on Euphemia by wanting to play it cool and not speak to her at the exhibition, but with the saddest look of disappointment upon my face.

It was the final day of February 1993, and I was agitated and not thinking straight. Reasoning things through correctly and logical deliberation were purely accidental because my decision-making processes were impaired most of the time. Moreover, through my behavioural changes, I had created a false reality that made me different from how people had known me.

My wife, family and work colleagues saw a change in my tolerance level. I became obsessed with testing my wife's loyalty because I was relapsing, and the actual reality of her love got knotted up in my false belief that she could not love me.

I came across the few love letters I had written to Euphemia before we were married and read them back to her in the comfort of our bedroom and asked her, "Did you see how I adored you and how I was obsessed with you?" She laughed.

Euphemia had never answered any of my letters, but she did write to me once when she went on holiday to St. Lucia. I pointed out to her that in all my notes, I misspelt her name. "Why did you not notice?" I asked, and Euphemia laughed. I asked her to write me a love note one day when she was ready and present it to me, but she just smiled. Finally, I reminded her that I wanted a love note from her almost daily because Euphemia did not show me love in the little things that make marriage spicy. She became a little angry. "For God's sake", she said, and on the 4th of March 1993, she rushed and got a piece of paper and a pen, and wrote, "Love, love, love, love letter, love letter love. From your wife".

I wrote her a letter to explain how I saw things, and I believed she was deliberately winding me up. I could not tell her face to face that I felt hurt by her not taking anything I said seriously and laughing. I was ashamed of her for what she had disclosed to the pension man who regularly collects the premium. I couldn't go on with her bearing little domestic responsibility and seeing her letting go of the person she had been before.

I told Euphemia she must leave because things were not working out, and we must have some time apart. I suggested she inform the children and tell them she would spend a week at her sister's. I had no place to go but my mother's. Euphemia wouldn't hear of it, and I could feel the stress of the state we were in worsening. I had stayed up all night writing that letter and handed it to her before leaving for work the following day.

I came home that evening after work and saw the dining table wonderfully laid for dinner. A single beautifully formed red rose full of scent in a vase with a note beside it that read, "Please accept this rose as a token of my love for you and I am sorry about everything. All my love, Euphemia". The children regularly saw me smelling the rose and saying how lovely it was. The perfume would die, and I wanted to preserve it forever — that spirit in which the rose was given. I liked the rose to remain permanently fresh always, so I took a photograph of it and treasured this beautiful moment in its original state. I kissed the note and carried it in my wallet until today, Sunday 13th June 1993, when it was stored away with other keepsake papers.

Euphemia had lovingly prepared dinner, and my conscience was talking to me, telling me things aren't that bad, and my heart softened, but I could not break up the incoming thoughts in my head that set my mind like concrete. I was too weak to win back the crown. My mind was so adamantly made up that I could not soften my psychological condition to win over my head, so full of solid mental images.

My heart could not overcome what was in my head. However, I had fought hard to change it by recalling or looking back at the past, seeing the present good time, and moving forward. I was paralysed by the specific psychosis that's coming, weakening and dimming my faculties at the molecular level, a genetic mystery of schizophrenia.

Euphemia went to see her mum with the children for a few hours on a Sunday afternoon, and when she returned, I had her bags packed for her to leave. Euphemia said nothing, and I felt I could not sleep in the same bed with an emotional batterer who still confessed she had a love for me. I catnapped on the settee, laid blankets on the floor, and tried to sleep there but could not. All night I stayed awake. In the morning, we took the children to school, and I told them when they came home from school that their mother and I were not getting on and their mother was leaving that evening. Again, Euphemia said nothing; the children cried all evening and well into the night when Euphemia tucked them in bed and left the house without informing me of where she was going.

All the children wanted to go to school in the morning, but I only allowed Katrina to go and provided her with a letter to give the teacher. I asked my dad to call in before I went to work, take the other children to grandmothers, and bring them back when Euphemia called in the evening. I told myself if only Euphemia could have agreed to stay at her sister's, the children's deep upset could have been avoided. Instead, Euphemia stayed with her mum and went to work and saw the children at dusk immediately after work.

I had trouble understanding people's behaviour and felt stressed by it. The first was concerning my wife, and the others were about work and work colleagues. Since putting up the notice at work, no one ever came to borrow my tools again. When they came to ask, I told them to read the note and give me ten pence towards school funds, and they walked away. Their behaviour rattled around in my head. I knew I was the only person in the factory with the tools they wanted to borrow. How were they able to do the job without them? That evening, I saw a freshness in my wife. In her eyes, I noticed that she seemed to want to put things right and stay in the house, but she did not verbally communicate it. My improper/ imposter biased thinking said, "but it is too late." I wanted Euphemia to stay away for as long as it takes. My heart told me that the one night away was enough. That was all it needed, but I was not obeying my feelings again. I watched television for a while that evening, and it was strange and confusing that the people on the TV seemed to be able to see me and read my thoughts. I left the room.

From this point on, it was almost impossible to have control of myself. I knew that everything would be out to destroy me and went straight to bed. Euphemia put the children to bed and came into our bedroom, and we talked warmly. I told her I was very seriously ill. Tears continuously flowed from the corner of my eyes, saturating the whole of my cheeks as I spoke to her. "You will have to stay now to take care of the children, for I am mentally ill. I need to go to work in the morning because the firm only pays sickness benefits of £45.00 per week," I told her.

Driven into the wildness of an unstable mind, I had once again entered a baptismal experience of problems and emotional and spiritual crisis. The pressures had broken through my normal defences, and I am writing about these real experiences without concealment.

I am willing to confront and attempt to understand and learn from the less palatable bits of my life. The first realisation that I was entering the schizophrenic world again was when I put the radio on. Songs always portrayed my sense of love loss and made fun of my predicament, laughing at what they obviously could not see me doing in getting ready for work. Also, what I saw on my way to work was strange and, finally, the television distortion. Newspapers became something I could not make proper sense of, and the only music that I could listen to without distortion was classical. The piece was unique. It spoke to my mind and acted as a pacifier does to a child. The sounds from pianos, flutes, violins, harps and other stringed instruments were so harmonious, so calming in orchestral music, and they relaxed me. The sensation produced in the ear by trumpets, trombone, drums and the rest of the orchestral instruments was triumphantly uplifting. The mix of these kinds of instrument devices seemed to bring forth confidence to face the day's trials with courage. The other forms of music feed on sorrow and weaknesses in the human spirit and the oppressed. My behaviour sought to act out inner hostile powers, and no matter how hard I tried to feel healthy, I could not help myself doing what I did or saying what I said.

I was close to insanity, but I would call it the tricks my mind played on me. The thing was, I had two levels or more of thoughts at the same time which produced feelings that opposed my true self, and during a conversation with other people, I felt weird and could not hold a coherent conversation. I was in a state of danger, and I needed to rediscover life's abundance, but a constant downward spiral was forming. It became an invitation to fulfil my destiny without God's purpose.

My journey back through the illness resulted in a vivid universal cry of fear as I encountered suffering bizarre thoughts coming through my mind telepathically. The voice entered my eardrums like a voice from a distance, far away from myself. I experienced a mixture of persecution and compassion. The mere fact that if they killed the body to get to me, I should still exist in my mind was mental torture.

In a bid to regain some self-control, there were times when suicide seemed the logical thing to do. However, I could not because even though I was conscious of a terrible vulnerability and frailness of the self, I could not end my own life. Now, it seems like a bit of a mind-bending emotional roller coaster, as I was going over the day's events in my mind, dwelling on what was happening during the night.

I became terrified to go to bed because of the repeated attacks of mental punishment and that they, the unknown people, were trying to kill me –not dreams, but real entities. On the night I told my wife I was mentally ill, I could not sleep the whole night. Tears continually cascaded down my face, and messages seemed to come between the music and the talk from the bedside radio. When the ninety minutes snooze time switched the radio off, high-pitched whistling sounds screeched like cosmic noises in my ears. I tuned in the radio again and switched it onto a foreign station. I still had the sense of someone wanting to communicate with me from the deepest space. Then the broadcast that seemingly was gibberish became a real live English-speaking voice. "Do you read me?" came a lady's voice from the radio waves. "We want to communicate with your world, earth." My mind was pumping out telepathic waves of friendliness and peace, and by morning, I was exhausted.

I felt weird, but not as if I was a danger to myself or others. I did not feel I was in this world, for the environment was operating much different from before, but I had to get to work. On my way to work, the light rain fell like hammer blows on my hooded coat, and people looked like they were walking above the pavement until I got so close that it became apparent that they were not. I knew that the feelings and perceptions of people's faces looking hostile and vehicles moving above the road's surface were weird. Logically, it was madness, but it was my internal reality – but how to stop this out-of-this-world experience? I had no way of stopping this terrible perception. As I slowly cycled to work, I thought I could hear communication noises in hissing pitches as if a frequency was opened but not broadcasting yet.

I then thought that I could not possibly last out the working day with such distraction. I felt nervous, internally shy, and unable to approach or speak to anyone, even people familiar to me, because any communication from adults would be misinterpreted. A grin, a smile showing some teeth, hand gestures, and the look in their eyes seemed threatening. I had to look away sharply and sometimes heard 'voices' saying I was a coward.

People's actions would be to harm me, which was increasingly riding over my logical consciousness. I clocked in at the factory ten minutes earlier than usual, after leaving the house more than twenty minutes earlier than I usually did. The communication noises I was hearing began to broadcast immediately, and I heard voices in the factory. My mind turned the chatting with workmates before our start time as a sign of them disliking me. I could not clearly understand the conversations in groups around the factory, which was not the only concept that was bizarre.

On starting work, I found that a measurement made on a piece of work with a one-metre rule yesterday was not the same length. It was shorter. I timidly told the foreman that the workpiece I had cut yesterday was too short today. He measured it, and it was at least 2mm longer than the finished size. I went back to my machine and measured it again. Again, it measured 2mm too short. I took the piece in my hand, shuffled my feet to my cabinet, stood there for some time, and then walked back to the milling machine to clamp the work to the machine bed. Thoughts of doing the job had disappeared out of my mind, and other irreverent thoughts were racing along in my head as I fiddled to clamp the piece to the machine bed. I then reached for the starter switch by the overhead motor, and my attempt to switch it on was suddenly halted by a sharp twitching pain across my chest. I unclamped the piece and held it in my hand, standing motionless as my mind was trying to get my concentration back, but I could not. My mind was rolling around in my head and not holding any thoughts, and I was almost a mute.

I had 'flipped' because from that point, I only spoke two words, "only two, just two, two, two!" and I was unable to look at anyone. The foreman saw me standing in front of the milling machine, holding the work and saying, "two, two" repeatedly and not seeming my regular self. As I was led out of the workshop to the reception area, a male voice suddenly entered my mind, which was not my thinking voice, "Karl, you are malfunctioning, you need a new implant. A new programme will be made for you", it said. Another male voice said in an angry tone of voice, "He holds up productivity – make him work faster".

The banging of the working presses, the sounds of machinery's running motors, the hissing of compressed air leaking through faulty hoses and nozzles, and the compressor's noisy cycle could not prevent the voices from being dominant. The voices talked of how workers functioned efficiently and repeatedly, without mistakes. I must be programmed to work without thinking. The sounds made 'hell' in my head. Yet, I did not rebuke it; at first, I just listened as it continued to say, "Karl must be moved from B.B. Enterprises (where I worked is called B.B. Engineering); he is searching for God – he is no bloody good here".

My wife and my dad came to the factory and took me home. Travelling in the car to home seemed to have become weird with time. The GP was called to the house, and he notified a psychiatrist, who Euphemia persuaded to let me stay at home on increased medication and go into hospital if I got worse. I did get worse, and I was continually saying, "I don't want to be controlled... I don't want to be controlled". Finally, I was admitted to the hospital.

I want to communicate further what had happened to me at the factory, at home and in the hospital. It was so personal and sensitive that it took me a long time to make up my mind to write it down without concealing anything from anyone reading this. Therefore, the contents may be shocking, offensive and explicit – but not deliberately rude. I want to thank my wife for being the most incredibly right, kind and loving person in my life. It seemed I had passed through a science-fiction sort of existence before finding the real in me and society. The experiences led me to think that I had lived out my imagination and experienced the weird and not-so-pleasant. My mind became the power that caused fear and created a battle between soul and sanity. I am a living fossil, bearing a record that extends far beyond what had happened in childhood. I became imprisoned in the structures of the creations of my mind.

Every white man and woman seemed to have a unique language, yet English and their body language were exceptional. I felt I had been fooled by the white race about the environment and my body. They understood me, but I was finding it very difficult to understand them, and it was not because of an accent - more about the various meanings they put on a word. The graffiti and the writings on the toilet walls and doors at the factory affected my psyche. I took the handwriting, 'Lazy fucking twat' and 'Go on, shit yourself,' very, very personally. The workmates' attack on me angered me, and I fought within myself to conceal my anger rather than air it.

My conscience was usually perfect when I made love with my wife. Sex was part of caring, something to be respected and treated with dignity, and I always thanked God for my wife, a good woman to love, make love to and cherish. So, the troublesome voices did not exist to degrade it for months.

One night, when I was at home before the hospital admission, I was woken in the middle of the night by a female voice being sexual, but I had no sexual feelings in my body. It said: "Fuck me, I am a real woman. We have been controlling your wife's vagina contractions for years, and black people got controlled, not real people; only whites are. It must have felt mechanical to fuck. You can have me, a real woman to fuck," it spoke. "I don't want to be controlled," I cried out in my head in my inner talk, the sound leaving my mind without any words coming out of my mouth. All the talk was my loud voice ricocheting in my skull. "We are human people too, but it does seem like black people are controlled – please let us go". A male voice then came on the scene saying, "You can't fuck, and you are not fucking good at the engineering job either". The speech had retreated, and my senses experienced noises and scents from sexual activity, an orgy happening around the dimly lit bedroom involving invisible people. The sounds of sexual climax and groans of pleasure were even coming from under the bed.

The bubbles of nervousness were in my stomach as I turned to switch off the bedside lamp to go back to sleep. I placed one hand over Euphemia's genital area: if the invisible man tried to penetrate her, I'd know about it. I went back to sleep nervously with the noises of lovemaking happening all around me. In the morning, I got out of bed and stepped as if consciously avoiding stepping on anyone. There was a genuine feeling at the breakfast table that other people were at the table, too, and chatting about the night's orgy. My raven eyes had no filmy surface and made gentle, graceful childlike blinks with a healthy glow because I'd had some sleep. Still, I had deteriorated and went into the hospital willingly.

In the hospital, my mind was, for many days, in transition. In the scenario of illness to wellness, change began with a fragile understanding of what was happening to me. Then, a permanent change occurred when the active schizophrenia condition was knocked right back by a regular daily dose of medicine.

I had experienced the voices of groups of people meeting every morning to discuss why I hadn't had the new implanted programme yet or why I hadn't been killed. They banged on the table in the room and shouted at each other. A chairwoman was trying to keep order and said that my death would, before long, come to be seen as a measure of injustice; "give him a chance with a new programme". "There is no death. I do not believe I can ultimately die because God is in my brain," I said to the voices. "When you are asleep, we will come and get you," they said. Then I was frightened to fall into a deep sleep and could never let myself, and I think a part of my mind always remained awake and alert. Whenever I awoke, I never felt that my conscious thoughts and subconscious thoughts ever wholly rested.

I sometimes called the foreman Captain Steve, and his wife was due to have her second child in the month when I was admitted to hospital. My mind was pushing out unlimited messages every night, asking him if she had had the baby yet. Then, finally, the voice that came out of space would answer, telling me to stop and not wake the Captain.

The staff seemed to know everything I was thinking by night and day. One of the women patients also had an insight into my thoughts. The running of the ward and the incidents on the ward were cosmic. I predicted them. One patient had died, and in a patients' meeting, we discussed death, dripping taps and showers, and the open abandoned wall sockets and ceiling row of missing lights. I talked about how the water pipes' plumbing noises and central heating were working on my psyche. The meetings were becoming less important to me. Suggestions from patients were overlooked because most were cuckoo ideas.

I began to write a few notes to the hospital doctor because I always felt that I was being persecuted and the environment was strange. As the hospital environment became more familiar, the troublesome voices disappeared entirely. I left the hospital with the active faulty voice-hearing, the auditory network in my brain suppressed, and I remained in remission.

I now have a great sense of reason, but it's allied to immense compassion for other people, and I have a secret personal view of the world which presents itself as thinking one thing while thinking another. It is because I guess what someone might want to hear, but I feel it first. The voices in my mind have entirely gone, and I am left confronting my thoughts as they should be. Euphemia had been a greater strength throughout the illness and recovery and is my best friend, making me laugh more than ever. Things can be defused in a jokey way, and we are good companions and, in her way, I know she loves me, for we sometimes become helpless with laughter and forget what exactly was the connection with the conversation. Thanks, darling, for your love and support. XX.

The Finished Painting
Written December 1993

I finished the painting. I yelled "Hooray!" to the family and imagined Georgina giving me a fanfare on her school trumpet. The townscape painting has enriched my life because I cannot stop going back to where it hangs and admiring it. There is excellent amusement that my artwork may not reflect the area as it is now, a year later. We looked back to when I first took the photo and began to re-create it in watercolours. This side of the town shown in the picture is due for redevelopment, and by the end of next year, 1994, my picture will show a bygone age. I will enter the piece in next year's competition and hope the judges are looking for a painting with nostalgia and see my art capturing the time's spirit.

My townscape painting was not only meant to be an accurate representation of the area – photography can do that – but it's to represent art. Through lines and colours, the image that I, the artist, produced cannot be understood through the visual and feelings and the unique quality of a painting. Taste walks a fine line, and my images are a definite statement of my taste. I priced the picture at £245.00, a grossly underestimated value. I worked on it for a year, hoping that the judges would see the subject's complexity, mainly in the architecture. Unfortunately, the medium I chose was problematic from the perspective of an amateur artist.

Nothing in the art world is built on concrete, but the satisfaction I get is to put my taste on the line for the judges to judge, and I hope with my adrenaline running high, my anxiety will drain when I win. The painting glowed beautifully with mid-autumn colours, made even more beautiful with vibrant, delicate flowers. My innovative use of colours and washes takes one's breath away. My eye roves across the painting and settles on a particular focal point. In my case, it was the litter bin that I had difficulty painting upright and keeping in proportion.

How is it for you when you look at the painting? I am drawn in by the picture because it shows a familiar locality. I recognise it's an exciting subject matter that possibly connects most people in the town. Gloucester Place is a major road junction in Wellingborough town centre. People visiting our house can identify the painting quickly. It's a painting that stands out and speaks to the observer, so one is drawn to make comments.

I feel a picture can change depending on where it hangs. It may appear lighter or darker, and it may be the last thing anyone thought is needed to have hanging in a home. My paintings reflect my taste, and if I give them as presents, it's the most intimate, special present I can offer. I hope it's not a painting of crumbling disappointment but a poignant visual delight that enhances their space.

I recently patted myself on the back because I managed to paint an image of movement, contrasted with stillness, and added to my pleasure. After toiling away in obscurity, I was pleased that I had plucked up the nerve to paint again after so long. I hope the painting will be the winning exhibit and attract more attention because I believe I am on the road to what I hope to be fame and fortune. Have a Happy 1993 Christmas, all of you!

Returning to work and the new pill
Written December 1993

I hoped to God that I would never again experience the open curtains of a mental breakdown accompanied by schizophrenia, even when supported with medication.

I still have a lot of living to do and, even with the help of God, there is no guarantee that I shall pass through the rest of my existence without the stresses of life bleeding me again. Believing in God does not stop life's trials and suffering from happening, and death in the family is the only concern I have that might knock me into the world of the person with schizophrenia again.

Death from illness or fatal accident seems to be the only thing that might knock my good emotional state. I know that my parents will die one day, but I do not want to bury my parents or children if fate takes them early. Caring angels at the pearly gates would insult my grief and my intelligence, and if anyone said, "God moves in mysterious ways", I would want to strike out at them. A child's death is not natural to cope with and, forgive me for saying this, but I would rather have to bury my parents than our children. I think I can just about come to terms with that, as long as wrinkles and old age accompany their passing.

God would feel sorrow, grieving with us at the end of earthly life, that ending being an absolute, unalterable fact; God would mourn for the loss of those who died.

The sorrow of death terrifies me: I have seen a corpse before, but I have lost the ability to deal with the stress unaided. So, I pre-visited my workplace on Friday before I returned to work. A warm welcome and happy-to-see-me-back smiles came from the boss and staff. I was allowed to visit any part of the factory to tell the workforce I would be back on Monday.

What I thought would be on Monday, my most awful, terrible, traumatic, mouth-drying, trembling-legs day, started and ended as a fantastic turn of human hearts, and I was alright. I was not even placed on a trial period to prove myself worthy of working again, as the doctor had signed me back to work. I have seen the most understanding of people and kindness, which still exists today in a selfish, envious, careless and greedy workforce. Everything has settled down as if the paranoid time of seeing graffiti that disrespected the factory, and the problem of my tools being used, were simply imagined. Things are in perspective now; the scars remained on the factory building, but I had seen a form of respect for me now that previously did not exist.

I had been visiting the psychiatrist monthly until now, but it's a six-monthly visit from here on. I had mentioned to him that, after taking the Largactil medication, I was sluggish and sleepy. I managed to do a day's work at the factory, but I had to go to bed at about 8 pm most evenings. I was becoming paranoid about going out in the evening and darkness falling when I was still out. I was frightened, not about night crime happening to me, but a feeling of terror and a lack of every kind of confidence.

I was supposed to be well, back in the community and working, but there were still periods when I had uncontrollable evil thoughts, and my mind was busy with things I cannot forget. So horrible thoughts just popped in and out of my mind, and I had to say, "Oh, God forgive me" or "God forbid", just to have some temporary control.

One day, when my way to a cousin's wedding with relations, my mind ran riot on me. My one inner voice kept up loud mayhem all day and night by repeating the same few sounds, like a mob chanting.

In my head, I was saying, "Oh God, oh God". Trying to pray was my only relief, but that in itself became like a further riot, and I had to go to the family doctor. My visit to the GP was not initially related to mental distress. I had picked up a hamstring injury from one of the few dance routines I had performed to impress and needed treatment, but then I let him know of the mental anguish. The doctor signed me off work for a week, and my psychiatric medication was changed to Sulpiride tablets, 200mg twice a day. It was the pill the psychiatrist had told me a month ago I may have to take if the Largactil no longer controlled the schizophrenia, the voices and my lethargy. I did not hear voices; I just hoped the medication change would reduce my repeated self-talk and night-time fear.

Within days, Sulpiride proved to be a great, fantastic pill. My fear had gone, confidence returned, and I could go out at night, stay awake for longer, and the chronic mental anguish didn't return. I spent quite a lot of time in my imagination, maybe too much, but anything can happen there and does. I have a form of peace and tranquillity that I experienced in my childhood, with the kind of confidence that brought me back to those carefree days of living with my parents, gradually gaining the assurances I needed to grow up.

Every day when there are changes, I want to change and grow, but not to lose! Losing would lead to mourning and grief, or just unhappiness, and without time to heal, the hollow places in my soul bring about terrible fears.

Schizophrenia has brought me away from the surfaces of life and into my depth, where I access the unexpected, unfamiliar mysticism of schizophrenia, a separate category of human existence and experience. I begin to wonder about the meaning, and I forget my immediate concerns as my creative impulses exhibit the pathetic dimension of phenomenological existence.

From one breakdown to another, I wonder what creativity has come out of it, ideas so weird that even someone with a good imagination would be left lame and wouldn't want to go there.

In my mind, there is a sort of struggle between happiness and sadness. Sometimes, melancholy responds to a feeling of twilight, a mood of autumn following a breakdown. Before a failure, I wanted relief from the weight and burden pressing me down into the earth when hope was gone, and the sense of a way out was lost to me, and schizophrenia appeared as an answer. In a sense, I am always going insane because of feeling sadness for the world, relationships, money problems, and I have no words but merely obsessing.

My soul knows of the buildings that are being destroyed, the up-rooted trees, and the spreading ugliness. Somehow, I am mourning for what is going on in the world. My children are to live their lives in the soul of the earth. I will become driven, obsessed, and sometimes wonder if it's a curse having a schizophrenic condition because things take over my life, and I have to use what I am and what I have and try to see the positive side of tremendous insights. The positive symptoms are fires that excite the imagination to go where it will, to unite my conscious and unconscious life. It is the warm heat flowing out with the capacity to see what is outside of my conscious control, what is extraordinary. My imagination drives me into an exploration of the weird and then returns to life's ordinariness.

In the schizophrenia world, I am reminded that we have boundaries and limitations, but I see an infinite horizon. There is a depth of reason and a vivid image in fantasising about the afterlife, heaven and hell that I can only achieve through schizophrenia. Often, the experience would be hellish. There is no literal hell; simply the old learnt Christian theology that the ego had about hell as an inferno, a damned state of misery, a satanic place of torture and pain. Hell sits in a place in the mind which is void. I have already eliminated it as a real place because there is no underworld. Life is full of mysteries, and I would not attempt to explain any of them, for I cannot.

My life has stressful moments, such as those present in this 1993 breakdown from which I am in recovery and can go back to work. Logic and sin were confusing me, and the psychotic medication did not damp my interest in them. I had no answer to why I had logic and sin dilemmas. I try to understand certain things, even with a frail mind; I thought I improved after the breakdown. That's all I can do –better the world with what I know and what I am. My mind throws out ideas that anyone with a good imagination could make up, but the tragic thing is, some of my thoughts and images have developed out of sickness of the mind. They form in the centre of my head, making the concept an audio-visual hallucination or a delusion that seems able to live. From one breakdown to another, the phenomenological – that cannot happen in a healthy mind – is metaphor framed to explain these distresses of psychosocial, cognitive functioning with negative symptoms that cause me to wonder, what the 'hell' happened, sometimes plays on the supernatural.

In all my writing so far, I had not recorded every bizarre thing that my mind was expecting me to believe, but now I feel I must go back a bit and tell the stories to be studied because they were so weird. There are stories of how an ordinary guy with common sense can end up bonkers and reveal the extent of his imagination and thoughts in a seemingly supernatural way.

One such time was when the leg with the hamstring injury suddenly 'gave way' again as I walked to the bedroom door one morning. I was frantic to hold on to something because my head was spinning too, and it was disorienting me. I was turning in the middle of the landing floor. I could see the children looking on as the noises I made brought them running to the bedroom door, and by then, I had just managed to get back into the bedroom and was sitting on the edge of the bed.

Suddenly, I was tossed about on the bed, head and limbs hitting the mattress at speed. My head moved from right to left in a turning action as my body jerked. My whole head felt like something had erupted from a region of it, and energy from my body was released violently, shaking me without my conscious effort, and I had chronic pain in my leg. I held on to my leg with both hands to give me extra support, as I had the sense of spinning. It may have lasted 30-50 seconds, and the children witnessed this freakiness.

Euphemia telephoned the duty doctor on the mental health community team, who told her to get me to relax, rest and see the family GP if it recurred. But, I thought, could it have been an epileptic fit? There was no foaming at the mouth, and it was not the room that seemed to spin – it was all the organs in my body, swirling around like churning soup.

Leaving earthly reality behind in psychotic breakdowns, I often feel in tune with, and close to, the 'stills' in nature, not the animalistic aggressive side, nor the scrounging for food from the natural world. But the low plant life and human state of meditation – what I call the graceful, still, peaceful, the quiet calm of the bustle-free passing of time in the environment. I love the 'stills' of a calm day, watching the clouds change from light blue and the certainty of sunlight bursting through and shining. The stillness of a plant gradually grows to be a tree and an expressionless face that will drop and wrinkle one day. Finally, the serenity of our human hearts gives a sense of inner harmony and calm; I feel a connection with nature's stills. I touched the plants' foliage and saw them gracefully lean away from the gentle touch of my fingertips. They sent a pleasant aroma to my nose from their blossoms. Plants responded to touch by swaying, lifting or bending their shoots and through this motion, friendly, peaceful energy was absorbed. I felt the heat, the warmth surfacing through my skin, going the other way, leaving a slightly drained feeling.

Then, the birds communicated with each other to announce their territory in the spring months; I experienced a deep connection with natural things and nature's sounds. Birds were chirping songs in the trees and others chirp-chirping on the ground as they looked for food or displayed a dance to attract a mate. Big black and brown birds, different species, just skipped up to me or dived down from the tree branches to land near me or on the corner of the bench where I sat admiring them. The air smelled fresh and sweet, tickling the fine hairs in my nostrils, sending breezes of calm through my body. I was at peace with myself, and for a long time, I would sensitively touch living things – plants, people, birds, insects, and so on – except the animals, as I did not want to invade their territory and possibly anger them. I would do this until no more special effects happened through the contact.

I had re-connected with the human-made environment, for I now have a rational perspective – like everyone else.

Happy New Year 1994 and the Summer's Spiritual Breakdown

Written in January 1994 – Wednesday 3rd August 1994

We move into an uncertain and unpredictable new year with our hope for prosperity and continued good health.

I believe that there is a providence working its purpose out as year follows year. Although I mainly treat religion as irrelevant, the exception is Jesus's life. We could have a relationship with God. The consequences of these loving relationships are to look after the earth and those we love. I mentioned 'graceful stills' in last year's writing. Having this 'still' centre in the depths of my being remains the most active element in my effort to cope with the personal and communal strains and stresses that I'll inevitably face this year.

Last year, I was strengthened by suffering, ill-health, and the miracle of medicine and my faith in the grace of God to offer the gift of peace. Expressed in some cases in restoration, reconciliation, reformation, regeneration or renewal, treated with indifference, was a miracle of healing for fundamental change. Prayer is my pressing petition for peace in the world. Meditation, relaxation, and other human techniques have helped ease worries about human cruelty, scenes of starvation, and watching the suffering of the innocent. I hope the divine gift of God's peace remains with us, always.

Last October, I bought my wife a used car for our 12th wedding anniversary. I borrowed £3,250 from the bank; the vehicle cost £1,995, and I paid outstanding debts with the surplus. The car was a bad buy, and I would like to change it, but I'll wait till summer and write extensively on sorting out my thoughts on images, reality, facts and metaphor.

It is summer, and we have fantastic weather, and my life is full of family joy. My most significant concerns are retaining good health and having financial security, and I pray and work towards those goals.

I want never to have to worry about money – not having enough is a stressor. I play the football pools now and will play the National Lottery when it starts in the autumn. I have entered the Reader's Digest big pay-out, and I have also applied for a secured loan of £10,000 from a building society.

Last month, I paid tribute to the actual credible 25th anniversary of the first moon landing on 20th July 1969, when Neil Armstrong set foot on the moon and uttered words destined to be included in every dictionary of quotations. Unfortunately, conspiracy theories are suggesting that the landing could not have happened. I had followed the Apollo mission as a boy and saw its facts right from the start, and now they are saying it was fake. I am taking this as weakening my trust with the world, and I distrust news reports as propaganda. I do not know what to believe anymore, and it is affecting my everyday life.

There is a spanner in the works, causing me not to trust anything I hear or see, for it might be a conspiracy. The Comet Shoemaker-levy 9 crashed into Jupiter. Twenty-one comets bombarded Jupiter throughout one week in July this year. It was tremendously exciting to watch the simulation on television, but was this a conspiracy? Only time will tell. I may have had a short spiritual breakdown seeing Rwanda and the foolishness of our world this month. I doubt a supernatural God in control of all phenomena, from giant stars to what is happening in Africa. I want to replace biblical images of God with abstract ideas – this would be advantageous for people trying to understand God. The crime of which I am guilty is the admission of doubt about the existence of a supernatural God in control of everything from His celestial tower. I questioned my belief in God and what I mean by God to determine the differences between images and reality, fact and metaphor.

In a sense, it is strange to be curious to know what is unfamiliar and inexplicable about God, which deepens and enriches my reactions to natural beauty, music and great literature. I may come to understand how the world works, but not why it works, not how we should live our lives, not how we face death or make moral decisions. In 2,000 years, lots of crap about religion has been revealed. I am at a loss to think of what God has achieved with people. People help people. Some people do not have a spiritual dimension and manage to get by. I question my mind to believe in a God that my imagination has planted in my head, making me sense being a part of something much bigger, like a cog in a massive piece of machinery. There is something extraordinary in the world that I try to contact in open-eyed prayer and stillness. While swearing by some spirituality that my consciousness gives me, I mistrust religion, seeing God as a 'He' with a white beard maybe... or something.

The firm belief in a spiritual dimension is a resource that should be tapped into by everyone. Rwanda's tragedy is profoundly depressing, seeing the pictures and reading the reports of millions dying from disease and starvation. Two million refugees fled from disaster and brutality into hopelessness in another country where people were mutilated, their bodies bulldozed up and buried in mass graves without decency or dignity.

The retaining belief seems to substitute for keeping an open mind and finding out what's what and what isn't true. I am worried if the prospect of having no afterlife happens to be accurate, and God is only a thick chunk of thought in a celestial control tower, monitoring everything as well as intervening when 'He' feels like it. Nevertheless, my soul must finish work on this planet before entering another dimension, so my God is somewhere out there, and I must retain my belief. It's a bit tricky trying to prove God's existence, but there was no reason not to believe in Him because not to believe meant that life was without purpose and meaning.

As a species, we have invented God, and by our faith, we know He works universally; he is somehow in us and out there. When humanity dies, God brings the afterlife. In the Bible, Job found that ultimately, God is a mystery, and nothing can be said of God that cannot also be denied about Him. It was noted that St. Augustine believed that God is mysterious and God is good, but we can even say that God is not good, for He is not right in the way that we are. Evidence of God's lack of merely human goodness is apparent in the bombs, the disease, the famine and the injustices of the world that He made. Since God is good and just, there cannot be a hell to consign millions of his creatures to eternal torment. That does not reflect well on his absolute unconditional love. I found it impossible to reconcile justice and honesty and the idea of 'hell'. Eternal damnation now has to be abandoned, but for the deserving cases who don't give a damn about 'life' – they will not come back into existence. If they already exist, they will die for the good, for nobody is all bad. We are a mixture of both.

In the wild imagination, God could see everything and punish everyone. His power extended far beyond the grave, but this life was only a preparation for meeting Him face to face, if just for a moment after death.

What God has done becomes more comfortable to answer: for people to help people, love and goodness exist in them as the product of God. Scientific discoveries have so far shown that God had created a clockwork universe that would run forever according to eternal rules and laws. Still, they remained puzzled that the pulse of life and love in all of us is an intrinsic essence of the Almighty.

The UB40 Concert
Written on 19th August 1994

Saturday 13th August was Euphemia's birthday, and I treated her to an open-air reggae festival.

We went to watch a UB40 concert at Milton Keynes Bowl. Sixty thousand were in the arena; from the start of the show, I was excited, and this built to almost fever pitch. I was whistling, singing loudly and yelling for my reggae idol. I was so engrossed in the whole programme that I was almost intoxicated by the end of the show. The reggae beat's rhythms were slow, with strong, regularly recurring sound vibrating in my stomach. So beautifully delivered with crystal clarity, the vocals had a sweet volume that undoubtedly made the live performance sound better than listening to music on a compact disc.

It was my first live outdoor music event, and it was fun to be among so many music fans and eating good Caribbean cooking. The atmosphere was electric, so hot with good music, so filled with piping good hits from their album and the splendid lighting of the stage after dusk was spectacular and hit me like something big and biblical. The crowds were enthusiastically embroiled in the band, and I, too, was transfixed by their music. Like some people in the group, I could not avoid expressing the happy feeling from hearing and seeing live professional singers and top musicians performing, and we danced. I marvelled at the performance and felt myself welling up with appreciation and enjoyment. The sweetness of the excellent tunes made the whole show liken to an intoxicating scent.

I was genuinely enjoying the concert, but, at the same time, something in my mind would distract me now and then from the whole spectacle. I first noticed the detachment from the concert's joy when my mind went off on a search and wandered. Coincidence had brought us to meet Euphemia's aunt at the festival, someone she had not seen for about ten years. From then on, I began wandering and wishing I could find my ex-girlfriend in the crowd. I became further detached from the live event as I walked from place to place, looking out for my ex, and as night came, I studied the darkening sky. I watched with admiration and curiosity the first quarter moon shining behind thin, slowly drifting clouds. Simultaneously, it moved and disappeared out of view, hidden again by denser, rolling clouds. There were a few twinkling stars in the night sky; as an individual speck in the vastness of space took my breath away, my mouth opened in awe of it.

Although the music played loudly, my imagination ran with it, touching outer space from the only known inhabited planet. I felt special in this expanding universe in the middle of the arena and believed I should be in prayer and not at a worldly event packed with people when church worship is declining.

The next night, Sunday 14th August, I could not sleep and felt I was coming down with an unpleasant illness that I attributed to the concert's after-effects. Being a born-again Christian in my recent past made me feel like a hypocrite, and I experienced a pang of terrible guilt for attending a non-religious festival – and enjoying it. I should not have experienced a worldly event when my preaching in my youth was to seek converts to Jesus Christ, and now it should be to God. In my past, going to dances and discos was only to seek converts, and I'd often talk to the young people at the clubs about Jesus Christ instead of dancing. I knew I was suffering from an acute guilt reaction, in which case, most of my symptoms might have been psychosomatic.

By the morning, I was going to the loo very frequently. The following night it seemed like the two coffees I'd drunk in the day had given me a caffeine overdose because I had worked out the problem and talked to my wife about it, but the symptoms persisted. I was again about to go to bed, fearing my illness was returning. I took an extra antipsychotic tablet and went to sleep with creepy creatures under my closed eyelids. My eyelashes get slightly moistened, which reminded me I was close to returning to the schizophrenia illness. All I could do now was let time pass until things were forgotten and not allow the past to control my present.

The extra tablet worked, but after two days, I was drowsy and felt weary. The pace of my work at the factory was extra slow. But now, on the 19th of August, I am back to the regular dose of medication. As I write, all the symptoms of ill health have disappeared. I consider myself to be blessed, but I have to make a deal with my God mind.

If something divine can bring about financial security for the family, we do not have to worry about bills and retaining good health. So I promise to give up my job, study theology eventually, and train to be a priest or minister to promote God.

Evangelical preachers paralyse the gullible with guilt, enrage everyone else, and parade their inner despair and lack of basic understanding of human psychology. When they preach to the congregation to be perfect and come away from worldly affairs, they dump unacceptable feelings like confusion, doubt, greed, and lust on any available passers-by who seek honesty. Now, fundamentalists are impossible to talk to; they leave me feeling confused and angry. I was thrown into guilt because of them, just because I wanted entertainment. There was a time when I was not to worry about the need to separate genuine necessity from a false desire to pursue spiritual values rather than riches and power because death seemed, in any case, just around the corner.

I am an enthusiast – "quench not the spirit". To restrain or suppress the source of my enthusiasm is to try to stop the activity of God. If my spiritual energy became stifled, my vision would be discouraged. I will do what I must do, work hard and someday, I will be heading for success. Such ministry is like the glory of life where you give and do not receive. To serve is better than to be served in times of need; be the strength in a crisis of weakness.

The Bible is not a record of what God did but how God has been understood by humanity. It seems that God has become less comprehensible as He has appeared perfect. God moves further from my theoretical understanding and closer to my heart when He becomes more powerful, as His follower grows weaker. God is becoming a casualty of the 20th century because an increasing number of people decided they could do without Him altogether. In contrast, others allow or encourage Him to retreat even further into incomprehensibility. People do terrible things to people in the name of God.

Both sides in the First World War claimed God's support, but after all the carnage, neither winners nor losers found it easy to forgive Him for what they had done to each other. Even more terrible things happened to His creatures in the Second World War. Among the poor and miserable, God's popularity and a sense of his presence never waned. Still, in the developed world, God was pushed away more and more to the periphery by the success of liberal capitalism in granting almost everything that people had ever prayed to have. The Being that had once dwelled beyond the celestial spheres is becoming a magnet to eccentricity. Theology has a description of God and deals with the ultimate meaning of creation, but the basis of theology has shifted, and now people sense it as meaningless and non-existent.

God the Father and Mother have dwindled into God the explanation of last resort, the Agent who acts outside the competence of insurance companies that compensate acts of God. Meanwhile, God the Son is a massive best friend, available in every circumstance of life, and God, the Holy Spirit, leads his followers into extraordinary places. I believe that the gender of God can be said to be male and female or genderless. Since Easter 1992, I have declared the Lord's Prayer in the modern explorations of God's feminine side; "Our Father, Mother, God, who is in heaven...."

Maybe for the first few thousand years of God's relationship with the human race, there is no denying that the Bible displayed a preference for the male gender. However, God is a being who combines every gender and excellence conceivable in himself, and I do not find it a disgust to call God 'Mother' or a woman. Nothing is horrifying or terror-filled about having a woman representing God. On the contrary, I would love to see the churches ordain women as priests and vicars and see women hold high positions of authority in the church and society.

Children and their schooling
Written on 8th October 1994

Georgina is in Year 4 in junior school; she is happy there, and everything is fine. In Year 1, Jonathan is pleased with the infant school and is doing well, and in the summer months, we had to choose a secondary school for Katrina to attend in the autumn.

We visited some of the local schools, and they were all co-educational comprehensive. The only school that seemed okay was Wrenn School, which appealed to us because we were impressed with how they taught the pupils, and they offer pastoral care for their pupils. However, Wrenn has a significant pupil intake, and the school has equipment that needs an upgrade. My wife and I wondered if a single-sex school might be more suitable for our child, having been educated in one ourselves. We would like to find out if, these days, that kind of schooling would provide an advantage in academic performance, building social confidence and allow growing up to be reasonable and not push children to adult sexual maturity before they are ready.

The closest girls-only school was Southfield School, a grant-maintained secondary school with academy status in Kettering, and we visited on Open Day. I was immediately taken by the integrated new technology throughout the school, with computers and other vital hi-tech teaching aids, things I didn't see in the state-run co-educational schools. In addition, the classrooms were spacious and did not appear overcrowded. I had almost made up my mind about Southfield before talking it over with their mum or seeing their past academic performances.

We weighed up the pros and cons of the schools we had visited, and my wife agreed there would be a significant advantage in sending Katrina to Southfield. It would cost more than if she attended a local co-educational school. The bus fares and school uniforms were only the beginning of the expense to give Katrina the best possible chance of success and happiness in a school where we believed she would strive. We hoped the school would encourage individual fulfilment, inspire her talents and make her feel confident of her worth, for Katrina is a little shy. Their aim is good work and high ideals with some fun in the process, and from what I have seen since Katrina's enrolment to now, 8th October, the school is a good one. The mix seems suitable for a happy and successful learning environment, without boys dominating a class, being pushy to achieve, and possibly encouraging sexual relationships early. I hope Katrina will find close friendships with boys when she goes into higher education in college or university.

Technology has revolutionised information-gathering in the past decade, and the school seems well-equipped to teach the subject along with music, drama, art, and design. The claim that boys dominate lessons and girls might therefore suffer educationally may be unproven, but I do not want to chance it and see my girls lose out or fail.

Girls may be as determined as boys, but I know my shy daughter and want her to have the best possible basis for setting out into the adult world. So they learn how to compete – even become a bit pushy – to get on in a male-dominated workplace and develop like female role models. In a girls' school, the pupils do not feel stressed to grow up faster than they want to, especially when it comes to sex. However, in a large mixed school, they may have boyfriends and feel pressured to become sexually active, which pressures them to look good – even glamorous – possibly becoming thin and unhealthy.

I like all-girls schools with their shared passions and aspirations for young girls. They have a career plan for girls, other than fashion, pop groups, and talking about boys, although these are all part of being 'girly'. If a single-sex environment provided quality of life with no bullying, it would give a good grounding for developing respect and co-operation with the capacity for survival in a macho world of work that they will face on leaving school. Here, they can live through the hopes, fears and conflicts in a community of girls, safe in the knowledge that they will not fail utterly or be lost from sight while experiencing the ups and downs that are the essence of living.

I am glad we had a choice and could send our daughter to the school we selected. But unfortunately, this is a myth for most families, an idea they hear about in political speeches, but an opportunity that does not exist.

The Dream, the Government, sold us

Written on 8th December 1994

We have entered the last calendar month of 1994, and we had hoped for prosperity this year. Still, it does not seem like we will bag a fortune because we have mismanaged our opportunity. It is why we are struggling financially and, in essence, causing an effect that must inevitably happen. Figuratively speaking, our predicament's causality is influenced by money, linking the sequence of cause and result in a chain.

We wanted to make money and free ourselves from financial insecurity, but strict laws govern the ethics of making money. Poverty as a state is to be avoided and is without virtue. Wealth is a blessing from God, enabling the recipient to do well, and the rich should redistribute some of their wealth back. Unfortunately, our financial situation has worsened. We did not get the £10,000 loan because our house did not hold enough equity. The National Lottery started, and I joined a syndicate with four people; three numbers came up, and we won ten pounds to share.

The Government has sold us a dream of great riches that bring eternal happiness through the National Lottery. I'll put winning a lot of money in the same league as the death of a loved one or discovering one has a terminal illness. The first reaction might be disbelief and the realisation that life will never be the same again.

I faithfully sent off my football pools coupon each week and played the lottery because I fondly believed in the dream of riches – not that wealth brings eternal happiness. Next year, whatever our financial fortune, we would handle it because I feel a supernatural intervention would have occurred to clear our debts quickly, or it would have been left to cause and effect. Winning a fortune will change our circumstances but not the person, me. I feel lucky, not because I avoid cracks in the pavement or touch wood or believe in superstitions. I am fortunate in most aspects of my life because I have healthy relationships and no life-threatening diseases, but I have no money yet. I'm working on it.

As I see it, luck is sometimes generated by my skills, mixed with genetically controlled or external forces. I have great faith in it. My spiritual path may have created God as a philosophical thought with an image. God exists as a first cause and first or final consequence, and I do not know what the phenomenon is that gives rise to this or that effect, but I assume a belief in miracles is of God.

Doctrines, I tell myself, are the icing on the cake of faith, and I struggle over certain lines in philosophy. The explanation of phenomena by teleology I find intellectually stimulating and spiritually satisfying.

As you know, I want to promote God. The problem I face is believing in a force that causes the perfection of the organic world. The God that I believe in has shown that all certainty rests on acknowledging causality, a genetic connection of the phenomena through which one thing under certain conditions gives rise to something else. I cannot think that any particular religion has a monopoly on God or how God should be worshipped. I sometimes have faith undermined when I see other people who have a passion for their teaching, but they are fighting and feeling that they must kill in the name of their faith. Maybe my search to find my God's embodiment and not knowing that model of perfection sometimes takes away my personal God and replaces it with a passion for good instead of a force for evil. I pray to be able to pray well and be a skilled preacher, ready to bring the news of God to life when the time comes. By my words and my life, God's love can be channelled into a world in search of healing and hope. Although I want to go to theological college, I do not think it will give me better access to God but a better understanding of Him.

We are in a material fate regarding our lack of money. In living away from our lives, we trust in God to assume an underlying purpose in everything. My spiritual condition is more critical than material fate, and becoming absorbed by material welfare sets my happiness because I need freedom from physical discomfort. I had allowed myself to be drawn into our lesser nature, and I worry about our problems, which affect so little of our essential spiritual life.

While other people appear to enjoy the Christmas holiday, I fear that our problems won't take a holiday; festive celebrations can rub it in, how desperate we are for money. I haven't bought the children proper Christmas presents, just a little stocking filler. I told them they would have their appropriate gifts in the New Year to buy cheaper during the January sales. I felt unhappy because I cannot afford to buy the children and my close relatives a present for Christmas. I kept up the hope for the tide to change, to be able to live comfortably once again.

Presently, I am aware of my ambition, goal, and what I most want to do. But, my children, if I can drum into your heads all the lessons I have learnt in life, that would save you all suffering decades of trial and error. I know your own experiences are supposed to be the only means by which you can learn, but if my word on some things can help and stop you from going through unnecessary heartache and pain, then I have succeeded.

New Year's Resolution 1995

Written on 4th January 1995

This year, I am making a sober-minded resolution to improve our financial management and keep within budget.

I look towards providing for the family better than in previous years, without having to scrounge. I like to think I'll make sound judgements in our family life and not worry so much. I want to be financially secure, so I can enjoy my family and maybe travel afar. I do not wish to have any worries to distract me from my enjoyment. In a way, I want to leave the rat race and be able to enjoy the comfort and freedom to do beautiful things with the people I love and have prayed to have hope in my heart. I trust in God that no severe illness will interfere with the plan I have for my future.

I am growing older. I feel different physically, and I have noticed that a younger reflection is staring back when I look in the mirror. Photos of me do not look quite the same, and my new beard hides the wrinkles. My love for my wife is not taken for granted. I look at young people always searching for something, and I see unhappily married couples hunting elsewhere for love that's missing from their lives. It's a never-ending hunt for affection and reassurance.

As the years roll on, I see so much more and realise how lucky I am. The love in my life is worth cherishing and not abusing, and I guess I am one of those rare people who can say I am satisfied with the love I experience. Time has taught me not to search so hard for the best things in life because opportunities in every area will always crop up. The things we do not look for, the things that just happen, are usually the best. I like all the good things in life to pass my way. I think horizons should be broadened with each passing year. If I still see life at thirty-eight as I did when I was twenty, then you can say I have wasted the last eighteen years. As far as ambitions go, I want to achieve them by my fortieth birthday next year, and much fuss and ado are to happen because I am focusing on a big birthday party. I am like a child who has found release, with the 40th year of my life being a milestone, and a new kind of adventure will begin.

Last year, God did not always meet my expectations, and prayers were not answered in the way or to the timescale I wanted. God has our best interests at heart and will eventually do only those things for our ultimate good, and I am experiencing a wait for prayers to be answered. Of course, I always want a 'yes' or 'no', but what is more, I still want my prayer to be answered now, and in precisely the way I thought it out. Earlier on in my life, I had known barren times when it seemed that all my prayers were bouncing off the ceiling or the edge of space. God looked far away, and everything seemed not to be working out. Everything seemed to be going wrong, and I thought that it could not possibly get any worse, and then suddenly, it got worse again and then again and yet again!

I have hit the bottom of the financial ladder. I hope the intense economic suffering will be comparatively short-lived because I am looking for healing and blessing through this difficult patch.

I had been reaching out to God for several months now with an extraordinary request. We must become financially secure. I do not doubt in my heart, and I believe that what was said will happen. I claim this promise for myself and believe any obstacles in the way will disappear because of the principles of faith and prayer. I am feeling an assurance that this will happen. I have done all I knew to do, and now I wait with a sense of expectancy. I cried out to God week after week in prayer and applied a lot of effort to the purpose, nearly bursting into tears as my heart overflowed with the expectation of winning the lottery. I think that, as we keep our hearts right and pure with God and learn to pray in line with God's thoughts and promises, we will be successful and win. My need for money is a genuine need for myself and to help others, not a selfish passion.

I am honest with God and have told Him where I was in my faith. I am not religious in the real sense of the word, but I have an active ethical code and moral lessons to tell my children and others. When I see or hear sad news, I say a little prayer and add, "God in your mercies, hear our prayers". Religion or faith is a little bit personal, it's something people do not discuss, but I want to explain mine. I have reached my conclusion about God. Humankind could smash the atom, rearrange matter and values, but humans could not eradicate original matter.

Therefore, if we cannot create actual matter, where did it come from in the first place? Once I had decided that God was beyond our comprehension, I stopped worrying. That is what makes me so sure that God exists and intervenes in our lives. God's existence is a certainty to me. Therefore, I can say that I have an inner conviction, and I believe in miracles and signs. Of course, there are always elements one does not understand, but there is a world of difference between complete comprehension and rejection of God.

For over two years, I had sung the hymns at the local church in my mind, and vocal sounds did not come from my lips. I stood still but was murmuring the tune in my head. From September 1992 to October 1994, I concentrated on the hymns' words in my mind and released them mentally with the music's rhythms. My wife and children told me I must sometimes sing out in praise of my God so that we can all have joint fellowship, and it's more socially acceptable. I no longer sing meditatively; I sing with the congregation, but I have combined both methods, and it helps me express my deep love for God and his creation. I learnt it was eccentric, not normally expected, but I was hoping my method will start a meditative trend in not sounding out the songs. Inward praise has the musical sounds monotonously entering into the mind, and your inner voice is singing to the origin in the depth of your soul.

I started an Adult Basic Education Class course in Basic English in September 1994 to prepare for my career move. I am enjoying the class, and I have learnt some basic English language understanding to GCSE standard. I shall attend the lessons until I feel I have gained enough knowledge of the language to move on and take 'A' level exams to continue to fuel my ambition of reaching the level of academic excellence needed to be a man of the cloth. Happy New Year to you all!

The Car Accident
Written on 8th January 1995

It is probably true what they say – "When you have a house and a car, you'll never have any money".

Since buying a used car for my wife, it always seems to need parts, and it failed the M.O.T. The garage carried out extensive and costly repairs, and it was re-tested again, and it passed. The car insurance was due to expire, so it has been renewed. Unfortunately, that same week, my wife was driving the car and was involved in an accident.

On 3rd November 1994, at about 6:55 pm at the Queensway roundabout in Wellingborough, Euphemia travelled towards town to attend a class as part of a 12-week hairdressing course at college. A car suddenly entered the mini roundabout she was passing through, resulting in a collision. The impact left her shaken, slightly shocked, and she sustained what turned out to be a whiplash injury.

The wing, one headlight, and her car's front bumper were damaged, but there was no damage to the highway signs or street furniture, so the police were not called out. The driver and Euphemia exchanged details, and a third driver, who had witnessed it but was not involved, drove off. Euphemia abandoned the car, and a lady on her way to the college saw her in distress and kindly took Euphemia home. I recovered the vehicle from the scene of the accident and drove it home.

My first thought about the accident was, why didn't I feel that an accident had happened? By telepathy, or in some other way, extra-sensory perception? I should have known an accident would happen that evening to have prevented Euphemia from travelling on that stretch of road at that time. However, I believed I had no notion of a pending accident because I was settling the children; they were on the go that evening. I was a bit upset and tired because they were noisy and more so as their favourite pop music show was on TV, Top of the Pops.

I spent most of the early evening wishing that I could sense it when something happens to my family when I'm not there with them. Then, finally, I came back down to earth before our bedtime. I realised I didn't have any special powers, telepathic or otherwise, to receive information other than human-made devices like the telephone.

A letter arrived on our doormat from the other driver's insurance company shocked us at first, then made us angry. It alleged that Euphemia was responsible for the accident because "she was changing lanes on the roundabout and did not indicate her intentions". Euphemia and I had never experienced such a feeling of nervous sickness in the pits of our stomachs as when we read that letter. It was as if every internal organ was vibrating; we were so shocked. That man might get away with telling his insurer untruths, we thought, because Euphemia had no witness to back up her version of events. We looked at each other, worried that we might never be compensated and may have to pay to fix our car. I then felt angered, so angered that I asked for a bolt of lightning to strike him. Where was an act of God to deal with people like him? I wanted him to suffer – no physical pain but a substantial loss of material wealth or possessions. His car will be repaired because he had a fully comprehensive insurance policy, but we had relied on our solicitors to prove his negligence.

I thought unsaintly thoughts for some time because we were hurting, and we needed the wrath of God to deal with people like this man, who makes other people's lives a misery when the courts are unable to do anything about it. After an assessor came and looked at our damaged car, we felt relieved that the driver who caused the crash may have, after all, told his insurance the truth. Now we wait for compensation, or they get our vehicle repaired.

Many anxious weeks passed, and we received a letter telling us the car was too old to be repaired and would Euphemia accept a market value for the vehicle of £1350? We became much happier. We felt pleased that the offer seemed reasonable, and I asked Euphemia to accept the interim payment. The uninsured loss and personal injury claims are still waiting for a settlement.

That money will come in handy to bring our finances back to a debt-free level. It must be how financial difficulties we have will be resolved, and we can again live without deep money worries. Although we would dearly like to have another car, we have no means of getting one for a long while, since the car compensation will have to be used to clear debts. Praying exclusively to God has invoked a natural answer to our money problems; nothing supernatural intervened, but the fate of things seems miraculous, considering the chain of events. There were terrible times when I asked, "How can a loving God allow this to happen?" I cannot give myself an answer. I have accepted a higher purpose at work, and this belief gives me inner strength, a fortress in which to shelter. I have a secure and happy family life and believe God enables us to withstand anything, even though I asked the question, "Why does God allow it?" when it is terrible or harms others. Does it not upset the status quo of why it is permitted?

The interim payment cheque came on Friday 17th February 1995, and a week later, outstanding debts and their burden were lifted. So, we can live day-to-day with the income we have, but no extras. Even so, we are happy, but if either of us, Mum or Dad, becomes seriously ill, we'll be back to square one.

I dedicated my national lottery and pool's coupon numbers in a religious way to God and vowed never to change them. I prayed weekly to be lucky so that history could be in the making. This weekend, Saturday 4th March, I had my second £10 win on the lottery with my syndicate numbers. It is going to happen. I predict that I shall have substantial success on the lottery or the football pools by the end of the 1995 financial year, without me paying too much into it. The money will help my family and myself and pay for my education in the new field I want to enter.

I do not know, but I have a sense that it is nearly within my grasp, and I have not long to wait before the miracle is about to happen. I know that I am often filled with anxiety, but this is different. I have a promise, and I have to wait patiently and stay firm and decisive in my wishful thinking.

Lent and wickedness and evil
Written on 5th March 1995

It was Lent. The festival runs to Easter, meaning Spring is here and relating to new life and spiritual growth. The popular associations of Lent are to give up something and be disciplined. Still, it's a time of inner growth through self-examination, constriction, forgiveness, renewal, commitment and the restoration of our souls' sincere desires.

I am striving for personal holiness, and it's an enormous task because evil seems to be so prevalent and infectious in our society. The level of what is acceptable is slipping ever downwards and recently, dramatically so. The political world is disreputable, and there is a massive increase in crime in the community today. There is a call for people to have self-discipline. The slums of human behaviour seen on television as novelty or comedy represent a plea for self-discipline and not a call for censorship. If society continued this downward spiral as the millennium approaches, there would be an ever-increasing number of panics. I think, every time there is an earthquake, a flood or a war, mystical scare-mongers will attribute it to the approach of the second coming or some supernatural catastrophe. Humankind can stop this spiral, but does it have to get worse before it gets better?

The cultivation of the beauty of holiness is a specific Lenten task, both for me and communally. There is a responsibility laid on us all, of whatever religious standing, to present in our lifestyle the beauty of non-fanatical puritanism and have a restrictive, moralistic temperament; the holiness that values the good, the lovely, the healthy and the wholesome. What concerns me is that so much that is trivial, trashy, and of no actual value shapes the surrounding atmosphere in which young lives evolve these days. The law seems somehow designed to take care of those who have done wrong and the minor injustices they may have suffered, as opposed to the significant crimes that victims suffer at the hands of those people. The topsy-turvy values of society! Victims still live with the suffering, and criminals are shown all mercy without paying back their victims. Murders and other violent crimes take away the freedom of life or leave victims suffering.

The Ten Commandments are the best laws ever, for they are never stupid and don't need changing. I get emotional, but I don't feel depressed when I read newspaper reports, catch TV or radio news bulletins on this world's evil. Instead, I go to a silent place to think and pray, and tears pour from my eyes; I reflect on the sad news items that portray the brutal wickedness of people's inhumanity. There are the injustices, the racial conflicts and the apparent breaking down of worldwide societies that used to love one another rather than deliberately committing acts of violence to inflict pain and suffering on others.

I should not burden my heart with what is out of my hands or what I have no control over, but I cannot help my sensitivity. It's a part of me, and when it gets too bad, I give up reading newspapers, watching TV news, and continue to pray and hope, in the wash of the tears I have cried, that good shall win over evil.

The world's situation, where evil seems to be winning, makes good people 'mad' and angered. I said I am not depressed but feel angrier and 'mad' as a figure of speech. Even in our local community, crime increases, and people feel less safe, even in their homes and neighbourhood streets. I praise the work of Amnesty International and other international organisations like UNICEF, who strive for human rights and safeguard the vulnerable. Those societies that look after abused and abandoned children have my blessing. I want to create something to bring down evil globally, as I wish the wicked people to die out or be killed. Capital punishment must be brought back, for there are genuinely some consciously evil people who fight for extremism and wicked concepts, and they need to be brought down. The force of evil in human nature is winning, and only in science do we see better. Faith transformed my views about wickedness and evil, which I wrestled with to formulate how I think crime should be tackled.

When I put my faith first, I have unspoken prayers of hope and redemption for the world and our community. Wicked, evil people were children before they became conditioned, and I do not want children to die but wish them forgiveness and love to be central in their lives. At the heart of the universe, God's unconditional love affects all areas of my life and leaves me free to work things out for myself, and if I get it wrong, I am assured of God's forgiveness. Evil men and women have twisted reasoning and blamed culture when caught out and may say, "It's not me; it's the society that has caused it". Hooligans, thieves and thugs blame society also, and the drug addicts might blame their parents. It seems to be an example of the culture of blame that is growing. There is blame on socio-economic circumstances that puts lives in a mess and when you trip up on a paving stone, do you learn to pick your feet up? No. You sue the council. Are we victims of forces we cannot control, or is it the government's fault, society, or upbringing?

Some people blunder through life, looking only for someone else to foot their bills and carry the can. In the past, people could blame a rigid class structure for their failure to succeed, and it's more painful to blame things on a lack of morals or merits. Television shapes a lot of people's attitudes with raw images of people as victims. A belief in personal responsibility is essential in a civilised society. Without it, people lose the guilt function and slip into moral anarchy. There is another thing needed in people's lives – spiritual sustenance that signposts us to enlightenment. When we begin to be dissatisfied with materialism, it fills the inner void. We cannot do anything about the life we were born into, but it's a struggle to accept it, whether you are beautiful or ugly, rich or poor. People who trust science, reason and materialism, and fail to nourish their souls are disillusioned and need to ask fundamental questions. By neglecting the spiritual, they reap the consequences.

Believe in religion, God. The modern world has allowed the importance of searching for life's meaning to be downgraded. And it seems ridiculous that we should believe that the big bang happened because scientists say so when spirituality is much more plausible than that. Western thinking does not encompass the concept that our consciousness is much more subtle than electricity generated at the neuronal level, impacting neuronal networks. It exists separately from the brain. Why do they think everything is a manifestation of the physical mind?

No one is compelled to believe in either God or the Bible; these days, anyone is free to accept or reject any bits of the Bible they choose. There is a pick-and-mix attitude to its teachings. Where are the holy men and women who are a fountain of charity and have an instinct for truth? They get paid to argue the case for God, but some support views that mean loss of faith. They are non-believers in the principles upon which facts are built. Is no one any longer ready to stand up for their God and the church's policies and beliefs? I cannot understand why even the clergy seem not to believe in God. Sure, most God-seeking people, like clergymen or more inclusive clergy members, find specific things and their conscience explicitly prohibits their conduct.

Nevertheless, God has existed for years as a word, and God is in our dictionaries as part of our language. Does the clergy suggest that God is an internal view of a conscious intention or idea, or is it an ideal moral principle? What are people to believe if the people who argue the case for God no longer believe in the perfect ideal?

I believe in Jesus, the man, and like to think his teaching guides me, but I hesitate to believe he was the Son of God. I do not believe necessarily that Bible stories are absolute facts and do not have to take them literally. I accept the Bible stories as stories but not necessarily as complete facts. The term 'Son of man/God' was a phrase used by other prophets, and Jesus also said he was the Son of man. Why are some liberal thinkers getting it so wrong? Some clerics who wear the frocks cannot believe what they say because they cannot give assurances. Some Bible stories are sublimely obscure, but I cannot worry about what 2,000 years of history have not clarified. It does not alter my belief that my Christian principles govern my behaviour. What gets me is clergy declaring they do not believe in God and the theologians' insistence on over-analysing religious texts.

I firmly approve of having women as priests, and people against women's ordination maintain that apostolic succession is divine and that the church is somewhat immutable. The church has a tradition of adjusting; after all, the church used to think slavery was alright. Humankind is the maker of gods and laws. How I see it, let the believer create his God in his world, let the atheist create his godless world but let neither seek to impose his personal and subjective world view on the other. People who claim spirituality imply religious belief because spirituality simply rejects the old pseudo-scientific notion that the physical and material world is the only reality.

Religious belief might be primitive, irrational and seem infantile, but it should not be derided on that account. Children need to believe in a loving, wise and protective father or mother. My spiritual uneasiness is primarily due to the growing rejection of organised religion's imposed authority and organised science, and powerful institutions are changing the social and political landscapes. It is because people can find the answers within themselves. We need a tolerant philosophical attitude and a tough modal shift. Nothing less than a mental and spiritual revolution can now save us from this worldwide social catastrophe.

There's a spirit not understood, a mysterious force that guides and directs men and women's affairs, which is available to believers. For many people, I suppose, belief in the theory of evolution by natural selection is no better than believing in a supernatural creator. Natural selection is not a recipe for the greatest happiness for the highest number of organisms. The universe we observe has precisely the properties we should expect if there is fundamentally no design, no purpose, no evil and no good – nothing but blind, pitiless indifference. DNA is DNA, and we dance to its tune because DNA neither knows nor cares. God help us if DNA cannot cure the peculiar contemporary theory of evolution. Although I believe in a supernatural creator, I also hold scientific beliefs that give us evidence, unlike myths and faiths.

What happens to Fatherly Love?
Written on Thursday 16th March 1995

This evening, an incident happened with one of my children, Georgina, who had me in a rage. I had to put pen to paper immediately after the event because I felt so sorry, so full of regrets to have committed an act of violence against a child. It pains me deeply to hear her cry and see her rub the injured area.

I am genuinely sorry, Georgina, for inflicting corporal punishment on you because I lost my self-control on a nine-year-old. It was terrible. I felt awful because I do not lash out when in an argument with an adult, and I lashed out at a child to gain the upper hand in a disciplinary matter. Let me say, I had made it a policy not to smack children, and I felt so guilty to use my hand and gave a smack to her bottom when I had a strict ruling not to spank. It was an extreme case to maintain control over her, and being in a temper made it seem acceptable. Still, the moment I hit her, it devastated me, and I immediately apologised and yelled secretly within myself, Oh, no!

Children, you can be so naïve and saint-like, as you should be, but you do not always do what your parents require of you. Tonight, Georgina was asked to have a wash and get ready for bed. She went straight to bed and stubbornly continued to say she did not want to wash. Usually, a good shout in my deep voice will bring her to tears, and she would carry out the task asked of her, but that did not work this time. I encouraged Georgina to climb out of her bunk bed by badgering her and yelled, "Do not let me lose my temper; go and get washed!". She stormed into the bathroom and locked the door, still refusing to wash. I allowed a few minutes to pass and asked, "How are you getting on?" A robust and challenging answer came back – "I am not washing!"

I felt initial anger that she was disobeying, and I shouted for her mum, who was downstairs, "Darling, come and see to Georgina because I am having great difficulty getting her to wash, and it's past her bedtime." I banged on the bathroom door and yelled, "Open this door!" Then I began to search for something to turn the latch from the outside. I opened the door and gave Georgina a harsh smack on her bottom, and pushed the wash-up bowl in her hand. But I had a devastating feeling. When

Georgina was back in the bedroom, still crying. I hugged her dearly and gave her my symbolic blessing, that is, making a kissing sound with my lips and touching her forehead and then stroked her face and said, "Mummy and Daddy love you and all the family; good night. God blesses!"

Two days later, I still felt ashamed for having attacked my loving nine-year-old child for her disobedience. If she were an adult, there would have been endless arguments but no physical contact. Georgina pushes the boundaries, and this time, I reached the end of my tether with her because when she says she will not do something, it is difficult for me to find a way to make her. I often leave it to her mum to threaten to smack or withdraw something she had wished to have. That usually works.

Children, believe me, smacking or withholding gifts no doubt hurts you for that moment, but it's a hated discipline I had to carry out that profoundly affected me. Katrina, you would do as I asked but under protest. You would make it known that you disagree, and we'd have shouting matches, but most often, you'll do as you are asked. Jonathan, you're no trouble. While hugs and kisses have helped our makeup, it nearly smashes me to the core if I have to strike any of you. You say you are sorry about your behaviour and I am glad to love you again. You are forgiven, and I am sorry for lashing out.

Finding out about my mind
Written July 1995

It has been said that the human brain is the most complicated structure in the known universe. From the secrets of the atom to the mysteries of deep space, all the great voyages of discovery would come to nothing without that lump of grey matter sitting between our ears. Life's ultimate mystery, our conscious inner selves, may soon be explained, not by philosophers, but by scientists with imparted holiness that alerts their conscience.

I think that humanity's survival and probably the survival of this planet depend on a complete understanding of the human mind. Philosophers enquiring into the human condition can no longer ignore the brain experiments of scientists. I am keen and enthusiastic to know about this last great frontier of human knowledge. The seat of experience itself got explored in a way unimaginable. Brain scanners, psychologists and molecular biologists are beginning to cross-fertilize in their search for a better understanding of evolution's outstanding achievement.

My interest in the brain is identifying how my brain activity differs from healthy 'normal' people. Being a psychiatric patient, is there something happening in my mind that can show different signs even with the medication? Understanding what goes wrong in the brain relies critically on a belief in the functions of the brain. I want to see a cure for mental illness. If I suppose we are indeed all ill and not just creative, conscious thinking affects how we live, our prospects for life and death and the thoughts are puzzling. Thinking and experiments hold out the promise that we may one day understand the universe in which we live and our potential as human beings. I probably would never understand quantum physics, and it's a test of the thought process that needs a great deal of imagination.

I do not know how to start to understand my consciousness. I only have an ill consciousness and an ordinary consciousness to compare, which might be the same. I have a clear awareness of the schizophrenia illness, and as I write, I feel as well as any healthy individual, but things in my field of vision are distorted as if in a curved mirror when the illness flares. Even worse was the demonic transformations of the outer world; people were out to harm me. I perceived in myself something people call a demon that had invaded my thoughts and tried to take possession of my mind and body in my inner being. The dreadful fear of being insane seized me. As it turned out, it was an illness, mind upside down and inside out, but without hallucinogenic drugs like LSD.

The illness that I have has become a scary ride into the inner recesses of my mind. I can still recall my fear of events that took place in a psychotic episode a decade ago. It was a horrible, terrible experience. I had the feeling of being out of my body, of being insane, of having lost all connection with reality. Indeed, consciousness is not a single intact entity! Chemicals in the brain do alter the doors of perception in quite disturbing ways. Has consciousness a physical basis, or is it merely a metaphor to describe how we describe ourselves? Defining consciousness is inherently tricky. Being sound asleep is not being conscious. Neither is lying on an operating table under anaesthesia, and I do not think consciousness has anything to do with being in a coma or being brain dead. There's quite simply nothing else like it, and I cannot define it in terms of anything. They say that – "seeing is believing", which is why sight should be prominent in the study of consciousness to see how the brain relates to viewing in our minds. Memory is so interlinked with the awareness that I don't feel it can be regarded as a distinct function and housed in a particular place.

I often wonder if being schizophrenic makes my consciousness more profound because sometimes, one train of thought impedes another. The theory is too readily distracted along some divergent path, and I felt either not remembering what I first wanted to say or what is said goes in through one ear and out through the other, leaving me with a blank mind. Understanding human consciousness is loaded with irony because the brain is trying to understand itself. It is so weird that it's a slightly spooky scary thought, but there are almost unimaginable ethical difficulties. If scientists know how the brain stimulates consciousness, the implication would be that they could manipulate it precisely. One could hack into another consciousness as others could hack into mine. You would not have the individual anymore. It's a slightly spooky scary thought the more I think about it. So, you think about it too, and you will find it weird also. Think about it!

I get sad when I have to tell white lies because it's a fluke in my character. Evolution put it there to protect me, and when the self is threatened, I know when I have to tell a little lie for escapism. I contact my higher self and say to myself, 'my God forgives me' or 'may God forgive me after telling the blatant lie'. I think I have an addictive habit or seem ungodly, and I pray and show my God; I received enjoyment from it. I do not want to stop the practice that is pleasurable and classified as a bad habit. So I say God allows it to continue the natural routine that people say breaks the moral code, but it is understandable to surrender to it, for it does not hurt me or anyone. I pray to God to prevent guilt and shame, the righteous punishment we feel when doing something wrong. I think not all ungodly things must go. Our human 'fall' makes us want these things, or we believe a human needs those things, and I think God understands. God forbid if thoughts of mine are not pure, I say. I think the worst is when I feel others threaten peace and goodwill. I am linked to evolution to bring to end evil and badness. I will try my best to survive, maybe selfishly, to maintain goodness, happiness and peace, through my 'walk' in life and my prayer life.

My brain has released some of its secrets, and it truly believes humanity was made in God's image. Therefore, how the brain works may offer insights into God's very work and creation itself, and it makes me think twice, or at least one thought for each hemisphere. Who among us imagines that human beings will ever be able to comprehend or explain the universe and their consciousness?

What has happened to the 'call'?

Written August 1995 – December 1995

In 1st Corinthians 9:16, KJV, The Bible says, "Yea, woe is unto me if I preach not the gospel." I feel it is a necessity to preach. Although I am called to the ministry by my God and convinced of the imperative of preaching, I still don't have the finances to start me on my way. It's money, not motivation, that bars the way.

The new term starts next month, and I want to move from Basic Skill Class in English to GCSE, but that course costs money, and I cannot afford the fee. I have not got a penny! And my faith in the lottery's big win is on the wane, and I am struggling to know if I will ever get to do the study this term, September 1995. Since announcing that I would like to enter the ministry, such an irrational decision has profound implications for my family and me, not least the abandonment of my engineering career. Nevertheless, I am convinced that this was a divine call to serve, and I could not resist.

A few years on, I hold that view but am sceptical. I cannot see my vision anymore because the term is to start in GCSE, and it appears I will not be starting the class, so yet another year will pass. I thought of resigning from the commitment to preach and concentrate on bringing up the family happy. Still, at my temple lobe and my forehead, I always remember, must remember, that it cannot lightly be laid aside. I feel I am a chosen vessel called to lifelong discipleship, but I need to learn how to discipline my thinking and take up the offer to preach.

The conversion process had been on the way for some time, but I feel that the suffering, the inner conflict, will return if I do not take up preaching in speech or written words. I need to communicate that we require God's exposition, a positive part of biblical theology and an informed pastoral sense grounded in recognizing the spirit's healing gifts. My mission is based on bringing blessings to the world by people experiencing personal spirituality. Preaching is a privilege to make known God to man and woman by promoting His presence to the world. I cannot make it my priority yet, because I need those vital exams to prove my wisdom and understanding.

189

My views need airing. Some are scripture-based, some self-taught, which should be called liberal theology, which must not be condemned. Any examination of the historical facts of the Bible creation is proper. I cannot take the full view that the Bible is written by anyone else from Genesis to Revelation but the pure Holy Spirit in humankind. Is there some unpure, unholy thinking substance that doesn't fit it together so perfectly? I was taught to believe that the world would get worse and worse, then Christ would come. I am no longer convinced. I think God comes through the mind rather than through the heart and makes us build a better future. The Bible's central teaching is the Atonement, and the cross is the centre of it all. It must mean I must accept the reality of heaven and hell, but I do not believe in the existence of hell. I can see there is a real place like heaven. It was said it's part of the revealed truth since the fall, and they will feel the wrath of God, but I do not believe in the 'fall story' as being literally true. - Jesus revealed it as the Son of God, but to me, he was a man - a preacher and prophet. Hell could mean only the absence of God because Jesus used the metaphors of fire and pain. It is a version peddled by most contemporary preachers.

I do not know if it's true that one's destiny is already mapped out when one is born. Therefore, I have dropped out of the necessary class. My decision to do so was because nobody likes a preacher instructing them to adhere to wholeness in preacher's sermons.

I devote myself to a sort of subconscious meditation and maintain contact with God within me. Since the decision, I have felt that God should be calling me elsewhere, but it will be out of the ministry and something more down to earth and something I can cope with better with any luck. To wear the dog collar makes me beyond reproach because we are God's representatives on earth. Some hypocrites are spreading his word, but their job is neither to judge or threaten people with God's wrath.

Today, priests, ministers, and vicars need to be reminded that they are in no position to dictate to the rest of us until they get their own house in order. Lately, across the religions, they have been at it like dervishes. We hear of bishops who have fathered illegitimate babies, priests who have been 'outed' after gay orgies, and suspicion of illegal wrongdoing in the church. If I were to be a preacher, doctrinal bits would but also goodness, kindness and honesty. If I am not a preacher, integrity, compassion, and reliability issues matter - not all the doctrinal bits. Once I have discovered my talent, I will use it.

The Bible has some magnificent stories, with tremendous application to the present day, but as you know, I do not believe the Son of God stuff. I was a great believer in the readiness to fulfil the call that the inner spirit says must be undertaken. I had a sense of adventure which lay between ordinary responsibility and indefensible irresponsibility. From a human perspective, being a preacher is irresponsible, but in the religious view, however, it's carried out in faith and obedience.

My spiritual growth for the sake of religion is on hold. For the cause, the sense of adventure is an essential element involving risk-taking. That is at the heart of creative irresponsibility. My faith with divine help and personal support will lead me to think that preaching is for me. I will have to work hard to recapture the sense of adventure inherent in discipleship. The spiritual journey with its risks and its experiences is, in a way, irresponsible, and I do not feel so committed to it anymore.

The Cloud of the National Lottery
Written December 1995 – February 1996

I have a piece of optimism because I am halfway to the bright side, which is a pretty shiny, happy place to be if you do not know it.

A few testing months have passed, and things have improved with the power of positive thinking and good luck. Einstein proved in his particular theory of relativity that everything is relative, including misfortune. I looked at the bright side of our problem by surveying the side of the road from someone's else's window. There is a saying: "what does not kill you makes you stronger". Therefore, things can only get better, even though we might think we have dealt with a dodgy hand.

I have talked of winning the big prize in the lottery or pools, but from last May 1995, I stopped playing the Football pools' after consistent failures to win any prize money. I have re-examined and eliminated; supposed paranormal explanations are the answers for this entire run of the mill experience of disappointing prize draws. The numbers are a randomness and probability theory test, with nothing to do with the paranormal intervention. I had a mistaken view and did not understand randomness. Coincidences get viewed as a 'spooky' result of paranormal phenomena.

My faith in the lottery win is on the wane, but I do not despair because it's a fun way to gamble with that loose change in my pocket and not with the money that makes up our financial future. I successfully applied for a loan for £6,000 to pool all my expenses and debts together. In June of 1995, I bought a used car and fixed what we owe better. Wow, I only have one liability to pay over five years and the mortgage repayments.

The national lottery has been running for a year, from November 1994 to November 1995, and I only play the syndicate. I stopped buying tickets for a sole win. I thought that the flutter activity is becoming compulsive by being intermittently rewarded by the thrill and excitement of winning small sums of money.

I felt myself encouraging a form of self-deception in which I am motivated, and if I win, it tends to reinforce my belief about the likelihood of having a more significant win. I have won twice, two ten pounds with my single numbers and five times with the lottery's first year's syndicate. I believe in 'luck' and the laws of probability and now only flutter the syndicate money away. When I lose, I place my faith in the rules of the possibility that a win must be just around the corner.

The lottery jackpots, 31st December, are expected to be £33 million; it's the second week. It's a rollover. I feel impulsive to gamble this week, just an extra pound; just to lay just one more bet is an additional incentive because it's such a vast sum of money. I hope it's not too puritanical to suggest that the potential for harm is considerable if the winner does not use the money wisely. Wish me good luck then! A Happy New Year to you all.

I spend £3.00 a week on the National Lottery. Since the jackpot of more than £30million was won by four people, an epidemic of lottery fever has broken out in the country for the double rollover of 10 million pounds up to February 1996.

I have gone beyond my comfortable means that we, as a family, spend on the lottery, just this once. I spent £5.00 on the double rollover. It would be the only time I would take a stab at the big win with money not allocated for the draw. I have made myself a gambler for the sake of keeping a sense of hope springing up in me and holding on to a dream of a better future.

I believe that randomness and probability work for us, and soon the big jackpot will be ours. I do not feel that I am an addicted gambler, but I cannot give up playing the game. I know I will have to reduce the amount I play by £2.00 again, but I still have the fever, hoping for an early win. The lottery encourages my hope; it sustains my dream of gaining some freedom from a weak financial present. If I do not play the lottery, there is no hope of seeing aspiration, the things we think of as possible and may need constant concern for results, like matching six numbers out of 49, spring the possibility of 'this time it's me who won. The social consequence of gambling on the lottery may be a nation of flutterers deluding themselves. Some may become addicted, but I hit out at lottery killjoys. But, in the end, it's fun, and at 8:10 pm every Saturday, life changes unmeasurably for the better for someone, and others, it's been bad luck.

I am looking forward to the next week where one's luck might change. Without the game, there would be no chances.

Saturday 17th February 1996, we won £10.00 on the syndicate, the first for the New Year. After that night's defeat, I decided to stop playing my numbers and only stuck to the syndicate numbers. This week, the lottery statistics were published, and the temptation to put faith in the pseudo-science of analyzing the lottery numbers gripped me. The graph did give me a riveting read that almost turned me into something akin to a drug addict, a lottery narcotic. However, I had to stop myself from analyzing because the odds of guessing six correct numbers out of forty-nine are still one in fourteen million.

I have abandoned playing my other numbers because I now feel that there are outrageous odds against winning. I am now beginning to oppose the entire concept. People like me who can hardly afford the one-pound lottery are buying the most tickets. It takes away money from those who cannot provide it and argues that it raises money for a good cause to leave me unimpressed. The National Lottery was established not to create millionaires overnight but to raise funds for deserving good causes. I thought of ending our money worries by scooping the lottery or winning the football pools before I stopped playing it. Instead, I downplay the lottery and only buy a ticket a week. Will I ever be lucky in getting a big payout? It's a chance in millions. I do not want to end up in the next century as I am in this one; hard-up.

I am thinking of how using a wise, shrewd, intelligent approach to our finances could work, rather than relying on luck on our side to bring me cash. The National Lottery is already a great national institution, and each week, millions of people take a chance of winning lots of lovely money in the jackpot. I know that my chances are slim, but I hope.

It will be lovely to have a little nest egg at the start of the next century, and I have been trying to put away some money for the future. Overindulging financially at Christmas and just not budgeting correctly always brings debt problems to us in February. We hope for the compensation money from the car accident to lessen the pain of February with its winter colds and icy roads. I borrow habitually to provide us with the things we need to live comfortably and pay on credit. We are not in such deep waters as we were a year or two ago, but it will be okay now that I have a shrewd way of living within our means. It's a bit like a sacrifice for me today, for a better tomorrow.

The sick world of terrorism
Dunblane
Written in April 1996

In mid-March 1996, one evil man massacred sixteen children and a teacher in Dunblane Primary School gym and killed himself.

Sometimes the world seems so full of violence and the horror of life's wickedness that I despair. Faced with such fragility of life and the apparent randomness of evil, it seems one cannot make sense of it at all. The tragedy of Dunblane had me paused, to stop and be silent for a minute, in respect for the children and teacher who died. I have deep anguish over the lives cut short and deep sorrow for those suddenly and cruelly thrust into mourning. I was deeply angered at this man's crime. He perpetrated it, and I sincerely regret to God that's what our modern society has come to be. "It was better for him that a millstone was hanged about his neck and that he was drowned in the depth of the sea". So, in Matthew 18:6, says Jesus to those who harm his little ones.

With the decline in religion, it seems that counsellors and those with insights into psychology are the ones who are forming peoples' guidance. The children will be grieving for their lost friends, and their effect will be fear and bewilderment. The children's faith in the world, their confidence in the ability to trust adults to protect them from harm, were all destroyed, and their childhood spoiled. I hope that many people will speak to the children about God, for there is comfort in religion, and I think children respond to it. They can accept the reality of a loving God and reap consolation from it even if, or perhaps because, they have lost their unquestioning trust in the small world around them.

The Bible is no stranger to tragedy, to the wicked, evil ways of humanity. With all this technology we have today, the mod cons, the heart of humankind is still smouldering within evil, which, once indulged, can unleash forces so uncontrollable that they become inhumane. Our ethical and moral consciousness is not keeping up with our increasing high-tech knowledge. The price of human freedom is always the same as the risk of wickedness and badness. The innocents' massacre poses deep and searching questions that challenge all of us to do something or say something with words that do not seem insincere or superficial. There are no words that can express my sorrow that a murder has cruelly and unfairly extinguished such a source of light as those children's lives were. A child symbolises hope, a fresh start, new possibilities, a life uncluttered by the failures and the wounds, the deep resentments adults carry.

Infanticide, the ultimate human abuse of vulnerable children, shocked me to the core. It challenged my faith to its roots; faith in God, and faith in others, my faith in humanity. How can one still believe in a loving and caring God if He allows such things to happen? Theologians have wrestled with such fundamental questions down the ages, which lies at the very heart of our human existence. Such madness sharply shows up the limitations of my understanding, and it punctures the pride of having some explanation to the mystery of life and death, good and evil.

The tragedy laid bare the raw frustration and helplessness which one feels. One lonely, disturbed man was responsible for the killings. Such murderers exist in mercifully small numbers and will always live amongst us if prayers are not answered in our time.

In-Service to the Community
Written February 1996 – 7th July 1996

I want my daughter Georgina to be a prospective pupil for an excellent mixed comprehensive school called Bishop Stopford School in Kettering. She is due to leave primary education and go on to secondary education in the autumn of 1997. However, I could not afford to send her to the same school as her big sister Katrina because the travel cost is not free; it costs £7.00 per week.

Bishop Stopford School is an Anglian church school, and it is known as the best school in the area, beating Southfield School, where Katrina goes, in the league tables. One of Bishop Stopford's criteria for a pupil to gain a place is knowing that the parent undertakes voluntary community work.

After reading the form, it twigged I should do voluntary work again, alongside my engineering day job. You probably can remember I had previously been a volunteer community worker before I was married and enjoyed it immensely. In unpaid community work, I saw my faith, kindness and caring love expressed in helping others in whatever way I could, to show that I was willing to listen and care about them. I have so much love and compassion to give to others, and I want to go out and present where love is needed. I thought of bringing up the children first before committing myself to the task again, for they are at a reasonable age where I can think of leaving them unsupervised for a few hours a week.

I found the work of befriending distressed people appealed to me, and I feel compelled to etch my character in the broader circle than just my family. So, in answer to an advert in the local newspaper, I applied to join the Samaritans Kettering branch as a volunteer. The qualities they asked for seemed to fit my personality, except I may need a comforting shoulder when dealing with calls which can be very upsetting. I studied the information pack they had sent me, and I am more than convinced that the work will test my human qualities of faithfulness, patience, sensibility, tolerance and confidentiality.

The Samaritans are not a religious organisation and do not seek religious commitment or a particular range of skills, academic or social. However, I have a clear motive for joining the Samaritans. I want my human qualities to show an exercise to my family and friends, extended into the wider community. Compassion and consideration must be delivered to all who were denied the opportunity to live life to the full for whatever reason. My listening and sensibility skills will give a sympathetic understanding to all those who come in contact with me. The considerable increase in suicide attempts these days is among young people, and I want to help prevent this disturbing trend and deal with this vital social care area today.

On Tuesday, 13th February 1996, the Samaritans interview me, and I passed this initial stage. Next, I'll be attending a series of six or so preparation classes, and at the end of the lessons, the position gets assessed. Then, if all goes well, practical training in the operation room under the supervision of an experienced Samaritan follows.

I have a secular approach, not a religious conviction as to why I want to take on that job, although the challenge comes from deep within my core self where religious feeling lurks. The ultimate grave concerns I have for people will be expressed and give me relief from inner torment. My faith plays a big part in myself for courage and strength. I will be dealing with people from all walks of life. The atheists and agnostics will be just as responsive to the healing of their broken spirit by my sympathetic understanding of their problems and my heart's secret prayers. In some ways, I am hoping to be like jump leads to a flat battery. It may seem too hard for them to live, but the battery recharges itself once the motor is going. The caller will be befriended and find that healing is taking place in their lives. Simply through sympathetic understanding and talking, the stranger feels that someone has switched on a light bulb inside them because their problem was shared, and they will be pleasantly warmed. That, I think, will improve their main symptoms of stress and unhappiness and may even relieve chronic pain.

I want to understand people's behaviour and how they communicate their distress, and I want to become confident and help support them. I hope that the glow that I carry in my heart, that tingling feeling when I seek to help people, but there is nothing one can do, will radiate that pure unconditional Love of God to them and get them hooked. The essential qualities I carry are patience, understanding and caring. I try not to be over-anxious. It's the month of May 1996, and I have been so passionate to join the Samaritans that I would have died a sort of death if I had been turned down. I have had practical training in the operation room under the supervision of an experience Samaritan. I am nearly at the point where I take calls by myself without the supervisor listening in. I am sometimes left to talk with the caller by myself if the supervisor feels I can cope.

Since I started taking calls, I feel a tiny instant of panic as the telephone rings. It's only a fraction of a second, a rapid heartbeat due to not knowing the caller's distress or problem. But by the third ring, my right hand was out to lift the receiver. My voice degenerated to calm and mellowed, and I spoke, "Samaritans - can I help you?" My voice conveyed my heart full of friendship, caring and love.

The calls are so varied. Here are a few I had to deal with: I am too fat, lonely, suicidal, relationship problems, fear, deprivation, unemployment, perverts and people with sex problems. I had training to listen in on female Samaritans calls, as some experience sex callers.

The act of suicide attempted or completed provokes in me a riot of emotions. I am moved with compassion by the thought of someone so despaired of life that they decide to end it. I was driven to deep searching thought to identify the failure to give meaning to another's growth. But, on the other hand, I am irritated beyond patience by the emotions implicit in someone's suicidal act and am threatened by what appears to be sensitive blackmail. This act is a serious philosophical problem, and it makes me reflect on just what or who it is that keeps us going, that makes life bearable, that sees us through the moments of despair and the occasional dark moments of our soul.

Some of the calls I had taken were from suicidal individuals who were psychiatrically ill but by no means at all. I do all I can to help suicidal callers to see reasonableness. However, wise people still kill themselves—the enormity of the impact of these final deeds is enormous, and the after-effects leave no room for reconsideration, no opportunity for apologies, and no moment for goodbye. Instead, they leave me measuring my compassion, knowledge, and expertise on how I could learn to identify and prevent suicide.

Now that I am experiencing troubled people, I realise that despair and suicide have no respect for people. Being in distress and perhaps wanting to end it is very much part of daily life's drama. Through the ages, people have demonstrated their power, the most significant human ability to kill oneself. One decides whether or not life is worth living by this final act. As a Samaritan, I am helping towards suicide prevention at its best by stopping suicide and assisting the person in believing that it is good to be alive. Helping desperate people who are suicidal continually reminds me of so many people's despair and unhappiness. The outcome of most of my encounters is uncertain, which means I have to cope with anxieties and bear them inconclusively.

I have discovered I have much in common with some of the callers. I share the deep emotional feeling of loss, selfishness, despairing and weakness as part of our human response. Like war, suicide can get given romantic, glorious and even honourable descriptions, when in reality, both are about death and destruction. Reader, you may know that once or twice, I have come to the brink of suicide, and then I experienced an inner stirring of hope in the grip of my black despair of clinical depression. I hope the caller's pain will be reduced, just through one intense encounter with me listening, but most probably, I will not find out the outcome.

I think that so many people in their desperate hours need to be embraced gently with human warmth, confidence and hope, but never get it. So, I pray in my heart that somehow this can be conveyed over the telephone, and the caller can feel they were helped.

The intensity of being a Samaritan and the emotional stress of many encounters make me aim to relax by talking to the team, having a good sleeping pattern and believing that God is working in the processes. I keep building up my confidence and learn to accept that each person needs some time to express their dignity, even in suicide. Already, I have had to bear emotional pains and feelings of failure, loss or guilt as part of the cost of providing aid for people who are feeling so desperate. Yet, the uniqueness of those passionate relationships seems to emerge from these struggles that I share a degree of empathy. Because we have a therapeutic relationship, there is absolute uniqueness about our togetherness, and I feel especially rejected and hurt when they want to kill themselves. I acknowledge that our special connection does not mean I had control over them, for acting as though we were the ultimate controller of human life or God is dangerous.

I always discuss the calls with my colleagues. I am not suggesting for one moment that I control human life. Being a pragmatist or exercising a reasonably democratic manner, sometimes more totalitarian, will bring about a better lifestyle, and people will not want to kill themselves. It seems evident that reducing suicide depends on education and positive social change. Doctors and cultures cannot treat social isolation. We should think of educating from birth to overcome all factors that increase the incidence of suicidal acts. Good mental and physical health, going to church or being involved in other social groups, fighting against being in debt, and total employment is potent factors against suicide. Suicide is a very personal act, but it is not unrelated to the environment. Improvement in the quality and the value of life is an essential part of prevention.

Since I felt drawn to providing help and support for those in distress, my psychological needs are being met, too, helping combat my depressive attacks. My motives now seem mixed. The heightened sensitivity and awareness of the needs of others provide me with psychological education in sensitivity and self-awareness. My personality does not prove more prone to depression and suicide. My instinct to preserve life is powerful, indeed, and I hope to finish my training to become a Samaritan by September 1996.

I have an all-important meeting coming up with the director to discuss my progress in mid-July. Then, if all goes well, I'll be doing my final training to become a qualified Samaritan in September 1996.

Last month, I made a mistake in dealing with a caller, and the supervisor said to me that I'm not ready yet to take calls by myself and that I'll be moved to see how another trainee has progressed. He says I often repeat myself in conversation, and he pointed out that this can be utterly devastating to a caller. I had the feeling that my chance of becoming a Samaritan might now have been dashed. I try even harder to get things right now, but I feel like a loser with defeat inside me.

I have not been to training for three weeks because of family commitments; the children's school held concerts, and there were parent evenings, so I cancelled my shifts. When I returned, I was not allowed to go on duty without my supervisor. I was feeling apprehensive, uncertain and dreading the worst. I am more a loser than ever because I did not think I had retained anything I had learnt; somehow, I had forgotten it all. I had just begun to hope that I would still be in the race and the Samaritans would accept me. My greatest fear is to fail in this vital task in my life, the one thing that I know I want to do. To be rejected, not become a qualified Samaritan, would be devastating.

As I tried to make blessed gifts useful, I was glad to be in that position that uses them to help others. Unfortunately, the opportunity to make a difference is now being taken from me because of the opinion of a body in the Samaritan organisation—a failure not to recognise my assets and only see my weakness. I keep repeating to myself, please, please, God, help me pass and encourage the Samaritans to identify and evaluate not only my weakness and failings. Ultimately, I know that this was something asked of me which I would not have thought of in any other situation, so I must try and try because it gives my soul and social conscience satisfaction.

Today is the 1st of August 1996, and the director and a senior Samaritan interviewed me on 16th July 1996. I was devastated to learn that I may have to leave the organisation if I do not grasp how to forward a caller. However, I did not think my problem was severely wrong to warrant excluding me from the Samaritans. I was told the sad news, my eyes moistened, and I felt despondent. They then decided to give me four more weeks' trial with a woman mentor.

That night, my anxiety from the sad news grew out of proportion; I felt much more anxious than I expected someone to be in my circumstances. I did not sleep. I went over what brought them to conclude that my performance was not helping the caller's needs. I thought that this was the right vehicle for me to express my care for others. The worry of trying even harder had no longer helped in sharpening my response but became a hindrance. I was worried because I was anxious about how my life would change again, and it became a vicious circle.

I looked at the problem hanging over me. I needed to grow in confidence and gain experience in handling tense situations. Still, I was losing something I hoped to succeed in, which made me lack self-confidence because I was failing. If it was only confidence I lacked in talking to callers, I could have accepted it, but I felt I was fighting to survive the caring nature of my soul.

In the second week of my extended trial, I faced a caller in pain and distress about her suffering, and I panicked in my response. That became the apparent moment when I could not be a Samaritan, so I could not hold back the tears and cried in a quiet corner when I got home and wrote a resignation letter.

I want to help people in their lives, and I am left praying for them instead of doing something practical. So, I am again looking for the right vehicle for my particular talents in caring for others.

Since leaving the Samaritans, I think my sensitivity has been playing me up. I wondered about the people I had contact with when I was with the Samaritans, including the past few days of worrying about the distressed woman caller. I am beginning to ask why God had made me so sensitive; for what reason? I am so sensitive that I had started to take on callers' problems and worry about them. What's the use of being keen only to be handicapped by it? I felt the only method I had for me is my dead body, which will become a donor of organs to help others.

I may not help people in this life, having sensitivity built into the essential makeup that is handicapping me. However, when I die, it will, in the end, give someone the help they need and will express my love for people and give them a good quality of life. It will show my prudent judgement and natural ability to value people as individuals and respect them because I became involved with someone's life in death. It is a privileged position, although it may not be for everyone.

Meanwhile, I am looking to put my sensitive self to fair use without suffering or developing ill-health. Please, please realise, it's not my wish to bring my death closer than fate has determined, but it's to use my sensitive nature for good and to go right through old age, still exercising choice over many aspects of my life to enable me to reach my full potential by then. I desire to serve my fellow human beings, but I am entering a time in my life where one has either done it or not.

Time seems to be running out because I will be 40 years old in September and still trying to serve people. It looks hopeless! We are in October now; I struggle to want to fight the forces of violence and despair. There's an urge to stand up and confront fatalism and hopelessness that seems to have taken over our world. I have a young family that I am bringing up, and I am committed to their welfare and happiness. I want the forces of violence to stop so my children and children's children grow up in a safe, caring environment that can be a source of grace and peace. Why can't more people be doing what's right and just? Even as a low-educated black man, I stand in resistance to those destructive forces in our world. God being my helper, I shall always stand for justice, peace and goodwill.

There are vast amounts of discoveries to be made in the next century that will shape the future in which my children will live. The nation is engaged in the process of reduction of values and principles. The benefits most promoted today are self-interest, wealth, success, and not getting caught. In a bid to end the growing menace of people doing wrong, right and wrong must be taught in the classroom and at home. Somehow, respect and caring are not instilled in the individual. So, children are unruly and rude because family life is not there or has broken down.

I am pleased that my children have laid down a moral code. They know their duty to society and responsibility to the self and commitment in a relationship and the environment. If only adults could be like God, parents to all children, supporting the families in raising kids, and telling them when they are doing wrong. If the crusade to boost standards of behaviour, led by the widow of a murdered schoolmaster, were taken up by everyone who wanted to see a positive change in society, it would happen. The main thing is to do with family values, and if that is right, we can see improvement in children in culture and our community.

One in 14 million
Written in October 1996

I pre-set the video recorder to record programmes from the Learning Zone, and sometimes I wake from my sleep and watch TV very early in the morning.

In September 1996, I watched a UNICEF programme and was brought to tears to see children's suffering in third-world countries. Children were working as domestic servants, no more than mere slaves, and working in carpet factories as child labourers, and there was an extensive spread of child prostitution. The film also told what was happening to children in this country, Europe and the developing countries. There is child abuse, children disappearing and even child prostitution.

And the evening news can make depressing viewing. A sixteen-year-old who murdered a headmaster was sentenced, civil war, victims of floods, earthquakes, displaced refugees, and crime, and so it goes on. I pray for the news, but it's depressing, even more, to recall them again to God. I am sick of seeing such images on the screen, but I only have two choices; switch off or try to help. There are appeals for money, but I have already dug deep into my compassion-fatigued pockets.

I cannot afford any more, but I will give away lots of it if I can be the one in 14 million. I have daydreamed regularly about winning the National Lottery draw. I still have my daily talk to my God about it and dream about looking after ourselves and our relatives and giving some to charity. Each weekend, I await the draw and picture the outcome in my mind of our comforts in a big house, but most important is the help I would give to my chosen charities.

The disappointments that I feel when my numbers, now £4.00 worth, are not read out, makes me think that my luck might be better next week. And so, it goes on. I sense my prayer has not been answered yet. I am earnest with God, and I believe God guides our lives, but I am genuinely perplexed. I do not want to take the alternative course and not play the lottery. How long can I pursue this path? The niggling question remains - Is God guiding me, or is it just my greed for money and material wealth? I have knowingly entered a game of chance which is costing

£16.00 per month. I have played my first entire month of £16.00, and the odds can be unfavourable, but the system allows replays.

UNICEF - a big cheque is waiting for you if I win, but I am also thinking about how many times I can continue to lose£16.00 per month. It so happens that the church I attend, URC, collects five pence pieces to give to UNICEF for their water purification project and help save starving children with a unique mixture for them to drink that cost five pence when the project started. The price has now risen to eightpence.

I put what I can in the UNICEF collection and put my name forward to volunteer youth workers. Later, at the request of my prospective employer, I was urged to apply for a paid part-time youth worker position, and advertised in the local newspaper was a vacancy for a part-time youth worker, three hours per week. I am still awaiting the outcome of my application.

The picture of my life of faith is a life of pilgrimage. The perspective throughout my life is to look forward, go somewhere, expecting something in the future. It seems God's plan will be not plain to me; there is an element of this divine purpose in God's overruling of my affairs, and I am perplexed. Life is often challenging, people misbehave, and hopes are dashed, and tragedies occur. Christ's sacrifice stands before God as an atonement for human failing, they say. Look at what they are doing to your children, God! "Deliver us from evil". The evil in question is not suffering but sin. God made the world in which they were experienced. He did not cause that suffering, yet he permits it. Part of the explanation is that suffering is an occasion for spiritual growth, but I can view pain without being affected by it.

I now ask about the confusion surrounding the afterlife of foetuses. I do not believe that a human soul exists at the moment of fertilisation. The soul enters the body with its first moments with the consciousness of pain. I am horrified by the notion of evolution without religion. God forbid that we should live by the revelation of evolutionary theory with unfettered competition and disorder. The world would be a petrifying place to be living in. If the carbons and atoms were not in exactly the right proportions, life would have been impossible. Finally, I voice doubts about the possibility of a virgin birth. There is a suggestion that the Hebrew for 'virgin' means young woman, and the doctrine of the virgin birth was developed to enhance the reputation of the Virgin Mary. Otherwise, it seems an impossibility unless the Holy Spirit was a sperm carrying the 'y' chromosome.

Science and Religion
Written in December 1996 – January 1997

Human beings have done unspeakable things to each other throughout history, and there are no signs that it will decrease. Even if it did, natural disasters such as earthquakes and famine bring their form of suffering. Thus, the problem of evil is complicated.

Knowing why God allows all this to happen, short of denying God's existence, there is no easy answer. So here is my attempt to explain how a benevolent God could have permitted so much evil, being all-knowing, all-powerful.

God must have known how things would turn out and must have the power to prevent evil, but evil still exists. It had been said that God gave us free will, which will account for what we do to each other and mess up the world, but how can one account for natural disasters and illnesses? It seems that I will always have doubts about faith in God. Uncertainty is a part of me, and having faith mixed with doubts brings growth because I found it very healthy to doubt and question. Science has doubt, and so has faith. There is much similarity between religion and science. The thing is, does the answer I have to lead me to heaven or its to cloud cuckoo land? I sense certain things are right when I listen to myself and find out through sensing it, feeling it and thinking about it.

The belief I hold now helps me find my scripture, and the Bible's scripture tells us about God meeting people at other times. There is also the scripture of my own life about God, here and now, with me. I do not believe everything in the Bible or everything in science; many are not believable. Accepting for me means loyalty to religion, not understanding everything in the past. That was my ancestors and my grandparents' faith, but believing is adding my truth to theirs.

Can science answer the question does life have a purpose? I doubt it could respond to it as part of science because meaning has nothing to do with science. We are dealing with the condiction of truth and its content that produces truth value. Their religion is needed to give a full, complete, truthful answer. Does the entity have a purpose? Eyes are for seeing, and ears are for hearing, but what is life itself for, what purpose? Does it serve any goals, or did it spring, quite by chance, from the primordial soup? Design and use are revealed in nature by the marvellous and subtle contrivances of living creatures. Few people can contemplate the wonder of the living world without a feeling of awe. They might, as I may find it difficult to believe that all the myriad life-forms with which the world is filled, are the product of a blind and purposeless process. I was brought up to think that doubt is the companion of faith, that he who hesitates is not lost but maybe about to make sense of something.

Science has tried to assume a monopoly over people's understandings. Religion and science have become separate because science has attempted to take over the natural world from God. It has fragmented the cosmos and relegated the sacred. Science has done the valuable service of showing us a world much more complicated than people ever imagined. Still, in its modern, materialist, one-dimensional form, it cannot explain everything.

As science becomes increasingly separated from ethical, moral, and sacred considerations, it sees God as a mere Newtonian mathematician or the mechanistic clockmaker. On the contrary, tradition reflects the cosmos' timeless order and anchors people into an awareness of the universe's great mysteries. While appreciating that the essential innocence has been destroyed everywhere, I believe that civilised values, as we have inherited from our ancestors, depend on the corresponding survival in people's hearts for that profound sense of the sacred and the spiritual. The danger of ignoring this essential aspect of our existence is not just religious or intellectual. Still, it also lies at the heart of the great divide between the eastern and western worlds over the place of materialism in people's lives.

Modern materialism is unbalanced and increasingly damaging in its long-term consequences. With its profoundly mystical and symbolic doctrine of the incarnation, the Christian message has been a message of the unity of the worlds of spirit and matter and God's manifestation in this world and humankind. But, unfortunately, people in the western world have lost a sense of wholeness of our environment. And their immense and inalienable responsibility to the whole of creation.

People are so much more than just a biological phenomenon; I sometimes think it's hard to believe in the existence of a God who appears to demonstrate cruelty by having living creatures prey upon one another through genetic determination over which they have no control. Children are brought into the world with permanent disabilities, and natural disasters destroy life on a massive scale, and individuals are affected with horrific illnesses. Many starve.

I suppose that complaining about the order of things reveals more about humankind and their demands and expectations than they do about God's nature. I spoke as if the world was fashioned just for people and as if anything that causes me pain is a violation of my entitlement to seamless happiness. I had to go back to the Bible, which says that God made the world and saw perfect for his purpose. I do not know what the goal is, not being a god myself. Please note, not being gods ourselves, we do not know what the purpose is. Humanity was established last; people were placed in an already perfect creation, so people must have become alienated from perfection.

I had only come to reject the concept of a divine being on the evidence of the existence of human suffering. People's humanity was raised from the rest of the created things and given the capacities of reason and reflection. There is a sense of pain, which must be the consequence of my alienated condition and my outrage that God did not exempt people from our material composition. Nevertheless, I go back to believing in God because it is human cruelty, not God's, the central event in human history. I reminded myself that the world as it is, is perfect for God's purpose and that it is people who make unreasonable demands.

With the precision of a military battle, I have planned the aim of this year, 1997, to keep in good health and make money. We need to have savings, put something away for a 'rainy day', and keep my prayer life and belief.

Making money can be like a business without a guarantee of success, but I will continue trying and making some. The most critical decision made last year was to continue to believe in the Supreme Being, God. The mystery of this must pass many people by quite contentedly without them once being troubled by it. I feel that the question of God's nature and existence ought to be obsessively crucial to every one of us. The modern world is not supposed to be less peaceful, and most people are perplexed about what they believe and whether they are willing to die for it. Until death approaches, people are eager to tick the box in which they profess some generalised religious belief, but they are jiggered if they can say what it is. There is a growing erosion of Sunday as a day of rest, worship and tranquillity. Strict observance of the Sabbath has become eccentric.

I did some of my Christmas shopping last year after Sunday morning worship. The day of rest as heightened pleasure is now Saturday, but Sunday follows it close. Let there be two days in the week for those that treat Sundays like other days and do not suffer morally from it. People should be allowed to take time off on different days to worship God, say Wednesdays, for a change. I shopped on Sunday because I ignored the edicts that one day is more sacred than all the others just because it was ordained to Moses that nobody and nothing, not even the cattle, did any work at all on the seventh day.

The Sabbath history has been one of constant erosion, which the vast majority of Christians welcomed. They allowed the law to lapse rather than repealing it gradually. It must be the combination of devotion and enjoyment that, throughout the centuries, has made Sunday a day to look forward to, but it can be said of any day in the week one wants to make a day of rest, worship and tranquillity.

Every time I try to define the position of God in terms of understanding, I find myself utterly defeated. I look at the world - and where is God? I had already developed specific theological worries; I was troubled by things inherent in having the Christian faith. No matter how much I wanted to believe in Jesus, the son of God, it is now, I found, exceedingly tricky.

It's the Christmas story that was not palatable, at least not all of it. My faith in Jesus, the son of God, has permanently gone. Although I am not an atheist, I'm not an agnostic either, but if anything goes wrong, speak of God and Jesus, and I'll listen. I won't return to the fold unless I get some explanation from God for the world's terrible events and my life experiences. Children should receive a grounding in Christian traditions to give them judicial and universal laws within the Christian tradition. I think of the Ten Commandments, the Sermon on the Mount, Isaiah's vision, and St. Paul's journey. Jesus Christ was ill-documented as a historical figure, but if he were not attached to the baloney, the hogwash nonsense of theology, he would rate a footnote in the histories of Roman times.

I have turned my attention to contemporary religious beliefs. I was persuaded that I am still aware of my nature's spiritual side, however incoherent one's religious beliefs and practices. It must be true.

Since spending £16.00 per month on the lottery, I have won £10.00 only once and continue to believe my time will come to have a big win, but when? This incoherent belief and practice have touched me like a spirit, carried around inside my thoughts as an unseen landscape that so precisely parallels the objective external world. Yet it's a giddy sensation of absolute mystery because I have no idea if I will win at all. It was daubed in the tones of my dreams with other wishes, and I can imagine the day will come. The purpose of a win has always summoned an image of almost alternate power guiding me. Still, as I look into the sinister, practically primitive darkness of the thought, I could hardly wait for the sight of this perception to happen.

The Christian faith was based on the idea of intervention. Humankind bowling along on its sinful ways and following it then, once and for all, the universe's physical rules receive a suspension, and God intervenes. I cannot see how, if the facts of Jesus's life are all true, they do not change everything. So many of Jesus's actions and teachings seemed to be profoundly ambiguous and prone to so many different interpretations and conflicting meanings. I now find it difficult to accept a man born of a virgin but insist that a corpse did walk out of the tomb, for this is my living hope.

I look at God differently than a Christian might. I do not worship a God who is represented as telling people that we will finally be rewarded or punished according to whether we are or are not willing to accept the terrifyingly intangible evidence of his existence. Life is not unjust when one comes into God's presence.

Is my marriage going to fail?
Written on 11th January 1997 – 25th January 1997

I think my marriage is failing because the wife and I are steadily growing apart. Not entirely because of the lack of love between us, more to do with her not understanding me, and I can't understand her money-related problems.

I cannot grasp how she looks at things, even now that the illness is in remission. I found the giving and taking has gone. Has my love become secretive about money? As I see it, she is putting as little as she can or nothing at all towards the family's financial upkeep. She is secretly saving, and I struggle to make ends meet and have to live off my bank's overdraft. Why does the wife think I am after her money? I am only interested in providing for the family. If only we could put money together again and work out how best to deliver the family's things and upkeep. I can count on my fingers the pocket money that I have to spend after receiving my weekly wage packet. Thirty pence is equivalent to fifteen cups of coffee at two pence a cup, but I feel no bitterness because I know that the total income I earn is used to provide or maintain our standard of living.

I was proud of my love in the past because when she had some money, it went into helping the family out financially, and we lived from day-to-day. I tried to show my appreciation, that I mean to look after her and the children, but I cannot do it by myself. My money cannot stretch to providing luxury, but I will invest in long-term goals and trust that she will see that I want to pay her back for the times when I used her money. I started a ten-year savings plan of £9.00 per month in her name on one of her past birthdays, and some years ago, I started her in a pension plan. I pay £22.80 per month to her pension fund, and just last Christmas '96, I invested in joint names in a National Saving Bond worth £1,000.

We argued again lately about money and seeing to the children's physical needs. I feel anger that my love seems to leave it up to me to remind the children of their responsibility when they fail to do their duties. However, I haven't seen it yet as trivial. I had made a mountain out of a molehill by screaming out angry words to

211

express my dislike, and my love retaliated with an angry outburst, "Why don't you go and boil your head in oil?" She knows she dealt a blow below the belt because when the phrase was first used many years ago, I told her it hurts my feelings to hear her say those words and still confess love for me when asked. I always take it to heart, and it feels horrible, horrible, but the making up in our relationship seems always to be left to me.

This time, I was gutted and distressed if she does not show remorse for what she said. I don't think my words to her were harsh; it was just repeated again and again and loud. Her words carried a great deal of hate and bitterness towards me, and she emptied in one sentence just what she thought of me, be it in anger that the tongue lashed out. It all seems to me that I am hated. Our communication with each other is cold now. No feeling of warmth radiates, and I have lost my bedroom confidence because I do not mind having space between us beneath the sheets. That had happened before I came back from the brink of celibacy, but it was not easy. Today, 11th January 1997, I am feeling rejected. I am looking for her attention in places other than the bedroom. We have grown apart so much that I cannot even ask my love to lend me money. Week after week, my pocket money is less than £1.00 as disposable income, and I picked up the courage to ask my love for a pound to put in the church collection plate. She looked unhappy, but she gave it to me. I asked the following week again, and she refused to provide me with a pound but later released it with words of protest.

From that day on, I have not asked my love for any money – it's some months now. We are losing common ground; our 'goal posts' have moved, and if I am not careful, my love for her might well turn to lovelessness. There might come a fit of anger that is not yet in me, loathing and scorn. My heart and mind genuinely love her, but if it's one-sided, it might become a loveless marriage. I could not tell someone I love what she told me and not apologise and make amends quickly! How could she? After fifteen years of marriage, her love must still be shallow. Perhaps I really ought to laugh it off, but this was directed at me by my closest partner. It makes me feel sick thinking about it. I plan to put it behind me so that we can love again and have a time scale for her to apologise to me. I hope it is done by Valentine's Day 1997 because I have a love treat to give her.

Since our difficulties, I have been looking at other women who might want to step into her shoes, be a shadow in an affair or be an affectionate friend. I think I have found someone who may go further than a flirt. I've become disillusioned with my wife. I feel I am wasting my time, and it's up to me to end the stalemate relationship because she won't lift a finger first to make amends. Every relationship has to be finely balanced, and when things become too one-sided, it makes me feel it's time to get out.

I have the responsibility of a husband and father, and even if I wanted to go with other women, I have no money to spend on them. My conscience tells me that I should spend it on the wife if I have money, with which I agree. I am broke. I want to be with another woman because the wife has hurt me so much that I feel sick inside and cannot physically mate with her.

I have played the incident in my mind's eye that has my marriage in a stalemate. Of course, I do not want our lives ruined, but every waking moment has occupied me this second week after the incident.

I am learning how to feel about myself and how I react to my feelings. I think about those feelings and what choices I could have had in response. For example, I read that I am abominable to my wife, and she detests me. I need to learn to have emotional intelligence and read her emotions correctly because it's not easy to understand my anger, sadness or fear. I want to be a passionate trainer to our children, much like athletes have trainers, to guide them about the world of emotion, as they see their parents with anger, sadness or fear. I want to teach them those strategies to deal with life's ups and downs. When they have these feelings, they should not object to them or ignore them. They should accept those negative emotions as a fact of life and their emotional moments as opportunities for teaching and learning emotional intelligence. When the wife and I argue, it's a lesson for the children, and I tell them, "Your mother and I have fallen out." When we are hugging or smiling at each other, "I have an announcement to make; your mum and I are in love," I say. They learn emotional intelligence; it was widespread for us, your mum and dad, to be loving and attentive. The children get hugs and kisses from their mum and me, and I say to them, "Mummy and Daddy love you and all the family".

Euphemia is never happy about the domestic conditions of the house, and it's always a painful experience for her, especially doing the ironing, which is the worst. She would like me to learn to iron so that I could iron my clothes. I am not too house-proud. We have children, and I am not too hygienic or orderly, but our home is neither dirty, compulsively in order, nor compulsively clean. Euphemia likes to see the house cleaned and daily tidied because the consequences, if it's not, reflect on her, and she wants me to undertake the daily cleaning task.

There is no pleasure to be had from cleaning a place that's already clean. On the contrary, I like to see the transformation and feel good when the home does need cleaning, and I am happy to help. But, from what Euphemia says, I think she would prefer to clean for a neighbour than for us, the children and me because she would get paid for doing it.

If I cannot see in Euphemia's face that she wants to say she is also responsible for our falling out, then there is no hope left for us. So far, she is still giving me the cold shoulder, and I am too resistant. Euphemia looks at peace within herself while I still suffer from sad emotions. Her voice drops to a crackling sort of near-whisper sound when she has to speak to me. Her face is just straight, with no signs of remorse over what happened. I do want the cackle of laughter to come back, to give way to wistful, craving expressions for me. But it looks like I will have to make the first move again.

It was just like all the other times when the culprit sticks out like a crab's foot in a lobster pot. Unfortunately, I am resisting my sincerest yearning to hug her, kiss her, and say I am sorry - let's get back to loving again! No more meat is needed on the bare bone of this incident, but you can see that if this marriage fails, it is both our fault. Yet, I ask myself, what kind of a union have we got when one partner cannot come to say sorry to his other trusted partner?

I am vulnerable to new relationships because there is no more romance in our lives together. I can see the factors that make me deliberate in letting our relationship lead to destruction instead of finding possible solutions. We both triggered the quarrel; why doesn't Euphemia do something to patch up this coldness I sense we are both experiencing? It will be a bumpy ride because I am unsure if I should try and save our marriage. However, the possible affair is tempting, and I feel I will deal better with someone who considers my feelings more in how they treat me.

The woman I thought to be my Ms Right is driving me to unfaithfulness, but things do not just happen. They happen because one wants them to happen. I do not know if I am strong enough or have the bottle to carry out those changes. My wife would deserve to lose me to learn from what has happened to me and teach her a lesson. I feel ashamed to give up everything with my wife for what may turn out to be a fling because I have bottled up the honest feelings I have for her. The good times are vivid memories that I don't want to fade, but I feel trapped.

I do not know if I want to save my marriage or commit to a new partner and break my marriage vows. If I have an affair, it will eat into my self-respect so entirely that it will crush any strength left in our marriage. I am probably looking for someone to confide in about how it used to be, talk openly, and know she trusts me because I am a good man, husband, and father.

My sexual thoughts about another woman are only incidental because a part of me wants to win back our healthy marriage. I want to work out my marriage problems and fix them with my brain, but I am working on hormones, and we need to have a serious talk, but my love cannot see it.

My book is the only way I can unload because my wife can do no wrong, it seems. All I want is to love and have a loving partner and a mother figure for the children. I do not want to lead a double life, but I got smitten by this other woman who does not flirt with me outrageously, but she made it evident that she fancies me.

Our relationship's future could end up out of control once I involve another woman, but it's hard not to.

The Other Woman
Written 31st January 1997

If not by my faith path, I was guided in my writing by a high moral code, ethics, and a purpose.

I am ashamed of myself now, looking for happiness outside my marriage because of my partner's inadequate responses. I feel that I am suffering appallingly, not physically, but mentally and I cannot see that my wife is also suffering. In this present time, I could only see my mental anguish just through being entirely misunderstood. I am not as strong as some men. I am more emotional, after all, which makes me not remote from human care. I want to do what is right, fair and not for envy, lust or selfishness. Reasons are only selfish if they're for self-preservation.

I do not know the punishment for sin in the head, but I have feelings and passion for a single black professional woman who makes me feel swell and always has a smile for me. There is a mutual attraction, but I do not know if I will ever let it develop into anything more. I can envisage us acknowledging the depth of our interest, which is growing. It's a matter of working out what we will do about it because I am married.

I have also acknowledged that she could not deny favour and told Euphemia that I was interested in another woman. I have always been open and truthful with her, hoping it would make her take more interest in me and not make me hold in my guilty feelings. For a bit of time, it seemed that she was, but it has faded. The difficulty I face is that we, the other woman and me, are getting to know each other within the limits of correct behaviour and decency and with complete discretion because of the public nature of her work. The conflict is brewing; it has to be faced but may be severe. I suffered to maintain happiness with my wife and break down finding common ground.

I want to behave correctly and not cause any waves or distress, but I have to think about the children and the consequences of falling in love and wanting to go off with another woman. What has happened to my morals? Did I sacrifice them for my happiness and feel guilty for the rest of my life? The only right thing is to realise that the only way to move is forward and for me to be happy with my children and a partner, wife or fancy woman. I will have to decide if my chats to my fancied lady friend grow into an affair, but for now, I will keep the woman's identity a secret to protect her and have my wife guessing who on earth she is.

It is most regretful that my marriage is failing, but I have no immediate plans to let it die. However, I do have re-marriage in view because I am falling in love again, not only because of her looks but because I like her personality and charm. I feel that I could make love to her if we become sort of close, but with my wife, right now, I have become temporally impotent, I think.

Suppose I continued to feel impotent near my wife. In that case, we must accept the truth that I am over with her emotionally, look into the issue open-mindedly, and then say that our marriage is now a celibate one. God forbid! At the moment, I am steering clear of my fancy woman and putting my energy into trying to sort out my life with my wife. However, I will have to talk to her soon and tell her I am still hurt inside and that my heart bled for my own sanity's sake.

Meanwhile, I am doing the little things to make my affection return. I make Euphemia cups of tea, take her dinner into the bedroom when she feels tired. And when she changes out of her daily clothes and relaxes watching television. I ask how she is feeling, and she tries to smile a little. I even ask her about work and make conversation that makes her smile. But, unfortunately, I can't rekindle our love life through kissing and cuddling because we are not kissing or cuddling in the family or social circles.

My love is not making any effort. A week or two more of this absence of kissing and cuddling will surely stop my engine ticking over altogether with her. Today is the end of the second week, and I am packed with strong emotions, realising that my wife seems unlikely to come to me and talk. I hope that she does because a new and rich understanding can take place. I am frustrated by having to have secrecy. I have never held secrets from her; we share our closest fantasies and dreams, but now I have a secret relationship and some undiscussed problems. Around Christmas 1996 was the last time I made love to my wife, and the following day, I could hardly bear to look her in the face because she was used in my fantasy, and I felt terrible as I imagined how she might feel. I was humiliated, in shame.

I could not get the other woman out of my mind during the performance, the act of love. My heart was racing as I imagined this had become one of the most exciting moments of my life. However, I felt I had demoralised the whole act, and my wife does not deserve to be treated in this way. Later on, my guilt was eating me out, and I wanted to cut away at the imagination to rip it out of my skull. Immediately after the fantasy, I was remorseful and could not stand myself for acting and giving in to the part of my lustful mind and its sin embedded in it.

"I am sorry, darling, but I wanted to be appreciated. " My imagination went wild a bit. I genuinely believed that I could never love anyone as much as you, my darling and I was wrong because I fell in love with another woman and exercised it in my mind with fantasies. I am sorry. It hits my self-esteem, which was hard to regain.

I have terrible doubts about whether my wife and I have a future to keep building together because I feel awful. In one way, I am so happy, and in another way, I am full of sadness. I cannot begin to judge how my wife will react to the truth. I love two women intimately, but one is at the moment in thought. I came to meet this attractive woman in her work in public. As she deals with the general public, her duty was to be considerate and friendly, but I caught a dear, warmer friendliness that made me feel like I was fancied. Then something clicked. I returned week by week, and before approaching her, butterflies were playing in my tummy. I first stood off at a distance, admiring her and then approached until we had eye contact.

She sometimes watched me, and her full soft lips, coloured with dark purple lipstick, gave away a charming, warm smile. When we talked about the product I was buying, she asked about me more profoundly than having a casual affair and said things about herself that only a good friend would share with a mate. My heart raced in this most exciting moment of talking to her, and I could feel trembling as I stood a little embarrassed and lost for the familiar chatty words.

I am now feeling crazy about her. In those meetings, we get on well when I buy products or ask for advice; she tells me more about herself. But I am scared to ask her out because she may prefer a more experienced, smooth-talker.

Somehow, I knew an affair would be seen to be wrong, but I cannot stop thinking about her, and my wife realises it. I get desperate to see and know a lot more about the other woman, but I do not want to destroy my marriage, and I do not want to see my newfound love ending up hurt. She is driving me crazy, and I do not think I can back off from her now.

The one thing that will cool the new relationship is when I consider the welfare of our children. There is no way I can get further involved with the other woman without jeopardising the family. This woman is free to love me, but I am not free to love her, so it will have to stop. I shall remember this time in years to come as a missed opportunity and may have some regrets.

Relationships do not come with guarantees, but I promised to love my wife forever, and for my children's sake, I have to keep this promise. It would cause irreparable emotional damage if I stopped loving their mother and got involved with the other woman.

I Had a Dream

Written 1st February 1997

In the twilight hours of this morning, I woke and remembered a dream that seemed to tell me something about my condition. So often, when I dream, I only remember it vividly straight after waking in the twilight hour, but when I fall back to sleep and wake up again at dawn, the dream is sketchy, or I cannot remember any of it at all.

This time, the whole of my dream in full detail was remembered last night— my last piece of writing on this page and chapter that came straight out of my subconscious.

The dream began with me standing, ready to travel along a long straight road that seemed to go on to touch the lowest point of the sky in the distance. I had a task to travel this road, dodging arrows fired randomly by bowmen who could see me at various points. I jogged, dodging and ducking. Finally, the arrows came too close to me and fell to my feet, nearly nailing my shoes to the ground. Arrows flew overhead, and near the sides of my body, it seems it was raining arrows. When I was about to realise how far I had travelled, I was back to the starting position again and again in a flash. I had gone over piles of fired arrows lying on the ground while more arrows were still getting fired.

Sometimes I slipped on them at the right time and missed that fatal arrow. Umpteen times I kept seeing myself back at the start of the journey. I was feeling scared and terrified that I might get killed if I attempt the journey again. I began to tremble, and my legs were giving way as I tried my hardest not to be killed. I got grazed a few times, and my heart was racing faster than my feet could pound on the ground of the fallen arrows. Then, suddenly, a flash occurred, and I was back to the start. My knees were on the starting point, and my head was bowed in my sweating palms. My feet had lost their shoes and were blistered. I panted and panted, feeling the blood from my grazed wounds oozing out through my tattered clothes, sticking some strips of clothing to my body. The next time, I would be killed because I am tired and full of fear and nervousness to do that obstacle again. Then, I heard a knock on the bedroom door that woke me out of my dream.

My eldest daughter, Katrina, woke to use the loo, and I always encourage the children to call me when they wake in the middle of the night because I see my waking up as a safety procedure. We have a saying at bedtime, "Good night, sweet dreams, see you in the morning nighty night boom, boom. Call me in the night if you need me, and God bless. Call me in the night, any time, God bless".

Leaving for work in the morning, I would call each child by name, saying, "Bye, bye, have a good day at school, tell me all about it when I get home. God bless, kiss, kiss!"

Finding Happiness in my Marriage again
Written May 10th 1997

Welcome back to the continued story of a life that throws up or brings out frustrations, worries, anxiety and sometimes depression. My heart's centre is the love and care I want to express to all without boasts or rewards.

The stories that follow will be as uncertain as those that have gone before. But they tell me what has happened and is happening in my life. So, although I do not have a crystal ball or any cosmic rays to see how things will turn out or what might happen, I can write with hope and expectation.

My life now seems to have happiness after the uncertainties I had a few months ago. However, the suspense and excitement that may have surprised the reader, if you are still interested, read all about what happened between January 1997 and today, May 10th 1997.

I feel happier, loved and appreciated; my entire life of heartache with my relationship with my wife has ended, and I shall write in this unforgettable autobiography how it happened. I believe I endured the suffering that has some delusional qualities that made me learn and trust. My wife apologized to me, and it made the difference between a marriage remaining just for convenience or a marriage life strong with purpose.

Four months had passed, and many actions, sensations, thoughts and feelings had crowded into that time, and I aim to catalogue some of them because I believe in some divine plan, so my story must continue. There is an ever-persistent urge to solve the cosmic mysteries, and my curiosity, learning, and philosophising give partial answers. I clearly recall the details of those moments when I thought my choices were destined to change my life. I feel compelled to share the incredible moments because I have learnt about myself and my partner.

This book is about my family, not just me. I want to give an accurate, honest account of how an ordinary husband and wife with three children live as a family. I realized I had come far in surviving within my marriage, but I am still enslaved and trapped by the sin of the flesh's emotions and immorality because I missed my friend who nearly became my mistress. I have just got over anger, guilt, resentment, and possessiveness and being released from being a slave to my desire. I am doing what I am fit for, ultimately being at peace with myself. But, like a musician must make music and an artist must paint, I must be true to my nature. I must become everything I can become; an excellent parent, husband and house owner, and satisfying love and esteem, including feeling safe.

I came to an abrupt decision to stop the new relationship I was developing because when I considered its effects on the children, I thought it was best to stay in my failing marriage, at least until the children had grown up. So, I passed the store and glanced in and stood motionless for a minute, admiring –the woman who had almost become my mistress, but at a safe distance so that she could not see me as I walked past feeling sad and heartsick. I kept going back to the store each week doing the same thing, looking in on her working and walking by at a distance so that she could not attract my attention. It was doing me no good because I felt mournful and so sad. I stood in a discrete place for quite a while and stared into the store, watching her at work. I suddenly seemed to have shocked myself because passersby looked puzzled, and I was beginning to get scared that someone I knew might pass and question me on my seemingly lost appearance.

I was shocked when I looked into the store, and she was not there. The first time I thought that it could be her day off. But it was persistently happening; she was not in the store. My feeling sank to the most profound depth of disappointment. It seems that she had left the job.

I had entered the store for many weeks hoping to see her, but she was not there. It had been a shock, and I missed her madly, even if it was just an apparent glance when I used to see her. It was something I thought would go on for months. Then, finally, I began to wonder if she missed me because I missed her image in the store. The only way I could imagine her was in my mind's eye. Missing her became so painful that I whispered her name in my head; Beverly. Somehow, all that could or might have been with her flooded my mind, and I was momentarily happy.

I told my wife that I had stopped seeing the lady of my fancy, but she did not believe me. On Valentine's eve, my wife told me she had read the writing in my book and felt hurt by it. I still could not believe that she had missed the point. Euphemia had hurt me by saying what she said and not apologizing. On finding the part that I wrote, saying I imagined my lover when making love to her, Euphemia saw me hurting her feelings, but I felt terrible about that. I told her again, and we talked for a good part of the night, and then it seemed we were developing common ground. And Euphemia said she was sorry, and I told her I was sad to have hurt her feelings.

The next day was Valentine's Day, and my wife gave me Valentine's card with the simple word 'sorry' written in it. Somehow, it made all the difference because we began to rebuild our relationship. I was surprised at myself that we were reconciled so quickly after her apology. I began to feel excited, and since then, Euphemia seems to come to me more caring and loving.

It is the month of May 1997. Euphemia has been warm and showing affection. We often greet each other with a hug and a kiss; she smiles more at me and twinkles her 'sweet eye'. That is a special wink with one eye. Euphemia gives me unexpected hugs around the house when I least expect them, and she sometimes expresses her sexuality. I love it all. We still have the occasional rows, but we can come back with no hard feelings. Sometimes she touches my hand warmly as we watch television and stays close to me. Our lovemaking is not frequent, but when it happens, it's extra special. When I am happy, I can tell the children my usual saying, "Katrina, Georgina, and Jonathan, your mother and I are in love". We all hug, we smile, and we laugh. They are happy about our marriage again; I am so pleased.

In periods when we relax, Euphemia's eyes light up, and she looks at me intensely. I can sense a sense of charm and flirt with me, and then she and I smile, almost uncontrollably.

The School Appeal
Written May 1997

Georgina entered secondary education in September 1997, but she was turned down by our first-choice school, Bishop Stopford, a church school.

The school governors did not offer a place, so we used our right to appeal against the decision and won. The school played no part in the appeal procedure, but the admission committee met after the appeal was heard. The panel thought we had a good case for admission and offered Georgina a place at the school.

The independent appeal committee consisted of four members, and two members contested the school's position, total capacity. One of the members was the headmaster. The appeal panel justly considered what we said and what the school said informally. It felt like, at times, we were on trial, us against the school. Euphemia was with me at the hearing, and I explained what I wrote in the appeal application to the panel. The appeal application letter said, "We were very disappointed to be told that our daughter was unsuccessful in gaining a place at Bishop Stopford School, for September 1997".

We felt strongly about our application being rejected because it's a chance of success and happiness for our daughter that has been dashed. She would have been encouraged to fulfil her potential in a happy, thriving learning environment, so that warrants an appeal. We sent letters from two mainstream Christian Church branches who conveyed that Georgina and her family are devoted Christians and regularly attend church. From reception to year six, all her primary education was done in a Christian environment, and she is now attending Church of England School. We strive to see all her education taking place in an ordered, caring community where she can learn, understand, and apply her abilities to think, create, and gain experience in everyday life and those moments when the human spirits soar.

My daughter is a black British citizen, and we wondered if she may have been discriminated against because of her race and having parents of a different culture from the school's usual intake. Unfortunately, we are yet to see a black ethnic minority in the school, and our suspicions may well be confirmed if, yet again, another year has come and no more racial groups who are Christians have joined the school.

"What is it? Must we all have pale skin, attend Church of England School and have parents or children attending that school? If the school is barring us because of colour or race, it's appalling. I have a son, who in the year 2000 will be looking for a place at the school. My son has no hope of entry if my daughter is unsuccessful because his sister was unsuccessful, so the spiral continues. I am placing my faith in the system, but if it's discriminatory, something should be done so that other minority Christian groups with children do not lose out like my daughter and possibly my son in the years to come".

Everything is now set for Georgina to go to Bishop Stopford School, and she had an introduction day on June 23rd 1997. There will be a parent's evening on June 24th 1997.

Money
Written May 1997

I am getting a great response from Euphemia, and she is contributing willingly to the family finances. Her giving is much better, and she seems a changed person.

What brought about the change? I am not sure, but it might be because my romance with the other woman ended suddenly. She gives me an extra income to help run the home and pays for a new loan. We have credit card debts, three years left on an unsecured loan of £7,000, and the house needs to be redecorated, but we cannot feed ourselves on our living wage; we have a shortfall.

I cannot think of getting money other than borrowing more money or seeking credit from primary lenders. The wife disagrees that we should acquire a large amount on a personal loan, but I need her consent because the building society will not lend me the money without joint signatures. I persuaded Euphemia that now, by earning £6.00 per hour, we would be alright in paying it back. We need some more money now.

I have felt so optimistic that last month, April 1997, I successfully applied for that unsecured loan for £10,000 over five years. As a result, I paid off our existing loan and will have the outer part of the house redecorated. It's the first time, and the family will be having a holiday to Legoland in Denmark, on the 24th, which is in a few weeks.

The children and I are excited about the trip, but the wife has no enthusiasm, and it has dampened all our spirits. It looks like we can manage the cost to Legoland, but we will not have much spending money. I am looking at the housekeeping again, and it looks like we will be in crisis whether we go to Denmark or not. Two weeks before we departed on the four-day Danish mini-cruise to Legoland, the tour operators cancelled the excursion. The operator said it was due to insufficient support.

Euphemia is unhappy; she wants to be a better learner and attend college to learn word processing, basic maths and English. Euphemia wants to educate herself further because she is not happy with her work. However, she is bravely sticking it out for the time being until something new turns up and until her newly learnt skills open up possibilities. Euphemia is not against the idea of me earning sufficient money to keep her at home as a housewife. We discussed that if I were in my first job, a toolmaker, earnings would be higher, and I must aim to be a foreman or hold a managerial position. But I am happy in my work and in the position I have reached.

Being a skilled milling machine operator, I only need to improve my reading of technical workshop drawings.

The Summer Break
Written August 24th 1997

I felt very disappointed that our first trip abroad was cancelled. So, I decided to use some of the refunded fees and book an excursion to the Isle of Wight.

We have not been on holiday in all these years, but the closest we can get to free time away with the family is a few hours excursion to an offshore island. We cannot afford a decent holiday, even though we have borrowed thousands of pounds and hoped some could pay for a trip abroad. I needed to get away and not think of the consequences of how our lives would be led without improvement in our financial position, even though we have borrowed £10,000. I hired a professional painter and decorator to repaint the exterior of the house.

The children had asked to go somewhere during their long summer break, and the day trip on a ferry, crossing the sea, had them excited. They were excited to see big ships sailing near small boats.

The navigation seemed very skilful, the way the ship thundered through the water and avoided the small craft gliding in the water without ever colliding. The coach drove on to the ferry, and the crossing was calm, and it was equally quiet going back across the Southampton waters. The coach drove around the island, and the driver was naming all the famous places, but without stopping. We passed coloured sand beaches and were disappointed not to stop off at the seaside and only had enough time to stop at one beauty spot, where we spent a short time buying souvenirs, glancing at the attraction of a picturesque beauty spot. Unfortunately, I had forgotten the camera so that holiday snaps couldn't be taken.

I treated the family to a televised Gladiators game show at the national indoor arena during the school summer break. It was the ultimate challenge of good evening entertainment in which trained celebrities versus national competitors competed on very physically demanding apparatus. The game's finals turned out to be an epic battle between the Gladiators and the brave contenders.

The Death of Princess Diana

Written on Sunday, September 7th 1997

Last weekend, Sunday 31ST of August, Diana, Princess of Wales, was killed in a car accident in Paris at age 36. It also claimed the lives of the driver and Diana's newly found companion, Dodi Fayed, the son of the Ritz and Harrods owner.

Much of the nation and the world mourned the memory of Diana yesterday. Euphemia and I watched the whole funeral on television with the radio playing sobering music in the background. As we watched the coffin travel to the Cathedral, Euphemia and I and millions of others who never even met the princess, felt they knew her because of the newspapers and publicity of her many good causes, and we became tearful.

The death of a reasonable person hurts. But, for me, it's not only Diana's death that hurts. It's destruction and the suffering of human beings and animals. Death brings a deep sense of loss, whether it comes as a release from long-term suffering, as the climax to a fruitful life, in war, accident, illness, disasters, or by another's hand. It brings pain. A sudden, dreadful road crash brought global sorrow last week. Mother Teresa, who founded an order of nuns dedicated to bringing hope to the poorest of the poor, died of a heart attack at age 87 on the eve of Diana's funeral.

I read somewhere once, "Amid life, we are in death". It is difficult to grasp that truth from a religious perspective. When faced with an accident, like that which killed Diana or the accidental deaths of children, the question that flows from my mind in such circumstances is not easily met by philosophical theory or theological dogma. Where was God in the events that took the life of the princess? How can a compassionate God allow children to die like that? If God has given human beings the freedom to do wrong, make mistakes and hurt others, can't that same God intervene to overturn the results of such freedom? Why are some people being healed and some not? I feel that God does not will such suffering. We all have to find our answers to these impossible questions.

While rooted in hurt, it is not the time to do it. Bereavement needs prayer rather than propositions, silence rather than words, presence rather than action, and touch and sympathy. Those who cannot take a religious view will find comfort and consolation, I suppose in the case of the princess, in the healing influence of someone never to be forgotten. She is someone with whose own pain they can empathise and by whose tender compassion they have been blessed. People in other faiths can spiritually feel the strength they know in the beliefs they trust.

In the long-term view, I believe that "all things work together for good" by sensing the blessing that can come from human tragedies. During the death, which hurts, I glimpse light, and life goes on.

There is a minority of people who say that nothing happens at the end of life. But, thank God, most people hold some belief that the soul passes to another world and that we may trust in God since all is in God's hands. That's my view. Others believe that we come back as something or somebody else.

It is not difficult to distinguish philosophers who have said that the Christian story of life beyond death lacks the courage to accept that death is the end, and it distracts us from the laborious tasks of doing the good we can, here and now. When a comparatively young person dies, like Diana, it presses with fresh urgency: is there life after death? What can we say for God about those killed amid growth, with such patently unfulfilled potential, such incomplete agendas? I feel ambiguity and incompleteness. Thank God that faith sets the uncertainties of all our lives against the background of two realities. God offers us a complete and fulfilled life, and his promise of authentic and discerning judgment is related to Jesus and his resurrection, they say.

My belief in the resurrection is that God's power in raising Jesus from death will bring us face to face with God in another world and then discover, with God, what it all meant and means to have died and gone to live in an eternal home. Belief in God's ultimate capacity to complete incompleteness, unravel muddles, and sort out injustices strengthens my commitment to do what I can while I have God's gift of time.

We grieved for Diana because it seems unfair when an excellent or harmless person gets cut off in their prime. So, part of my emotion at yesterday's funeral was an attempt to express dissatisfaction, the unfairness of her life's ending.

Youth Club

Written October 19th 1997

Since August 2nd, I have been involved in a youth club on a Saturday afternoon.

The youth club is situated in a Hindu Community Centre, and primarily Asian young people came. Before taking up the youth club's place, I get sent on an introduction course on counselling skills. Then, as a Youth Service member, I can take up any direction that the Northamptonshire Youth and Residential Service arranges. I am now on a certificate course in part-time youth work.

I am not sure if I shall continue on the course, because the youth club has closed and at the moment, Tuesday evening is the other day the club runs. To maintain the direction, one must be connected to and regularly go to a youth club. I am not sure if I could fulfil the commitment on a Tuesday evening between 5 pm and 7 pm. Before the youth club closed, I hoped to set up a discussion period for my part-time youth course project to share their ideas on current affairs and things that affect them, express their opinions and values, and affect change in the community.

While I was at the Saturday afternoon club, I did not have any difficulties. All the young people wanted to do was play sporting activities. Being an oldie, I had fears if I would get accepted as a youth worker. I had my reasons for wanting to do youth work, which I will come to in a minute, but my fears of unruly youths, disrespectful and harmful images of today's youths, filled my mind.

I was pleasantly surprised that the youths were well-mannered and had good behaviour, and I began to think culture had something to do with it. I felt part of their community, and the Asians only spoke English in the club, which allowed me to interact and befriend them. As a result, I entered youth work as a self-made, confident role model.

In the scene and the issues that young people have to deal with today, their guidelines are blurred or non-existent, so they find it hard to say 'no' to the temptation that may be harmful, sinful or involves wrongdoing.

I come into the youth service consciously attempting to help young people develop self-awareness, self-confidence, spiritual and cultural awareness, and make informed decisions and independent judgments. It is a challenge that I enjoy working with people who, like me, try to broaden their horizons with young people and empower them to understand and act on the personal social and political issues that affect their lives and others' lives in the communities in which they live. I am out there to make a difference, fight prejudices, motivate, build self-esteem, respect, be non-judgmental and guide them away from crime.

November 22nd 1997.

Early this month, Wednesday the fifth, I was introduced into a mainly white youth club, where the standard of behaviour and discipline was well below the Asian youth club's middle standard. The youth club is on a deprived housing estate in a building in poor condition. The skills I talked about will be most helpful because they need to divert young people from non-law-abiding activities and come off the streets. The youths were unorderly and smoked and spoke mainly foul language when communicating. One saw evidence of no knowledge to understand the consequences of some of their foolish behaviour and poor social, academic and personal development skills. I could identify areas of need, but nothing was getting done because it is such a big issue that involves the whole community.

The young people are fun. I always want to be there for them, interact with them, and help meet their needs. I try to be open-minded, but it is hard not to be judgmental. These young people are disadvantaged by the broader society because they are council estate youths. And in general, because of one-parent families, poverty, lack of better facilities and social background, other cultures and races tend to think of white western youths' attitudes as naughty, mischievous and don't give a damn about anything.

I dropped out of the part-time course because I would have two projects to complete shortly, and it would be too stressful to try to finish by the deadline. Furthermore, I needed more time to get to know the new youths and ask them to help in the project, and I hope to return in the new term of 1998.

Resolve To Improve My Wealth With A New Year Financial Resolution.
Written on December 30th 1997

Most people pledge to go on diets or give up cigarettes and alcohol in their New Year resolutions.

At the beginning of 1998, my priority is to do a financial makeover and revamp my finances. I am looking for a natural feeling of economic well-being. I want to spend less this coming year and clear debts, and take up more exercise. I have to reduce deficits, credit card bills and bank overdrafts. It seems like the interest charge on owed money is higher than the interest on money saved.

Debts look like they are out of control again, and I have used the £1,000 investment bond and received £48.00 in interest. I have now no rainy-day money left in a bank account or national savings account. I am not sure how to prepare for the unexpected, but I hope to make financial gains, and I feel a spirit of good luck working in my circumstances. I cannot say what makes me think this way, but I sense an excellent feeling of good luck, factors beyond my grasp in my prayer life. I wish so hard to end the circle of debts and low finances that I feel the development of wishful thinking, ready to create external factors to evolve into wealth in the core of my mind.

I gamble more on the National Lottery because I think I have lucky numbers, and it's because I am desperate to win, to improve our lot and others. If such events ever happen while I am in good health, as debt becomes a real burden, I will never again question the existence of a God. I cannot sensibly say He exists, and I cannot wisely say He does not. I like people and enjoy sharing my discoveries, and this book has a prediction of God's will for me. However, I must seek to escape the hold of rising debts first.

I write in a cosy room with my imagination telling me what to say. I have examined my heart for ambitions and felt it's too late for God to use me for his glory, but God is unique, and I am short of language for explaining. The world situation demands a loud voice, which can only come from believers who are guided by God and devoted to God. I am not qualified to tell people anything.

When I think like this, I wonder if schizophrenia is kicking in. My consciousness is creating a power that is at the disposal of God. I believe that prayer poses philosophical problems, but I am sceptical, and I am seriously putting it to the test. I hope to fulfil my thoughts' conditions, and the issues will be met in the indisputable fact of answered prayer and the joy of conscious fellowship with God.

I try to pray, but I cannot pray well, and my soul loses some of the vision of moral duties. I am reluctant to say that prayer always works. However, it comes to me as a dominant feature of life and a joyous necessity. Prayer is a drain on me; it could cause depression. I am aware that loud crying and tears give me a faithful intercession into an unpleasant sacrifice. I labour earnestly for our world in prayer and think of our future. Still, it is utterly weary, and it's a wrestling agony to see evil winning over goodness in our community and the full-wide world.

I do not know how to pray as I should, but some feeling helps my weakness. My prayer may be psychical rather than spiritual, but I am thinking about how to master the technique of worship and understand its philosophy. I plead earnestly in religious worship because it comes from the activity in the soul. My heart and mind's human energy can achieve only social results, but praying from my soul's operation releases supernatural resources.

The preliminary thoughts are doubtless not new ground, but it is very easy for intellectual apprehension of spiritual truth to outrun my practical experience of reality and power. My prayers do not influence the heart of men to stop doing wrong. It is the God to whom I pray that I must be able to move through the intercessor's prayer to control humanity wickedness. Prayer seems a burden, for it rests on my heart, and still, I keep praying because it's God's purpose to grant the answers.

By the power of prayer, I think that the command of the power of God comes into play. I am responsible for the circumstances in which I find myself. One can give up in depression or look to the sovereign God who has everything under control, who can use the experiences for our ultimate good by transforming me. God engineered circumstances and uses them, as well as my loyalty, to prove He is the creator.

Wouldn't it be exciting if the next lottery winner was me? It could be divine intervention. I miraculously became a winner when all the odds were against it. What a miracle! We'd all be excited and praising, thanking God. It'd be something we could confirm for ourselves. We'd share my deep thoughts and hopes, and now I hold the winning ticket; we may think we have seen the wonder and power of God.

Wouldn't that be thrilling? I poise my pen. Visualise that scene; the money that will clear the debts, the money that will help the families, the money that will go to my many charities and finally, the funds that will allow God's work in the churches to heal souls and preach salvation. That will be exciting, indeed. You see, that's exciting because it's God's money, and it would get used to help his kingdom come. From the standpoint of eternity, 'souls' can be saved and live forever if only the money came through his intervention.

My body is only a flicker in the time-span of eternity; then it dies. I want to carry people with full bellies beyond their physical needs and creature comforts. They should seek God sincerely as they receive more of God's blessings or be 'zapped' out of existence and the world to go to where Evil and badness has stopped. God's kingdom must come or be created on earth. Humankind must be the one who makes evil. Since God does not deal with us according to our sins and iniquities, more should seek his kingdom to come.

I am waiting for the spirit to use my particular thought-out numbers as I pray to win the lottery for God's purposes. If only one person got drawn to know God through my experiences, then my life has done its duty and souls rejoice. But, unfortunately, people do not always listen to the experiences of others and learn from them. The thing that will get noticed most is the lottery win, but do not forget that God is working in all areas of our lives and those of other believers.

I know that God does not give everyone special attention and intervene that way in their lives but allows most people to go right ahead in their tracks. God does not interfere, even though He knows they will ultimately destroy their lives, health or happiness. I hope God will guide me where I am going wrong or getting the message wrong. I also hope people will learn from my experiences when I was granted money to further God's kingdom, help people and do works to save souls.

A great flood of personal joy comes to me when I see the wife and children happy. Of course, we had our ups and downs in 1997 when our marriage nearly ended. But there is a strong bond of love now, which ties us together again as a family. Since your mother's relationship with me is alright still, her strong character and loving personality are working as hard as mine to see that we have a happy home. Our evident love for one another has reflected in the children's lives and made them feel secure and wanted by both of us.

I plan carefully for 1998, which means setting goals, developing a budget and reducing expenses wherever possible. The turning of the year can be a moment of great hope and anticipation. The new year implies new opportunities, and we hope that things may be better than before. I have the desire, which I trust is not wildly naïve. It could be a good year that should enrich us as we seek to be obedient to God and as a witness to our faith. It has not proved a comfortable journey so far, but I pray for a listening spirit, as well as a passion for God's will to be done and for greater wisdom, as I seek to discern the right path. Happy New Year, and God bless!

The New Year's First Thoughts
Written Sunday, January 4th 1998

Life is like a series of injustices; I have not won the lottery, and my motives are misunderstood or misrepresented by others.

The good that I try to do somehow rebounds and produces negative consequences. I only wish our lives to be marked by opportunities that should have opened up but did not. My ability and hard work go unrewarded when others seem to forge ahead in the stakes of worldly success.

After years of providing security with some upheaval of the market, or whatever, it robbed me of my protection, and now I have no rainy-day money. Sickness has been a very random incidence so far. We have escaped severe illness lately, and I realized that health is not an entitlement but a cause that senses injustice if one is not well. The feeling is accurate enough to convince me that good health is a gift from God and not an entitlement.

As time delivers us into being more aged and older, life as a whole can be seen to have been a disappointment sometimes, as a collection of unfulfilled ambitions and as unrecognized efforts get remembered. They are, however, attitudes of my own making. I should not feel injustice, but objectively, my treatment at the hands of fate or others is sometimes undoubtedly unfair. Being that I am a person and not an object, the world is a catalogue of the benefits which will fall to anyone. I see fewer worthy people flourish, less excellent in my definition and perhaps really so by some absolute standard. More and more, I know the truth is that life does not owe us anything except the chance to use our time in the cultivation of spiritual consciousness. My expectations were determined by a desire for worldly recognition, happiness, security and release from pain, but I am disappointed. I look ahead to glimpse the evidence of the unseen world in the fragments of my hopes that deliver us into an eternal life that extends far beyond my experience of earthly things. The essential part of me, the role of us which is to survive, that is to say, has no practical test by which it gets recognised. It is the part that has the quality called eternal. After all, in the end, nothing matters beyond kindness, love, good manners and humour because each moment of the day is a gift from God. Time is life, measured out for us to work for spiritual formation in our minds.

My mind compels me to believe in something outside myself and within my body for some strange reason. I have this belief because I need to worship, and I do not idealise anybody. I came to believe in my religious belief because I took a leap of faith in somewhat incomplete evidence of assumptions and then stuck to it, and then at that point, it was not open to argument. I am a free thinker, but authority and dogma make me obey a higher being: - God, the phenomenon.

I was destined to obey a higher authority. At first, I bought it, but now I cannot escape it, because it has come. If I serve God that way, I must no longer draw away from the task but do it. I have a definite conviction, and a clear sense of mission to see visions and achieve. I need certainty through God and the church because the world is uncertain and only follows the trend; today, it's unfashionable to marry.

A large part of my sentences could have ended in question marks because this is an uncertain age. Job's insecurity, street violence, even meat may be dangerous for us, but I am hopeful. The circumstances of the world seem pretty discouraging; the pollution, the economy and the wars. There will be no Armageddon, and there will be no sudden ending. Year on year, we will see our children grow and grow; growth will continue in the broader world after them. I look to the future with fear, but knowledge overcomes some of that fear, for we know so much more today. Technology and biotechnology have taught us much about our world.

For a long time now, I have been awaiting the future or the path to the next millennium, and it seems sure to be lit with technology to brighten the millennium doom. Yet, as I lift my gaze, I see we have almost made it to the year 2000 and beyond. My mind is no longer filled with intense fears but with something just as frightening. I see a slow decline of a world that thinks we are victims of human evolution. It is going a particular way, and we have to take it or leave it. Sometimes, I feel we know too much about our planet, each war, and each needed stranger and no dogma or belief can claim to know all answers. Yet, I yearn to find a vision to hold on to, something substantial to carry us ahead.

There is something we always carry - inventions of mechanical things and the applied sciences and arts. As we look towards the century's end and parts of the world are in disarray, we see biotechnology making us able to control our evolutionary destiny. It tries to determine what sort of people we want to become. But now, voices can be heard. Technological change is moving swiftly, and I fear I might be left behind because it's not buying into my dreams of worshipping a superhuman being with power over nature and human affairs, who is the creator and ruler of the universe.

Humans are intrinsic in themselves and are not merely a biological computer programme written in their genes. I retain the notion that human beings are much more than the sum of their parts and cannot be reduced to a DNA strip of three billion base pairs long. They have a value that transcends molecular biology, but who believes people like us?

The ranks of the persecuted have not grown thinner in this century. As we approach the millennium, technology has also presented us with more recent and sophisticated weapons to crush even more masses of our fellow human beings. I pray for the world's problems, whether political, economic or social, and I build up huge expectations of prayer. A failure in an answer results in real anguish and devastation.

All my life, as far back as I can remember, I have prayed for world peace and to gain everlasting life. It's been over three years since I prayed for a change in my financial life, but is prayer incapable of changing the material world? Prayer feels worthwhile, but it gives a different answer to my desperate state and people affected by war, famine, and diseases. I am frustrated with prayer and disillusioned with the power of prayer because I prayed hard for all kinds of sufferers in the world, and it is a pre-scientific recipe and is a form of charm power that does not work very well.

I still repeatedly pray for an advantage I believed would happen but feel a failure in faith. Maybe little faith prevents a miracle, but my belief is more significant than a grain of mustard seed. From my observation of prayer, advantages for answers, whether or not they occur, tell me that God is a God of surprises, and beautiful things shall happen. It may come through financial experts or medical ones, but I am still looking more directly to answer the mysterious prayer beyond our understanding. When I pray, it does not occur; I wonder if I lack faith or my spirituality is low. I have to remain spiritually close to God, so that spiritual powers increase. Hard as it is to believe, nothing will be impossible. The emphasis is not worldly and outer, but it is the power of love and is inner. It was based on the truth, love, peace, proper conduct and non-violence that govern my life.

Wife's Baptism.
Written in April 1998

The notion of sin has evolved a fair bit since those Garden of Eden days. For example, a get-out clause in the holy book says, repent and be baptised and be born again.

I am delighted about this because it makes a place in the kingdom of God for everyone who truly repents. The righteous ones feel like saying 'praise to God'. The state of being saved from sin and its consequences appears to mean that you can commit any crime, big or small, moral or not moral, and God will forgive you if honest regret and the right resolve lead to a new life. The marvellous invention, Jesus Christ, gets you off the hook every time if you have salvation through baptism. Look at this - deathbed repentance allows you to sin all you like, cop a plea, then waltz off into the sunset wholly absolved. One can get saved even just before death after cursing all life if the get-out clause gets used. Through the swinging sixties and the permissive seventies, sin started singing an entirely different tune, and now in the nineties, the whole concept of sin has gone out of the window. After 2,000 years of civilization, it seems like it was twigged that the entire point of sin was to take pleasure even more pleasurable.

People readily accepted that baptism is the sacrament of Christian enterprise. Euphemia committed herself to Christian baptism on April 5th, 1998, after soul-searching to fill the void she felt in her life. I have to go back a few years to put you in the picture of how Euphemia came to accept Jesus Christ as her Lord and Saviour.

Euphemia was brought up as a Catholic, married me in a Catholic Church and christened the children in the Catholic Church, but never thought genuinely about Christianity and her faith. Until Catholicism had her dumb by the news of unfaithful priests, child abuse in Christian churches, she found that the Catholic Church's service was repetitive each Sunday and that she could not find anything there that touched her heart. Euphemia came to worship with me at the URC, but nothing grasped her mind or emotions, and Euphemia found the service dull. She yearned to find something that made her think God is there, and she can feel Him in her life. So she looked more profoundly for feelings about her Christian faith and ousted Catholic theology.

Euphemia then looked at Protestant theology through the eyes of a Jehovah's Witness. A friend of hers regularly came each week to pray and give Euphemia bible-study lessons. Finally, something clicked because Euphemia read the Witness version of the Bible. But not everything happened as truths to her, and the Witness ways were too cultist for her.

Another of Euphemia's friends was a Pentecostal in a mainly white Pentecostal Church. She attended services with the friend, and Euphemia said, "I felt touched; a warm feeling came over me, and I was happy at the worshipping. The people seem to get filled with the Holy Spirit". Since that time, over three years ago, Euphemia has kept up her attendance and has joined in church activities such as prayer meetings, home groups and bible-study classes.

In the last year, 1997, I saw the beginning of the Holy Spirit's spiritual work. It was the springboard to her blessings and fulfilment in her commitment to baptism. There is a transformation now that she practices the Christian faith devotedly. She gives herself time and space to pray, but we found prayer challenging to say in each other's company. I think it's such a private personal thing, talking to God. We feel shy to pray with each other. We spoke to each other openly about it, and we pray for our wants and needs for others and ourselves, but not for long when we are together in prayer with God.

When the family is at the dinner table, and prayer is usually said before a meal, I stick to the traditional Grace or the Lord's Prayer. It is challenging to say a prayer as a blessing like a preacher, but I do not add more words to the vocabulary. At a hearty Sunday lunch, I asked everyone at the table, the children, my wife myself, to say special thanksgiving grace and then eat.

A lit candle is a symbolic beacon of hope for peace in our days of wars, terrorism, and crime at Christmas time. We hope the future will be politically, economically and socially better for all of us. Over the twelve days of Christmas, the Grace was said every day over dinner, and we brought to our thoughts and prayers for the poor, lonely, starving and other needy people. As we prepare to eat, I silently prayed for the persecuted, those with little freedom and fear for their lives. I consciously thought of them and also for people's repentance. I openly asked that we think about the environment and pray for the proper nurturing of the land and animals. I recently introduced a 30-second silent meditation over Sunday's dinner to transmit our positive thoughts and send optimism and good feelings and hope to give strength by our mind being relaxed and getting a feel-good factor by the silence. We hold each other's hands and form a ring around the table, which gives us a sense of constant energy flow and has our heads bowed and eyes closed. As we visualised in our minds, the moment felt very spiritual, the energy going further than ourselves to our relatives and friends.

I don't think the family fully understood what I was trying to achieve, but they enjoyed the 30-second silence, and we all had a big smile on our faces afterwards. I then touched the children's foreheads and cheeks and said, "Mummy and Daddy love you and all the family". Then, I suddenly felt the wife's face while uttering the words, 'God bless you, darling' and kissed her.

As I shared in Euphemia's spirituality since her conviction and baptism, she reminds me of myself as a young, new Christian. I sensed the 'fire' she had experienced in church and seeing the communion of Christians praising God and getting moved emotionally to the point of tears. The prayers of the faithful, causing ailments to ease through the laying of hands, made us cry out thanks to God, hallelujah.

The disbelief that talking in tongues affects the person until she fully accepted the Pentecostal way and saw what she thinks as another line of truth was utterly transforming. Like me, when not in church, Euphemia thirsted for more words on Jesus, and her palate was quenched with songs, religious music tapes and reading spiritual books.

A new Christian radio station now broadcasts programmes that help her fill the appetite for Jesus. It was a blessing, and she was indeed energy-filled and alive with the Holy Ghost. Nevertheless, I clung to the idea that nothing happens without purpose, and the experiences in Euphemia's life have given her strengths that I never saw she had. I believe she can accept the Pentecostal theology because she studies the Bible privately, feels good about herself, and her life has changed into becoming fulfilled. She is growing active in every area of her life, not only spiritually.

That has been wonderful. Euphemia's temperament has changed, and she is not ashamed to talk about Jesus Christ in her life which a meaningful faith gave her. I would say Euphemia has true Pentecostalism, and myself, I am just a believer in the mighty God, for I do not hold to one doctrine because doctrines and dominations are labels that divide and separate. People of different faiths can share a coming as one unit because there is only one God almighty, so I am pleased to go to the Pentecostal church on occasions. I would not even mind if worship were in a mosque, temple or church. They all satisfy my need to worship - the kind of place does not matter.

Katrina, our eldest daughter, no longer likes the Pentecostal church's worship style and comes with me to the URC (United Reform Church). My other two children, Georgina and Jonathan, do not mind either worship and attend the churches. I am not a regular churchgoer, so there is no conflict about which church to pray in. The Sunday morning worship on the radio and television takes up my meditation period when I am too lazy to go to church.

It's when the strain of the week begins so often to anguish in the pit of my stomach that the waking thought on Sunday morning is that I had a bad dream. Then comes the realisation that needing the church is a reality. So, then I make an effort to go, and I feel much better afterwards.

In the theology about baptism and church rule, it is essential to know what we believe and why and this is clarified by St. Paul in the early church. In the study of scripture, the environment of contemporary Judaism, and the early church's practices, we must understand. The doctrines we hold when the emotions are damped, and we believe in our mind we can fall back on, will help us live a life of high principles. I think Euphemia understands how to walk with God, even though she has not learned to follow New Testament theology fully and the cardinal truth of our faith. She believes it in her heart and wants to walk in the light of it, which is sufficient for her. An intellectual inquiry does not come into it because she feels her heart guides her actions.

The coming to baptism has led Euphemia to tell me about a problem that I knew nothing about until now. She took out a personal loan from what can only be described as a 'loan shark' company because the interest to pay back was not reasonable but highly inflated. She has two hundred pounds left to pay off the loan, but she cannot make any more regular payments at the store, and she suspects an agent will call round to harass her because she has already been sent a letter of default.

Euphemia knew the problems we are in concerning money, and, with her money worry, it's an increased burden to sort out. I thought my money problems were also hers to help because family needs had led me into financial trouble. But, instead, she committed to her money problem rather than jointly sharing mine. I told Euphemia about my financial planning, but she kept hers a secret until now.

I was not angry with her when she told me but was disappointed that she needed help with the payments and had not even mentioned that she took out a loan. Euphemia wants to live and act as God's representative. Her baptism was a public declaration to allow the Holy Spirit to help her live an honourable life and one that is pleasing to God, so she felt it only fitting for me to know. Her Christianity style is dynamic, sacrificial love, praise with thanksgiving, and living a suitable life obedient to God's laws. God does not work by magic to help us in spiritual and material events with our problems and the dreadful imperfections of humanity. Still, the laws of the very matter that He, the author of all things, had exploded into existence, shows that He cares.

Now that both have joint communion with God, living problems do not go away, but we seem to develop our inner strength and an inner core of peace. The awareness of God's presence enables Euphemia to face life with new vigour, though, as I said before, living problems do not go away. Being a human being, she will still make mistakes in her newborn-again life.

Today is April 12th 1998, Easter Sunday and a Happy Easter, everyone. In this hope, the expectations that arise from Easter to see the prospect of life beyond this life and eternity are God-given truth. God bless you, darling Euphemia, my lovely, on your baptism.

Unanswered Prayer
Written APRIL 1998

Not having success in prayer may sometimes be the result of ignorance or the wrong motive.

I must have been very foolish to suppose that it will undoubtedly get done because I asked God about this and that, such as debt getting paid by miraculous means. I have a right to ask for anything God has promised me, but if it goes beyond the range of the divine promises, I also go beyond the scope of certainty and confident expectations. When one gets fancy in one's head, I suppose that God is there in my fancy. I have recognized my ignorance of divine will, and delay on unanswered prayers may become a training school for me.

The feeling that I am not receiving answers to prayer suggests that God is telling me something entirely different from what I expect, and I am not picking up the message. I cannot find any consistency in my spiritual pilgrimage. By being conscious in sleep when I dream or awake, I feel spiritual without finding time to pray. My God-consciousness is always with me, and even though the bustle of modern living makes it challenging to pray, I feel alert to God's power and will without taking time out.

The spiritual dimension is squeezed out of people lives by the pressures of timetables, phones, work and family. But, even with demands on my time, I pray without any consistency. I am communicating something to my thoughts, and they enter deep into the mind and mingle in my head among the prayers within the crowded hours of earning a living and raising a family.

My work time was no different from my prayer periods because, from the time I woke to go back to bed, I am as aware of God's presence as when I am still. In the noisiness of machinery or the bustle of everyday living, I possess God because I do what I commonly do for the sake of God. I was troubled in mind because I was making things for the military at work. After a while, I stopped feeling guilty about it and just did my duty, and the Holy Spirit blessed me with peace.

In earlier times, I spoke of digesting hymns to feel spiritual. The accolades and spiritual melodies have been like devotional reading books from those days to now, which let me feel great spiritually and give therapeutic value. Reading hymn melodies as prayers is inspiring, and learning about the lives of great Christians has been a source of inspiration. I stilled my mind many times in the day, like when I went to the loo. I still breathe deeply, let the breath out and relax, close my eyes, and then in mind, in God's presence. Nothing else matters that moment of peace in the presence of God, which is the beginning of the order that passes all the understanding.

When I am in bed under the cocooning warmth of the bed covers, I spend a minute and pray and fall asleep. Then, in the morning, I wake up like a lark, fresh and bright and out of bed and only say good morning, God. My desire to pray is nothing intellectual. I'll pray longer; it's more in the gut, like a wave of emotion that swamps me. There are times when I am completely overwhelmed by it, and all the time, this voice inside me was going, boy, oh boy, it's intense, and I prayed on and off until the craving ceased.

There were times when welling up with sadness and worries of the day made me anxious or desperate. My thoughts were not orderly. Days go by when I am unable to think about anything other than my anxieties. The problems keep coming back to me, hanging over me. I try to get a sense of order in my mind and pray in terms of sections. Prayer for the health of mind or body is the first section, family and friends next and environment and money are the last part. Then I see what I can do about the problem, do all I can, and leave the rest to God.

There is no use worrying about the things that I can do nothing about them. When I conclude that there is nothing that I can do anyway, I become grateful for all the blessings I already have. I ask for guidance in the problems and the solutions that I have thought about, and I say the Lord's Prayer embraces everything. I find the weight of anxiety then begins to slip off my shoulders.

I am convinced even more and more that prayer is a way of life and needed in life like air. It is not so many words as an attitude to living and breathing. This state of mind that always has an awareness of God in all experiences, good and bad, this state of consciousness enables me to cope with trials and difficulties. In this state of mind, I appreciate the love of God revealed in the people that God has given us to love more. It sees everything with the eye of faith and fully appreciates everything in creation with fresh and grateful eyes.

When I hear the birds singing melodies at the break of day, I feel like shouting aloud for joy for the creation of a new day when the birds awake me to it, but then at least in my mind, I will let my prayer sing for joy. My prayer is usually a phrase, released as quickly as an arrow, sometimes when in a rush, a blessing occurred to me. God is in my mind and on my lips. I am reminded of his presence almost by accident sometimes, by looking at the sky. When I look up at the sky, since the time at the reggae festival on August 19th 1994, I woo day or night, no matter what kind of atmosphere it is, swirling grey clouds or patches of light blue ones smiling at me. It's like the spirit of God is ever-present, and I smile because somehow the sky tells me that God is with us, watching over us, loving us. Believing in God gives me an awareness that intensifies life's moments we live until we meet God and eternity. God could transform ordinary events into exquisite experiences.

I am just beginning to believe that there is no such thing as unanswered prayers. All prayers are heard and answered. Either we might receive a miracle or be shown how to cope with the job using our gifts. Ultimately, if we can trust in the love of God altogether, we can accept that sometimes. God says no. I am coming around slowly to the idea that every prayer is received, heard and processed. I suppose they are because the question should not be, 'Does God answer prayers?' so much as, 'How do we perceive the answer to our prayers?' I do not think the age of miracles has passed, but nothing less than a miracle does happen in the prayer asking for things. Sometimes, my problems with God and the answers do not involve a blessing. I do not require a gift to change the situation. I can change the situation myself. It feels like God's answer is that I have the talent, the ability to cope with the problem, and, given the strength, can change the case for myself. Prayer could be answered without a miracle, which would dramatically change things.

I have discovered that the amount I spent on the lottery increased and increased week-on-week until the spending reached £10.00 a week and credit card spending reached its credit limit.

I am bound to practise what I pray to have. It was going beyond what was expectable. I am in this crazy world of expecting my luck to change and a much better chance of winning when I play more lines, but we were suffering because of needy things we had to do without putting on credit until the debt was out of control. I could not see that I could pay the rising credit card bills. There was no getting away, for the day of reckoning was coming because income did not meet the outgoing expenditures.

I am currently fluffing credit money to pay for the essentials, and this practice is temporary. However, it gives a breathing space to find a more permanent solution. I am trying to reduce expenditure and bring in more income, but average spending is not falling but rising, even though I am conscious of what I am doing. So, in the words of St Paul, "Be not anxious about anything, but in all things, let God know of your needs through prayer with thanksgiving. And the peace of God that passes all understanding will watch over you". Amen.

God knows of our needs, but God knows answers are not always heaven-sent. God is not the answer, it seems. He has become a problem too. He does not mean to be, of course, but once I invited God to the party over at logic's place in my mind, reason climbs out of the window, and after the party, much of everything that's a problem remains the same – an unsolved problem. It may be because I had introduced the creator whose work is apparent in all things, but my issues should not be overlooked. I wait on God. It is the head-scratching time because, yes, why are things not working out? That was a bit of rotten luck, or God cannot be relied upon to change the material world but only bring comfort, joy and morality to people.

I start thinking and never know where it ends because up until I recognized the influence of an unquantifiable super-being, I lost the plot and fought back the tears and thought He had disappeared from my life.

Neighbour Dispute
Written May 1998

It was probably three years, say 1995, when our current neighbours moved in.

Our first impression of them was that they did not seem a friendly couple, and the man appeared like a thug, even though he must be over forty-five-ish. My wife thought she saw that sinister face of the man somewhere in his car, involved in soliciting. Within weeks of moving in, confrontational arguments raged in their home. They battled with harsh, lousy language and shouted at each other. Our children soon told us the neighbours had sworn at them not to play there on many occasions as they played ball games on our driveway. My driveway is directly in front of both houses, semi-detached, and two garages face the drive, but our neighbour's garage and parking area are at the side entrance to his house. So, the total length of the driveway from leaving the road belongs jointly to us and our neighbour opposite. The neighbour's only legal right is the right to have access to his house from our driveway.

I played down the possible tensions that could have arisen from the neighbour's verbal abuse of the children. I continued to allow our children, friends and related children to play on the driveway while I looked on and observed. If the ball went onto next door's land, I would go and fetch it. I looked for them to come outside and start swearing at the children, but neither one appeared.

My wife told me the truth about the man and how his face began to look familiar. Now that she has remembered, she does not talk to them, and they avoid her eye contact. I would still greet them with the word 'morning' or 'hello', even though Euphemia told me she firmly believes that the man next door is a pervert and has suddenly changed his car to avoid detection. Euphemia said, on her way to work, she gracefully thanked the man with a nod and a silent thank you with the movement of her lips as he allowed her to cross the road in front of his car, and he drove slowly away. After that, he went slowly by in his car most mornings as Euphemia walked the usual route to work. He raised my wife's suspicion and tried to change the direction

250

of getting to work, but still, he managed to meet her walking the road she must take to reach the workplace.

Once, he drove so close to the pavement, winded the car window down, and had his trousers flies unzipped and exposed himself. Although Euphemia turned and hurried to the nearest advice centre, Victoria Centre, they rang for the police. A policewoman interviewed her. During the interview, Euphemia felt uncomfortable with the questioning. The police alleged that she had egged on, did something that encouraged and caused him to expose himself sexually to her. Unfortunately, the policewoman lost the plot. Euphemia came away from the centre more upset because she was being judged guilty, and her explanations and details of stalking had not been taken down sensitively or seriously.

Euphemia told me this story again, the week this man and his wife moved in. She immediately said that man was the sex pest who had followed her and exposed himself to her, but I could not believe he would risk living next to his victim. Surely, he has a twin? I did not know what to do precisely, but my feelings told me not to cause a confrontation and see how my relationship with them may develop.

He used to talk to me about the garden blooms and invited me to come around to his house for a drink sometime. But, of course, I never took him up on the offer; deeply seated in my mind was the allegation that he is a pervert. But we must get on as neighbours, and I talked to him only when he spoke to me.

As seasons passed and years rolled by, the allegation was at the back of our minds, but the children continued to tell us that foul language was said to them when they played when I was not outside. The children were beginning to be frightened of them and ran indoors immediately to let us know. The wife went straight over and told the culprit not to swear or say insults at her children and informed the police of the neighbour's behaviour toward the children. When the husband appeared, my brother attempted to talk to him about his foul mouth, but he got dismissed with highly abusive language. Finally, the police said to let them speak to the neighbour, and I assumed it would frighten them into leaving us alone.

For months, things had been quiet until spring came again, and the shrubs in his front garden were growing out of control. Mainly one bush had grown into a tree. It restricted sunlight to our property and overhung the place where the downpipe of the gutter divides the two properties visibly. The previous neighbour had asked us to maintain the shrub that can grow into a tree. They told us to prune it if it was beginning to get too big.

The rains came in April, and it was the worst monthly fall since records began, and raised the fear that the tree, which is very close to the house, might grow so big that it would affect the foundation of our home. So, knowing the couple next door would not agree to prune the tree, I cut the main shoot to my waist without their consent. I was ready for a confrontation when I met the man a few hours later, and he chatted with me about how beautiful my running flowered vine looked, climbing up between the two houses, without realising his tree had been pruned. Then, as he began to put new shrubs near the grass verge boundary, he became aware of the cut plant. I was in the garage pretending to be busy, and he shouted angrily to me. Then, with a smirk on my face, I said, "I thought you would not mind because you can see it's blocking the light, and it has grown too big".

The flower bed that was designed to have low-lying shrubs had got a large plant in it. Two days later, as I arrived home from work, the male neighbour had planted more shrubs in his front garden. As I strolled to my front door, without warning, he gave me the most insulting verbal abuse, and with the fury of a madman, he made racial remarks with threats to provoke me to be the aggressor to a physical assault. He egged me on to see if I dared to attack him and used callousness to try to insult my intelligence and my family. "If you had brains, you would be dangerous, but you are f-----ing sh—t". That was some of the provoking foul languages he used to urge me to fight him. He bickered with me that he would not let the matter rest because I had damaged his property, and I would hear from his solicitor. When he threatened to take up violence, I said to him, "I am not a man of violence", and I sensed he saw my remark as a sign of weakness and fear of him. Then, using the common ground that he can relate to in conversation, swearing, I used strong language to describe him as a pathetic man. I will destroy him if he lays a finger on my family or my property.

The language was learnt in the workplace and is used freely in general conversation without people taking offence or seeing it as abusive. It's foul language, but it expresses extreme adult speech. The Queen's English was not getting through to him until I bombarded him with Anglo-Saxton words that I would not like my mother to hear me say. He laughed and said the F, B and C words, and we threw a raging battle using bad language. He looked comfortable using foul language as a weapon to hurt my feelings. Finally, I resorted to the Queen's English and made it clear that I would kill or lose my life in protecting my family. He threatened our very existence on the planet, which terrified me because it seems he could do anything. After all, he talked like a thug and a bully.

I hypothetically imagined him attacking me. I would hit him twice as hard and then let the law deal with us. I cannot think straight enough during an angry scuffle to know reasonable force or behaviour; my instinct to defeat him would likely permit me to kill him. I believe his threats to kill my family are not bluffs because he looks capable of committing murder. I often see that the law does not dish out proper justice, so I will do the maximum damage to him and let the judge sort us out how he pleases. I have not abandoned my Christian principles, but since our existence was threatened, I will defend my God-given right to live on this planet until He calls us into the eternal world.

Fundamentalist Christians showed me that in their method of standing up for what they believe in and the great danger of finding it, you have the right to be self-righteous all the time. I was probably guilty of a fair amount of self-righteousness by not asking my neighbour's permission. I was wrong not to have asked, and I apologise only with a pen on this paper with a lump in my throat.

Today is Sunday, 10th May 1998. I have not come across the neighbour since the threats last week, Tuesday 5th May. The tree was cut on Sunday 3rd May and caused the confrontation. I know that I haven't a leg to stand on legally for pruning next door's tree because it is on his land, although I was looking after his and our interest. The tree could grow too big and affect the foundations of the house, I thought. However, in our quarrels last week, he said that he would not have given consent to cutting the tree if I had come and asked him. He is not an amicable man or the type one can confront. He is particularly good at evoking fear, and his aggressive behaviour showed he is incapable of showing mercy. In the end, I did not have any doubts about what I was trying to do, but, regrettably, it came outside the law because the law asks one to have permission.

Our Child
Written Sunday 12th July 1998

JONATHAN

Our son is nine years old, and he is a good, polite and loving boy. He loves receiving hugs and kisses equally from both parents. He is not shy or embarrassed to be kissed or cuddled by his father or mother like other boys are in public.

Jonathan makes no actual demands on us; although he likes to have designer labels, he is not so upset when we cannot buy the things wanted but is joyous and forever pleased when the gift he asked for is given. Jonathan understands the need to consider the feeling and opinions of others and offers a view. He is conscientious and loves playing football and the violin. Although father and son rarely play ball games together, his sisters contribute to his physical activities and development by engaging in ball games and board game skills. Jonathan practices ball control skills by himself and sometimes cycles around the cul-de-sac close with his youngest sister. He has had his first season of playing football with an under-nines football club called Westfield Rovers YFC. He trains with them on Saturday morning, and on Sunday morning, he plays in a match.

He suffered asthmatic symptoms during a football match, which are mild enough to be controlled with a puff on an inhaler. Nevertheless, he's been a brilliant player because he has a dominant right foot that shoots accurately towards the goal. His position on the field is usually as a defender, and he tackles the opposition skilfully and removes the threat that the ball will end up in his side's net. Most weeks, he saved his team single-handedly from losing disgracefully and was named man of the match. His team drops a staggering seven goals to nil, and Jonathan's defence brings respect to the side because he shows good ball skills. In contrast, the other team members display a poor understanding of playing football competitively.

The coach selected him to be the person to take all penalties, free kicks, and throw-ins and to take corners in a league tournament. Unfortunately, the team was losing discipline and was not taking the coach's instructions, so Jonathan got chosen to carry out all the particular duties in the competition. The team was bottom of the league. Nevertheless, each group member received a medal for participating in the Weetabix League sports; they had fun even though they were defeated and outplayed. They are all looking forward to next season.

Jonathan supported the famous Manchester United Football Club. He had a day trip to visit the home ground, Old Trafford, with Georgina, myself and some other pupils and teachers at Freeman's Primary School.

It is the World Cup '98 contest, and all the children support England in their playoff with Argentina. The game was tense and packed full of exciting football entertainment, and we felt our spirit crushed when England just lost out on penalties: four goals to three. Before the match finished, Jonathan had to go to bed, but he learned the final score before falling asleep.

He is excited by football, watches live televised matches intensely, and says he picks up tips to incorporate in the football club games. He goes outdoors to practise the moves soon after watching the game, remembers football's rules like the professionals, and dislikes a player's deliberate fouling.

Jonathan has been in the URC Anchor Boys Club. It's like Cubs, and he has been going since he was young enough to join. Jonathan received a small silver-plated cup for being helpful and has moved on to Boy's Brigade, where he was presented in his first year there with a big silver cup for good attendance and best turned out in uniform. He enjoyed the programme's activities of the Brigade and tried to get his friends and family interested. But cousin Leon, Daniel and a school friend, introduced to the club, gradually stopped going.

Jonathan's schoolwork is above average, and he has represented his class on the school council and got merits for outstanding subjects. He was in a national curriculum year four, and his end of term report was pleasing. The teachers said the things we expected of our good, loveable and obedient son. Jonathan enjoys reading storybooks; the Stench-Scented Horrible Book series such as those on History, Horrible Science, and Bart Simpson's comic strips are his favourites.

After a good read, Jonathan turns his attention to the digital handheld game called the Game Boy that thrills him, or he plays on Nintendo and does not realise that the number of hours spent playing exceeds reasonable time. I tell him it's time to stop, and he is obedient to the request, and his sisters play the game too and sometimes do not understand when time is up for the day. They like to play for hours, and I have to halt their play.

It will be School Sports' Day in a few days, and he has qualified in the heats in which he gained places in the finals on Sports Day. Granddad Willett was a spectator at the Sports Day event and saw Jonathan run the flat race and win. He came second in the relay and fifth in the three-legged race. Well done, Jonathan. Well done.

Our Child
Written Sunday 2nd August 1998

GEORGINA

Georgina is our second daughter; she is twelve years old and a beautiful, loving child. At the starting of the new term in September, she will be in year eight.

Georgina is an active child who has many out-of-school activities. She attends Girls' Brigade and has won medals in playing netball and rounders in school tournaments. The other sport that Georgina is a keen enthusiast of is playing football. She plays for an under-thirteen all-girls Football Club, also known as Westfield Rovers FC. It is the end of the second season of playing with the club, and Georgina is one of the up-and-coming hopeful players. She showed great potential, and the team is up against equally good competitors, and they beat off stiff competition to reach runner-up in the Weetabix Youth League. Unfortunately, Georgina has suffered asthmatic symptoms for two years now and needs a reliever inhaler during matches.

Georgina is enthusiastic and likes making cupcakes and biscuits but tries to sneak out of the washing up. When her school homework is completed, Georgina chills out and relaxes by playing with her brother on the Nintendo almost continuously until bedtime. I have to limit their playtime on the Nintendo at weekends, or they spent playing the game the entire weekend. I set a time to play-learn by doing small light chores, tidy their room, and set the dinner table. Then, they partake in the shopping experience with a mini child-sized trolley shopping with us at the supermarket, buying things, counting money, and receiving change.

Georgina is generally a happy child, and we are pleased with her progress through the first term in comprehensive education. She excelled in being taught the German language, her first modern language, and had a day trip to Germany. Georgina has shifted through exploring musical instruments to discover which ones get liked best to learn to play. She has asked to play the piano from the early humble beginnings of playing the recorder, keyboard, trumpet, violin, and trombone. I talked to her about

257

the affordability and how it's outside our reach to have her tutored, and I asked her to improve her playing the violin, the current instrument she has learned.

Georgina is a Manchester United supporter and shares a bedroom with her older sister, a Manchester United supporter too. The walls of their bedroom are covered with posters of their football team's favourite players. But, unfortunately, they cover the wall like decorative wallpaper with so many advertisements, and the original plain wallpaper got obscured.

Georgina is polite, and we rarely have crosswords. However, they can be a breakdown in discipline, as she needs speaking to twice about clearing up when she has finished playing. She needs more talking to, more so than her older sister, mostly to tidy the living room and wash up a small load of dirty dishes.

She has a full circle of friends from those in the Pentecostal Church Youth Group and Girls' Brigade connected to the URC Church, her school friends and those from the girls' football team. It is not surprising then that Georgina gets invited to many birthday parties, sleepovers and even invites to call round to play at friend's houses for a few hours. Georgina is a popular girl among girls, and her face has an almost constant smile, and in communicating, she is very jolly. She has been dubbed with a pet name, smiley, "My little smiley" - by her aunt Lorna.

Since the earlier days at junior school, Georgina has been singing in the school choir, and moving school was no exception. She sings in the senior school choir and plays the violin in the junior orchestra. Georgina has been to Gavilan in Wales to undertake various adventures under controlled, supervised conditions. She tried all the apparatus even though they seemed risky; she went on them and enjoyed herself.

Our Child

Written Saturday 5th September 1998

KATRINA

Katrina, our first child, is passing through her teenage years. She will be sixteen in two months and is a wonderful, loving adolescent daughter who challenges my judgement about what I think is right and wrong. Of course, I am happy to answer why, but Katrina sometimes cannot accept my answer and becomes vexed and argues with me. It strikes me that Katrina's reasoning has not developed sufficiently to see my points of view, and she shouts aloud mainly at me and says I do not understand her points of view. I then deepen my voice and speak loudly to her, not in a rage of anger because my inner self was not perturbed, and the wife says, "The two of you, stop your shouting."

I love my daughter, and shouting is a way of making her listen, I thought, nothing to do with anger management, for I never felt my shouts would escalate into being a raging temper. I saw her shouting as a method of owning her space, expressing her feelings and points of view, and allowing her to do so in the controlled environment of the home where we can tell her that's enough or that's taking things too far. She learns the boundaries of acceptable behaviour.

It is incredible how the media and peer groups greatly influence her attitude over what she wants. We thank God that we have helped shape her personality and awareness of actual needs, respect, and meaningful goals.

Katrina's school report for June 1998 has been highly variable. She attained above-average marks in media studies and geography to below-average attainment in science and art. The teachers had made it seem like Katrina chose not to work to the best of her ability, and for us, that does not sound like our daughter's conscious attitude to school work. The teachers' ability to teach the subject to make her able to grasp the concepts should be more in question! Katrina said she wants to achieve higher standards but cannot always understand what is taught strictly, and the teacher's time is limited to how long they can explain to an individual. Katrina was sad not to have fallen in the grade of an average pupil in science or art and feels now that science has become too complicated.

The wife and I think the girls' school is failing her at this time of critical learning, for up until year 10, Katrina was excelling. We asked her if she would like to change school to the mixed comprehensive that Georgina goes to, known as the best school in town, but Katrina did not want to leave her friends. Furthermore, as there is a rivalry between school pupils, intimidation and bullying may occur if she changes schools.

We thought then that she has time before her GCSEs to improve her standard in art because it will help her towards her first career choice of being a graphic designer. I am worried about Katrina's education because it seems the school concentrates on the brightest pupils. Students or newly qualified teachers are the primary tutors to those in the lower stream. The school rating in the league tables has dropped further down the scale. Although the school is not preparing most students to enter into a man's world, she got poor GCSE results in subjects that can help her career choice. But does not make it impossible to excel when a college education follows the chosen career with hands-on training. I hope Katrina will prefer college rather than sixth form at Southfields to continue her studies after GCSEs.

We are pleased that she has excellent numeracy skills and excellent literacy skills. However, she needs to ensure a consistent effort to do justice to her abilities in next year's exams. Katrina's life outside school revolves around football, not necessarily playing it, but being a dedicated, enthusiastic follower of her favourite football club, Manchester United. She has a crush on the attractive players, and her sister, brother and herself all cheer England or Manchester United on in their competitions.

When it comes to a championship match, they are so excited for the team that their glorification could almost bring the house down. They stamp their feet, scream and shout when goals get scored, they sing the football songs of today, jump up and down and wave their hands in the air. All because of the excitement the game gives them.

The World Cup '98 had an atmosphere in the home like a fever. For four weeks, while the football World Cup was played, nothing else was watched on television. Katrina could speak about football and the adorable Manchester United players like data on a computer. She remembers everything about their private lives that got known through media gossip or interviews. Katrina has been to Old Trafford, the home ground of Manchester United, and met Fred the Red, the team mascot. She bought merchandise and books on the players, and if one asks her about her favourite players, Katrina can tell you their whole lifestyle, possessions, money, and love.

Her crush on Manchester United's football players starts with blushes when David Beckham plays and when his behaviour may have caused England's defeat in the World Cup because he got sent off the pitch. To her, Beckham can do no wrong. Nicky Butt and Teddy Sheringham were equally adorable to her, and her shared bedroom walls were covered with posters of these men. Magnolia-painted plain wallpaper cannot be seen in any part. The signs and all kinds of merchandise clutter the walls, and the room resembles a place only for fans of Man United, and no other colours are more prevalent than red in the room.

I do not know if going to a single-sex school gave Katrina an appetite for crushes because she was starved of the company of boys. She is in company with girls with boyfriends, but she has not said yet that she fancies a boy enough to be her 'boyfriend'. The ratio of girls to boys will be more balanced if she takes a college place, rather than the sixth form. She will, we hope, make relationships with boys and find in them a good friend or partner.

The three children are supporters of Man United, and when matches get televised, the house is full of noises, team cheering, song singing, waving of scarves and jumping. It is all part of their expression of love for the team. Katrina leads her siblings with bursts of joy and laughter, almost unbearable to the ears, as the game grips them and gets them frustrated if the team might lose. Mum and I could not hear ourselves think because the entire children's loud shouts blocked the brain's messages and the TV commentary. One can almost see the walls shake, but it could be the floorboards.

The children were ecstatic and full of joy as they watched their team's performance, and even in defeat, they were proud of the group. However, the game between England and Argentina in the World Cup 1998 made the children over-excited and almost overstimulated their acclaimed voices as they got hoarse. The children had nervous restlessness as the penalties were taken, and I could see they were catching a fever because their body temperature rose, and they were hot.

Katrina's next best-loved sport is Grand Prix Formula One. She is a fan of David Coulthard, a driver in the Mclaren team, and a fan of Eddie Irvine in the Ferrari team. So, she gets thrilled when Coulthard or Irvine clinch victory from the reigning champion, Michael Schumacher. This fast, furious, four-wheel motorsport hooks Katrina like a thriller movie. First, she must watch the qualifying laps and videotape them. Then, when the grid for the actual start of the race unfolds, Katrina's attention is held from start to finish. The competition is furious and can have some dramatic developments. She watches intensely, and her concentration stills the air as the track is mayhem from the very start. Finally, the drivers rush off to a position where they can maintain a lead from a chaotic start.

She has seen every race so far from the world's top circuits, such as Silverstone to Monte Carlo and Rio to Monza; They all set her pulse racing. Even when the race is broadcasted live at three o'clock in the morning, she wants to stay up to see the live-action. I cannot permit such late viewing and insist she goes to bed. I do not allow her to set the video recorder because she will wake up early to view it. Instead, she can watch any two repeated shows later on TV at 1 pm or 11 pm. Katrina asked us to withhold the race result, for her entertainment would get ruined if revealed. The latest race she has seen was the Belgian Grand Prix, and it sent her adrenaline pumping like no other sport except football can.

The race took place in poor visibility due to heavy rain leaving surface water, and the rain clouds still hung over the track as the race ran. Eight cars out of twenty-two finished the race, and all the leading competitors' cars crashed out of the race. Still, Damon Hill emerged from what must be the most fantastic race in Formula One history and clinched the most remarkable triumph of his career. Behind Damon Hill's glorious run lay a trail of destruction, devastation and despair in perhaps the most incident-packed race Katrina had ever seen. You should have heard her shouts of terror as she witnessed one of the worst shunts in Formula One. It was the worst nightmare imaginable with potentially deadly debris, but nobody was seriously injured. Thirteen cars were left wrecked all around the track. Katrina cheered Damon Hill tirelessly as he mounted the rostrum for the Jordan team and sprayed a giant bottle of champagne.

There are three races left in this year's championship. Katrina regularly reminds us of the following track dates because the world's highest-octane dynamic sport makes Katrina's adrenaline run wild. It inflames her passion; it excites her like nothing else can, except football, which triggers arguments with the TV, as she sometimes disagrees with the commentary and referee's decisions.

Like this years' 1998 Belgian Grand Prix, the very best performances raise the hair on her back of the neck because these heroic races on high circuits, where drivers seem to have clinical and skilful ways of passing each other, are thrilling. We promised Katrina driving lessons on her seventeenth birthday, and she is anxious. Meanwhile, she daydreams that David Coulthard has driven her around in a two-seater McLaren, and as her thoughts come back into the real world, she wants to pass the driving test and have a superb Aston Martin DB7 to be her run-around sports car. I said to her, "Katrina, you are still dreaming; you have not even a few dashes of realism thrown in!"

Katrina loves to wear the latest designer clothes. She loves T/sweatshirts, tracksuits, bootcut trousers, trainers for footwear and would rather wear tracksuit bottoms than skirts. However, she can distinguish between when to wear comfortable casual clothes and innovative garments with parental guidance.

Katrina wants to show her individuality and is very conscious of her identity clashes with her sister, like wearing similar clothes. She gets annoyed when Georgina's garment is the same as hers, though the colours may differ. Katrina becomes very angry if Georgina likes to buy the very same outfit in her smaller dress size. She would say all she can to persuade Georgina to change her mind. Georgina's selections and taste must not be the same as hers, but Katrina never sees that she may have to change her mind when Georgina selects the same clothes as for herself.

Katrina has a work experience placement with the engineering firm I work for and will be employed as an office junior for two weeks. From the 14th September 1998, she is to carry out duties unpaid, including word processing, filing, using the fax machine, knowing how to use the photocopy machine, and reception work.

We have a Packard Bell home computer which she uses to brush up her typing skills, and all the children are learning to use it. They use computers at school, and the home computer gives them further practice. Katrina has tried to get a placement with a graphic design company, but they only take college students. So, Katrina stayed on at the girls' school and went into the sixth form. She wishes to continue studying with her best and closest friend, Michelle, and the sixth form at this school has what she wants to learn in its curriculum.

To All the Children
Written Sunday 6th September 1998

Mum and Dad want the best for you all, and we are striving to get it. We love you all, but it can seem like we can never do enough, and I certainly cannot do it right.

As you all get older, you will never tire of letting me know. We are working hard not to feel or be a failure as a parent. Instead, we get you educated to be wise and happy. You all have vast, enormous needs of your own and Mum and I are putting your needs first because we love you all so very, very much. We want you to have the opportunity for a better life than ours, not necessarily through money, but through the wisdom, you have learned from the mistakes you have made.

I am happy and proud to say that we had you, and you were not a mistake that happened. We wanted children to love for life and not just for instant self-gratification. The greatest and most intense moments of our lives have been the births of you all. It was an extraordinarily humbling and, at the time, phenomenal experience, and we feel in awe of the power of life.

My daughters and son, you will, one day maybe, in your teenage years, find a boy or girl with whom to form a relationship. Take contraceptive advice and stay clear of sexually transmitted infections, adolescent pregnancies and fatherhood. Britain has the highest rate of teenage pregnancies in Europe, and teenagers are not emotionally equipped to raise a child. They impose on a child all those things which make them unhappy—something like social deprivation, the lack of opportunity, lack of success and the lack of self-worth. Don't fall into the trap and imagine that the mere act of childbirth or being a father will raise your self-esteem and magically transform you into a brighter, desirable person. You may think having a child makes you feel successful, influential and less of a failure. Regularly you may feel worthless because you cannot achieve the same as the next girl or boy, but having a baby would not be the answer. I suppose it's easier than passing an exam or getting a job, but tough babies are not living dolls, and babies need parents who understand what it means to be an adult. When you take responsibility for yourself, realising that nothing in life comes free and its endeavour and effort reap the rewards, then you are grown up enough to exercise self-discipline, restraint and concern for the lives of others. I hope you all turn out in life okay and make us proud.

My Sister In-Law's Death
Written Thursday 17th September 1998

People regularly face the possibility of grief, and it came to us in a sad, tragic way.

My sister-in-law, Elizabeth, died of an overdose, and our loss made Euphemia's and my reactions change for the worse sometimes. But as time passes, our response is better.

The death happened on Tuesday 9th June 1998, and it threw the whole family into shock. I had to rebuild my beliefs from the foundation up. This traumatic experience of sudden death in our family pushed me to explore how I and others have approached and viewed God. Have our views changed? God is still beyond us but awaiting some different description. I was angry with God for allowing her to die. Why did He not let someone find her in time?

Early in the year, Elizabeth had attended a revival at the Pentecostal Church. Why wasn't she 'saved' through the preaching of the word? She lived with a drinking problem and had days when the bottle was her only comfort, and it seemed she forgot about her two lovely children. Why did the message not convert her from the bottle to looking after herself?

No words can describe our feeling following Elizabeth's death. In the presence of our nieces' broken lives, my shattered mind tries to understand what must have been an accident because she could not have meant to kill herself but try to seek attention. I had shattered faith because words seem especially irrelevant to explain where Elizabeth is now. Heaven, limbo land or the suggestion of a so-called hell! Where is she? If intelligent life can evolve on earth, it can elsewhere, and my intelligence tells me that our soul must go somewhere! What can be said in the face of our loved one dying? The grief and such pain on the day of the burial? Tears spurted out of all our eyes like water leaving a fountain and splashed on the wearer's shoes, softened them until the tears trickled and made a damp patch where the feet rested on the floor. The family wept and wept until the weeping made some weak at the knees, and they were unable to stand on their feet, and they buckled.

The Catholic Church was packed with mourners and also with those who wanted to show their last respects. The coffin was positioned in front of the altar's first step, which I was within inches. The intense emotional weeping and wailing did not trigger my outcry but kept me feeling extremely sad. Staring at the polished teak coffin, knowing it was my dear sister-in-law who was at rest, had my heart needing comfort, and weeping erupted. We all received support from the moving singing of redemption songs. Still, gushes of my continuous crying damped all my tissues, and the tears were unstoppable until the hymns triggered some therapeutic effect, assuring me that Liz was in good hands and that there is a destiny for her. Then the crying stopped. Mucus in my nose still got released, and I kept sniffing like a hound dog during the rest of the service. The hymns that affected me profoundly and told of the human condition and the welcome hand of God were Amazing Grace, Abide with Me and The Lord's My Shepherd. Again, the hymns provoked some powerful, sensitive emotions.

At the cemetery, we stood as motionless as stone pillars as the grave was filled with earth. Choruses were sung, and I said my last goodbye by throwing soil into the grave and placing my hand on a wreath, murmuring the Lord's prayer through deep breaths in and out of my nostrils. As I stooped forward, my heart was filled with a kind of peace and sadness over Liz's departure. There was no weeping for me at the graveside, but I had wept bitterly during the church service.

Euphemia and the two nieces without their mother suffered badly and needed comforting and physical support throughout the melancholy. Their bodies buckled, and they wept without ceasing until, at the reception, the tears stopped, and their bodies relaxed to a healthy posture.

They had plenty of support the day of the melancholy, but soon after, some few weeks later, and now after months had passed, nobody asked Euphemia and the children how they had been coping since the loss of her sister and mother. It is as if Liz never existed. The close family said nothing, and friends said nothing and got on with their lives without finding out if she and the nieces were moving on and coming to terms with Liz's tragic death. We thought that there would never be a time when our lives and our nieces' lives would get back to normal. After such a sad and sudden event of their single mum's death, how will our nieces cope with that experience alone? Somehow living goes on, and it's only those of us amid their suffering that find it hard too, but we are learning how to help them cope and encourage them to continue their lives, however complex, with the grace of God.

I have learned many theories about being mortal and life after death, but out of necessity, I want to know that our loved ones will meet again. We are not just atoms without real meaning to life and purpose and no other existence when life on earth has ended. Shared grief strengthens the bonds in the family, and some friends and the church fellowship enable us to come to terms with her death. It is not the theories about suffering or death that comfort, but the holding onto faith. The knowledge and practical experience of Jesus, who wept over the death of a friend and endured agony in Gethsemane and cruelty on Calvary, showed me that there is no answer to the problems of death and suffering. There are no explanations for how human beings can be so capable of cruelty as in Omaha when the Real IRA planted a bomb and the blast killed twenty-nine people or the depressed take their own life as the only way to escape anguish.

Judas committed suicide to free himself of the hardship he was experiencing. Why did Jesus not forbid him from taking his own life and tell him he forgave him? For Jesus was supposed to know the heart of man and should have picked up that Judas was genuinely sorry for what he did and would end his life.

In due course, I realised that God was there with Elizabeth in the darkest hour of her life, and she has gone somewhere good and is well. The difficulty for the human soul's destination led me to weep for those left behind because the moral argument about our conscience instinctively knows what is right and wrong. And the knowledge placed in our souls must have come from a good God who is behind all things; tell me the first tears are God's tears! Words fail.

I felt both anger and pain with God because the most familiar theme was if only God had done something in the early stages of her drinking problem, an overdose of tablets with alcohol may not have happened. The pain was the guilt over believing that failure to take action might have prevented that fatal situation. Martha made the plaintive plea in scripture, "If only you had come, my brother would not have died". - Jesus wept. (John 11:21)

The sins of remorse will linger, perhaps forever, over things I believed I had failed to do concerning Elizabeth's death. The reality is that we did what we could at the time. We are not omnipotent and may have been able to act differently in the circumstances in which I feel we failed. It's only with hindsight that possible alternative, if any, can be seen. I am pleased that our faith believes in the forgiveness of sins. In the infinite divine mercy, the failures of the past lose their power to hurt and destroy. I know I can move forward. Rest in peace, Elizabeth, and I think it's safe to say she has gone quietly into the afterlife, where hellfire and eternal damnation do not exist because hell as a place does not equate with God's infinite mercy. Hell is a part of Christian dogma, and I do not believe in it; the church has got it wrong.

Life Blows.

Written Wednesday 23rd September 1998

Life has a habit of striking the cruellest blows. We have not yet gotten over our financial crisis when one of the wife's sisters dies, followed by expenses to buy new clothes and travel costs for a family wedding.

My Aunt Lorna is terminally ill with cancer, and Alistair, my sister Joan's husband, is critically ill with kidney disease. Euphemia has changed employer because she found it challenging to work for a boss who showed no sympathy while grieved for her sister's loss. She has worked for the company for over twelve years, and for the boss not to say anything, not even to send a sympathy card while she was on unpaid compassionate leave, she felt he was brutish.

Euphemia started her new job manufacturing curtains on Monday 13th July 1998, and we got through those weeks before her new employment wage by living off the credit cards. However, the curtain factory pay was reduced, and we still need to have subsidised the financial position with credit card purchases to live our daily lives.

I was lucky to get paid employment with the Youth Service to work one and a half days at £5.30 per hour in a neighbouring village every fortnight. I remained a volunteer at the local youth club, where I attend on alternate weeks. The youth club money helps provide income, but it doesn't significantly affect our inferior financial being.

I am off work today, 23.09.98, because of a stomach bug that sends me to the loo as frequently as a tennis ball getting hit back and forth. The loss of a day's pay will affect my pay packet next week. I am worried about the implications.

On Tuesday, 15th September 1998, my wife was involved in a car accident; she had no severe injuries but was shocked. She went to the hospital with her knee and the sides of her neck in acute pain. Then she was released and told to take painkillers. No other person was hurt. However, the other driver caused the car crash due to not taking care and paying attention and bolting through heavy traffic. Our car had to be towed from the scene to our house, where it stayed for six days until the insurer collected it and loaned us a small car, an 'R' registration Fiat Cinquecento.

We have no idea if our car will get fixed or if it will be written off and how long the courtesy car is on loan. The accident happened as Euphemia moved off from a newly laid-out road called Cannon Street, now controlled by traffic lights. As she began to travel along this built-up area's primary way, suddenly, from her right side, a car moved from an entry to a council depot and bolted between slow-moving traffic, through to the other side of the road and into the path of the wife's car and a collision occurred. Euphemia had no time to react to prevent the accident but only brought the vehicle to a standstill and immediately applied the handbrake when she heard the smash. The car went across Euphemia's path, and the passenger's side of the other vehicle was severely damaged. Luckily, the driver was not carrying any passengers. The careless driver's car fell under a shop on the window sill on the adjacent street corner. Euphemia's car bonnet had wholly caved in, leaving only the wings intact.

I wrote a prayer for travellers on the road and displayed it on the dashboard of our car. It was written in 1994 when Euphemia was involved in her first car accident. The prayer had been symbolically on display in the vehicle, suggesting God's watchful eye would bring us safely to our journey's end. The words of the prayer are as follows:

As we are about to depart, O God give us a fair journey on the highways in whatever places. Guide, we pray, with wisdom, all who are travellers on the road. Those who drive along the street have consideration for others. Those who walk on them or play beside them, thoughtful caution and care. So, without fear or disaster, we all may come safely to the end of our journey. Amen.

I had found it a quarrel with God, for I supposed that God had not protected Euphemia in the car accident, but Euphemia felt she had escaped serious injury because God was with her and enabled her to do the right things. Symbolically, I displayed my thoughts of trust and care in God's hand by the prayer in the car, and I thought we were safe, but I miss how God protects us, even though amid danger.

Euphemia was shaken up by accident and was nervous about taking to the road again, but six days later, she went back to work and believed that God held her hand for her to drive another car so soon confidently. I am very proud of her. It was a courtesy car she had never gone in before, but she braved it and said, "The Lord is with me; it's the Lord who drove it".

Euphemia gets flashbacks of the accidents, of this recent one and the previous one, when her mind drifts and recalls episodes. It makes her nervous. She is very cautious and always drives with extra care and attention, for she looks out for the fools on the road. I do not think she is comfortable driving yet, but she needs to get her confidence back.

I almost thought that my prayer had stopped working because after four years of safety, believing in the power the words conveyed, had it let me down? Well, no, my loved one is safe, and the spirit of God was with her, and we will continue to display the prayer in the cars that we drive. It is a symbol that we do trust our God, and I have learnt that, whatever happens, we will be in safe hands. I believe that the good vibes and the aura of the thoughts were in the car, and the good Lord, working in the prayer, shielded her.

Our financial difficulties are more profound and worsen. I daydream, ending our money worries by scooping the lottery, but is it going to happen? Few people are ever that lucky. It's a chance in millions. We have no more money coming in other than two pathetic wage packets, a monthly child benefit allowance, and the youth club petty cash going through the account. I have a £5.00 Premium Bond somewhere, issued since my teens, but no lucky strike yet.

I am going back to gambling excessively again on the lottery because it seems it is likely to be the only means of coming into the money before the savings plan matured in 2003. We need wealth urgently, and I have convinced myself that the lottery is a money-spinner. The implication of this is that I believe it must work out and give us a big win. I hope it will happen soon, or how can we manage to keep the little luxuries in our home and a roof over our heads? It will be the most difficult decision I will have to make about my family's future.

Nevertheless, we should not conclude from this that all is gloom. God only knows how things accumulated to impoverish us. Atheists might say there is no God to help us, but belief in the mythical trappings of our faith has diminished because confidence in the solid core of my religion clothed God in humanity to redeem us. So, theological statements have meaning, and God cannot only be described except by analogy. I go along with the possibility that He exists and will help us through our difficulties. Our imagination seems vital to lifting gloom to see certainties and when good luck will happen. God is incarnate, some say, a human being approachable through prayer, and I feel a link to the Almighty, like soil and vegetation. The various stories of life's blows require endeavours and hope, and God only knows how we can keep them going because it feels like we are losing the war on living to the full in whatever circumstances we find ourselves. Our events look bleak. We have received knock-downs again and again. Now with the situation worsened, it's a kick in the teeth as well. I am glad that I still retain the spirit to get up and fight. We are down but not out. The gladiatorial fighting spirit is in us, and we will see these problems through to the end.

We do not know how our financial problem will resolve itself, but God forbid we will lose our home. We are without economic security, but it does not spoil our happiness or shake our love for each other as a family. I have the protection of my wife's trust, respect and our God. Us working together to see things through by sustaining our hopes and optimism shall, over time, come to see there is light at the end of the tunnel and that every cloud has a silver lining.

At the moment, we are in a bleak period in our lives and need some good luck. We need some more good luck, and luckiness comes from a spiritual force and is in tune with my aura and vibes that enter our adverse conditions or circumstances and change them through dreams and, in due course, life itself.

Turn Hope Into Reality And Yet Unfit Financially To Beat The Downturn.

Written, Friday 6th November 1998

I am in no doubt that I was walking in circles by trying to force a lottery win, and I have to try to make sense of my decision on how it's my big break.

After many years of playing the game, I had enough of trying to figure out the winning combination and kept failing to discover it. I used my thought-out numbers for years then changed each week's numbers when a midweek draw was introduced with a lucky dip option. Finally, I opted for the computer to randomly select the numbers for me. Still, that has not worked, and it came to me that I am wasting vital money and am angry at not winning.

I bought my last individual lottery ticket on Saturday 17th October 1998 for that night's draw, and since then, I have pulled myself up to say, "get a life", and the game's hold on me has diminished. But I remain deeply committed to the syndicate. I play in the union because I still want to be part of a win and do not want to see lottery luck slip altogether from my grasp. I pay £2.00 a week into the syndicate for fun, for its close friends that we join with to share the fun event of a win. But I now think it's an utter waste of money; the success got delayed, and a feel-good factor is pressing me to continue playing against all the odds.

On the other hand, something unfathomable happens when I play the lottery alone and check the winning combination. My heart feels a terrible numbness, and I wrestle with the fact that I was a loser. I do feel a tremendous sense of abandonment, and I cry, "Lord in your mercies", because it's so hard, week after week, to accept that I have lost again and again.

I continually search for sense in a situation with apparent logic but an absence of supernatural power to project my faith forward. I felt some bitterness because there is a lack of financial and spiritual working out in all the years of playing the lottery and using consciousness as a guide. I still have unsolved dilemmas.

A festive fighting spirit will be instrumental in helping us beat financial problems, and I hope that this turns into reality so that we have more wealth in a usual way, rather than faith beyond reason. Of course, I'm not suggesting that just by hoping we can cure our money problems. Still, in many cases, there is a slight chance that positive thinking and determination to sort the problem out have given us a better chance of surviving this debt burden around our necks. We will be lucky to survive this strain, where others have not, for they have lost their house, possessions, and possible relationships with partners or friends have broken down. The sheer delight will come when we have beaten the problems and see ourselves as lucky in our lives again.

The thing with money is that I want to make more of it, spend less of it, and save it, and by having my financial affairs in order, it will raise funds for charity while having security. I think that opportunity will come our way, and we will get what we need. Still, at the same time, incredible opportunities are disguised as insolvable problems, and I need to continue, partly by faith and belief. I have this ship, my family, and it is up to me to steer it. I follow my instincts and make decisions based on our judgement, and I wish for strength in this immense challenge to get it right so that the debt problems are solved. I am optimistic and do not understand depression when the outlook seems pessimistic because I do not expect too much from the world. I won't be too disappointed.

Euphemia has shown symptoms of phobia since the car accident. Unexpected surges of anxiety come over her when driving the courtesy car on rural roads with plenty of traffic on them. The journey becomes so unpleasant that Euphemia becomes fearful, has a panic attack, and shakes and trembles behind the wheel. She can only drive on the local road close to home, with me at her side. We had the courtesy car for seventeen days. We received a cheque on 17th October for £1300 because our car was written off, and I found a suitable vehicle almost immediately. Euphemia told me of her worries about driving, and her lack of confidence is misery; just talking about it becomes upsetting.

Like the bruises on her internal organs and pain in the middle of her back, the physical wounds are worries. However, it's the psychological trauma that's worrying her the most. The solicitor told her about research carried out to help people get back to normal after accidents, and she will be assessed from a questionnaire to see if she has the type of symptoms that the programme was designed to help. If she is, a more detailed assessment with a clinical psychologist will follow. Euphemia is on edge, easily startled and enjoying life and activities less independently. It has become so painful and distressing that she does not want to take up driving again. My psychiatrist gave her some helpful tips on overcoming the phobia, carried out as a form of self-help therapy.

I have bought a used car, a Proton, costing £1295, but Euphemia has not driven it yet. So I asked her to have the courage and attempt to practice the tips my psychiatrist suggested to expose herself to the car gradually.

This weekend is her first practice to learn to relax and systematically carefully use exposure therapy. The anxiety should die down with me in the front passenger seat and her in the driver's seat with the engine immobile. It took another attempt, and as she sat there until the ensuing stress died down, the fear started to go away within a half-hour of exposure. Week after week, she remains frightened with daily repetition of this prolonged exposure to the agitation for one to two hours. However, the desire to avoid the problem is gradually disappearing. It's restoring her confidence, and I hope she soon will ask me to take a spin with her, for she seems to have lost the intense anxiety she had handling the wheel.

For months, there has been economic speculation that Britain may be heading into a period of economic slowdown. The month is November 1998. It's becoming likely that the country is in a short step to a severe economic downturn. It's a blow below the belt because, after years of unfolding financial crisis in our life, an outright recession will make matters worse.

I am in a rush planning to survive and maybe prosper in this challenging time ahead, for I assume that life will be turned upside down, at least financially. I am trying to slim down our spending and debts because it is twice as necessary. But I find I am not able to do it. I spend more and more. I daydream that it may take many years before we are financially healthy because I still use credit to get by. A pre-crash money diet is an obvious solution to meeting payments, and I have the ideal financial detail, for I keep a folder of all incoming and unpaid bills. We can see how much is to go on our mortgage, loans, credit cards and other fixed outgoings and when we paid them. I make a note of it. Kept in a separate folder are bank statements, paid bills and receipts. Being organised with the bookkeeping lets me see where the money goes, and there is still regular overspending. Money coming in and money going out do not equate, but on the positive side, some financial assets were tied up until 2003. We might usefully sell hidden assets because one man's junk is another man's treasure, but I have not sorted out unwanted possessions for car boot sales or garage sales.

I feel calm about finances and facing what we owe and decide what to do about it and how to act. Debts are about as attractive as visiting the dentist, but they cannot be put off. I calculate how much repayment money can get negotiated with creditors after costing out all the essential spending on mortgage, food and bills. I can reasonably do what I am doing because I have identified the priority debts such as mortgage, gas, electricity, and water. God forbid that I shall ever be summoned to appear in court about our obligations. I shall undoubtedly take free debt advice from the Citizen's Advice Bureau or other fee-less money advice centres.

I do not want to say that I have been here before, but mainly around Christmas time, we get poorer and poorer. Christmas is only a month away, and our wealth has not changed like the seasons. We were no better off throughout seasons past, and come the festive season, growth in wealth has never happened. If I had wealth, it would be a great thing because I'd improve my family life, spend money on education and travel, and I would invest in worthwhile things. I would give money to noble causes and to help neighbours and relatives too. My life would be better if I were rich, and I daydream, wishing I had wealth as a tool, nothing more. I cannot eat or drink money or wear it, but I can accumulate it like many tools and use it for good.

The lottery is four years old this month, and its jackpot is over twenty million pounds, but I am not interested because I am too fed up with losing four years where I did not win. It regularly tested my patience playing for four years without a big win. I am not playing, not even on the game's fourth anniversary. I will not backtrack on my promise that I shall never again play the lottery other than paying the stake I have in a syndicate. The syndicate is testing my patience rather than moving me into profit; it's dodgy. I think this may not be a good gamble.

Physicists and statisticians may have confirmed that the draws are fair and random. Still, it's just based on cold probability theory, telling me that buying lottery tickets is a foolish gamble and that human behaviour is no good at picking numbers. I need to have something that allows us to outwit the laws of probability. It's hopeless. I have not found a set of numerical circumstances or conditions in which the win is more significant than the initial lottery investment in four years. I have put everything into finding an equation that will make me win, and it's a no to having success in the probability law. I may have to wait 900,000 years before moving into profit, and by that time, asteroids will have hit the earth and destroyed all life on it.

I sometimes wonder if God does not believe my heart's feelings about wealth and how I use it. God's intervention is not yet apparent in helping me to create wealth. I yearn for God to read my heart and mind, discover my longing to get rich, and pour back more significant benefits to society. If God reads me, He will know that I would like to get rich through hard work and wise investments, not necessarily having it given me on a plate or in a lucky strike.

I feel one day, my life will be freed of debts, and I'll burst forth to enjoy wealth's great benefits. I know I cannot solve all my life's problems, but I should solve my gross material deprivation problem. By making the most of honest hard work in the free market, economic liberty will create wealth, and I hope to God that my idealism becomes a reality one day.

What Is Going To Happen, And Looking On

Written, 26th December 1998

Soon, a new year's arrival is likely to be greeted with mixed anticipation because there are no fresh opportunities and optimistic predictions for our lives.

Nevertheless, we have never before in the history of humanity been so unprepared for the latest technological and economic opportunities, challenges and risks that lie on the horizon. Our way of life will likely be more fundamentally transformed in the next few decades than in the previous thousand years. I suppose, by the year 2026, our children and we may be living in a world utterly different from anything human beings have ever experienced in the past. I believe that in as little as one generation, our definition of life and the meaning of existence are likely to be radically altered, and the long-held assumptions about nature, including human nature, are plausible to be rethought. Many age-old practices regarding sexuality, reproduction, birth and parenthood, could be partially abandoned. Equality and democracy ideas are expected to redefine a vision of what is meant by the terms 'free will' and 'progress' and a sense of self-changes. Society will change too, as the epicentre is a technological revolution unmatched in all of history in its power to remake ourselves, our institutions and the planet. Scientists are beginning to reorganise life at the genetic level. The new biology tools are opening up opportunities for refashioning life on earth while foreclosing options that have existed over the millennia of evolutionary history.

Before our eyes lies an unchartered new landscape whose contours are being shaped in thousands of biotechnology labs. I do not want to give up the belief in God, but will I be forced to do so? My human response to existence began with the acceptance of mystery, but now, new technology is challenging my belief. The speed of discoveries is phenomenal. After thousands of years of fusing, melting, soldering, forging and burning inanimate matter to create valuable things, scientists are now splicing, recombining, inserting and stitching living material into economic utilities. This radical new form of biological manipulation changes both our concept

278

of nature and our relationship to it. The organisms and species no longer command our attention or respect because we begin to view life from a chemist's perspective. The creation of God is natural and self-sufficient for divine purposes. Humanity is a part of a divine purpose but does not know what those purposes are. Through the use of reason, we are inseparably a part of matter and not retouched agents.

I am contemplating my place in the arrangement of things and devising an explanation. Still, God's conception is hugely unscientific, and I need to release my understanding of Him from superstitions and the perception of place for magical powers. I am sceptical of things that may not be subject to scientific verification, and as we are earthly, our lives are not exempted from the way the universe works, but what will happen?

--- If a mountain collapses on me, I am crushed, and if I fall out of the sky, I break into pieces. I am saying that whatever happens to us has value, which I choose to endow with moral attributes and emotional significance. Technological revolution brings benefits and costs to disruption and destruction of ecosystems and social systems that sustain life. Until the last couple of centuries or so, people had expected growth to be hazardous and were brought up to understand that the world was a dangerous place. Natural afflictions, combined with human savagery, make the conditions of existence unreliable and unpredictable.

What's happening to us financially? What are the fates that await me? God's proximity to me reduces Him to the demands most people expect Him to make in life. There is no pain and suffering, no dreadful illnesses, no victims of natural disasters and no interruption of human happiness. Life itself then seems like a series of entitlement from God. Still, as knowledge can inform us, we exist in the middle of a gigantic explosion, and the universe is a transient phenomenon, seemingly a blast in a void. I can see only dimly now that I can sense where biotechnology leads us from believing that creation was the expression of a super-being (person) or a creative Will alien creature that gives us purpose and meaning to the universe. Human life has momentarily coated a speck of hurtle cosmic dust debris materialism existence in space-time. The unknown fate awaits living things, the creator of all things we can know in unconditional Love, calls us to share with the Almighty in the creative process. Now scientists are beginning to reorganise life and are playing God. The sheer majesty of God gave me the sense that life was intended to be fragile and transient and has spiritual beauty, and is not designed to be scientific.

I carry out a stock-take of my life for the year 1998 and weigh up the possible fate in the months that stretch before me. I see global uncertainty, and many of my problems are still old ones. I thank God that I have specific purposes because I believe in a higher destiny than the low ground of materialist consumption that is all about immediate self-interest, with little to encourage pursuing higher goals. I seek a level of protection from uncertainty and the ordinary hazards of living, but that level is not available. No matter what I or anybody else may do, life on earth will always be full of uncertainties, and our unreasonable claims for personal exemption will, in the end, constantly be ridiculed by fate.

In a seemingly darkening near future for us, I fear our security because I cannot perceive growth in the New Year. We need superior divine guidance henceforth because I am passing through unreflective in consequences. I got rebuked for my past mistakes on poor judgements, poorly calculated risk-taking and wrong choices. Far into the future, near pensionable age, according to the truth of my imagination, the pattern of living which evoked risk-taking and ethical judgements today will result in less stress when I am old. Mistakes are a fact of human life. It is, indeed, one fact with which everyone has a daily acquaintance. It is not just that I fall into the commission of doing wrong, but that our very being expresses the inherent presence of sinfulness.

Mistakes are universal; the level is the same in everyone, but variations get expressed differently. For instance, there are minor mistakes and major ones. After acceptance of God's forgiveness, my inherent sinfulness remains united by God's mercy, and my shortcomings will be judged with wrath, as well as with outstretched hands to forgive me. The love that moves the sun and other stars chose, as Christians believe, to be a human being for an extraordinary period of human history, they say. He suffered death for mortal sin upon the Cross. He rose again and proclaimed the infinite significance of every human individual in the scheme of things. People who lack the imagination to believe the whole story, myself amongst them, see it merely as the greatest and most ennobling of all human myths that society should fashion the values of Christendom. Dying to Live is quite unlike any secular form of goodness. I can do lots to promote it when I have money and worldly success.

Myth or truth, the Christian idea, is woven into the fabric of political, social and ordinary lives. It reflects on a new beginning in human history since time, and I suspect most stories about God's son Jesus are accurate. I like the Christian package, especially the part about eternal life, but Jesus the Son of God? I do not believe a word of that supernatural part. I wrote about this earlier on, yet I need to add that my conscience is clear between truth and fiction if the subject comes up.

Some people believe the truth of specific stories, while others do not. I positively like other people to believe in the divinity of Jesus because I do not disbelieve out of choice. On the contrary, I wish I could understand the whole Christian package, but it seems fictitious.

The bitter victory of intellect is that one does not just believe. We look for evidence to show us that life is meaningful and everlasting. The whole Christian package has flaws and only in parts makes complete sense. To have a new belief in it has some blindness. I have a natural longing to believe that life is meaningful and everlasting, and I can see it is. As long as other people want to stay in ignorance, the delightful possibility remains that the gospel truth is, in part, myths. I encourage people to take the whole Christian package and accept it as gospel truth and not part myths, but for me, who has got enlightened, to be honest, cannot carry the self-delusion anymore. But they don't want to hear it.

Education showed faults in Christianity that do not interest the man in the street but to know the truth and nothing but facts that God's godliness is seen in Jesus and humanity. The universe created by the divine designer is not a delusion. Still, the message and teaching were a godsend and could not fully be believed.

There is a paradox at the heart of the Christian religion. It makes me think ---- No 'material' exists about Jesus in his early years, and nobody showed interest in collecting life records of Jesus, so stories developed and myths got formed. What, then, is the truth?

Can you blame my mind for rejecting the conservative, widely spread gospel stories that my heart likes to accept? Other gospel writers were not included in the Bible. The fantastic events that shook sleepy Bethlehem 2,000 years ago heralded the single most dramatic intrusion of the most God-conscious man in the world of all time. None of the leaders of that time had the slightest inkling about what was unfolding right under their noses.

God did not work through the political structures, instead has revealed himself to utterly untrained people and not in power corridors. So on the fate-filled night, the world was shaken, but most grunted in their sleep. So the birth of Jesus was revealed to a group of lowly shepherds working out in the fields while the religious leaders slumbered in the Temple at Jerusalem, and their sleep was not disturbed.

The first part of the truth relates to specific historical events in Palestine during Pontius Pilate's procuratorship. It was 500 years after Christ's birth that anyone thought of celebrating Christmas, and I read that over 1,000 years were to pass before any Christian, rather than seeing the Cross as a triumph of God over death, would begin to meditate upon the passion of Jesus Christ's hanging and suffering. No crucifix existed before the high Middle Ages in Europe.

The earth-shaking event of Jesus coming into the world, his life, death and resurrection, went mostly unnoticed. It is a sad reflection of humankind's warped priorities, and it remains the same today.

Often, I pray that God will do something so dramatic that it will wake the nation up and force people to give God the glory and humble themselves enough to stop and listen to Jesus Christ, the light of the world, instead of mainly ignoring the message. Are they not troubled by their sins? I want to offer insights into a better caring world, but how can others share the visions with me when the imagery of a perfect world or the afterlife in heaven is all in mind? My imagining is magnificent regarding the things I'd like to see a place in our lifetime, but it suffers from a complex internal logic because of impatience. I look heavenwards and hope that he does not order my departure to float heavenwards and leave my family in even worse hardship without me.

Although I want to take up the afterlife offer, I want to live to finish the call to serve God and raise a loving family. Therefore, I want to live life to the full-on earth, and dying is not an issue because only being with the family, believing in beautiful things, and praying for the world's peace occupy my dreams.

The reality of having a wife and family makes me reach for the Kleenex, for I am so happy to have changed my life around from a void. I want to create a new year's resolution in 1999 to reach goals and maintain good health and happiness. The rock-solid union that my wife and I enjoy now that the days in the year 1997 when the course of true love never ran smooth and our romantic travels were collapsing are behind us. Whatever the uncertainties in life, we can count on each other since there are only two certainties: we die, and things change.

The good thing about change is that we make room for something better in letting go of the past. The wonderment of the world's beauty gives me the spontaneity to cultivate a lot of fun, stop taking life too seriously and not be too severe with myself. The passion for things gives me enthusiasm, and I find enjoyment in restoring positive thinking, for things are never total gloom. The stretching of the mind and effective planning makes me go on enthusiastically, especially when it clicked; that's the answer.

There is a purpose in our existence that transcends our priorities. I can barely manage this year, being well wrapped up in anxieties about security and money and still, the problem is carried over into the following year, 1999. However pressing the priorities seem to be, I escaped for a moment and wondered about the eternal drive to stop the worries. Where will the money be to pay the bills and buy food for the table in 1999?

Religious thinking focuses on me. It's all a journey that gives rise to hope and progress in dealing with problems, engendering optimism. Optimism believes that things will get better, and hope is the courage to make them better. I cannot tell if hope or optimism shall continue in my spirit. I am sure that, unlike optimism, faith will survive in my mind in tough and confusing times. I lose confidence because I become depressed, but during the depression, hope was still there.

Being poor is too tiresome. I look for guiding principles for attaining spiritual and material wealth. I am happy and miserable. How can I get rich and stay satisfied? I suspect that being poor is our natural state because being poor is thankful for health, happiness and vitality. I am working on a sort of 'wealth consciousness' and believe that I shall be prosperous one day in my life. Then, I am sure to experience more feelings of joy, happiness, vitality and hope.

Fulfilling my wish to be productive does not mean just getting more dosh, but I got hooked on searching for money through higher earnings or investments. I got hooked because the state of being wealthy is solely upfront in my mind, and I am absorbing the fantasy that in the real world, it's nothingness, but not negativity, no not negativity. Are you baffled? Well, I say no to negativity in the fantasy and think it's good to be aware of wealth in my dreams, and I am reaching out to touch it.

The spiritual side gives me the most comforting sense of where I belong in the universe. Science shows that the world is a less predictable place than we have previously supposed, and the laws of matter involve more arbitrary aspects than mechanistic thought had allowed. Therefore, reality must now be seen as an original series of phenomena. There is no need for a supernatural explanation because God has revealed his purposes in creation, and it is our only source of knowledge.

Dazzled by the ability to devise technology, humans ignore the fact that they cannot reconstruct themselves. Still, if they could, they would not know how to begin to agree about a programme. God gave us reason to explore the world from which our sensations were derived. Science is, I believe, holy work, as all authentic extension of the frontiers of knowledge enlarges human participation in the divine scheme.

On the surface of this unstable planet, the human inhabitants represent an environment chosen for us by God, an entire climate of hazards and chances that provides the challenges needed to stimulate intellectual advancement.

As we acquire knowledge, it becomes clear that it belongs not with us only; it belongs to other people. It was developed for a purpose, and it should produce the maximum amount of good. Therefore, we have a global responsibility to help relieve human suffering, alleviating it through science and be good.

MILLENNIUM
Written, Saturday 9th January 1999

The millennium is a Christian moment and a landmark in Western civilisation's history; two thousand years, arguably, since the birth of Jesus Christ. It seems since then that the modern human is journeying towards a destination.

The idea of linear time has a profound error because it gives a distinctive orientation towards the future. In early civilisation, they longed for a world in which stability ruled over the natural catastrophes, floods, famines, earthquakes and droughts, which seemed like the battles of the gods. The gods were forces of nature, and there was a high drama of myths and the struggle for cosmos against chaos.

Time is defined by those things that never change, like the movement of atoms or planets, the cycles of the seasons, the eternal recurrence of birth, growth and death. All things return to their source and begin again. Mythical time is cyclical time. God was no longer identified with nature, nor is his image humankind. Instead, we are a fusible mixture of the dust of the earth and the breath of God.

I think I conceptualise because I talk and can imagine a world different from the one that exists. So, can you! The system of society was written into the architecture of the universe. Being a free human makes us capable of choosing between good and evil, if not alone, in partnership with God and our fellow human beings. I see time as a biblical vision, a journey, never totally eclipsed by forwarding motion, driven by science and human rationality.

This millennium is causing some people to imagine a horrible catastrophe before another 1,000 years of human history passes again. On the contrary, I think we can build a contemporary society that honours all persons' equality and dignity as citizens under God's sovereignty. From the millennium onwards, the status quo will be transformed. Instead, it will become the stage where the high drama of humanity failed to respond to God's call was played. People are no longer held captive by the past, and we are not destined to repeat our ancestors' mistakes. Our vision is not bound by what is because a new emotion was born and understood. I believe that dreams are not small waves that break as they reach the hard rock of reality but are, in fact, hopes. My hopes and other people's democratic aspirations are not in vain; though the way is long and hard, we are not alone. People today and those of the past fight one another in the name of God, making religion far from bringing peace instead it bringing conflict.

Far from pursuing truth, religion seems sunken in prejudices which it was prepared to defend tenaciously. As we approach the end of the 20th century, our certainties have been shaken because technology has given us the ability to destroy life on earth. Progress should have, through science, conquered ignorance and reason and banished prejudices. Trade should have developed all nations' wealth, and the growth of tolerance should have spread because of democracy.

The 20th century ends with human ingenuity taking over where evolution has left off. We are going into the 21st century with cloning and other revolutionary biotechnology methods of manipulating life, making headlines every time human ingenuity makes a breakthrough.

The Human Genome Project will soon finish mapping the billions of 'chemical letters' on our genes, giving us the potential to transform our descendants' genetic make-up. Of course, there are setbacks, digressions, wonderings and false turns, but these are not grounds for the death of hope. The millennium is one way of forging a sense of destination to another 1,000 years so that we can be a just society, a heaven's kingdom, and a world, having human dignity and grace.

I sense, children and their contemporaries, an urgent need for a coherent narrative through which to make sense of our head-long journey into the future. In a world that seems to spin ever more rapidly, whose certainties are fewer by the day, they search for solid ground on which to build their lives. My guess is they will say that we are guardians of a world. In part, people are formed by traditions, institutions, families and communities, and moral life. Ultimately, these rest on a sense of transcendence that binds us to one another as fellow citizens in covenant with God. Science sounds infallible and, in parts, gives a chilling insight into the future of genetic engineering. They are changing genes of the sex cells which will be carried on into the future and altering the outcome of millions of years of evolution. It's the beginning of the last year in the millennium, and I am bracing myself because I am not ready to face the future when every day is a struggle and our reality is like a dose of poison. Facing the future serves those best who adequately prepare for it. It is a tough challenge with lots of self-examination because the gap between the reality of my life and the fantasy of my future, sadly, is too broad a gap.

The time has come to face the future and bridge the gap, but not until the basics of time start clearing up money matters like the morning mist. Otherwise, the lingering financial difficulty is poverty. Although I try to plan, I can only concentrate on my first daily 'to-do' list and vow to resolve the problems that blight my future vision of the 21st century. I already have to face reality and adapt to it.

Today is Saturday 23rd of January 1999, and I have to pay bills instead of spending the already decreased amount of money on buying food. It does not seem like it will get easier soon. I am constantly forced to examine our future, making for more stringent economies in our weekly orbit and one of the future's trends. Meanwhile, I have adopted the Scouts' Motto 'Be Prepared'.

Even though modern living has the potential for misery without money, I am happy because I have inner peace through self-acceptance, loving relationships and peace of mind. The hard reality is, we might never be successful in having material things. But, as the wife follows Christianity, she is happy with herself, and success can never equal happiness. It's moments like these when I feel lifted above the problems, and they are no longer the focus and drain of our lives. Our pleasure has less to do with life circumstances than the joy experienced in the Christian walk surrounding us with God's unfailing love and favour.

The product of life's reflection and learning the truth led me to deny the full divinity of Jesus Christ, and I think the radical transformation will happen to God in the future. In historical fact, a cold dose of reality is not always pleasant and cannot dismiss divinity. There is a pervasive sprinkling of errors in history. Suppose you find it baffling that I still want to talk about God and mention Jesus, well, in the end. In that case, belief in God can never be a matter of history, rational argument or imagination, fashioned to fulfil a need. It is rather like trying to argue someone into falling in love with me, but that is not how love works. All the arguments may sound convincing, and the balance of advantage and calculation indicates a decision for falling in love, but that is still not how love works.

Ultimately, I decided to say that there is an external force of divinity other than the mind's longing. We are answerable to a truth-being that we did not create ourselves. There is some praise and tribute to human creativity in spotting external creativity. With all its present faults and the appalling blemishes on its record, the Christian church still does its best to witness creatively. So why does Western Christian civilisation, uniquely among world cultures, produce more and more people with the ability to deny God's idea? This culture has a massive division between evolutionists and creationists because independent choices are possible now, being shaped by science and information.

I am an evolutionist and, in part, a creationist because I believe God created the heavens and the earth by evolution, but it's hard to omit doubts about it that can damage. I think all my questioning days about God are over. I am sure to have fresh doubts in the millennium because parts of the Christian ideas still perplex me.

I will never again question the existence of God when I am in good health, and debt becomes a lessening burden because, quite honestly, I can't sensibly say God exists, and I can't wisely say God doesn't. In its full context, read the writing, Resolve to Improve My Wealth, written in 1997. I no longer put God on trial what we will be, and by going down the honest, straight forward and admirably clear road, it's true, everything must be all right. A force of divinity exists, and when I am in the departure lounge of life, the next flight out will take me straight to our Maker, who will give me all the answers. Let's leave the questioning at that!

There's no doubt in anyone's mind that the year 2000 is going to be unique. It's a time when great things could happen and a time when there could be more opportunity. But, again, God is our helper in our dedication; it could be a time for lifestyle changes, but realistically, there may be more issues to face and painful trials to endure.

Human life is short. Seventy to eighty years in this grand, elaborate and astonishing universe is not long enough. Undoubtedly, life expectancy will increase for all, and I find the whole heaven and earth thing fascinating at the end of a few more decades. Heaven on earth or a Heaven elsewhere would be an excellent place, but I have to think it out for myself. I could either be a passenger in life and go where one is told to go, believe what one is supposed to think or try to figure out what life is and the truth.

As you continue to read this book, it must be apparent what I am trying to do. So, think with me and learn the truth because I find discovery and new understanding exciting. The most significant revelations have been my unfolding understanding of Jesus Christ and the processes of evolution.

I try to make our life happy for us by creating a comfortable home. Moments of truth and unexpected freedom also make me happy. My inner self smiles in this pleasant environment, and outwardly, it shows to family, friends and colleagues, but really, my life has ups and downs, as anyone else's. It's sometimes happy and sometimes unhappy, but I certainly try to be honest and straightforward and stand up for what I have come to realise are excellent and worthwhile.

The millennium will be an exciting moment, for there are goals to complete. However, I am not too concerned about completely fulfilling goals; I am pleased when I can see plans ahead of me and within reach, hoping I'll live to see them.

The coming millennium can serve a purpose if it compels a personal, spiritual stocktaking and gives the world a fresh look at the need for true godliness or God-inspired morality. Thus, we can take into the year 2000 the traditions of lasting value and an openness to new ideas in every part of life, not least theological and ecclesiastical, and a determination to forward the lovely and good things.

Debt Mountain
Written Monday 15th of March 1999

I have used up a large amount of credit money to repair the car I bought six months ago. It needed a battery, exhaust, brake pads and two new discs. Unfortunately, last week, the chancellor's budget has made it harder to run a family car and have a mortgage. Petrol has gone up, car road tax is up too, and MIRAS, the Mortgage Interest Relief, has been scrapped.

I know that I cannot meet the increasing outgoings, and I am trying everything in my power to stabilise things, but spending is still spiralling out of control. All four credit cards have reached their credit limits, and many more everyday items are still needed. God knows of our needs, but God knows answers are not always heaven-sent. Every working day I am anxious to check the morning post. I get a little uptight if I miss the morning post and have to wait until evening to open the day's letters.

The post is crucial in our home because it brings personal news from family, friends and all sorts of organisations. The story may be good or bad, but its information and information is essential for making good decisions. The right kind of letter arriving on the doormat can cause life-changing decisions to be made, or a message could shatter our expectations. In both cases, anxiety gets the better of me. The first letters to be opened are not the regular brown envelopes of bills or junk mail. I target the unexpected official white envelopes because I have entered free money-winning competitions and free prize draws, so I eagerly watch the post.

The laws of probability ought to govern my decision-making, but sadly, mostly, I rely instead on hunches and guesswork. The crisis has driven me to gamble on the second kind of lottery known as the Irish Lottery. Gambling is foolish, but it gives a feel-good factor at the point of putting on a bet and, in the end, hearing about the win. So, I am going to flutter, starting this coming weekend, on the Irish Lottery. The Irish Lottery is slightly different from the National Lottery because its odds and the probability laws might work better in my favour. I hope it will be a lucky shot and I shall only pursue trying to win for up to three months. I shall play indeed for no longer than three months because my purpose is to play purely for economic reasons, win some money, and not be addicted to the thrills of gambling. Win or lose, and I shall stop betting when the period is up.

My debt crisis is so bad that I will try any law-abiding and natural way to get some money. At the moment, the natural way is letting me down because God has become a problem. He does not mean to be, of course, but once I invite God to the logical place in my mind, it becomes a matter of waiting, and reason climbs out of the window. Introducing the creator, whose work is apparent in all things, makes me unable to find out why my problems look like they have been ignored. It's the head-scratching time because, yes, why are things not working out? Could it be that it is a bit of rotten luck, or God cannot be relied upon to change the material world to bring comfort, joy and morality? I start thinking and never know where it will end because up until I recognised the influence of an unquantifiable super-being again, I lose the plot and fight back the tears. I thought God had disappeared from my life. I do not trouble God much; I have accepted that I do not know the details.

The Irish Lottery can only be played at the bookmakers (betting shops). Vivid childhood memories appear in my mind, going to the betting shop to drop off my dad's hot horse betting tips. Written on a bold slip of lined paper, the bet on his favourite horse got chosen from the tabloid Mirror newspaper's top tipsters. I would take the petty cash and the slip of paper to the counter staff on a Saturday afternoon while Dad was busy doing DIY around the house. There was hardly a time when my dad went back to the bookies to pick up winnings. Still, to this day, Dad uses petty cash to have a flutter on the horses, and again, he loses more than he wins, but he never looks disappointed.

Other childhood memories are flashing and bursting like visible soap bubbles. They are beautiful yet contain hurt, failure and experiences that make me understand my sensitivity and makeup. The need to release them in writing gives me a sense of well-being.

At the age of eleven or twelve, in the RE lesson, discussing the meaning of life, I consciously muttered to myself, 'If men and women of intelligence and sound mind can believe in an invisible God, I would like to be a man of faith when I grow up.' I got so smitten by the New Testament's message that I wrote an essay for my CSE course work called The Character Study of Jesus Christ when I reached age fifteen. (Search the bookshelf for my CSE English folder and read the contents). I should have had a church career because I thought of why I wrote it, and it didn't buzz through my head. I felt I had a job to do, to make the world a less cruel place, but I did not want to leave school to participate in a world that I noticed is not obedient to the law.

Adults seemed to do what pleases them and feel no guilt for disobeying the word of God. I wanted to grow up believing God is genuine and not sin against him and achieve lasting good by faithfully living my life as I become a grown man.

I learnt quite early while reading the New Testament that we were put on this earth for a purpose, and there can be significant rewards and terrible suffering. Still, we are not born to have a comfortable life, and because I follow goodness and godliness, I thought I would die young and probably wouldn't see my 30th birthday.

I am setting aside my ego, for I am working for future generations to live in obedience to an invisible God. However, it offends some deep-seated sense that religious explanation for life's meaning and the universe is no straightforward certainty.

I was primarily concerned with its truth and certainty, but nobody knows the meaning of life and God's nature, and in my youth, I accepted the Bible teachings as the only truth. As a result, I denied knowing what I wanted to do when I left school and settled into engineering. Now it feels like my faith in God is being tested, and I must trust no matter what career path I have taken or the problems I am facing.

As a young apprentice engineer, I practised for almost two years to be truthfully honest and not tell a lie in and out of the workplace, not even a white lie. I obtained perfection in being accurate and truthful, but there came times when brutal honesty hurt the very person it was meant to free. So, I dropped the practice, and the phrase, 'Oh God, forgive me', followed after every lie, like a whispering little voice in my head, automatically deploying it. (Please note this was not a schizophrenic experience; I had all my faculties.)

Nowadays, I say my penitence before I attempt to sin. When it's in my heart to make up a false story to get out of a situation, I ask God's forgiveness first and feel no glory over it, only a sense of shame. I conceal the truth about how I humanely can, but most times, people see straight through me and say, you are lying, and then I own up to it. I get tormented by guilt, and sooner rather than later, I squeal because my conscience is weak at deception. I am a man of God and had practised building my character on honesty, truth and holiness. The difficulties I face today are that I judge people on my degree of reliability and character worthiness. I am naïve when it comes to understanding sarcasm and 'only kidding'. When I catch on, I realise the conversation's light-hearted intentions and sense of humour, and jokes were neither substantial nor had any literal truth. By not recognising what I was missing, I was laughed at and asked to chill out. I looked at life so seriously, observing and learning about the more significant questions, that I laughed very little and missed out on clean, funny, harmless humour. I made no time to enjoy the other things life had to offer because I had a mission to clean up humanity and be righteous.

At college in PSE study about the Civil Rights Movement and its leader, Martin Luther King; I was moved so much by the film and voice recording of the struggle that I wanted to be revolutionary and combat injustice. At first, I had a sharp sense of sorrow, and then a deep tumbling of positive emotional waves went through my body. Finally, my mind was full of prayer. The enormity of it was that he inspired me to peacefully fight discrimination and racism and take up other human rights issues in this country, alongside proclaiming God's love and forgiveness.

I had such strong feelings to show love and peace to all people that I felt like I'd explode if I don't spread this peace. I felt mightily challenged but rebuked the call that sat in my heart, which unsettled my mind. I refused to do it because my education standard was low and complained to my inner self, saying, "Who will listen to a poorly educated black man?" I felt as if the love in my heart for all people was 'screwing' me up because I could not give that love away to those lives shattered by evilness or purely with no freedom. After all, one need educating to get to the position where my voice is heard and work on the ground.

My heart was suffocating with the love that I could not share with others. My valves needed to release some pressure, so I made up my mind to channel part of that love by loving one individual, marrying and raising a family and bury the rest far from the surface of my mind. There is a reason why I needed success, but there are things that we do not understand and never will. Though I'm married with children, I have not achieved all that I wanted to make, but ultimately, success or fame is not essential in my life now. My family and real friends matter first and foremost. My relationship with other people and my ability to love and be loved is paramount.

I haven't always been very confident, and the 'call' was a flipside to my character that struggled for strategies to help people. The fantastic feeling of a brave, loyal leader was one way of building high self-esteem levels. I almost needed to tell the world that I am a leader in the making by the will of God.

Having a loving wife and family gave me a true calling to be a good husband and father and serve them with my heart and soul. I have not lost my ambition to help all people, but I am less self-obsessed. I have chosen family life over a single entity devoted to serving countless people.

The way I run the family finances needs to be more efficient. I have not gotten any better at spending much more than I earn, and I have been quite a serious person. My father and mother are solid as a rock and give me my underlying stability. However, I have lost my confidence that our earnings could one day lift us out of the financial drain hole and plug it by itself. My belief is only returning because I am to take up gambling and wish that mega dosh will reach my account before the end of 1999. I choose to gamble but can least afford it - it's a chance!

I also feel optimistic because I have a perception of self-fulfilment in the role of being a family man. Though there are risks and uncertainties ahead, discontentment seems to be focused only on money. It seems remarkable, but I am satisfied with most other areas of my life and feel happier. I do not know how things will work out, but I love my wife and family and do not want the terrible dissatisfaction of having any money. Being fulfilled to a greater or lesser extent has dough mixed up in it. Since we have no money, I have no economic power as a primary provider for the home and feel frustrated. I have spent over twenty years working and should be in the high noon of my earning life with money in the bank, but there's none.

I have grappled with the natural world at that time. I am now vigorous with tons of valuable life experiences and brutally worried about money, but not about satisfaction. Incredibly saddening, I fear that I am living off false hope, expecting to win from gambling. I am fighting to keep our heads above water because we have floated into a new poverty trap. I've been learning to live on wages that do not suit our usual lifestyle, and it is weaker than previously, leading to lower aspirations. Our immediate expectations and future goals were reduced because we have no money, and it's easy to imagine poverty is only a few weeks away if no more cash gets found. I hope that my children do not have to learn to be deficient in their lives because aspirations and expectations get curbed to nothing, and one feels locked in and trapped.

Life's Perplexity
Written Saturday 29th May 1999

Much of it is true that a great deal is written and said about the complexities of life in human society. Human beings naturally mate for life, but our modern way of living is so distorted that we put so much pressure on ourselves. Moreover, the pace is so fast that it influences relationships very adversely.

I feel exceptionally well-suited to my wife, and I believed in our rightness for each other from the start, but we have our ups and downs. Now it feels like we are sailing in calmer waters, for our love is on the up, but I find it hard gauging her feelings and seeing her natural points of view.

In a conversation sparked by reminiscing, Euphemia expressed her sorrow for not recognising my outpouring of affection to her. She had blinked at it. Still, I noticeably saw my lady's backtracked approach to the domestic tasks, and Euphemia saw red after that at everything I did. She approached me with looks of flirtations to make up for the past, shared her affection with me, and said, "Karl, I love you". Euphemia took my catchphrase as her own and spoke to the children, saying, "Mommy and Daddy are in love".

For once, it seems it is not I who is sending out love signals. I acknowledge her affections with kisses and laughter and tell her my love for her has not changed, but please never ignore it again. "I give you all my love and support, trying not to be lazy or be a non-productive husband and father."

It is great to be sailing into calmer waters with our relationship. The pressure for wanting to please her still exists, and it's all noticed. These days, when I do anything romantic, my darling sees. The warmth in her eyes makes it worth it. We rarely argue, and although Euphemia finds that I cannot provide her with a life abundant in material things, she is blessed to have my love and said that she is happy and content. But I only half believe it. She is not asking for the earth but wants the money problem side of our life sorted because it's all she worries about most of the time.

We talk very candidly about what we hope to build and want out of life. We agree that we want the same things for ourselves, the children and our nieces, who have lost their mum. At the centre of our views is a statement of regeneration. Still, it's merely about coping with the immediate problem of life daily and look to prayer as a means of rearranging reality to achieve our desired end.

Reason and reflection, I believe, alter perception, and consequent discoveries account for earthly phenomena that increasingly exclude the likelihood of supernatural forces determining the actual outcome. I have prayed until I was blue in the face, spun around like a bluebottle fly, and wept bitterly because current events have overwhelmed me. But, unfortunately, I cannot find a solution to the shortfall of money.

Since Easter, our son has had frequent headaches, and it's a worry. The wife has car-accident-related back pains, and the bombing in Belgrade has me worried sick. I suffer agonisingly for the love of people and my family. I pray for changes to personal dilemmas and world conflicts. I cry for the innocent ones who suffer in Kosovo's killings, where civilians have been used as human shields in front of Serbian tanks, which is shocking. The Balkans' conflict's language seems to reflect a descent into hell because of unstoppable killings and the reported execution of refugees in their thousands. The western world has rushed to Kosovo's aid but largely ignored the many other killing fields worldwide. The tribulations of Albanians in Kosovo mean they have unleashed an attack that Europe thought it would never see, the new world order bequeathed to us by the collapse of communism and the end of the cold war. Kosovo is only one of a string of ethnic tension points spanning the globe. Brittan and NATO want to demoralise the Serb army generals with continued bombardment, since late in March (25th) 1999 until Yugoslav President Slobodan Milosevic accepts that it's futile to refuse to make peace.

I am uneasy about the conflict in Kosovo and ethnic violence around the globe. There are never any good guys in war because war tends to drive both sides beyond humanity. The world shows no signs of wising up to this. There may sometimes be such a thing as a necessary war, but it's the stark realities of war, the human suffering, that had me weeping over the pain of our world until I once again realised the ascent from hell should come. I shed emotional tears over my service's failure to the 'call', the ambition to combat injustices. Somehow, the world's darkness affected my happiness because the ascent of misery to lasting peace in a world without end required higher powers. Almost intuitively, I find myself saying, 'God help us'.

Today is the 29th of May 1999, and President Milosevic has not buckled under the NATO air-attack bombings. It is the most significant human disaster in Europe since World War Two, and the truth of the post-cold war world is that there are vast areas of the planet which do not march to the western drum or any particular drum. History has not run out of killing fields; they have come to our doorstep because Albanians and Serbs are recognisably European.

Over some time of effective relaxation through listening to music, mild exercise and a good night's sleep on the problems, I am tension-free. Although no solution to the issues has emerged - I cannot believe in fate or blame fate for items that happen in my life - I have to say that it must have a cause, and then I'll try to find out. I accept things can go in a particular direction 90% of the time, but I must be prepared to change course when something else seems right.

These periods of money matters and world conflicts make me feel powerless. It's the worst drain of my mental energy because, beyond a point, it seems nothing will work, and it's fruitless to search for answers. Leaving things on the back burner and often waiting for the development brings unexpected results. There is no need for supernatural explanations. There are no mysterious intonations or visions which do not derive from our material constitution. God has revealed His purposes, but in His grand design, we cannot know. This intellectual culture supposes that all things can be explained and somehow are owed or entitled to explanations as a kind of birthright. God is represented in mysterious paradoxes, rendered in human terms, but quite unlike them in operation. The God, whose unknowable purpose hurls galaxies into space, is the same power whose tender concern for his creatures extends to us. He operates through His material creations.

Telling the story of my life that contains my travels in life and my walk with God might not have excitement on its pages, but I continue to write to feed your curiosity and make you want to turn the page to find out what happens to real people like us, who live humdrum lives. One can do something worthwhile, never being too cynical, because I want to do things and make good things happen, but I have made a big mistake in handling money. It seems like I have to live with debt problems for the rest of my life because I may not get a second chance to put things right.

Life is not fair. It blighted me with the possibility of extreme hardship, poverty and ugliness, but not if I can help it. Good things only come from passion, but it takes so much out of me, yet, at the same time, it's therapeutic. I want to bring myself to the top of my life, but I have a complicated relationship with money, as complex as my relationships with people. I feel not having enough of it is pulling me down, and it's a shame that I'm the creator of this crisis because I always saw myself as level-headed and would not get trapped. I am scared that, 'this is my life', low-income provider, watching every penny, a non- achiever and a dreamer. I worry that

I might reach middle age and not get what I want out of life, especially what's money related and, as a pensioner, get it, but be too weak to enjoy it. I can see the point in constructing the grand edifice of belief. Living should be about living in the moment intensely and comprehensively and not allowing the present to be blighted by fear, worries about the future, or regrets about the past. I tell myself that I can have what I want, as long as I have the nerve to try and try for it. I scoffed at the idea of being a loser and thought I could begin to change those beliefs about myself that are not gutsy and that life would change after that.

Still, some things do not come easily, but the lingering financial crisis means I am addicted to seeing these debts as history. I expect a lot of things will change, but the basic stuff shall stay the same. To change something takes more considerable and more significant effort, but I think my life looks like it has been mapped out in parts like pre-destiny. Take money as an example; it appears money talks, and it has clout, but I have never experienced the use of its pleasures because I am hard-pressed to find enough of it, which seemed to preordain us to financial hardship.

I am forty-two years old, and I have not felt that I have altered inferences or changed how I handle money in all those years. It tells me one thing in all those lifelong learning years - get into poverty, and you'll be trapped. There is no charming my way out of it, except by earning more or inheriting wealth. I want to do things to break the circle and make exciting things happen, even when I stop praying and believing. Damn hard work, a bit of luck and getting the timing right is probably essential. Out of these, the impossible task causes the connection between body and mind, manifesting illness. There is a saying, 'you are what you think', and my thoughts are negative sometimes, and that's when the physical condition appears. When I remind myself of my positive qualities, I feel better already as smiles surface on my face from the endorphin kick that positive thinking gives.

Last week, Wednesday 26th of May 1999, Manchester United, who had already won the premiership and FA Cup, took just one minute to score the two goals that brought the European Cup to Manchester and euphoria to the whole nation. It was a minute beyond belief and an unforgettable moment in the children's lives as devoted Man United fans. It had looked hopeless with ninety minutes of play against Bayern Munich, energetic and seemingly impregnable, still holding the one-goal lead. Then, Man United snatched in the game's final minutes and scored two goals. It's almost incredible that two goals came in the last minute of play. The game was played in Barcelona, and it was the substitute player, Teddy Sheringham, produced a dramatic equaliser in the 90th minute. Then, incredibly, in injury time, Ole Solskjaer snatched the winner.

I have looked at various analyses of this magnificent victory and concluded that the appearance of manager Alex Ferguson and his strategy worked. He had inspired determination and persistence into the players from the dressing room to the pitch. They played keenly without slacking up, giving Man United victory on the final whistle. I began to look at my money problems in the light of having seen working strategy, and suddenly, I saw a way forward that did not rely on chance, like playing the Irish Lottery, which I promptly stopped after four weeks.

I have not bought another ticket since I was gutted that I didn't win even once during the trial period. Though I asked for dreams in which the winning numbers were revealed, there were no revelations as I woke from a deep sleep. Then I tried deep thoughts and picked the numbers that came out of my consciousness on the same day of the draw, and again, this didn't work. So finally, in absolute desperation, I crossed my fingers and drained my prayer thoughts into the open air under a high blue sky and still nothing supernatural or otherwise happened in creating a win for me. In theory, the Irish Lottery is supposed to give a higher probability of success, but it faired no higher than betting on the horses. As a result, I had impaired vision for the months ahead, and it is too bleak since playing the Irish Lottery to win did not work out.

I worked it out roughly, consolidating the existing loan and credit cards into a £10,000 new personal loan over five years. I put the rest in the house's equity — secure homeowner loan of £5,000 over the mortgage's remaining period—the place I had assumed to be worth £52,000. The figures seemed close to what the new borrowing would be, and probably there would be no cash reserve when the debts were settled. So I talked to our mortgager, Britannia Building Society, and the consolidation was approved.

This solution to our money problems has taken a weight off our minds. My whole self felt immense relief and, through the months and years, God willing, we can retain the money in our pockets as spare cash. Our immediate expectations and future aspirations are coming back because it is an option that I thought would reduce the outgoings by over £150.00. When the settlement sum of £7,060.64 was required to redeem the loan and four credit cards combined, debts were £9,590.97. I realised the figures did not add up, but I had already cashed the cheque for £10,000. I have not received the home loan yet; being secured on the property will take several weeks to come through. I needed to make a U-turn but didn't know how to!

I told myself I had been foolish to run up such debts and plunged us into the edge of financial disaster or possible bankruptcy. The whole disastrous episode saddened me enough to reform our obligations. I grieved all the time when I looked back at the initial start of us being in debt to the way it is today.

We are one of the thousands of ordinary families earning well below average. I made the initial mistake of having a flexible lending facility on the credit cards, which means running up debts of hundreds of pounds and only paying back £5.00 for every hundred pounds spent. The credit card companies reduced the minimum required to pay back to 3% of each month's outstanding balance. That led to my poor debt management for managing the payments for the personal loan taken out without insurance, and I had three years left to repay it. I was level-headed at one point, but I saw a lot of credit offered when the money was tight, which led to much unwise use of the cards, which has me severely indebted. Credit cards only require the borrower to make a minimum monthly repayment, the equivalent to 3% of the outstanding balance, which blinded me to the debts I was mounting up.

As a family, we were rarely far from the haunting fear of debts, and I fell into the banks' lending policy that seems to encourage indebtedness, which cannot get repaid. It was not that I wanted to buy desirables but just wanted money to keep buying the essentials. The children are aware of a money shortage and are naturally sympathetic to the idea that we need to economise. We are trying not to spend too much money, but still want money to spend on leisure, and to save to go on holiday is in the rounds of dreams.

I am looking at this financial mistake as a significant blow that it seems I'll regret for the rest of my life, for it is difficult to amend finances when they get wrecked. It is very convenient to draw the curtain across this problem and say, I shall move on beyond that curtain, but I have no idea what happens. I am leaving this page knowing the entire debt follows on, but I profoundly believe that somebody is organising everything that happens on this side of the curtain.

By the grace of God, we go on.
Written Saturday 10th of July 1999

My half-baked, weird idea that money will come our way utilizing the senses deep feeling, and the struggle to make ends meet shall then disappear has not happened. I haven't sensed anything of the sort. It is just foolishness said in utter desperation.

We are desperate for extra money because outgoings still exceed our income, resulting in a debt spiral. At one point, I had let my finances fend for themselves without proper control, and debts escalated. I badly want to be back in control of our finances, and regaining control is led by dreams and hope. I am working hard to find the solution, but I have no relief from this financial headache. I guess that it's years away before I can have complete control again if I ever do, but I want it now. I believe in hope and being positive and continuously pray and fill my mind with expectations. Although I have failed, a significant part of my success will come from my failures. Quietly, I hope, and I think my family agrees. I do a lot of self-analysis and writing this book is like talking to family and friends, and it keeps stress at bay.

I want to stop myself from turning into a nervous wreck ever again, be it at work, in the home or outside relationships, avoiding confrontational situations and shutting up when faced with potentially dangerous scenarios. So instead, I spend a little time each day alone, listening to calming music and trying to prioritise. I strive for a balance in my life, and the inability to tackle and resolve outstanding issues means I am stressed. I recognise the challenges may seem like obstacles, but I'll be alright so long as I can cultivate a positive attitude and sleep.

This year, 1999, is a very difficult one financially because halfway through the month, nothing is ever left. I have concluded that if current trends continue, I cannot provide for the family when the school term brings added requirements. We cannot afford it already in various areas of need, like paying road tax, maintaining the ageing car, and essential repairs to the central heating system before winter. Also, there is no money for the care of the house and replacing our worn garments and shoes. We can't live like that. We'll be losing everything before too long. Sometimes

I wonder what it's all about, particularly after being fed up that those prayers weren't getting answered. Using the ability to think, I first thought I would develop a new financial start plan to make a significantly better future on the card. Still, it gave a reality check - while in unfortunate circumstances, learn the actual value of money.

Money could not buy happiness, and we did not become happy through cash, but if I can be aware of getting wealth in my natural state of not having any, I will giggle and giggle and never forget the moment and bank it. I will control money again, and it certainly won't be left to its devices and spend, spend, spend. When the time comes, I'll look after money, and money will look after us.

The other thing that occupies reasoning and my dream scope are worries. Our son's frequent headaches and our nieces' home security and happiness since their mum died. Our children are growing up and expressing their need for their own space, and since our nieces need home security, the idea came to move to a five-bedroom detached house on a distinctive development being built in the town of Kettering, where our daughter goes to school. Five houses out of seventeen were constructed, completed, and I wished and wished, hoping that we could get a mortgage for the home at Chestnut Grove, London Road, Kettering offered at over £150,000. The Somerset style house was expected to be completed by Christmas 1999, and I continue to hope, almost daily, that we'll be the occupiers.

I have turned to chance again to bring the money that can change our lives. Last week, on the 3rd of July, I played my numbers on the National Lottery after nine months of abstinence. To the God that gave us life, sustained us and blessed us with family happiness, I pray for this new fulfilment in our lives. It is easier to believe in God, whose power created the universe than to think that He involves himself with the work of his hands. I guess my prayer for a suitable partner and having children are a gift- blessings and other promises of benefits are waiting until the due time. I hope I can win the lottery so that I won't have to worry about debts anymore, and the house of our desire will be materially ours. Every week, my heart feels pressure, and gravity pulls when letters arrive, and the lottery results are known. Wishful thinking, that belief founded on what I hope for and not facts, as I crossed my fingers. I linger for hours in a state of perceived change by a phenomenon that senses the big win from the depth of the mind, but it's yet to come true or materialise. "Yes, yes, yes," I said. Thank God, the numbers come nearly within our grasp, but I did not get to touch the money to do what we need to do because they aren't the winning combination, just close to them.

Life can seem unfair, can be perplexing and annoying, but by the grace of God, we can gain the strength to overcome the problems we face and experience some joy because life is not a straight line. I still believe that I will get things like a big win through prayer and hard work. It makes me feel so full of positivism that it's sickening, but it will work, believe me. It's going to work because when prayers get answered, coincidences happen.

Lord, How Long?
Written Saturday 28th of August 1999

My anxiety is growing more and more because I am worrying at an alarming rate. There is a deficit of £165.00 a month, which is accumulating into one massive debt burden.

I was unable to tackle the shortfall in the money that accumulated each month. It is almost September, and the children are to return to school, and there is absolutely no money to kit them out with all that is necessary to start the new term. In addition, there is no money to meet future expenses, i.e., the car MOT, car tax, car service, birthdays, Christmas, and money towards Katrina's first driving lesson on her 17th birthday.

A circular came in the post from the wife's bank about applying for a personal loan. With our backs up against the wall, it was clinging to a straw that we thought about carefully. There was no alternative to bringing more money into our immediate lives. The loan was a definite temptation to appear as an instant quick fix. A credit of £10,000 over 48 months at £27.75 per month without insurance was accepted this week by the bank. Of the £5000.00 received from the Home Loan last month, £4800.00 got invested over three years with interest paid yearly. Putting the Home Loan money towards the debt problem would have been like throwing a grain of sand into the sea. In other words, the money would not have made any significant change to the debt crisis. There would still be a substantial considerable debt to pay but, £45.00 would have been saved from the deficit of £165 a month, leaving us always having to find £120.00 a month if the entire home loan got used on the debts.

Each waking day I feel in my heart, achieving the goals that I have set for myself can be accomplished, but when another day passes and time seems to be running out, my anxiety grows and grows. It is getting to a point where I say daily, "God forbid". It appears that we are heading towards the worst financial scenario we are ever likely to face if more money is not found to offset the shortfall. It is frightening to realise that I am doomed to live a life in poverty and financial suffering unless I can manage money in the real world.

Theological intricacies are of no immediate comfort to me, and I am distraught. There is no practical purpose served by an academic discussion of suffering in whatever form it takes. I am nearly crazy with worries, agitated, at one's wit's end to know how we will survive this financial struggle. The deep roots and firm foundation of faith teach and train my soul in faith and trust that the wonder of the divine reflects the loving heart of God and to the cry, 'Lord, how long?' there is no answer because my life is to experience the wonder of the joy of the divine surprise.

Faith provides insights into ultimate meaning and truth, and the sense of purpose is driving me to overcome obstacles, trying to ride the crisis undeterred and undefeated. I found no emotional satisfaction in believing in God; God's existence makes actual demands, implying a set of obligations to God. My jury is out on God in Christ. I see it more as a God force, unconditional love, than God in human form. Materialism was expressed in the brutality of market forces, and the dominance of money makes spiritual sensitivity and ruthless materialism unable to live together. The equilibrium of life is seriously disturbed by materialism because physical, emotional, and religious circumstances cannot triumph in financial consequences.

I am, therefore, beginning to think that we create our destiny by making decisions. Making a decision and committing to it moves the chance in our favour because life moves from moment to moment, and each moment is like a choice. Therefore, although I thought that my life would get blighted because of bad decision-making in the financial circle, I feel a pastoral responsibility for those with bleak and blighted lives.

The immense outpouring of grief since my sister-in-law's death was for the victims of an earthquake in Turkey when the earthquake's death toll rose to 13,472 confirmed deaths, 27,164 injured, and a total of 40,000 suspected dead. Six hundred thousand need rehousing. I felt the need to attend prayer meetings with Euphemia to pray for a sick elder, for friends and family and those I don't know. I also prayed for starvation and our problems. The destructive hurricane, the devastating floods, the catastrophic earthquake all took place on the earth in a year and claimed many lives. When a geological fault and human failure combine to destroy thousands of people's lives, we are staring the realities of experience in the face. Here, the mystery of suffering tears at faith digs deeply into doubt and frames the question of the integrity of a God of love.

This planet is for learning lessons, and life will be as good as it gets when 'God's Will' happens, but as I wait, the chatter in my mind plays on my nerves. So, I focus my thoughts on achieving the goals that I have set myself, meditating on them, and feeling fulfilment from within myself. I have learned that I should listen to my inner guide, but I can only hear it in my mind in perfect silence and when there is no constant chattering inside my head. So, I try to make sure I do not cause internal discussion by living up to my standards and doing what I know I should do, and also by forgiving myself when I do something that goes against my sense of right and wrong, or else I'll end up torturing myself. Now, I'll never have days when I'm too tired or irritable because we each possess the power to have our lives the way we want them by the grace of God.

I possess the truth of my life within myself, but I have not got the fulfilled life I want now, but I feel it's coming. I think that it will be God-given when all kinds of obstacles along the way have gone. Problems occur time after time, and if I can see them as obstacles, which I learn and grow from, they are gifts. Sometimes something defeats me, and then I catch myself being victimised by it.

The most excellent show on earth
Written Saturday, August 28th 1999

There was a solar eclipse on Wednesday, August 11th 1999, at 11:11 am, and it was an impressive, wondrous sight.

The last time a solar eclipse happened in Britain was in 1927, and the next in 2090. The weather pattern on the day of the eclipse differed around Britain. It was sunny with scattered clouds high in the sky in our region, and within minutes the whole country saw the change in conditions the solar eclipse brought. The sky went dark, like a late evening's eerie dusk descending, and the birds fell silent. The temperature dropped, and the eclipse was 95% over our town. I saw the sun almost extinguished through protected welding shields at the industrial factory where I work. Millions of people watched the total solar eclipse of the millennium as they saw nightfall before noon.

I was thrilled and yet surprised at the suddenness in which darkness fell, and the temperature dropped, causing a shiver in my body. It was an unforgettable experience to see the sun and moon play hide and seek, peeping through gaps in what was becoming an overcast sky. It was awe-inspiring because it was pretty impressive, and the eclipse sparked a deep spiritual fear of events in the universe that signalled an apocalypse. Interpretations of Nostradamus and the Bible had fueled the anxiety. It was easy to understand the ancients' terror because even equipped with knowledge of solar systems, orbits and velocities; it had a sharp, distinct end-of-the-world feel about it. For a little over two minutes, I stood and stared at the newly bizarre surroundings the eclipse had created in the environment. Then, as suddenly as it began, it was over.

Nature's most beautiful, spectacular event, what for many would have been a once-in-a-lifetime celestial phenomenon, was over. The moment of totality I saw later that day on television. But when I was outdoor at the workplace watching the stunning spectacle, it had been like a bad omen, only because the sun is vital for life on the planet and its disappearance was a prophetic sign. We are pretty blessed in this generation to be around to have seen three once-in-a-lifetime events. We bear witness to the experiences of seeing Halley's Comet, the eclipse and the millennium.

There is an explosion of knowledge, an enormous expansion of information about life's nature and the context it has set. Still, the quality of the wisdom available to humankind has not changed. Nor, I must emphasise, has the timeless level of human sin. People are, by their very nature, able to share in the divine scheme of things. Perhaps eventually, they will reach out to the extraordinary creation beyond to develop the planet's life.

Knowledge without wisdom is the seat of human pride, and if we do not wise up, we shall multiply our errors and make a living hell of reality. I asked myself a series of questions about knowledge, which I might answer if I can learn. Is there knowledge to match our goals of painlessness and comfort at the expense of moral conduct? How far can we humans use the expanding pool of expertise to engineer life itself? To what extent should human inventiveness set terms to procreate life, to its preservation, to its termination? Is there a limit to how far humans may go? The poise of questions has made my thought close-minded that there is a line beyond which God's will for creation cannot cross, and in the same breath, humans are to probe and probe continually. Honestly, it is becoming difficult in our day to perceive with the mind or senses exactly where the line lies, that's because probably there can't be a line as such, for people were built to serve and learn to know the mind of God.

God, thou have forsaken me.

Written Sunday, October 31st 1999

I have run out of patience with myself. I understand what I have done wrong that has got me into this financial mess, but I feel disillusioned and angry because I have fallen deeper into crisis.

I was in my living room in the middle of the night, just searching my mind for answers, when I began writing a letter to two of my creditors, telling them I cannot pay them any more money. To one creditor, I had only made one payment. It has all gone so very wrong.

I went to my mortgage provider to help me sort out my debts, but they advised me to take out a personal loan to pay another loan and put our house as a security to a home loan. It was ultimately the wrong advice, and every day I question my stupidity, and I cannot forgive myself for the error. I revisited where I went wrong and cannot move on. It's haunting me like a spook - though I look to find a better way forward in the mist, I drop myself deeper and deeper into crisis. I clearly cannot think straight with the ghostly memory.

I have found a way of having peace with myself; though I am frustrated by this failure, I eventually forgave myself. Unfortunately, failings are more and more frequent because I have fallen below what I would like myself to be. You know, I believe in God as the energy and life force that is life itself expressed in and through all of us, but why has his spirit forsaken me? My belief in myself has been shaken because of bad decision-making, and the meaning of God's Spirit working in me has diminished. He appears to be failing me because His spirit is fading out of me though God is not of my early mythology of punishing, condemning and very judgmental. I doubt I'll ever be free from this debt, for God is creeping out of the equation.

God's gifts are given to each person, regardless of whether we believe in a particular form of God or not, and I doubt God is with me because I have gone a little foolish. Reading about atoms or the universe, I feel that there must be something at work beyond humankind, but does it involve itself in human affairs? What happens to ourselves brings to mind that the higher power, or a more complex one, may have lost interest in my case, for I feel abandoned. When we die, we still exist in some pure form, indeed in this flesh. He takes an enormous amount of interest to see us right. I do not know anymore if this higher power involves itself in human affairs. I may never understand what makes things work, but I feel that, as we learn more, we might eventually find out how it all began and why certain things work out the way they do. That does not necessarily mean that there is no God.

We may be a collection of atoms, but sometimes I have these moments when I think there is something else to it all, some reason why some people exist to suffer in this life or, like me, to suffer the worst through bad decisions consequences.

I have been to the local Citizen's Advice Bureau and requested money advice. I was in shock when they said I might have to consider bankruptcy to solve my debt problems. I am overwhelmed with the vision of many years of debts that may take me beyond retirement, and to abort it, employing bankruptcy is cowardly and merely a cop-out and failure on my part to tackle the debts responsibly.

On the other hand, bankruptcy would be a responsible decision to make. Bankruptcy seems an easy way out, but I cannot think of it lightly. In my heart, it feels very dramatic for an ordinary man in the street like me to declare himself bankrupt through the courts. I would be shattered and sad if that were to be the outcome. I need to know that bankruptcy is not an illness, and worse things can happen to people. At the moment, I feel my character will get blighted, and the credit score rating agencies damn me. Right now, my conscience is to the fore because I believe it is always there and always a guide, along with my gut feeling, but it is seldom correct.

Even my gut reaction is letting me down. Take the way I first reacted to the advice to declare myself bankrupt - it made my stomach churn. I think circumstances make me a fighter; well, I have to because I am an eternal optimist, and we shall come through this. But, let's face it; there are far worse things than not having any money and having to be declared bankrupt. So I want to say, "Right - that's not going to happen to me, but I am in that kind of mess that may lead to becoming bankrupt".

I hope to God there is an alternative, and thankfully, it can sort out this financial mess, and I never go back into that mess again ever. But it is really about choosing bankruptcy or not. There may be, there is, an alternative if I take up crystal gazing to find one. Seriously though, in the same way, that from the gospel of Jesus Christ springs hope and the love of God's indwelling Holy Spirit (which I thought had left me temporarily), my heart is being pointed in one direction that seems to be like gazing through a crystal ball.

I am asking for help from three fronts. First from within, then the third party and thirdly, calling on heaven to give me a break and this time to recognize good or bad advice and not drop myself even deeper in the sh—t. God of the beckoning future, I wait for your surprise help that's to come when I hear your call that someone becomes my miracle.

I am reaching out today, 31/10/1999, and tomorrow because we cannot live in the past, but we must grow from it, and I intend to keep moving forward though I have debts weighing on my shoulders. I want to shoulder all the burdens of my financial problems and let fate favour my effort to help myself. I cannot handle my creditors, and they are too big an organization for me to interfere and fight on my own. I want to share the reward of proper debt management when the advice centre pulls it off. Citizen's Advice has the muscle to talk to my creditors effectively, and their involvement has eased my anxiety. All correspondence from the creditors goes to them, and from the financial statement, they have the power of credibility to show evidence that there is a monthly cash shortfall.

My wife is getting depressed and tearful because modest spending in our world of being broke is still an overspend. The domestic debt will soar if we buy Christmas presents or buy anything extra, other than remain committed to paying our creditors and significant expenditures. So, we are budgeting as best we can and play on caution rather than optimism. Despite all the tears that I had shed and those of my wife, nothing had changed.

Euphemia feels that a doctor's visit may be necessary if bursting into tears and not sleeping well continues after the Christmas holiday when off work and relaxing could help. I am saddened to see my wife looking pale and worried about the lack of spending for Christmas. She fully understands the problems, but I do not want her to lose where cash is concerned. I have crippled our spending due to foolish decision-making. I would love to have let her spend like a monarch of the past and let her have treats, but I have made her feel sick. Euphemia hoped that married life would bring a sparkle of gold dust in our direction as we pass through life together and spend to add comfort, holidays and security, but that has not happened! I have messed up her hopes. We are forever struggling to turn a corner onto the route to prosperity, and it is delayed in this our eighteenth year of marriage. Neither of us expected our wedding vows to be challenged by the most demanding test to a couple's love because, for worst, more impoverished and in sickness are not conditions one expects to endure till death do us part. Where is the good life that was supposed to come to be better, more luxurious and in health? I labour on, knowing that I am storing up goodwill, which one day should repay intangible dividends and generous gifts for the wife. I cannot rely on the notion of the universe or other dynamic initiatives to make the positive happen in our marriage. I am out to put the finances on a sound footing by having the right festive touch. I know I cannot fly solo and rely on my partner's cooperation, but she suffers when I get it wrong. We all suffer when I get things badly wrong. I probably get it wrong because my emotions are tied to the financial decision, and secure judgment basics get obscured.

We aim for a lucrative end to 1999 and probably, in the year 2000 and something, when fairer winds are blowing behind financial hunches, we will see a much better outcome. I have changed my mind to a certain extent about money not buy happiness. The wife is sad, and this episode of sadness is directly linked to money. Spending power is central to a state of well-being in some people. My wife is happy with the overall quality of life but saddened that money can buy happiness because spending power is central to a state of joy.

Our Millennium Dream

Written on Monday, December 27th 1999

The lack of cash is preventing us from doing what we intended and stopping things from being accomplished. It is frustrating for us to change our lives for the better in the new millennium, but it's a shame that money troubles hinder us still as we go into the year 2000. I could realise our millennium dreams if only our finances were in order.

So, here we are, teetering on the edge of the millennium with just two days before entering. I am excited by the century I was born in and the next century because I witnessed such beautiful advances in human achievement in the 20th century.

I hope the new frontiers waiting to be explored with technology give me financial, social, and economic growth. Most people are going into the next millennium hoping to live to one hundred, and this century has given us penicillin, TV, central heating, cars and computers. Twentieth-century technology has also brought us electricity, air flight, electronic communication and space travel, not forgetting this internet age. However, less comfortable gifts in its sack were nuclear weapons, progressive eugenics, pollution and harmful rulers having a broader canvas to paint their evil deeds. The hole in the ozone layer and creating a greenhouse effect could cause environmental devastation in the coming century.

These aspects of modern life inspire my optimism because of technological marvels we take for granted, but Europe has plunged into a catastrophic war twice this century. Civilization is still under threat by terrorism and the ambitions of rogue states. Every generation, it seems, is forced to confront evil. It looks like science in the new century can work for good for humankind, but understanding technology like genetics must get understood before letting it loose in our fragile world. My biggest hope is that we learn to be more tolerant and show greater understanding so that the twentieth century's violence gets left in the past.

I am excited by these formidable new frontiers that await exploration in the next hundred years, but I cannot keep up with the latest technology. Therefore,

I encourage my children to grasp the modern internet age, making the world a more accessible place for everyone.

In the last few days of the twentieth century, the lining of my stomach was touched by what was believed to be one of the century's worst natural disasters. A week or so before Christmas, 50,000 people were killed in Venezuelan floods. It almost ripped me inside out because I ached with sorrow and mourned the victims. Yet, despite faith, prayer and long commitment, deliverance has not come to us or for people who suffer because God did not will it. My dilemma is the conflict between an obedient desire to believe in divine omnipotence and the harsh realities of life or other human suffering forms tie faith in knots.

There are some things God cannot do. Let me point out that massive human suffering, whether corporate or personal, always makes me ask how a loving God can permit suffering. That accusation will continue. More trying is the profound crisis of faith and doubt that pain can bring to genuine believers, who were brought up to accept everything possible. Not infrequently, he, Jesus, accused his disciples of having 'little faith' and criticized their failure to believe that all impossible items with men are likely with God. Having given the gift of free will and freedom to human beings, God gets bound by the present and cannot necessarily prevent the result of that freedom. If human freedom is a reality, human suffering is inevitable.

It was not only frustrations alone that made me cry over killing fields in the world. Turkey's earthquake and now the sadness of Venezuela's floods. I also felt profound compassion. Are there some things that are too hard, even for God, such as disasters that were caused naturally or through human failure? A combination of both leaves me with the mystery of suffering unsolved. There has been human suffering beyond comprehension through the conflicts of the twentieth century. In the forty-three years of my life, starvation still stalks the earth. There are wars, destructive hurricanes, devastating floods and catastrophic earthquakes, which are headlines for a day only to be forced off the front pages by the trivialities of celebrity relationships. So often, it seems, it is ill-health and death that dominate life.

Against such a backdrop, it reminds me of the wonder of the joy, the divine surprise. "God has brought me laughter," said Abraham's wife, Sarah, in Genesis. The reason for such hilarity was that God had promised Sarah, well advanced in years and past the age of child-bearing, a son by her centenarian husband. So, she laughed when the promise was made. I would love to laugh my way into the millennium, but this world travel seems to be a less joyous journey, more a vale of tears. The birth of Isaac reminded me that when there is a time to laugh, laugh I must, and when there is a time to weep, weep, I will, either with others or alone. The reason for my hilarity is the promise and the millennium hope that would be infectious for everyone who hears about it. We are born to live for a while, and then we die. What's it all about, creation? I have to believe in an optimistic future for humankind, for humankind will create divine inspiration and possibly, God's involvement is to confront evil.

We are moving into the third millennium, and on January 1st 2000, I'll raise a glass to what the future holds, not what might have been, and hope to God for prosperous years ahead. A completely new understanding of historical Christianity had come to light after reading a book written by Barbara Thiering called Jesus the Man when I had the sense to pick it off the bookshelf and read it. Its hypothesis quenched my thirst to discover the man Jesus. He was born and lived in an ordinary way, which I suspected about the real Jesus. It presented records of his life and gave a new view of the origins of Christianity. I was so engrossed in the book that I did not put it down until I reached the chronology. It was 4:30 on December 31st 1999, when I went to bed with an excellent feeling and a terrible wonder in my mind, as the book affected me so profoundly that I felt I would wake up without the Christian faith.

I woke with no actual change in my belief in a Christian God, but some other things have changed because I had been suspicious that the church was covering up. Nobody challenged the church's supernatural claims. Lay people are not told the whole truth about Christianity, so if the hypothesizes brings out the literal truth of historical Christianity and stands the test of reason, then a completely new understanding has come to light, making the faith in the Christian God more meaningful.

The book's controversial new interpretation of the whole story of Jesus Christ rightly upholds the fundamental faith of Christianity but challenges many of its most ingrained supernaturalism beliefs. I have lost the confidence in the virgin birth, which I had my doubts about all along. It's missing the faith in Christ's resurrection that would have been the most painful if I was able to give up the belief, but I could not, no matter what the book said. I maintained the thought and the idea of resurrection and hope for humankind, for the Christian God has the power, but was the resurrection of Christ a natural and human event? It seems strange to ask this when I do not doubt that God can raise the dead and give believers eternal life. It has to be recorded that I interpret the resurrection of Jesus as a matter of symbolism and imagery, some metaphor. I think God has the power when He is ready to bring about a transformation from the dead, and we can triumph over death in our natural bodies. Christianity's foundation is on the resurrection. I think it is possible to have a transformation. Still, the acceptance as the truth of the testimony of those who, through successive centuries and in different cultures, have received the assurance of the first disciples based on the emotions of individual believers' direct personal experience is not literal fact. It depends on the reliability of tradition, for all the knowledge of salvation and authentic events are all teachings about God.

I am sorry, but I have to choose according to sensibilities or tastes, conditioned by our age's needs, priorities, and intellectual disposition. I certainly have to represent the truths that God can bring about resurrection after physical death. He had, so to speak, told me so because I do believe it's possible, but it has not happened yet in human history. Jesus has gone the way every human being has gone in the past. I do not have the language to describe what or who God is. My belief does not rest on human understanding, but my submission to the divine will proclaim His truth and Jesus as an ethical teacher. He has gone the same way every human being has gone and awaits the mystery of the faith in God to raise them and do on earth as it is in heaven.

On this eve of a new century and a new millennium, December 31st 1999, we are all privileged to be part of a defining moment in human history. People who insist on strict adherence to the literal meaning may point out, with accuracy, that the twentieth century does not end until January 31st 2000. However, biblical scholars could undoubtedly argue that the real millennium has already passed since Jesus Christ was probably born in 4 BC.

Katrina, our eldest daughter, thinks that we are dull because tonight, when the world waits for midnight chimes in exhilaration in house parties and clubs, we will be in a church. The price of partying has rocketed for the millennium. So, after leaving the church at 12:30 am, we party amongst ourselves until late into the morning.

By near-universal consent, a millennium is an event of genuine significance after 2,000 years of the Christian era. In our lives, the deeper meaning of the truth about these celebrations will not be overshadowed. It is a time of renewal and hope for the churches and everyone. Though we live in a secular age, western society is still steeped in Christianity and Judaism values. Religious impulse remains a permanent part of our human make-up even if the church-going habit is waning. The way forward is through meditation and prayer and not always through the cry, 'Lord Jesus, Lord Jesus', or traditional worship.

Tomorrow is the dawn of a new age and is a challenge in the new millennium for humankind to fulfil its potential, develop and thrive and reach for the stars, but not to abolish the past. The human race will not start from scratch in 2000, and anyone who acts as if it will condemn themselves uncomprehendingly to repeat past errors. Despite every evil perpetrated, never more horribly than in the twentieth century, it is unusual to make 2,000 years of a universal civilization a celebration. Nevertheless, it gives a reason for the blessed hope, and it's joyful and solemn to be embarking upon the third millennium.

Happy Millennium
Written on Saturday, January 1st, 2000 AD

Our celebration after leaving church continued at home and ended at 4:30 am this morning.

It is January 1st 2000; brilliant, not just another date on the calendar, like no big deal. It was as if the world would change or just a lot of people were drunk, and governments wasted millions of pounds of public money on fireworks and silly projects. The whole world partied and first to celebrate was a remote South Pacific island, and over the following twenty-three hours, the rest of the world welcomed in the new millennium. Events were held across the globe, and each nation competed with the following country to see in the year 2000 in spectacular style.

At midnight, it felt like the digits finally ticked over from one millennium to another, and the world went collectively crazy. For one magical moment, we had stood poised in no-man's-land — balanced between our past and our future. Then the chime started, and the world hurtled onwards again. This morning, ever so slightly, something has changed; the morning looked the same, but my perspective has changed. To the birds in the trees and the fishes in the sea, the midnight bell meant nothing. This meaningless, human-made concept of time defines our lives, and thanks to the invisible but momentous threshold we crossed last night, I am not looking back anymore.

We are looking forward to optimism, not pessimism.

We collectively prayed together to mark this recent change, something we did not do before. We hope the future can be better than the bellyache of worrying yesteryears at this dawn of the age of destiny. What should be, or what did not happen, is not a concern; only what can be. Figuring out how we can make the best of tomorrow made us realize that the future can be better in just a different way. The twentieth century has armed us for the journey to come. At our disposal is learning from past mistakes, and ahead of us is an undiscovered virgin territory or the possibility of the same things happening again, but not if we wise up.

Technology is capable of bringing prosperity to all if it gets used wisely. Over the horizon, breakthroughs in physics and medicine promise yet more progress, accelerating decade by decade throughout the twenty-first century. It is humankind's destiny to explore. Astronomy and space travel will undoubtedly take us on the next step in our journey to the planets and, who knows, the stars. Maybe this will be the century when we finally discover that we are not alone in the universe, which I suspected, as scientists learn about more and more planets circling distant suns. Of course, some of the changes will be frightening, and I already feel inadequate to use new technology, like mobile phones and computers. Still, I educate my children for the 21st century in this brave new world, not the one we have just left.

I leave the 20th century behind us with mixed feelings. A terrible century, which was scarred by wars and famine and man's inhumanity to man, was also a century blessed by scientific, social and economic advancement. It has been the best time to be alive for some people, and I am glad that I was born in this century rather than any other before it. For we built democracy, defeated Nazism, founded the welfare state and witnessed the collapse of communism. Only by aiming high has humankind advanced. The only limits to what humanity can achieve in our next hundred years, let alone the millennium, are the ones in our imagination. Our target should be to banish all diseases, poverty and war throughout the world. But, unfortunately, humankind shows the same tendencies to the wickedness and to be wicked that it always had. The most exciting thing about humans is that they never change, and at heart, they have not gotten better or worse. Fundamentally, people are the same as they were in AD1. Two thousand years is a scratch on the scale through which human beings have developed. Evolution takes place very slowly in the genetic sense, and it could not change us in twenty centuries, less so, since we have begun to overcome the cruel selection of nature.

Technology changes rapidly, people change slowly or not at all, and evolution moves even more slowly. That is strangely comforting, for it means the contrary is authentic, that we can aspire to the highest levels of thoughts, music, heroism and storytelling. My futurist view of the world and our lives is incredibly positive, and I am not even making a prediction. I am merely saying that things have the potential to be good if we do not screw them up.

The growth of knowledge and ideas has to be looked at differently in this new era: economy driven by technological advances and nourished by global capitalism's triumph. I look for peace on earth, as soon as possible, because war is too terrible.

The process of globalization will interconnect all nations to such an extent that conflict will become unthinkable. The communication revolution will transform the world where frontiers and language barriers are replaced by a common interest in achieving a single society through global communication.

This third millennium of people is the last generation to die if the earth remains and is not destroyed by space debris. God takes us to live in a spiritual form out there and reforms us again into the flesh on a new world if humankind's home is destroyed. The technological golden age will unite all the dead generations and give the world to come those who had died.

The Bible has futurist scenarios which end the human story with Armageddon. The book is a closed one, but our hearts and mind must be left open.

Although it's a book of redeeming, not of despair, it rarely saw optimism as a beautiful future.

Yesterday was supposed to be the millennium night of all nights in the holy city of Jerusalem, awaiting the second coming of Jesus Christ and all that would result from this momentous event. No Messiah, no apocalypse, definitely no end of time. It's hardly worth the 2000-year wait by the Messianic Christians, doomsday cultists and Christian fundamentalists, who now have egg on their faces. Since Nostradamus's day and before, perhaps, pessimists have held the platform that the planet is doomed, and we are all on a short slide back to barbarism.

I have tiptoed for forty-three years of my life, believing this is so and the 20th century will be the last decade. As the new millennium approached, the fear that the world's end was nigh gradually disappeared and was replaced with optimism. My knowledge assured me that the future is coming, and if there's to be an end to the world, it is millions of years away. It is time to listen to the optimists, or perhaps take a deep breath and accept that the only sure thing about the future is that it's coming, and the second coming of Jesus Christ is for the pessimists.

It is odd that when people consider such prospects, they tend to be so optimistic or pessimistic. I get obsessed with the pursuit of personal security, which extended into fear about the planet's future. After two thousand years, it's time to be free, and pessimists have had their day. They will see the possibility of an unimaginable future good because of technology. We are almost suffocating through technology. It has us enveloped in a culture of health and safety, where ecological preoccupation stimulates an ambiguous materialistic world, though quintessentially moral. The future looks promising, for medical science has made considerable strides in the past century, but new research promises to give people a vastly improved quality of life. I get entranced by the prospect of scientific, commercial and technological advances, but human beings' inherent sinfulness is seen, on the other hand, not only in darkness. There is an extensive opening up of problems and solving human beings' sinfulness by permanently supplanting ignorance and superstition. New knowledge is not a source of chief evil to heartlessly assault humanity's uniqueness, but perfection should still hold human dignity.

Thanks to the Bible, from creation to destruction, human life is depicted as inseparably linked with all things fate, and to the pessimist, a cataclysmic end of humanity. A large part of Jesus's teaching was concerned with judgement and the end. It gets reckoned that, just as each life terminates in the personal cataclysm of death, it was pessimistic to think that the certainty of decay, like everything else, would happen to humankind by the coming in 2000 of Lord Jesus Christ.

We now know that human life and its terrestrial vehicle exist in the middle of a monstrous universe due to successful scientific investigation. It's a transient phenomenon, and our sense of time is a frame caught in extreme slow-motion. The twentieth century teaches, better than almost any previous period, the ambiguity of what human beings do, and it seems that there is no gain without loss. The motor car is a good example. An image previously considered unchanged has vanished because of this technology. One thousand nine hundred years ago, Jesus, a good shepherd, was understood, and it's getting heard for children who have never seen a shepherd in modern urban society.

The educated and the ruling classes cannot fail to feel nostalgia for the twentieth century's passing. A tolerant society where people have the right to be wrong is not what everyone uncritically accepts. Everyone chooses for themselves, which makes us all accessible. However, freedom is not a mechanism guaranteeing happiness. It is a collective cultural construct that exists not in the abstract but can be understood by the history that created it.

Perhaps the next millennium will see the end of our planet or the end of the human life that coats its surface so substantially that maybe it will not. There is no way of knowing yet. What can be calculated are some of the possibilities. Jesus has never promised worldly comforts. He spoke instead of appalling events to come. So, I watched and prayed that the bleak future Jesus painted of the earth would not escalate more with so-called signs of his second coming. Those who do not understand humankind's inherent sinfulness will deny that the symptoms of our time are telling us that Jesus is returning in this millennium. I will only say that humanity gets set upon an adventurous and dangerous course of discovery, calling

God out of themselves to share in the earth's progressive development and reach out to places beyond.

The new age, the 21st century, is based on evolution, but there is no literal truth behind it. Evolution is an unproven theory, and the idea in part is comically daft. Nevertheless, in conjunction with the incredible Bible stories not having literal truth, I believe in some of it. Evolution theory has a strong following in the west, and many people are leaving out God because they have lost reverence for Him. I am not sure if evolution theory will survive the passing of time as the Bible has. It gets said that lonely, frightened people want to expel God from the universe because they found the idea that God exists profoundly uncomfortable. Knowledge of evolution is very young, and new ideas about creation will not last if God gets blocked out of the processes. I know that the Bible will survive its onslaught because it says God exists, and that is a profound form of fact for every generation to examine and come to its conclusion.

The Education Struggle
Written on Saturday, May 27th 2000

We received a letter about Christmas time last year, 1999, saying our son did not get accepted into the secondary school of our choice for the autumn term of 2000.

Our youngest daughter is already a pupil at the same school, and we immediately launched an appeal. It's the same way we had to have the agreement heard independently over our daughter, who was initially rejected from getting her education at the school. We never thought for one minute that the school would reject our application to educate our son in the school that successfully raised our daughter's attainments and has developed her as a rounded individual and a team player. But unfortunately, the school's points system had scored Jonathan very low, and the application was instantly dismissed and never considered.

Unleashing an appeal, I clarified in the letter why it's unequivocal and emphatic that Jonathan should have a place at the school. Furthermore, it would be economically and socially difficult to maintain two children adequately in various schools in different towns.

We attended the appeal hearing on March 14th 2000, and a hollow feeling was in my chest because our appeal hearing would be the final one to be heard on the last day of a two-day trial of appeals. People coming out of the request expressed that the school was making a good case. The school is entirely at capacity, and the appeal judges refuse applications because the school gets oversubscribed. I hoped the appeal panels would look at the whole picture in our case, see our desperation, and make us a particular subject. I put over our circumstances to the board very well. During the deliverance of our views, the panel seemed to show sympathetic understanding because they nodded and looked in agreement with everything I expressed to them.

After we stepped out of the hearing, I told my wife that I was confident that the panel had listened and would throw out the school's argument. But she felt it was a show that will have no bearing on their judgement. However, within minutes of expressing my confidence to my wife, it was immediately shattered by a female, not

323

of the panel, but helping out in administration or security. She approached us, began to talk, and mentioned that her child did not get a place even though she works for the school. Well, what then were our chances?

There was virtually almost no hope of our son getting a place; that was the scary reality. Two days later, on March 16th, 2000, I recognized the envelope that came in the first post containing the appeal decision, and I felt a little shaky-handed as I began to open it. I read the first sentence of the letter, "I have to advise you that the appeal panel has decided not to uphold your appeal against the refusal of the school to offer Jonathan a place in September". I stood stiff as if just being stunned by a high volt of electricity that entered my body, and my automatic reflexes moved me towards a place to sit. I read the whole letter very carefully, looking for suggestions on getting the decision reversed. We knew that the school was the best one for our son, so the judgement was wrong and had to be overturned. My anxiety grew to a suffocating level, making me feel I must do something and not just accept the decision.

I was due to start work at 8 am that morning, but I delayed going in until I had spoken to the appeal panel's secretary, so I made some plans. I anxiously watched the wall clock as the hand moved minute by minute and listened to the seconds' ticks that seemed louder than usual. Immediately, upon office opening time, I picked up the phone and contacted the secretary. He told me that the decision was final and could not be overturned, but I could appeal to the ombudsman if I felt the panel was prejudiced and I had grounds to believe that the committee was unfair. On hearing that, I built up an inner resistance. I was not allowing what he told me to penetrate my heart and make me give in to the system that, in my opinion, was damaging to the whole family

My next move was to contact the Education Department to determine if any good schools had vacancies that offer outstanding ethos learning and good pupil relationship and behaviour. Unfortunately, the schools that the department told me about, which had a vacancy, were not desirable. I telephoned the local MP's office and, in my desperation, asked if he could try and influence the school to change its decision. His secretary said the MP would be in touch, but he failed to contact me or invite me to his surgery for talks.

My final telephone call for the morning was to the district Racial Equality Council to see if they could find that the school operated in a discriminating way on race. The percentage of blacks and other ethnic mixes in the school is meagre indeed. I was given an appointment to discuss it with a senior adviser. I went into work with lapsed concentration because part of my brain was thinking about contacting famous people in the community who could be influencers.

I had a strong belief that some way would be found even though each avenue I had followed so far appeared closed. I could see an urgency to work quickly to change the decision, and I had ideas to pressure the school to change its mind. When I came home from work that evening, I said to the wife, "We must put up a stiff fight to get our right for a good education for our son, and we must be determined to do all we can do, for we know a Christian education is the only right choice for Jonathan. So, we must exhaust all means to get him into the school and then we can say we did the very best we could with God's help to get him in. We know our son; the state school system would not suit Jonathan because attitudes are different from church-inspired education. My biggest fear would be that Jonathan might be subject to bullying in a state mixed comprehensive.

In-state schools' choices, pupils' personal and moral development with excellent pastoral care is slack or lacking. Their school reputation in the community is not exemplary, and they have abysmal academic reports too. We truly believed that it's God will that Jonathan should go to a church school. How can it then be that we will fail? I feel surer that this is the right decision to get our son into a church school, and I cannot stop the drive to see it accomplished. I take the stand to determine that I am sure it is the right choice we have made, but the wife feels defeated and doubts that it is God's will when the corridors are closing instead of opening. The latest passage to close was the Race Relation Council to find racial discrimination operating at the school. They couldn't find any biases on racial grounds. "It was unfair, but life is unfair and a bitch", the male adviser said.

The first weekend has passed, and throughout, I have been working on a strategy to keep up relentless pressure on the school until the right decision is made to admit our son. In addition, I have a campaign in mind to write to influential people in the community.

The disappointment Jonathan experienced by not getting into the school with his sister made him worried and forgetful. He was preparing for the SATs and was having headaches, and his concentration dropped. The first Monday of the new week, I posted a letter to the school's headmaster and the Bishop of Peterborough, the diocese of the Church of England Bishop Stopford School. Further on that week, I gave Jonathan a letter to give to his junior school headteacher, and I wrote one to give to our GP for the next day. Euphemia contacted her pastor for an appointment to discuss if he could send a letter to the school, mentioning that Jonathan is a good

Christian boy. That afternoon, Jonathan returned from school with the message still in his bag; he had forgotten to hand it over. To further move the campaign, I would type letters from a drafted one asked relatives for their approval and sign. First, I brought it to my mother's attention. I am asking her to have a say on how her grandson is affected by the decision. Aunts and adult cousins would be the next asked to sign a letter.

If the bombardment of these letters does not bring results, I would finally ask friends to write in their handwriting from a drafted report. On the day I was to post the GP letter, I forgot and left it in my pocket and took the note to work to post it in a nearby post box outside the factory at lunch break. I received a phone call from Euphemia just before lunch, informing me that the headmaster of Bishop Stopford School wanted a word with us, but he did not reveal the reasons. Nevertheless, we suspected it was because of my letter, and I was ready to defend its content.

That day was Thursday, March 23rd 2000. After Euphemia called, I immediately thought to abandon posting the letter to our GP, at least until after the interview. Instead, we rehearsed what we were to say to the headteacher. The reinforcement of my written words about Jonathan was sure to act as an excellent role model in the school and outside. His career choice may well be that of a vicar because he is a good Godly minded boy.

The headteacher warmly welcomed us to his office where, in his second sentence, he said, "There is a place available at the school for your son". Euphemia and I looked at each other as if we had just had our first surprise kiss in our relationship because we felt so good about it. On March 30th, 2000, the Bishop of Peterborough wrote and said he was pleased to hear from the headmaster that the appeal's decision had been reversed. Euphemia and I were delighted that there had been a satisfactory outcome, and we did not try to analyze how it had happened. Instead, we thanked God we had the correct result for our child, and we felt sure he would benefit the school.

Our Neighbour from Hell - Part I

Written on May 28th 2000

In the term 'our neighbour from hell,' I do not mean a place of punishment for my malicious neighbour after death, but a state of supreme misery they have caused in our lives.

Euphemia had to have a weekend away one time, and we both had an extra-long weekend. We did not return to work until Tuesday because of the suffered stress and exhaustion that our neighbour had put us through. I made blunders at work because the neighbour's problems worried me so much that I could not think straight while engaging in engineering processes. I took another Monday off work because I was sure to make other blunders and I was not fit to go in to sort the catalogue of minor errors that occurred on Friday.

We reported the neighbour's nuisances to the police, and a community police officer called round on Monday. I lay in bed due to the weekend's intolerable behaviour by the neighbour. I had just awakened up when I heard the doorbell ring, and I hurriedly dressed. I suspected my appearance at the door looked dopey; my face was drained of colour with dry dribble marks at the corner of my mouth. My sleep had been interrupted because of what was going on with the neighbour.

Things have become so bad that I asked in prayer for his death. Night after night now, I prayed for my neighbour's husband's death so that it would put an end to his threats to our lives and the continued onslaught to try to take our rights away. The only way I thought he would halt his malicious behaviour was to provoke fear in his mind, not what I may do to him, for he is not scared of me, but what can happen to him when I ask a divine source. I suspect he will think I was practising black magic or voodoo to harm him, but in truth, I was actually asking the living God to kill him by natural causes. I told him he would fall sick if he kept violating my right to park my car on my property. "You'll be a dead man because I am praying for your death".

In this post-Christian society, where white people move towards a post-God society, they negotiate their way through life without reference to a divine figure to fix their moral compass to know what's right and wrong. I was surprised that he called the police to arrest me for causing him to believe the fear I suggested in his mind. The police turned up within minutes to warn me of the possible offence because it got taken seriously. They have entirely overlooked the anguish he is causing my family. I pointed it out to the policeman, and he said we could both end up in police custody and put in a cell. I had called out the police about this man's behaviour towards us, and they said they would talk to him. The police did not come back to tell us the outcome of the talk. But when a black man threatens a white person, immediate action is taken. I have put the fear of God in this man because the material facts did not shift his attitude. Spiritual uncertainty deludes and raises mental and emotional illness, which will make him stop his threats and harassment.

A very long period had passed without any more incidents until he became active again on Saturday, May 6th 2000. He cut off the branches on our conifers that overhung his garden at the rear of the house and threw the branches directly on a clearly defined area by the boundary fence where beautiful flowering shrubs and draft plants grow. He had to walk a few yards and look over the wooden fencing to drop the branches on the floral bed.

On Tuesday, May 9th, he parked his car near my car's rear bumper, blocking my car. I would have to ask for his permission to move off my driveway. He did that last thing at 10:30 pm. I said nothing to him as I noticed his dirty tricks more and more and worried about what might happen if I needed to pop out after 10:30 pm in an emergency in the middle of the night. He departs for work at 7:30 am, and his car gets moved in time for when I leave at 7:40 am.

When I called upon God to kill my neighbour, I was at the end of my tether and had abandoned God's traditional view because the change took place in my mind due to the problems I have with my neighbour. I chose my own God, father/mother almighty and looked inside myself and out to God for direction, but the desire was intense as I asked for his death, like asking to let me have a big lottery win. The lottery win has not come about, and I suspect my neighbour's death will probably not happen. The all-powerful God is in my daily thought, and I am begging Him to have this man eradicated from the face of the earth. The suffering is killing me with worry and will probably cause me to be sick in my mind, physically as well. God may have already answered the prayer in a way unknown to me, but I cannot stop the process of divine intervention, and I come to believe that his death is as sure as the daffodils in spring.

In the same breath, I asked and prayed for his forgiveness to restore his soul and not be lost in all eternity and perish. I think there is something after death, and we are not just a biological organism that ceases to exist at death. Science may tell us of natural phenomena, and the belief in God tells us of human behaviours and how to behave in a kind light. Indeed, God protects his people, and I often read the psalm verses that said to be of courage!

The ongoing dispute with my neighbours had me employ a solicitor to stop them from impeaching our property rights. A physical assault on me by the husband took place on March 29th, 2000. He was swinging an offensive weapon, a kitchen knife at me, and we got into a brawl. He attacked me and came at me, wielding the knife and mouthing terrible language and racial abuse. One of my lower front teeth got chipped as we engaged in a fight. I managed to disarm him in the combat, but as I retreated after punching his head to a pulp, he located the knife again and caused criminal damage to our car by dragging the knife along the car doors.

I went to the police station and reported it, but the police did not charge him. I live in fear that this vicious man, who has no good nature, has got away with the crime. I threatened him that God's wrath would stop his worldly onslaught on us, and it worked for a while. Until I suppose it clicked, God's actions cannot be wicked, and I do not practice black magic.

Since the affray, I have taken more security measures to secure our home and property. I regularly check the car for tampering signs, and thanks to my vigilance, I found 3-inch nails propped under the car's back tyres. He threatened again to harm my family and burn down the house. I leave a security light in the house all night and place smoke detectors in vulnerable places, like the entry hall. The letterbox on the entry door could be targeted, sending missiles into the house, and a smoke detector protects that area. The radio is preset to come on automatically and play music moderately loud to simulate the house occupied during working day hours.

I get sleepless nights because he came out with threats again and his aggressive shouts of racial and verbal abuse make him a man not to mess with, for he seems capable of murder.

On May 11th, after further incidents filled the night, I called the female community officer to call around the next day, and she brought a male investigating officer with her. The latest incident happened on May 13th 2000, when the man next door said he would block my driveway repeatedly and the police could do nothing about it. He added to the sentence a chilling reminder that he is a man not to be messed with at all. "I will take you out, and I have friends who will, too; I am a vicious man." Words of this nature cannot be taken lightly, but they only told me to record what he says and film what he did when I told the police. I was disappointed with the response of the police. I would have to buy equipment costing hundreds of pounds for the police's benefit to prosecute. There must be another way.

I wrote to the superintendent of police explaining the incidences in a letter and that no action had been taken to stop the neighbour's harassment. It was causing us to lose confidence in the police. I received a letter from the police chief saying the investigating officer is making a report to send to him, and the officer would keep us informed.

Today is May 29th; we have heard nothing more from the police since their visit on May 11th. Facts about the neighbour's conflicts get recorded in the letter to the police, and a copy is in my solicitor's hands; I need not give fuller details in this book.

I am racing with my neighbour; he is trying to drive me out of my home, but it's a marathon in a sense. It's a stressful road adventure, and it's by not retaliating and treating others as I would like to be treated that has turned it into a test of myself. The demon in the neighbour seemed to pursue us since they moved in five years ago. It has primarily quietened down again because I did not compromise my rights to this brute of a man. A massive, strong storm had ripped out three fence panels, and that was another problem that had them fuming and insisting it must be fixed immediately. They stormed like the weather that blew the fence down, regularly shouting, using foul language, every day talking about fixing it, fixing the f—ing fence. We did not resolve it for many months until the fencing we had was strengthened with concrete pillars. It had new attractive trails added to the height of the fence, which gives our vine a place to climb on and stops the possibility of peeping in over the wall.

The police called round on Wednesday, May 31st 2000.

I Tell the Truth, Nothing but the Truth.

Written on Sunday, May 28th 2000

I take my autobiography to be a personal narrative, distinguished from narrative fiction by the assumption on its readers' part that it adheres to the standard of truthfulness, honesty and on the part of me, the writer, to an aspiration to tell the truth.

This book was not intended to be only a kind of writing of history, but rather non-fiction concerned with events, thoughts, and feelings known to me. It required an element of trust on the reader's part to be reliable, and there has to be an understanding that the truth is getting told, and I shall never lapse for any reason. It will only be too shameful to make the public feel I have destroyed the reader's reasonable opinion of me. Therefore, I shall tell the truth. There is a complex and exciting reason for surreptitiously breaking the pact. Still, I serve to tell the truth and not invent stories that encapsulate the truth more neatly, more pointedly, than strict adherence to the facts. Autobiographical revelations are bound up in soul-searching and the confession of sins. It's idle to try to hide the truth or tell lies because the ultimate reader of one's autobiography is God. There is no point in hiding the truth since the autobiographical endeavours are ultimately for one's benefit.

This book will not be a history of me, but stories about people and the information will be the truth and have truth-value, probably mixed. That is to say, some historical truth and some poetic truth in which the poetic truth is the work of the imagination; you will be able to tell the difference.

Writing is a way of reliving the past by retelling its story and bringing the past into the present. The momentum of the information is pushing and presently appears to be moving fast. I still have a good stretch of experience to come in front. Thoughts flowed from that – the most important fact is that life is concise - it's time to focus on priorities. So much of life rush past us without ever being entirely transparent, and for me, understanding things is one of the big joys in life and love. I talk about myself at length, and there is prestige attached to authorship in western culture, primarily when one writes and publishes the one story that I alone in the world can write, which is the story of my life.

This year, 2000, has already brought me far from my humble beginnings to stories that seem to exaggerate one's difference from other people. I know the feeling of my heart, and I think I know men. I was not made like any of those men I have seen. And I venture to believe that I was not made like any of those in existence. I am not better than other people; at least, I am different from everybody else even though I feel connected to humanity's river. I am conscious of the tug between social and individual behaviours, between unjust laws and just practice.

With the willpower in men today, is there anyone but me whose works have virtues and steadfast honesty? I have beliefs that are mine, and they have been forged in my fire. They were tried in me in the court, nurtured in my own heart and cleared in my mind. However, through a thoughtful review, I must take my time, go gently through the learning curve, and trust that what's opening up is in a new way, despite its scariness and the aggressive edge, a gift, not a punishment.

The Matter of Wealth
Written on Tuesday, May 30th 2000

So far, my financial story's shape in the course of the 21st century seems suspiciously similar to the year we have all just emerged from a few months ago. In May, when a cheque for £7,000 compensation settlement for Euphemia's car accident in 1998 was finally awarded, things began to take on a "sexy" shape.

The finances finally began to look attractive, but the bank account was like a bath, which bothered me more about the drainage hole than the water supply. The money is draining away though I am keeping an eye on the plug. A degree of leakage is unavoidable, but I suddenly have to worry about getting more money in as the pool is draining. I want to hang on to what is left because most of it will pay off debts, and it seems I would not have any in reserve. I looked at the pool of money again and allocated £2,000 in a High-Income ISA investment account and flirted with the notion of prosperity. Another investment from the past is yet to mature. The combined investment may represent our eventual destiny as being prosperous. An indulgent purchase of an ISA is seemingly sizeable, but it will be an intelligent investment. With a constant call on the £5,000 cash, there will never be much in the way of a surplus.

I did not use any money to clear debts on utilities, gas/electric, water bills, council tax or the principal personal loan repayments. The quick drain on the money came when the bank instantly took £1,000 for overdraft repayment. I have now reduced the overdraft limit to £650. The money disappeared quickly again for the redemption of Euphemia's new loan and overdraft payment. The amount taken was £1,257.53 to redeem the credit and £551.81 to clear a single account overdraft. Day by day, there is a new demand for money, especially for household repairs. A total cost of £134.20 was spent on video, vacuum cleaner, violin repair, and headphones. I gave Euphemia £300 to spend as she wished; after all, it was her injury compensation money. Travellers took advantage of me and received £200 for partly cutting down a row of conifers that stretched down one side of the garden and along its width.

They hacked the trees down close to chest height, leaving badly damaged trees and left some debris they said they would clear the next day. They asked for payment and came with me to the ATM to withdraw cash because they do not take cheques.

I was terrified to challenge the standard of their work, knowing the reputation of the travellers' community; I thought my property, and probably my safety, would be at risk if I did not pay up. But unfortunately, these people are low down on the social scale. So I choose them to give one family of Gypsie's a chance to earn decent money for a skill they said they had, but instead, they messed up by leaving, botched job and scampered with my money and did not return to remove the rest of the debris from the garden.

Money gets put aside to erect the fallen fence and pay solicitor fees. Still, I may have to dip into the overdraft to meet the total payments because miscellaneous spending has eaten into the funds put aside for them. The miscellaneous expense totalled £1,047.06, which became essential items and not off-the-cuff purchases. The cost went on school trips, dentist fees, optician's, home security light, car service/maintenance, children's clothes/shoes, and a passport fee and paid for a second-hand settee.

I tried to budget the money carefully, and I clearly saw where the money was most needed, but there was a constant need to divert some of the money for miscellaneous expenses, and now the dough has finished. To be accurate, only £509.40 remaining for two significant projects — rebuilding the fence and paying the solicitor's fee. So I had not squandered the money except the unfortunate loss to the Gypsies.

From the day I started to handle money on my own to the day I die, I see myself as a slave to the great god "money". There was great hardship in the 20th century when I needed to shake off outmoded ideas on money.

As the Citizen's Advice Bureau got involved, I no longer postpone life. I am busy making plans other than thinking about unmanageable debts. It seems it's getting sorted, and I can do what I want to do now. That's living in the here and now. It's the "real moment", rather than projecting my hopes off into an unattainable future. I am living in the present and have stopped worrying about the past or the future. I am trying not to regret what's gone before or get anxious about what's to come. Life can then be approached with a sense of wonder and fascination. That is easy to say, but I will try to implement it because those milliseconds of those thoughts brought moments of joy and increased inner peace. I am thinking happy and trying to banish negativity from my life. I am reaching out to understand my mood and question my judgment when making decisions in low moods. It's incredible not reacting until the feeling passes me to see life realistically. It brings a spirit of adventure to everyday living, and the world seems new and fresh.

The Citizen's Advice Bureau has handed control back to me in handling money and keeping on top of my debts. I still owe thousands of pounds to creditors, but the negotiated payments are affordable, though there is no realistic vision of when the debts will be fully paid off. It might take us to our graves because it got settled to pay £28.00 per month for nearly £20,000 worth of debt.

Some people at work are getting difficult to get on with, and working is integral to my life challenges. I would like them to change, but I have come to accept that everyone is an individual, and I cannot change others, only myself. However, it takes less effort, is more exciting and make me happy, showing kindness in relationships and watching its contagiousness.

Each of us sees life from our separate reality, our interpretation, our personal experience. None of us questions our version because, to us, it always seems to be true. So, it's futile to attempt to change someone else's thinking pattern, but I try to change any negative results from their separate reality. Respecting each other's views is essential too. I am glad to come home when work is done, with all the pressure globally, out there. I always make sure that our home is a sanctuary from the world for the whole family and never a show home. I want to feel comfortable at home, house-proud, cosy, relaxed, playful, but not exceptionally proud because the children must always feel safe, comfortable and happy in the sanctuary of home.

I have a fantasy that one day I will win the lottery, giving us everything we want. The idea is so fantastic that I watch the magic winning numbers getting announced every week, and it's enough to provide me with a delicious momentary thrill, a glimpse at a possible future devoid of problems and filled with joy.

I buy tickets for the lottery solely to win because it's a desperate bid for prosperity and relief from debts and old-age provision. However, it's not just any game I find myself interested in, and I hope it to be a way to receive fortunes.

The real-life recipe for fortune and prosperity is solving debt problems and spending whatever gives the most satisfaction. Some people believe that they can never have enough in the bank, while others say that as long as they can get by, they'll be happy. It's not how much money one has that is the key to happiness, but how one spends. I have been worried about paying the mortgage and debts, affording the children's birthday and Christmas presents because I have no money to spend on them. Such poverty causes great misery, but following a guide to resolving financial problems is progress. Money problems only get worse if they are ignored. Tackling them is the most effective solution.

My happy levels may seem to go up and down with circumstances. In reality, it's my thoughts, not my circumstances which dictate how I feel. We produce our opinions, not the outside world and negatively thinking will make them low and vice versa. I cannot take my thoughts too seriously because they can change, but the feeling comes afterthoughts. So, my opinions are a sure barometer of my thinking. I often try to work out our dilemmas like a maths problem on a computer but put the back burner's issues in my mind, the quiet place where solutions can develop and answer will soon pop into my head within the time scale I give myself. Rather than racking my brain for answers right away, I forget it, and like magic, a solution pops into my head.

I feel superior because a mixture of contentment and wisdom laced with inner peace and satisfaction has, through the realization of patiently waiting, made life seem less complicated, and our problems appear smaller and appear more straightforward to solve. I feel better inside, for I have access to my wisdom and common sense.

There are times when it is hard to smile, and there was such a time again. It did not occur in my personal life, but human tragedy struck in the world in August 2000. Horrific pictures appeared of human drama in Mozambique. Floods pushed my ability to watch and absorb it to the limit, as the sight of suffering was brought into my safe and comfortable home by newspapers and television. It is suffering on a scale so vast and unbelievable as was the holocaust of sixty years ago.

We are here on this earth for a millisecond in infinity, the tiniest dot on a radar screen and life is a gift; it puzzles me that it can end at any moment through an accident, illness or natural disaster. Therefore, to spend time rating money, material goods and criticizing others seems a shame. Psychologically, we are all wired up the same way. We all think we all have moods, and we all have feelings. But equally, we are unique individuals. I cannot believe your thoughts, and you cannot feel my feelings. People need to appreciate and understand the similarities and differences and the way we all connect.

My take on life is happy in the universe, and my place in it all is a question of learning to access the site inside myself where serenity already exists. I am learning to rediscover my natural feelings, remove the obstructions keeping me from them, and learn through malicious processes that I have pretty innocently come to accept as necessary or inevitable. It means I can play my part in the vast puzzle of life and enjoy small things, like a smile from a stranger, a word of understanding, a shared joke and the sun on our backs. I'll give my joy freely to other people.

There is always sunshine behind the clouds, so thinking of solutions is to think positively, not negatively, and problems are generated more by how I feel than by my circumstances. My soul positively sings because I am re-connected consciously to an inner potential for joy.

Our Neighbour from Hell - Part 2

Written on Saturday, July 29th 2000

I have tried to start this write up for days now, but the continued stress of my neighbour's behaviour on us interrupted the first mark on this page. However, I cannot put it off any longer and make a mark today, as I need it written down to diminish my stress.

He appears to have a defective brain cell because we cannot get through to his understanding of how to discuss this problem like an adult. His behaviour has startled me, so much so that I am looking at taking out insurance to cover me if I die by this man's hand or become seriously injured by him. How will my family manage without my income, and how would they financially cope if I suffered a critical illness? It's pretty hard to control what's coming in now and with debts already hung around our necks, how can the family have a more comfortable life if I die or become ill? It is only a matter of time before this stress from the next-door couple breaks out into something chronic. I try not to think about the appalling behaviour and get on with my life. Still, I employed an independent financial adviser to research adequate life insurance because I have not adequately covered my eventual death or critical illness with an insurance policy.

These diary entries should show a celebration of life, but this period is partially stressful, and it is nowhere near over. I am a bit morbid and worried about my family because of intimidation and hostility from the neighbour. This stressful period seems extraordinary and exceptional because my cry as a faithful believer in God is occasionally frustrating, and it stresses me more. God's existence begins to puzzle me.

God, Christianity and the Bible are working their way out of my head. The neighbour seems to be getting away with his dastardly acts, and I am left victimised. God witnesses it and does not bring deliverance from this madman. I am acutely aware of the purpose of God in everything that happens to me. My neighbour is causing me much stress, and faith in providence should lie at the core of my experience, but it's not clear if God is present as a silent witness or to bring deliverance. God is not acting to relieve my stress.

It appears that the neighbour is taking away our rights, and we are not getting justice. God working with and through his people is just wishful thinking! I called earlier for my neighbour's death to end his bullying and his hate for us. My neighbour hates us, but where is the unusual kindness in him that all humans are supposed to possess? Where is it? He shows love and compassion to his wife, friends, and, of course, he loves himself. But, unfortunately, he has made my life stressed to the extent that I suffer daily with a headache and tummy pain with fluttering butterflies and the possibility of vomiting.

Each time an incident occurs or when he deliberately displays contempt for living in peace with us, I feel sick and angry and need sedation to sleep well at night. He assaulted me and damaged my property, and through these actions, he thinks he can gain rights by bullying us to accept his warped views on property rights that are not based on law. We argue over our property rights, and I told him to resolve this through mediation or a solicitor. Still, he throws the idea out in a hail of words of frightening vulgarity and then said I only need to accept not to park the car under his window.

I long believed that kindness exists in the evilest of people, but in the experience with the neighbour, he has shown me he cannot share understanding with someone he dislikes, and somehow it is not present in his heart. I do not think it's his perceived enemy who can do it, but can his kindness be drawn through his loyal friends telling him to make peace with his neighbour? I want to reconcile and be at peace with my neighbour but to be at peace, I then have to give up being right.

As the problem with my neighbour continues, I cry, 'Where is God in the distress of his people?' I am a lover of God and look for his intervention. God saw his faithful people perishing in wars, natural disasters, incidents in crime and other conflicts and witnessed their brutal deaths at the hands of evil men and women and stood back.

Josef Stalin, Hitler and Fred West show how bloody and stained with wickedness the past millennium has been. Last century, millions were murdered by evil men, but body counts do not define immorality. Each of these wicked men perfectly encapsulated a deadly sin. Their terrible acts symbolized the worst that man can deal with, the darkest demons that lurk within the human soul. I half expected Him (God) to step in and protect his people from such violence and death, but history does not show He gives deliverance but presents himself as a silent witness.

I want to see the marvellous glimpse of the inherent goodness in this man, or else it will force me to believe that the world is a cruel place and that it has little good within it. Since my thoughts and prayers for my next-door neighbour's death, my wife has talked to me about returning to Christian teaching fundamentals. Love God and love thy enemy and pray for change in his heart and for him to ask for God's forgiveness. These are the chief virtues my heart aspired to, but my mind cannot patiently see the difference in people determined to harm others. Their head rules their heart, and the seat of their emotion does not trigger love and kindness through their bloodstream.

I thought that humans had a fundamental capacity to be fair. I suppose I am illiterate in human complexity because my wife said I must have patience, and in God's good time or God's willing comes deliverance. Wanting the neighbour's death would not allow me to glimpse God's inherent goodness in this man. My born-again Christian wife has focused my wandering mind on the purpose of faith, even though she cried to find out where God is leading her.

On the 26th of February 2000, Euphemia cried and prayed diligently about having lots she would like to do for Christ, but the abilities do not seem to be there. "Where are my talents?" she asked. She lacks academic skills, and because of that, she feels talentless. Euphemia told her feelings to me and retreated to a quiet place, begging God for positive growth with academic success. One day, she wants to testify to the church that it gets achieved through the indwelling of Jesus Christ's spirit, building up the needed expression of confidence and having greater inner joy gained with new skills.

The greatest talent one can acquire from the Almighty is resilience, and somehow, we will adapt or turn things around. Learning to roll with things and always be prepared that a great deal of life will be random is the hardest thing to accept. I never know how things will turn out, but faith makes me believe God works out his purpose.

I am fully engaged with life; I would rather be alive than dead, but my life has been threatened by the man next door, and he has already displayed he is capable of committing a serious crime. Yet, I feel enveloped in God's caring hands, and the beautiful aroma of his presence gives a ring of confidence that we are protected, and the neighbour will get what's coming to him to make him learn how to be good.

For one moment, I thought to carry out a revenge attack or retaliate on him by either damaging his property or causing something brutal to happen to him. I tell people, or they get to know how the neighbour is disturbing me, come and say to me, give them the go-ahead to injure him, beat him up and damage his property; he doesn't know us and would not suspect a thing. But I could not. At first, I thought to have him roughed up, but my alert conscience quickly dampened my thought, and I felt sick in the pit of my stomach within minutes because I can imagine the brutal blows of punches to his face and body.

The truth of the matter is, I want to bear witness to the foundations of faith, the doctrine of providence, the inherent good in human beings, the reality of suffering and our deliverance from the evil of vandalism and racism that grips my next-door neighbour. I cannot order others to attack him. I want to make a massive claim about this stressful time that it presents a microcosm of our life because I am too curious about the here and now and cannot see into the future when it will all end. My tummy is like a jigsaw puzzle getting worked out; it churns because the answer to the struggle for our survival in this house is reconciliation, and it is very far from that. If the home insurance policy does not cover taking the dispute through the civil court, we will sell the house. For most, if not all, of our journey so far, I have been a scarred and struggling traveller. "There but for the grace of God, go I."

I believe in how important it is to know oneself and realise that so much can change. For example, if one is bad-tempered, one can try to make oneself better tempered, and if one is intolerant, one can decide to make oneself more tolerant. But the inherent bad that one can do nothing about by oneself needs prayer and conversion to God to get rid of it.

I pray and ask God for my neighbour's conversion to living like a Christian believer and suppressing his inherent badness. The hostile forces within him overwhelm the goodness coming from being created by a good God. The intrinsic merit wrestles with the negativity of his badness. It's as if it's a futile struggle praying for him to be reasonable when it appears he has a personality disorder or something seriously wrong with his brain. I quest for grace to help me deal with his unreasonableness, leading to God again, and I ask the question again. "Who shall deliver me from this injustice and the badness of this man?" Biblical analysis feels irrelevant, if not unreal, but turning to analytic psychology and its exposition of the meaning of the unconscious, the psyche's shadow side manifests those same negative pressures from repressed feelings. It makes more sense to think in these terms. As the prodigal son discovered, the unconditional love divine is waiting at the end of the journey where all will be truly well. If the imbalance between good and evil in him is corrected, and his behaviour begins to show redemption, I would not guess whether it is an organic or spiritual issue that has caused the imbalance.

I would think nothing of the turbulence and the turmoil he has caused in our lives when all will be indeed well, God willing. I am out to do the work of my faith and live out what I believe. Don't do wrong to others that do evil to me and overcome their wrong by doing good. I am determined to live fair in this most difficult time because I am a good, kind, nice guy. Good, nice, friendly people get walked all over. Nice people get ripped off and pushed around. Lovely folk, though, don't care because they enjoy being kind. When nice guys, in turn, stand up for themselves, it makes them just as horrid as all those people that they do not want to emulate.

My ability to be kind is now severely compromised by someone or something best described as not very nice. The only way I can continue to be compassionate is to turn nasty, at least briefly, in a limited but critical context. I want to show some teeth and stick up two fingers at my neighbour today, Thursday 24th of August 2000, because I experienced rage when he spoke to me over the garden fence as he stopped gardening for a moment and said he would again start to block my car in on the driveway.

Twenty minutes later, I met him again, this time at the front of the house. I pretended to have something to put in the locked garage, but I went out to snoop on him. He raised my suspicion because I could hear, from inside the house, water jets sounding like a hose pipe being used very carelessly. The path to the front door was entirely soaked with water, and there was also heavy jet spray on the whole area of the car that faced the little patch of garden to the front of the house. He had deliberately targeted the water jet stream at the vehicle because watering his flower bed could not have made such extensive spray reach all over the vehicle's bonnet, roof, and boot. I watched him spray the jet of water that shot off at the height of the plants. Instead of directing the jet stream to the plants' roots, the water went through the plants' leaves, wetting the car considerably more than a light sprinkle that may occur from regular use of a hose pipe. "You are in for it; wait and see; you got it coming," he said. Before I prompted myself to say something to him, a thought stopped the forthcoming rage. There remains the 'call' and comes a time, especially in painful personal situations, to reach a level of sensitivity more exceptional than we usually show as part of our attempt to try to have the same attitude to life like Jesus Christ. I needed strength to respond without anger as far as I could. I asked in a calm, quiet, passive voice, "Did you have to soak my footpath and car with water from the hosepipe because I would not do as you wished and move my car into the garage off my drive so that it does not obscure your view from your window?"

I could not expand on my words physically and emotionally because sufficient curbed grace stopped what could have been a fiery tongue, but there was an ache in my tummy. I think I have wised up not to cause affray because being wise is to discriminate with available knowledge and recognize that the capacity to act is not the permit to perform. Nevertheless, I feel I am being pushed around and walked all over because I am a nice guy.

Our Neighbour from Hell - Part 3
Written on Sunday 12th November 2000

"Continue to love your enemies and pray for those persecuting you".
- Matthew 5: v 43-44.

I have seen myself use the quality I value most in people; courage. I do not mean physical courage; I mean moral and mental grit. The capacity to do what I think is right and without question is fair and just.

The problem with my neighbour took an inner journey. I realised what a complex mixture of light and darkness we all are. It nearly got me mildly depressed about my dark problem because I calculated and planned to sabotage my neighbour's property. The plan only got spoiled because they did not create the usual mischief. Nevertheless, I planned on that day to carry out criminal damage to their property.

Wednesday morning of the 25th October 2000, the wheelie bin is placed on the driveway to block in our car by the neighbour because it's the day the council collects the refuse. Wednesday the 25th was the day I planned to commit criminal damage to the property, but the weather turned stormy torrential rain, and gale-force winds created a morning of severe weather depressions that lasted all day.

All the problems we have with our neighbour would be sorted out with the sabotage. For a long time now, I thought his action must stop because the wheelie bin's location directly behind the car is a manoeuvre problem, and I usually move it out of the way before driving away. I am at the end of my tether now, for they have harassed me for too long. Come winter, when snow is on the ground and time is limited to get to work, this will be a more considerable inconvenience to me; I cannot tolerate this tactic anymore. I want to get in my car and drive my car off my driveway without this hassle. I have been tormented and my access compromised for far too long, and I am determined to make him respect my rights. I had moved the car further away from his fence and sometimes parked the car closer to my garage door, but my neighbour noticed none of my compromises. The criminal damage I intended to do involved pulling up plants out of their front garden bed and pushing over or breaking the tree's trunk to bend more on their area, or better still, uprooting it and allowing the whole tree to fall on their land. Then, I would chop off the vine that runs along the back-garden fence. I am fully aware of what I was out to do but did not think thoroughly about what harmful consequences may result, only what I would positively gain as I faced the challenge squarely. There is more to the individual than just the material; I was out to destroy some of his material processions, but I also wanted "a pound of his flesh" to break him. Still, there is a spiritual aspect that lies beyond men's or women's power to destroy.

The wife had no idea of the plan in my head, but she saw an unusual pattern emerge on Tuesday evening. First, the frequent picking up of the Bible to read passages, then as the night rolled in and bedtime was approaching, Euphemia asked, "What has drawn you to God's words? You seem restless. Again, you picked up the Bible". "I want to know what the Bible says about right and wrong and avoid doing the things that displease God," I said. So, I settled down and read the whole of Psalms and Proverbs for wisdom and saw how David cried out when he was faced with his enemies, and he, a good, righteous man, looked for deliverance.

I needed strength and protection. I felt I had to do something terrible to my neighbour to get some justice. I am a good man who always tries to do what is right, and I came across Psalm 92: v7-13 - 'For surely your enemies, o Lord, surely your enemies will perish.' The Psalms expressed humanity's heart and soul, and I felt the whole range of human experiences shown there. The psalmists had risen from the depths of despair, and it was comforting to hear them sharing honest feelings with their God. They asked God for help in times of trouble and praised and worshipped Him. I could associate with them, for it touches my true feelings, reflecting a dynamic, powerful and life-changing experience to discover the power of God's everlasting love and forgiveness. Will God forgive me if I carry out sabotage? I have asked God to forgive me before carrying out the show of destruction. I confessed a sin that I had not committed yet, for I had the intention to carry out the act. A little voice in my head wanted me to turn from it, but I said we would not see justice unless I tried to do something to damage my neighbour's property.

I felt physically broken, worn out by my neighbour's persistent aggression. His wife had alleged that I had assaulted her, and the police had been investigating it since July 2000. I received a letter from them last week saying that no further action would be taken. It was blatantly untrue about the assault. As far as I can remember,

I shouted at her not to swear at my children or prevent them from playing on the driveway, and she made up a story that wasted police time, but she was not charged or cautioned.

On the morning of the 25th October 2000, I left the house for work, and the neighbour's wheelie bin was behind our car. I did what I always did, relocating their wheelie bin to the top of the driveway—that time without the anger in my heart, just a calm inner self. As my plan began to unfold, I protected my identity by wearing gloves when moving the bin, but then came a rush of anger, which quickly drained. I rushed back home at 8:10 am, expecting their wheelie bin to have moved and been positioned carelessly on our driveway again. I changed out of trainers and put on an old pair of shoes, just yards from the turning to the driveway. As I glimpsed, I walked closer and saw that the wheelie bin had not been moved from where I placed it. I sighed and was generally pleased. I sighed again when I got into the house, but it changed to a disappointing feeling. The thought remained a wrestle in my head amid my clear conscience.

My mind said I should carry out what I planned. It was unfortunate, bad luck, that the terrible morning storm that had brewed kept the neighbour from moving the bin back to obstruct me. A bit of me still wanted to vandalise, but I froze close to the patio door, still holding the kitchen knife to make some mischief to the problem vine on our fence. I stared through the light mistiness on the inside pane of the double-glazed door with the keys in my hand, looking out at the problem vine as the rain was beating down and the droplets on the pane accumulated and dashed down the glass door. "Cut the vine and pull up his plants and fell the tree," I devilishly said to myself, but my usual low voice was silent in my head; something different brewed in my thought's seconds later. "Conditions are not right; it's too muddy, and it would be easy to trace who did it because of the bad weather; footprints and other visible evidence would be retained."

I walked out of the house, stood under the canopy for a while, and stared at the problem. As the wind gusted and the rain beat down on the tarmac driveway and flooded the drains, the rainwater soon overflowed the drains and poured like mini streams to the bank. Splatter, splatter, the rain pounded; the tree and shrubs swayed violently in the wind, and the grassed areas were so saturated that a film of water layer above the shoots.

The rain eased, and I ran carefully to the car and drove back to work, losing only thirty minutes of the working day. My behaviour towards my neighbour's property showed that there is the capacity for both good and evil within each of us, and because we have a conscience, we can choose between the two. I also respect the fact that one cannot set out to beat nature.

I say that things will work out; though nothing happened that day, a mighty force on our side is hope. I hope that things will work out. The confidence gets built into a faith that does not carry trappings or doctrines surrounding religion for intuitional expression. The heart of my faith has to do with a pilgrimage to discover the truth about God and myself. That is not always a smooth experience. If I do not, I have to believe that I would be unable to have faith in any aspect of our lives, and no religion would help. Then there is a charity with different levels, and I do not mean writing a cheque. Kindness, loving and giving is the kind of charity I am speaking about that. I concentrate on the here and now, rendering thoughts of eternity irrelevant, for I must get through this tough earthly life first, and when I am dying, I may again see the profound mystery as real as life on earth. For now, I left it out of the equation, for I am not looking to go anywhere. I am neither looking for an eternal home nor a move away from the neighbour from hell.

I want to win his soul, for I feel that there is a profound mystery at the heart of every person and the universe's centre. It cannot be rationally explained by science or expressed in satisfactory terms by religion. Nevertheless, at least religion points to this mystery. With each discovery in the secret of peoples' makeup and the mysteries of our world and the universe, the extent of the unknown grows more substantial, not smaller.

I think I am living but cannot live well as the neighbour is causing me to worry. My instinct tells me to get out of living near them, but I cannot take flight and move away before fighting to keep my property rights from such an aggressor. I am not a coward and ready to defend what is rightfully mine in a peaceful diplomatic way, but I may have to leave the territory if we cannot live in peace.

I had seen silhouette images of the vandalism I intended to carry out in the darkness of my mind, and it's only now I am free of them. Until recently, the evil thoughts have haunted me to try again. The dire, bad reviews of sabotage have left me. I have a limitless appetite to update you on the events of our lives. During the height of the dispute with the neighbour, the police contacted Victim Support, and I had a worthwhile hearty conversation with one of the staff at the local branch. It was comforting to see that the cops saw us as the victim. I understood that the neighbour did not get asked to see Victim Support or talked about the organization. Disturbances caused to us by the neighbour had not improved over the months. Their behaviour led the police to say that we would get dragged through the courts and summoned to keep the peace. Going down that road will achieve little but hit our pockets in fines and court costs. The police referred us for mediation in early August 2000, and the wife and I were delighted that the argument would get heard by someone independent. We would at least be in dialogue to resolve the disputes.

The neighbour was unwilling to go to mediation, but the police said they persisted, telling them this could bring an end to the strife before someone became seriously injured. Then they said they would cooperate. So, the mediator came to our home to hear our side of the story and borrowed my correspondence file that showed the evidence and facts of what the neighbour had done and read that the attempts to get legal advice and financial help to see we got justice had so far failed.

The insurance company turned down the claim because they calculated that the policy had not been held long enough to qualify. I disputed the calculation's inaccuracy in a letter to them, but no answer from them yet. Finally, two weeks ago, I telephoned the mediator, concerned that there had been no communication between us since the first meeting at our house in September. "When will we all be seated around a table to thrash out the dispute? They are still a nuisance," I asked her. "Your neighbour has not answered my letters to talk, and the police are investigating," she replied.

A week later, on the 7th November 2000, I sent a letter to the mediator telling her I had run out of patience waiting to see something develop from her intervention into the neighbour's quarrels with us. So I would continue with my defensive action and relocate their wheelie bin to the top of the driveway every time it was placed behind our car. I asked for my file back, and today, Monday the 13th of November 2000, I have still heard nothing. My financial adviser has secured life assurance for £100,000, which began on the 6th September 2000 for twenty-five years. It omitted critical illness because the combination of both would make the premium too expensive.

Our eldest daughter, Katrina, sat the learner drivers' theory test on her 18th birthday and passed. The concerns about our son's recurrent headaches of several months' duration gave us much anxiety. Still, after a brain scan, Jonathan's head showed no abnormality or feature suggestive of any raised pressure inside the brain cavity, according to the consultant paediatrician. That was good news; it is reassuring that he has no apparent cause for his recurrent headaches of a severe nature. The general hospital's orthopaedic department offered a bed to Jonathan to have an operation to remove a growth on his left tibia called excision of exocytosis. He has a pre-assessment before the surgery on Wednesday 15th of November 2000.

Georgina is being baptized by complete immersion in water. It is to take place, God willing, on the 26th of November 2000 at the Christian Centre church. It's the same church where Euphemia worships, and she also had an immersed baptism in 1998. The church has given us food from its pantry to help us when Euphemia is short of an entire month's wage. They advised her to use the service whenever she feels in need of food, and we strongly feel we would contribute to the service when we become able to. However, it is stressful that we are so close to outright begging that it is not very comfortable taking the product and trying not to let on that we can't feed ourselves. Moreover, relying on some food handouts makes me feel devastated and ashamed that I haven't sufficient money to feed my family.

In the past few months, the incidences had me thinking, is it only us, my family, who want to be honest, truthful and fair in the world and practice this goodness unselfishly? I feel alone in dealing with my neighbour, facing him and trying to change his attitude. Of course, I put into practice what is fair, what is rightfully proper to help bring about a better individual, but the perspectives of communities worldwide need to change. People should do their part when in a position to help and sacrifice self-interest for the good of all. It's not because of our religion that we should do it. I do not believe it; I do it because I love God and his laws that make my conscience sharp to his will.

My wife, who follows Christian teaching and I, had adapted our education with evolutionary psychology. Sometimes, we are torn between self-sacrificing charity to others, looking after our interests, and letting others be damned. All the knots of thought get smoothed out when I acted with a conscience. I kept resisting the hardening of my human behaviour for revenge, retaliation and vengeance as it is terrible, but it's natural. I must be selfish for survival, and I do want to do these ills. I have practised unselfish love for too long, and I am alerted if I contemplate doing wrong. I follow the impotence of learning and developing spiritual morals and social good that links me right to my gene of less sinfulness and selfishness. That may seem incredible, but it's alarming because if I continue teaching and showing my children unselfish love, we will not survive in this world of harsh realities. It is not surprising why they say the good die young and go to heaven. I am concentrating on the here and now, which renders thoughts of eternity irrelevant and having to bring up children knowing we cannot make the world change with our good deeds is sad, but I might help change one person.

It's beautifully clear that the product of evolution, the factual chronicle of my migration and our descendants, had reinvented themselves in genetic diversity. Humans being intelligent is natural, but being unselfish is impossible unless it is from God. I do not try to do right simply because of my thoughts of being a citizen in paradise for eternity. It is most important to act justly in this life because it is the only right thing to do and see that we have much in common with our fellow DNA-based life forms on this planet; we all exist out of this life the same way. The world cannot grasp the essential lesson of the centrality of sacrifice and the pursuit of truth above the individual's advantage. I am urged to make sacrifices for others' well-being or to secure justice in human relationships. Still, I continue because sacrificial living is the consequence of surrendering to God, which would otherwise bring me pleasure or advantage. My heart is so tuned to acknowledge sin, and sin decides that my life seems to lack comfort and security so that I might discover the will of the creator. It is not deliberate that I stand without anything to my name. No growth in getting money and material things get annexed to that of sacrificial living. God exists independently of our needs, and the universe was not created to fulfil them.

So far, I have included little of what has happened to us in the past few months. I will soon reflect on what has happened as accurately as possible, but first, you must have gathered that I have made up my religious system, and my wife is in correspondence with the institutional church. What is our faith? I would say my wife is a Christian, and I believe in God, but I would not go much further than that. I heard so much bigotry and unpleasantness preached from the pulpits and churchgoers behaving outside the teaching that to go to church is not essential, but pray I must.

We do not seem to be moving on. I thought faith should cater to my personal needs rather than reflecting on the nature of religious traditions. There is a certain restlessness about me that I must contribute to greater harmony in the world. From the rank of injustices, I have to experience the neighbour who needs tolerance to volunteer my service to the needy. Euphemia was encouraged by church people to pray harder, ask for prayer, discuss problems with trusted members and believe there will be change. It's frustrating to understand and keep faith when life is such a struggle. Still, for Euphemia, her obligations towards Jesus Christ should make our problems shrink because she'd systematically study religious ideas in the way I used to. That way did not work very well for me, and now I choose to accept ideas from various sources. From the Bible, I randomly picked up information through chance, thoughts in my head and pursue solutions like drawing perspective lines and targeting the vanishing point. Though I was prepared for blessedness, I hoped for better things in the same token of consequences, and I find God difficult to square because of what I have seen with a belief in a benevolent deity.

To the Devoted Reader
Written Monday, November 13th 2000

Few autobiographies count as important; fewer still count it like art what happens in peoples' lives.

I think I can write, and I assume that it may not be helpful because I have a literary reputation with spelling and grammar errors. Still, I hope the result will be readable as an engineer who wrote his memoirs with no writing experience. The unpredictability of change will happen to turn our misfortune around, which is much of the appeal. But, unfortunately, it taxes my patience, and it is a terrifying lottery for the most devoted reader of this book because what mostly happens is by the grace of God and chance.

I dished out my thoughts and actions without knowing whether the result would change what we desire in our lives. I often pray for good luck and written-in-blood sincerity. The phoniness of the passages will lead to sensationalism and adapting the work of good novelists of fiction. There is always frustration and an unforgettable anchor to some soundness of sense. This book is written with affection and self-love, making it pretty amiable, not wild and wacky.

The peripheral writing so far has taken me beyond my own experiences of what I think and do, and it has enlarged my sense of the complexity of life. It was not because of the pleasure in the art of writing that got me this far; it's because there is something to be said, just as science is defining what it is to be human, and humans could lose control of their world. Placed in the world, changed by new knowledge about our genes, brain chemistry about intelligence, animal, human, and artificial, I still seek to please God and be sinless. Science is killing off religion, and there will only be a few of us who have maintained our belief without religious bigotries so that our descendants might at least live in a world at peace with itself.

Bereavement

Written Monday, November 13th 2000

Alistair, the husband of my youngest sister, Joan, died aged thirty-nine in summer 2000. I sensed that he was still within reach by telephone call because I spoke to him for months, and the sense of extinction from this life was absolute and did not come to me immediately after he died.

At the wake, the reality that I will not see Alistair again in this life hit me like a ton of bricks. And the service at Kingdom Hall beforehand and the cremation were reminders that every living creature who has ever existed has to go in just the same way. He disappeared like a match going out. His death was sudden; although we knew he had kidney failure, I did not expect Alistair to die yet. I felt incredibly sorry for Joan for the sense of loss and the possible knowledge of the loss of identity. Joan has to establish a new way of being, which is the odd thing about grief.

Stop on the Syndicate playing.
Written on Tuesday, November 14th 2000

I found out that the two pounds I pay towards the lottery syndicate had to stop because the money was needed for housekeeping. So the little pleasure I had in playing the lottery in a coalition has now waned, and it's upsetting that we cannot be a part of a win if it happens.

Since paying towards our daughter's driving lessons, the first lesson was in March 2000, and the two pounds lottery money is needed to go back into the housekeeping. A superficial amount of two pounds means the difference between spending it on a loaf to feed us or putting it on a chance bet to win millions. I have to provide for ourselves over a chance bet that has not won us big money. I decided to stop playing many times, but I continued to tell myself just one more week - this is the last time. But it was not. I had wished harder and prayed earnestly that the win would come before I stopped for definite. I felt rage, and without a doubt, I wanted to stop after such a letdown in intensive prayer. The universe knew how difficult things are for us, and it did not allow us the chance to work to change these dire circumstances. I use to slightly tremble when I checked the lottery numbers twenty-four hours after they were aired. In those absent hours, my heart felt like it was being crushed with pounding beats. I was anxious, but I stayed in dialogue with God and believed that I'd be amongst those who won hundreds of pounds when I looked up the results. I played the same record to my niggling thoughts that I shall win one week, but the weeks passed and yet no win.

I knew I had to stop playing for two main reasons; first, it's harder and harder to find two pounds to give each week, and I was fed up with my tactics because nothing I did put me closer to a win. The draws on August 12th and 16th were my final syndicate games because I have not played since then. I had waited near the telephone on each occasion in case the team leader of the syndicate rang. Part of my strategy was not to immediately check the numbers when they were aired and feel the adrenaline rush stop. Instead, I spent the time near the telephone and watching the clock's hand tick past the time of the draw. It was as if my heartbeats were pushing up against my ribs as I stayed in dialogue with God. My prayer seems to reflect a conversation with myself because there were no divine interventions to the prayers, for I didn't win.

I made my last good luck prayers on the mid-week draw and became indifferent. It is now the end of an era, for since the lottery started in 1994, I have played in the syndicate and thrown away hundreds of pounds, and on Wednesday 16th August 2000, it was indeed the last time I played in the coalition.

Today is Tuesday, November 14th, 2000, and I have not looked back, but I flutter a pound occasionally on rollovers when it is lottery fever across the nation. The belief that I could win drives me to play one line a week, but drawing a pound from the housekeeping budget is challenging. When I squeezed out the pound other than when it's a rollover, I opted to buy a lucky dip instead of using my numbers. Computer selection, I profoundly believe, has the probability of better odds. As I approached the terminal to buy the ticket, I started a silent prayer, and when it was placed in my hand, I folded it away without a glance at the selected numbers as I continuously muttered to myself. When the results are aired on television and radio, I cannot be holding any winning combinations. The ticket is often left in my wallet for days, for I'll not bother to check the result until curiosity begins to eat at me. I take a casual approach until I feel deeply anxious to check the results out of sincere interest because I expect prayer and probability to have worked out.

When our outgoing expenses are more extensive month by month, I try to scrape a pound a week from wherever to play the lottery and speak with God through prayer to meet the expenses with lottery money and see our lives improve. It feels I am in conversation with myself; it is as if by magic we pass through a day, a week and then a month and survive them because nothing is ever left over to ease living on the edge. I cannot find the presence of God in communication, that spell of intervention in a way that will handle our debt-stricken lives. The reality is damaging my contact with God, and my material needs mean I am tireless in pursuit of money, money, and money.

I want to balance the scales and get a sprinkle of prosperity on the weights that got tipped on the side of deepened debts and poverty. Virtually, the sole purpose and end means of playing the lottery are vanity, security, and a second chance to manage money properly. There is no indulgence of pleasure for its own sake when I play the lottery and do not play regularly. A single pound is hard to come by. In desperation to get more money into the house budget, the pound disappears from bank overdraft credit.

I need a win, but I cannot win unless I continue to play. I have lost the compulsion to play the lottery week by week and no longer feel out of control and fear the worst if the big win eludes me. Before I could not break the circle of playing week by week, I almost reached severe withdrawal symptoms that nagged my mind to continue, and before the results of the draw were known, I had resorted to claiming the prize as mine through faith and dreams. I have displaced the truth of reality that chances are I have not won.

The purpose of organising my life is conveyed in religious and philosophical truths, even though I want to sustain and extend my material welfare. God, who has given me meaning despite the waywardness of things, made Life's quality eternal, and I prayed. Worship is all I can do in the pursuit of transcendence and thus a thoroughly materialist new order. I believe in an afterlife, although I have no clue what that will be. I am trying to live following the right way of God and awake in the afterlife in paradise. Many people in the western world have become atheists, and eternal life is provided by medicine rather than religious belief. Medicine postpones death. When mildly depressed, instead of looking at life's problems and sorting them, people look towards medication. Medication cannot postpone death forever, and the loss of hope could imagine that they could. The white race is becoming atheistic, and the few faithful fight to restore authentic belief.

Scientific discoveries and modern intellectual culture have de-mystified everything largely, but the de-mystification of reality is an enormous advantage. We no longer expect the world to be moved by hidden forces, and it's hard to see individual lives directed by a supernatural agent. By some, religion has come to be set as merely a human phenomenon invented by a race that lacked our capability today to account for the mechanics of existence, give social control, and secure their significance in the universal scheme of things. God was disclosed through his creation, through the very materiality of things. The world was not an illusion, and it was not directed by mysterious forces but by forces for which an explanation was not available at the time. The Universe expressed a great act of creative will, and God himself was not an arbitrary and unknowable force, an unknown first cause, but the one who operated through laws He had set up. It is those laws that disclose the nature of the creation but not its purpose. Discoveries about the establishment laws have, in some people, removed the need to believe in a creator God.

God invites people to probe the nature of reality and, in doing so, has begun to define both themselves and the very substance of this material environment. My inner voice is very much in tune with my destiny and intuition; call it instinct. So,

I have remorse for playing the syndicate all those years and not winning the big money prize, but lost money that could have helped buy small extras instead of going without things.

It has knocked sense into me, for I cannot dwell on it; I need to stop regretting the past but create the future. All dreams and all achievements have started with a thought and end with results. So, I can begin to visualise what I want to do, and I shall be taking practical steps to see it come true.

Falling into a Black Hole
Written on Saturday, November 18th 2000

The course of my financial story has been managed well for the last five months. I gradually emerged from a financial black hole by using our joint overdraft to settle annual bills and emergency expenditures. However, we live close to the bread line because an escalation in demand for extra cash has us falling back into the black hole from which I cannot see a way out. Suddenly, there are more mounting debts, and things are going so badly wrong because appliances are breaking down, and there are things that need immediate replacing that have strained the wages and the overdraft.

I have no means to prevent us from becoming impoverished. School music lesson fees, car MOT failure fee, car tax, the new iron and the family birthdays are this month's extra drain on the already stretched resources. Our son has been asthmatic, and Euphemia had to take four days off work without pay to look after him. The petrol cost is soaring because the truckers who deliver to petrol stations had the pumps run dry in September to force the Government to review the tax on petrol. The family car is expensive to run, and its maintenance bill for upkeep has reached beyond digging a hand in our pocket for petty cash. The vehicle has developed gearbox problems, and it's expensive to fix. We are an impoverished family because we cannot afford the day-to-day running of a necessary car and cannot make ends meet without dipping into overdrafts.

The overdrafts were our last means of emergency money that should not get used to their limit, but this crisis will inevitably push its use beyond the agreed deadline. I have a poor track record in managing credit cards and personal loans and cannot borrow again. Our little savings are tied up in investments that might prevent us from retiring in means-tested poverty. I do not want to borrow on credit or have a loan, but I want to earn a decent wage and gain the skills to control expenses better at an ever-increasing cost of living. I want a second chance in finance management, not to go back into borrowing though we are nearly on the breadline, for we struggle to get by on our joint stipend of just over £17500 a year.

I have applied for the new government benefits called Child Tax Credit and Working Family Tax Credit to have more income put back into my pocket from the Inland Revenue. I am hopeful that we will get it because our joint earnings are below the threshold. So far, I have received an acknowledgement letter that the application is being processed. People who work for God have launched a campaign for a pay rise to bring clergy in line with other professionals. The clergy need the state's worldly laws to get them employment rights and buy equity in the church houses they occupy. As the law stands, clergy do not count as employees and therefore have no pay rights. We had coped on our wages with great difficulty, and the clergy on their stipends reported the same sort of challenges, and they are finely in tune with God. There is hope for the rest of us when praying to God about money. The clergy needs state laws to be made so that equal pay and human rights are obeyed.

It seems like every problem in human life is solvable by the law, and we must believe that blessed are the poor is only for religious pacifists. I now have life insurance, and the family don't have to leave the family house if I die. We are only just managing to pay the mortgage, and Christmas is only five weeks away. The wife feels our pennilessness and refuses to glance around the shops with Christmas stocks or engage in watching shoppers with Christmas gifts without a moan.

The easiest and most productive way for my family to get money is for their father to get knocked down by a bus, but suicide is not an option. Life is already too short a span, and I see how the children and the wife love me, and I love them, but it's easy to imagine ending my life for financial security to have a future of prosperity that I cannot give as a living being. I do not want us to live in poverty, and as I cannot kill myself willfully, I am looking to have an accidental death. Love and loss go together, but it will be too devastating for them to be brought up without my fatherly love. I do not want to miss out on grandparenthood either or any of the new life that comes in retirement, but if God can give a hand in an accident that causes my death as the means of ending my family's financial hardship, I am prepared. His gift of my life was to be fruitful, but God can stop it promptly by his direct supernatural agencies. In all honesty, I do not want to die before my children grow up and live fruitful lives. We are a happy family, within ourselves too; even though our material environment needs improvement, we love one another and are glad but not contented. I see it on the children's faces and in the wife's eyes. Life together is more precious than the material things I cannot get.

The family's closeness brings the true meaning of living that sterling currency cannot buy, and that's love. I have a problem with our needs for the basics to feed the body, clothe it, and shelter ourselves. The thing is, God is not known to work magical effusions to help the flesh, and I need help to maintain all three so that I do not feel ashamed and less of a man for making us live on the bread line.

An active belief in God's direct intervention by mysterious presences has moved to the fringe because modern scientific discovery has de-mystified everything largely. Our lives could be an unfolding accumulation of evidence of His presence in working out the nature of things happening to us, good and bad. I actively seek writing to achieve a culture of understanding that glories in a God of authentic revelation, that the Universe itself is God's handiwork and expresses a great act of creative will.

I feel I must die, but if I tell anyone, they will talk me out of it and think I must be depressed and suffering from mental illness. I only want to help my family; I am stressed but not depressed. Though I would like to talk about how I may willfully die, it is not because of insanity. Death is a taboo subject in our age, just as sex was twenty years ago. I mention death because when I die, the family get financially rewarded. Perhaps the biggest challenge we will all ultimately have to face is not killing ourselves for money. That may have sounded ambitious, but I would eventually give my life up for love. Usually, I would hope to live to an old age knowing death can, of course, happen at any time. I cannot predict when my end will happen, but I can begin to prepare myself. On an emotional level, I remind myself not to harbour any anger, guilt, resentments and jealousy, and a Will should be written on a purely practical level. I guessed I would be even more unlucky than I am today for it to happen, and it will save all from guilt and blame because death will appear accidental or by natural causes. Either way, God has intervened, and if I live, God is also responsible.

There is no depression creeping up on me making me say those things, and this is not merely being morbid, but at its simplest, I am stating the most basic fact of living, that of death. I have an enthusiasm for living with a twinkle in my eye. But I am thinking of my death as the way to financial well-being for the family. So I am analyzing the fears and consciously attempting to remove them to walk coolly into death without panic. I can imagine being alive at one moment and, in a flash, gone, fully transferred into the afterlife.

The whole purpose in one's sense of living experiences and lessons is life's way of making us change. I owe thousands of pounds to creditors, and I will never, ever let it happen to me again when it's cleared. But, unfortunately, I cannot manage to wipe the slate, and I get more and more in unmanageable debts; that's why self-sacrifice would be necessary for insurance money to wipe out the debts.

Our House Is for Sale
Saturday, November 25th 2000

Nothing is holding us to remain in the neighbourhood that my heart has grown to dislike. The children have been successfully placed in schools in the town I want to move to, Kettering.

The neighbours' ongoing problems and parking difficulties in the close for visitors made me dislike where I live. The semi-detached house itself is still lovely. Most of the original occupiers, in the end, have moved out, and the whole dynamics of the place have changed. We are worried that we may not get a new mortgage or retain a mortgage with our existing lender because of poor loans and credit history, and we have a tie in a lease until July 2001. It's conceivable that we will need a bigger mortgage, and I have spoken to a mortgage consultant for advice. The maximum we can borrow on a mortgage is £55,000, which is the exact figure we owe our lender. House prices for semi-detached properties are well above this figure, leaving at least a further £15,000 to deposit on another house.

We are working on a zero return; property with a garage needs no refurnishing in good decorative order. The house was registered on 31/08/00 for sale with a corporate and general relocation property specialist whose advertisements are spread throughout the country but not the local town. They aim to introduce a buyer and agree to a sale in eight weeks. If it takes longer, I will not be charged commission upon completion. The registering fee was £95.00, and I valued our house at £75,950, which I suspect is the maximum the market could bear outside the local property pricing, even less inside the region.

I want to generate national interest in our property from people who want to relocate to Wellingborough. House prices have been stable in September, and modern semis like ours are fetching £60,000 to £69,995. We need as much equity out of the property as possible, and £69,995 would buy us a down-market property. We can barely make a sideways move to a similar modern semi without putting down all the equity as a deposit. The only affordable house is a terrace which will leave us with money in our pockets. I am not looking to buy a terraced house because it feels like I would be returning to the bottom end in housing, and it's not an improvement in living accommodation, but it shows failings to be housed again in a terrace with first-time buyers.

The house has been on the register for six months, and so far, there has not been any national interest. To get an accurate valuation of our home and sell it through an estate agent, I contacted a local estate agent who valued the house at £64,000 and said it's a realistic price to attract buyers. I disagreed with the valuator and told him that the minimum I would sell at is £69,995. He talked to his colleagues and telephoned me and said, "Houses of this type are getting offered at £61,000 in your area, and the best we can do is to offer your house for sale at £64,000". I could not accept their valuation because I think it's dramatically underpriced. The house is worth, in my opinion, £69,000 to £73,000 as prices have increased in the last months.

I searched for estate agents who can give a valuation I can accept. I needed the house to go on the housing market at that sort of price to buy another; any lower, and we would be priced out of affordable housing. It just seems sensible that the local market could bear the cost in the region of £73,000 because prices are steadily increasing month by month, which may price us out of the market if we do not act soon and put the house on at the maximum amount the market can bear.

On October 25th 2000, I contacted another estate agent after turning down the first estate agent. I immediately informed the valuator how much I expected for the sale of our house. He looked around the house and, without hesitation, priced the home at an asking price of £71,995 to test the market. I was delighted and signed the contract for them to be the sole agent for eight weeks. I told the evaluator that we have a problematic neighbour who we think is a racist and that we do not want to erect a 'for sale' board outside for him to know our business.

He returned to take the photographs of the house while the neighbour's car was off his drive, which indicated he was likely to be out. In the first week with the local agent, a black couple, mother and daughter, looked around the house and were interested in buying. They came a second time to make an offer to us, and I decided to mention the neighbour's difficulties. I thought it was fair to warn them that the neighbour does not get on with us, and they probably would not get harassed if it is only a personality clash. However, we learnt that the female sales negotiator broke the breach of trust by contacting my neighbour and asked him if there was a problem with us as neighbours and if there were any racial elements to it? It came to light only because I told her I would like to speak to the manager to discuss the moral dilemma should we tell prospective punters about the problematic neighbour. I was shocked that she answered that my neighbour said there's no racial problem between us, but our parking on his property is the problem. Later that day, I went to the manager's office and discussed his employee's breach of trust, but the complaint must be written.

On the same evening, I wrote that we were distressed by the negotiator's action who told our neighbour our business and would like an apology. Another sales negotiator showed a prospective buyer the house on Thursday, and as soon as they left at 6:55 pm, the telephone rang. The person responsible for unprofessional conduct apologized, but I told her I required it in writing. At the weekend I received a letter with a written apology.

I was stunned by the attitude of colleagues, friends and the church, and relatives too, who I told the story. All except that of an atheist man. He saw how difficult it would be to square it with our conscience if we sell without warning potential black families of possible problems. We do not want another family to go through what we are going through with the neighbour. We interpreted his behaviour as racism, but we would rather like an ethnic minority to buy the house if they choose to think it would not be a problem. We stand alone in allowing informed choice for the buyer, an immediate risk that may stop a sale going through, which has happened with our first black family who wanted to buy. The messages I was getting from all my peers and community people were, "Don't tell anybody anything; you want to get out of that place, so black, white, Chinese, do not say a thing to them so that the house sells without hitches". The wife saw we lost a buyer because of our keen consciousness, but we can feel good about ourselves where others see it as stupid.

We have worked out another strategy that still allows us to mention that the neighbour and I aren't getting along, and we keep ourselves to ourselves, having nothing to do with him. So far, five sets of people have viewed the house as their possible home, and we are expecting another tomorrow, Sunday 26/11/00, that will make the sixth. The market continues to bloom in the best housing areas where we would like to live in Kettering, and we are getting priced out of affordable housing. My affordability for the right quality house gets reduced because of monetary considerations. I am on the mailing list of estate agents in Kettering for details of homes that come on the market. Nowhere in Kettering could I find a brand-new, four-bedroom or suitable three-bedroom semi-detached property under £69,995. To get less than the asking price for our home will put us in a challenging position requiring me to negotiate skillfully on stuff that interests us. Each week, the local newspapers' property pages show the whole market, and we view the ones that look suitable.

To date, 25/11/00, there has not been a house we have seen in our price range. We comfortably viewed properties as if nasty surprises await us, like structural repairs and significant renovations, which will get noticed when a survey is carried out. We are frightened of having a house with nightmare defects that will blow our tiny budget.

The Neighbour from Hell
Has Raised Trouble Again
Sunday, November 26th 2000

On Tuesday, November 21st 2000, the neighbour caused trouble again. At 10:15 pm, I called the local police station from my mobile phone and asked them to intervene, and they replied it would take a while for an officer to come because they were busy, but they would respond as soon as possible

The situation got worse, and I felt I could not contain the explosive bad feelings I have for my neighbour and asked again for help from the police. At 11 pm, my wife phoned the police station from the landline. They told her they were busy with two emergencies and would not be able to come. The situation had gone on long enough, and my patience began to run out, and someone was likely to get hurt if the problems do not get defused by authority or by third party involvement. The cold night air was heated by fury because my nostrils exhaled gushes of hot wind in a steady burst until they increased to a forceful blast that could not be regulated until I cooled myself down with deep breaths.

It had just passed midnight when I rang 9 9 9, the emergency services and asked for the police and explained the problem. It was classified as non-emergency, so I should again contact the local police station. I again called the local station very obediently, for I was worried about my safety. Although I intended to use force to make the neighbour conform, I did not know what else to do. It upset me before I hung up on the call, and I became furious with the police because they said they would not come out until it was an emergency; they can only deal with emergencies. The police are waiting for serious injuries or death before taking action, and I shall respond now with brute force to my neighbour's aggression and fight as he retaliates to the response I have received from tit for tat. I may get hospitalised if I attempt to bring peace and reconcile later to our lives, but the action is not cowardly but courageous because I know I may get hurt by simply walking away. He might collar me.

That is the story of my neighbour, who again placed his wheelie bin in the location that would cause me the most inconvenience, and I reacted, producing the highest explosive situation so far between us. I left the house and walked towards the car and immediately noticed the wheelie bin behind the car's nearside rear braking light, and before I could move the car, I would have to move the container first, and it's so annoying. Our other neighbour has a vehicle standing in front of their closed garage door, and our car is next to it, making it doubly challenging to reverse. So, I moved the wheelie bin to the top of the driveway, clear the drive and placed it on the path. I was furious because it seems he is doing this just for the hell of it, but I will not put up with this anymore.

I drove to collect Euphemia from a house group meeting, and when I got back at 10:15 pm, the wheelie bin was on the tarmac, directly blocking the approach to my garage space. I drove halfway down the drive and pulled up just short of next door's access to his garage, and Euphemia got out of the car and went into our house. I remained in the vehicle. Twice, next door's wife deposits household waste in the wheelie bin, which stood where I should have access to park my car, and she was aware I was waiting in the car both times, which followed in quick concession, 11:05 pm and 11:08 pm. Within a couple of minutes, the husband appeared with a rubbish bag and placed it in the wheelie bin. Their front bedroom light was on, and from time to time, peeps came from behind their curtains. It's annoying the hell out of me. Since arriving at the car, the engine has been switched off. The vehicle is stood in the middle of the shared driveway anchored under the number four house window. Our house number is eight, semi-detached with clear boundary ownership to respect and its number six neighbour causing us grief by not adhering to them.

12:10 am: I got out of the cold car and stormed down the drive with the momentum of the chilly busty wind propelling me sharply into the wheelie bin, which I got hold of and heaved over the neighbour's front low garden-level wooden fence. Most of the contents in the container were emptied into the garden. I tried to snap the tree trunk with my foot by pushing and stamping hard on it, but it did not snap off. I wanted to make it lean more to his property than ours.

I was satisfied with the result and went back to the car, locked the doors and phoned Euphemia from the mobile phone. The man next door opened his front door dressed in his dressing gown, saw the overturned wheelie bin with its contents on his garden and looked in my direction, finger-pointing in vigorous hand movements that could cut like a razor. His stare was sharp and penetrative; if facial expressions could kill, I would have been dead. And though the lighting on the drive was by house lanterns, I saw a neo-Nazi type racist thug who has hatred on his face. I have never come across body language that expressed so much anger and hate before.

I was some distance away from the house, and my mind filled in the blank empty face that was obscured, and I believed I saw a look that could kill, and his terrible language made it sound like war had broken out. "You will not get away with it; you'll see," he spoke. It was the only part of his speech without swearing, and he disappeared back into his house. However, it was not long before he appeared again and used his side door to get to his car, which he reversed across the drive.

"I have called the police; you will get locked up."

Just then, the mixed-race female neighbour in house number ten came out of her house with a man I saw earlier collecting things out of her car at about 10:45 pm. They walked through the back way of their home. They went down the garden path to the gate which opens onto the forecourt. I came out of the car and approached them, and talked to them. Euphemia appeared out of our house and joined the conversation, then both women separated slightly from us and chatted amongst themselves. I asked him if he saw the obstruction of the wheelie bin on the driveway?

Now my neighbour's car was parked across the whole of my drive blocking my access. We then observed my neighbour moving his vehicle back to his forecourt space, and my space became vacant. The woman from number 10 suggested that the tension between us and next door might ease if she drove our car onto the area, rightfully our property. Euphemia and I agreed and gave her the key. She moved our vehicle to in the space, and the husband and wife badly abused the woman verbally, swearing, name-calling, and gesturing prostitution and goings-on at her house. The husband then said the police had told him about the dangers of living near blacks because there is a purge on with incidents with black people, and they have to be careful. Euphemia and I were an arm's length away from the woman from number 10 as our neighbour quarrelled with her and the husband came in physical contact. It appeared our neighbour had blown cigarette smoke in the woman's face and flicked cigarette ash on her; they held onto each other and struggled like in martial art combat. Finally, the male friend rushed across and pulled his girlfriend away and stepped between them. As the neighbour retreated with backwards steps to their house, his wife also remained with argumentative bad verbal diarrhoea. We walked towards our home, and the woman and her partner walked back to their home, and the only decent words our neighbour said were that the police were coming to lock us up. All the rest was foul language.

It was almost 2 am when we got to bed. Although my eyelids felt heavy, I could not sleep, as they never closed completely, and I lost consciousness. Euphemia caught a glimpse of sleep, but it was not enough because it was hard to get out of bed by dawn to get ready for work. At work, Euphemia felt sleepy but just managed to complete the working day and came home shattered. She said she could not cope with it all; her head felt peculiar and severe headaches had developed, and she felt out of control of her life. My head was clear, with no trouble, but my body was not acting normal. The left side of my chest twitched, and a constant steady pressure pain had developed there.

Working for both of us under this immense stress is damaging our health. I lack concentration at work, especially when using digital readout data on machine monitors. Errors could take the workpiece outside the tolerance limits, and the job may be scrapped, which is a worry.

Today, 26/11/00, I feel fine, but I am worried that it might flare this week again when the wheelie bins are to be emptied by the council. My wife still feels peculiar, as if her life is in limbo, and she has no clear idea of how to ease that distressing feeling. Yesterday, Euphemia went shopping with the children and said she felt blankness, numbness, tensed and frightened, a need to let out screams as if out of control. Euphemia was in a daze in the shopping mall and picked up more than one item that she needed. Euphemia could not remember how the extra things ended up in the shopping basket, and at the checkout, her mind was in a spin. The crowds in the shops seemed to spark a need to rush out screaming, but Euphemia cried when she got home.

I telephoned the insurance company and asked that they re-examine my claim because the area of land that is being disputed is ours. The problem is just getting worse with the neighbour's false delusions that it's part of his property. "Look at the claim again," I told them. They told me to return the file to them and clarify in writing the problem, which I did yesterday and sent by recorded delivery first class post.

Testing Time
Saturday, February 17th 2001

A sense of expectation, excitement and enthusiasm filled the year 2000. However, there were many failures in the country and on a personal level. There was some success in some sports for Britain in the Olympics in that year. However, the millennium dome closed its doors in December 2000 despite millions of pounds being fed into the project. The Millennium Bridge across the Thames remained closed, too, as it is unstable and needs modifications to its design. There was social chaos as the Hatfield crash and flooding affected the railway systems in many parts of the country. The rain fell persistently heavily, and the National Health Service is fraught with problems. The year 2000 was challenging for the Government and us; it's now part of history.

We have entered into the year 2001 feeling uncomfortable because subtle happenings affect our sense of security. There is also insecurity in world news bulletins on the international scene, but I am most worried about my feelings of helplessness over global destruction. El Salvador had earthquakes that killed eight hundred people and left around 750,000 without shelter, and a month and a day later, on February 13th, a quake hit again, killing 283 people, and more than 167,000 are homeless.

As I write, the radio news is broadcasting that a third earthquake has hit El Salvador tonight. The shock has shaken our society which is accustomed to violence, both factual and fictional. It has seen two tragedies with the death of Damilola Taylor and little Sarah Payne murdered. Gujarat, the second most industrialized state in India, was devastated when an earthquake hit on Friday, January 25th 2001 and measured 7.7 on the Richter scale. Today's death total was 18,000 confirmed dead, and the suspected number killed ranged from around 30,000 to 100,000. The exact figure may never be known because of the number of bodies buried under rubble. People are reporting deaths of relatives retrieved from ruins of collapsed buildings every day that passes.

Perhaps nature deeply resents the abuse received at human hands in the 20th century, which is still happening; maybe that's why there have been many more terrible natural disasters. I have subjective feelings of insecurity, so the analysis may overestimate our time's anxieties, but not what makes us anxious in our living.

It's the second month of the New Year, February 17th, and it's not an easy time for us because we have ever-present worries about the mischief of my neighbour that has disrupted our lives. Its testing time undermines inner security that involves risks in selling the house, finding another suitable property, and sorting out the children's schooling, career, and employment; all these challenges will be a leap of faith to change our lives.

Our son, Jonathan, has missed most of the term's teaching because of hospital treatment and days off for feeling ill. Georgina is getting ready for GCSEs with projects and a test-taking place, and Katrina is sitting 'A' level exams next month. She is aiming for grades that can get her into university to study sociology at Manchester Metropolitan University. Katrina did not gain entry on the media course but wants to find employment on television or radio behind the scenes. Katrina works a few hours a week and part of the weekend at a retail store called Matalan and Christian Nursery. Katrina helps us support her by earning money for fashion and social life with friends outside the family circle.

Euphemia left the machinist job, which has poor working conditions on Friday 9th February 2001. Euphemia's stories about the factory sound like the workplace were in a third world country, not the first world modern Britain. The firm failed to provide adequate heating in winter and ventilation in summer. The workstation had cheap, shoddy chairs that caused back pain, and there was inadequate lighting around the sewing machine. In addition, an automatic aerosol system sprayed scents that masked the smell of rising damp, making Euphemia feel sick and bringing on headaches.

On Monday 12th February 2001, Euphemia started a new job at the Christian Nursery as a nursery assistant, where Katrina works three hours a week. Euphemia has told me that she has wanted to work with young children and move out of textiles for some time now. She has become more certain since she worked with children in the Church Sunday School and crèche. However, I have persistently told her to wait because the wage is inadequate in care work, but it was not so much of a fall from her machinist wage when I did some calculations. So, I began to encourage her to take this opportunity to move out of machining textiles and apply for the current vacancy at the church for a full-time nursery assistant. Euphemia has a three-month trial and gets paid monthly by cheque. I have never seen her happier in her full-time job, but she realized this is a period of uncertainty because we are in a deep crisis.

We are in crisis because we cannot find a buyer for our house. Fifteen people have passed through our doors, and they have not made an offer. We are in crisis because we cannot find an affordable family house, and we are in trouble because we have to manage for a month without the wife's wage. So I asked myself what will happen to us, our world and the earth; those are worrying things. I hailed the New Year as being the chance of a new beginning and expectation, for I have long waited to rejoice in the opportunities we have prayed to have. But, unfortunately, the pressures seem to be increasing, and I need to experience deep-rooted confidence more than in the theory of things and say, "I know whom I have believed".

The year has already tested the inner resources, which makes crisis also an opportunity. God usually comes in our hour of need, and security means safety, and we are yet to feel safe now that our world has been turned upside-down with the hope to move and live in a new community. We do not know how we will be accepted; I began to see the realness in my concerns, for they can become a reality if I cannot get out of the crisis. I hope we get the house sold, find affordable housing, and get a new car. I hope, too, the solicitor from the insurance company gives the go-ahead to fight the neighbour with legal documentation that states ownership of the land and wins the argument. Other hopes are that our children are unbeaten in their studies and employment and that we can find the money for school trips and fix failing worn-out household products. Finally, I hope to pay off all our debts and always do good in the world. I also hope for money. The final word on hope is that I hope for material blessings, and I have stuck my neck out to believe hope is at the heart of faith, and as I walk in faith, God will see me through whatever happens.

Will God see me through because I am living on a prayer, have faith, and believe in the hope that whatever happens in our lives are for the best, although we struggle in life? The Gujarat earthquake has caused me upset like the Venezuelan floods of 1999. It feels like there is nothing I could do to help. If I had money, I could give generously to the appeal fund. Where natural disasters bring death and suffering on an unimaginable scale, I get grief about faith. From my ascent from hell, I will testify to extraordinary grace when I have finished travelling through the awfulness of life. I want to witness our lot improved and the world growing safer. Still, there is precious little money in the house to feed ourselves, and there are more significant needs on the planet that I feel empathy for as a part of humanity, and I would be courageous for the family and the people of the world.

I have my last two pounds in silver and bronze coins and bought two National Lottery tickets from different independent retail shops to increase the chance of a win. I know that I cannot 'will' anything happen just by thinking about them, but I am always desperate to have more money. Things need more money, and I got forced to 'will' myself, like a burning desire, by thinking hard and uttering prayers. Unfortunately, household running costs drain my wages, and creditors are chasing me to increase instalments. It's a vicious circle, and we have been at the stage where we cannot meet outgoings for a long time. Outgoings exceed our income, and at this stage of financial trouble, debt is an emotional problem, a burden we carry.

On Saturday, February 10th, 2001, the day of the draw, each lottery ticket had three lucky numbers, and it netted a total of £20.00. I gave £8.00 to the appeal fund, and £12.00 was deposited towards a school trip. Jonathan raised money for school funds in a readathon, and Georgina was equally successful in a Polo Mint-sucking contest to raise funds. I yearn for the things of my thoughts to come true, but they are beginning to appear in dreams because I think day and night about the blueprint of what my heart desires.

The blueprint is made up of a collage of pictures and words of what I want from life. I do practical dreaming at night, and upon waking, I know something valuable and creative has happened, but I do not always remember them. I wake in chaos sometimes and daydream later and explore our life quality, living by choice instead of defaults. I find I am trying to reaffirm those thoughts over and over positively, and my visions I feel can turn my dreams into reality. I am trying to expand my horizons and keep an open mind while gathering as many relevant images in my mind's eye that express my innermost wishes and fondest dreams.

Something deep inside me told me that raising myself and my family out of poverty is a way of introducing myself and my family to prosperity. I do not know what it would be, but I shall grasp it with both hands when the opportunity comes. Nothing comes easy; I have to work for it and have to inspire to it. I think fate will intervene, perhaps not an almighty person but a mighty power that drives us through life, sending us in different directions. It's entirely out of my control, but I go with it and have to learn from it. It could be coincidences that happen, for it's the house key to the future. Even in simple mundane ways, accidents influence our lives, but coincidences are a random set of chance events that may seem strange, but it's a fluke in mathematical terms.

My dream crosses a random set of chance events that imply that hidden rules may work on the horizon of credibility. My subconscious is manipulated because choosing which of the many realities I experience seems to respond to physical reality. I suspect the laws that govern how truth comes about in the cosmos, and my subconsciousness is searching to find answers in the working of prayers. We hope that they eventually come true.

My dreams often influence my behaviour because I act out of ideas I can hardly remember too well. I have a psychotic illness that places my belief as paranoid rather than mere neurotics. Even a traditional faith in God is neurotic. I am a logical person and feel I have a code to live by, a set of values that obey and speak to God because God is everywhere, a solid, tangible thing translated into belief, if not a person. It hurts my head when I contemplate the afterlife. Not everyone will get restored, but I am optimistic about my prospects and those of the people I love. No one should be missing from heaven. Even the wicked can be redeemed, for humankind has come of age, and people are trusted as adults to make their own decisions. Adults choose to believe in God or not and believe heaven is a real place or not. I do not know what will happen in the afterlife; I know something will happen spiritually because of a higher force. I understand that there is only one secular world where God acts and communicates with people, and as I see life in the light of love, no one should miss out on being in heaven.

Under new Estate Agent
Wednesday, February 28th 2001

At the beginning of the New Year, I instructed the estate agents to erect a sale board at the front of the house. However, this month of February, I have severe doubts that the estate agent can find a serious buyer for our home. Seventeen people have passed through our house since contracting them to sell it, and none of the viewers was serious enough to make an offer. So, I wrote a letter to the estate agent explaining how I feel, and the contract is to be terminated on 27/02/01.

Today, 28/02/01, the house is under a new estate agent, and a board has been erected to attract passers-by. The home is advertised on the Rightmove property website and the local newspaper's property page. The solicitor acting on my behalf in our neighbour dispute has told us that bringing court proceedings against my neighbour could take up to a year and affect our house's saleability. I fought so long with the insurance company for a solicitor, and we will have to make him redundant because we cannot wait another year for the dispute to reach court. Since we do not intend to be at this address for another year, we decided to concentrate on selling the house and stopped the solicitor from taking any action. I want to see something positive happen when we move, which I hope may be before September 2001, the first twelve months of marketing. I contacted the police on March 9th and asked what had become of the mediation.

Disillusioned with God
Saturday, March 10th 2001

The story of my life is an enchanting account of ordinary dead experiences. However, I believe that there is someone out there who is specifically interested in my future.

Things are not going well personally, but I am out to get it right, and when I do, I want it to carry on like that. So, there is an adrenaline rush as I work at it, but there is a downside. I get disillusioned.

We need more money again for the day-to-day running of the home because many essential bills have become more expensive. Euphemia asked her bank for an increase in her overdraft on Saturday, February 24th, 2001, and they declined. She is already getting a maximum of £650; the bank allows the ratio to her earnings. Something is running through me like the lettering in seaside rock. I need to bleed it out or relieve the pressure of worries.

Staring at a pile of bills that there seems no hope of paying is a scary, frightening experience, but it need not be the end of the world. So I retained a degree of optimism that things would be all right. It will begin to get better because it's okay to believe that life is a mixture of good and bad fortune. It's a lottery. The universe is so immense; so much went into making it that I have to say to myself, it's metaphysics; someone or something did arrange this and made creatures.

God should be entering our affairs to fix them, but it is easier to understand that God has set the stars in the sky and more complex to see him acting in human cases. Religion is in my genes, and I cannot abandon God, even though prayers are not answered. Thoughts on God are like a magnet, it just pulls you in, but its human agency defends us against gross negligence from honest mistakes and genuine accidents. I cannot blame the 'act of God' for wrongs or collisions for how the universe works.

I am uncannily predicting that our misfortune is about to change. I am pragmatic. I developed an understanding of cause and effect, and I am putting the ideas into play. The key is probabilities acting on ideas with faith and hope in the mix.

Tonight, and mid-week for one month, I will play three lucky dips on the lottery, which will cost £6.00 per week, in an attempt to make money. I get disillusioned with God, and I act in the scheme of things to engineer a miracle. Buying a lucky dip lottery ticket makes the chance of a win more probable. Still, God is mysteriously working in the big picture, and a lottery win is, anyway, a probability one day.

A lottery win's primary purpose is to let you live happily ever after debt and buy hope for the poor. The thing is, when God is present in events, 'the best is yet to be'. I remember that God is still creating, and the Holy Spirit is like the free blowing wind, active in the world. God's promises for tomorrow are yet to be, but I feel I shall have them today.

Since January 2001, I have been searching through the job market in the newspapers. I am interested in part-time evening or weekend work as an additional income. Years ago, the bitter experience of fatigue while doing a second job reminded me that I could not do any more than a day job. So, I thought of changing my career and doing something with higher pay. Working nights is where the money could be made because it's an attractive option with night allowance and bonuses, but this is not appropriate for me. It will cause havoc to me before I can adapt to the changes to the night hours. Economically we are broke, and my chance of a good motor car, a beautiful house and a life without debts is a dream until I can build economic power by earning more.

The total capital we need is more than we can work for, and with everything considered, what's left but to bang one's head against a brick wall or continue to pray, keep steadfast with faith and play the lottery? I hope to God that a miracle will halt the trend of declining standards in our lives. I cannot see any other way of helping some of these people worse off than ourselves and having a new beginning than to win the National Lottery.

I woke this morning still asking God that in one month of spending £6.00 a week on lottery tickets, the chance in millions should work in our favour. I have seen the lottery numbers for months now; my numbers were either side of the lucky dip numbers that the computer selected. I want to know the reality of this working out, so I hope to God for luck and bet on the chances. I fund the lottery out of the Working Family Tax Credit of £7.84 I get per week, and oh my God, I can imagine the probability of it acting out favourably for us. I heard the lottery terminal rolled out its selected numbers, but they did not look like good numbers as I looked at the ticket. I murmured to myself as I ticked off the sequence of numbers, "Oh, God in your mercy, hear my prayer", and handed over two pounds to the cashier.

I have not dared to listen or view the lottery result for tonight yet. I hope that when I write to you again, the good news of a massive lottery win will be the main topic of conversation.

Deluded
Friday, April 20th 2001

For five weeks, I had become a compulsive gambler in the hope of making a fortune.

I could not bet as I had intended after two weeks of paying £6.00 to the lottery because I was short of money and the usual stake for the next three weeks became £2.00 a week. However, I would not go without food and clothes to find the money to gamble or engage in illegal activities to see my theory work.

Betting is socially acceptable, and it has changed from a specialized activity for professionals since the National Lottery arrived. The only gambling I do is the lottery, and advertising has made me think that I have a good chance of winning the jackpot rather than the one in 14 million opportunities. It played upon my charitable instincts, giving me the feeling of altruism. I deluded myself into thinking I had won the jackpot or it's going to be me the next time.

I have been reduced to buying two tickets a week, but sometimes, when it's a rollover, a further two more cards are brought, and I get upset that I have lost, and I moan that I have not won again and again. I am a mug to this harmless flutter that can so quickly turn into hardcore gambling, but I do it in the hope of winning a fortune.

On Thursday, March 22nd 2001, I asked the bank for the maximum overdraft on the joint account. It was £800, and that's our new limit. We are over our necks and stiffening with the debts right under our noses, leading us to drown. I do not need to force-feed you the evidence because you, too, can see that we cannot keep living off the overdraft. The money will soon not be there to pay the mortgage, and then we'll be kicked around by people out to make money from our vulnerability. The mathematics are correct, and we cannot continue to live like this. No, nearly 65% of our earnings go to creditors and bills. I yearn for my death from this debt-ridden society so that the insurance money brings my family out of our debt, as my earnings could never be sufficient. Still, if an accidental death could get recorded, which attached no one to blame for my end, it can be believed that God has called me home and left my family with a financial blessing.

I have insecurities and doubts, but I have to make peace with myself and live on a very balanced level instead of thinking God should manufacture a time soon in my life when I get killed for the greater good. We are in a deep hole, and I am trying to climb out of it, but it is getting deeper; even though we moved on and are clinging to the sidewalls, the bottom has dropped further beneath us.

The house has attracted a buyer on April 9th 2001, bought subject to contract, at £71,000. It is likely to be a few weeks until the contract's exchange makes the sale legally binding. I am incredibly excited about this, but I am under stress with one thing and another and need to balance health and life quality. There is a cosmic chance that I may die early by being in the right place at the right time. Nobody is to get blamed, not even God this time. It's just a tragic accident that will eventually benefit my family in a way that they would not have if I lived.

I am making plans to end my life, so my voice and touch are messages of trust, compassion, patience, understanding and love, all conveyed every time I touch the children's faces and talk to them and the wife. I feel very fortunate to have a family, and I am passionate about you all, but life is harsh when who I am and what I bring to life are possibilities that are not entirely open to me. It will be time to exit so that money and whatever else money can buy is in the lives of my wife and children, which will come easier through the death of my flesh. They should have no more worries because money will pay for everything. It's the way of the world, the harsh reality of the world. Without money, we are weak and blighted. I want my family to get the full richness of material things and happiness, and I don't seem to bring those things to them. Though I think the children are happy with us, I cannot get complete satisfaction and contentment from their mother. I would rather die in the knowledge that money will be available to the family than walk out on my wife and kids, leaving them to cope on their own without sufficient cash and becoming an absent father who starts a new life elsewhere.

Spiritually, you know I am with you, always. Children, you accept a faith, but you will struggle to understand my physical extinction from the world as unselfish love. I played a big part in your growing up, and I know you all need my guidance, but we cannot have everything. My fatherly love and my love for your mother should never perish when I have gone. It was done so that you can have a better life, full of all that you want, except no father to share them. I am sorry that it has come to me giving up being, but it is my choice to bring a swift end to money problems so that you can all have a better life. Don't misuse the gifts with which my life has paved the way towards a better future for you; a holiday you never had, education fees and education requirements can be met. The four-bedroom house with a double garage in a good location will come true, and I am sure there will be enough left to buy a nice car. I am not forgetting to keep back money for saving for your future or when a slump comes in your economy. The most beneficial thing to come out of the death of a loved one is that we will all be free from debts and the misery of day-to-day expenses people take for granted. I want nothing more than to be a loving, loving father to my children, a friendly, alive husband, an existing friend and a loyal, loving companion to all, but a dead one can have its benefits that a living body cannot give. I will not be there for you, tragically, but you will get the material benefits I could never bring to you.

Sadly, 'life' is inescapably unfair, and I am sorry that you will be acquainted with grief that cannot be more painful than to hear of my death as children or as a young adult. It's right to cry, sharing the pain of grief when death has made tears flow from the overwhelming loss of your father and of a husband. It is not by taking my own life that your future vision changes; it is forbidden for me to commit suicide. I imagine accidental death as part of my fate, and this will come about only if no one were to get blamed for my fatality; even carelessness would not be in the equation. I take great care when I travel, and, in all tasks, I do a risk assessment to allow me to think of extending the boundary of my experience of adventure. In the meantime, I will play and laugh with you and do my daily fatherly, husbandly things while all the time my heart has tugs with the head to rethink and stop imagining the cosmos is working on my timely death.

Nobody would notice anything wrong or think I was depressed because I will continue to create the pleasant atmosphere we always enjoy, and my moods shall not waver. My conscience is clear, for I am convinced it's for the greater good, and my life will be taken when I least expect it, and as I think it through, it would not be depression that brought me to the brink, but the thought of a healthy mind, choosing self-sacrifice. I will be sacrificed to get what I want you to have, and I am prepared to pay that ultimate price, which is the price of my life, to wipe out debts so that you can have a decent living, not just an existence. I have to go by the will that's in the heavens, that controls cosmic forces. My death will turn your world upside down for a while.

Within the pain, somewhere lies the seed of giving thanks for the gift of my life, which I deliberately took away. The writing I leave behind is just a fragment of what I was and the range of horror globally, which is sometimes too much for me and my problems. I saw no point in refusing to face the worst. I am getting nowhere in living; it is a constant struggle to survive on the basics that we cannot be sure of tomorrow. Shelter, food and clothes will get provided.

I have not gone any further in life than baby managing ups and downs, but understating or softening things seems cowardly and dying for what I believe in is brave. Ethics will always fail to justice the human condition in an omnipotent force and life after secular death.

Easter has just passed and being a conscientious man, it is tough to accept the whole Christian story because it flies in the face of reason and scientific evidence. The Easter story of the physical resurrection of Christ from the dead flies in the face of everything we have said about the kind of society and the world we occupy. I believe that the dead will rise because only God can do it and carry the soul to a world where consciousness's survival goes after death. It means that there are scientific grounds for not dismissing the existence of ghosts, but I do not think they can come into this world's reality unless by chance. Spirits formed as ghosts' lives outside the space and time of this world cannot affect it, but the soul's energy radiates on leaving the body. I protest that the world is not as it ought to be, and I cannot change it, but collectively it's possible to change the world. The whole thrust of modern thought has been towards reducing the sphere of individual moral responsibility. I feel I should die on another account because I am a righteous man in an unrighteous time, and I am not really for this age. It is challenging to live in holiness when I am the only one practising the high godly principles. Dishonest, non-virtuous and aggressive bad neighbourhoods are widespread. Society will have to change so that I can live comfortably. I cannot be a part of evil-doing because I am hurting as the world's people become uncaring and wicked.

I hope God sees accidental death as the way to take me out of here because I am too sensitive for this age. I hope my children are immune and do not carry sensitivity or restraint, for it seems they will lose out on personal development and good fun. Life experiences are necessary for growth in confidence and wisdom, and all I have been doing in my life is to be a good example, living faithfully to God's will. But, unfortunately, I am not as accessibly free in my conscience as the world's people to indulge in worldly pleasures and risky projects.

I have been pushed over the edge, and it all boils down to economics and money. I cannot see a decent standard of living without the economics coming right, so I am expected to be 'called' in a short time. I have run out of patience. No matter how prepared I try to be, I am never ready for death at the frontier of my mind.

You may remember my philosophies and advice to pass on to your children when I am taken to the other side of the universe. Having your love and affection and the love of a wife is one of the greatest pleasures in my life, and I do not want this good feeling to end, to be honest, but I am just too sensitive for growth. I have not forgotten that my part within the family is irreplaceable, and as a man, only Dads do things that a dad can do. Politically incorrect, maybe, but I take the male role seriously in raising my family and protecting my wife and children. I am in an impoverished situation but do not want to hurt my children's self-esteem and confidence; it's undoubtedly a blow that will hurt my children, and they would be scared and in trouble for the rest of their lives.

Writing enables me to communicate more meaningful with the wife and family, and above all, myself. I like to re-establish my family, and I want money because of what I could do with it. Life is supposed to be full of opportunities to take, but one makes one's luck. I must succeed in my abilities and not trust wishful thinking. It's stifling that probably 65% of income get paid out in debts and other bills. Our house purchase is moving steadily in the solicitor's hands for completion, but we cannot obtain a mortgage at the present rate believed to be 7% from mainstream lenders. Joint income can only get us a mortgage of £47,000, and mainstream lenders will just lend us that £47,000 and lenders know a bigger loan may lead to a mortgage crisis if the debt cannot get repaid. So, we cannot find an affordable house, and we do not want to make ourselves homeless.

There was equity in our property of £20,000 when the existing mortgage and secure loan was paid off, but our unsecured loan amount is over £20,000. By almost clearing the debts, there is nothing left for a deposit on another house. Property of reasonable standard is on offer from £69,995, and the asking price of homes on poorly managed estates is almost as much as those not maintained in a good state of repair. We saw a house we rather liked at an asking price of £78,500. I talked to a mortgage consultant to advise me on options and what might be best in my situation. After speaking to him at length, he advised me to get a copy of my credit record files and not get a mortgage of more than £50,000 for we would be overstretched. In his professional opinion, depositing £10,000 and negotiating with my creditor to cancel the rest of the debt if I paid back £10,000, taken from the house sale and trying to buy a home under £60,000 is the best way forward. He also wanted me to determine if our endowment policy grants a loan on the terminal bonus and get the policy unassigned from the mortgage company interested in it so that it becomes ours solely. We would have raised money, but the idea was slightly flawed. Norwich

Union's policy can grant £4,155, but Standard Life refused to speak figures because bonuses are not guaranteed to make a surplus. Standard Life does not issue loans on terminal bonuses. At the start of our house hunting, we looked at properties with an asking price of £60,000 to £80,000. I realized houses priced under £60,000 are at the crap end for housing and in a down market. We are not looking for anything extravagant, just wanting to find a house similar to what we live in with the same upkeep in standards and a good location.

There are tragic foot and mouth disease outbreaks in the country, putting farmers' livelihoods at risk and causing chaos in the countryside. Current distress is causing a high suicide rate in the farming community. The trauma of witnessing the slaughter of flocks of sheep and lambs, together with cattle and pigs, pushes them over the edge, and it all boils down to economics and money. They cannot see a decent life as I, in the same way, cannot and see my death to bring the money to the family.

Thursday, April 26th 2001, I checked the midweek lottery tickets I bought from various retailers and won £75.00. I bought £7.00 worth of lottery tickets for the weekend and £4.00 for the next mid-week draw. Wishful thinking made me think that God had engineered the £75.00 lottery win and paved the way to the big one, but when I won nothing in the subsequent draws, I was angry and couldn't understand where God's involvement had gone. I am determining now never to buy more than two tickets a week and wait for cosmic evolution for the chance to win big. God, thank you very much, I would say when I have lots of money.

Money comes first and then its profits, and again, I thank God for the wealth. In this unfair world, one is either a predator or prey, and I do not want to end up as prey, so I have to become a predator. Not being prey makes me come out on top, and as I want to be 'good' in terms of winning, yet there is something else slightly more subtle that lies behind it. 'Good' also means being accepted, feeling confident, knowing how the landscape lies, not being beaten down by the forces of the world that will get me if I do not understand them. 'Good' also means feeling secure because you have won, and as good people, we are artists. I see the tough as having sold their soul to evil and having gone through the fire of damnation and come out wicked. Being an empathetic and vulnerable person, I have to persist in the face of difficulty. The long experience of uncertainty continues to boil inside me because things are not looking any better as we reach the end of April and enter into May.

Today is Friday, May 11th, 2001. We have to be firm believers in self-reliance because the most helpful and profound things in our lives are usually the most difficult. We can help and heal ourselves because, ultimately, our lives are our responsibility. The estate agent has told us we must vacate the house at the end of June. We have to move out of our home in under two months, and we feel panicky because we have not found a suitable house or a mortgage. We are certain the buyer for our house desperately wants the place, but the wife rethinks and says stay put, and we will live through the difficulty with the neighbour. We asked the acting neighbour's dispute solicitor to proceed in legal action; we have changed our minds again and want a court proceeding, no matter how long it will take. I have been working hard to persuade my wife that we have no future at Kennet Close, at this house and try to buy a home somewhere else in Wellingborough since Kettering housing is more expensive. She is not keen on upheaval and makes it dramatic, adventurous to move to a new town.

We do not have enough capital to move, and it looks like we will have to buy a down-market house in our home town after all. Moreover, disregarding the problems we already have with the neighbour, it would be impossible to cooperate with them if our semi needed repair and needed access to their land or property, such as fixing guttering, roofing, or drainage.

Moving and starting a new life somewhere else is a must. I want to make a completely fresh new start like a migrant, but my wife wants to stay in Wellingborough among familiar surroundings and people she knows. Euphemia views houses with our daughters. I never view the homes in Wellingborough because I am not interested in living in Wellingborough anymore. However, should they see one with characteristics, I would seriously consider staying in the town.

The wife and children could not find a house they were keenly interested in bidding on. On May 17th 2001, our house survey and valuation were carried out, and the sale of our home has advanced, but we cannot find an affordable, decent house to buy or an acceptable mortgage offer. The mortgages available to us were 9.45%, APR 11.1%, which was too expensive. We looked at mortgage after mortgage deal until May 24th; a mortgage illustration was prepared by a mortgage agent, giving a variable rate of 8.87% but fixed at 7.65%, a 1% discount, until June 2002. The mortgage can be 85% on the purchase price or valuation, whichever one is the lowest. We only have to deposit 15% of the assessment, and the lease can be any size.

Yesterday, 23rd May 2001, I received a letter from the neighbour's dispute solicitor asking for more information and a self-drawn map of the properties' plans to evaluate the problem further. My wife and I think the solicitor should travel to see the problem and not rely on plans and how good I can explain the issues in a letter.

However, we felt deprived of justice and ignored the solicitor's request because the house sale is now so advanced that we are waiting for our conveyance solicitor to confirm a moving date. When we know the actual moving out period, which we expect to identify within weeks, the solicitor will be told the house was sold, and unless the sale falls through, the request for the plan and more explanations will be shelved.

How Success came in buying a House
Written on Sunday the 3rd of June 2001

After having no success in finding a suitable house with big enough bedrooms in Kettering and my wife's attempt to search for a home in Wellingborough ended in frustration, we thought to look at village houses between Kettering and Wellingborough. Isham and Burton Latimer were the main villages that we thought might offer homes priced lower than the two towns. So on Sunday, 23rd of May, we viewed a detached house in Burton Latimer. We fell in love with the place because it was all that we were looking to buy. Spacious bedrooms, a modern detached with off-road parking and a garage. The asking price was £81,950, and I offered £80,000 to the acting estate agent on the May Day Bank Holiday Monday.

£15,000 needed to be deposited to buy the house, and the mortgage would be £66,000. The sale or surrender of one of the endowments is necessary to bring in minimum cash of £5,877 to make up the deposit shortfall, 15% of the purchase price. Tuesday 29th May, they accepted our offer, although the owner conveyed to the agent that although he wanted the minimum to be £81,000, he would take £80,000 because our house was not in a chain and was well advanced in its sale.

Wednesday evening of the 30th, I filled out the mortgage application with a cheque inside for the £175 valuation fee to post the following day. That evening, the agent telephoned and said the house owner had offered £81,000 to a friend and asked if we wanted to equal the offer. After a lengthy discussion between the wife and me, we thought carefully about the house, which is actually on leasehold land for one thousand years. We decided not to offer any more money as it was not a freehold which was a significant factor we had first overlooked. Instead, we looked at the property newspaper that came out that evening. We went through it with a fine-tooth comb, examining details, and eventually came across two houses in Kettering we were interested in viewing.

It turned out that the two properties were unsuitable, and we thought we would never find the house before the evacuation date. However, as the mortgage can be

£80,000, we asked an estate agent in Kettering to see the images and details of houses up to £85,000. Unfortunately, only one of the places on the system took our fancy at an asking price of £79,950.

Yesterday, Saturday the 2nd of June 2001, we viewed it. The house is an excellent sized three-bedroom 1900s-built semi-detached at Roundhill Road, Kettering. It is less than ten minutes' walk from the children's school, and it's the best 1930s semi we have seen in Kettering. It had some renovation works done to it to make it somewhat modern. It can be lived in as it stands, with only cosmetic work needed to make it to our complete liking. I asked the agent to negotiate with the owner our first offer of 79,000, up to our final bid of £79,500. I explained to him why it would be difficult to exceed the figures we saw as reasonable, but that we did not want to lose this house, so it was a possibility that we may, after all, go up to the asking price if a buyer is challenging the request. I contacted the agent, eager to know if the offer was accepted, but they could not reach the vendor yesterday or today.

Monday 4th June, the estate agent had contacted the vendor and confirmed that they agreed to the £79,000 purchase price subject to the contract. The property would become vacant in the week, and the owner would like completion within seven weeks or as soon as possible. I had to borrow the £175.00 survey fee from a new work colleague who had become a close, trusted friend named Gurpel Singh. I surrendered the endowment, and when I received the money, I paid him back and put £2,360.00 into another bank account towards Katrina's university annual room fee.

The children have seen the house and liked it, and things are beginning to fall into place gradually.

The Catastrophe on 9 11
Written on Sunday 16th September 2001

There has been a great thirst to write down the events in our lives as they happen, but I want to present the whole story at once, and I resist picking up the pen and writing in between stories. A global event has overshadowed my life events that I mentally retain to share with you. I have come to the table with a pen and paper to record thoughts and feelings on a catastrophe on Tuesday 11th September 2001, which overrides the personal events momentarily in our lives. I gave in to my sense of distress.

Terrorists launched a bloody and brutal assault on America. First, they hijacked four passenger airliners and crashed two Boeing 767s into New York's World Trade Centre's twin towers. Both buildings, 110 storeys high, collapsed into the busy streets, with the loss of thousands of lives, and New York's skyline changed forever. Minutes later, in Washington DC, a third hijacked aircraft, a Boeing 777, crashed into the Pentagon, the heart of American's military machine. Finally, a fourth plane, a Boeing 767 believed to be heading for Camp David's presidential retreat, crashed near Pittsburgh.

As the news came to me at 3 pm at the start of a coffee break at work, I had just had a few sips of coffee when colleagues began discussing it in their informal group in the canteen. They had heard it on their radio, and I overheard them. A few empty chairs separated me on either side of me, and one person was facing me on the opposite side of the table. When I feel like engaging in conversation, I talk or read the newspaper with close people around the table.

My immediate thoughts burst out of my mind as a loud voice, "Oh my God in your mercy!" I said as a response to the catastrophe. It was a complete horror that people could do something so brutal, and it's the stuff of fiction and nightmares. Hearing of the astonishing terrorist strikes sickened my stomach, and I felt an anxious feeling for humanity. I silently prayed for the injured, the victims and their families in the last few minutes left of a ten-minute break. I was not going to vomit, but my nerves were on end because the knowledge that terrorists can strike at the heart of the largest western democracy in the world was utterly horrendous. It's hard to imagine what organization or individual could carry out such an appalling attack. The radio broadcasted bulletins every 15 minutes throughout the day and night, and television screened live coverage of how things were to the minute and repeatedly replayed how the atrocity began.

I was transfixed by the awful images from New York, where the atrocity was meticulous in its coordination and horrifying effect in hitting the Trade Centre. America suffered the worst terrorist attack in history that day, and I became saturated with the news of barbarism which flowed through my emotions. I could not bear to watch or listen to frequent and constant updates anymore. My mind replays events seen on TV over and over again, and my imagination is remorseless. To this day, I only listen to two news updates a day and can only watch brief visual coverage in the evening on television. Radio provided the morning news bulletins and TV in the evening, and then I switch the channel. After the first two days of the atrocity, I avoided all regular news coverage because I was so saturated in grief that my everyday life would have been affected if I had not taken breaks from the news. It was a tragedy, and my thoughts are still with the people and families who have been devastated.

My children had never known anything like this in peacetime, and they told me how terrible it was. It was difficult for the whole family to take in the scale of the slaughter, and it's horrific to think there are groups of people out there who are so ruthless as to have no care for the sanctity of human life.

This disaster overshadowed telling you about my family affairs. I had in mind to write about the move to the house in Kettering, birthday celebrations and our daughter, Katrina, moving into student accommodation yesterday, 15th September 2001. She is in the Manchester Metropolitan Hall of Residence and will study Sociology and Cultural Studies at the Manchester Metropolitan University. I am still so horrified about the brutal assault on America that, though my personal life is happy, I empathized immensely with the people of America. My happiness is overshadowed by my feelings of sorrow for America's people when I celebrate moving house, my birthday and Katrina's success in gaining a university place.

Those tragic events happening to the American people result from human evil, but how can faith in a loving God be sustained in the light of these brutal assaults? I would have liked God to stop the heart of the terrorists who have killed, to date, 5,000 people and struck at the very heart of the free and democratic world. God can only share in our grief and stand alongside all who suffer; thus, a tragedy, and He grieves with the bereaved and injured. The impressive scale of 9/11(September

11) has a growing determination that evil shall not prevail and life will go on even though the terrorists dealt a heavy blow to the global economy. Those who perpetrated destruction in the horrific events in America, the suicide pilots, were all too clear about what they were doing.

As many as 90% of American people to date demanding vengeance and retribution because the clarity of vision has departed, perspective is disturbed, and rationality is endangered. In a world as battered as this, we need a clear vision, but I can imagine they feel a sense of divine abandonment. The American people need love and light combined with the clarity of vision and profound wisdom to take them forward. It is the essence of the faith to believe that in every human situation, God is present. Blind retaliation by the military force is what Americans want to see, but it risks escalating the conflict and provoking different reactions. How America responds will be a measure of western world democratic convictions and what they mean by justice. Mortality has felt uncomfortably close in the past five days, and with it came a heightened awareness of the preciousness of life and its fragility. The images of those jets gliding noiselessly into the World Trade Centre's twin towers with such relentless intent have etched themselves onto the collective consciousness of the entire world.

I am happy that I kissed my children good night and lingered over a bit of tenderness with them, and held them tight as usual. The world with such ingenious barbarity buckles the mind. Words flutter uselessly against the stark fact of such physical and emotional devastation; thousands of innocent dead, but the many others left living on in a state of acute sorrow. Of all these living victims, the most heart-wrenching is undoubtedly the young. Children lost a parent in last week's terrorist attacks on America, and for every one of those children, life will never be the same again. The shock of such a loss is almost impossible to imagine. Not only have they lost a person who was of fundamental importance in their lives, but the manner of their parent's death will rob them of much of the security on which happy lives depend. Innumerable other children will also have had their confidence in life severely shaken by the events, and its long-lasting effects on those children should not be underestimated. Maybe the young were too young to have lasting conscious memories of their own, but we should not lose sight of what each of these losses means to a living individual.

Reassuring the mildly troubled is one thing, but comforting the brutally bereaved is quite another. To have your life devastated for no particular reason other than that your mum or dad was in the wrong place at the wrong time is hard at any age and to ponder man's inhumanity to man is hard at any age too. The cruel twists of fate put some people in the way of falling buildings and kept others safe in distant traffic jams!!! I don't know. I struggled to translate the images from the television and the numbing effects of witnesses' reports of the indiscriminate slaughter of unsuspecting ordinary people in the attack. Indeed, surely there is no cause so high that it justifies the random killings of ordinary people. The organized attack on the United States and the Trade Centre and democracy must be called to account by the international community. Seldom in our lifetime can there have been, within two weeks, tragic events in the world that invaded my heart with such intensity that tears wanted to flow, and sickness cannot but try to erupt from my stomach.

The second awful atrocity was that frightened children from Belfast were abused and spat upon for walking along a Protestant street to go to a Catholic school, all because they were Catholic. There is nothing more awful than the suffering of a child, and my emotions were in a spin as their tearful faces imprinted on my memories. It's a crying shame that the community could inflict such damage on children, all in the name of so-called adherents to religions, Protestants and Catholics. They continued to bring pain and death to human beings and suffering, perhaps irretrievably, to children's physical and emotional health.

I begged God to keep the world in peace, but some horrible injustices are still being carried out in the name of peace. It's more prudent to act than to be passive, but all believers ought to unite their efforts to ensure that justice is carried out in the name of God and horrible injustices are avoided.

I dislike fanaticism and terrorism, slandering God's name, disfiguring the actual image, and taking God hostage for their human ambitions. The feeling of certainty of retaliation for America's attack creates uncertainty prevalent in a world under threat. The implications of such a development are beyond knowledge. There ought to be a blissful feeling to be alive every morning because much good has begun to shape our family life. Instead, with the present overwhelming sense of catastrophe, the world is desperate to retaliate. There is a profound unease and fear despite conscious attempts to overcome it, and a new day only reinforces it.

Autumn has started bringing its annual beauty. The evening sun lights up the changing leaves. Children return to school, and the routine activities go on as they must. The awful irony is that it does. This year, 2001, under a dark cloud, there is a sense of foreboding and apprehension over an unknown world future.

The Sale and Moving House

Written on 22nd of September 2001

The most stressful, worrying period in our family life was probably selling our house and buying another. The whole family felt the strain when it appeared that we were falling into significant problems with the exchange of contracts. What were we to do? We were given seven to eight weeks to move, but we had to plan for the likely event of not having anywhere to live, for the house was sold subject to contracts. We neither had a mortgage nor a home to move into at the time and had eight weeks to move. Anxiety crept in as days went by. When it ran into weeks, tension reached a level where I felt I would panic. Still, I anxiously learned about container storage facilities and asked my relatives for support to accommodate my family. My parents were willing to assist us with two spare rooms, and Aunt Lorna, whose health was feeble and worsening, was also ready to help with accommodation.

Our application for a mortgage was accepted by a specialist mortgage company, giving strict terms and conditions that our solicitor had to make sure we fulfilled. On 16th July 2001, we discussed the mortgage requirements with the solicitor and signed what I thought were contracts. He found our lender challenging to deal with but assured us that the hope for completion by the end of July was realistic and possible if he could get the seller's solicitor to act and release the relevant documents. Our solicitor made several telephone calls in our presence and confirmed the actual date for the exchange of contract would be Friday 27th July. We naively thought this would be the day to move out of the house and have it vacant, so I set the ball rolling by beginning to tell people we were driving out on the 27th of July. As the days came nearer and nearer to the 27th, we became concerned there had not been any correspondence from the solicitor. For some time, we assumed a letter to come before the 27th. I had re-directed our messages to take place from the 27th, booked the removal van, booked the council to remove the unwanted bulk objects and arranged for the telephone to be cut off at noon on the 27th.

On the morning of Thursday 26th, I read the gas and electricity meters. I continued to pack things in boxes while waiting for the morning post, eagerly anticipating news from the solicitor, but no letter was in the postbox. In the afternoon, I telephoned the solicitor's office, and the secretary answered my questions of concern. "I thought I was to vacate the property tomorrow?" I spoke. "You thought you were to vacate the property tomorrow? I do not know why you should vacate your house; you would not want to be made homeless. The buyer of your house is not expecting to move in on the 27th, and it's the exchange of contracts that are expected to take place," she said.

I raised my voice in anger as I explained the predicament we were now in, with everything in place for the move tomorrow. I asked to speak directly to our solicitor. "He will be available in the morning." I immediately hung up on her and vowed, off the phone, talking to myself loud enough to be overheard by eavesdropping snoopers, that I would be speaking to the solicitor in the first minute of office opening hours. The realization hit me sharp the moment I calmed down. We made a mistake in our understanding of what the solicitor had said. "Oh my God, how foolish; it's my fault".

The exchange of contracts does not indicate that the completion date is the same day or date when the contracts are exchanged. After negotiating contracts, time for completion is made when monies are electronically transferred, and the house transaction is complete. Then keys can be collected from the estate agent. I informed the removal firm that I may have to postpone moving on the 27th because we were under the impression that we must make the property vacant, and with less than 24 hours to go, it's clear that it was a misunderstanding. We stopped packing the remaining things, and the whole family looked at me very worriedly. Finally, the children's voices spoke out together, "What are we going to do, Daddy?" I told the wife that maybe our best option was not a U-turn and embarrassed ourselves by not moving when we had told almost the entire community we were moving. I could not face the people in our neighbourhood and telling them without feeling humiliated if we stay. As I aired my views to the wife, we agreed to put the house contents in storage and stay with my parents, and the two youngest children were to stay at Aunt Lorna's.

It has been some time since the house was sold subject to contract, and our buyer has been patient. If the storage firm has an empty container, we will call the removal firm to take the house contents into storage. The next day was the 27th. I got on the phone to the storage firm as soon as the office opened, and to my joy, they had an empty container I could hire. I then spoke to my solicitor and said we might have misunderstood him, but the house would be vacant today. The next call was to the removal firm, and I told him to put the things into Rusden's storage, six miles away. I asked him for a quote that included me shifting the stuff to keep the price low. The children were a week into their six-week summer holiday, and it was the first Friday in the factory's fortnight shut down for the summer holiday. Within an hour of calling the removal firm, he arrived. We managed before they came to box the remaining things and dismantled most of the bigger things that could not go into boxes. Loading the van quickly got me exhausted. I did not realize how physically demanding the task would be. It became too much for me, to and fro between the house and the truck and making two fully loaded trips to the container. He had misjudged the van's capacity to do the job from the range in his fleet. On the second trip, I was physically unable to load and unload the cage that the forklift raised level with the platform. I was also getting vertigo because I was unpacking into the container on the first floor from a height. My feet had buckled, my waist, back, shoulders, and neck ached, and I walked, stooped, barely able to put one foot in front of the other. The forklift driver took on the task I could no longer do and received a cash tip from me for generously helping out far beyond his duties as a forklift driver. He did some manual lifting and carried some things up a manoeuvrable staircase with a safety cage attached.

On Saturday 28th July, the estate agent for the seller of the house we want to buy contacted me and said, "The contract has not been exchanged. You should contact your solicitor because the requirements have not been met". We wondered what the problem could be with our new house all through the weekend; we went over the survey report from our mortgage lender, which showed no significant issues. I had told our solicitor of our temporary address and feared the worst when Monday's post did not include a letter from him. We speculated our buyer might have pulled out, even though he would have a hefty penalty fine for not exchanging. I was more concerned about our house not being sold than our proposed house deal falling through because our home's sale gives us equity and puts us in a better position to buy again, and we'll not be part of a chain. Finally, the news came to us from our estate agent that our house contract had not been exchanged either, but should take place on Wednesday 1st August. If the agreement does not get transferred next time, we will be doomed because it would be too embarrassing to return to the neighbour from hell. I was nervous and prayed to God to forbid we would have to return to the neighbourhood. I crossed my fingers as a gesture of good luck, as I discussed it with my mother.

On the exchange of contract day, 1/ 08 /01, I was tempted to find out the outcome before the close of that day's business, but I again crossed my fingers and waited for tomorrow even though I was worried. I telephoned the solicitor's the next day and asked the inevitable question, "Did the exchange of contracts take place yesterday?" "I do not know, but I'll find out for you". The phone was put on hold, and it became the most nerve-wracking wait for a phone call I had experienced. Blood rushed to my head as my heart raced. The receiver was pressed tight against my ear lobe as I concentrated hard to be ready to listen carefully to the secretary's reply. My chest rose high under my chin, and my shoulders began to climb even closer to my ears, and then came the answer, "......Yes, and the completion is to take effect on the 10th August when you must vacate the property." What a relief. Everybody began to relax, and the delight about the news was expressed with, "Thank you, thank you, thank you!" I placed the receiver on the hook and a thank you, thank you remained on my lips as I continued to delight in the news. Finally, a letter confirming the exchange and completion date arrived in the post on the weekend.

The estate agent contacted me that morning and told me my buyer wanted to enter the house the day before completion was due to measuring up for curtains. We thought it was an unusual request and wondered if it's because he may want to change his mind and use that as an excuse. A last-minute final look around to cast out doubts before completion! Since the contracts had been exchanged, the chance was slight that he might pull out, but it was a risk; we told ourselves and said yes, he could enter the house before completion. On the night of Thursday the 9th, a thought came to my mind that I might experience my worst nightmare if he had changed his mind, and, on the 10th, I was aware that I had not had a good night's sleep as I was still awake at dawn. So thoughts mingled on the possibility of the good and the unfortunate things that may result from this new day. Euphemia said, "Not to worry, and things will work out as planned; in God we trust". Such confidence, I thought, and I too earnestly wanted it to be so. She trusted in God, and I hoped to God.

Our house needed a certificate for the significant alterations of the living room and dining room into one communal area. The council inspector examined the structure, and on the 9th, it got given the all-clear. It was not until 3:40 pm on the 10th August 2001 that a call on my mobile phone from my solicitor told me that the transaction had taken place and the sale and purchase had been completed. If you could have seen my face and how delighted I was, you would have believed I had a sexual climax. A massive sense of relief just expressed itself like pleasure, and I was eager to tell everyone the happy news. I picked up the key from the estate agent, and Euphemia and I went to see our new house. We looked at the home up and down, from chimney pots to the step at street level, and as we entered the property, Euphemia gave a big sigh! – "Thank God for this," she said. I silently murmured amen to that and interrupted my inner prayer, thanking God when we arrived outside the property. Then I spoke from the bottom of my heart, "At last, at last, it's ours". We walked through every room in the house and thought there was a blessing upon us because we sensed we'd be happy and have peace in this house.

On the 13th of August, the day of my wife's birthday, we moved in. The same removal firm took the things from the storage containers and loaded two small vans. I watched like a supervisor on-site, and when they had finished, I paid the boss and gave him the extra cash for the additional person and dumping at a refuse site the items that looked unworthy to be brought into the new house as they were old and worn out. The wardrobes that had fallen apart and the double bed and mattress were dumped; we'd had them since our wedding day. My wife was first to meet the next-door neighbour from the other part of the semi-detached house. We found that we could hold a good conversation with them, not a feeble cold-shouldered 'morning' or 'hello', but the casual meeting over the garden fence was warm, friendly and showed genuine concern, and we shared in humour which had us bursting out in laughter. They are such good-spirited people that a bond of neighbourly love has already formed. Within a month of our move here, they told us about where they are going on holiday and left us a contact number in the event of any concerns about their house while they are away. The other neighbour I met at the front of the property immediately spoke to him about damp patches on our wall that seemed to come from the cracked porous concrete flashing, which requires leaded flashing replacement for the roof. The garage was built using our house's existing side elevation structure as a supporting wall. The neighbour was pleasant and cooperative in a way I did not expect because he seemed not to accept what appeared to be the obvious solution to the problem. Seal the porous lead flashing where the roof meets the wall. Instead, he said he would look into the possibility that something in the garage is causing the damp to be only noticeable in the middle of the wall and not at the top where the roof begins. We have now greeted many people in the neighbourhood, and they all seem warm and friendly.

Today is Sunday 23rd of September 2001, and we met with people in our road as we walked to the nearby convenience store, and in the shop from time to time, we have seen nothing less than friendliness in their faces and charming smiles. The move to this, our third house, had stressed me endlessly. I cannot remember having had so much anxiety about buying our first house and moving into the second house we bought years later. The purchase and move into our third house brought almost intolerable stressors to bear likened to bereavement.

My daughter goes to university, and the international affair causes me to worry

Thursday 11th of October 2001

I picked up my pen today to start writing about the historic event in our family's history. Katrina is the first child in Willett's family to gain a place at university. I begin to describe the overwhelming joy in my heart, and a worry of an international nature has me paused my pen, off the paper and in the air, dangling through my fingertips.

The radio news bulletin had just stopped the flow of my concentration when the information was announced that the United States had carried out its fourth night of bombing raids on Afghanistan. They had repaid Osama bin Laden's organization responsible for the suicide attacks against the World Trade Centre and the Pentagon on September 11th. Since Sunday, Britain unleashed sustained military strikes in Afghanistan, and most of the international community thinks the USA has the right to bomb Afghanistan. The Taliban regime became the first target in the war against global terrorism. The Allies' impressive firepower bombers pounded targets in Kabul and other Afghan cities for the fourth time. They think that Osama bin Laden's terror network, which got accused of killing 6,000 people in the U.S. a month ago to the day, will be destroyed, or it will strike again.

I do not think bombardments end terrorism, and it merely encourages it even more. Bombs cannot create conditions for justice and peace. Has the twentieth century not taught us anything? People's hearts turn evil in high poverty of spirit and hostility and hatred from the centre of humanmade ways for reconciliation and peace. When God is present in the middle of suffering and misery, a cult of evil thrives on human suffering. Inhumane attacks awaken the scourge of terrorism. People who carry out acts of this nature are instruments of iniquity who are not weakened by tears but feed on the worst kind of cruelty. When they die, either by the action, they carried out or eventually by the fate of all mortals of humanity, they are dead forever and in vain. They can never be part of the after-life, the regenerated spirit. My head prompted me to suddenly write my feelings on international affairs, which I have no control over. Now I am working on the new worries that affect us personally.

I have again begun to release the fillings of my heart's joy by writing about Katrina, reading Sociology and Cultural Studies at Manchester Metropolitan University, which made the whole family proud. The threat of terrorism is disrupting city life, and my number one concern is my daughter's wellbeing in a big city like Manchester. I continue to keep in touch with international affairs because it can signal major alerts to threats on British soil. Political protest, racial matters and religious violence in the city streets overseas can bring instability. Terrorism is like cancer on the human condition, and it can spread, but we must oppose it wherever it is. My innocent daughter is going about her everyday business living with the threat of extreme violence erupting in a major city. It's an ever-increasing danger for her. I prayed to God to look after her, protect her from every concealable danger, and bring her safely through trial and temptations to everlasting happiness. Katrina, a threshold, is looking to fulfil her ambitions and dreams in a world that seems to show the future vision as a catastrophe and at other times as bliss; I beg of you, God, to maintain the excellent views of the optimist in her. Continue to visualise the coming reality where good shall always win over evil and badness in a world without end. I continue to pray for peace in our time and a crimeless society that I may not come to see in our time.

Within a week of Katrina going to university, I had written to her. I said we missed her like crazy in the letter and wrote a fatherly talk about taking care of herself in this new environment. Katrina launched herself into the big outside world without a family to hold her hand like when she was an infant. It makes us proud to see her grown up and ready to let go. We hope we brought her up well because we nurtured her and allowed her to resort to the power within herself. As Katrina begins her journey as a young adult, I beg God's guidance to follow her and keep her safe. Katrina spent the last week before departing for university meeting with friends and family. The previous day at the nursery, happy tears filled her tear ducts and flowed down her cheeks. Her mum worked there too and got caught up in the emotions and shed tears as well. Katrina spent that entire week weeping while saying goodbye to her friends and burst out crying when it came to the day of departing from us, Mum, Dad, sister and brother. Sniffles from the nose came first, then were soon met with tears and hugs, and finally kisses summed up the final feelings of having to leave the people she loves and knows best.

Alternative arrangements had to be made quickly that week to get Katrina to Manchester because our car developed a faulty clutch at this vital time. A family friend used her car and Cousin Bernadette, a former student, showed her the Hall of Residence. Katrina did not find a life away from home easy; she returned home on the first weekend, and after the tricky feeling of insecurity passed, she found it a worthwhile goal to mix with the new students in residence. Homesickness became a thing of the past because she gained confidence as the weeks went by. Independence is a goal in itself now as her lectures and studies make the weeks seem to go by fast, but the weekends drag. As a threshold eighteen-year-old student, our relationship with Katrina makes all the difference in helping her deal with stress and loneliness. She telephones us regularly, and we phone her straight back to keep her cost down.

Katrina is in the threshold year. We acknowledge there will be times of unhappiness and financial problems. The trouble is that being grown-up means coping and getting on with things. It's difficult to admit being out of control with expenses because she does not necessarily burden us. I want her to know when problems arise or she 'messes up', it's not up to us to bail her out or fix everything, but to be supportive and forgiving. The somewhat frightening prospect of almost guaranteed debt is a significant cause of stress and anxiety as she thought she would be financed. Katrina had the experience of doing the family shopping and budgeting for the haves and not to have, but it is the first time she has had to pay bills, juggle student loans and an overdraft, with the temptation of what she would like and what she can afford. Katrina mentioned she bought a pair of shoes that may have caused a problem with her finances. She will receive £4,000 from the student loan company over the current academic year and must buy books out of it. The lessons are being learnt quickly as the costly expenses of life at university begin to unfold. Katrina wants to look for a job after Christmas despite the immediate feeling of isolation and financial bewilderment. The sympathetic tutors and we are telling her to resist going to parties. Managing money is likely to be as much a part of her undergraduate life as socializing, drinking, and of course, devotion to studies. I want her to experience all the good things that life has to offer, but the challenge is studying and finding love, stability, and learning to accept that there are things that innocent young women cannot possibly know about yet. I beg her to be careful, take precautions, love herself foremost and strive towards the goals that make her feel fulfilled and happy. It is a journey she has just started after leaving school and going straight into the adult world, bearing responsibility and seeking pleasure. Katrina has a boyfriend named Philip, who appears to be a promising young man, yet I think he is too old for her. Katrina wanted a sexual relationship with him, took a mature, responsible attitude, and asked to take the contraceptive pill. I saw my first offspring grow into an attractive woman and reliable adult in a brief period. For my first little girl is in courtship and fighting with the type of irresponsible boys out there, she might be tempted to surrender herself.

Katrina said goodbye to Philip forever because it became clear her moving on into higher education has made them incompatible, and their visions were not merging as one. They remain friends, and he remains in contact with us, but Katrina wants him not to be. The lecture room is full of females, and only three eligible bachelors are on her course. So it is, pretty much like the girls' school when in lectures, and her ideal mate will not be found in the lecture theatre.

The Yobos Attack
Written Monday 15th October 2001

Yobos and drunken thugs in our society are not just a small group of people who brawl among themselves and do not affect ordinary people. Their behaviour is a problem that affects others and can bother us. I rarely go near those crowds of people and try to keep clear of trouble. As parts of society increased in violence because of alcohol abuse, we got caught up in a brawl after a family night out. In the present age of science and rationality, I wondered why it could not answer why we fell into the hands of thugs. The old idea of fate, mysticism and superstition gave me a sort of explanation. We brushed with what's terrible in part of society, generated by coincidence; it's an unconscious pattern of what already exists in my picturing of society's breakdown. In other words, it was just a matter of time before I got personally involved in some violent act in the community because statistics say so. Maybe, after all, it was a science to have fallen into the hands of thugs because it predicts it.

On Saturday13, October 2001, we attended an elegant evening as part of Black History Week. My brother-in-law sang in the amateur soul band Mid Sensations at the venue and wonderfully entertained the crowd. A black poet read some of his poetry, and we all enjoyed the tastiness of Caribbean food, but we were craving to dance to my brother-in-law's appealing singing and group playing. Space was limited, so we had to sit and listen. Our children, Jonathan and Georgina, were in the car, with the wife in the front passenger's seat as we were going home. I was driving up to a road junction, a drunken young man, probably in his late twenties, was in the middle of the road and on the left-hand side of the roadside at the edge of a small car park was a woman and two drunken men. The woman was yelling and screaming. It appeared to be an argument to do with their drunkenness. The man's feet in the road were firmly anchored to the ground, and his upper body was swaying. It appeared he would not move out of the road and was more likely to fall over. I lightly pressed the car horn once as I drove slowly up to the obstruction. Suddenly, the drunken men were arguing with the woman; one of them emerged at the curbside, then jumped onto the bonnet and the roof of the car. I jerked the car forward to dislodge him. I heard a bang on the boot, and I suspected he had rolled off it and hit the ground. I put the car in neutral when it came to a stop, just short of the crossroad junction line where the man in the road had been standing. I began to get out of the car to see if the man who rolled off the boot of the car was hurt, but the swaying man got hold of the car door and aimed to throw a punch at me as he said, "You tried to run my mate over". It became a brawl, a fight between us where my clean forces, energy punches and not so swift feet movement worked against me, and I got floored. We fought like animals on the tarmac and rolled into the road gutter as I fought 'girlie' without an ounce of anger. As the brawl continued, my head became lodged between his feet, and the pressure of the restraint foot lock was suffocating me. The wife saw I was losing the fight, saw the distress and stepped in to break it up. She tugged at the man's clothing, hit him around his head, screaming, "Let him go, let go of him!" The man broke the headlock as the wife dug her fingernails into his neck while wrestling with his head. The wife's fingernails were broken and may have lodged in his throat, and the man's injury had made release possible.

An older man with a walking stick stopped and verbally condemned the drunken men's behaviour and got punched in the face. The whole moment was like an extended clip from a trailer of an action movie. It was all a horrid, unpleasant and upsetting thing for the children to see. The incident seemed to have lasted a long time. Yet, no peeping neighbours called the police. In this real-life physical human assault drama, I was caught performing poorly. I felt the effects of strangulation on my throat. The power in my body was emptying, and feeling like I was being put to sleep. My skin's blackness, areas darkly golden brown too, was being drained of these darkish colours. The wife later told me I was going pale.

I had struggled to stop myself from slipping into unconsciousness. I worked more and more to slip out of the lock, but I could not release the tight hold, and I imagined being vegetative state when it's all over. Finally, I became too weak to continue to release his grip. I barely heard my wife call out, "let go of him, get off him" - the cries must have been loud. Held in the foot lock, I was dazed; the blows and tugs from my wife made the man release his lock against my throat. I had pinched his leg and tried to grasp his thigh, but it made no impact on him because, by that time, I was too weak. The actual squeezing on my neck was not a bother. First, I thought. I could quickly release it, but as the pressure increased, it was taking my breath away. Again, I struggled, trying to get free, and my darling intervened and got me free.

The woman partner stopped, the men retaliated again, persuaded the men to cool it, and allowed us to walk away. She then said to us to drive away. I did not look back even though I had thoughts about the older man who had to defend himself with the crutch as he got hit in the face by one of the men. My children said they had called the police on their mobile phone while it was going on. I estimated that I was in combat for ten minutes and at the scene for about twenty minutes, and there had been no response from the police. The police station was only yards away in the next street, three minutes' walk tops. I told work colleagues about the incident, and a colleague I know lived about four doors away from where it all happened and witnessed most of it but did not call the police. His reason for not getting the police involved was that disorderly behaviour is typical in that street when Yobos drink alcohol in the pub and display unacceptable behaviour when leaving the pub. He heard the troubles and saw a man in a smart suit defending himself, but he had no idea it was me.

My wife thinks I should take up training in self-defence and attend classes to learn restraint techniques. I do not want anything to do with using physical force, I said to her. I hate fighting, I hate it, hate it, but I thank God that aggression and violence existed in humane passive people to fight off hostility. My assault was mild-natured and controlled, and my punches were delivered in a series of slaps that hurt my fingers. I cannot seriously hurt anyone, even my worst enemy. I aim for simple ways to discover my enemy's inherent goodness. If a weapon had been used, I would have been killed in a world that hits out first and asks questions after. Although instinctive aggression will kick in and override my consciousness and make me fight for self-preservation, it would be hard to survive using words alone. I am living by faith, and I want to act to help bring about heaven on earth, a place of love, peace and goodwill, and I want the change to bring an end to violence and an abusive world too, where the rich get more productive and wealthier, while the poor are poorer. I am a man of peace, a dedicated pacifist. I would not like any form of aggressive physical contact with anyone unless sports competitiveness is played in good nature. I believe the savage man fought, but the civilised man should talk. Humans should not have to fight another human being; civilized men do not need to fight, except direct aggression in good sportsmanship and give a handshake when the game is over, which recognizes fair play over the idea of a winner-loser. Civilized men only fight in virtual reality worlds. As human knowledge gets to know how to eradicate sin, we shall indeed just fight to compete for tactics that will resort to good sportsmanship on a level playing field. As humankind evolves with the Bible messages in its head and the planets and stars move further apart, and our world is lonely, humanity will come to see it's safe and sane to live as brothers and insane to have conflicts on the one planet we share. We have learnt by then to work towards a mutually acceptable outcome, a win/win outcome for all parties and avoid a win/lose as a way of dealing with conflict. Humankind will evolve clear and specific skills on how each party's perception lies, and both define and share their understanding of the match and their desired outcomes. People understand people in this new world where they take responsibility for themself and avoid blaming and accusing others of how they feel and what they think.

The behaviour of thugs tried to weaken the foundation on which I built my optimization of a good society. I carry on as usual, for the way forward is to be different, although I tend to wonder about the growth of violence in society, and it's hard to find role models in the media who are not bad boys. My stand is to get on with my life and be an example of good citizenship. My encounter with violence in the street and in this modern time, seeing the world plunged into its worst crisis in years of terrorism, means there are good reasons to fear, but carrying on, as usual, is the best way to beat the thugs and terrorists.

Despite recent events, including anthrax outbreaks in the US this week, Friday 22nd October 2001, we have seen off a whole raft of global threats and are in the process of seeing off a whole load more in our lifetime. I am optimistic because the principal threats to this planet remain what they always were: famine, pestilence, war and death, especially in childhood. Biological weapons are in fashion, the latest in line stretches back millennia, and anthrax disease can be controlled and contained. I take pride and comfort in rational thought that made it possible to see off a whole load of evil but not the accidental or deliberate acts that humanity did to the dodo. Evil thoughts are undoubtedly likely to genetically engineer viruses because nature has failed to develop a way to stop wrong ideas. The technology to make such a virus certainly exists, but we have faced countless challenges from Ice Ages to nuclear annihilation threats over time. Each time, we have peered into the abyss of extinction, and each time, our God's ingenuity and wisdom have seen us through. We should never lose faith in our ability to find solutions to nightmare scenarios that are now a reality. I guess that humans are best at learning from experience, and my dream of an apocalyptic kingdom of heaven would materialize in the lifetime of you, the reader. Still, this apocalyptic vision rests in the assurance of faith's unquestioned truth, which is extraordinary. In my life, I want to be a more effective witness and exhibit the portrait of the beauty God has created in us; although pointing out the end of the world as we know it is optimum, evil is what paints a bleak picture of human degradation. The best thing I can do in moments like this in the world is to amaze people. What can be more unusual to the world than believing there is a better way to get people to care about the environment and truly love one another by being a fantastic example myself?

I am drawn with Christians to pray for world peace and the success of war aims. I do not know if all conflict between people was produced by uncomplicated self-interest or by sheer wickedness applied in apparent evil. Press coverage has drawn my attention to conflicts and individuals who carry out evil deeds. Most disputes are incredibly complicated, and the appearance that they are not may derive solely from accepting one party's controversial assertions. We pray to reconcile differences and significant ideological differences and have strict principles involved in their purpose. History shows the Nazis and the Jews' ideology was irreconcilable, and righteousness had to be achieved through brute force. It was then right to pray for the success of the war aim, but today, as I look at the USA government on its fight against terrorism, it bothers me. Governments exist in societies as God's providential way of allowing humans to cope with their corruption's terrible effects. Because we are fallen creatures, we need governance to preserve social order to live a moral life. People have always differed about how government should conduct its stewardship of the people over whom it exercises a control measure. In our society, these differences have a sophisticated inquiry about a philosophical basis. The 20th Century saw the first mass education, the first large-scale democratic practice, and the early widespread dissemination of knowledge. The result was the most horrific warfare and a single act of sheer human nastiness the world has ever seen. It makes me think that evil people need their genes manipulated to become competent, but on the other hand, people are thinking creatures and can choose between right and wrong. We are not animals to be mollified because God's peace is a condition of our hearts that shows compassion. We must recognize that vast differences in views are the raw material of human advance.

The Digital Age and the predictions
Written Friday 30th November 2001

The familiar confine of analogue television shows the world has little interest in a conflict and does not tailor to my interests, hobbies or moods. I hardly see a schedule that shows interest in happy things happening in the world. At our new house, we have digital cable TV. It undoubtedly restored my intention to be informed of good happy things happening and programs designed to educate or stimulate the senses without making a drama out of a crisis. The analogue TV had very linear programming, and much of what I watched was the same dull entertainment. On the other hand, Digital TV offers documentary channels with a broad spectrum of fascinating documentaries on National Geographic, Discovery and the History Channel.

I subscribed to a package that includes an extra £5.00 a month for God Channel, bringing spiritual uplifting into our hearts. Their program tells and teaches about God's glory. The 700 Club and Turning Point are inspiring curricula, and so much of the God Channel challenges my standard of belief or makes me ask who they are trying to kid, especially when they go on about the actual existence of a place called hell. The program can be informative, but most often, they are dumb. Then I switch channels. Digital TV also provides sports coverage, children's diverse delights, top films, music, and 24-hour news. I am much happier watching the TV showing so much good work in our world done by good people who may not have sinned as the cause of the problems. It's a matter of principle and ideology irreconcilable in world conflicts that make righteousness be achieved through brute force. I hate the good having to take up arms.

Tonight, I am trying to be open to the Holy Spirit, and my head is working hard to receive fresh insights, learn from experiences, benefit from contemporary ideas and sift and weigh up new aspects of truth. I am convinced by the supported Holy Spirit-led ability to learn and grow that God is to astonish me with the awesome reality that He signals I am ordained to carry out the work I vowed to undertake.

When we are materially blessed, I promised to buy hope for the poor. God laid out his nature and his commands through some very worldly events, so He will help me fulfil my solemn promises.

There is, unfortunately, no magic solution to the most significant single event in the year, Christmas, which pushes us to spend more than we can comfortably afford. I am reaching another Christmas again, and debts are more than 20% of our monthly income. There will be no getting carried away with a spending frenzy as Christmas approaches. Christmas after Christmas, we have amassed excessive debts. We considered how much we could afford, but income has not increased enough, so we are trapped. There is not enough money to spend on gifts and just sufficient to buy food and pay the bills. That often means prioritizing when things are so tight, so we go without some hearty meals and make late bill payments, which incur charges that we must pay. No amount of calculation can stretch the money to serve all the most essential requirements. We are trying to live within our means, but it stresses me to see that basic things can be out of reach. We are glad about our house's location and its potential to be the right family home. I have run out of money to put in some basic furniture. We wait for the time when second-hand wardrobes, cabinets, damaged dinner tables and chairs can be replaced and modernizing the kitchen can be done, as it has become an eyesore. I have spent some money on the kitchen to give it a more acceptable look by having new work surfaces and replaced the units' doors. I am longing to do something about the bedrooms that are not to our liking. The removal of old, unattractive wallpaper and discoloured painted woodwork is a decorating job I want to take on. Still, the single cost of the few materials to do the work is out of reach of my pocket. The weekly wages are for everyday living, and nothing is left that can be used for those basic comforts. I do not want to wait for years before I can begin to see savings for home improvements. With no money in our pockets at present, peeling off the wallpaper to make our home look beautiful is the least of my worries.

Behold, the trigger is cocked; I feel my nerves expect a change in circumstance so very soon. We hoped and prayed so hard and long to be blessed with the items of our dreams, one of which is a family holiday abroad. In more than thirty years, we have never travelled to another island or continent on the face of the earth. Since leaving the land of our birth, we long for a holiday to recharge our weary selves. Still, the coming of Christmas 2001, which is less than four weeks away, it seems will turn out to be the most brutal festival season of our lives because there is no money at all to spend on gifts for the children, the family or friends. I cannot see where the money will come from to buy a new Christmas tree or decorate it to show a festive spirit. It's a nightmare to plan for festive joy when gifts are not included, and with less than four weeks to go, spending power must improve to make Christmas joy and less of a burden on an already weak financial position.

I am hurtling towards pensionable age, but I still retain my dreams and aspirations. However, I have a feeling that the next twenty years may be just like the last twenty. Yet again, the costs of Christmas do not correlate to the household income. Nevertheless, I have triggered a better feeling in myself, I am calmer, and I believe in healing myself with the thought that my dreams will come true. My views or prayers to the mysterious universal life energy source called God have a cosmic consciousness on all creation; please improve my feeling of doom and gloom. As I continue to write, I am feeling better, less anxious about how Christmas will pass. It's a form of peace that is subtle, but my rational mind says things are happening. Through subtleties, which are coincidences that are difficult to measure, I feel that my slow-changing circumstances and changes generally will set up a vibration that may lead to the materializing of personal fulfilment and world peace. I have great hope in prayer for peace, justice and prosperity, but there's little expectation of achieving them in any society in which sinful human beings are in charge. Is God not listening? I am resorting once again to lottery games; at least, it gives the odds of having prosperity and peace and justice in the world. God only knows.

I parted with three quid for the lottery draw on Saturday, 1st December 2001, because my dreams still focus on winning a giant lottery. I bought two lines on the lucky dip and wrote down random numbers that floated in my head on the third line. Three pounds! It is not surplus money but money taken from the shopping budget for tomorrow, but I hope to recuperate many more than the three pounds in a win. I have a strange feeling I'll be lucky tomorrow, a feeling that is not linked to common sense, so I bought tickets. I want to win and must win. I have not yet begun to play the midweek lottery draw; a simple single quid is hard to find at the best of times. I buy newspapers or bread and butter with it. I am proud when I play in the weekend lottery draw as searching for one pound a line gives me the sense of nearly winning, and I challenge myself to at least buy the one-pound ticket to be in it to win it. It gives me a psychological boost, suggesting that the real win is just around the corner, and it's another day of the week when I can sense that wish of winning what is set to be ours may come true.

I had deluded myself that I had a near miss. It sometimes depends on my mood on how much I risk a flutter, knowing I have got no money to waste and each pound spent on the lottery is part of the daily bread and butter money. It must be the tricks of the mind that makes me carry on playing and betting more than a pound sometimes. Throwing one pound away on the lottery is no fun. I sometimes cotton on that I will not win and miss a week's play, but the lottery is about hitting the big one to bring a swift change in our lives. I believe that we will benefit from profits or a lottery win by Christmas for some God-forsaken reasons. The tide must change, and we will give generously for the first time this Christmas.

I have a real sense of mission, for I promise my God I will live by faith and good works. So, I do my duty to praise Him and humankind through the revelations given, experienced, or learnt from my unique position of being one common man walking with God who avoids taking up a job in his church because I have the madness disease schizophrenia. I am a churchgoer, living with it out in this world's harsh reality with a soft, putty heart that is full of feelings of others' suffering mixed with the cause-and-effect pain of my own making. I need to escape from living, leave benefits for the family early and stop their worldly sorrow. Rational men say they speak to God and hear God's voice. It's even more challenging to be a known schizophrenic and say such things from the pulpit. I struggle with the thought of staying out of the pulpit because my life experience has something to say to ordinary people. I wrote that I wanted to escape living because I think my death will release my family from the breadline and constant foraging for money. I will make sure the life assurance premium is paid so that when death comes, the family benefits from my loss with a financial reward—no more monthly bills to worry about, no more having to stretch. The payout will be substantial enough to keep the family in comfort.

December 2001, and we are in crisis, the worst that I have ever known, but yet we must pull through. I have stopped paying for life assurance, so I am not thinking of doing anything silly to test my character. Still, I have no idea how to make it through Christmas into the new year, let alone celebrating. As day follows night, I rejoice that I am alive and continue to work and pray to make things better instead of throwing in the towel for a seemingly more comfortable life for my family. I prefer to hold out, but because I began to think the economic struggle was too great to pull my family through, self-sacrifice is the only power I have left that I can use selfishly and bravely. Dying leaves only a legacy of grieving relatives, and when you lose a parent, you do not just lose the person – you also lose their involvement in your life, the past, and the present. My voice breaks in mid-sentence when I talk about my ridiculous vision to end my life!!!! I had paused my pen on the paper for the same reason, and it should be unthinkable. I love you all unconditionally and love unexpressed, or things left unsaid will not put things into perspective. Nothing quite prepares you for the sheer visceral shock of it, but like pain in childbirth, it will be forgotten almost immediately, while death goes on and on, and you do not want to forget. I am sorry to have shocked you with my morbid thoughts. I almost made you lose the relationship you share with me, the part of your life that you witness. If I continue to look at it as something that may happen in the future, the landscape in my head would not have changed, and part of you would have felt numb. I am trying to look at the future more positively and be glad that I have not deprived you of future memories with me. Be assured; I will be around until God lets me go over to the other side of the universe. Grief is the loneliest thing in this world, and shared sorrow is no consolation. I could not bear the future unfolding ahead without me in your lives.

Dear Aunt Lorna's Death.
Written on Saturday, February 16th 2002

Cancer has taken our dear Aunt Lorna after suffering long-time with the disease. It deteriorated her quality of life continues until she then passed away in her sleep. Euphemia and I saw Aunt Lorna on Christmas Eve 2001, and she was skinny and ate very little and told us all she does is wake a while and sleep. We sensed Aunt Lorna was going to depart soon.

A week later, we heard that Aunt Lorna had stopped eating altogether, and on Wednesday, January 2nd 2002, she died in the latter part of the day as evening was about to fall. The time of death got recorded as being at 5:30 pm. We had known since September 2001 that Aunt Lorna had not long to live, as cancer had spread, and the doctors told her there's nothing more they could do. Aunt Lorna never admitted to the advanced spread of the tumour to the family so that she and we could prepare for her end and funeral. Aunt Lorna had been on the journey to death for a long time, and when she finally arrived, the destination was reached. I believe that Aunt Lorna passed away, aware only of a slow and peaceful fall into the state of unconsciousness. Her death was not a profound shock but freed us from seeing her suffering cancer pain and losing mobility. Death took place in the relative anonymity of a hospice bed, where the administration of pain-killing medication eased her suffering. The stark truth came when I recognised the breath of life coming to an end in her mortal body, but I encouraged Aunt Lorna in the ward of the dying to have a prospect of survival and promised we would come and see her again new year. It was easy to manipulate Aunt Lorna to imagine continuing to live, for she never mentioned that she was dying.

I offered Aunt Lorna a kind of false assurance about the possibility of survival, but in my mind, I knew she was close to eternal blessedness. Aunt Lorna's body was placed in a chapel of rest, laid in a coffin dressed as a 'bride of Christ' for the mourners. We visited the chapel on January 12th and touched Aunt Lorna's corpse. On the touch, I had a complete feeling that Aunt Lorna was neither in existence now in her dead body, nor was she floating spiritually in a sphere above our heads. The body was rigid, the skin appeared pale but highly polished and smooth, like wax on marble, firm to the touch, and the skull was cold as ice and hard like stone. Her corpse made me aware that beyond the grave lies a fate which, for so very many, may prove truly terrible or truly happy, depending on their Christian beliefs.

The redeemed is glad for salvation that comes to the mortal mind to work in preparation for an eternal existence with God and His host. Those who ignored the spirit's thoughts can't pinpoint self, you, in the body or the mind and where it comes from, remain in death zapped out of the eternal existence of an afterlife invitation and can never enter the new creation, the glory God wills to faithful systems in people. They don't believe the truth part in the God made thinking creature. So, through the simple belief system that guides us to free salvation and plays on our minds to be competent individuals when we are addicted to sin, it makes sense to accept the promises that God implants in us to be born again. The Christian creed tells societies looking for the resurrection of the dead and the world's life are to come to the substance of faith and not believing slips into the unconsciousness of death. The invitation ceases for the living when the world sees the second coming, but being in the unconsciousness of death and not surrendered to the universal spirit of truth in faith spells doomsday for the conscious self. Death either destroys the person or frees it, but nothing remains excellent or bad for those killed.

As we stood in silence around the coffin, a momentary, short whisper of the Lord's Prayer passed our lips, and thoughts came to me that Aunt Lorna no longer existed in the material world but was elsewhere, in the cosmos of things not seen. Spiritually, it's on the outer side of the known universe. The living knows nothing of its structure or its actual existence but can theorize over such a heavenly place. For Aunt Lorna, the best part of her remains; having lost the heavy burden of the body, she is free to explore entering the world God wills to the faithful that beckons her into the more divine, higher light of eternity.

Auntie's funeral took place on January 14th, 2002. A crowd of witnesses gathered at her local United Reformed Church service with the family, and then her body was laid to rest in Kettering Town Cemetery. The funeral service celebrated Aunt Lorna's life honourably and splendidly. I wept a bit in the church when our dear aunt's personality and vitality were expressed and summed up by the disabled woman preacher. An essential thing in life is leaving it because, for all of us still doing the earthly pilgrimage, the marvellous light of eternity's paradise is an unknowable filament until we die. The final attainment of blessedness is the heavenly consequence of those who have commended themselves to the mercy of God. I thought that Aunt Lorna did not want death to happen because it wears the look of an abomination, for we all share a love of self and a survival instinct.

Therefore, Aunt Lorna rebelled against dissolution because it removes us not only from what we consider good but from what we know, and we have a horror of the unknown and the dark. Death will take us into darkness, and the strange and fear is the consequence. I am sure that Aunt Lorna's Christian faith reassured her that Christ Jesus would take her into himself by the power of resurrection, and she would be with him in paradise, as the Christian story suggests. The death that was feared is not our last and not our only end. Daily, portions of our lives are taken from us. Even when we are small children, our lives are growing shorter. We have lost, in succession, infancy, childhood and youth. All the time passed is lost, and we share death because we were born to die. It is the fate of our mum and dad and all who come before us and the future of those who follow us. Death is a precondition of being born, and we will have to live on those terms and use them to honour our life. After being in the presence of the corpse of a deceased and seeing the arrival of death to a loved one, I seemed not to be distressed over the one thing we can be assured, death.

The Stable State may be coming into our lives
Written Saturday, February 16th 2002

In my second write up in 2002, I have to report a stable state within our life. We experienced some recurring positions and reference points which return repeatedly. One such aspect of the text is Christmas time, which has always been challenging to manage. The commercial side of Christmas should be abolished. We work to make ends meet all year, and provision for Christmas was still at the back of our minds. I moved it to my frontal cortex in September and worried about how we could afford Christmas. A surge in expenditure at this time usually forces the expense to impossible heights. Last year, Christmas 2001, was exceptionally bleak because no extra money existed, but we pulled through on what we had. The children had small gifts, and a card went to my spouse, and we had plenty of food to eat on the table. The joy of Christmas just naturally flowed through our spirit as we forgot our hardship momentarily. A peace and prosperity candle was lit from Christmas Day over Christmas dinner, re-lit each morning, and extinguished at bedtime through to January. We remembered the lighted candle's symbolic message, which symbolizes prayer for the less fortunate people in life and the world's coming hope.

We are into February 2002 and have seen the passing of Christmas 2001 with no thrills in the house, but we did erect a fresh Christmas tree, and our bellies were full. Welcoming 2002, believing it will become a financially stable year for us, I still feared I could not go into the future without trying to change it. It looked like one hell of a struggle, and two months on, still not a breakthrough sign of financial stability. I want to make self-sacrifice for the good of the family unit. The family will get insurance money to see them through and set them up financially, happy for life, but I would not be there. I have given the final price for their freedom from financial hardship: my precious life. It seems like every pound I have has to meet two pounds of pay-outs. More items have to be bought out of the one pound, and it's impossible to stretch a pound to buy things it's not designed to pay. The coin's face value is one pound, but the pound buys less in goods because of inflation. I looked at the bank account mini statements and saw there was not a penny in the accounts, and all the bank overdraft allowance had been used up.

Suddenly, worry stopped plaguing me. I put it to the back of my mind and preached to myself the unimportance of material wealth and began to feel the hurriedness to live and measure life in each day, being contented and seeking the health of my soul. It is taking my whole life to learn how to live and conquer the consensus of how dreams come true. My hope for the future is that things level out; it's all so below the margins I had expected to be devoted to God. I am looking for higher heights and not staying on the margins of life. Is that so bad? The aspiration to do one's duty as a father and husband raises constant dilemmas when making ends meet. Death could come to us accidentally through sudden heart failure or God's decision to relieve us from earthly suffering.

I am not afraid to die because I feel programmed to use instant and dramatic violence to end my life, but how can I teach my children that death is not evil but that giving up one's life is terrible? I thought that if I give up on life, it will serve the family's every whim and satisfy our bank account. There is enough money in the bank - hooray. I hoped it would not induce the family to lust for more and more. Greed has a low IQ, and getting what I crave for us has cost me dearer than cash. I may have to pay with the loss of my life itself. Natural desires are limited, and I have to accept life is on the same terms as the weather, and sometimes I want to escape the conditions of life because I cannot deny them. Living is a choice business, which I happily give up for the ultimate good of my family. I began on life's long road on which I have stumbled, and because of life's twists, I fell and got tired and wished and pretended to choose death. When the dice are rolled, things happen without my participation. I anticipate the blow that will do the most harm and cling for all I am worth to never giving in to adversity but aiming for prosperity, but I can never trust it. Money buys us things, but the fact is that the effort spent in getting what I crave costs much more than cash. I am ready to acquire stuff like money at the price of doing away with anxiety, danger, freedom and time. I want to hold on to my self-respect in the process so that I die knowing that I behaved honourably and that no one's freedom was lessened by my actions - least of all, my own. I have never considered myself a danger to the public, my family or myself. Still, when my thoughts begin to focus on death, the afterlife, God and the universe, I wonder if I am sane enough to see that it's a natural process in my mind to examine the meaning of life. Why is my thought on these matters so possessive in the imagination? It's sparking into elements of the reality of horror and unpredictable devastation of oneself or others.

I gave an insight into some aspects of my thinking to a previous psychiatrist who thought me to be a philosophical thinker. I have written to the area's Health Authority for a copy of my psychiatric medical records. I am curious to know what the past doctors recorded about my state of mind from 1979 to 2001. I want to explore the content of their writings over twenty years of psychiatric assessments. My move to Kettering from Wellingborough put the responsibility for my community-based psychiatric care into the hands of a psychiatrist, with yearly outpatient clinic visits as long as my wife continues to agree to it. In this new town, Kettering, my wife and I felt that the previous arrangement would still work well, understanding that if I thought I was becoming ill or my wife thought it, an immediate appointment would be made. I must be seen that day by my consultant. Only if he were away would another psychiatrist at the clinic see me.

Little by little, we are getting what we need but cannot always get what we want. It seems we have so little at this time that I yearn for more and feel impoverished. I weigh everything I want and need by natural appetite, which is easily satisfied because I am on good terms with poverty and can count ourselves as productive. I am no longer a passive poor but an active poor. The contents of our house have grown since Aunt Lorna's death, only because we selected some items of sentimental value and usefulness from her processions in her home to furnish ours. Unfortunately, the main wardrobe and dressing table were too big to fit in our house, but the neighbours who lived next door to Aunt Lorna put in a wall-to-wall wardrobe unit in their home and gave us their easily reassembled wardrobe and dressing table. It was our first second-hand item ever taken from a stranger. It was not perfect, but with a coat of varnish, we felt it would appear beautiful. I have stopped wanting what I do not have, and instead of multiplying wealth, I subtract my desires because nature requires that the belly is filled, not flattered.

Natures only wish is that our thirst should be healthily quenched and whether or not the glass is of the most beautiful crystal makes no difference. It's the unnecessary things I toil to create a comfortable living and make me feel I have achieved something. It is getting to the stage where we have to choose between eating or heating, and I feel paralyzed by debt. I cannot seem to get financially fit because of the paralysis. It's not only past debt that we still pay; it's everyday living expenses. I say to myself that it cannot get any worse, but it does. Both of our bank accounts are empty, and the overdraft limit was reached, and the bank will not permit a further increase on the overdraft without evidence of more income going through the account. Food needed on the table, council tax two months in arrears, NTL bills are not getting paid on time, and neither is the mortgage paid on its due date and occurs extra charges; that's only half the story. I hope to fix some things tomorrow, but others will take longer, like decades longer or more like the length of our lifetime. We need to buy stuff for vanity and smarten up at the hairdressers/barbers. Our very selves are almost neglected because of the cost of beauty products, haircuts, and black ladies' hair treatment at the hairdressers.

On top of that, new clothing and shoes have to be bought, but how without money? There's simply no money, and the need for these things are great. When money goes into the bank, it comes straight back out within days. Child benefits, tax credit and wages are all pooled together, and I try to budget the demands to equal the income.

My family tax credit was reduced halfway through the year 2001-02. I had full entitlement from 1999-01, but I was informed that our income exceeded the qualified limit on applying this time for the benefit. My wife had changed job with a slight reduction in take-home pay, but I had a pay rise of twenty pence in the pound to make my hourly rate £6.60 per hour. The government had reduced the tax burden by taking less tax out of earnings and set a new tax threshold that year. My slight wage increase had made our family tax credit cease, and the other support, child benefit, was reduced when my eldest daughter reached eighteen. We have less money now, and overall, our income has fallen. Since buying our first house and settling down to raise a family, there has never been any disposable income for anything we desire. It's not surprising that I turned to loans, credit cards and overdrafts right through life to make up the shortfall. Today, the fridge freezer is nearly empty of perishable food, and there are no non-perishable foods left stocked in the cupboards. The dinner plates have less meat and vegetables than before Christmas. Tomorrow's bills, not yet generated, are set for due payments per month, per quarter or yearly and are becoming today's problem on top of having little food to feed ourselves. We do not have enough money to live on; all debtors have sent out reminder letters asking to make a payment. They all want their money. The last amount, £372.00, for our daughter's university accommodation, has to be paid by April, and the school trip fee, violin course fees etc., cannot be met. Those require advance payments to be made within fourteen days.

Longer-term planning looks likely to be jeopardised because my hope to achieve has eroded from forward-thinking to expecting home improvements. Having a short holiday break and helping the children with their financial education requirements will be a nightmare without sufficient money. The Proton car that we own has been serving us well, but today, its reliability, condition and performance are a worry because the vehicle could break down at any time. There is no money for any kind of mishaps, least of all transport requirements. But the need is great for an excellent second-hand car when the Proton is scrapped. I yearn for the right, reliable used car, and my research led me to a Honda Civic, which had been a favourite of mine anyway, but if I had winnings of a million, I'd choose a nearly new Audi; it ticks all the boxes, and it looks so appealing to the eye.

The thinking about the possibilities and the dissolving away of my worries are all tied to hopefulness. I walk with a crutch now because a long-time limp with debts needs support, not to be crippled by the recent debt requirements. I know we may have to carry liabilities for a long while, but not being paralyzed by the outgoings like we are today will take a lot of hope and determination. I have been financially crippled for some years now, and more problems have arisen to burden me more. For example, the central heating system needs an upgrade, including the boiler. Many years ago, all the investments I placed money was due to mature this year, 2002, not 2003, as first thought. I checked the paperwork, and it reified that investment money will be coming from July 2002 through September. The outcome of it all can only place us on an English holiday beach if some were used for a well-deserved holiday. The central heating boiler and upgrade quotes are £3342.63 and five months before the first cheque arrives. Still, I have begun to anticipate returning to the investments because I need to work out if it's only utility bills and other bills to cover or if we could afford a short break to Europe.

Our son's birthday is next week, and there are no celebration plans with his peers on the day he becomes a teenager. The likelihood is, he will cut a Tesco chocolate cake and spend the time in the house eating it. The bleakness of our present lives has damped my expectation of me being the right provider. We should not still lack the basics because it's high time we should afford what we need. It's not fair that we are still fighting to afford the basics of food, clothes and shelter. We need to buy food each week to have some in stock in the cupboards is not within our means. Budgeting for new clothes and shoes has to be delayed so that urgent requirements can be met. The roof over our heads may soon be under threat if the arrangement to pay the mortgage seven days late goes beyond the seven days of grace.

Today, Sunday, February 17th 2002, our cupboards are nearly bare, and the freezer is running with little content, and they are becoming buried in ice. There is no money in the bank, and we need food and drink on the table and petrol for the car. The debit card is abandoned in times like these, and cheques are used three to four working days before payday. Cash-in cheques take three to four working days to clear, and I am experienced enough to know which shops process their cheques in three days and those that take longer. My wage is paid a week in-hand into the bank by bank giro credit every Friday, and I spend on a Tuesday or a Wednesday to avoid having bounced cheques. I have been lucky the money from the cheque cleared on Friday when my wage is automatically paid into the bank. I am aware of how much I earned a week, and I make allowance for the cheques coming out of the account, the direct debits and the bank fee and the money left is taken out in cash. I calculated, to the nearest pound, the entire income and the known necessary expenses. I hope there is sufficient money left to make some cash withdrawals. Usually, cash withdrawal can be as little as £50.00 per month, and cheques are a godsend to give us instant money in the week, but technically, I am paying for them later. It's a constant battle; the money goes in, and it immediately leaves the account through direct debits, debited cheques, and if I earn a little extra, I withdraw some cash. So, it goes on - money credited on Friday is all out before the following Friday. There's absolutely nothing I can save or put away for unseen events. I have to identify anything new that comes out of the money allocated for shopping each week. I cannot wait for Tuesday when it's safe to use the chequebook. I need money now, but Monday (tomorrow) is the earliest to speak to the bank.

I contacted the bank and asked desperately to consider raising our overdraft limit by the absolute maximum because more money is going through the account. The bank giro was set up to go through the joint account, and the vision to do so was innovative, and it showed up on this month's statement, and when the bank did its calculations, a further £150.00 was granted, making the new limit a whopping £950.00 overdraft. I made the withdrawal of £150 on the same day it went into the account and shopped at the supermarket. The kitchen cupboard was stocked, and the fridge/freezer was filled with food, and I had £20.00 left.

The certainty of twenty-four hours in an earth day comes without fail, and the circumstances that shape our everyday remain the same since faith and hope seem to be as emptiness acting on it. To have enough money to live on, the shift we are looking for is without substance based on hope and faith to enter the equation. I pray in my heart, believing that God has a will for each person, and each person's life is integrated with a cosmic drama with a catastrophic ending. I do not know what's going on, but it seems the risk is necessary for us to progress, and I asked for God's wisdom to show us how to live without losing my life to premature death. Life is not getting any more comfortable or bearable, having commitments I cannot fulfil and a lifetime of uncontrollable debts. I am losing patience. I want to use money when I get enough; I will not boast about it but use it sparingly, remembering that it's only a deposit. I will hold ready the gift granted to me and restore them without complaining when called on to do so. Doesn't God believe me? Doesn't He know my heart and my spirit? I do not praise poverty enthusiastically in itself, and I understand the vast difference between the things we want and the things we need. Still, I am not a greedy person and do not covet the belongings of others. I simply do not know why I have not yet been pulled out of this financial hole.

Science teaches that even the simplest of things, like the atom, is hard to understand. Religion also does not give a quick explanation for anything. Since our move to the house in Kettering, I have not been to church, apart from the time at Aunt Lorna's funeral service. I enjoy going to church for a mixture of cultural, social, aesthetic and ethical reasons. It's also because I have no dogmatic beliefs, and I respect the traditions of the Christian church and value participation in its rituals. I do not think you can expect anything more than an incomplete understanding of my issues and what my faith tries to address. Something personal seems speckled with darkness, and it causes believing to be shiftier than it should be. There are an enormous number of things that I do not have an adequate talent for and want to do in God's name, and married with children was 'a default option'. It has made me the happiest man in the world, though. I have deep domestic contentment, and I suppose I would have liked to have done more, but that may lie ahead when I get sorted out financially. The universe is fine-tuned; we are fortunate to be alive at this time of spectacular advances in knowledge of the world. As humanity lives in a temporary state of affairs, the universe will expire and living things with it. So, time, therefore, is precious. There is a limited life span, and my thoughts on shortening mine to get money to support my family is an act I feel I will do. I left a financially secure family and donated my body to medical science for research from the motive of love. I desire to contribute to humanity's quest to understand the organ of the seat of knowledge, the organic brain. Also, other body parts in a donation will benefit others suffering from some dreadful disease or genetic disorder.

I have thought about the consequences of what I want to do, but the dilemma is not just by applying logic, concrete thinking and ethics. I still may go through with it. The God of my knowledge called me to participate with him in the development of the planet. I cannot kill myself. In Christian understanding, God's nature includes his love for his creatures and his promise of immortality for those who respond to his call to faithfulness and who live life sacrificially. Taking my own life would be devastating for my loved ones, friends, and the planet that seems short of good living people. My imagination generates images from my mind's recesses that tell me I have everything to live for even though I am sometimes torn between spiritual ambitions and the pressures of the external materialistic world. I am begging for a miracle, and looking at it means that chance, luck, and supernatural power can bring about changes. It needs people with resources to come into our lives and develop events to help us.

I want to learn the virtue of patience because I am tired of waiting for the results of my strength. I need the power of the supernatural God to intervene to help my efforts and empower me to be able to say, "Truly, truly, all will be well, God, I believe; help my unbelief". Though I don't know it yet, the words' full power in my desperation may bring solace, for I will repeat them over and over until the evidence breaks through and faith pours out. I can hear my voice, the self, "I feel alone and crying in the wilderness, desperate to find a solution." Then, suddenly, at the last moment, I scream out loudly, "GOD, I BELIEVE; HELP MY UNBELIEF," because I am frustrated.

Like the Samaritans, there are sympathetic groups in the world who will listen and one is comforted by them. But it's practical solutions I am after, not a shoulder to cry on. God is a better listener, but His communication method is as ancient as time itself, and I do not think the message has got through. I feel my problem; it's to get worse before it gets better. I have dwelled on the issues too long and fought my thoughts to develop solutions, and my mind was never calm or relaxed. When I am quiet in meditation, answers come to me sketchily based on 'And Ifs.' And if that should happen, the problem would be solved. And if a relative or a friend left money or property in their will, everything would be fine. 'And if I won the lottery, or if I can manage on what I earn'... and so it goes on. Some of these things are already in the equation of circumstances and events.

Hope, carried on in faith, brings about the desperate materialization of works, and the biblical quote comes to my mind, "Faith without work is dead" in James 2:14 KJV. My entire life is based upon faith, hope and love, and the most significant test will be trying to climb back up out of the pit we are in by the effects of these three things. The consequences are entirely right because I have prayed on these things and continue praying for solutions with them in mind. We are sure to have deliverance; we have hit rock bottom in my world, and if we slip through the bottom, we shall 'perish' and lose everything. The only way out is up; I am counting on my intellect, or someone else's, to come up with the solution by God's grace. With all that in motion, we have a good chance for some things to start to become good this year, 2002, so that our lives will not have to be miserable. I feel that this year, we will discover if we are moving on, in a stalemate or slipping through the bottom. I will not be defeated in running financial matters and living life in general; I try to put substance to my visions and work my dreams. Economic issues have eroded us to dust, and we exist in the order of things that cannot be destroyed. Therefore, I shall ask my employer for £380.00 advance in wages and pay back £30.00 per week for 13 weeks as a deduction in my take-home pay. The money will go towards the final payment for the university accommodation fee.

I have an inner voice saying inspirational quotations and dictating texts from the Holy Scriptures that I have learnt, and they come through in murmurs. My mind adapts to sentences to suit my mood, giving me the confidence to take informed risks and stretch myself beyond being a brave man. I run the risk of being brave but foolish. In rehearsing this verse over and over inside my head, it states my strengths and my purpose; "Greater love has no man than this, that a man may lay down his life for his friend/family" in John 15:13 KJV. You may have thought that life is extraordinary, but it's not for animals and bacteria; they live without knowing this. What's remarkable is to die honourably and splendidly, which is rare. I have given myself a time scale when things should start to become profitable. We are in the middle of this period, and at any moment now, we will be free one way or the other. Each time I pick up the pen, I am writing about episodes in our lives that have been unfolding. I have tried making predictions, but you'll realize as you read that they are far from the mark. There is no saying that prophecy will collapse this time, but we are in for a surprise, whichever way it goes.

Today is Thursday, February 21st 2002. It is our son's birthday, and I promised him entertainment and a gift or money when money goes into the bank tomorrow. But, unfortunately, the stark reality is that we cannot afford to. It's "the story of our lives."

Text message to my wife
Monday, March 25th, 2002.

I started an argument with my wife, insisting she should leave me for another man. She thought my 'I Love You' was just words that rolled off my tongue so often that she felt them meaningless. To her, I was not backing it up with anything, and she is tired of hearing them. Nothing symbolic with the gesture gave her the feeling that I do mean it. It is easily said, and it cheapens the meaning to listen to it so often. My wife had no idea it was part of a farewell and a push to form another relationship with a man who can provide for her and give her romantic things. I hate that I have no money to keep her, and I felt her love is shallow and needs gifts from me to sustain it. I was heartbroken about what was said and could not hold back, apologising for sparking the argument. I waited for the next day when at work and sneaked writing down thoughts to text my wife. Unfortunately, my mobile phone battery failed during texting and needed recharging, and the message was lost. Luckily it was written on paper. I asked an excellent single work colleague to borrow his mobile to text a letter to my wife because we'd had a marital quarrel. The message I texted said, *"Darling, I am sorry that it seems I was driving you away into the arms of another man, but I felt hurt by you expressing my endless showing of affection as merely meaningless words. I love you more than words can say, but I know it is possible to lose you because your love is shallow. After all, I have no money. I hope your love for me can grow because you are a good partner, and I want to be good for you. Money is not everything, but you mean everything to me, and we should try to always be in love with one another. Yours ever loving, Karl".*

I am very stressed in my life, and coming up is the six-month review meeting with my psychiatrist on Tuesday, April 9th, and I made notes on lined paper to remind me of all that is stressing me and that I want to speak about to him. I outlined four things on the notepaper. The first was: Computer/text, working CNC machines. Stressed; by new technology being introduced to use with work equipment. I feel overloaded, can't take in details, ask to repeat time and again in different ways. I want to learn it. Confusion with numbers and the spoken word, figuring out how to type. Secondly: The concerned wife is feeling depressed. She said, "I don't feel I can make it through to the end of this year". She feels no proof of my love through not spending on a special thing for herself by me. My excuse; We are broke, with no money in the bank accounts. Thirdly: I do not feel depressed but stressed, and my thoughts are negative, rational. Without a change in this vital year, I think I cannot make it through to the end of this year either. Fourth: A positive, rational, possible change when received investment money of £4000.00 and two ten-year savings pay-outs between July and September 2002.

Only Seeing the Blues
Written Tuesday, June 4th 2002

We are struggling to meet our day-to-day existence costs and having to juggle priorities. I truly believed that if I practised goodness and did all the right things, the miracle of wealth will come to us - it would happen. Only, it did not. I am angry and disillusioned. I have shut down in the past three months. I made myself numb to not feel the pain and fear of what's unfolding day by day. I have a great need to express myself and write of our overwhelming hard times each day in a period of headaches. Emotional health is the last thing I have to get me through this bleak time, and if that too is fading, my God, where will be the strength to allow us to be transformed or move in a new direction? Although I always feel that love and family are more important than anything else in our lives, I have a sense of complete bleakness, and I only feel at peace with specific aspects of my life. Love is the one word that expresses my highest and most positive emotions. Hope, peace, friends, faith and unquestioned loyalty all have to do with love, and I feel I am failing my family because I struggle to meet our day-to-day existence costs.

It posed the question of my dying in despair over spiralling debts. My wife had a touch of the 'blues' and started to figure it was no use going on, but it made sense to struggle through her beliefs. We remembered the tragic death of her favourite sister, Elizabeth, who accidentally died of an overdose. I begged Euphemia not to bring an end to her life by her own doing. In April 2002, my wife and I felt depressed over our finances and our relationship; we did not have enough money to provide us with a good living.

One day in April, we tried to work out our options, but we both sensed the loss of power and control to do anything between us. Fate will take us where it may. We have lost influence in our own lives. We are alarmed, and fear hopelessness is the consequence of doing nothing. We feel defeated, and either of us may have to lose our life, for the strain is becoming unbearable. It is scary because, in our opinion, we aren't getting anywhere, and we grapple with hopeless situations. My wife cried, and

I consoled her in my arms. I received comfort from our embrace too, but Euphemia seemed to lose the mechanism to calm herself. A headache followed, and I was mindful and saw her take the correct dose of paracetamol tablets, and we went to bed. There was a déjàvu moment when Euphemia said, "I will not make it through to the end of the year". She had said it before, and it was a sharp reminder because I was also experiencing similar sentiments again.

On Tuesday, April 9th, I was travelling in the car to attend the meeting with my psychiatrist and the moment I drove out of the work car park, I was on autopilot. I was occupied in thought about risking my life in a road accident involving a lorry. I attended the clinic, but the psychiatrist did not pick up on the clues I contemplated ending my life. Instead, I joked around, not want him to pick up on the hints and ask if my intention was suicide, which I would have had to answer truthfully. The intention of driving the car head-on at speed into oncoming traffic and colliding with a juggernaut remained firm. I look out to spot juggernauts, but my life was spared because the condition was not perfect for dying. It was the day of the Queen Mum's funeral, and the country was in mourning, and the roads were quiet, and I had not spotted any travelling juggernaut lorries either on the way to or from the clinic. I had abandoned taking any riskier action by the time I returned safely home. I did not tell the wife. I behaved like it had been an ordinary day, but I am rapidly advancing towards that fateful day when I am killed. If I am brutally honest, I have always had the urge to end my life. Day by day, frightening scenarios evoked me to be brave enough to value life, not throw the towel in the face of an inevitable future. Remember the good of the past and look at the excellent product in the present. I almost abandoned my human dignity or nature as it currently exists, unaltered by drugs or genetic tampering that give us moral value. Deep in my soul, I felt a duty to obey because I am confronting suffering and death, but the act makes me a brave person, and I would have avoided the compulsion if I could. The environmental factors saved me this time.

Debt is a nightmare, and there are no quick fixes. We suffer anxiety, worry and constant stress, and it has effects on our entire life. I always try to fulfil my duty to my wife and children by securing their financial future in a very uncertain world by ending my life. I do not believe that the price is too high for this kind of security. I have accepted that it won't be me who will win the life-changing multi-million-pound jackpot from the National Lottery. I had made room for a supernatural accident to occur over the last eight years of the National Lottery - to have an unexpected win. It has not made us a fortune; I was only lucky on occasions to win a tenner. I have just won one ten pounds since the start of 2002, and it is now June 2002. Despite being a pathway to riches, the odds of one in fourteen million hitting the jackpot meant I have little chance of winning without the Almighty intervening. Since the day of the new name launch as Lotto, I have stopped playing the game. I was fooled in the past and misjudged the odds. God is not acting in the game to sway it; it was a pound to dream, but it's a lottery, which means any win was luck. I am tempted to buy my first scratch card to try my luck on the launch in March this year. The lucky ticket guarantees £10,000.00 for the duration of the winner's life, but scratch cards cost £2.00. So far, I have decided not to buy one because of the cost but am tempted to find the money from somewhere. I have ideas on opening up other pathways to riches—entering free competitions with no obligation to buy products and win prizes from supermarket ranges of promotional labels. One such title up for grabs in the biggest ever lottery-style supermarket competition is to win a car, free food or cash when one spends over £25.00 in the store. There is a one in ten chance of winning a prize.

There are problems with our old car; the radiator is leaking, and I temporary sealed it with compounds, but it needs replacing to maintain reliability. It's another worry on the list of things that need the money, and without money, it's impossible to secure our travel requirements. So I return to the 'And if' scenarios to ease financial difficulties. One such example is £50.00, which my sister Joan gave me on February 27th 2002, when her insurance investment matured. It went solely on the fee for our daughter Georgina's residential day out with the six formers. My employer had advanced my wage by £480 for twelve weeks and deducted £40.00 per week, and the last deduction was due on July 5th, 2002. So, £108.00 went directly to buy shopping to put food in our mouths, and the rest paid the university accommodation fee. The disappearance of £40.00 out of my wage each week has taken hardship to an unmeasurable level for the take-home pay is like taking peanuts; we do nothing with it except learn to manage on it.

As you continue to follow my life, it may appear my past can still justify itself in my present. I am determined not to let my history explain itself in my future because my determination to have debt freedom has added substance to my future vision. Although I pursue happiness rather than the total fulfilment of duties, like a fool, I allowed myself to be a victim of my desire to want and want. I am haunted by things that need doing, and everything seems overwhelming. My head is a free space, and the control of all those critical voices, dim memories, imaginary arguments and fears, got through, but they do not belong there. I have stumbled on revolutionary thinking that I must consciously embrace good when evil, bad, and good thoughts come into my head. By taking control over my thoughts, choosing the right one as I identify my passion, I hope to notice happy coincidences that take me nearer my goal. Life is fantastic when I come to think of it, but the trick is I have to think of it as often as possible. Everything is miraculous if we pay attention to it, and it takes my mind off my internal monologue when I fix my gaze, looking hard enough on the ordinary things in front of me in nature; it stops me from brooding.

To have faith, complete trust in my religious belief system, in this scientific culture, makes it a substance that can be investigated and debunked. There is a peculiar notion that faith is equated with believing obligatory doctrines when it originally meant a struggle to find ultimate meaning and value in life. Doctrine principles are assumed to be statements of irrefutable fact instead of myths. A myth now gets regarded as something untrue instead of a way of expressing a truth that is too elusive for ordinary logical discourse. Since my sister-in-law and Aunt Lorna's deaths, the response to the specific knowledge of being dead has me imagining some form of a heavenly afterlife. It's paradise, splendid and marvellous, in which the afterlife will be in conversation with the angels. These paradisiacal visions suggest childhood ideas of heaven, a blessed state in which the individual soul enjoys intimacy with the mighty creative force or that happy bliss in the sky is a real place crowded with embodied spirits in a garden or city. My imagination favours that heaven cannot be described with conventional language, and I am speechless without resorting to metaphor and analogy. Jesus compared it to a mustard seed.

I endlessly determine the imaginative visions of heaven as wishful thinking, myths of paradise in my emotional and creative response to death. Convinced it's a reality that heavenly happiness place was constructed in the scheme of things, but hell is ruled out as ever being co-existent other than the hell suffered on this earth. My views on heaven, hell and Jesus Christ are unorthodox. I decide my creed and do not focus on technical points of theology that no one understands. It has been an eye-opener, fascinating and breath-taking to discover truths which I yearn to tell, but I have a feeling it's so radical that Christianity would not exist as we know it. The ideas are thought-provoking, and I can only write them down to speak them out. It's murder to the Christian church. With my discovery, I cannot go back to being in the dark. I live a lie in public going around as an orthodox Christian, but I am an utter liar in the light of my knowledge.

I deny the divinity of Jesus Christ and the possibility that God could become incarnate and deny that Jesus is the saviour of the world. I have been upfront about my reformed beliefs to my wife, and she increasingly feels this is why we are not getting out of the rut. We are opposed to each other's struggles to understand the nature of God and us in his creation. I think that Jesus was just a remarkable man who was a member of Israel's ancient community. His death could not have saved humankind because to require a human sacrifice for forgiveness and salvation is suggestive of divine sadism. God's nature is love and ethics, both in our belief, but I tell my wife that we must talk of God from our common ground. I no longer qualify as a Christian, but I love God and the church. God, who is excellent but hidden, has no special revelation through Jesus. Incarnated, the so-called creed calling Jesus "Perfect God and perfect man" is misleading because the human race makes up all peoples' ideas about God and his actions.

My ideas were formed on what is understood, not on what we cannot comprehend in theology. The sky at night fascinated me as a child, and I never once failed to look up and wonder about what I saw in the heavens. As a young man, there was still the fascination, and today, the heavenly bodies capture feelings in my heart of wonder and mystery about our universe, and it takes my breath away. There have been startling images from the Hubble space telescope that showed space is truly the final frontier. In May 2002, the Hubble telescope captured real pictures of the wonders of space, and each was breath-taking in its scale and beauty. The Hubble telescope is at the forefront of scientific exploration of our universe and our origins. The images provided even more proof that the world is infinitely stranger and infinitely more beautiful than we had ever imagined previously.

Latching onto Probabilities
Written on Saturday, August 24th 2002

I have resumed playing the Lotto to make me feel a little happier. The Lotto is a living hope, to bet a pound to win. I know that change must occur in our circumstances, but I cannot see that it's happening at all. It seems nothing has changed since the financial crisis. I am again latched onto probability to help bring about the change. Still, I am running a significant risk of changing my job to pursue more money and a career move into social care. There's much more to life than work, food, shelter and sex, but I am not experiencing much more than this. Although I do not lack the theoretical basis of modern materialism and humanist interpretation of human life, which says we have to advance, I can see that humanity's wisdom remains the same.

I have bought two tickets for tonight's draw, but I will not examine them at the draw time but later when I have completed this writing. I am fed up with being too poor to escape the reality of our lives. As yet, we cannot afford to go on a family holiday; home improvements need to get done, and that too can't happen. I would love to give money or donate goods to charities to do my bit to ease their plight. I want to support a recently launched campaign to help 12 million people facing starvation in southern Africa, but I cannot recommend it by giving them money. I have nothing for today, but I start thinking about tomorrow because I am fed up with waiting and attempting to make change happen faster before I sink into depression. I continue to assume that there is a God, for without assuming God exists, I would have given up on the core of my dreams.

Thoughts just dropped into my mind from heaven that make me conscious of specific faults I have, either habitual shortcomings or, in the more acutely, self-analytical fissures in our nature which allow grave characteristics of error and sin. Under the New Labour government, the chancellor puts more squeeze on my already troubled financial situation. Last month, I was worried about the range of issues New Labour wants to introduce before the next election; problems ranged from higher university tuition fees that bring the cost of completing a degree higher.

That could mean I cannot afford to maintain Katrina, Georgina and Jonathan in university. They all told me they were interested in studying for a degree after the sixth form. Georgina starts her A level studies in September to prepare for entry into university. Katrina resumes her second term of study at university. I worry about the future education prospects of my daughters and son. It would be a real tragedy if I could not send them to university or maintain them because the university had become the preserve of the elite again. As I look at how we can realistically manage today, I also project our economy forwards to predict sustainability or improvement under the chancellor's comprehensive spending review. He announced increasing National Insurance payments, slowly chipping away at my wage packet and threats to axe Child Benefit for sixteen to eighteen-year-olds. I get buffered by today's low-interest-rate of 4% that substantially cuts mortgage repayments, but not ours. House prices have rocketed, jumping 20% in two months. The spectrum of a 1980's style collapse into negative equity is returning.

As I craved to live comfortably, they stopped Family Tax Credit, and another child benefit stopped. Then the Council Tax rose, and national insurance increased. So I am not growing in wealth but losing it. I am guilty of working hard to provide a good standard of living for ourselves and being squeezed too hard, as I try to edge into what's called Middle Britain. The government is penalizing us homeowners to help lower-income families. They are giving on the one hand and grabbing back with two, and all I will soon have to live on is my wife's and my wages, and they have not kept pace with national earnings. It's frightening to live on lower income and survive because progress can judge our ambition and successes as breaking the mould of our declining standard. I suppose we are classed as middle-income families because we do not qualify for state support anymore but cannot pay for private services without enormous sacrifices. There is a health and education lottery out there. We are not unfortunate enough to rely on the State and not rich enough to pay without financial pain. For the presence of many regular financial pressures and added pressures paying car insurance, road tax, council and income tax, life's purpose is just on a survival plane. Our daughter will leave university and go into work, struggling to pay off her student loan and getting onto the sliding property ladder. We get caught in the middle. A bewildering array of stealth taxes and means-tested benefits has left us seeing double and paying twice for everything. We are not extravagant, but it is an uphill struggle. I had curtailed our spending, but I blame my woes on the high cost of modern living.

It is socially acceptable to be in debt and too easy to slip into it, especially as my daughter is an undergraduate; banks throw credit cards and overdrafts at her. I do not think Katrina thought carefully about finding herself in the real world and about paying it back. In 2002, Katrina booked to go on holiday with a girlfriend to Ayia Napa in Cyprus using her bank overdraft and student loan money. She had to be given cash from her mum's saving plan for her holiday spending money. Euphemia had just acquired the wealth from her ten-year saving plan, and on July 12th 2002, Katrina went for a week to Ayia Napa. Katrina now finds herself in the real world, and the money has gone, and she was unable to find a summer job to tide her over until her second-year student loan comes through, amounting to another £4000.00. Katrina now owes over £8000.00, including overdraft, when she returns for the second term.

The dark tunnel had crept up on her spiralling debts, and I had argued with her to be careful, not to get trapped. I had preached to her to think carefully about spending her money and budgeting. When I learnt about the booking, I told her that a student loan is not meant to pay for a holiday. Becoming so severely in debt means everything is a hassle, and you have to watch every penny you spend. I spell out to Katrina our experiences and what the family is going through; it's a nightmare. Katrina said that now she had experienced a bit of life, too, she would be more careful with her spending. Money worries are one of the worst problems one can have because you cannot escape them. However, it is her life, and I know she has to do what feels suitable for her. I did not like Katrina's use of borrowed money to go on holiday. I may not like some of the decisions she will make, but Katrina, Georgina, and Jonathan are entitled to make their way and make their own mistakes as they come of age. I think Katrina is respectful and assertively explains what she wants to do; even if I disagree with her decisions, she appreciates my blessing. I am reluctant when her planning does not match what I imagine is proper planning, carefully thought through, but I allow her to control her decision and praise her for taking a firm stand. It's all life experience, and she would continuously kick herself if she did not do what she feels to be correct. If things do not work, there is still a home to come back and pick themselves up.

I think Katrina thought her student loan would last longer than was realistic, so it was a shock when she discovered that it was all gone after the first academic term, and there were other months to get through before the start of the new academic year. Finding any job to tide her over was more challenging than she thought, and the cost of living came as a dramatic shock. Hanging on to her cash had been tricky when Katrina enjoyed clubbing and seeing her new friends were in pubs having a great time and her old friends, who did not want to go to university, had more spending power. I also think Katrina now realizes she must use skilful money management. We do not want to see her dropping out of university because of financial difficulties. I stress that we have no money to help her if she does not carefully use the next student loan. As a student, we are aware of her money troubles, and we asked her to carefully plan in case of financial mishaps by trying to get a job with not too many hours to supplement her student loan. All her borrowing must primarily go on her study and give her an allowance each week to stick to it. University gave Katrina the first taste of real independent life away from home and the struggles to make ends meet. I asked her to prioritize her most significant expenses, living accommodation, food and drink, travel and course materials, mobile phone bills, clothes, and entertainment are big income-drainers.

I look at Katrina's academic year's achievement, and I am pleased and excited about her passes. Georgina has also done well at school, passing with good grades in all her GCSEs. We are incredibly proud of them. I fret about the future as a parent for my daughters and son. I can keep our heads above water financially, and I am building up pictures of things in my writing that shows a wealth of experience to leave them, but in place must be the purest form of financial protection, Life Assurance. Georgina had a work experience placement with Giles Sports Plc, a retail store. The deployment ended on February 20th 2002, and she was offered Saturday employment, which she accepted. Georgina earns her own independent money. Her working days now include Sundays, bank holidays and sometimes on weekdays during the summer holiday. It helps her buy clothes and things. When she joins the family queue to university in two years, Katrina will be finishing her final year. I am telling them this message: Don't bury your heads in the sand; learn to work out skilful money management. There is no avoiding the sober reality of life on a student income, and it's hard. Do a budget, balance the amount of spending with the amount in the bank (incomings).

Katrina is no longer in the Hall of Residence for accommodation. In this new term, she will be sharing a privately rented house with five fellow students; £212.33 per month for a full twelve months rent per student, which does not include bills. I was the named guarantor on the contract. Our son has had a paper round since March 20th 2002. Jonathan's distribution of newspapers and magazines are along streets that are close to his neighbourhood. The paper shop and his paper rounds are within a short walking distance from his house. He asked me to save his £9.00 per week that he earned, but it got used in household spending. However, I ensured that his little heart desired soon met as I adjusted spending to incorporate his realistic request. One such proposal was for a mobile phone which Jonathan patiently waited for, and now he has one.

I am attempting to get more out of life by changing my job to get a better wage, but Warehouse Operative requires working nights or a rota pattern of day and night shifts. I have applied for the job and now wait to hear from the company. There must be more to life than work, food, shelter, and sex. I am not experiencing much more than this. I do not lack theoretical reasoning to understand humankind's basic needs, but underlying modern materialism and humanist interpretations of human life say we have to advance. Advancement in my personal life is a challenge in itself, but rather than looking outside the box for wisdom, and humanity reminds us to look after one another. I want to develop our future and accomplish the things that will bring us more happiness and, of course, maintain myself in good health at all times.

Last month, July 2002, £7016.37 was paid into the bank, and £7638.90 was the amount of money that left the account in a single month, which still has us remaining in the red. £3,000 was given to us by my father as a gift from Aunty Lorna's life insurance pay-out. We had dramatically cleared the priority debts and bought a used car, a Honda Civic 1500cc costing £3495. It was purchased on July 8th 2002, and it seems to be a most comfortable car, and we hope it turns out to be reliable. As recommended by most car journals, it is a reliable model. The reality today is that I could not keep up payments on Katrina's accommodation. I had to pay more money to taxes like the poll tax, car tax and, insurance to maintain the new car with its 6,000-mile regular service to keep the car guarantee valid.

Last month, we saw the neighbours sell their house and move away to live in a bungalow near their daughter. The new neighbour is currently modernizing and refurbishing the entire interior before moving in. There are two men, probably in their late thirties, but no one is sure of their relationship. We ruled them out as being brothers and pondered on them being straight housemates. The wife was surprised when it was revealed that they are gay partners. She was very disappointed that the new neighbours are not a mixed-sex couple, to see them have children, but she replaced the initial thought and said it does not matter after all. One of the men called round to discuss their requirement to alter the fencing or erect another higher fence by the existing one to make it more private between the gardens. We had no objection to the idea.

The idea of two gay men are in same-sex coupling is not a problem for me. Even though it's supposed to be immoral, same-gender bonding is a matter of in-built preference. It may have presented as a surprising point of view, as perhaps it sounds worthy of headlines, but theology down the centuries before this one, the 21st century, has been regarded with particular respect and as the moral landscape has shifted to this age of sovereignty of humanity. Human welfare and human love assessments are essential to same-sex mating, in which candidates are seen as acting immorally. However, they are as much as us, creatures of the earth but claim exemption from one of our moral codes, the natural rule of law. I could never accept this condition because I am an honest man genetically engineered to be straight and be least affected by environmental factors to alter it. Still, I can understand what makes people wilfully separate this rule that may look like it tarnished God's original purpose, and it is suitable for the State to tolerate gays and lesbians. After all, not all immoral acts are against the law. One can tell a lie about the weather or one's whereabouts last night and offend God, but not fear secular prosecution. The law's purpose is to prohibit evil acts that disturb society's peaceful state, like theft, murder or perjury. There is the same timeless experience of mortal sin's permanent mark on each human life, and it causes trouble.

Nevertheless, we often choose not to identify it as such and blame instead of external causes, like nurture, or it just happens because I cannot help myself. Sexuality is primarily self-induced and is inherited from a mix of sexual genetics. The origin lies in priorities for pursuing pleasure rather than fulfilling moral duties to God, and there are wrong estimates of our entitlement. What gays and lesbians could say to the heterosexual community is that they are victims of their desires for gay partners, rather than the beautiful union of men and women having different genders. Yet it's no business of anybody what orifices same-gender partners use and make heterosexuals feel disgusted.

Ok, I'll leave that debate there, and before closing this chapter now, tonight, Sunday, August 25th 2002, I have examined the Teletext lottery results for last night, and the news of a lotto win has eluded me again. Neither card held a drawn number with two tickets bought to bring double blessing on my return to the game. I was so disappointed that I swore, "Damn it" - as my hand slammed across my knee.

The faith needed to get through more Living
Written Tuesday, September 24th 2002

We had reached the dates of two birthdays, my daughter Georgina's and my own. Our gift to her was a course of driving lessons, the beginning of her driving experience. Jonathan had given up doing his paper round on 21/09/02 because of after school activity and the commitment he has to complete homework on time. However, he involves himself in the community under-fourteens football club and training on a Saturday morning.

The last investment money went to buy a top-of-the-range personal computer for Katrina to do her university study. I began to think about Christmas and beyond and mentioned early to the family that the outlook of this Christmas and the new year was bleak, but they did not believe it. They said, I always say that every year as Christmas approaches, I concentrate too much on money matters, and I should leave room for faith and unexpected good things to happen. I feel I know the deadliness of what lies ahead if our circumstances do not change, for it's an economic forecast of gloom that is overshadowing the other areas of our lives that are well. There's not enough money to buy presents and food. I can already see that the sums in September for December and beyond do not add up, but it feels like it's a tradition to say we are without money at Christmas. We scraped through all those past Christmases because of certainties. We bought things and paid later because the funds were due to come in, and I was as sure as the sun rises in the sky every day, that money would be in the bank. Now there are no known funds to enter our bank account, no money whatsoever from here on. We can only rely on faith alone to see us through that which is coming. I plea for cash in my prayer, knowing that it's the only certainty of the promises of God I must come to rely on entirely. Still, I find it hard to believe that the unseen God makes money appear and wants nothing of me to do other than believe it gets done by His will. I feel I need to put worldly certainty into the equation at this time. However, it comes to all living things in due course. It will come in the time of my expectation when my gloomy economic forecast cannot bear the reality of my family getting poor and more impoverished. It leads me back to the question of ending my life so that they can live in comfort.

Right now, I remember some words that Steve, the foreman, said to me when my performance in my day job was deteriorating. I was doing two jobs, engineering in the daytime and a shelf packer at a supermarket in the evening and working overtime on my day job. He said, - "After all, it's only money. I am not telling you how to live your life, but after all, it's only money". A biblical verse clicked into my head - "The love of money is the root of all evil". (1 Timothy 6:10) I want to know that my financial prayer request will be answered with blessings, but I need complete faith and good luck to get through any more living because I have stopped seeing visions. I need complete trust in God to maintain my ambitions, for I feel I am losing it. I considered the things that might take five, ten, fifteen, twenty years, or even near the end of a life span to accomplish. It appears to be disappearing from my dreams; I am left empty without hope, all because the blessing of prosperity is missing.

Society is based on prosperity for a few and poverty for many. That's the facts of life, but I used to imagine the reverse. We are broke but broke as never before without glimpsing a light at the end of the tunnel. It has caused anxiety to spread throughout the body, and I am asking my nerves where the money will come from to meet today's requirements and tomorrow. We have no more investments and cannot put anything aside for now or the rainy days of eventuality. I can wait no longer; never will I see the new central heating system installed or the modern furniture needed in the bedroom and the living room. Worst of all, I'll be absent from having involvement in my daughters' and son's futures.

No longer would I experience the eternal love of my wife. Luckily, writing relieves the symptoms of premature death, taken wholly rationally, to obtain the blessing of prosperity. I am writing what I think. The motive comes out of unselfishness. What may follow soon cannot make you assume I am mentally ill but committed to a rational suicide with emotional, physical and spiritual stress factors. I cannot go on scraping a living when there's an easy way to bring riches to my family. The eternal God who made the universe with a world full of suffering, pain and sacrifice made us infinite; though my organs perish, consciousness lives on to get clothed in an eternity of bliss. My senses tell me that I must continue to live in the God-made world.

I cannot make sense of continuing to live on faith only, for I could have chopped myself by now because my faith is thin, and the pressure to obtain a better standard of living for my family is intense. I believe in God's promises to his good people. He wants us to prosper, but, in my eyes, earth time is running out. The present-day is hard to get through without sufficient money. The needs for today and tomorrow have blindfolds. I am in that needy condition; no longer can I assume it will get better rather than worse. If I do nothing, it seems things are worse, and to carry out the actions that should bring certainty of prosperity will be the death of me. By the time I conclude this chapter, I expect to have sprung back up to optimism because the knowledge of God is encouraging me to live, rather than having a negative self, forcing me into an early coffin.

The call from God to exist in this world on his terms means that I have to complete a purpose-filled life before my consciousness exits this mortal body. Live rather than exit life demands faith in a supernatural God or being who created and sustained all living things. All are riding on religion, and I sometimes cast doubts on whether I could continue to stay on the faith train. To live meaningfully, one must believe in something and do for others out of the goodness of one's heart and not expect rewards from others heaven or on earth. There is no alternative but to maintain oneself selfishly in a meaningless existence without expecting anything earthly or heavenly and relying on one's strength because there's no acknowledgement that the breath of life comes from God. I am all for everlasting existence, which begins when a good or repented soul leaves the body and maintains its presence by God in the burial sphere of nothingness until it is a beacon to have formed again and exist supernaturally in a euphoric new world.

Sometimes I think I may be bringing devastation to my family if I carry out the thoughts of how to rescue us from financial ruin. It might come to represent both a family tragedy and a loss to society. Outstanding men are rare in the community because they are committed to all goodness and building a world so just, enlightened and rational, without violence, that we expect a generation of people to live in it one day. Good men reasonably hope for dishonesty in the human species to die before the natural process allows weakness and cowardliness. Courage and strength are found in a good man, and he endures to the end because he believes in God and goodness. My life has taken this turn to self-destruction because financial pressures make me want to do something more original than giving in, but to do something more faithful to myself is not to quit. It's a challenge to write to tell how things are unfolding, and it's in my mind to be a hero who remains sensitive without being wimpy.

I owe organizations thousands of pounds, and every week's existence needs me to shuffle the little money around to pay the requirements. That is the present predicament, and yet I have the future to think about too! Where's the money to come from to service the car, pay the insurance and the MOT? Where's the money to come from for the school trips? Where is the money to help my daughter through university? Where is the money to come from for my nephew's wedding in the summer of 2003? Where is it to come from for the urgent home improvements and to make a will? Where's that money to come from to invest for when the danger of this torrential rain that is falling on us stops washing us away? The present time is hard enough, and I cannot bear to think about the future moments other than the distant future. The danger zone is the torrential downpour of things that are required or need preserving. Only faith allows me to think we will find the money and believe that God is acting in the middle of things, and the solutions are already known. So I continue to work nights to increase earnings and not discount the luck of a lottery win or an inheritance.

By the grace of God, I believe one of those three things will see us out of financial hardship. I can think of no other way under heaven of being debt-free and having enough that we can feed, clothe and shelter ourselves.

I am also providing my children's education; helping them pay back student loans is also part of this money-envy priority. I am no longer thinking of bringing a personal tragedy and a loss to family and society. Most of this writing gets assembled from jotted down thoughts on a piece of paper at my day job, 8 am to 4:30 pm. As soon as a thing that harasses my mind forges itself in the centre of my mind, I force them out in writing. The sudden thoughts linger and are built up upon other immediate ideas and cause an explosion. I write them down and manipulate them to suit my mood and feeling at the time. I try to eliminate as many lousy grammar and spelling mistakes as I can. These thoughts were the results of yesterday's manipulative thinking, and I am glad to get rid of them from the core of my brain because they kept my soul searching to the extremities, allowing money worries to take over the whole of my life.

I want to shatter the illusion and see myself develop fully rounded in all areas of life, no longer trapped by what I classed as the end of everything because little money cannot breathe big money. Not having your finances in order does not mean the end of everything. I have discovered the illusion, and there is plenty of life to live out of the mist of falsehood. From my collection of memories, I remembered this message, *"God sent one of the highest members in Great Britain, the former prime minister Harold Wilson, to get a poor Bible smuggler out of a Czech Communist prison. And what thrilled me so much was that the prisoners used to say, why do you read your*

Bible? Why do you pray? God can't answer prayers. But do you know, the only one that out of prison was the one who believed the word of God and prayed"? This message was allegedly made in 1970 by an evangelist preacher in an underground evangelical organisation. One of their supporters was thrown into prison for smuggling Bibles, and the message has inspired my life.

My wife went to a prayer meeting this evening and regularly attended Sunday morning praise and worship. On the other hand, I am numb to praise the community of 'saints' and am not going to church because my life is miserable. Although I am thankful for my life, and a daily requirement of praise gets given for that, nothing else can be said about God's involvement in our lives making a sufficient difference. I still have anxieties, being unlucky or have lousy luck, terrible things happening, and pain. Saints in Christ cry out in testimony and announce what God has done for them and with songs of praise, prayer in worship to the living God in whom I seek financial deliverance. I wait for the change in my life to send me back to church and proclaim that the living God has done something for me which can be accurately measured. Our life should involve some supernatural power to fix it because we can't do it ourselves.

Meanwhile, my worship became slackened because I feel no positive evidence of the spirit as I battle with money worries. Devotion consists of silent prayers and internalized hymn-singing in my home with radio and TV religious broadcasts music. I have a heavy heart, willing to learn to believe and obey the immortal, invisible living almighty God and explore how consciousness got created. Still, maybe my religious faith is a misconception.

Scientific ways of thinking will give the solution to the problem we face personally and in the world. The curiosity that drives science might have sprung from the same source as faith because it has the same desperate desire to answer questions. I have not had the spirit to praise God because I lack energy. I am worried and tired, and it seems that religion does not provide answers to my questions. I want to stop my negativity and grow in positivity, but science makes the world more uncertain. Science today is more potent than at any time in history and has paradoxically made the world seem a more uncertain place. Nuclear power, overpopulation, pesticides and cancers, the ozone layer, the greenhouse effect, cloning, genetically modified food and animals, and so on – these are all fuelling my anxiety, and it's scary. The pace of technological change created a sense of heightened uncertainty, even though the world is, in reality, a much less risky place for people than it was one hundred years ago. Risk, uncertainty, vulnerability and trust are the human condition, but the enlightenment made me believe that progress can be achieved via the pursuit of knowledge. I stand in awe of the products of recent scientific progress. Science is not magic, and scientists do not possess a collective magic wand; they did their calculations and verified the experiment. Still, modern science has not removed our fallibility. The growth of knowledge does not guarantee human happiness. Evolution is a prolonged process that sees species develop to an advanced stage eventually. Still, there is a halt in my progression as I experience more of life to make me an all-rounded individual. Science is a way of asking questions about the world that has extraordinary power. The earth is doomed physically, it cannot last forever, but it's touch and go for us humans if we outlive this century.

I can find no more to say at this time, but be sure to return to read what life has dished up to us and if we can handle it. Today is Wednesday 25th September 2002, and I shall write to you again soon. I am sorry to have had you worried because it's not a fictional drama but complete writing of a nonfiction crisis.

Pray to be like Christ, and I prayed to be different.
Written on Friday 27th September 2002

Hello! I am back sooner than I thought because, after a couple of good night's sleep, which were as deep as a baby, I am refreshed, but my thoughts are racing with ideas and nostalgia.

Today, I went into work confident that nothing can happen through the day that noble Christ and I cannot handle. By the end of the day, minor errors occurred on the factory floor, but none of my workpieces was scrapped. Instead, they just passed within limits, and with minor adjustments made to the overall assembly, the components I made were in place on jobs worth thousands of pounds. It had been a day where my mind was in two areas at once, concentrating on a vital piece of engineering to be made and tackling intruding thoughts that took up a part of my concentration. My thinking was multi-tasking, solving practical analytic engineering problems, and at the same time, holding theological discussions in my head. What made me, me? Where do you come from in the material world? If I can believe it, the Christ story, all things become possible for me.

The distracting thoughts multiplied more as the working day ended, and I could not understand my paradoxical consciousness coming up with paradox answers. I am confused and feel tiny bits of myself are going wrong. How do the few ounces of spongy stuff in my skull create the experiences of being human? I am malfunctioning, bombarded with questions and lessons from the past lead to confusion. It seems my seemingly unique mental capacities have turned off and developed tricks to only believe in invisible entities. I am a born believer and again want the attribute of the phenomenon, God, interacting with the physical world, to stay. Still, it is a default state of my mind that has stopped the theological argument raging and told me to accept God absolutely and have no more discussions.

A significant part of how I am today is rooted in a tangent of how I have perceived life and my decisions made at a young age. At the age of fourteen, it was critical to consider CSE course options or leave school at fifteen without academic qualifications. Two years later, after CSEs and barely ready to choose a career, I had to pick a job out of my best CSE results because sixteen was compulsory school leaving. I had fears about going because everything outside the cocoon life of the school seemed scary. With the desire to have adult pleasures and love, as the Bible teaches, my maturing masculinity gave me a choice to obey the spirit of purity and resist the temptations of sinful desires. I had formed concrete ideas based on biblical teachings by the age of fourteen, and as a maturing man, I made a vow of chastity and washed and rinsed my whole body in running cold water if I self-loved. I felt ill-prepared to cope in the big broad world environment with all kinds of mechanical inventions that can be dangerous in a child's hands and work with talented mature men and women. Also, destructive social issues scared me, and no one wanted to adhere to man's law or God's law. Adults seemed to view the code, not in my child-like perspective, where breaking rules leads to punishment and condemnation. Like Christians, they should try to fill their minds with God's grace and not sin or break the law. But as young adults, Christians do not always practice what they preach. The obedience to the spirit is not sustainable in a Christian's life without a daily call on God to forgive us our trespasses.

My CSE results guided what I wanted to do in life, but I had no precise aim other than a blank no to a church career or becoming a skilled carpenter. I did well in two subjects, religious studies and carpentry. Still, I was sure and afraid that I'd lose my identity and personality if I became a carpenter or worked in the church as a preacher. I assumed in the developing age that a career in the church or training to be a carpenter would make me a copycat of Jesus, and I'd lose who I was and what I was born to be. I wanted to grow up faithful to my oath, a good, just, honest man of faith and felt courageous to live as a commoner with conviction and ridiculed for my moral standing. I was not shy to speak about Jesus where I worked or in a social circle like a dance hall, youth clubs, and open spaces like parks, towns, and city pedestrian areas. Over the years, when I was a young man, confident in the word of God, I took the gospel to those places. I was passionate about Christ and not ashamed to speak of love, peace and non-violence in the context of biblical teaching.

Somewhere along the way, I became mentally ill. While the Christian church was praying to be like Christ, God knows how I prayed for some differences between myself and him and be my own man. I learned in my psychosis that I was destined to be an unconditional holy man. In a parable, I was kneeling and praying like a monk, all day and night in a unique community of believers showing total reliance on God, with unquestioning belief without a doubt that the world would be put to rights just by prayer, meditation and fasting. The message was about faith and opting out of an economic ruthlessness that characterizes contemporary society, like the sale of arms for profit, abuse of children, the intolerance of ways of living other than our democracy, social injustice and selfish competitiveness. I believed it could get sorted, and faith would take care of things. Personal problems would be solved, and mutual love and profound respect for others aim for the notions that God's belief will address. I wanted to walk in faith but be proactive in the world, not stuck in a community of worshippers waiting upon God. I had the zeal to be an excellent example of biblical teaching and spread the good news of God's love that teaches us to love and respect one another.

In reality, I saw faith was not comfortable to hold on to when one expects the results to be in by now. I wanted to make a difference. I had worked hard on belief, but now I think of stopping believing because of poor results. I feel empty, lonely and unhappy as I dare to face not believing. It will take a lot of effort to be an atheist, and I would need to find new ways of filling Sunday mornings. I am a born believer in God's creation, and the mechanisms in life's inventiveness evolved my brain to be only susceptible to God's word. Though my results have not come in as yet, I need to be patient. I had shaken my belief system as I looked to find the supernatural and biological gifts that change the natural world and the human-made world without physics. I am worried that believing has no substance; the foundation of the belief is based on an external force working to bring about personal stability and put the world into shape. My financial world has not seen change for years, and I thought of giving up on the notion that all things are possible by faith and change can miraculously happen. Back in the days of my youth, I saw the church always cried, Lord, Lord, Lord, Jesus but their lives and their actions in the world did not seem to show God's activeness and protection so that all could come to believe. I stood with a conviction to see the world do as I do in Christ as a true believer, for I practised what I preached insincerity. My mind was saturated in God as I focused on the unsaved in prayer, begging that all would accept the revelation of the teachings of Jesus. I sensed something must be wrong to get me so possessed in worry for people's souls to be saved and was announcing to God that the people do not want to hear. Still, I was so driven to live in a spirit of truth and see others follow, creating a universal brotherhood of love and peace if everyone prayed and believed.

I went to the doctor and told him that my mind gets saturated with God, God, and God all the time, and I am not getting answered, but I have to believe that war and famine will be no more. Violence from human to human and the destruction of nature will cease if everybody believes in God and miracles. Today, the reality of faith is still hard to know and is baffling, but healthy living and not overdoing things are essential to me. My biological make-up insists that I hold on to faith and believe that one day if I take life in moderation and live to the full, the content of my dreams will come to pass.

I retained something from the spiritual quest during my youth when the thoughts about God, the Soul, and God's actions and life were more baffling. It showed a predestined journey, and some people are fated to face more difficulties than others. If I am right, I was never given anything I cannot deal with, so I'll pull through by holding onto faith and letting go of the baggage that burdens me, and I must learn to be patient. The belief is a clear commitment in my heart that I believe God is at work in the world. Our God wants to change the world into the kind of place He intended it to be when He created it. People of faith are here to continue after Jesus's making of his kingdom and believe in His promises of a society without poverty, racism, sexism, militarism or environmental destruction. We are all called to form this paradise kingdom of God again by being an excellent example of Christian love. Believers are empowered with a vision to reflect on justice and aspire to share in events to change society for the better.

Now, I have said all that has burdened my heart, and my problem seems shrunken. This immediate sense of feeling the Holy Spirit near seems sedative because it broke my worry pattern. I am having a break from my worried fears, and I feel better about it, but it may take some time to fully recharge my battery from the stress because there's no getting away from it all. Nevertheless, I now have a kind of peace because my mind gets settled physically and mentally. When my battery gets fully charged, my problem and the relationship with the broader world will look ordinary, and I will return to church and praise the living God. I'll probably go to church this Sunday. I hope it's not self-deception; though I feel relaxed, joy and a deep sense of worth and happiness, I know how easy it can fade.

The Readiness to Receive New Insights
Written Thursday 26th of December 2002

I am ready to receive fresh insights, learn from experiences, benefit from contemporary ideas, and sift and weigh unique aspects of truth. The pressures of 21st-century living need a mature and enthusiastic faith to cope with a spirited ability to learn and grow. I now want to stay alive to enrich and understand reality and further explore the mysteries of religious truth. Life is a gift of God, and I come to see it is not to be treated as if it was at one's disposal but entrusted to us to use our time on earth as an education. Next year, I'll be looking for a better life of joy and enrichment that means a growth in wealth, and the joy of living is fashioning me for pleasure and eternal bliss.

I could not stand the pressure that forced me to enjoy God solely by myself in the comfort of my living room on a Sunday and not go to my local church. I want to experience God worshipped in a church and not just from worship in the comfort of my home. I want to approach religion in church again to characterize my enthusiastic love and exuberant faith with pleasure. So, on Sunday 20th October 2002, I was back in church, the local URC and Jonathan came with me, but he did not go into the junior church and stayed in the primary church worship. Staying at home to worship is no longer an option on a Sunday morning; that option is down to laziness and not because it's hard to get out of bed and not having money to contribute generously to the collection plate.

The weather that Sunday was stormy. The rain that overflowed in drains and winds that picked up debris had us struggling to walk forwards at a rhythmic pace risking getting blown over. During the first four continuous weeks of attending church, sometimes with our son, I was as generous as possible with the £3.00 a week collection. After the fourth week, I found it harder and harder to budget £3.00, and it's the minimum my conscience will allow me to pay for the pleasure I get out of a church service. It was impossible to maintain giving £3.00 generously to the collection plate. The church provides a staffing service, so be it spiritual or not, they need money. I enjoy the real sense of celebration, hear the church vibrate with songs, and have living themes relating to real people's problems like despair, doubt, deprivation, exaltation, prayer, and preaching God's beautiful word. I enjoy God thoroughly in worship; the church ministers to many needs, and I cannot go without paying the ministry. The URC and the mainly white Christian Pentecostal church, which my wife goes to, offer the authoritative word and contain the physical, mental, emotional and spiritual pleasure to let you enjoy a relationship with God and people. They operate as one united body in Christ with diversity in styles to bring the message across.

The Christian churches seem to fight for supremacy, and there is no unity within them, which saddens me. I am spiritually blessed in diverse ways of worship because some services are more geared to the intellectual effort, which has the mind wrestling with the deep things of faith, often divine passive, while listening to the sermon. Others are wholly submissive without philosophical inquiries. The united church would better serve the people with its active involvement in multi-Christian beliefs under one roof.

For the first time, we had opened our hearts to people serving us directly through the church about the extent of our debt problems. We were enrolled in the Pentecostal Christian Church community's free and confidential Debt Advice Centre in Wellingborough. Our relatives did not know the full extent of the debt because I was ashamed to tell them of the figure owed to creditors. Finally, Euphemia forced me to admit that there's no harm in allowing the debt advice team and the people working for them to know; they promised confidentially. But, I thought, there's nothing they can do but see why debts are not managed and give the advice to cope with the worries. They could not reduce the amount paid to creditors because the non-priority debt repayment is low at £28.00 per month for the £20,000.00 owed. The priority debts are getting hard to bear because money is not coming into our pockets but is redistributed to debtors and leaves us out of pocket with no disposable income.

I had a meeting with the Borough Council in early December about the three months' arrears in community tax. They said I must pay as much as possible, but their computer would generate demand letters if it did not comply with the minimum. Although I could produce something, I tried to tell them I could not pay the minimum, but the council was not listening. "Give me more time; put an end to the letters and extend the payment over 12 months instead of the usual ten months, which will give me up to four more months to pay the total debt instead of two months," I pleaded. They said it was a priority debt, and I could be summonsed and go to prison for not paying community tax. I told them that I know it is a priority debt, but I fell behind with payment, and I want to pay, but I have not got the money. It all fell on deaf ears. The council's following letter will be for county court action if the debt is not arranged to be fully paid off by 1st March 2003 and will incur further costs and possibly involve the bailiffs.

The debt advice centre could see the predicament, and a budget planner was filled in with our current outgoings and incomes. Community tax was listed as a priority debt that must be paid no matter the circumstances and must be placed second in importance after the mortgage debt, to which I agreed. Still, they could not develop a budget plan that would work without accepting essential food donations from the church pantry. I struggled with the thought of having handouts and was not comfortable with it because I am a proud man who wants to provide for his family on my own merits.

Twice, on Wednesday 3rd October and Saturday 30th November 2002, I won £10.00 on the lottery, and I thought I was close to a mighty jackpot. On the other hand, my wife felt that I was taking the lottery too seriously to cure all our ills. Since September, I had not missed a game, most often only a one-pound stake mid-week and at weekends, with the vision of maintaining future good health and winning the battle of the debts. I will have to change my job to working the night shift or have a lottery win. I was interviewed for work on the night shift in a warehouse earning £8.02 per hour in the week. I was informed by letter at the weekend that I did not get the job and thought immediately I read the word 'unfortunately' in the message that the world might as well give up its spinning. I had convinced myself that the interview went very well. I did the best I was able to do to persuade them I needed this job. I am the right man for the job. I was overqualified with a career in engineering. I would have risen above my debts with an increased wage, and I became instantly depressed when I read the letter. I flopped into bed. I did not see any more daylight until 4 pm, when I took my buried head out of the pillow and uncurled my body that was tensed up on top of the duvet.

I saw no way forward to having a Merry Christmas and a Happy New Year. I was depressed for days, imagining there would be month after month, then year after year without the changes we are looking for, which is devastating. I said to myself, 'Will we always be broke? Will we still be unable to afford new clothes and to feed ourselves properly? Will we ever live comfortably and get to enjoy activities in life that money can buy?' I had prayed; God gives us a lucky break. I am looking for a solution. The job failure had snapped my spirit, and I felt hope had gone.

I can't get a well-paid job, and the one I have makes mainly military equipment for the MOD, and it is on my conscience. I want to leave, but I am not getting a lucky break yet. Debts feel like they are destroying my life. I live my entire life with ever-increasing uncontrollable debts, but I guaranteed that debt problems and money worries would soon be over. Instead, I would not spend the next decade not coping adequately with priority debts and having an ever-decreasing standard of living. But, I'll note, I'll not! Some people have horrendous times, and they've killed themselves.

You know, suicide has crossed my mind. My money problem is not like a walk in the park, so self-pity goes out of the window. It would be pathetic to imagine that my situation is not so more desperate this coming year 2003. I have no choice but to get on with it, believe that it almost certainly will end, and I can start living in the fullness of life again. I can think of nothing that changes things as there isn't any pot of money squirrelled away. We are already natural by God's will, but we still go off trying to find a way to live in euphoria. In reality, security, individuality and independence secure my sense of a happy self, and I am a free agent, ever-expanding my search for the objects I need. I shall evacuate selfhood in return for family security and not have us dependent on others. I recognize the whole of my environment 'exists as God's will' and that I am unconditionally reliant on God. Therefore, I should not worry about providing and trying to make sense of the psychological insecurities I see around me, stopping me from coping. Practical, down to earth remedies need to be applied to ensure having enough to live adequately. I approached my employer to advance my wages by £300 and deduct £20 a week for 15 weeks. I am doing overtime, sometimes until 7 pm, and I work the half-hour lunch break, but it does not show a much fatter wage packet on payday. I still have not any surplus money because of the taxman and spending on essentials.

After negotiation with my employer, BB Engineering, they were happy to advance my wage, revise the £300 in 10 weeks and docking my wages by £30.00 per week. I asked if I could make the repayments starting on 10th January 2003 out of the new year's first earnings. The accountant said it could not be guaranteed that the deductions could be arranged for the 10th.

I've discovered this plan 'B' and have faith it will secure us a happy Christmas. I would have struggled much more to afford Christmas dinner and give out presents if I hadn't connected £300 from my boss in the season of goodwill, allowing us to have a luxury this year, Christmas dinner and give gifts. Food and presents are now luxury items at Christmas as we face financial oblivion and cannot be taken for granted. Begging for a break of good fortune has not happened; it was a case of hard luck. No lottery wins, and it's two weeks until Christmas. Christmas would inevitably prove too much of a recession, being that we were hard-pressed struggling to fight our way out of the personal debt economy. A brief double-dip recession next year is likely because we cannot recover without further cutbacks, spending cuts on food mainly, with the possibility of reinforcing hope later in the year as supporting mechanisms begin to work. What could be right about all this stress? I do not want to be alarmed about this, but the evidence is pretty conclusive. We had to borrow and hope and remain hopeful even though my employer's arrangement has us tightly squeezed.

Two of Euphemia's terrific church friends organized a handout with Euphemia's consent. Cheryl and Buki coordinated it, and I did not know how conventional food and traditional frozen foodstuff filled our half-empty freezer and cupboards. They planned an intriguing strategy to prevent me from suspecting the food parcels. They said a friend's fridge had broken down, and she needed to store some frozen food. My suspicion arose when only frozen food arrived at the house. I then learnt it was a goodwill gesture from the church in Wellingborough. Preparing for Christmas 2002, we put the traditional ornaments up a week before the festival day. I told the wife not to bother with any decorations, for it would be like any ordinary day. Euphemia disagreed and said we must buck ourselves up. The house was sparing of anything Christmassy, except family Christmas cards on the dining table that came in the post. I began to grasp the Christmas spirit as the house took on colour. Euphemia and the children dug out and sorted the past year's decorations and hung them up. The living and dining room looked moderately different, with the decorations being up. Last year's Christmas tree was erected, and an inadequate quantity of items fashioned it, and it formed the central focus under which presents would lie.

Katrina came down from university on Sunday evening, the 22nd of December, and I rushed to open the front door before her key turned the door lock completely. I burst out singing, "Welcome home, welcome, come on in and close the door. You've been gone too long, welcome, you are home once more", as I hugged her, making our way in a tightly squeezed hallway through to the open space of the living/dining room where her mum, Jonathan and Georgina were waiting. They repeated the song 'Welcome Home' altogether, singing in harmony. They gave her hugs and kisses, happy to see her. Katrina had been away for three months, the longest she has been away without making physical contact, though we regularly speak to her on the telephone.

The stereo music centre with its CD and tape does not work, but on Christmas day, the radio provided the Christmas music, and we entertained ourselves chatting to the children about their growing up. They talked about what they could remember, and looking at the family photo albums had us all overjoyed with laughter. In the flickering light of a candle, the atmosphere of shown love, touching the children's foreheads and cheeks, saying, "Mummy and Daddy love you and all the family", is a feeling of love and being loved. We were happy there was an atmospheric glow that seemed to radiate out through the walls, and despite everything, a little more spiritual realism, the real meaning of Christmas was achieved as we sing carols. The exclusive tableware, usually in the display cabinet or stored away, had dressed the dining table. The top table had plenty of food on it for the Christmas feast, with all our popular favourite dishes served on our best china plates. A larger than average-sized turkey and a bottle of wine were given to all employees at BB Engineering. The only alcoholic drink on the table was that bottle of wine, and a plentiful supply of tap water kept our glasses filled. The turkey provided a tasty meaty feast that gave us leftover portions for a few days; combining the rest of the bits gave us chilled pre-cooked food for four days. I had symbolically placed a lit candle on the table at mealtime from the first day of Christmas until the 14th day after Christmas. It represents the longing for peace in our days, prayers for the need for food, shelter and care for the environment and its creatures—a candle for light in our world illuminating God's presence in an iconic form.

Before the meal, we held hands around the table. We prayed the table prayer (the Grace written for blessing the table) and additional prayers to bless our family and bring the long-awaiting prosperity into our lives. 'Continue to bless us with good health and strength'. We remembered all sick and lonely patients, and we prayed for our relatives and those without families. We asked for success for the children in their education and help in their learning and understanding. We invited a special blessing to our parents and relief from suffering, especially for my dad. He was diagnosed with Parkinson's disease just before Christmas and later diagnosed with progressive supranuclear palsy (PSP). The candlelight had wilder flickers as the breath of laughter reached the flame. The dining table atmosphere showed family love filling the room with an aura that radiated a happy family's sounds through the walls. The season for overconsumption and indulgence lasted until Friday the 28th of December 2002, and we had an excellent traditional family Christmas and had not indulged disgustingly.

As the new year approached, a question stewed in my mind. What are we making of our lives? Debt burdens are not easing. We helped Katrina pay for her accommodation fee, and we contributed up to half of the £212.33 needed per month. In 2003, I will not be making life-changing decisions but more life-enhancing choices. We want the opportunity to come where we can do more things together, travel perhaps and make more time for things. Money gets called upon, and our health needs to be good. The approach of Christmas saw Euphemia come down with ailments that needed four prescriptions from the doctor. The lack of money made us only buy the three important ones, and she will have to go back to the doctors in the new year for a blood pressure check. It was high on her last visit. As for my health, I have gum disease, which has my left jaw swollen and an excruciating toothache over Christmas. The tooth still aches a bit, but I have developed a cold now as well, with a persistent runny nose and sore throat. I could not afford prescription charges if I went to the doctor or dentist fees for examinations and treatment. So, I'll sit it out, hoping it will clear up by itself like it had done the last time. The children's health is excellent, and my next thought is, I am so lucky to have a wife and family.

Feeling lucky is hardly an emotion one would expect anyone to experience under the circumstance of struggling to make ends meet. I am fortunate with a capital F because I have a loving family, caring, working together and filled with God's love. It allows my customary daily praying to grow from an ordinary spiritual baby into a spiritual Saint. I have made a vow to find the money to keep up a frequent attendance at church, and Euphemia hopes to settle in the Sister Church in our town, Kettering, in the new year with mainly black people worshipping. My mother had somehow sensed our financial difficulties because she had already given me and Euphemia clothes for Christmas presents and concealed £20.00 in a Christmas card for us before I said we have no money for Christmas, we are skint.

On Saturday 29th December, mother and Dad had supper with us and spent the whole evening with us until 11:45 pm. Mother handed me an envelope containing £50.00 in a secretive manner as she passed me in the kitchen to go to the loo downstairs. Mother asked me not to mention anything about the envelope to Dad because it was entirely her money, and he knew nothing about it. I was reluctant to take it, but my mother said they wanted to help. Thank God for parents, for the money was handy for buying fuel for the car for the rest of the holiday period and getting me to work on 2nd January 2003. The payment was also used to play a small part in reducing my community tax arrears by £40.00. Mother and Dad are pensioners, and I believe Mother used her pension money to see us through to New Year because I had said we are broke. So, I understood her motive to give. It's hard for parents to see their children on the breadline and not make personal sacrifices to help them get back on their feet. Thanks, Mother; I am very grateful for the sacrificial gifts you have given, past and present, and that you had not told Dad. I found it hard to fathom my mother secretly giving me money and not speaking about it to Dad. I felt sure Dad would approve, but my mother kept giving me money, requesting me not to tell Dad, so it remained her secret.

Confronting God with suicide
Written Monday 28th April 2003

Years of prayers, watching, waiting and searching, doing all I felt I could do, have led me to want to confront God. I want to face God about the deep crisis in our lives; though the world does not owe us a living, I see my family struggle year after year and have to pull straws; we cannot live life like that anymore. I watched my family sink deeper and deeper into poverty while I still assumed God would help reverse the trend. But God was doing nothing.

Christmas 2002, I had to accept third-party charity handouts to get through the festival, and as a proud man, it was the last straw turning outside the family for essential everyday living support. I was deeply aware I could not provide for my family, and it would only be a matter of time until I would sacrifice my mortal body to have an encounter with God on the other side of the universe. In the new year, a letter dropped through our letterbox that said the council had rejected my plea not to pay the outstanding arrears and enclosed the new demand for 2003-04 council tax. It gave me a sense of hopelessness because feeding the family and paying the bills was already outside my means. To divert more money to this would mean less for buying our food. There was no money in our bank account, and critical spending was still needed; we needed this, we needed that just to stand still. We needed money for school trips, food, clothes, a new boiler, car service, petrol and installing home entertainment. So, when Katrina sent down her student money to pay for her student accommodation rent, I spent it on food and household bill payments as emergency payments. I had asked for an advance of wages over Christmas and paid it back in instalments taken directly from my wage packet. I spent half the fees of Georgina's driving lessons, and the stream of demands on money seemed never-ending. Our nominal wages have no more stretchability and have finally snapped as the flows of financial requirements multiplied. Our income was reduced because of leaving work when one of our children was ill at school, getting to work late by fifteen minutes each day, or when the wife fell sick and did not turn up for work. I rejected a lifestyle where I could not live comfortably and fought for the only way to benefit my family, even if it meant my martyrdom. I would give up my life as a survival gift for them to have a good quality of life.

On the weekend of 1st March 2003, I needed a supply of antipsychotic medication for just £6.20, and I could not afford it. From the beginning of that week, I was weary and moody, day and night, in constant prayer. I went to strategic places for moments at a time to pray and press God for change to our circumstances. I had many ideas about God and his actions, and I was optimistic I had a chance of seeing a self-fulfilled prophecy and a significant breakthrough in faith. But, instead, I cried - "Merciful God, forgive me for the way I choose to bring about a swift change in the life of my family. I planned my exit from life on earth by suicide because there were also too many harsh realities which, even though I have no control over them, were causing me distress". Why does God not intervene in human affairs?

I was heading to the other side of the universe to find out why, knowing there was no way of coming back. I thought of myself as a man of faith, but nothing seemed to work; even believing in God gave me no credibility. On the morning of Sunday 2nd of March 2003, I woke from a deep sleep with sketchy dreams that convinced me my life had glimpsed heaven and eternity in my mortal flesh, but I could not remember anything about it. I will cause myself to be where God is prematurely and ask the biggest questions that had affected my life. The belief that God stands on the other side of the universe with Jesus, the saints and all the angels are an excellent assumption and makes me want to take a spiritual leap off the edge of the earth by deliberately having a fatality. I would experience another place that faith says exists and momentarily stand there with the great heavenly host and disappear back to the world with not human-made memories.

On Sunday, the 2nd of March, I regularly hugged the children and talked calmly to my wife about insurance documents and essential housekeeping paperwork. I cuddled up to her on the settee, smiling more to show a loving bond. It had been missing due to tension in our relationship in the week. I was snapping at her for days, and she retaliated and snapped back, and it was all to do with my anxious state in putting my affairs in order without directly letting on what was disturbing me. We warmly touched each other's hands, gazing at each other with twinkling eyes. Euphemia began to feel very comfortable and a bit suspicious of the attention. We have shared hugs and kisses on the lips and cheeks in front of the children watching television. I was doing everything I could to make my family feel cosy that evening, knowing I plotted to end my life in a cowardly violent way. Children, Daddy will not be there for you or mummy anymore because my motive is to meet the creator out of a sense of complete bleakness. I cannot provide basic needs and believe a single parent with insurance pay-out can better head my family. Society's systems are geared toward the survival of women and children without their male partners.

For many years, I had convinced myself that the only way to ease poverty and give the family a secure financial future was to fight for change. Still, I became disillusioned as change did not happen over the time scale I had expected. So, at 9 pm, I left the house, feeling brave and confident to carry out an act that would not see me returning home. I told Euphemia a false story about going down to the pub to get a soft drink for our son's lunch box, as the corner stores would soon close. Usually, when I say I am going down to the pub, it's a family joke. All I'd ever do was to walk through to the hallway to the front door, open it and close it firmly again and they all knew it was a hoax because shortly afterwards, I'd walk back into the living room asking who wants crisps or a pint.

I became remorseful overnight when I almost made all those who care and love me lose the relationship they shared. I almost took away a massive chunk of my family's future memory, a family that loves me, because I attempted suicide and escaped death only by God's grace. The morning of 03.03.03, I deliberately, foolishly, braved walking on a non-pedestrian road, the A14 dual carriageway. I collided with a 39-ton articulated lorry when I willfully strayed into the path of the vehicle. Today, 28th April, eight weeks on, I am well enough in the local hospital, Kettering General, to be writing this report. Due to my folly, the injuries I sustained were stitches in a wound in my left palm and right arm, a fracture to my right leg and a broken ankle, and multiple fractures to my left foot, including the heel. I had a skin graft taken from the inner area of my left thigh to repair a large area of open tissue on my left foot. I also had a surgical plate inserted in my right leg. They were no facial injuries or internal organs damaged, but I had blood in my urine, and I found it difficult to pass water. The medics intervened with an abdominal catheter and asked me to drink plenty of water, sorting the problem. I cannot bear weight on my right foot, but the doctors don't know why yet.

I could not feel anything but angry at first that I had survived the attempt to put our welfare in order by my death. I immediately worried when I realized I had survived the collision. It had made every process and everything in our lives so much harder than before because I was damaged; things would be an even greater struggle. The worst of the worries as I lay in the hospital bed was that I had left Euphemia in the lurch with a financial mess, and she would leave me. I had no insurance policy to cover this 'accident', and the insurance that I had classed this as self-harm. If I had died, there would be no pay-out, I learnt from my hospital bed, and I was eager to pick up the pieces, sort the mortgage arrears and the children's education that may have suffered because of me, as I wanted to put things right. But they told me I had to get myself better physically and mentally.

My family and close relatives came to see me regularly, and the relationship with my wife was not in tatters; she was angry at what I had done and called me a "foolish man". I was ever so pleased that she was not thinking of leaving me. Euphemia said she would only find it necessary to separate if things continued without free time together and if she continued to feel she was not getting my attention. As a couple to our offspring, the care and love we can show collectively are not only for the children. She wants more attention from me. I have caused Euphemia much pain, and she was angry with me for leaving her on her own with three children and no real support. It was a selfish act of escapism, and now she has to survive with me, the primary breadwinner, in the hospital.

It is incredibly hard on Euphemia. As God is my witness, it was not my intention to make things harder on the family, but it was difficult to see anything other than my death-bringing victory over almost all stress-related life problems. A male family friend had seen Euphemia's vulnerability as I lay in the hospital, and Euphemia told me she had dinner with him. He offered her a dirty weekend away. I was jealous, and I felt even more useless because when I was able-bodied, I had no money to dine her and provide for her. This man can offer her wealth and successful life as a professional businessman, but his marriage is on the rocks. I would not blame Euphemia for falling for a better life with another man who offers holidays. I had twenty-one years to improve our lives but only made more of a hash of it, but I'll be sick if Euphemia were to have a sexual relationship with this cheating predator so-called friend of ours. I think Euphemia is feeling pity for me, and our marriage cannot survive with this emotion. But she came back at me to say she was angry, furious. "I am not bothered about us not having money; it's just that I want someone to love me and be there for me. It will take time to see how things will go and if I'll feel any different." I held back tears, my eyes moistened and biting down on my lips, and my whole self filled up with sorrow and remorse. I sensed what Euphemia said was right, and I looked at our marriage from her perspective for the first time instead of observing how and why our relationship was failing. I have deluded myself that it's because of the lack of wealth and lack of power - power in the sense that no matter what I try, it's bound to fail. Euphemia cried and could not stop when visiting time was over and left crying, suggesting that our relationship would sadly end. I had misread her signal of sadness to be one of abandonment, for she told me I'd see her in three days because she had things to do.

For three nights, I occupied my mind on saving our marriage and cried myself to sleep. In the waking hours, I was thinking up ways in which separation could work. When Euphemia came to see me again, I thought out a practical method to separate. It's a sad fact that Euphemia has another potential partner with money to improve her happiness. I asked Euphemia to take up to six years, when our son is twenty, to make up her mind to return to me after enjoying the life this man was offering her. I could not see that my logic and rationale were not working well because I pushed her towards separation, hurting us terribly. I love Euphemia so much that I promised her I would wait and never form another relationship but, for her to have sex with another man, I am not sure that our bedroom manner can ever be the same when she comes back to me. I told Euphemia over and over, 'I love you; I'll wait to have you back, whatever happens, you will always be my best friend'. I would have to scale down my romantic tendencies when I meet her on the street and exchange only a hug. On the other hand, I said to Euphemia, "I will never give up on the friendship we have shared for so many years".

Honest to God, I want Euphemia and me to have a holiday rather than head for separation. I bet if we had a break together, we'd be alright, but for that to happen, it boils down to having money. I've got none, so I am bound to lose her to a rich man. I am trapped, unable to provide for Euphemia, yet want her to keep our companionship when it is clear another man can offer more than my wishful thinking of seeing us jet off somewhere on holiday. He told Euphemia that he fancies her and isn't rushing her for closer involvement until she wants it. Euphemia revealed what had happened so far in her relationship with him. I have learnt he has separated from his wife now and is waiting to see if we will break up or work things out, but at the same time, he is on stand-by for Euphemia. I am terrified that my wife is deciding to separate. Still, I gave her an ultimatum -to take until I come out of the hospital and go into rehab to determine what direction she wants our relationship to go. Euphemia has the strain of looking after the house and the children, and I have added pressure to collapse the family unit. Still, I needed to know which way our relationship was going to get over the pain.

My suicide attempt, if it had been successful, would have been an opportunity for Euphemia to be in a new relationship with someone who has enough money to look after her and the children. I wanted to die; I saw it as a way of making things final and easy for Euphemia to be free from me, as I am making her unhappy and can't provide for the children. I had thought all would have come right with death, but now that I have survived it, I am glad to continue sharing my life with Euphemia until natural death does part us. Euphemia is unsure what she wants and asked me to give her more time than just up to my hospital discharge. Euphemia is fancied by another man who enjoys her company, and this may go far beyond friendship. I wanted her to forget him and concentrate on making our marriage work. I would like their obsession to fade, but they meet and go to the pub, and, therefore, it seems the relationship will grow rather than disappear. Euphemia comes to my hospital bedside and looks stunning, lovely and happy. I pressed her to end the meetings because the time would soon come for me to leave the hospital. Euphemia said she is unsure what she will do and needs space and time to reach the right decision. She was still angry at what I had done and doesn't feel I listened. My trust and respect for her had faded, and I took her for granted well before the accident, she says, and she likes enjoying this man's company.

It came as a sad surprise that's beyond belief that I was taking Euphemia for granted and had decided to kill myself selfishly. My motive to kill myself was driven by love and my ideology. I've undertaken a reality check and hope there is a possibility of redemption. I am trying not to continue down the road of self-delusion, for I cannot repair this situation unless I am truthful. I want to change to please Euphemia because I love her; if I do or say anything that irritates her, I am working hard to stop it because I want her to come back and love me, or I have to face up to a failed expectation of life. I am incredibly sorry for what I have done, as it has made matters worse. Also, I am enduring extreme pain after the operation to fix my foot. The problem seemed unbearable for many weeks, and now the pain is better controlled, but the left heel continues to give me shooting pain like a stabbing sensation the moment pain relief wears off. As I lay in hospital, my parents paid the immediate bills to support us, and they also gave the money to pay Katrina's rent of £300.00.

The Third of the Third 2003 suicide attempt

Written Thursday 1st May 2003

I am a fortunate man because I'll not expect to see my family again. I had closed the house front door on the night of Sunday 2nd of March 2003 and walked off to commit a suicidal act that was supposed to have shown no greater love from a father for his family. I looked deeply into the night sky and muttered the words, "Here I come, God. Prevent my action if it is not meant to be, oh God, amen". My spectacles, mobile phone and the main bunch of keys were left at home. I did not take the car key or remote either; I only had the spare house key and my wallet. I did not want the fatality in our car and cause mobility problems for Euphemia later on. I did not wear my spectacles because I did not want to see the calamity I intended to have. I am short-sighted, and having blurred vision would make it difficult to judge the vehicle's speed that would knock me down. Put me on the other sides of the endless universe to meet my maker in an alien form or see what eternal unperishable is, and the first cause is us in us looking in us.

An hour after leaving home, I expected to be dead and enter the unknown, another side of the universe, where good and faithful people go when deceased. I went to the corner shop and bought bottled water, and meandered through the streets, stopping momentarily every so often, looking up at the stars and mumbling, expecting a cave in of my determination to go through with it. Instead of feeling sad, unhappy, tearful, depressed and lonely, I grew in strength and courage. If I could not go through with it, where would be the sign or something to make me change my mind? I walked about one and a half miles away from the house until I reached the Trading Post pub, close to a bustling road, the notorious A14. I sat in an obscure corner of the pub with my hands clenched up to my lips. I engaged in prayer and communicated to God that I must die and the way it would happen. "Right out instant death and, God, do not let me down on this one." My face was now buried in my hand with my eyes firmly closed as my thoughts deepened, pleading to God to make my death an accident instant death. Not let the incident affect people, including the paramount vehicle driver ordained in my mind to help me exit from this earthly here and now. "Please prevent the suffering of any psychological damage or physical injuries." I pleaded to God for this to be the condition of my death. My life would end in an instant, and the power of God and the mind would prevent harm to the afflicted. I believed I had that assurance from the living God, and hearing the traffic noise and seeing the vehicle's headlights from the pub window flicker. My mind had great clarity over my fate.

I left the pub at 10:30 pm, and I strolled down to the main road, a dual carriageway without a hard shoulder, just grass verges. I steadily inhaled deep cold air, took a breath of courage and exhaled a warm passive prayer breath of, 'Should I be doing this?' The temperature had dropped, and frost had begun to form on blades of grass and everything around me. By the time I said to myself that there could be no turning back, it was midnight. So, the nature of my prayer changed to asking God to stop me from doing this between midnight and one o'clock. From one o'clock, the ground stood hard, and the condition had worsened. Frost clung to everything, and my whole body was cold as I continued to walk to get to an all-night service station and ask for help.

I reached the service station by 3 am and stayed a few hundred yards away from the area. The road was much quieter at three in the morning, and I started to practise playing 'chicken' from the verge of the road to a raised cover of the maintenance drain seen above the height of the damp grass. It was no more than ten steps to the maintenance hole cover, and I marched to and fro to keep myself warm. From the grass verge to the utility hole, I would sometimes just come short of advancing further than the white line-markings at the edge of the road in an attempt to be mowed down by the selected road vehicle. This long lorry was passing at a considerable speed.

I saw police cars on both sides of the carriageway, which sent a bit of nervous tension through my body. Some had cruised their way through the service station and had glanced at me, marking time on the top of the maintenance drain cover. However, they never caught me near the edge of the carriageway. I thought that 3 am would be the ideal moment to collide because traffic was not frequent, and I could quickly identify a roaring lorry with dip twin headlights and extra lights around the front of the cab. I listen to hear the incredible noise the truck made as it came. I imagined it would be thrilling to be in front of it and get knocked down swiftly—that time passed as I waited to glimpse the vehicle that would take me out of this world.

Dawn broke at 5 am, and the night sky started to disappear. By six o'clock that Monday morning, in the east, the sky glowed bright yellow, golden orange appeared above the horizon, and it was a chilly climate, but I had peace of mind. Although vehicles travelled incredibly fast and furious in all lanes, bulky goods vehicles and vans dominated the nearside lane. The traffic rumbled my stomach, my shoes were soaking wet from the dew on the ground, and my fingers and toes were freezing. I could see the flattened grass where my feet had trampled a track during the early morning. I moved from the roaring traffic and stood on the maintenance hole cover, and stopped the dodging back and forth in an attempt to give up life. I watched the traffic from the maintenance hole as I made a mental calculation of distance and speed, then I moved swiftly to the edge of the road when a lorry was approaching with a determination to end it there.

I had missed a few chances and now began to walk on the white line that determines the road's edge in the direction of oncoming traffic. I leaned more to duck into the traffic with one hand on my hip to support my waist, which had a very painful stitch. My posture was weak. I could feel the agony of my strained side, back and neck, and I was bent like an unfolding pen knife. Two policemen in a patrol Land Rover pulled up beside me at 6:10 am. The flashing hazard lights were too bright, and it dazzled my eyes because I could not see their faces for a moment. They stayed in the patrol car, and one of them asked me where I lived and if I was waiting for someone. He had seen me standing in this area throughout the night. I said my address, and he asked for my ID. I showed him my driving licence, and he asked me to give him the direction to my house. I suspected the policeman thought I might have lost my memory and I answered, "I am waiting for a friend travelling from Birmingham to make our way to Huntingdon. He should be here soon, and my house is very close by". I had hoodwinked the police; they believed me and carefully drove off and joined the stream of fast-flowing traffic.

Within seconds of the police patrol leaving, my throat swallowed saliva, my stomach sunk and churned over. My sincere desire was to go home and ask my family to forgive me and take time off work to evaluate my life and ideology. It shocked me that they, the police, were like symbolic guardian angels, coming to give me a chance to stay with my loved ones and people who care about me. I felt low in mood, disappointed with myself, and wished I had my mobile phone to talk to my wife to let her know I love her and am on my way home. I realised that I was within distance of a telephone kiosk as I was yards from the service station. My mind slipped back to the idea of prematurely ending my life, and I felt I must go through with it. My nerves were as tough as steel, and I was ready, and I felt a coward to back out of it and a brave man to commit myself to what I believed. At 6:20 am, I had no hesitations; I stood confidently on the white line, ready to have my life taken from me. The conditions became perfect, and there was a gap in the traffic; I identified a lorry with no vehicles following close behind and aimed to collide with it. I stayed calm as my short-sightedness revealed tiny sparkling lights on the truck, and they were getting more prominent as it approached. I began to whisper a verse of The Lord is my Shepherd, then a line from the Lords' Prayer, and I called to God, "Here I come, oh God". I leapt off the white line into the road in a split second and collided with the truck. The driver steered toward the central barriers. I had looked at the driver a split second before the big truck impacted my body. The sudden unexpected leap gave the driver no time to sound the vehicle's horn, only to swerve the truck to a halt. I felt a cushioned impact with the corner of the lorry's cab, and I saw a flash of bright white and orange light as I was being thrown further into the road. I lay almost straight across the width of the two-lane carriageway without feeling pain or suffering any loss of consciousness. As I lay on the tarmac with my face to the side, I could only see the ground under my nose and had no idea of the posture of the rest of my body. I did not know whether I was under the lorry, and the rest of me had got smashed to pieces, but I had imagined the worst until I moved my toes and could see my palm.

To this day, I do not know how I escaped death; I was momentarily angry because I had not crossed over any domains, and I thumped the ground with my right hand saying, "Damn it, why didn't you let me die? Why God? You let me down again and let me live." I was fully conscious and had no pain whatsoever throughout my body, but I noticed clotted blood on a wound on my left palm and sensed I had grazed my right arm because of more significant bleeding, and I thump the ground with my right fist again and again with fury. Why hadn't God let me die? The collision had stopped the traffic passing through, and it did not seem long before the voice of a man came onto the scene, asking me to lie still; an ambulance would be arriving in fifteen minutes. Unfortunately, I was not in a position to see who he was. Instead, I heard the roar of the heavy traffic flow passing by on the other side of the carriageway. It sounded like both carriageways were in use. The paramedics arrived, assessed me on the ground in no time, and told me I had a fracture in my leg and foot. They placed a brace around my neck, put me on a stretcher, took me into the ambulance, and then to the hospital.

I suffered a great deal of remorse; I was very sorry because things would be more brutal and worse to sort out. It had been tough before I tried to take my life, but now I cry, for I am happy to be alive. However, as the doctors fixed the physical damage, I wanted to improve the emotional injuries, which included damage to my relationship with my wife.

On my first week in the hospital, I asked for my psychiatrist to visit me. He came, heard my brief account about the road collision and left about ten minutes later. He stated that he felt the ward lacked privacy and wanted to see me at his clinic. An ambulance was booked to take me to his clinic on his instruction on 25th April 2003. When the day came, my legs were in a plaster cast, and I was wheeled into a private room on a stretcher, but the door could not close because the room could not accommodate the entire bed length. The psychiatrist explored the problems of my life with me and what led up to my attempted suicide. The most remarkable thing about the session was his lack of understanding of my explanation for my ideology, why I did as I did, and why I am as I am. He asked for my permission to invite specialist doctors and nurses to speak to me when we next met.

He also asked me to trust him because he wanted to change my antipsychotic drug to modern medicine for no other reason than having a newer drug. In addition, he said it would be more effective. Although he did not say that my medication was ineffective, he felt I would benefit from the recent advances in antipsychotic drug therapy. His manner in his request made me think it was in my best interest to have the new drug, called Risperdal, and for me to deny it makes me a fool, so I gave my consent.

It seems to go against my better nature because I have broken out of the psychotic mound and no longer hear voices, see things and sense things that are not there and I think the drug I am having now remains adequate and effective with no noticeable side effects. So, there was no need for the change from the Surpride medication. Last week, I was moved to a rehab ward, which meant I did not require much nursing care.

Today, Thursday 1st May 2003, I was told of a new specialised rehab centre, located in Wellingborough, called Beachwood, that should help me be more effective in mobility and looking after myself independently with or without added equipment. It is the place where I am to go when discharged from the hospital rehab unit. I am getting weaned off my usual antipsychotic drug, Surpride, and tonight will be the last dose, and the new drug called Risperdal replaces it.

I was discharged from the general hospital on Friday 30th of May 2003 because I had progressed well from a pulpit frame, gutter frame and Zimmer frame to walking with crutches. A place at Beachwood rehab was not available when my mobility increased, and I had progressed so well in the rehab ward that they let me go home. The OT department equipped my home with chair raisers, a high stool, and a toilet raiser, and I regularly have physiotherapy at the outpatient clinic. Doctors and especially nurses were angels to me, incredibly hardworking with long hours working shifts from 7 am to 9 pm and nights from 8 pm to 8 am. They were devoted, dedicated and their energy-efficient spirit and the care given falls into the category of remarkably efficient, professional people. I want to thank them from the bottom of my heart for how they looked after me.

Today is Monday 16th June 2003, and the antipsychotic drug Risperdal is giving me embarrassing troublesome side effects. I was leaking urine in my sleep (bedwetting) in the hospital setting, which continued when I went home. I leaked urine at night in bed next to my wife, and I have sexual potency problems. I wrote to my psychiatrist and told him of the issues I am having with Risperdal tablets, and he changed it to Amisulpride 400mg tablets on 19th June 2003. He appointed me a male psychiatric nurse to oversee things, and what is a remarkable coincidence is that the nurse was my nurse in 1990 when we lived in Wellingborough. I said that I did not need one.

Looking back on fresh-cut grass
Written on Saturday 16th August 2003

Euphemia was targeted by a new man who came into her life when she told him her husband was in the hospital. She may become a statistic of a failed marriage because Euphemia is risking an affair. He was supposed to be a family friend, a friend of both of us. When I was in the hospital, he came to my home and said to Euphemia that he had always fancied her, and Euphemia did not seem to see that the friendship with him was spoiled. He had wooed her, and Euphemia didn't understand how hurt I felt when she noticed him and tells me he's only a friend. I do not think Euphemia is strong enough to resist his charm, so an affair is inevitable.

My relationship with my wife is at an all-time low because I am suspicious of her and believe she is cheating on me, but she tells me that she is not unfaithful, and I struggle to see it as not so. I suggest that we try to rekindle our love, although my suspiciousness stopped my libido, and Euphemia had said her love for me was becoming more like the love of a sister to a brother. I ache with jealousy that Euphemia has a lover. How can we rekindle the spark we once had? We are dull, and there is no spark left because her Casanova manfriend aims to split us up; they still keep in touch, and Euphemia has lost her desire for me. In an attempt to win Euphemia over, I was willing to make changes to see us flourish in ways familiar to couples but alien to us. I talked to Euphemia about us putting a small amount of money in a jar for the sole use of going to the pub, eating out or going to the cinema. But she seemed to disapprove of the idea by not saying anything.

I have no evidence that my wife is cheating on me and suspecting that she would do because I have lost my trust in her, which presents a problem. She has become less open and stays silent when I talk to her about her Casanova. I need the reassurance that she is not playing around with this man and will run off with him. Instead, Euphemia holds me in suspense by her responses, silences. Did I want to hear her reveal my worst nightmare that she is having an affair? Euphemia broke her silence and muttered, "Why can't I have male friends without you thinking they want to get into my pantie?" The evidence was not there to raise the suspicion of cheating, for Euphemia comes home from work on time and says where she is going when she goes out. Indirectly, I know when Euphemia leaves the house because the children get told their mother's whereabouts by their mother, and they tell me if I ask them.

I am becoming so insecure in myself since my wife will not reassure me and say things that will allow me to feel she wants me more than anyone else; she stays silent. At my nephew's wedding, I showed my fully blown-up insecurity by watching every man who was eyeing her on the dance floor. Euphemia, along with the wedding party, was dancing near me and showed no direct eye contact with anyone, but I found any man a potential threat to take my beautiful, attractive wife away from me. I talked to Euphemia about my feelings and said she brought insecurity into my life because I can't trust men who make advances towards her. A bad feeling welling up instantly in Euphemia worsened an already bad situation with us. Euphemia probed me to get to the truth she thinks I am getting at. "You will never be able to trust me going to clubs with the girls, will you? You think me a slut?"

The product of the relationship with this man was that it destroyed my trust in her. I think it's up to her to build back that trust by telling me our marriage is safe, not on the rocks;

saying something reassuring so that the twenty years of confidence and feel secure in her company can continue. Euphemia defended the friendship with him, saying they were just friends. He has told Euphemia himself that he wants to be more than just friends, so why doesn't Euphemia tell him where to go? But Euphemia does not! I detailed our relationship's sorry state before her birthday on 12th August and kept talking about it after her birthday too. However, there is no reconciliation; my gut and emotional feelings damage us, and we both have anger and bitterness. The thing is, deep down, I feel I have so much love and warmth to give, but I can no longer show Euphemia that affection because she says that she wants us to be like a brother to a sister. I was stifled because I got trapped within an ocean of love that I cannot express. After all, Euphemia is cold and uninterested in me. Euphemia denies that she will reject my approach to release my need to touch her and have intimacy, and I suggest we go to Relate, a marriage counselling service.

I went to talk to my parents yesterday to explain to them for the first time why I tried to take my own life and how my relationship with Euphemia has broken down. Euphemia was not in the room at the time, and they believed it was essential that Euphemia was present to be part of the conversation. So, Euphemia was called into the room and explained her views of our difficulties, and my parents did not take sides; they were mutual in response. Euphemia's point of view seemed to have won points with my parents at first, but their conversation with us favoured the two of us making up and making our marriage work. They never judged us or condemned us.

On the contrary, they listened and summed up with supportive advice, equally valid for the two of us, but we still went home and quarrelled. We argued well into the early hours of the morning, and Euphemia told me my angry shouting would wake the children. "Stop going over the same things and shouting." Euphemia became aware that one of our kids was awake. Our daughter, Georgina, whose room is next to ours, got woken up, and she moved her bedding downstairs and slept on the settee. I went downstairs at 4 am and gently woke Georgina and apologised, and encouraged her to go back upstairs to bed. Jonathan, whose room is the back bedroom, said that morning he had heard us arguing, and he did not get to sleep soundly; the noise kept waking him up. I told Jonathan I was sorry for interrupting his sleep last night.

This morning, 16/08/03, neither of us had the desire to say good morning to each other. I did not want to talk and felt awkward being in the same room as Euphemia. In the evening, I started arguing again, and she ignored me, and I got frustrated. At that time, our eldest daughter, Katrina, came down from Manchester and entered the house at the height of my frustration and mouthing off. Still, Euphemia would not get to loggerheads, and I was forced to calm down and keep the peace for the sake of the children's happiness. I explained to the children that mummy and I were not getting on, and it was the final straw. I said, "We cannot work out our differences alone, and we are going to see a relationship counsellor on Monday 18th August to help us resolve our difficulty." In a joking way, I added that we might end up divorced to make light of a serious matter, but not really.

It doesn't feel possible that we can get back from where we are now in our relationship. I feel like we hate each other's opinions, which selfishly affects our liking. As time fell to evening, we had a short distance between us as we sat on separate armchairs and relaxed in front of the TV with the children in our midst. Our eyes met the moment we glanced away from the TV, and our gaze locked firmly, and neither of us looked away. I felt my tension release by the fixation and automatically released a smile. Our brains had synchronized, and we began to smile at the same time as if the turning of the same switch had triggered it, and we laughed for the first time in ages.

I thought of waiting till tomorrow to take her down to the pub to celebrate our breakthrough, and I had the money from payback from Family Tax Credit that put us in an excellent financial position. I generally thought this is a good sign, that smiles and a laugh had built a bridge to move forward on, but it was a testing time tonight. It looks like we have made teeny weeny progress. We were still smiling as we went to bed, and I asked to be hugged, and as we held each other in a long embrace, I said, "Will you try? For I am trying, and I am sorry". "Yes, Karl," Euphemia replied.

That night, quarrelling between the sheets did not happen. I cuddled her; Euphemia didn't come onto me. So, it did not feel like a pleasing of two minds, but the surrender to one partner's emotional need.

Today, Sunday 17th August, I asked Euphemia how she was feeling, and she came and embraced me for a considerable time. Then she kissed me, and she broke the embrace to go to church. We were brought to hugs again after church for peace had replaced frustration, and after dinner, we lingered at the table, relaxed in general conversation with our daughters. Jonathan was absent from dinner because he went out to play football with his friends on a floodlit playing field at the leisure centre. I could not fulfil my want to take Euphemia to the pub because Euphemia began to help Katrina unplait and remove her hair extensions. Euphemia never knew that I had hoped to take her out for a drink.

I am aware of the extra stress on her. Our relationship is the most significant stress factor because Euphemia speaks to no one about our relationship, so the burden never gets released. It must build up in her. I hope the counsellor tomorrow, 18/08/03, will help her release her pent-up feelings and thoughts because she does not tell me about them. Maybe it seems I do not listen well; I need to be smacked in the face with a wet fish for feeling so insecure. Now I am sick of my voice, banging on about how vulnerable Euphemia has made me. This misconception is the obstacle stopping our relationship's growth and happiness, just when I thought there had come a time when one knows there is a right or wrong thing to do to make myself happy. Be it debts, illness or relationship problems, life can still be sweet unless I feel out of control with compulsive, repetitive thoughts, and things are going pear-shaped. I am my own worst enemy. I have been foolish, draining my energy on what I think might happen without clear evidence and stressing the ones I love. I vowed to listen better to Euphemia, give her time to speak, collect her thoughts and prompt her to tell me them. I suddenly thought we would be alright when I thought we were heading for the divorce court moments ago. I did not physically raise my hand to batter my marriage, but I had illogically beaten it with my mistrust. I am so, so sorry, Darling. I felt changes, and I guess giving you the time you asked to sort out your feelings will let you decide what's right for you. I hope to God she does not cut me out of her life.

When Euphemia rang Relate, we learnt we would have to go to Northampton for the consultation; Kettering has a long waiting list, and we'll have to pay if we do not receive the qualifying benefits.

The invaluable Support
Written on 18th August 2003

Joan, my Jehovah's Witness sister, has dug deep into her life savings to help us. We had a brand-new boiler installed; Joan gave £400 towards it, and my mother and dad gave the rest, including paying the council tax arrears. Joan also gave another £300 for Katrina's accommodation which totals a massive £700.

Joan is aware that looking on the inside of our lives, we are struggling, and the general public only sees the outer appearance of elegance and our happy faces, and they cannot imagine we are finding life tough. Joan commented on the family's elegant looks and the luxurious appearance of our home. She especially picked out Euphemia's elegance, and I don't know how to understand her. Joan's colour television has stopped working and is beyond repair, and she watches TV on a small black and white portable set. I am indebted to her for her constant help to us and want to return her generosity. She needs an injection of cash, but I have not got any, making me feel sad. My relatives had regularly come to see me in hospital and at home and gave invaluable support, but Joan was exceptional in her visits and Christian Witness's charity. After work, she travelled twelve miles on the bus to see me without a bite to eat. Joan carried only packed sandwiches and a drink and sat and chatted at my bedside at what would have been her dinnertime.

Joan and I differ on the principle of religious belief, and it is well-known in the family circle. We argue on theology differences and agree to disagree because opinions don't get shifted. Family members warned me Joan would lecture me on Jehovah's Witness views on the serenity of life, and I suspected she would. Still, Joan did not mention religion but said only once, "Jehovah" - Joan was able to comfort me and made me feel I can survive this without having a lecture or sermon preached to me. Joan's visits actioned the gospel's truth by visiting me in hospital and not stressing to talk the gospel's truth. Her action spoke stronger than words which was a powerful working of God, a central belief. Joan has a sympathetic attitude and uses encouraging words that ease stress and anxiety. She explained how Jehovah has worked in her life, and Joan knew I had my human story of His involvement. She said on leaving, "You must not worry; things will be taken care of. You just think of getting yourself better, and when you are on your feet again, you will see things will work out; Jehovah will help".

The Christian Debt Advice Charity has provided a valued service. They gave food at Christmas 2002, helped Euphemia with more food aid this year, and supervised her in making financial statements to creditors and minimising our outgoings without a shortfall of cash. But they cancelled the contents insurance and suspended or reduced the payments owed on the essentials. Then suddenly, they withdrew their support as I recuperated at home. It was a devastating blow to our stomach and a kick in the teeth, which hit us when we were already down. This self-righteous evangelical Christian organization who self-praised themselves and advertised 'no strings attached' had not the decency to be truthfully honest about their decision to end their support. My wife was employed as support staff at the Church Nursery and worshipped with this community of Christian believers and helped out at the Church crèche on a rota basis. They decided all this when the suspended payments and reduced mortgage payments were coming up for review. A chief committee member called round at the house and told us the kick in the teeth news that they could not deal with our case any further because "It was inappropriate to take insurance money". Through our debt advice meetings with colleagues, he had been aware that I did not get a pay-out for the road collision. I had an insurance policy called Hospital Guild that pays £20 a day for twelve weeks for an inpatient stay in the hospital. It was ludicrous and outrageous to class this money as wrong to accept, as we had paid the premium for many years, and we had a legitimate claim. He hid under the insurance umbrella and could not be honest enough to say that his church people had a warped mentality towards us that pulled the rug from under our feet and punched us in the gut. We believed the real reason was that it was not ethical to attempt suicide, and therefore, their foolish, silly-ass rule/law that takes the moral high ground prevents them from adhering to the working of Christian conscience. Silly ass.

We are grateful to Kettering Citizen's Advice Bureau for immediately taking up our case, drafting a recent financial statement for our creditors and mortgage provider, and reinstating our contents insurance policy. In real terms, we are in credit. How ironic; I am not working, off sick, and have surplus money for a better living. After years of foraging a living, ironically, I could get by with only one wage and benefits when I could not balance income with the expenditure in work. The consultant says I am likely to be off work year.

Today, Monday, 25th August 2003, Euphemia had just come back from a most welcome break, a getaway from it all from Friday 22nd. Euphemia attended the 2003 Grapevine International Festival of the Lord Jesus Christ with a religious companion, Buki, held at Lincolnshire showground. Euphemia drove Buki's automatic medium-sized car to the showground. It was the first time she had driven a vehicle more prominent than the average family hatchback. They took their food and camped out in a tent on site. The site had all amenities that included loos and hot water for showers. People were there from all parts of the UK, Europe, the USA and South Africa. The gathering of people lifted their hearts in one accord, and Euphemia was caught up in the whole spiritual experience and enjoyed being impacted by the Holy Spirit and enriched by the word of God. Euphemia brought back gifts, gifts for the children and me, luscious chocolate and a coffee mug with printed words on the outside which read, 'Trust in the Lord with all your heart'. It is a beautiful mug that I am delighted to treasure.

A Message for each child
Written on Saturday 23rd August 2003

Children, my road collision happened at the peak of you doing revising, and I had been hospitalized in the months since revision and school examinations. All your energy was needed to concentrate on the exams, but I had caused you a great deal of worry and additional stress when you had to focus. All of you have said the accident has affected your concentration and caused you immense concern. As a result, Katrina, you had to retake one of the university exam test papers. Good luck, Katrina, on the retake, and my thoughts and prayers are with you at this challenging time, trusting you'll get the grade necessary to map out your career path.

I am sorry, children, for the emotional and immense pressure you had to bear because I made an unwise decision to take myself permanently off the face of the earth. I internalized world tragic events and saw complete bleakness in my ability to cope with life's demands. My conscience was less purposeful and goal-oriented because my internal dialogue that had governed my wisdom had failed to interpret my foolish self. What the 'voluntary' action of the 'free will' intended doing was harmful. Conscious processes could not have created the information I perceived in my consciousness to attempt suicide. My mind experienced an awareness shift through an urge before the physical act of attempted suicide resulted.

As a father, I look to serve you and be a good father to you, for I know we love one another. Forgive me for surrendering to the part of me that was the foolish self. I am here for you as long as I have breath, for I have seen the error of my ways and promise never to do that again. However, I do seem to become more incapable and more mentally ill in every decade that passes. I hope the future will belong. I want to be of sound mind to see you grow to mature adults and have a family. I hope mortality will get pushed back, and I can live with a good quality of life while continuing to take antipsychotic pills.

Katrina: Katrina, you studied Sociology and Culture Studies at Manchester University and told us you have fallen in love with a white male student called

Robert, who studies Physics. You told us your romance started about five months ago when you began part-time shop work at a WH Smith store. It appeared to be in the same period as my road accident. He has been there for you during times of stress, and you are in a physical relationship with him. You stay at his place of accommodation and Robert comes over to stay at your home sometimes. Robert has given you a lot of support. You spoke to us about him and your relationship, the romantic aspect and the realistic one. I gathered you are taking one day at a time and not taking today's moments for granted.

They are growing happily together and making a steady relationship. Nothing significant is in both heads about their relationship, which shows realism, but they are in love, which goes a long way to building trust, commitment and faithfulness. Katrina sent us a photo of Robert attached to an email. The picture showed us a warm, friendly-looking, mildly handsome young man. Robert is moderately cute through my male eyes but has the face of an attractive young prince in the eyes of the beholder, our daughter. I took a closer look at the photo. He looks of average height but quite a big-built young man who appears relatively fit.

I was trying to judge my daughter's steady relationship on how he looked on paper, which is funny because Katrina has already told us so much about him that I had approved of him dating her in my heart. Still, it was questionable in my head until I met him face to face. We met Robert for the first time on 19th July 2003 and what was remarkable about us meeting him was that I told Euphemia afterwards to wait. It felt like we have known him and had familiarized ourselves with him before this face-to-face meeting! Robert has such a friendly face, and a warm heart and plumpness make him look all the more loveable. Naturally, we liked him, but I became interested in what he may be thinking of us. I quizzed him a lot in our conversation indirectly, and Katrina said Robert did not sense it; I believe I had subtly incorporated it into the general discussion. Robert looked like he can hold his pints, and I know that Katrina likes alcoholic drinks. I hope they keep a check on their alcohol intake and do not binge drink too often, and think of the risks it may have on their health. Two intelligent people seem like they may well be suited to each other, but the testing of their relationship will come when romantic love has fizzled, and I hope that Katrina and Robert will continue to pull through.

Katrina is in new digs, a shared house with three friends from the last home on the same course as her. The landlord of the last place in Fallowfield had died, and it's up for sale. It was her digs after leaving the university Hall of Residence. The house had been robbed twice while Katrina was living there. On the first occasion, Katrina's room did not get broken into, thank God, because I worried about her safety and the cost of replacing uninsured things like her computer and stereo. The second time, the burglar climbed through Katrina's downstairs room window, and at that moment, Katrina was out of the room in another area of the house. The thief escaped with Katrina's mobile phone and her purse, which was on her bed. The police made Katrina aware that the domain is notorious for burglary and crime, and she must be extra vigilant.

On 1st July 2003, Katrina moved into the house on Doncaster Avenue, Wethington, paying £222 per month rent by standing order. As I acted as guarantor, Katrina gives me the money. Katrina's contents in this house are insured this time, and although the area is known to have a high crime rate, it's not as notorious as Fallowfield.

Georgina: Georgina, since turning seventeen, has blossomed into a rounded, balanced young lady who will soon be a young adult woman on her 18th birthday on 19th September 2003. What a remarkable change in such a short time. I know I had nearly eighteen years of seeing her growing up, but my second little girl seems to have grown up faster than I saw the seasons changing. She appears to be emotionally more challenging than her older sister. Tears do not flow so easily for Georgina when she meets with disappointments. Being upset or adapting to change may be risky to be involved in, but it challenges them to succeed. Georgina's GCSE result last year was above average. She gained a 'B' in seven subjects, two at 'C' and excelled in physical education with an 'A' grade. We were all very proud of Georgina's academic achievement, for she did well in the subjects that are so important in living skills.

Georgina went out celebrating with friends until the early morning of the next day. I knew she might binge drink as she was with her influential peer group and was full of joy. When Georgina returned home, I could see it was an enjoyable time was had and Georgina did not overdo the drinking. Georgina showed us that she acts sensibly. We allowed her regularly to go to the pubs and into nightclubs because her late teens years looking eighteen years old is a compliment. However, I did not encourage the nightclub life, so I told her to stay out of those places until she gets a little older. I let Georgina have her freedom to enjoy her independence safely at student nights on Thursdays, relaxing with friends and drinking in pubs, knowing she is coming of age in a few weeks and is legally responsible for her actions. I was not pushy or strict on her but reminded her to take care, be safe, try not to overdo things and allow her the space to continue to test out the adult way of life.

Georgina went into the sixth form to study at 'A' level rather than going to college and is looking forward to the next chapter of her independence, moving further away from our apron strings. We are proud of her; Georgina has new challenges, and the choices she has made are the ones she felt most comfortable with and made with a very mature attitude. With the help of her career's advisors, Georgina chose some new subjects to study at the 'A' level. The topics were not directly relevant to a job now, but the idea was to get the right balance and keep options open. Georgina has made a big decision in her life to go into the sixth form. Although I do not yet expect her to plan out her whole life, I expected her to have a pretty good idea of what she wanted to do. Georgina loves physical education and is thinking of going into something to do with sports activities and needs four subject options for the 'AS' level. I felt she was a bit lost and did not know how to choose suitable subjects. In the end, Georgina wanted to study Economics, Psychology, Biology and Physical Education. Still, the first two had her worried because they sound challenging to research, and as entirely new subjects, she did not know how she would fair, but she set her heart to the challenge.

Earlier in the year, 10th January 2003, the school arranged a presentation evening for the children to collect their records of achievement, and Georgina was amongst them. The guest of honour was Lord Dearing, and he gave an inspirational speech that reminded the children to believe in themselves and have faith, for they are only at the beginning of their lives and will meet with challenges. "You are tomorrow's people and could change tomorrow," he said.

Georgina had a difficult time in June sitting the 'AS' exams. Therefore, she feared she had failed in psychology and would not get the points to send to UCAS. Georgina collected her 'AS' levels last week and was pleasantly surprised because there were no failures. She gained an E in Psychology, a D for Economics and a D for Biology. In Physical Education, she got a B. Georgina, and her friends celebrated their exam success by being out all day at the pub, then went back in the evening and drank until closing. Georgina arrived home at about midnight under the arms of two of her friends. They were on each side of Georgina, trying to bear some of her weight. They said Georgina had begun to stagger through the streets on her way home. The moment Georgina entered the house, she headed straight for the loo to vomit. Georgina slurred her words when saying goodnight to us as we lay in bed. Her friends took off her shoes as she flopped into bed. Georgina woke at around 4 am and used the loo, then changed into her pyjamas. She slept until late afternoon and felt the need to be sick on waking, and she was fatigued. Georgina lost her appetite, and her eyes looked dreadful; she had experienced drunkenness.

Georgina has a full circle of friends, male and female, known to her through her part-time job, school and the gym. She tells me she has close friends but is not in a relationship. Georgina knows that she is fancied by boys and liked affectionately by both genders. Picturing herself in a year, Georgina tried to map out in her mind if all goes well and she was rated 'C' and above, the next chapter in her life would be studying at a good university, and she will work hard to get the grades. Georgina needs to study three subjects at 'A' level. She dropped psychology because it was her lowest mark at the 'AS' tier, and she found studying psychology very difficult. Georgina had researched her choices thoroughly and is aware that a wrong decision at this stage can have a detrimental impact on her career plans. Faced with large piles of prospectuses, where is she to start? The local careers advice and education organization came into the school to plan with the students for university placement. Georgina attended the UCAS West London Higher Education Convention at Earls Court and chose to do a degree course but worried about the better universities' entry requirements. Georgina does not have to decide yet but will have to travel soon to check accommodation and facilities before applying to UCAS early next year, 2004.

Georgina wears top and bottom braces on her front teeth, not diminishing her confidence and attractiveness. The bubbliness of her energetic personality strikes one before one notices her striking good looks and her dress code of fashion-conscious clothes. Both my daughters are gorgeous, and neither needs hair extensions to improve their faces, but at the moment, it's the fashion to have extra-long artificial hair, which is easier to manage combined with their natural hair. They wear a small amount of makeup, highlighted eyes and lip gloss, and no coloured lipstick, at present, to further their image of themselves. The clothes girls like to wear have not changed since I was a lad. They still love short skirts, skimpy tops, high-heeled boots, or fashionable shoes uncomfortable to wear. The thing about my girls is that they know when the garments they choose look gaudy, too revealing, and appear worn to seduce, which might give an impression of promiscuity. It is as rare as eagle's eggs if I ever have to tell them that their clothes are unsuitable or inappropriate.

Jonathan. Jonathan has made the first big decision of his life by choosing the subjects he wants to study at GCSE. They are English, Maths, Science, Art, Graphics and Electronics. He told me he wants to be a computer games designer, but only 20 years ago, there was no such thing. It's a growing field today, and Jonathan is rightly ambitious and wants to have the skills and knowledge. However, he will need to go through higher education after 'A' levels and gain a degree. Still, Jonathan is unsure if he will take the pathway to university to get a degree or do higher education at 'A' levels or apprenticeship.

When we moved to this house in 2001, Jonathan played in a football team called Ise Lodge Football Club. For over a year now, Jonathan has found other interests and does not train with the football club anymore. Still, he plays amateur football at a leisure club with his mates, including some severe Gaelic Football training to compete with other Corby teams. Up to my road collision when the cricket season started, Jonathan played cricket for the Old Grammarians Cricket Club in Wellingborough. I used to take him to train and also to perform at venues around the county. Jonathan is very competent on our home computer and is knowledgeable about emails, the internet and word processing. At the beginning of his teenage years, Jonathan knew how to programme and tune in the television and radio. He helped me set up our home computer all those years ago, and he set up Katrina's equipment.

Jonathan regularly helps his grandparents with how to use the TV remote-control programmer. He fixed the colour and settings problems, put them right, and showed them simple steps when the technology was too difficult to use. We tried not to let Jonathan lose out on the technology he loves, and eventually, he will get the game console he wants. It would develop his hand-eye coordination, dexterity skills and concentration, which I think is right. The first electronic game he had was the handheld Game Boy console. Then, his uncle Simon bought the children a Play Station console for Christmas 2000, and despite our financial difficulty, he received an X-Box console last month as a pre-Christmas present for 2003. Jonathan told us he wants to do a newspaper round again or find part-time work to help pay for his video/computer games and consoles. Jonathan barters with his friends over games and the shop manager at the game store where he exchanged games or sold the fun games at knockdown prices. There were two times when Jonathan's entrepreneurship surprised us. First, he sold his unwanted games to the games shop manager and bought an X-Box Extra with the money. He believed he had got a reasonable price for them. Then there was another time when Jonathan sold his skateboard. He bought it for £15.00 and no longer wanted it and sold it to a fellow pupil at his school for £50.00. That money helped us to buy him the latest X-Box console.

The games Jonathan buys are 15 rated, and they disturb me because of the violence. After a time of playing with the fun games, ordinary life seemed similarly dangerous. I found it chilling to play war games, the horror in fighting games such as Blade 2 and Smack-Down, even though it only pressing buttons to shoot and kill or chop off body parts, be it monsters or whatever; It blurs my understanding of the real and what's not so practical. As for Jonathan, he is so well-balanced that he knows reality from fiction. He knows realism from fantasy and make-believe. I can only play rally car racing and certain other sports games, for they do not trigger nausea or squeamishness. I am sure that Jonathan has no hang-ups, and his developing mind is excellent. He would not get led to experimenting or trying foolish things he saw on videos, television and computer games. Our boy shies away from the extreme, thank God, but loves to watch outrageous, hazardous behaviour on TV, such as Jackass and Dirty Sanchez and gets a good laugh.

I am concerned that Jonathan says he wants to ride a motorbike when he reaches sixteen. I believe that he will ride sensibly on the motorcycle; it's not that, but the thought that other motorists are foolish and with the heavy traffic flow on roads, I would always be wondering, heart in hand, 'Is my boy safe? Will he come home to us without calamity?' It's hard to give my consent to having a motorbike when the roads are so dangerous. I think he must go for training with a recognized school and ease some of the anxiety. I told Jonathan that I am aware of his eagerness to turn sixteen, but I am not ready to think of the consequences of allowing him to ride a motorbike.

One big constant worry would be when he mounted the motorbike until he returned home and dismounted outside the house.

Jonathan has gradually changed his image. To me, it appears it's not just a fashion statement but how he sees himself growing into a man. I made sure it's not only the trend for teenage black boys that he is following and that it's to do with expressing himself, which he will always be happy with right through to adulthood. The last time Jonathan had his hair cut was in November 2002. He has grown his hair to get it plaited into cornrows, and when it was at a reasonable length, his mum doubled it in the cornrow style. In the first few months before, Jonathan had tried to keep his hair looking neat, but he had a job on his hands because his hair grew to have tight and knotty curls. Jonathan groomed himself without the use of scissors to shape the unevenness of his hair growth. Jonathan spoke to us about having a stud in his left ear lobe and a tattoo on his arm.

Georgina also asked about having a tangible symbol on her 18th birthday. My answer was that I would consent on Jonathan's 15th birthday to him having an ear stud but cannot allow them to mutilate their body with a tattoo. They can wear outrageous clothes that reflect decency and moderate piercing in the ear lobe, not the body or tongue. They can also have streaks in their hair of outrageous colours, but I am against body piercing and tattoos. They are permanent deformation of the body, and when the fashion has dwindled, they will be left with an unfashionable permanent eyesore on their bodies. I would like them to grow up to be the individuals they want to become. So if they wish, I ask them to wait until they are twenty years old, more mature, so that I can be sure that tattoos and piercings are not fashioning statements but a part of their character-building that will make them feel happier. Jonathan looks after his appearance and goes to the gym, not the same as Georgina, though, and he looks physically fit with his gradual growth spurts and broad shoulders. He is a handsome youth who uses scented shower gel and perfumed deodorant and wears comfortable clothes, designer garments not being essential. Still, he asked us to buy clothes and shoes that are of his generation. Jonathan likes shorts and trousers of the baggy kind, oversized loose sweatshirts and baseball caps that one does not have to wear backwards. Jonathan isn't so comfortable in an innovative, bright shirt and ties anymore, but he goes along with what we say when we decide his traditional clothes should be worn. Jonathan has a circle of mates he plays computer games with at our home, and they are the ones that called around for him to come out to play.

He is yet to tell us of a relationship with girls, although he says he has just mates and friends. Georgina comes and tells him of the girls that fancy him at school, and he blushes and laughs. Jonathan has made significant progress in becoming confident and outgoing. A year ago, we could not send him to the shop or town centre without him wanting someone to come, but now he has learnt how to be safe and wise about the decisions he makes.

Message to my Children: You all know of the difficulty I have communicating with your mother. You tell me I am too angry and upset to hear anything your mum is telling me. It looked like we would be heading for the divorce court for a while, but things are generally improving, and I can see us remaining as a couple. Children, we do not want to scare you or make you decide which one of us you'd like to live with, as we will have a separate house. You will always be a part of us, and we will always love you, but if the worst comes to the worst and your mum and I have to part, do not blame yourselves. Your mum and I have just grown apart and want different things and have fallen out of love. We continue to love you equally and pray for your future happiness. We are incredibly proud parents to have such exceptionally good and outstanding children who participate in making us a happy, loving family. It's no secret that higher education has become an increasingly expensive affair. It looks like an unmanageable prospect when the financial help currently available, such as the student loan, is not enough to live on, and you turn to Mum and Dad for help.

We are aware of the financial difficulty with Katrina. Georgina and Jonathan, when you too have student financial difficulty, do not be afraid to ask us for money, and we will give what we can.

The long-term benefits of further studying and keeping you in university outweigh the cost. Don't let the cost of studying deter you; try and do part-time work during the holidays and term time. It would be a great way to earn extra money, but perfect for your prospects. As Katrina has learned, balancing a job with studies can be tricky, but it's feasible and helps minimize her overdraft size. Katrina, you need to continue to try and stay within the overdraft limit. The scary thing might be when you finish your studies, the prospect of owing thousands of pounds as a graduate might make you think twice about going into higher education in the first place. Please realize that graduates earn more throughout their working lives than non-graduates, and it does seem more feasible that you can pay back the student loan in a certain number of years. As a graduate, you will have a much better chance of achieving your career ambitions than if you have gone straight into work at eighteen, and therefore, you would have a better shot at a good standard of living and more job satisfaction.

Not only will you have learnt skills, but you will also have gone through a vital rite of passage. As well as the prospect of earning good money, the experience of moving away from home, making new friends, watching the pennies and having a pretty leisurely lifestyle will be challenging for you. But keep a tight hold of the purse strings; you'll have money to spare for frivolous activities while pursuing an intellectual or vocational ambition, and it will all make the financial struggle worthwhile. We want you all to excel and be financially better off than us today. Your mum and I have struggled all our married lives so far to be financially better off and have not lived a pretty leisurely lifestyle or relaxed. We work hard and only survive to this day. We got married with a £500.00 loan from Yorkshire Bank, and we are still borrowing, using credit to put enough food on the table. Life seems like an exercise of survival; we had had no fun entertainment other than television and rare outings. We wish you all best wishes and good luck and hope that you all will graduate, and we ask God to keep you safe and his speed and blessing upon you.

It's a challenge to provide you all with an excellent education that shall give you good earnings prospects and make you into rounded individuals. All your mum and I ask of you are to do your very best, and your very best can be a first, a 2:1 as a pleasant surprise to yourself or a 2:2 degree which is nice. If you happened to end up with a third or a pass, we'd want to buy a bottle of champagne, for it's still a good bet it will not be a drawback. Do not worry about getting a third or a pass; life does not end because you didn't get a 2:2 or above. You can be proud because merely having a degree is the most crucial thing in the job market right now, regardless of the classification. Even though more people have degrees, more and more employers are looking for degrees, so demand for graduates will outstrip supply. I want you to understand that research has shown little correlation between degree class and career success. What counts, children is how determined you are to get a job. You can earn a bit of money and learn something about life before you are successful in your career choice. Okay, early in your career, maybe a class of degree matters, but what counts more in interviews is that you must have evident enthusiasm for employers who do not take the tick-box approach to recruitment. They are more likely to look at your personality profiles and other skills, such as working with people and showing common sense. You might need to use some lateral thinking to get into your chosen career by doing some relevant work experience or getting into another related field first. I want you to know and be convinced that we will not think any less of you if you gain a third-class degree, and it does not necessarily consign you to a third-class life. It will do you no harm, for more people must get firsts than thirds or pass grades, and we want you to be pleased with whatever you come out with because we know you worked hard and there is nothing to be ashamed of you. There are six tips I came up with as I researched on 'How to get a first-class career with a third-class degree' if the worst happens.

1. You must be positive. Do not assume that your life is over because you did not get the degree that you wanted.
2. Take some time to re-evaluate your options and talk to advisors and us about it.
3. Do not skirt around the issue; bring it up yourself and explain why you got the result you did. Do not try to lie about it.
4. Think laterally about how you can get into the job you wanted. It might mean doing something else initially, which leads to the position you originally wanted. You could take a year off to get some work experience in a relevant field.
5. I am not sure what is meant by 'networking', but it gets said that networking is vital, and many jobs come from networking rather than advertising.
6. They say most employers do not specify the class of degree, especially smaller companies, so those might be a better option.

So, there you have it, whatever happens, you can still make a success of your life. The main thing is to be happy and love yourself so others can love you and look at life as a mixture of opportunities and disappointments.

The check-up, disability and daughter's engagement

On Wednesday, 24th September 2003, I had a physical check-up at the hospital related to injuries sustained in the road accident. However, I preferred to use the word collision because it was my fault, not a random act. My ability to support weight on one foot and take a few steps was causing pain down the leg. The doctor suspected that I had sustained a further injury to my body in the collision. On examination of the x-rays taken of my spine, knee and hips, the doctor discovered I had fractured my left hip bone and growth on the side of my knee called exocytosis may need removing because it contributed to pain in the knee. Physical examination of the left foot showed that reconstructive surgery would be necessary. I am waiting for a hip replacement, removing the exocytosis and reconstructive surgery on my foot. The operations are to be carried out over some time, not all at the same time. That has made it impossible to know when I shall return to work.

Our income comes from Incapacity, child tax credit, living allowance, child benefits and Euphemia's working tax credit. My employer pays £180.00 when holiday pay is due, and the total government benefit each month is £829.57. It has made our lives feel like they're more being lived instead of trying to live day-to-day and feel we were only surviving. We qualified to reduce council tax, decreased water rates, free prescriptions, and all health care, including dentists, opticians and trips to the hospital. I hold a 'Blue Badge' because I have no mobility without using a pair of crutches. It enables Euphemia to park the car in the disabled bay or park in Town Centre restricted zones for a limited time if I am the passenger. Road tax was free because Euphemia sometimes used the car for my mobility. The freebies and the benefits system seem to do us better when off work, but I am determined to return to work, earn my living, and not live on state handouts.

I have found that the public is more considerate of my disability. People who help open doors seem pleased to lend a hand when they notice I am in difficulty as I used the crutches and accidentally drop my shopping or my crutches fall to the ground. Without hesitation, someone always asks if they can be of assistance—privileges as a disabled person range to more than just not queuing to get spacious areas for sitting. The public makes it easier for me to struggle through a crowd than an able-bodied could most time. I have never been knocked about or pushed over, and access is relatively smooth. I never play on my disability and let others do things that I can do if I am patient. I try and do as much as I can independently, but it's only the impossible tasks that my condition does not allow; that's when I ask for help. I do not expect my family to recognise the job I can't do or need help with without saying.

With so much free time on my hands, it has caused boredom to set in, and I sometimes feel lonely. I am in the house in the daytime by myself. I have asked my son to help me learn to use the PC, but I found it incredibly hard to study. My mind seems to forget the information quickly, and I could not successfully practice what I was told. Somehow, my brain has disconnected or connected less efficiently to learning because I cannot think logically. Enthusiasm fades. It feels like there is a pull on my brain to learn. I have decreased energy, and consciousness shifts away from the urge to learn. I get abnormally negative symptoms of low concentration and lack of motivation which curb purposeful and goal-orientated desires. The road collision has forced a change in my circumstances, and I could have so easily been killed, but I believe in miracles, that the mysterious God has saved me from a premature death for reasons only known to me through insight, and I am to respect it.

This convalescent time is cosy because finances are better controlled; it's not unlike a long holiday break, for I am not back at work and have plenty of leisure time. That is a blessed time, although we cannot go away on holiday. I am pleased to see we are managing, and it's time for preparation and prayer.

Katrina told us of her engagement with Robert on Wednesday, 03/09/03. Katrina spoke to me during the daytime on the phone. My first initial thoughts were it's too early to be engaged, and it's only been months since she met him. Katrina explained they had seen each other most days since they met, and the days swiftly multiply into lengthy together time. They share their space and live under the same roof at times. Their time together probably amounts to more than my three years spent with your mum before we were engaged, and it was primarily weekends when I saw your mum. Katrina's engagement pleased me very much because it's a better public showing commitment to true love than just making plans to live together and explore their relationship to see if it works out. Being engaged shows us and the rest of the world that they are genuinely in love and willing, both of them, to explore, experiment, and commit themselves to find out their compatibility and relaxing in their relationship. Katrina and Robert have shown they have eyes only for one another, and the link feels safe. They can build on having lasting happiness and not worry that they have to experiment with other relationships or flirt. Their engagement tells me that neither wants to find another mate, and they want to live the rest of their lives together. And that is the first authentic step in commitment before marriage.

I did not reveal the engagement to the family but informed Euphemia that Katrina had spoken to me during the day and would like to have a word with her. When Euphemia telephoned Katrina that evening, Euphemia sensed Katrina was thrilled and asked if she was about to tell her that she was engaged to Robert. Euphemia was hugely excited and delighted; we all were, and congratulations and best wishes were showered down the telephone by all of us. I posted the biggest engagement card I could find to her, and when it reached her, it got severely buckled and creased because the postman squeezed it through her mailbox. Katrina said they planned to have a long engagement of four to five years because she and Robert were still students, and she wanted to be in the job market and have an established career. Robert is thinking about a career in teaching and has further training to do after his finals. He wants to start a family early when they are married. As I learn more about Katrina's and Robert's plans for marriage, I find out it's expected to be an extravagant big church wedding. I am all for this because I want to see myself walking my daughter down the aisle to marry the man she wants to be with for the rest of her life in the most significant fairytale blessed church wedding in the history of our family. Katrina says they will certainly wait for me to get well enough to walk down the aisle to the altar with her without the use of crutches.

My niece, Dorrell, married recently, and it was very extravagant. Dorrell got married in Jamaica and held a blessing ceremony in her new home town in England. They made a video of the occasion, and the still photos captured the story of their Caribbean wedding with incredible beauty, liveliness, and a well-organized ceremony. It was a perfect wedding on a perfect tropical island on a sunny day. Katrina's marriage may be four years away, but I am already planning for it. A remarkable miracle is needed to pull off a spectacular wedding on a low budget. Dorrell's father had a tailor-made suit, and it looked stunning in the photos. I have imagined myself in a well-made tailored suit as I daydream and hope we can plan the perfect wedding for our daughter. No expenses spared; the money will come in, from where I do not know, to pull off a marriage which it seems, right now, we cannot afford. We have no savings to pull off a wedding that is extravagant or without frills. Even a budget wedding would show us up as paupers.

Nevertheless, I have high hopes that we can rise to the occasion, for I pray to God to bless us with prosperity so that our daughter, whom He created, can be proud and happy. I am in prayer also over the financial support Georgina will need when she goes to university. So many things need praying for, and it's not only personal matters but also elements of the world and the planet itself. Finally, I am asking God to help our student children and future son-in-law succeed in their studies. I have told Georgina to resume having driving lessons from 17/10/03, and they cost £68.00 a month. How ironic it is that I could not sustain sending her to driving lessons when I was at work, yet, from government benefit, I somehow can.

I prayed in a term that acknowledges God as father and mother, Jesus as a unique man of God, the saints to be spiritual people, and all the angels as people given to us for protection and guidance. I ask Jesus, the near-perfect man, the saints in Christ, past and present and the angels to pray with me to God himself as I say, "Our father, mother God, have mercy upon us who art in heaven", and I continue to say the Lord's Prayer to the end. I genuinely believe that the saints and the angels are a kind of heavenly people or people of spiritual perfection who can help our prayers travel to the ears of God. I am looking at unrighteous areas of my life because I believe it's not until I am righteous enough that God's promises of blessings will magnify themselves. When all areas are of rightness, the benefits of God will flow, and I will be able to be more generous to people and charitable organizations.

Is our marriage in tatters?

Written 15th September – 03rd November 2003

*This chapter contains themes of an adult nature

I wrote, in my own words, a direct friendship card to Euphemia and sent it through the post to our home address to communicate the words that I had said to her, but she doesn't believe, hoping this time they are taken seriously, and she makes up her mind about staying with me. The card reads:

> I want this card to tell you exactly how I feel, I try to say to you myself, but you do not seem to believe. So that you will know and understand my love for you is accurate. You are very, very special to me, more than you could know.
>
> I think about you all the time, no matter where I go, but you have found a mate to take my place since the road accident. Although I am aware you do not love me as you used to, that does not bother me because I love you.
>
> There will come a time when a choice will have to get made. Do you love me enough to have intimacy, so we both can feel we have a marriage relationship that brings us fulfilment and happiness?
>
> I am sorry not to have sent you a proper birthday card on your birthday, and it's because I felt rejected by the one I hold so tightly. When we have a tiff, the love inside my heart remains constant, so true. Sometimes, we say things we never mean in heated moments, but it would be a lovely blissful scene if we could kiss and make up.
>
> Not everything is perfect; that's a simple fact of life, but no one could be happier than me to be in your life. So perhaps we'll drink a toast later to love and absolute commitment to the one who means the most to me, you, my darling partner.
>
> Yours ever,
>
> love Karl XX---x.
>
> September 2003

I am disappointed that we had our anniversary. I could only present Euphemia with a giant card that says *Happy Anniversary* and a synthetic voice saying, *"I love you"*. I wrote these words on the card:

I have shown you in some ways that you are an essential part of all my happiness. You have shown me, with some affection, that I am someone to whom you can turn for fundamental understanding, loving concerns and someone you think of fondly. Darling, this gift and warm greetings bring wishes for joy, cheer and happiness on our Anniversary, and I hope we will always grow in love. Therefore, there is no need to weigh words and no need to pretend with someone so special. This card comes to wish us happiness and to tell you too - "I love you".

Another card entitled **'Love like ours can overcome any difficult time'** was given to Euphemia when things had got tougher a month later. It was written by a well-known poet named Joanne D. Cobb. It says:

I know things haven't been easy for the two of us lately. It seems that no matter how hard we try, nothing comes out of my mouth right. But I believe and have come to know honestly, I love you, and I always will. You are the one I want to work things out with, the one to whom I give my love, my support, my desire and my heart. But I know we can do it. We can have a fantastic future if we try to remember why we fell in love with each other and how we wanted to love each other constantly. Then, we can weather this storm in our lives so that we can share the unobstructed sunrise of a new day and the hope of a renewed love - and a stronger love - together forever.
Love, Karl XX.

As I clutch at straws, I wonder, have I watched my marriage eroding because I cannot provide? I know another man is interested in Euphemia, who seems able to give her a better future. I will not blame her if she leaves me. I would instead go through suicide than to see her go for a new partner. I want to win back her confidence and fight for her to want to stay, but it's up to her to make up her mind.

On the 1st November 2003, our relationship had come to an end because I found out Euphemia had lied to me. On Tuesday, 02/09/03, Euphemia and I promised a new beginning, a fresh start in our relationship, and I gave her my heart again. After finding out Roy's mobile number was frequently called since I had been hospitalized, she denied cheating on me. When I found out that Euphemia was still contacting this man after we had said we would make a fresh start, it bruised my heart and gave me a sad feeling. I had peeped in Euphemia's address book that she kept in her handbag, and I checked mobile numbers on the itemized phone bill on Monday 03/11/03 and will check all areas of her life with me after that, I can trust her again.

We had our first meeting with a Relate counsellor named Sandy. The one-hour session would usually cost £40.00, but it was free because of our circumstances of claiming benefits and our poor history of financial deprivation. I got upset and raised my voice to her as she began to take to one side of the argument without listening through my reasoning and being mutually understanding. She was aware that I have an enduring condition called schizophrenia and thought I might become a threat to her during the consultation and asked to obtain references from my doctor, psychiatrist and CPN before accepting us as clients. However, another appointment was made for 24/11/03. Though I thought it's unorthodox to ask for these references, Euphemia figured I should give consent, for she might be able to help us.

On 3rd November, I wrote a letter and asked Euphemia to give Sandy the follow-on consultation because I was not going. The message was in an unsealed envelope and stayed in the letter rack until the appointment date, and I have no idea if Euphemia sneakily read it. She said nothing about the letter, and I assumed she had not peeped inside the envelope. I wrote the following message in the letter:

Dear Sandy,

I find I cannot resolve the conflict with my wife because our perceptions are always opposed. Euphemia deliberately tries to make what I say damaging to her and blame me for saying it when I did not say it to have a wrong meaning.

She does twist my words and can only remember the negative things I say to her. Euphemia is cheating on me and can no longer tolerate my advances to her. On 2nd September 2003, we pledged to each other; we promised a new beginning to our relationship.

When we came to see you on 15th September, I thought we were making a go at making our marriage work. We were intimate and doing heavy petting, and our communication I rated as excellent. But, to my surprise, I have just discovered that soon after our pledged promise, Euphemia contacted her manfriend, whom I know is her desired lover, not me. On the 5th, 20th, 25th, and 29th of September, she contacted him.

My heart was broken; I am hurting. Euphemia is in denial that she is in love with someone else. Euphemia continues to say, "I love you but not in that way". I have told Euphemia I will always love her, and I love her to bits no matter what she has done.

However, her behaviour has me in emotional turmoil. I was rendered numb, and my heart and mind wait for Euphemia to return to a relationship that gives free unconditional love. If I am realistic and have learned anything about life, Euphemia may never want me again, and I think we should divorce in that instance. I enclosed copies of things I wrote to her sometimes in a card, sent to express how sorry I am that things are not working out, and I am desperate to get our relationship back on track.

Sandy, if you think it will help our relationship, please read this letter to my wife, but if it seems to be thorns in the side and could damage our fragile relationship, keep it to yourself. Yours sincerely.

On Sunday, 7th December 2003, I asked myself the same question: Is our marriage in tatters? Unfortunately, my relationship with my wife has caused me to hang out our dirty laundry in public as I began to write about the things kept locked away in the closet.

Please believe me when I say that they have not been written for spite, to be malicious or for revenge, but to bring healing and be open in the darker side of our relationship. The stories may show impairments involving how I think as I lose much of the ability to rationally evaluate Euphemia's surroundings and our interaction. The result is to write the most intimate stories in our relationship, which may seem bizarre to the casual observer. Still, they are consistent with my perceptions, ideas, and beliefs that may say my behaviour is delusional in the events. Without context, these stories reflect my irrational, illogical reactions because, often, it is difficult to understand my wife. Still, she is a wonderful, enduring woman, and I have difficulty accepting what she sees as the 'true' reality.

My behaviour has caused profound disruption in our lives, and Euphemia is a good woman who is a long-suffering spouse. I thank God she is in my life, but due to impairments in insight and judgement, I cannot judge and control the temptation to come out, resulting in disclosing the most extraordinary kinds of things. At this time of writing, it is unclear if our marriage is in tatters because of delusions, which reflect distortions in my perception and interpretation of reality. What is clear is that my good lady has no misconception or prejudice over me. On the contrary, she copes with my odd behaviour and strange ideas like dealing with cancer. She is compassionate, non-judgmental, understanding and treats me as a whole person and demystifies the grave prognosis by how she loves me day in and day out. However, I have a belief intensely false about her.

I have been seeking a solicitor to advise me on how to dissolve the marriage and what grounds. I say I love her, and Euphemia says she loves me. I believed that my spouse does not love me, and recognising this has led me not to hold back on our relationship's private and intimate secrets. We had sought counselling with Relate. On the second meeting on 24/11/03, I did not go but handed Euphemia a letter to give Sandy. My letter illustrated how I felt Euphemia was treating our relationship, and it presented my argument, and the words speak clearly to Sandy. I hoped it would show that Euphemia needs to own up to the truth that stopping our relationship from growing and say things as they are. Last time, Sandy seemed to have empathy for Euphemia's half-truths and false memories. However, it led to misleading understanding from Euphemia's remarks about our twenty-two years of marriage and how being married to me had made her feel.

For twenty-two years, Euphemia held some disturbing feelings about our marriage but did not tell me she felt unhappy in our relationship. "Just for the sake of keeping the peace and being obedient to my husband," Euphemia had said to Sandy. It was a shocking revelation that I could not get my head around; I could not believe that Euphemia resented me so much that we could not talk about how she felt our marriage was working, or, as the case may be, how it's not working. Euphemia spoke of giving in to me, and all the wedding was about was me, me, me, and what I wanted. I did not take her feelings and thoughts into account; "What Karl wants, Karl gets," she said. Euphemia revealed more false memories saying, "I never really felt loved by Karl because all his love and attention was directed to the children; we never got to do things together. He's saying, 'I love you, darling' it is meaningless because It did not show in his behaviour. I could never feel like part of the family. Not even as a mother". Euphemia's argument was I did not allow her to say how the children were brought up. The children took directions from me, and, in Euphemia's own words, "I am only a maid in the family to do the cleaning and washing". It's an incredible revelation; my whole world has been turned upside-down. It's all a shock for me and feels like a stake in the heart, but I am trying hard to see it from her perspective and can't. My world, which sees me as a good husband and father, making a happy family with my wife's contributions, has fallen apart.

Nobody in the community could say we were not a happy family. However, all my efforts over the past twenty-two years of striving for the family with no disposable money to give Euphemia gifts makes her imagine I do not love her. I think Euphemia could find no love for me because of the lack of personal possessions and blames me for her unhappiness. Euphemia never once spoke to me about how she felt about things; I had no idea she saw me as an obstacle to her happiness. I tried to make her feel happy but gauging her mood is poor until it gets to the point of shouts that become so upsetting that Euphemia wants me out of the house or does not talk to me. Can Euphemia not see I supported the family unit, including her, the best I could with an income that couldn't contain luxuries? As soon as I found I could not give them anything, I wanted to kill myself!

I did sense that I could not bring her happiness and wanted to die so Euphemia could remarry. I never thought of walking out on her; I chose to die rather than agonise about leaving her in a rut and living out a distant dream elsewhere without her. There was another reason why I tried to commit suicide, which I mentioned in previous chapters - claiming my life insurance money and having no worries about future financial matters. I even had a written plan for my wife to follow on my death, giving full worked-out details of reserves when all debts were paid. On death, we part, and Euphemia can go to the man I thought she would go to on hearing of my death. Come to think of it, it was two years ago, 2001 when it first sparked in my head that I could not make Euphemia happy, and since that recognition, I had worked hard to satisfy her. However, I still have no money in our marriage, and it's frustrating just to be satisfied with a poor husband. I don't think Euphemia could be happy with a poor husband, a home and a family who loves her. I must escape bringing her happiness but secure them financially when I do so. I could not get my wife to be happy because I never have enough money, and these days, we do not speak of each other's earnings or use the joint income for the best possible outcome to help the family purse.

We have lived through so many things, happiness, sadness, arguments and care, and I think about everything we have been through together and love how our love won every battle so far. We came together to be together, and we have come a long way in our relationship, but today's marital difficulties have decided it's the end. Euphemia has been in touch with her ex-lover, a man of her parent's generation she loved before meeting me. In the seventh year of our marriage, Euphemia was almost unfaithful with this man in the seven-year itch when we tried for our third child. I was unsure if Jonathan would be my biological son, but I had to take her word that nothing sexual had happened. Love is all about choices and forgiving. Euphemia told me of her near infidelity, and I was prepared to bring up her child if it had turned out I was not the father.

I had always been aware that Euphemia held his telephone number and his address to this day. In 2000, Euphemia and I had a bitter argument, and she left to go to London to spend the weekend at her aunt's, I suspected. Still, Euphemia revealed on her return that she stayed at her ex's and slept with him without a sexual encounter taking place. Even when the infidelity does not cross the line sexually, the effect is just as damaging, if not more so. I want to give Euphemia the freedom she deserves from me but could not get with me alive. It seems she wants to love another man since she could not put any more of her energy into helping our marriage work. I cannot ask for a divorce because I still love her and want her always to love me as I love her. I have chosen her again and want to do the same again, but I don't think she likes or wants me. For many years, Euphemia had me as the only man she would try and love since I was the one she chose to spend the rest of her life with, for all the time.

Her ex reappeared in her life when I was hospitalised for attempting to commit suicide and sustained some severe injuries. I did this to allow Euphemia to have the man she constantly desired, but that was just one of the reasons. I remember telling Euphemia she was playing with fire when the man, a friend of ours, became her focus of attention during my recovery. I would have been happy if the encounter had happened and I was in my grave, but I survived, and I am jealous and hurt to learn this other man was taking her out, and her ex-flame is back on the scene. People have told me I have a good attractive wife and a loving family. I was fortunate that the wife regularly came to my hospital bedside at visiting times to see me, but they did not know that Euphemia was dating another man. She told me not to worry; he was there as a supportive friend. However, I think Euphemia meeting with him gradually turned into an affair and caused her to reject all that was going for us. The people in the hospital, mainly the patients, told me that I should not have tried to kill myself due to debts because it appears I was being selfish and did not appreciate my wife and our children, for money cannot buy love. They were unaware that the second most potent reason why I wanted to die was the feeling of failure as a lover that can't provide for his family. There was no support for males who find they cannot provide for their family, so self-sacrifice seemed an attractive unselfish way to help the family get the government's help and for Euphemia to have a new partner.

I am always struggling with Euphemia's disappointment in me. I would do anything to see her happy with me to the point of becoming homeless for a weekend to get out from under her feet and give her space.

During the summer of 1999, when Euphemia was so upset with me over a domestic task I did not do, it got her so frustrated that she made a movement to hit me. It was a horrible time, and without thinking things through, I told Euphemia that I would go to a friend house in Kettering when the weekend came to get out from being under her feet. It was the middle of the week when I asked Euphemia if she could use the car to drop me off at the train station on a Friday evening. There was no friend in Kettering I could stay with, for all people known to me were acquaintances only, and I could not ask favours. I had no close friend in the world other than the wife, although many people know me. So I decided to take the short journey to Kettering and stay at a work colleague's house.

I had in mind to spend the entire weekend as a homeless man in Leicester, the nearest city to where I live in Wellingborough. I bought the train ticket in advance and only had £3.00 left to last out the weekend. Euphemia had dropped me at the station, unaware my train journey would take me further than Kettering, and I would end up in the city of Leicester. I stayed on the city streets from 8 pm on Friday to 3 pm Sunday, with only a rucksack and a thick waterproof mackintosh on my back. I spent a long time at the railway café until the station closed. I slept in bus shelters, shop doorways near the hot vents, and concrete benches in open spaces. The city was lively all the time; in the daytime, it was bustling, and at night times, it was still bustling with plenty of people. I walked from one street to the next to pass the time; I window-shopped, visited the museum, the library and fast-food outlets and looked at the movement of people outside nightclubs at what seemed to be a thrilling nightlife. I had anxious moments living on the streets when drunks approached, and gangs of youths came close to me, appearing to want to threaten and harass, but instead, they either spat, threw litter and kicked cans in my direction to cause a reaction of affray. I walked the extended distance from Wellingborough train station to home on a Sunday afternoon, and the children were thrilled to see me and ran up to me for hugs and Euphemia watched and smiled.

I have since told Euphemia the full extent of the truth about my going away for the weekend. I have come to think Euphemia does not love or respect me, respect me in the sense that she would not fight for her man or say she takes delight in trying to love me. Instead, Euphemia would prefer I left her not to be the one at fault that contributed to our marital break-up in the public's eyes. I would feel shamed and gutted if we broke up because it takes two to tango. Without knowing how, somehow, I am adding fuel to a volatile situation for which I cannot be without blame. I share the responsibility for the failings in our marriage, although I cannot see I am responsible for it at this time in history. In time, the part I play will become apparent to me; I hope we can get through this challenging period and have no regrets here and now and in the future.

I had a face-to-face conversation with Euphemia and explained my motive for attempted suicide, money for the family purse and a new relationship for her. Euphemia could not accept my explanation and be angry at me for being so foolish and believed my sickness, the schizophrenia had flared up, and all the pressures in me led me to give up. However, I shouldn't try and blame her. "You don't appreciate me; people are talking, and you are selfish to have tried to end your life. You weren't thinking of the kids and me, and you were selfish; you were thinking of yourself and how you could escape the problems in life without a thought on how we would cope without you." Euphemia did not try to assure me of her love for me; instead, she confused me by saying, 'Can't we be friends?'

In my overarching plot of telling her the truth and her real thinking, I never thought that what she said indicated weak or crazy. On the contrary, I have worked hard so that you can imagine I was at the perfect state of normality and showed real grit, courage and heroism. I asked myself daily to try and understand, and although you probably can't tell, I'm having a hard time with it. We have faced strong arguments during the years of our marriage, but in the end, we solved them, and so here we are fighting when our love should be assured. I felt like a useless married man unable to provide for my family and the things she needs, such as going to the hairdressers, buying clothes and particular food we could not afford. It breaks my heart to see Euphemia and the kids suffer because of my pennilessness. Sometimes I cannot buy even a Valentine card, birthday card or anniversary card. I didn't even have enough money to buy a two pence cup of coffee from the vending machine at work. It must have become evident that I could not provide for her, and I knew some men could better provide for her than me. Euphemia never seemed to show me she loved me, regardless of not having anything, and I worked so hard. I know it was hard for her to be so long in a relationship and with nothing to show for it in wealth. So I had to share my thoughts that I love her and prayed for changes in our lives that attracted wealth and prosperity. I have looked for this side of our lives to change for many years, and I hit rock bottom when my near and distant future projectile lifestyle predicted more gloom. So I tried to help, along with change, by an attempt to take my own life.

Euphemia always knew how much I earned and what all the money got used for and brought. She knew I had nothing left after sorting out the family needs and her needs. I had not bought myself anything new for years. I relied on relatives to give gifts on my birthday and at Christmas. I gave Euphemia all I had, my heart, my soul, and she damned me for what I attempted to do. I wrote love notes regularly to her, sweet words to melt her heart with passion. I think she wanted proof of love in holding romantic objects. It was rare when Euphemia got a small present from me, but I always tried to budget in the occasional organized dance and pay her store card bill to acquire new clothes. I felt like I was on a cliff's edge, desperately trying to hold on to her knowing I could lose her at any time because what I had was not sufficient.

I have telephone records of up to two years that showed that Euphemia contacted her ex-flame twice a month, and the other man's emotional affair started as a simple friendship. She may never have intended for it to become anything more than just that. However, a thin line between friendship and an emotional affair may lead to a sexual encounter. Euphemia denied sexual encounters, but I have told Euphemia that I cannot trust her as I use to because she was cheating on me and didn't admit it.

I have been having very little sleep during the nights since discovering Euphemia's secrets. On Saturday 8th November 2003, from 2 am until 4 am, I generated powerful emotions to argue about in the morning. My thinking is going wrong somewhere, and I can't make it out. The argument escalated as I expressed the hurt our relationship issues were causing me. We are losing structured conversation during which we talk about what's on our minds. We are not connected lovingly, and I significantly challenge the relationship/communications with the men damaging our intimacy. I want a divorce to stop the hurting but do not want to be the villain divorcer. I still love her with all that is going on but cannot trust her again sincerely, and she should serve me with divorce papers. I am plagued with doubts and frustration because Euphemia has not said anything suggesting she wants to divorce and is asking forgiveness or feeling sorry. I told her she never asks for my forgiveness, but I give it. Euphemia, you can do no wrong because every time you transgress, I will come back and forgive you without you asking.

She admitted nothing, and I fear our relationship has ended. It feels like it's all over, and I thought the pain would cease, but it has increased because I cannot be without her. I vowed for better or worse and continue to feel love for her. Euphemia has been remarkable in my life, and I do not want her to accept what I said without a challenge. Doubtful over the rebuilding of trust, Euphemia then agrees it's best to end our relationship. Hearing her decision, my soul went empty and drained of love. Euphemia spoke calmly and looked unaffected; no palpable sadness, it came out with honesty and mutual respect and spiritually, it killed us. I fought to win her back because I tried to open up that private behaviour that fulfils a unique need. I begin to see that her basic psychological needs were not being fulfilled. I had caught up thinking that I would give my spouse a hard time about every single thing. I am not meeting her needs for love, belonging, power, accomplishment, freedom, independence, survival and fun. I am confused with where the delusion lay, for my mind is mixed up.

In public, Euphemia played the part of a smiling, content wife and mother. Privately, she was distant from me, and I felt ignored and invisible. I had to create a way for practical solutions to emerge, trust to grow, and the return of emotional and physical intimacy between us. I gave Euphemia a card entitled 'Love like ours can overcome any difficult time' and a CD of her choice. Euphemia kissed me and – thanked me and carried the card in her handbag. I have been glad that Euphemia has not contacted a solicitor so far, to my knowledge. It appears that she is not seeking out divorce as the option we should take.

Euphemia, to me, it's God's will that we met, and it continues to be the will of God that we should be together and bring up a family. In my suicide attempt, God did not let me die to start a new relationship. God saved me for a purpose, and part of that purpose was to stay in a marital relationship with you. I fell in love with you almost effortlessly, and from the first time we met, I have thought of you when I wake up when I fell asleep and mostly anytime in between. It started in my mind that you were destined to be my soul mate because, emotionally, we connected. Some minor conflict exists because of the difference in views on petty things like a newspaper questionnaire on dating and relationships on which we disagreed. Still, we reconnected with each other lovingly and maintained good feelings. I do not know how I fit spiritually into how you see life with me, but for me, even with our challenges to deal with regarding each other's emotions and arguing, I feel connected to your spirit, and I am blessed to have you to share my life. Our intimate relationship issues, the bond of physical, emotional and spiritual togetherness, has been on hold since February 2003. I want us to rebuild or start again because we both produce chemistry for our bodies to perform. The desire and emotions are there during stimulation to arousal, but our brains do not let us lose our self-control because our spiritual feelings are not quite right yet, so the state of celibacy remains.

On Sunday 30th November 2003, our progress in our marriage up to that date had suddenly stopped because I began a conversation that evening by asking Euphemia if she valued me. Euphemia blurted out hurtful, suggestive and alarming things that she claimed I had said about her and was doing to her out of the blue. "It's not true!" Why is Euphemia acting awful and saying I want to hit her? I stamped my crutches on the floor and harnessed myself to accept the hard truth about myself. I am willing to acknowledge my behaviour, own up and take it, and then work to change it. I have made a solid choice and am putting in the effort to improve. Unfortunately, Euphemia brings some things up again, some things that I thought the two of us had worked through, like trust, faithfulness and the frustration of not having a quality, happy marriage. Euphemia was taunting me to hit her, for I would feel better. "Take a look at yourself. You banged the bed and banged your crutches on the floor, and you are outraged, extremely angry. You must want to hit me; listen to your voice." "I do not want to hit you," I said, but Euphemia insisted I must hit her to feel better. My legs froze in my stillness, and I broke down in tears and covered my face with my hand and repeated, "I do not want to hit you; I do not want to hit you. Stop it; stop it, please. I do not want to hit you."

I cried heavily, could not control the flow that poured out like a fountain. I sat on the edge of the bed, hands soaked from the tears, and the tears fell on the floor. Euphemia came over to me and hugged me and said sorry to me. As my head touched her shoulder, I burst out sobbing again like a child, and the tears kept flowing uncontrollably with more incredible intensity. I sniffled and sniffled and got tissues to wipe my eyes. I blew my nose a few times, then the tears began to dry up, and my eyes were as red as a beetroot. I developed a headache and had exposed my insecurity and inferiority and had to come to terms with how I, a grown man, acted subservient in a verbal attack by his spouse over their marriage.

My reaction was not out of the pit of guilt; sometimes support can look completely unsupportive, and lines get blurred, resulting in this flip-flop of re-evaluating our relationship. That night in bed, Euphemia kissed me goodnight and said, "I am sorry to have hurt you; I want you to be happy. I am so sorry to have made you unhappy; I want us to be happy". I responded to Euphemia by using the exact words, repeating what she had spoken to me and adding only the word 'too' to the ends of the sentences. We knew that we made each other unhappy unintentionally. We're human, for we've done things that hurt and try to make amends feel even worse, but once we had waded through all of it, my goodness, did it feel good!

The most significant leap forward to happiness together has goals attached to negative emotions anchored to it. I nag myself to do my best to make amends, ask Euphemia to forgive me and reduce those negative feelings of guilt or shame by forgiving myself first and accepting her forgiveness which I was powerless to make her do. That was entirely her choice.

Today is Sunday night, 7th December 2003, and we appear more compatible, and we are learning each day to love again. I am feeling that my darling is now trying equally to restore or convey happiness in our marriage. It has only been a week, and

I think things are better; communication is no longer harsh and damaging. I do not feel there is a risk in our marriage because my trust in Euphemia has been restored. We touch! Touch often, casually and intimately. Touch, kiss, because it eases our anxiety as we reach mindfully, rather than absent-mindedly. We hug for longer than we usually do. Hold hands while we walk. It's a great feeling when there is no tension between us, and we look to the future, intending to continue to be happy.

I left this year 2003 with a toast to our happiness and renewed love. The page marks the end of chapters in our lives, and it has brought the events that presented themselves through the years 1997 to 2003 closer. See you next year, 2004, God willing, in the continued episodes of our lives.

The Love I cannot see leads to a tragic Incident

Written Saturday 27th December 2003

I didn't expect to write again before the New Year. Euphemia and I have been having a good sense of togetherness since I last wrote on 7th December '03, and the dust has settled on the things that had made our relationship hard. Last night, we came back from visiting our niece's new private house, which she and her boyfriend are buying through a mortgage. We had a lovely time there, for we adored the music played and were regularly smiling and looked into each other's eyes. Finally, we said goodnight and covered ourselves with the duvet when we went to bed, and Euphemia fell asleep.

As I lay in bed, my mind raced over settled dust, Euphemia and the affairs with her ex and the man who was a friend of the family. I woke Euphemia, and at my heightened state of frustration, my behaviour amounted to emotional abuse and harassment. I hurt the person in my life who I love more than anything. I had done such an excellent job of reaping uploads from the past that it had devastating consequences. "I did not want to hear any more about the men because it's over; why can't you drop it?" I continued to say that we must talk it out before moving forward because I love her so much that I'll be paralyzed by not knowing the truth, for she has been lying. I pulled a few more skeletons out of the closet, and Euphemia marched out of the bedroom, saying, "I cannot take it anymore." I went downstairs twenty minutes later and asked her to come back to bed, and said, "I only have one question to ask you. Give me one reason why you are still with me". Euphemia looked up at me, and her jaws hung, and her face drooped. I stood standing by her, but Euphemia did not answer. I slowly walked away, locked in this irritating thought that not answering was a positive impression that Euphemia could not admit she does not love me, and I was only a functional piece.

I shall cut to the chase and tell you that last night, between 3 am, and 7 am, Euphemia attempted to take an overdose of Ibuprofen to make me see that she loves me.

It would be easy to blame her for the destruction I had committed, putting her at her deepest low because of the complete instability of my mental health. Still, I don't believe that mental illness is an excuse for I feel very healthy. Sometimes sorry isn't enough, and I blame myself for challenging again what has already been done and dusted and laid to rest.

Part of the road to living well with the illness has been making amends for what I have done and taking responsibility for doing wrong. I decide my subconscious attitude has worked that out. My mind played catch up in properly working itself out prioritising positivity instead of holding on to negative boundaries and settings. However, with the amount of damage I have done to Euphemia in my wake, I have to walk the walk to earn her trust and forgiveness. It had just passed quarter past three in the morning, 27th December, when Euphemia came back to bed and said, "Karl, I do love you, and I did not mean to hurt you". "Why didn't you say that when I came downstairs? I was looking for us to make up," I said. Euphemia turned to me and said, "It's because I know you would not believe me. You are the father of my children, and you are a foolish, silly man for not believing me". Gradually, she turned her face away, crying, and spoke solemnly, "I have tried to cut my wrist, but couldn't. I took some tablets not to wake up". Then, a silence, "My God" - exploded through the receptors in my brain, breaking the silence ever so quickly. Finally, I shouted out, "You foolish woman!" I rushed to her side of the bed and shook her shoulders, and told her not to go to sleep.

Euphemia, with her eyes firmly closed, still cried, and her body was floppy. I asked her how many tablets she had taken as I gently lifted open her tearful eyes and then shook her again and again. "Please, please, open your eyes; don't die. Please, darling, open your eyes and try to vomit. I will call for an ambulance." Euphemia grumbled the number, 'six' like she was snorting it out of her mouth. I then had to decide if six tablets in twenty-four hours was a life-threatening cocktail when the box said six is the maximum dose in twenty-four hours. "I think you will make it, and I will not let you go to sleep in the next four hours," I said to her.

Love is not always logical, and last night, I did not see the illogic of what I said to Euphemia before and during her suffering. I said, "Can you not see you are not showing me you love me; you are telling me you want to be out of my life. Please keep awake, and we must get through this". I asked Euphemia to try and talk or moan and to drink plenty of water. I continued to speak to her and allowed her to groan, but when there was no response, I shook her gently and wiped her tearful eyes and her brow. I spoke quietly about the future. She would have no involvement because she could not think of being around—the general things to do with Christmases and New Year's she would miss. "We need you around, darling, and I need you; your children need you and your nieces. I promise not to mention the men's names ever again, or the things that hurt our relationship - that is all past and buried".

This morning I looked back at how we might be seen as a foolish couple. I feel sadness over the product of a series of uncredited thoughts bypassing my conscious brain processes. We wanted to convey pure love to each other, but we used a negative emotion, guilt, to make the other own up that they were responsible for their unhappiness. We chose not to exist and, by doing so, burdened our partners with guilt that would last the rest of their lives. Suicide suggests the spouse contributed to their partner's death because they did not listen to them or believe they did that to them. I cannot explain why I tormented my long-suffering wife leading up to Christmas; I organized what I called a love week. I expressed my enduring love for her each day by giving her small gifts or creating a treasure hunt from articles I hid in her things. Each day, items could be found in various places, and the rewards should come as a surprise. I may have been expecting Euphemia to be ecstatic over the first week of original romantic love, including traditional flowers and chocolates. Still, she said nothing else but thank you. She appeared low-key in her approach to what had taken a considerable amount of thought and organizing. It was meant to show that I love her and appreciate her, and I am trying not to take her for granted. My romantic week started on Thursday 18th December and ran through to Christmas 25th December 2003.

On Thursday morning, I got up early and made Euphemia scrambled egg sandwiches for breakfast, and each morning, a cup of tea would be by her bedside. From there, it snowballed to texting her romantic messages or simply saying words like – "Thinking of you. Have a nice day, darling. May God be gracious to us and bless us and make his face shine upon us. Psalm 67v1. All my love, your ever-loving Karl xx". Another day, I presented her with her favourite cracker biscuit with the words 'I Love You'd scribed into the cookies with a clean hot implement. I placed a small piece of paper with the words 'I Love You' - hidden shallow in the jar of her decaf coffee, hoping the first scoop of the coffee would reveal the message to be discovered during her coffee break. In the days to come, another piece of paper again with the word 'I Love You' was placed on the kettle's spout. I wrote 'I Love You' on the surface of her Philadelphia soft cheese. I placed a mini box of chocolates in her handbag and a single red rose. I put notes in her coat pocket, complimenting her looks and hairstyles. Under her pillow, I hid a small 'to you from me' teddy bear for her to find when she went to bed. I put love messages with biblical texts that inspire me in between the daily Bible passages she reads. The Bible message got taken from Psalm 75v1.

"*Unto thee, o God, do we give thanks, unto thee do we give thanks: for that thy name is near thy wondrous works declare*". Then, finally, into her handbag, I dropped a fridge magnet that summed up my feelings in a few words, and it says:

Darling, I love you so much, and I hope you can see that you are, and always will be, the only one for me. Your ever-loving Karl. On Christmas day, Euphemia received from me a colour television combined with a DVD player and a card with the original word changed to read,

"*I believe in Santa Claus Almighty God, I do. Who else could bring a Christmas gift as beautiful as you? To share the joy of Christmas with the one who shares my life, to know my every dream fulfilled in you, my darling wife. Who could have wished for me upon a Christmas star so that every Christmas spent with you would be the best by far? A desire that every part of Christmas would be filled with loving cheer, and I'd have the best of Christmas every day throughout the year. Happy Christmas and Happy New Year.*

I had things awfully wrong about my spouse, and my write-ups reveal the extent to which 'I Cannot See' the depth of her love for me. It is tragic that, in my view, it was concealed until, all of a sudden, in self-sacrifice, she hoped, at last, that I would see the extent of her love. The previous twenty-four hours had shown that my interpretation of her overdose would have been wrong. Thank God she survived to tell me the truth.

The Bickering, why has it not stopped?
Written Tuesday 17th February 2004

I sat down in the armchair, and I have memories from the first two months of this year, 2004, that will fill pages. When I left the blank white pages in December 2003, I wondered what in 2004 was in store for us, enabling me to continue writing a book.

The blank white paper that my pen is engaged in writing will reveal my real-life stories that came out of the blue and could not have been predicted. So, I am glad that you can re-join me again and get into the action and feel the fantastic moving stories from what is the experience of an ordinary man with a mental health issue who has an enduring wife and family.

I do not deliberately set out to make things difficult for my spouse and make a mountain out of a molehill, but our bickering has not entirely stopped. In hindsight, I am the one driving our love story up the garden path. I do not want to play out a drama in our lives because the stress and pressures may kill me and hurt the ones closest to me. Everyone is a product of their upbringing, and I project my belief or perspectives onto my spouse to follow my lead, but I cannot tell when I am illogical. She has a different way of doing or seeing things that do not make them wrong, but it is hard to take on board. I must remember that my darling is much more sensible than me and has plenty of common sense, and I should see she has a vital position in my life and stop the bickering. I have trouble knowing my place in her life as productive, but I can't see how my step-by-step moves advanced our relationship. I always think I have failed and often fail this wonderfully kind woman, and I push her to go to another man because she deserves a better lifestyle.

I am working hard to change the mental ill-health that is fueling a downward spiral of hardship. My mindset needs to change; I need to use minor variants in my language to make a big difference in our communication, and my mental wellbeing should not be so shifty. So, I start this new chapter writing about past events that have put an incredible amount of stress in our lives. I cannot find a better way to start than with the words; Love conquered all. Some calendar dates left lasting memories on my love life, while others have no more significance than to say the sun rose again and our life passed through twenty-four hours, and we age. I have decided I do not want them to be news or to make the news. That might be a good motto for my life. I do not want this book to have headline news other than its spreading in popularity because of the religious, educational, anti-stigma and discrimination-busting effect on the readers.

Another thing is if I lie, cheat, and steal, that's headline news. But, by living honestly and morally correctly, I hope an unnoticed yet significant spiritual influence will occur on people around me or with whom I come in contact. My religion is there to please God in everything I do; it makes no difference whether anyone applauded my actions or not because I get called to be faithful, not famous. Bad behaviour and sex sell newspapers and books; although they may contain lies, deceit, unfaithfulness and anger, the Lord God wants people of honesty and integrity. So, I aspire to lead a quiet life, mind my own business, and walk appropriately towards people outside of faith. I may still talk of fame, but the worldly applause cannot compare to God's approval.

On Monday, 12/01/04, after pre-assessment on Thursday the 8th, I was admitted for the total left hip replacement operation, which took place the following day. I had been in great pain from the hip and around the knee beforehand. The process took two hours, and I woke four hours later, although it seemed like I had been put to sleep for only fifteen minutes. Unfortunately, I had to have a blood transfusion, and I had a high temperature that delayed my recovery by a day.

My relationship with my wife still did not feel right, and we bickered about almost anything. I kept feeling Euphemia wanted our relationship to end. If I am not in my right mind, how can I give a valid account? I know it is challenging for her to start again and set up a home. Making conversation with her annoys her, yet she says nothing to me. Even on the day of admission for the hip operation, we had bitter, turned-down mouths. I also felt so stomach-churningly sick of the situation of bickering that the voices in my head cried out, "for God's sake, stop it". I had not associated that the bickering, arguing from inside my mind that was focused externally on the wife as odd or acting schizophrenic. Hearing voices and responding to them seemed to be that of a frustrated self.

To my recollection, when Euphemia came to visit me, which thank God was frequently, her eyes were in different places analyzing other people or looking at the hospital equipment, rarely concentrating on me. I needed eye contact from her, but I did not see much. I found it disturbing that her glances at me were so few. Another time Euphemia came and saw me alone when she had promised she would bring the children with her. She arrived near the end of visiting when she usually spent the entire hour with me, but she left swiftly. When I asked why she did not phone to say they could not make it, she said, "What have I done now?" Euphemia got up and left; the end of visiting time had not been called. I could not make out why she was on bad terms with me. A hunch in my head wanted me to telephone her that night to tell her sorry that her visit went so badly, but I was not clear why, so I persuaded myself to resist the temptation to call her that night and waited till morning. I had felt mentally restrained, for I could not act on my will to phone her because a part of me was convinced that Euphemia had not thought twice about our falling out. During that night, I was anxious and hardly slept. I eagerly waited for the morning, but tiredness crept up on me, and I slept through to 8 am, missing the nurses' first wake-up call. By then, it was too late to call her; Euphemia had already left for work.

I was discharged from the hospital on Friday, 23/01/04. On Saturday, in the bedroom, I glanced across to Euphemia's bedside cabinet. She was not in the room at the time, and I saw a leaflet with bold writing designed to attract anyone's attention. It was entitled, 'I want to get a divorce' – what do I do? I was shocked, but should I have been? All along, I had thought she wanted a divorce. I stood motionless and breathed deeply, picked up the leaflet, stared at it but did not read the contents and put it back. For months, I had felt my marriage was going down the pan. Then, the symbolic reminder, my wedding ring was cut off my finger in March 2003, after the road collision. Euphemia was wearing hers as a necklace because hers had become too small for her finger. I missed not having a ring on my finger to touch and rub because it conjured up and symbolized eternal love, and I delighted in showing off that I am happily married.

I had a craving for a ring. Euphemia could not understand my need to have a new ring because she wanted me to feel freer, more accessible. I calculated that we would struggle with budgeting for rings because I wanted to replace hers too. However, Euphemia said it was unnecessary because she was satisfied to wear hers on a chain. I managed to get interest-free credit on two rings, and I proposed giving them to each other on Valentine's Day. The combined price of the rings was £469, and I paid a 10% deposit and signed the agreement to pay, by direct debit, £68 per month for six months, the last payment being due in July 2004. I had in mind to plan a grand Valentine's evening, eat out and go to the theatre and watch a love story, then end the evening at a nightclub.

Euphemia thought I would still be convalescing from the operation, and my legs would be weak, and possibly travelling in a car would be difficult for me. So Euphemia proposed that we stay at home and she would make us a romantic dinner, and we could enjoy time together. Sadly, it did not click that my good wife was considerate and thoughtful because I ignored her well-meaning positive contributions and thrived on letting her know that my brother's wife and her good friend, Pearly, was going out of their way to please me. Euphemia could not care less. My brother's wife fussed over me when he came around with her, their son, and our dad. Euphemia was in town shopping with Georgina. Pearly made sure I was comfortable, placed my slippers in front of me before I got up from sitting. She had the footstool ready to put in a position when I sat. Pearly made me a cup of coffee that was too sweet, and my sister-in-law did not hesitate to pour off some of the coffee and add more hot water to it. She had even baked me a cake.

With Pearly now, although she was a visitor in our home, I only needed to say I want something, and she would go to get it; it was the same at her home. I liked her hospitality and that special attention. Revealing those things to Euphemia led her to say, "What did your last slave die from, ah? You married the wrong woman". I thought she had missed the point, but in earnest, only in hindsight, I was cruel and insensitive. Euphemia carelessly placed her things around the house without thinking, and they were near to tripping me up. I am still using sticks to assist my walking and felt that the obstacles were deliberately placed to annoy me most of the time. I had not considered Euphemia's rushing, bustling about when running late or when she misplaced things and turned the house upside down looking for them. On the night of Sunday, 25/01/04, I struggled to understand Euphemia's ordinariness and perfectly normality when I did not ask for help. I fought to fix my pillows in bed as she lay next to me, which I thought she would have given me some help. Maybe sleepiness or something more sinister prevented her from doing so. There had gradually been a change in my behaviour alongside my different way of thinking. I never looked adequately at Euphemia putting on clothes or undressing in the bedroom. I put the bedsheet over my head or went out of the room before she changed her clothes. I switched off my attraction, and now 17/02/04, I don't tell her she looks splendid, gorgeous in her clothes, or I admire her looks. I couldn't put my eyes on the profile of my wife's prettily clothed body or naked one. Although I still fancy her, I had stopped saying, "You look lovely, darling".

Before then, Monday 9th February, I had held back from revealing my natural desires. Finally, I glanced at Euphemia and said, "I have something to say. I cannot bear it anymore; it's too hard sleeping in the same bed as you, and we do not explore our sexuality, and I do fancy you and love you. I cannot go on as we are, seeming on the outside as if everything is alright, and I have to live a lie. I cannot do it. I think we have to separate. As soon as I am financially able to, you or I will have to move out of the family home. I am aware you do not like this town, Kettering, and it seems like you would prefer to set up a new home in Wellingborough where your old friends are. I will help you all I can to provide the things you need and help you to settle. I know it might be a long time before we can do this, but I expect a windfall from free competitions I have entered, or it may come from a win on the lottery, and things will move faster."

I took action to get the ball rolling and bought the local newspaper on Thursdays when properties are advertised for sale or rent, diligently searching for a house for her and didn't tell her. "I do not know the divorcing rules, but I think we need to be separated for three years before a divorce can get granted. I will then look for a partner who will love me, understand me and have sex with me because she fancies the pants off me."

I could not look her in the eye and say any of these sentences. I was seated in the armchair, and Euphemia was sitting on the settee. I glanced up at her and saw her head hung down, and she was staring at the floor. I waited for a response and asked if she would look up at me and give me an answer. I stayed there and also stared at the floor. Knowing that Euphemia had not interrupted me at any time during the talk, I thought she must have something to say about what I had just told her. Again, I waited and waited for a response, not taking in her visual clues. My left hand was on my chin, and I continued to look down at the floor. Probably she, too, was staring at the floor. Still, Euphemia had said nothing, and time seemed to stand still.

Nothing was said, and I couldn't hear her breathing, so I looked up and made eye contact. Then I had to keep that visual contact and wait again. Time restarted when I asked Euphemia, "After listening to my talk, have you got anything to say to me?" Euphemia quietly spoke, "What would you like me to say?" Her reply sounded extraordinary in my mind. I could not make out her response. "Karl, it's bedtime; it is past 11 o'clock, and I have to get up for work in the morning. I'm going to the bathroom" Euphemia was so calm and collected it had my mind in a spin; I was puzzled with flashbacks.

For the next six days and nights, my mind was overactive about every conceivable thing that had ever happened in our relationship. I had good feelings, bad feelings, good times, and harmful mixtures in the brain as chemical soup. My endorphins were losing the battle. I was weeping in bed, and messages in my head with twitching impulses were waking me and alerting me that I would become ill if I didn't stop this emotional waterfall pouring out of my eyes every night. Euphemia became aware of my terrible sadness and restlessness and reminded me to take my medication if I hadn't done so because she did not want me to fall ill. How and why Euphemia could not see that her withdrawal from me was driving me crazy; that and not telling me anything she's thinking, but allowing me to suppose things and say nothing to challenge my belief and make me change my mind. I do not want to accept or believe this distinct form of my thinking, but it poses itself as overwhelming evidence that Euphemia and I must separate so that I can have peace of mind. Yet separation conjures up fear; I would have to be in a mental institution to get over her for the rest of my life. I love her so much I could never come to terms with losing her because it's insane to leave this lovely caring, beautiful woman blessed with compassion, empathy, kindness and love. I am not thinking straight; which of the two ideas/beliefs is a delusion?

On Friday the 13th of February, I rang my CPN and asked him to visit me. However, he could not call around until Wednesday 18th February, when I suspected it would be too late because my relationship with my wife would be at an end by then. My emotions continued to overwhelm me; if tears did not come during my night's sleep, in the daytime, home alone, my cheeks were saturated with them. I tried to stop crying by calming myself by listening to religious music and love songs on DVDs, but they appeared to intensify my sorrows. The songs had empathy for my low spirit and had me closer to tears than drying them up. I can think of nothing other than the Valentine dinner Euphemia was to prepare; a part of me was sure she'd forget. Where is the logic that your spouse would not have dinner on the list on the most romantic day of the year? And the thinking is not going away, and I cannot decide what my right thoughts are.

On the morning of 14th February 2004, Valentine's Day, I sat in the living room doing nothing but breathing automatically when suddenly, black and white images flashed through my mind like still photographs from a developed film of happy times; I laughed out to myself. It changed to sad times with grainy pictures of people and places where I encountered stress, mainly my school days and working in factories; nothing from my marriage was in these grainer images. Tears made their way through the corners of my eyes. All week I had thoughts and flashbacks of my life and mental images created in my head. Just sitting, I was provoked by pictures from the past. Finally, I got up and kept my mind off my agony by doing something around the house. I washed up the dirty dishes from last night and this morning, but as soon as I had finished them, my face screwed up, and I sank quickly into a low mood. I found more chores to do and vacuumed most rooms in the house, although I had been advised not to bend over to 90 degrees or stand for too long because of my hip's recent operation.

I am in my fourth week since the operation, and I feel fine, with no pains from the hip, and daily, I feel I am getting more flexible and more reliable physically. Keeping myself busy stopped the crying, and I had hardened up. All the children had woken, and I said daddy would have something to say to them when we all got together for dinner. In the week, I told them that their mum would make a romantic dinner on Valentine's Day, and they could either stay upstairs or make themselves scarce and plan to be out. In the afternoon, Euphemia and Georgina went shopping. When they returned, I looked for signs that the evening was under control and panicked because I could not see anything from the shopping list to suggest foodstuff for a romantic dinner. I sharply hardened up again. I told myself no more crying, Karl; I have to show strength and have emotional restraint to talk to Euphemia later today. The time had just passed 4:45 pm, and my mind said silently to me, be damned with it all. Not another tear will pass through my ducts over her. Euphemia came into the room just at that time and smiled. She looked for our best china and glasses in the cabinet. I sighed and blew a belly-load of air through my lips and spoke quietly, "Thank God for that". - When Euphemia had left the room, I lifted my hands in the air and rejoiced for being wrong about Euphemia and the planning for the evening. I was crazy about the evening. I was glad to see sense but foolishly had the determination to deliver a damning speech without softening up and letting my emotions get the better of me. Selfishly, I thought of how it might affect me but did not consider how Euphemia would cope with the devastation. Even though we had sorted out things, I continued emotionally attacking her for some unknown reason. I do not understand the mixture of thoughts acting on my good conscience. My good conscience lacks the strength, while the opposing side brutally tells me what to do and stresses my brain, even though I am taking my medication.

The dining table was set for a two-course dinner, lighting was low, a lit candle on the table and a bottle of bubbly. Clear crystal glasses and cutlery were neatly positioned with napkins shaped in a neat triangle, and our best plates were on the table mats. Our best coffee set was taken out of the cupboard and placed on the kitchen worktop, ready to supply the later refreshments. Smooth jazz and classic soul music played in the background. It was a perfectly relaxing scene set for a good evening. To my surprise, Euphemia changed out of the clothes she went shopping in and prepared the meal. She came into the room to take the plates to warm, and she looked stunningly sexy in a brand-new skirt and blouse. Her elegant legs looked smooth in black tights, and her feet pushed into a pair of comfortable-looking stilettos. I looked at her pretty face with the least amount of make-up necessary to enhance an already naturally good-looking beautiful woman and her beautifully arranged hairstyle. Then, looking stunning, Euphemia presented herself for dinner.

Still, I did not want her to know I admired her gorgeousness because she would say thank you, and it would appear all was alright, so I avoided looking into her eyes. Finally, I dropped the resistance and had to tell Euphemia she looked gorgeous, and she replied with the predictable, "thank you!" While Euphemia was in the kitchen, my good conscience kicked again for me to change my clothes. I wore an elegant shirt, tie, and Trousers with crisp front seams. Euphemia called me and was on her way upstairs to get me when we met on the staircase and smiled. I asked her, "How do I look?" Euphemia replied, "You look fine!" I then said, "You look lovely - my lovely, thank you". The feeling of love was welling up in me, and I realised it had never really gone away. We entered the dining room and approached the table where the food had been set out on a bone china plate. The way the food was arranged made it attractive, appealing and mouth-watering. On the plate were boiled potatoes, carrots and very finely sliced whole beans. A portion of salmon covered in a white sauce was first class, and the taste of the food was spot-on. I was handed a glass of bubbly, and Euphemia picked up her glass, and we interlocked our arms, and the glasses touched.

"To us," I said. Euphemia replied, "To us, cheers". "Cheers, darling, the meal is delicious". Then Euphemia presented me with gifts. A soft toy, 'from me to you' small teddy bears, a keepsake card and the new wedding ring. My attention moved away from the food plate and focused on my lovely wife's adoring looks. As I looked at her love-filled eyes, my darling was looking back at me adoringly. Euphemia said to me, "Karl, this is for you. Would you be my Valentine and accept this ring and marry me again?" Her pleasant manner with kind expressions nearly had me bound to keep this kindly contact going. Still, foolishly, my eyes gradually moved away from her expressive eyes, and my head bowed. I gazed into my lap, and I started to cry. I used up my pocketful of tissues and wept uncontrollably. (*What on earth could be wrong with me? I am just plain stupid, and something is stopping my learning.*) I reached for the napkin and the Kleenex tissue box, and Euphemia was sat fiddling with the cork, the silver foil and the wire from the bottle in her hand. I spoke out between sniffles and sobbing about what my uneducated depressed conscience was hanging onto, false burdens that were ruining the evening. I said pathetically, "I cannot accept this ring. I have one to give you too, but I will hold back from giving it to you. I wanted nothing more than for us to exchange rings and pledge a promise. The ring symbolized our eternal love for each other and us growing more and more in love, but for a long time now, I have felt you wanted our relationship to be over, and you showed me nothing that persuades me you did not want our marriage to go down the toilet. Now you give me this!" I placed the gifts back on the table. Euphemia took the card off the table, handed it back to me and asked me to open it. I opened the credit size card, and it was titled 'I'm sorry.' I bawled as I read it; it felt like the last pool of tears was emptying fast like a constant flow from a leaky tap. I was damaged and cried like an infant denied his feed. I am embarrassed now to have shown you, the reader, my collapse. It shamed me to the core. It would be interesting to know if Euphemia thought this was an act of self-pity or performance of courage, but I had lost the path to reconciliation. Partway while reading the card, my vision became blurred because tears were distorting my vision. I wiped my eyes clean with the back of my hand and read on. It was a joy to read the words that expressed her heart's feelings for me. The time was 8:30 pm, and I was beginning to feel in control of my emotions, but my behaviour was not normal, although the tone of my voice and my thought patterns seemed normal and calm. I showed no sympathy or thanks to Euphemia for her tolerance; instead, I said to her, "All I was guilty of was trying to love you and be your best friend, but you see me as someone who was taking away your happiness". Trapped in the nonsensical world of my bizarre thinking, I continued to punish the one I love. "I do not beat you up or act aggressively towards you, but you only see I am a good father and cannot see I am a good husband too." Euphemia began to answer my observation of her behaviour. "Karl, you aren't a bad husband, and I do love you, Karl, but you do not want to believe me. You have already made up your mind about me." I want to be wrong about what the wrongs I think of you; prove me wrong instead of allowing me to believe what now comes to look natural to me. I want to be wrong about what I think is not making us work well as a couple. I crawled back into self-pity and opened up to Euphemia that my life would have been distinctly different if I was not married. "I should not have married. I don't deserve you, and I should have remained celibate. I made a mistake to marry and have children, for it was not my vocation. I am not middle-aged, and we cannot go further in this marriage because I am a holy man. You may not think so, but I am religious, although not connected to organised religion. I call my faith multi-denominational Christian faith. I am consecrated in behaving in a morally and spiritually excellent manner, for I believe in holiness. I want my saintliness to stay sacred, and my life expressed my belief in good overcoming malicious wrongs and became a follower of truth and honesty. Darling, because of my complexity, I cannot show my sexuality to any other woman. I have to stay celibate and not marry again. I cannot express what we do in the bedroom outside the marriage. I will not marry again. You may feel you can do nothing right for me". I began to sense some discord in my thinking, and it's not only self-punishing but insensitive and is wounding Euphemia. I can't be in my right mind because I am battering her with talk that's crap-chat off my tongue. So comfortable with her that I can self pitied cry and let go of my inhibition. I couldn't do this in front of any other person. I am a man of God and a sensitive man but dammed with that. At that point, Euphemia began to clear the table and took the things to the kitchen, and I got up from the chair visited the loo. When I got back, Euphemia was sitting on the sofa watching television. Inappropriately I said in anger, "We have not finished talking; nothing sorted yet, and you turn on the tv.

I do not know what to do; I am confused. Are we getting back together or not?" "I am sorry", Euphemia said without raising her voice and straight away, she switched off the television and tuned it back to the radio and came and sat back on the chair at the table. Euphemia drank from a glass of water and asked, "Karl, would you like coffee now?" "No thanks, darling, I would like to know about the leaflet that explains divorce. Do you want a divorce because you are having an affair?" I asked. "No! I don't know", Euphemia said. Euphemia began to look bleak and withdrawn. I held my tongue.

Silence hung over us for a while; Euphemia stared at the wall and then gazed out of the French door. Then she bowed her head close to the table. Euphemia then opened up, went completely sad, broke the silence of her inner world, and slowly revealed her deep personal secret. "My mum was right; no man will love me. And your mum was right; you should have married a well-educated woman." I stayed silent and listened. "I am not taking care of myself. I should have been the one who died instead of Elizabeth. (Her sister died of a drug overdose) I want to die. I know I shall die from a stroke." Once again, like Christmas 2003, 'Oh my God,' loudly exploded in all cavities in my head. Shouts of, 'Oh my God, oh my God, oh god' exploded like fireworks. "Are you taking your blood pressure tablets?" I asked her. "No, I have chosen to have a stroke and keep my hair; the pill thins my hair.

You don't want me, and I am better off dead," Euphemia said. I was thinking hard to think up something positive to say that would snap her out of her low mood.

Before I spoke again, I tried to sort out my mixed-up thinking to mean the right things. Euphemia was crying intensely. I put my hands on her shoulders and brought her body close to me, and cried too. "Please, please, darling, don't do this. Please, I cannot let you do this to yourself; I need you. Promise me you will take your blood pressure pills. Let's put the rings on our fingers and make a promise."

"No! You do not want me to have the ring. You don't want me," Euphemia said. I asked her to think of what she would be leaving behind and what she would have no part in doing. The lives of her children, having a mum in their future, would be affected. "If you are not called yet by God and deliberately cause your death, think of the effect, how they'll feel, and how they will take it." "The children will have you. You are a good dad," Euphemia replied with a hoarse voice, and her tears were so plentiful that a handful of tissues was soaked with the tears and were soggy as she wiped her eyes with them. "I am a dad, and the children need their mother; your role is different from mine though we both care. Please, darling, don't think of doing anything silly. We love you!"

I gave Euphemia a load more paper tissues; those tissues were saturated entirely and disintegrated to mush from the tears and blowing of the nose. Euphemia complained that her head was hurting but continued to speak softly and emotionally, saying, "God would not forgive me; only God loves me, but He can't keep forgiving me." I talked to Euphemia about God's forgiving power and his love. He knows our heart and our nature, and in her low mood, that did not allow her to think too straight and be full of life. "It was my fault that caused this because I was pushy. I caused you to feel this way. I'm sorry. Darling, I love you too; the children love you. Please do not give up; we all need you to stay in our lives. But, please, will you promise you'll take the tablets?" I pleaded. Euphemia sniffled and nodded her head. "Please speak and promise you'll take the tablets," I asked. Euphemia shook, nodded her head a few more times. "Darling, please tell me you'll promise to take the tablets." Euphemia breathed in profoundly, sniffed and breathed out slowly and said, "I promise to take my tablets." "Thanks, darling."

I took the ring I had for her out of the box and suggested, "Let us hold hands and place the rings on our finger and make a pledge." Euphemia took the ring she had for me out of the box, and we placed the rings on each other's fingers and said to one another, "I give you this ring as a symbol of my eternal love for you with the hope we'll grow more and more in love." We hugged and kissed deeply on the lips and smiled and smiled. We kissed passionately again and again, and I half-opened my eye during kissing. It was beautiful to see Euphemia was enjoying it too. We smiled and smiled as we picked up good feelings from each other, but our independent happiness released uncontrollable smiles and giggles. The wall clock chimed the last automatic chime for 10 pm, ringing out that stressed period and ringing in a breakthrough for happy times. We danced late into the night to smooth jazz, talked about our anxieties and fears, and made fun of some of our foolish situations. We laughed together, then went to bed engrossed in a love in which Euphemia could share her heart, and I had a better understanding of it.

The next day, 15th February, I eagerly went and told the children to forget that I had something to say to them yesterday for it was no longer of importance because, "Georgina and Jonathan, your mother and I are in love." Euphemia looked on and smiled, then we got close and kissed on the lips in front of our children. Georgina said, "You have been having a difficult time. Does that mean you and mum won't be splitting up?" I then said, "Mum and I have made a breakthrough; we'll be alright now." This week, Euphemia discussed Valentine's Day's success with our eldest daughter Katrina who is expected to get married in a few years.

On Monday, 16th February, I jumped to the conclusion that Euphemia had broken her promise to take the hypertension tablet and had gone to work without having it. I had uttered my daily devotional catchphrase, "Have a good day at work, take care on the roads, and God bless. Bye, bye, my lovely," as she left for work. I panicked when I saw her medicine had not been taken that morning and telephoned the doctors' surgery. I had a call back from Euphemia's doctor. I discussed the challenging times we had been having in our relationship and Euphemia's attempt to overdose on the day after Boxing Day 2003. She had thought of dying from a stroke by not taking her hypertension tablets. The doctor asked me to encourage Euphemia to come and see him at the surgery. It turned out that Euphemia had genuinely forgotten to take the pill that morning. Before afternoon that day, Euphemia telephoned home and talked to Georgina about bringing her tablets to her workplace when she came into Wellingborough for her dentist's appointment.

Today is Saturday 21st February 2004, and it's our son's birthday. My relationship with my wife feels good and promising, but I wonder how I can maintain it. Yesterday, at the start of dinner, Euphemia put a keepsake card by my dinner plate, which read, To My Soul Mate. I cannot thank her enough. I appreciated it very much, and I hugged and kissed her again and again. "Darling, thank you!" The latest change in our relationship; I hope it will last forever. I do not know how to maintain this happiness and not slide back into unhappiness and rejection feelings. I hope we work together and want the same things; we will love through eternity or until death do us part. Euphemia gradually tells me of her inner feelings, alien to me because she had bottled them up. I am learning when she is grumpy and wants her own space. I am learning to gauge moody, happy, sad, and depressed, can't sleep at night, or feeling tense. I discovered all of Euphemia's range of emotions in one month, and on Wednesday, 25th February, Euphemia maintained her happy feelings. She gave me a small box of chocolates with the words "I love you" written on the box. It means Euphemia is showing signs of expressing her inner feelings in words and deeds. "Thanks, my darling."

Today is Sunday 7th March 2004, and Euphemia talks to me and tells me about the burdens, especially the money problems and how she feels about them. Euphemia may not be sure of the reasons for her varying moods and puts it down to tiredness.

The desire to stray
Written on Tuesday 11th May 2004

Everything I discovered about lovemaking was with Euphemia. But, unfortunately, although I wanted us to continue exploring the beauty of intimacy between a woman and a man, things in that department have failed quite sharply. So, unfortunately, celibacy is the order of the day.

I wanted to stray and have a sexual encounter with other women, and Euphemia's reluctance was a gateway to having an affair to make things even. If I have a new relationship, I would agree with the partner that it's purely for sex, no emotional involvement, only goosebumps of pure sexual pleasure. There is soon a blip in my communication with my wife, and it's taking negotiation skills to get started the initial round of dialogue to say we understand each other and what we say we want the other to do. For example, Euphemia asks my permission if she wants to hug me. Why? I cannot understand! I think the affection has disappeared, but Euphemia quarrels with me that I am making our relationship hard work. It's so sad that I picked up the vibes of intimacy dying, and I cannot get practice becoming a good kisser.

The marriage feels one-sided, and it's not passionate. I pray to God that our marriage explodes in the two of us, putting enough time and energy into the relationship to not feed my mind with the persistent rumble in my head that I need an affair. Euphemia still bewitches me because I love both her external and inner beauty. I am always in love with Euphemia. I am full of remorse and want to apologize to her for what I have not done but simply thought about – namely, infidelity and thinking about having affairs. I briefly have the idea to leave her to have a fling, but the overwhelming richness that being married to Euphemia gives my life is denying me a momentary sexual thrill. I am getting back determined to work things through with Euphemia because I can remember the romantic dream of the long and happy union.

I need to free up the energy to enjoy ourselves and achieve what we want out of life together. Euphemia says I want to control her; I always want to have control.

I do not understand what she means, but she gets angry when I expect something of her and fails to do it, so she gets reminded again. Then I got angry too and asked myself, why do I bother? Euphemia thinks I have a problem with the balance of power and can't see correctly the love expressed by her, but I believe Euphemia is not clear that there has to be a trade-off. It comes down to real business; the reality is our marriage has much less to do with the romantic dreams of a perfect match. Instead, it's like a whole company with notions of investment, resources and negotiations. So I can't prevent myself from acting on nonsense, quick ideas that emotionally batter my marriage.

I invested in our marriage, and we both got returns on the investment. I expected difficulties, grey patches in our marriage but not snubbing resistance to change for the better that may positively grow our relationship. I have been working hard to arrest the disillusionment cycle, to reconnect and become happy together again. We should be in the maturing phase of our marriage by now and have the security of a comfortable and satisfying relationship. Still, Euphemia does not feel keen about my thoughts of having an affair. The marriage union needs a lot of maintenance. We have no deep resources because earlier and recent conflicts are remembered and bankrupted our relationship. Instead of making hardly a ripple, we have to rebuild our relationship. The important message I would like Euphemia to understand is that I respect her; I wouldn't violate her body or take advantage of her and go against her will.

Saturday 5th June 2004, I am so pleased that our relationship is functioning normally again and the previous thoughts of having an affair have been squashed.

The days of favours
Written Saturday 29th May 2004

Through prayer, I have been asking a favour of God, to appoint a time when my financial situation will be without worry. For two months now, our finances have been overstrained. I was expecting prize draw money to come in by now. Each week that passes since then puts us nearer and nearer to a crisis. On Saturday 1st May 2004, I asked the bank to increase our joint account overdraft to the maximum of £1,150.00, and on my account, I got given extras on my overdraft of £100, which will run for three months. The overdraft period will end on the 1st of August 2004. The money is meant to cover costs incurred for ordered items necessary to be a prize draw finalist or secure prize money when the parcel is delivered. There will be no money left in the bank accounts to pay direct debits or buy anything after 8th June. I desperately need the prize to draw cash in our favour. I rely on being lucky in the prize draw to bring in the capital to balance the books and provide for us. It is predicted that the account will be overdrawn if extra cash does not enter our bank by then. The overdrafts would be used up, and my benefits would not reach the account in time to avoid a total meltdown.

On Thursday 27th May, I received the prize draw winner's cheque for £5.00; it was minimal. The prize draw should have netted me up to £60,000 for taking out Hospital Plan Insurance. I shall stop the plan to save £4.15 per month because I did not receive a significant cash award to secure the policy's running. Yesterday, I got the expected parcel without the winner's £5,900.00 cheque. It was another disappointment; The product came with a claim form document that confirmed a winner but no actual cheque award. I had bought products in my desperation for money. I do not want to use it immediately, but it will come in useful. I had accepted things like an ice pack, steamer and a decorative wall-mounted butterfly for external walls to secure prize draw money, but I may have been scammed. They do say, 'If it looks too good to be true, it probably is,' but I put my faith in receiving a cheque from those lovely people who are not from Premium Bonds. I had prayed daily to

God, saying, 'please let it not be a prize draw scam, God'. My heart believed some truthful prize draws out there just waiting for my authorization as a winner. In a sense, I took a risky gamble with some unsolicited mail that asked for purchases in response to prizes and required a short time to respond, which should have raised my suspicion. I saw prize draws as a quick fix to money because we solely relied on one low wage and inadequate benefits to living off.

I calculated that the chance of winning was great because the event releases God's power through the favour of faith. I denied the reality of consciousness, which made me suspicious, and I assumed a scam could not happen because I felt spiritual and owned my private thoughts. My action stems from my conscious choice to take the chance, although I felt strange when I did so. I imagined a click from the universal life force could discharge enough energy into my round of circumstances and cause a blip that would change our entire lives.

Katrina, our eldest daughter, gave me the last two months money of £221.00 to pay for her student accommodation from her final student loan money. Still, I allowed her to use the money to help her, and her fiancé put down a deposit on a two-bedroom flat. Katrina had given up her part-time job to have more time to study for her exams in May 2004. She hoped to find work now that her reviews are over but not necessarily a career choice. The relatively stable financial position I had enjoyed since I gambled with my life in 2003 and won has come to an end. As I look at this new financial year from April 2004-05, income was expected to drop dramatically because Family Tax Credit would be halved. My second child will be out of further education, and Child Benefit stops for her. Euphemia's Working Tax Credit was said to have been overpaid, and it would be clawed back, leaving her with, if I remembered correctly, 76 pence per day in tax credit. My employer has sent me my P45 due to my long-term absence from work, as they cannot keep my job open. When my doctor advised me I was fit to return, they were pleased to hear from me. I seek employment rights advice from Citizen's Advice because I should have received vital holiday pay to boost my Incapacity Benefit during the annual holidays.

Total recovery to full health certainly seems far away, but I have made speedy progress in the movement of my limbs, and my consultant gave me an appointment on 15th September 2004 for the next check-up. Our mortgage was expected to rise since a succession of rates rises, three in the last six months. Utility bills, gas and electricity, are the latest household essentials hit by soaring costs. Four pounds per month more is expected to have to be forked out on an average electricity bill. Petrol prices are forever rising due to the unrest in the Middle East. The £886.71 council tax bill, thanks to God, we are exempted from paying until a review of our circumstances in October 2004. Also, the £400.52 water usage demand has been reduced to £10.50 monthly.

I am being dragged off again into worry as the essential commodities get more expensive, and I shall find it hard to find the money for them. Our lifestyle won't improve as we struggle through a financial emergency. We have no long-term accessible saving pot, and short-term economic costs are driving us into severe difficulties. I trust God to make it all work out right and give us a favour because I have to be in it to win it. All my prayers couldn't fill the bellies of starving children, stop wars or help desperate people who are worse off than us. Then I wished, and it changes nothing but prayer has a shift in the decision. I decided to give to the poor as I experience a leap of faith to believe I will be blessed with a good life because my love of life has never been so strong. I can see how beautiful the future will be, and there will be an appointed time, sick or healthy, when money will allow me to bless other people through my giving to charitable causes. Next, the funds will allow me to pay towards my children's higher education and weddings and refurbish our very mundane house, garden and fence. It matters not a jot that I have no money to improve our lifestyle or cut out what appear to be essential luxuries. The vital things are to believe that God will work miracles and put enough bread in our bellies. We love, give thanks for family and good health as the cosmic chaperone, God, watches over us. However, I worry when we don't pay promptly enough for debt repayments and paying essential bills such as those for food and heating, and we use credit cards to clear them.

Life is to be enjoyed whether we have a lot or a little, or are sick or well, but when one has nothing, somehow life goes on, and things happen, and then I get excited about them. The best vehicle to have at times like these is faith in God that we'll pull through. After all, we know that this physical entity, God, set off the big bang and made the universe eternal, and He has the power to intervene. I am hoping that the door of opportunity will not just open but fall off its hinges. I believe God wants me to prosper so that the more He gives, the more I can provide. By being blessed, I can bless others.

Today is Saturday 29th May 2004, and my faith is just about holding out after losing out to scams. There is, however, an excitement that I can almost touch, but it is elusive. The financial blessing was promised, and I have to wait for the Almighty to exercise the promise when ready. I use my faith to create and increase my resources and release favours. The vow of fidelity is directing me to do something within the laws of God and man to be richly blessed. I am not supposed to repeat the season of not supporting the family and not putting money aside in a rainy-day fund, which will protect us from unforeseen expenses. I again see life is not easy because it's not fair, but faith is, I think. I am about to find out as I walk on purposefully. I anticipate the worst but expect the best and, in my actions, may be more harmful than in my reaction. I vowed to God to keep faith to do something to increase my resources and help others because I care about right and wrong, even if doing the right thing is not in my best interest. I have the compulsion to react to sad news in the media and respond to the tragic personal moments that life throws at me by pouring out my deepest feelings in exhaustive praying. In the end, I shed tears and say, 'God in your mercies' or 'Thanks be to God' if the sad news had a good fortune and turned to be the good news as it resolves. I am happy again.

I get incredibly anxious when the world turns cruel, and the planet crawls around in injustices, with a lack of freedom and morality. I have to switch off the news from the television and radio and don't read newspapers. Although it is transparent national and international affairs, I have no sense of peace and worry, and I cannot fully understand the dilemma.

I am making it a duty to attend church each week and set aside £3.00 per week for the offertory plate. I want this minimum contribution to multiply when I have 10% of my disposable income or grow concerning my wealth. The things I say might seem foolish, but today I have taken money, £1.00 from the church's designated money, and bought a National Lottery ticket. I have no disposable income, even for a national newspaper that costs 40 pence. In the ten years of the Lotto, it is the first time in its history that there is a triple rollover, and the estimated jackpot is twenty-one million pounds. The church and other charitable organizations would benefit if I won that amount of money. I will go to church tomorrow, God willing, to give reverence, adoration and devotion to a deity that is the all-powerful God. I will ask for pardon if my expected lucky flutter on the Lotto provokes change. It seems wrong while I try to understand the nature of God. I shall repent and pray for the good of all. Despite there being an all-powerful God, it seems somehow necessary in the universe to justify punishment. I have a moral sense based on the assumption that I am a master of my destiny because I'll not get stripped of free will. I take medicine even though I believe God is controlling the course of my illness. I had steadily increased in weight from 13 stones a year ago, 2003, to 15 stones 9 pounds today. I look like a barrel with this protruding stomach. I must bring myself back to eating nutritious foods and exercise to restrict the weight gain associated with the antipsychotic medication.

The Appointed Time
Written Sunday 6th June 2004

I lie in bed and pray to my imagination because my everyday experiences give rise to extreme anguish, for it feels like God is not near when life is beating us. For example, in 2003, when I attempted suicide, God saved my life so that I could live faithfully and be true to myself, but I am asking again, 'Does God exist?'

Religious belief has always been regarded as inseparable from the supernatural. I am one of those who have adhered to religious tradition and have expected some paranormal experience to be a possible accompaniment. Jesus Christ is an applicable invention; the whole of my environment exists at God's will, and I am unconditionally dependent upon God. So why on earth don't events come at the appointed time to ease worry? Instead, they remain in the pipeline or don't happen at all. As creatures, we are already what we are naturally by God's will, but I still go off to find ways to prove security, individuality and independence. I leapt too far because if I released my inner power, I could change myself, and what I expect of faith would be the norm and not the super standard. I see a way of improving myself and the possibility of changing my whole environment by learning life skills. I have enrolled in a course module to improve my word skills with Learn Direct to help me achieve my goals, and I am also on work-based learning for adults in free computer training. I would not lose government benefits, and it's a 26-week course with a work placement. For twenty-one hours per week, I will get training and gain qualifications in ECDL (European Computer Driving Licence). The classes start tomorrow, 07/06/04, and my goal is to improve my life skills, IT, brush up on reading and writing skills and build up confidence in looking for a job as a disabled job seeker. I was advised to declare my mental health to employers and my disability which requires me to walk with sticks. If I need employment support, practical ways to help me keep a job can be explored.

The computer training has been postponed for a week, and the new starting date is Monday 14/06/04. I believed in God even before talking, but I have a hard time reasoning if God exists. I should have had success due to my faith. Now that my career is being turned around since the road accident, it instils this belief even more deep-rooted. I've always been kind and want to give to charity, but it has proven that what I receive is directly related to what I offer. It has never been my intention to give to get, but I can see that God has blessed me when I should have given up on something but did not. There is much more I can do, and everything is a blessing, even if it's a blessing in disguise. I wanted to kill myself for the family's financial gain, and the situation did seem right to die; I should not have lived, but I take advantage of the blessing that I am alive. I believe God does not discriminate or judge unfairly. I want to be an excellent example of living by faith more than ever, and I need to make decisions based on my education and religion. I am educating myself by going to classes, and it brings fulfilment and freedom. Life is hard, and I await the appointed time to ease the restless struggle to get by. I am nervous that the financial blessing may not come to pass in my lifetime, but God is not worried because He knows. 'Thy will be done.' I pray to maintain a relationship with God and corporately with the church. Sometimes, God got addressed as She and personally known in the Christian doctrine of the Trinity as He. His nature can be abstract, but I sometimes conceived Him in the images available to me. Knowledge of the divine derived from my conditioning by life's circumstances and conveyed in language, symbols, and culture.

In the Judaic-Christian spiritual culture, God is understood to have revealed his nature and purposes or, at least, enough of his character and intentions for us to enter a relationship with him and establish laws that enable humans to obey his will. In the Christian revelation, God Himself came into the world. This generous act of self-giving not only provided for redemption but also confirmed that God could be known in Jesus Christ as a person. That is primary Christianity, but I think God help my unbelief. The accomplishments that appear to elevate emotional sensations led me to imagine that prayer can be addressed as a therapeutic species to an abstract spirit of goodness. God is encountered in meditation and can be resolved directly from persons in adoration of Christian religious worship. I do not believe in all of Christianity's claims because God is getting known to me in ways established by Him outside of Christianity, in a distinct spiritual interpretation. Christianity is teaching us to learn about God from traditions adopted from the ancient world recognised as mysteries. Truth in this modern world about God's working in our society is outside customs, and the understanding of the Divine perceived in nature.

Understanding God today occurs at the press of a computer keyboard or viewing a television documentary show. It contrasts with the modern expectation that the spiritual truths revealed to the ancients are not self-explanatory, and we can get revelation today, which needs interpretation. I have thought and prayed that I would experience a phase of wealth and opulence as I have never known. It surprises me that I have not received it yet, and I feel so sure of myself. I have experienced a rare intense phenomenon that gave a message from the destiny that alerts me that there's absolutely no doubt that I can win as much money as I need. I have continuously thought about this expected wealth all night long, and as a result of sleeping and waking up constantly throughout the night, I was exhausted in the small wee hours. I decided to pray, and it felt like destiny had finally decided to do something for me. God knows that life has not always been kind to us, and He knows the hardships we've suffered. It all feels like God has shared our discouragement and the weariness we face. We certainly had more than our fair share of issues with such an unfair lot of our constant money problems and difficulty making ends meet. All that will soon be just a bad memory because it is guaranteed through my thought processes. The centre that corresponds with the Almighty and the laying down of favourable circumstances will allow the powerful thoughts to control all events and bring about the pre-ordained.

I would like so much to live the life I should have, an experience where I would be financially well off, where my debts would get paid off and where fear of the future would no longer exist. I am continuing to have life difficulties, and the stresses can be intense. I am not so much worried now but excited that this real life is within reach, within my reach, because as soon as I have complete trust in the vision, I'll improve my position significantly and realise some of my dearest dreams. I want to give to charity, see my children through education, and financially help them get married. I also want to redecorate the house, take a well-deserved holiday and make those dear to me happy. As day breaks through my window this morning and after a long night of reflection, I am now sure that many good things will happen soon and change our lives radically.

Today is Monday 7th June 2004, and the positive transformations I will see very soon have to happen within days, or else it's merely bad luck, or success will be delayed. Why the delay? God only knows! Maybe I am impatient to wait for the appointed time. The delivery of cheques to my doorstep must be imminent because it came to me like an absolute truth that I'll live a life of opulence, luxury and riches. If the cheques do not come, I shall give an anguished cry, "My God, my God, why have you forsaken me?" - Darkness for a while will cover my unfolding story and the weight of the dark and the days during it give me no reason to believe that even on the best of days, God is with us. I was getting through the second day of the shock of not receiving anything created a more significant relief. The surprise, puzzlement and ultimately, the joy of my resurrected spirit in all its glorious splendour will get me through this weeping for prophecies to be fulfilled and promises redeemed.

After today, the following ones are non-event days indeed because it's only a time of waiting in which nothing of significance would occur and of which there would be little to be said. I am only assuming the days to come are an empty void, nothing days, shapeless, relatively meaningless and anticlimactic, simply because the 'appointed time', as it unfolds, is happening without turning to the last page in this book. I have come to the end of this write-up, and I expect that the next time I write, the strife would be over, and the battle between me becoming prosperous or not would be won. Hallelujah! You will hear from me in a few days if my prediction is sound.

Reflecting on my mortality
Written Wednesday 9th June 2004

In my previous writing called 'The Appointed Time,' I expected riches, remembering my relatively imminent death. The pursuit of wealth made me stand back and reflect on my mortality. The thought of death can bring authenticity to social life, and it can also be a relief from anxiety. The death of other people who have achievements such as fame, riches, status, or power loses much more than their power at the end of life. The thought that everyone will ultimately end up as the most common of substances, dust, gives a melancholy message, but arguably more so for me anchoring my life around the pleasures of wealth. It seems to be the rich, the beautiful, the famous and the powerful to whom death has the cruellest lessons to teach. I do not believe it, except that choosing worldly goodwill take me farthest from God. I am anxious that Christianity emphasised this can happen.

Beneath my flaws, there are two ingredients, fear and a desire for love. I do not want to feel absent from God's love or that of my family. As creatures of God and loved by Him, my acquirement of wealth would not see me stepping away from God but moving in closeness and constant celebration of his blessings. It is best to emphasise that we all will die; everyone we love will vanish, and all our achievements and even our names will get stamped into the ground. So, I instinctively recognise how closely my miseries are bound up with the grandiosity of my ambitions. Still, people will be under the brutally descriptive title of 'loser' or a 'nobody' because they are unable or unwilling to follow the dominant notions dutifully to achieve.

So far in human history, we know we only get one chance at life on the planet, and if my life is to be the best it can be, there will probably come a day when I need to change it, but I find change deeply troubling. Whether good or bad, it is usually stressful and my natural reaction is fear and resistance. But the change I have found has been easy to think about and difficult to make. I actively see myself living out my dreams, and I imagine myself doing everything I have said in the chapters. Visualisation is a powerful tool because the more influential the 'picture' of my goal, the more excited and motivated I become. The life I want is not going to fall out of the sky into my lap. It feels like hard work, but I must stick to time frames and commitments and eventually, I'll get the life I want. Though there's no guarantee that I will succeed, I try to be realistic and give myself the right amount of time to change my life.

One possible way of getting the life I want is to complete my computer training. I am anchoring my life around the pleasures of a high position in a suitable desk-related job. I have returned to education to realise my dreams, and if I am persistent and systematic in getting the lessons in my head, there's no end to what I can achieve. My new status now that I will not be a factory worker carries no moral connotations that what I do says strictly nothing about who I am. It makes no sense to believe that one's place in the social hierarchy reflects actual qualities. Though I expect my new job to afford earthly things because this life is only a prelude to a far more critical next breath, the vanity of material things is not essential. More serious is love, goodness, sincerity, humility and kindness over pursuing fame and riches. Being aware of my inner dialogue, the way I silently speak to myself - "I can do it, I'm allowed to try things" - and not having to get things right the first time that's what is essential. Each time I relapse, I take a step back towards my old life. It's a risk, and I tell myself in therapy that negative talk is 'self-limiting beliefs' because I end up talking myself out of doing what I want. I wouldn't fail! It's an exciting assignment, and I can pay the mortgage, but unfortunately, life is not like that. We do not live in a controlled environment, and I will need to deal with the unknown. Of course, I would not be reckless but be willing to accept the consequences of my decisions and actions.

After all, even if things do not go according to my plan, they may still turn out well. I can picture myself at my 80th birthday party, surrounded by my friends and family. The sun is setting, and I have a glass of red wine in my hand. It's been the perfect day, and I stand up to make a speech about my life, productive and fulfilled. I've achieved my dreams by marrying and having children, loving my wife for my entire life, and having responsibilities that structure the commitment, visiting other countries, going back to education, and writing a book. That is my personal obtainable dream life. My conscience forbids me from ever, I mean ever, attempting suicide ever again.

Back to the future
Written Wednesday 11th August 2004

In the past, we had financial problems that are still with us to this present day. They hold on to our future, but I can see time back to the future where business problems are better controlled or don't exist. But, wait, the day is not yet here now; it's in a tomorrow to come, not here.

The reason I attempted suicide is still here with me today, one year and five months on; the inability to support the family is bothering me. I again cannot feed the family adequately; cash is hard to come by, and we struggle endlessly to cope with our existing resources. I have to move the little money I have around, reduce the reasonable amount we need to buy food, and direct it onto essential direct debits to pay bills. I am again cutting back on food bills, and transport costs need to be reduced. An overhaul is required on our mortgage to put it onto a lower interest rate and buy an adequate life assurance for the mortgage and ourselves. We have a decreasing sum assurance on our mortgage, which is inappropriate since we changed the mortgage to interest-only payments. Our mortgage rate is 8.15%, and mortgage rates could be as low as 4.99% if we did not have personal loans and credit card debts. I am looking to re-mortgage with them, Kensington Mortgages, or re-mortgage with another lender who does not access income. My mortgage advisor told me it could be more challenging to get a lower rate mortgage because I am unemployed with high outstanding debts. I am still suffering the injuries caused by the road accident in 2003.

So Life Assurance will be expensive since I had attempted suicide and I have a diagnosis of mental illness, and I'm on medication to suppress it. So it will be harder to get life cover, so I want to outline further the problems that are mainly money-related and tell you how worried I am if money does not reach our bank account soon.

We stemmed off the last meltdown because something just suddenly turned up unexpectedly. I think my worry will disappear soon because I anticipate the blessings and luck smiling at me. My sister Joan surprised us and left a gift of £50.00, a religious magazine, and a bottle of wine to collect from our mother's house. An investment of hers had matured, and Joan shared this with the family. This £50 came just in time to stop our bank account from exceeding the overdraft limit. So, my struggle to free ourselves will not remain pipe dreams but a reality that the enormous millstones of debts and the battle to manage with current resources without having to squeeze in our bellies anymore will come soon because it's an eagerly anticipated blessing.

Each month I reflect on my dream of wealth. So far, I have been receiving letters. I am guaranteed thousands of pounds, and I believe them because I have received many delivery notifications from various reputable companies in the last nine months. I think God has willed it because it offers us hope. Some might say it's a false hope, but it is hope under God's will for us to escape debt and start to manage better. We cannot get the money we need any other way but through luck, hope and prayer. So, my post gets swollen with promises of prize draw money, and I play the lottery whenever I can squeeze a spare pound out of my resources.

On Saturday 7th August, I won £10 on the lottery, and I could see our misfortune was changing. I stopped attending the IT course on 6th July because my legs could not be elevated during the day. Hence they swelled up by the end of the day, and walking became painful.

Our daughter Georgina was registered on the car insurance on 16/06/2004, and she drove the family car for the first time on Sunday, 20/06/04. Georgina regularly drives the family car and displays the 'L' plates on it. Either her mum or I would supervise her driving and her manoeuvres. Georgina's driving is excellent, but more practice is needed for parking and reversing; she is just short of being good at them. For the next four weeks, Georgina will be getting double lessons with the driving school to sharpen her skill to take the practical test on 3rd September 2004. We wish you every success, Georgina, in passing the first time next month and good luck in the 'A' level results that come out next week on 19/08/04.

Katrina is taking driving lessons in her fiancé's aunt's driving school car. She is a qualified driving instructor, and she gives Katrina driving lessons for free. Katrina has not got a job yet, but she is not entitled to a Job Seeker's Allowance, although Katrina has had no means of income since the student loan company's last final pay-out. The Job Centre and the Benefits Agency told her that the State would not support her with Job Seeker's Allowance because she cohabits with her fiancé and works over 16 hours a week. Katrina is exempt from all government-assisted help unless she is expecting a child or has a disability. We attended Katrina's graduation on Tuesday, 13/07/04, and have photos and a video that captured the whole happy ceremony. Katrina and her fiancé, Robert, graduated in the same month by gaining a 2:2 in their degrees. To my reckoning, their graduate bill has a degree of pain because Katrina will owe the Student Loan Company and bank overdrafts up to £13,000. They are fighting to make ends meet, and Robert works in the early morning, but there is a threat to his ability to keep a car on his earning and support Katrina. He had already given up some leisure pursuits to save money in his pocket to keep Katrina and himself comfortable. My prayer is with them, for Katrina had said to me, "We should not be going through this financial difficulty when neither of us has financial independence yet. We are in love, so we get no help from the government; they look for us to mess up our future together or our own lives." They say that the cost of university is an investment in the future for graduates' earning potential. However, Katrina cannot get on the job market because employers still ask for experience over degree achievement. Earnings are a later worry; getting her foot in the door by getting a job is the genuine hurdle. They are getting into a deep crisis because Katrina and Robert are fed up seeing their circumstances crumbling before they have even begun their married life; they crave the independence to use their own money. At the moment, Katrina is not looking for a promising career, and she is desperate for a job that will help adequately pay the bills and give her disposable income. We never anticipated, nor did Katrina, that she would still be out of work after graduation. Going to university had made her happy because Katrina found her true love near the campus and achieved independence from her parents. Still, she waits for the ultimate from a university education, a job, a good job. Katrina has applied for work in other fields she is interested in, like child care, The BBC, and a university asking for a graduate to do research work. As yet, no luck in finding a career, but we continue to pray for her success to come.

My daughter is experiencing the harsh realities of life, a quote from my writing to celebrate Katrina's birth. I sincerely pray, hoping she and her partner ride the storms of these difficulties that lie before them and that their relationship grows strong in the face of adversity. There's an option remaining; Katrina could come home and tell the authorities she has split with her boyfriend, and that will enable her to claim Job Seeker's Allowance when she registers with the Job Centre in her home town, Kettering. It would mean that Katrina would sign on at the Job Centre every two weeks to receive about £44.00 a week, then she could travel to Manchester to be with Robert. I have been sending Katrina £100 a month to help her support herself. She says Robert is accommodating and supportive because when she gets low and cries to end unemployment, Robert says, "Do not worry", and they hug. Katrina looks for jobs on the internet, in newspapers, and have regular bus rides to the Job Centre but does not ease her job search.

I will receive benefits from September 2004, £496.05, as I am between benefit adjustments. This month, I received a Working Tax Credit of £614.13, and they will claw off £105.00 from Euphemia's earnings. Euphemia's wage pays the monthly mortgage of £437.00 and petrol at £25.00 per week so long as we do not exceed £90 a fortnight for shopping, and that leaves my wife with very little of her own money for her personal use. Our shopping bills exceeded £550.00 some calendar months, but now we shop every two weeks, and in the week when I use my benefit money, we cannot exceed £200, so it's usually within that figure. We have reduced our shopping bill from over £550 per month, giving up good cuts of mutton and a bottle of wine to the present day where I cannot afford to exceed £300 per month for shopping. Look at our shelves, look at our cupboards, look inside our fridge and freezer, and there are missing essentials and empty spaces where foodstuff was stored. We have rationed the supplies because there is not enough money to stockpile or buy necessary food items. When I considered what cash gets used from our income for motor expenses, the M O T and the car needing two new tyres, along with the graduation photos and videos, we have insufficient funds. We also have to consider the cost of driving lessons, subsidising Katrina, the increase in the mortgage, insurance increase, and the finding of £148 to pay household bills. That does not include direct debit/standing order payments of £217.60 each month. To add to the misery, Sky, the satellite company, has told me we have been underpaying for Sky Talk's use, the service's telephone side, for three months. Their computer had made errors on our account, and we have to pay £194.45 this month of August 2004. Also, an advance payment of £200 is to be made to secure a university campus accommodation place for Georgina. Jonathan has a school trip in late September costing £180 to go to Gavilan. I had applied for a grant to subsidise the journey and was successful and only have to contribute £50.00 toward the trip now.

As you can see, I am anxious to secure more money in the bank as before, back to the future, but I am not in despair this time because I am doing all I can and not giving in. I believe that all good things come to those who wait. I have written to one of the long-running promotion prizes draws that guarantees £10,000, and I fibbed a bit about having a heart condition. I cannot believe that all the prize draw promotions I have entered were scams. I am holding out that this one is genuine, and they will reply to my letter.

On Wednesday 11th August 2004, my mother and dad's golden anniversary and all of their children were invited, along with friends, to an exclusive restaurant for dinner. Georgina has passed her 'A' level exams and has her first-choice university place at Middlesex University to study Sports Rehabilitation and Injury Prevention beginning on 20th September 2004. We wish you all the best and God's blessings, Georgina. On 17/08/04, Katrina came home, and on 25/08, she intends to sign on at the Job Centre and go back to Manchester on Friday 27th for two weeks. Katrina is now on the car insurance, and on the 18th August 2004, she drove the Honda car for the first time. Her mum took her out on the roads.

Déjà vu
Written Friday 3rd September 2004

There was a period in August 2004 when my marriage went through a period of déjà vu. I cannot understand why I am stuck in the repetition of attacking my wife's sincerity in our marriage. I find it hard to accept the past stays in the past, and I can't let go of her near infidelity and the secret communication with a past lover.

On Sunday 15th August 2004, I attempted to liaise with Euphemia to cooperate with me to trust her fully again when she only told me she is popping out without saying where exactly she was going. Euphemia was furious and went ballistic. That humble beginning of a conversation turned into a marital breakdown. "You do not trust me, so it's over!" I felt my heart deflate, and the air was squeezed out of me, but my heart also felt I had not been fair to her, and I see I am damaging our marriage. I was devastated; there is no pain to compare with a relationship that breaks up. Suicide comes close because nobody healthy wants to die, and nobody healthy wants to burden their loved ones with this kind of pain. My relationship break-up is like measles; once you've had it, you're immune from further attempts, but to be in love is not enough when I am also ignorant, so dreadfully ignorant. I thought I had to accept that Euphemia's decision was made in a heated moment and make the best of what must become a separation request.

"I want to be with you for the rest of my life; I am sorry and want to do what I can now to have a happier marriage," Euphemia said to me the next day. I had wiped away tears from my eye's night and day with my hands, and sometimes, when the tears were massive, with tissues. I had spoiled our marriage and was not subordinate to the pain. Euphemia's message was trying to bring back hope into our relationship. Still, I thought our relationship is best being over because I was getting pitied; my foolish self wanted me to accept the decision that it was over. I will give our relationship another chance because it's too painful for me to have her leave.

I have the assurance I need, and I begin to feel I am acting normal as our relationship begins to return to normality. I stopped sleeping on a single folding bed on the floor in our bedroom and switched back to fancying my wife. What had nearly been the end of our relationship has sparked a new beginning. We both agreed that we could not take another emotional battering to our marriage; we both want the same: a happy marriage. It feels like death when our marriage breaks down.

My challenge is to revoke the damaged part of myself that provokes a voice that attacks my deepest cares, and I will gain a sense of personal accomplishment if I manage to stop that interfering voice. The view digs deep into the part of my soul which inspires me and continues to search. Like my wife without a "broken" self, ordinary people, a unified sense of self, are taken for granted. Ordinary people sit comfortably inside a body they feel is theirs; seeing, hearing, touching, and smelling belong to themselves alone. Happy or gloomy, we own our bodily actions whether we reach out to shake someone's hand or play cricket; it is uniquely a part of our life experience and imagining our future. This 'self' appears seamlessly and effortlessly grounded in the body as a whole in ordinary people, but as it seems my unity of self does fragment, it leads to actions that shock or are odd. It is always an astonishing journey when the 'ill self' experiences depersonalisation, and I am in the phenomenal self that ordinary folks cannot experience unless their brain is diseased. I cannot say why I struggle so much to get the correct answers out of my head and seemingly categorise my loving and caring wife under the title of unloving. Mismatches between the senses or wrong constructions of reality can leave me struggling for the correct answers.

This new beginning in our marriage feels like we are still dancing like newlyweds. Our rapport has changed with the awareness that we, and our children, are all we have got. We are a family, and like any right loving family, we protect and nurture each other. I have a giddy sense of celebration that comes from making a hard choice and then discovering our secret; we enjoy the same things, kiss hard and often. For all that Euphemia has gone through with me, I would put her on a pedestal because she is a beautiful, loving soulmate, nurse, best friend and red-hot lover all at the same time. I am not worthy of having such a wonderful person, and I will do all I can to make up for my shortfalls. Euphemia has exceeded my expectations, and realistically she is an excellent, caring spouse and remains an exciting person to be around, someone I built a stable emotional life with, and her love for me plays a big part in the equation. Emotions could cloud reasons, but I have good reasons why we should try again in our relationship.

There are times in our marriage when I feel so fulfilled that I want to spread our joy, and this fresh start has awakened that feeling. Euphemia may not have known when she fell in love with me that a handsome man could be combined with sensitivity and be soulful, but now she knows. Euphemia is an excellent companion, a brave, courageous woman, a woman before her time who loves a person with schizophrenia in an age that fears us, stigmatises us and discriminates against us. I wish us well in what seems courageous, hoping that our relationship will never hit the rocks again. I cannot un-know what I know, but I can move on. What I do know is that I want to be with Euphemia for the rest of my life.

Happiness, Good luck, Love and Riches
Written Sunday 3rd October 2004

I am pleased to announce that Katrina will start full-time employment at Barclays Bank's branch in Manchester tomorrow, 4th October 2004.

Nobody deserves to have less good luck than others in this world, and everybody has the potential to be happy. So far, I have not succeeded, and I struggle to improve our lives by being truly courageous and strong in faith. I call upon God and think He can change the course of events. Things are not getting better, but I am making the most of things and feel I can work my way up, providing God is my helper, and I get a chance. I have to hold onto my inherent goodness and kindness, which makes me exceptionally sensitive. I think God heard my silent cry for help, and I sense everything I touch will be a success soon. Nothing would ever be the same again, and it would change the way I think and the way I view the world. Unless my belief is flawed and the truth is scientific and less biblical, I will be forever a Godly person.

Our finances are growing worse, not better, but the fierce battle for love and extreme happiness is sufficiently disarmed, and I feel like I'm floating on a cloud. I am surrounded by joy in my love life. The pursuit of good luck and riches, money, success and even glory uses up my energy. My family life is a joy, but I cannot fight off the defeat I feel when tackling those problems that anguish me. God senses my anguish and despair over this, and as a most desperate soul, I believe our lives will be transformed. For years, I have been speaking to God, and I feel His care for our lives because we have been protected by an aura, something in God's will for us which will, in good time, automatically attract fantastic good luck, happiness, riches and success. The hurdles in our life concern money and fortune; although my visions expect a blessing from heaven, I am collapsing under the strain of every day's need for money and good luck. Each time I strive, I awaken the qualities that hold on to my worth and trust God to deliver a new life free from debts if we endeavour.

A brand-new destiny in all areas of my life has started. Love, money, luck, and happiness make me more satisfied whenever any one of them succeeds. I believe

God offers us stable and enduring strength, and I can open the doors to pure luck, material wealth or spiritual wealth. He protects us and guides us towards blissful happiness with a capital H!! The course of our lives will change, and I will live out a beautiful destiny that I so richly deserve and which experience has denied me until now. Life has not been too kind to us, and not many fantastic opportunities have come our way.

I think more than anybody else, I deserve to enjoy good luck, and I feel injustice and anger because again, a prize draw that could have netted us £30,000 put only £5.00 through my bank account on 31/08/2004 and nil pounds and pence in another prize draw which should have given us £20,000. I am bitterly disappointed, and my cry for help is so desperate and sincere that God decided to offer his full attention now, and I have no reason to despair. Up until now, I have had not much luck, but all this is about to change. My financial problems will not continue. It has become a real plague in my life. Not a month goes by without asking myself how I'll be able to pay such a bill, and I had to deprive myself of things to continue.

Nevertheless, I have all the necessary potential for my life to dazzle and glow with immeasurable joy and to be showered with beautiful things. Although this is extremely rare in many people's lives, it will happen in areas of all of mine. Money, luck, happiness, love and success in my present life will grow, for my period of great disillusion, which preyed heavily upon me, is coming to an end. You can imagine I will be sceptical about what my mind is telling me because you'll understand why! How many times have I been deceived? There have been reasons to believe my life is about to take an essential positive step, and I dared to suggest that my world may be in for a dramatic turnaround. It has not happened, but soon I am in line for more money than I ever thought possible, and I'll be able to purchase practically anything I ever desired. I think I have finally crossed paths with a heartfelt thought, and at last, my destiny and luck are about to change for the better.

At the moment, I am continually struggling with difficulties from everyday life and confronted with an experience that has never really offered me great things. Although I feel drain spiritually and physically, I am now calm, optimistic, and cheerful under the circumstances. I faced up to the reality of harmful waves that have gradually surrounded me, leaving no room for real hope or positive waves to wrench me from the vicious circle to enable me to fulfil my realistic goals. Miracles do exist, and it is not by waves of a magic wand that our life will be transformed but by real help from God who blesses us.

Contrary to what my family believes, I have come very close to a grand fortune several times. I was always getting very close to chance, but always that touch of good luck was missing. God knows our financial difficulties, all those bills waiting to get paid, all those necessary expenses which leave us with nothing left over to afford things that would please us or make our lives easier. It's a feeling of solitude as if heaven has forsaken us. However, I am reassured that we will soon forget this challenging time because divine intervention will make situations where the money will not be an issue. Debt will totally and enduringly disappear to leave room for our lives to overflow with riches and prosperity because faith is a living organism. I must put my trust in God. He is the one who is holding out his hand and who has the power to transform the excellent luck that lies dormant within me. My future is now as golden as the brilliant sunshine in a summer's sky. I feel inner peace and tranquillity and am well prepared to embrace the fantastic future that lies before me.

Every Thursday morning since 2nd September 2004, I have been attending Said Eucharist at St. Michael's and All Angels Church on the corner of our street. My spiritual life needed a boast because I am too ashamed to attend my usual United Reformed Church on a Sunday without putting money in the compulsory offertory plate that gets passed down the pews. I am stressed and feel uncomfortable going week by week and cannot contribute a generous visible donation. There is no offertory collection taken on a Thursday at St. Michael's Church, but if one wants to make a monetary donation, a wooden plate is discreetly placed at the back of the church to use before or after the service. Since I don't go to my usual church, I look for ways to be spiritually filled. Some of these ways I am listening to Christian radio programmes, religious programmes on television, reading books, and go to St. Michael's Church. I love the talk or sermons on God, Jesus and on the people who follow faith, but I do not at the moment take the Holy Eucharist at St. Michael's, an Anglican Church, although I am baptised. I think it's barbaric to enact eating human flesh and drinking human blood. In the United Reformed Church, Eucharist gets known as communion, and it is carried out once on a Sunday each month. The Anglicans carry out the rituals of the Eucharist in every service. It's revolting; I cannot take the communion/Eucharist without disrupting the symbolic act by re-interruption because it does not sit comfortably. It leaves a sickly feeling in my stomach, and I cannot get my head around the traditional view. I reformed in my mind the eating of the meal. Taking the wafer/bread, I pray to the Almighty God to bless his world, feed the hungry, and forgive us for the inequality, injustices, and I wish the kingdom will come. Taking the water/red wine, I pray to the Almighty

God that people who thirst can have clean water, and our bodies get nourished with the bread and this wine. I remember Jesus's sacrifice, the Saints and generations of people who gave their lives for the world's peace and who now sing with the Saints in a place of glory out of this world.

'Merciful mother/father God of the universe, the source of truth and love keep us faithful and united in prayer, and the symbol of the breaking of bread and drinking proclaim our souls and bodies to be a living sacrifice. Send us out in the power of your spirit to live and work to your praise and glory in joy and simplicity of heart. In your name, God of all creation, we pray, amen.' That is the format my thoughts take when I take or watch the Holy Eucharist/ Holy Communion administered.

Today is Saturday, 9th October 2004, and I bought three lottery tickets for tonight's draw. I checked the tickets soon after the draw and noticed I had won £10.00. Unfortunately, the big win has not materialised. It's a tragic disappointment because I scraped to find £3.00, and the return was not high, but after all, it's a small win and gave me more money than I put in to play the game. The luck growth in my life with the divine inference will lead to immense fortune for my family and me.

A week later, Saturday, 16th October, I increased the number of lottery tickets I bought to five lines which cost £5.00. I bought them from various retailers, and three lines had two drawn numbers and the bonus numbers. The other lines had numbers close to the actual lucky draw numbers. One ticket had one random number only, but the last card had three lucky draw numbers, which won me £10.00. I put £5.00 worth of lottery tickets on the mid-week draw. The tickets had to be bought on the day of the appeal. So, the energy of that day is locked in a fight with varied powers on that day. Making the rounds of chances with the daily bustles, mixed with natural luck that God has created running throughout the cosmic universe, might guarantee I win millions. Though it may seem odd, I have no worked-out formula to ensure I gain a million pounds in cash. In my spirit, the random sharing of my desire to benefit from winning has nudged me to tell others of the faith to pray for a successful result. It put pressure on our circumstances to change amid prayers.

I informed my wife that, God willing, I shall telephone a prayer request to Prayer Line so that the whole nation prays with us on the coming Wednesday. I intend to be in prayer all day and night until sleep catches up with me, and on the next day, Thursday, I shall go to St. Michael's Church with the tickets in my pocket and pray in anticipation. Then, with the tickets blessed, I shall return home to check the numbers. I believe that dreams might turn to dust, for there is darkness in our own making, but the reality is much brighter when we share our ideas with others because the night of our fears is released. I offered up prayers to God, but it appears futile until I sow the seeds, the purchase to the maximum I hope to afford in tickets to make prayer work.

The harvest has come, and it's a God moment, for as I check the ticket now, after church on Thursday 21st October 2004, I almost begin to tremble. My body's nerves have tightened, and I was forced to remain calm and relax them through controlled breathing and relaxation techniques. I strongly sense the sudden shifting of the gravity centre when the first ticket showed no lucky draw numbers. I was looking for the big prize, but as I revealed the next token, I thought I would hardly be able to live to fight another day because it was nearly a prize-winning ticket but not quite good enough. Never mind, ha, still three tickets remaining. The following three cards revealed two lucky numbers. It's a blow; it's not sufficient to secure any prize money. The minimum needed was three numbers to get the minimum prize of £10. I am very disappointed; never mind, I must live to fight another day.

I could only muster up £1.00 to play on Saturday 22nd October's draw. So, there is a slim chance that I'll win the big prize on Saturday; I hope to God, let it be us - let it be us who wins since prayer this week has not yet shifted our landscape.

Yesterday, 20/10/04, I didn't manage to telephone Prayer Line because I didn't hear the telephone number they issued in time to call them for support. Every Wednesday, one hour of choral songs and prayers was aired on the radio, and I am a frequent listener. This week was marvellous at lifting my spirits.

There are demands on my purse again to produce cash. Our son would like to go on his school trip to Austria in February 2006, costing £615.00, and the school requires a non-refundable deposit of £100.00 by half term, October 2004, then further deposits of £100 in March 2005 and May 2005. The remaining balance of £315.00 will need to be paid by November 2005. How can I raise £100.00 by the end of October? I want Jonathan to go on the school trip because it will be a fascinating, enjoyable experience for him. All his school friends have already deposited the £100.00 to be sure of a place.

I need to have deep pockets. Come on, lottery, please, please don't fail me now (Saturday). I pray to be able to see some way of meeting the constant demands on my purse. The stimulant today was too much, and my reaction to this school trip has caused me stress. I rehearsed in my mind a prayerful script and hoped what is getting offered will heighten both my understanding and enjoyment of the love of God and His will for my life, but after today's prayer, 'prayer sucks'. Once again, I have not won anything on tonight's lottery draw. I have gone wrong somewhere along the line because of how I perceived now, and the future almost wants me to take up holistic behaviour. Our son, Jonathan, came to me with a kind, thoughtful suggestion and said, "Daddy, I know you cannot afford this trip, although you said you'll try to raise the money. Save it instead for you and mummy's silver anniversary in 2006, and probably Katrina's wedding could be in that year, and you will need the money." I hugged him and smiled and thought, oh, bless!

My reaction to getting nothing on the lottery, when I had prayed so hard, caused me stress, and I am again trying to take control because I am changing my reaction to how I suddenly perceived God. It feels like God is not mindful of what is happening in my life. That is the Christian religion, and when we pray, it should be alright; things should happen. I have many important and urgent things to be sorted in my life, but how to know the difference between them to do the right ones first? By the end of this chapter, the stress would have terminated because I became reasonable with myself, avoided perfectionism, and began to feel completeness again. I will not panic because of the stress symptoms I know, and I am putting my whole life back in balance, and I have the drive to succeed.

Mortgage
Written Monday 1st November 2004

Several mortgage advisors worked to find us a reduced interest rate mortgage with capital and interest incorporated. Unfortunately, not one of the three advisors approached me with a satisfactory product. So, I searched the market for myself and stumbled upon Intelligent Finance, who seemed to give the best deal, so I re-mortgaged the house with them.

Although we had not raised any surplus money through re-mortgage for home improvements or paying off debts, we have a new lender to take over the old mortgage. The mortgage is £64,500, paid over 16 years and 11 months. The rate was fixed at £460.67 included interest and capital for two years and a further year after that discounted. After that, it's a variable rate, or the mortgage is reviewed again. The mortgage repayments were protected by a 100% mortgage protection plan costing £22.94 per month, and the life assurance on our lives has completed the financial planning for now. However, the future looks like a budgeting nightmare. Euphemia Has life insurance with critical illness cover, and the premiums are very high. She has to pay £86.33 per month, and the underwriters postponed a decision on my life assurance for 12 months. Intelligent Finance had asked, in the event of my death, how would the mortgage be paid off? They can reasonably see how the mortgage gets paid off in the event of Euphemia's death, and there would be surplus funds left, but how can they be sure that the debts will get paid if I die?!

I had cancelled and then quickly reset up the £50.87 direct debit for the decreasing mortgage insurance with the critical illness, which, from this year, 2004, would payout on death £48,259.00. The endowment policy would pay out £16,000, and life assurance on my pension plan would pay £5,512.28. The total sum of death benefits is £69,771.28, whereas the mortgage is £64,500. It leaves a surplus of £5,271.28 for the family. I told these details to Intelligent Finance, and they were satisfied with it. When death comes to me and money is needed, it>s to help with funeral expenses or money to leave for the wife and children. I want them to have enough cash, an easily accessible lump sum, or a large enough quantity of savings that my loved ones will undoubtedly appreciate and can live comfortably on for the rest of their lives. I measure financial success as not only having enough to get by. I think financial 'know-how' is the best guarantee of becoming wealthy with luck, education and family backing cited as other factors.

For the most part, there is a myth about my want for money; it's not a get-rich attitude as many might be thinking, but more that I aspire for comfort rather than excessive wealth. I hold the values of hard work high and have a cautious approach to money. For the past two months, I've had to pay a hefty amount in bank charges, and it was only last weekend when my wife and I shared in the utter hopelessness of our financial situation. Euphemia said to me, "Although we cannot see how improvement can come through our own doing, stay positive, believe that God can deliver us. For after every storm, there is always calm." We talk about the deep crisis of not having enough to get by and how our nieces and nephews live their lives without contact; they are on our minds. We have fears and worries that are keeping us from having a good night's sleep. Thank God, soon after talking about the anxieties, a call came from one of our nieces and a text message from our nephew. Our hearts rested in having the assurance that they are alright. We have not heard from two of our nieces for a very long while now, and we can only hope and trust God that they are living safe, happy and enjoyable lives.

The only thing we have to fight the day-to-day battles of existing is good health, but is our good health about to go too? It takes me a long time to get off to sleep, and I wake twice in the night due mainly to money anxieties and a weakened bladder to empty. Euphemia spends hours awake in the middle of the night and feels fearful, and it's only God who is enabling her to have enough energy, she says, to help her last through the long working days. Euphemia is so glad for the weekend to get back some calm that does not come during the week. Yet again, at weekends, Euphemia is restless in bed, and a flood of anxieties crowds her mind at bedtime. She says she knows she believes it will not last. "We are going to be all right; our trust must continue in God, and we must have faith." Euphemia has worries but continued to say, "We can only leave them in God's hand now and try not to worry because we are doing all that we can, and we do not want to go down the road of borrowing again. We have not been ex-communicated from our nieces, and we love them, but when they are ready, they will call. Other relatives and we do not know where they are to be able to make contact."

I think financial success is coming; Euphemia believes it too, but at what point in time? We do not know. For me, it's not a question of if, but a matter of when! I have tried to predict, but the marvellous wonder of living with enough is still elusive. Last month was our twenty-third wedding anniversary, and we were only able to exchange cards of how we felt about each other. And I added I was sorry for not providing material growth.

As I look towards Christmas this year, 2004, it seems it will become the bleakest ever. I cannot anticipate giving out gifts to anyone, not even to our children. The money is not there to adequately feed ourselves, let alone to buy Christmas presents. I hate Christmas because it represents money, but God's creation is fundamental and operates according to laws, He has ordained for it. So I will try very hard to see we have a blessed life and a happy Christmas time.

Belief Examined

Written Thursday 11th November 2004

The situations I am in have forced me to examine ideas and presuppositions on faith. I catch myself as just existing, and as I explore my life, it's a life that's worth living. I love wisdom, and I often see myself as a truth-searcher. I need to examine the general philosophical problems about religion and God, religious utterances and explore the nature and existence of a God who is supposed to interact in the world.

I came into an experience of something beyond the natural order when I survived my suicide attempt. It has been a long time now, and still no deliverance from debts; that is the truth. Is there no God? From severe personal problems to shocking problems in the world, events have become the daily news. God does not seem to respond because He does not exist or He does not care. I am trying to avoid a spiritual crash,

and my natural response as I encounter the hazards of living is to navigate life's journey by reading the manual, the Bible. There is no proof other than the teleological argument that puts God in reality in existence, so I am in a spiritual crush. I formulated God's presence based on life's experiences and miracles, which claimed that God exists. In an instant, I can imagine the coming about of my marriage, our children's births, and the attempted suicide, as all being in some way a mysterious and significant experience in religious miracles. Incidents like those shove me to believe that God exists and shapes my future or takes an interest in it.

Moments continue to be added, but since the beginning of my adult life's history, I have existed barely able to make a living because of mental ill-health, and a year ago, I tried to cease to live. Still, God sustained me, and I see life is for living. I understood the idea of the sanctity of human life, and I even contemplated suicide. The act was not necessarily a matter of total condemnation and voluntary death when one got low—the desire to meet the creator, quiz it, and repent likened suicide to secondary martyrdom. I was in constant contact with God; he knew my heart and motive was just, and I expected that life after death would still be offered through a sense of being a voluntary martyr. If I had thought that eternal life would be jeopardised, I would not have attempted suicide. I felt God understood the state of my mind and my altruistic behaviour. I tried to escape this world's terrible surroundings to a life of inner riches and spiritual freedom. Hope has become the most crucial emotion; though I have struggles, I must not lose hope but keep the courage to believe that the hopelessness of our efforts does not detract from its dignity and meaning. Someone looks down on each of us in difficult hours, -- a God or other being, and they would not expect us to disappoint them. I was given a second chance to live out my days on earth. Is it a brutal fact that the universe has no ultimate explanation, so there is no God? Or is the absolute truth that there is an explanation that the universe could be contained in 'God'?

The universe cannot account for its existence, order, regularity and purpose. They are marks of design, but Darwinism accounts for natural changes and has a theory of natural selection to account for those changes. I accept the basic idea of evolution; I am one of the few who reject the creationist's opinions of the Bible because development does not eliminate God. The old notion of exterior design has been replaced by inner-self regulation. I see God designing evolution to show how He achieves his purpose, guided by God at critical stages. It comes to me as misleading or untrue that order and complex systems can be self-arranging. My human experiences concerning moral consciousness and moral obligation require explanation, but the only satisfactory answer I can give is God's existence. Once I perceive something to be correct, I can no longer view it neutrally. There is pressure on me to respond, and God is required for morality to achieve its end because we are obligated to Be excellent or virtuous human beings. I believe there is a power to ensure that merit is rewarded or coincides with happiness bringing it into harmony.

It is difficult to achieve happiness in some areas of my life, like not having enough to live on and relationships outside marriage with other people who have the wrong motives or are evil. I had every kind of inward communion or conversation with the power recognised as divine and the only one who takes an unmeasurable amount of time to give the result when I asked for things. Praising God, confession and thanksgiving are prayers that get immediate attention, but a petition is a prayer that does not get answered with a direct response but ideas of how it can come about. I live by prayer, believing that God provides and through religious life, I should experience 'coincidences' that make it seem that my life is being guided. Being interested in the origins of life and the origins of human beings comes naturally. Most such explanations centre on a supernatural creator; it is a matter of faith with a bit of science thrown in that make up my belief. I found it difficult, and some thoughts were painful to write, but I feel I must set them down.

I can say with reasonable certainty that God exists; there is life after death. Some of my life experiences and the terrible violence in the world always bring me back to question if there is a God, but it's the truth; there is a God. I am distressed by shocking events in the world, which I do not write about anymore. In the year of our Lord 2004, wars still rage, conflicts between nations and individuals eat away at humanity. Pestilence and other illnesses, environmental issues, and religious scenes of hate form a global pattern that has real significance to what's happening in my personal life. I wonder why God does not intervene to prevent such human suffering. I concede that violence in the world has more to do with human instincts than any absolute religious observance, such as what one can see in the crisis of war in the Middle East and the war on terrorism.

I am full of hope for humanity, for many good works are being done to stop the slide of a doomed world. But, first, the faithful recognise what works in the society in which we live and an ethical framework to protect life, uphold justice, accept human equality, and believe in mercy. God, observes humans and the ultimate manifestation of an evil act or wrongdoing are in their selfish genes. As inseparable from the matter of creation, I perceive certain truths in the images of the earthly things known to us. I would have expected to explain terrestrial phenomena and ourselves in the ways explored by science. But the origin of all things was a mystery – a miracle. The world was created, as the Bible relates, out of nothing. When God intervenes directly in our world, He comes in the only way possible to communicate with mortals - as man, as Christians believe.

I have been sceptical for most of my life of these miraculous occurrences, preferring to interpret them in terms of the same human values in ways the secular world of our day sees them - God, and indeed, the man in the incarnation - Jesus. Jesus, I suppose, was conceived by an ordinary human agency. Still, I believe in resurrection and Ascension, an essential Christian belief, but I am not a Christian because I do not believe Jesus was divine. They tell me I am a semi-skimmed Christian, and that's okay with me. I hold certain specific Christian values fast, but that does not have me recognised as a Christian. It does not bother me because I know in whom I believe; just the one God, maker of heaven and earth, offers everlasting life to those who believe in It/Him/ Her and want to do Their's will. God in heaven gave us the incredible reality that He/Hers, the creator, can raise the dead. Jesus's disciples remember his life and personality, and the Ascension is an excellent manifestation of God's power over creation. Christ rose to a throne in glory in the celestial kingdom, but I have scepticism to adhere to a judgement day for the world. I can conclude about Jesus Christ from living my own life in God, my intelligence and heart, and perhaps being in error, God forbid. Still, Christian truth lies in the faithful's consensus because the people of God collectively can never depart from the authentic message.

Christianity is the religion of the flawed and the corrupt, and that describes the whole human race. My view of things gets more than compensated by a supreme optimism about the great love of God. The sign of its presence is when people love one another, not because they are cute but because they share the universality of sin in our selfish genes. My devoutness - the ability to feel spiritual - may be inherited, and it gives us Homo sapiens an evolutionary advantage to this day. Voltaire wrote, 'If God did not exist, it would be necessary to invent Him.' Like my consciousness, I cannot allow science to explain everything; of course, I do not in any way deny evolution. However, it is clear that knowledge of the inborn pattern of behaviours and view of development alone by no means explains our existence or how I am, or other people are. We in the cosmos are most remarkable. It's beautiful in design. It has physical rationality and is populated with human creatures possessing insight and divine intelligence, making our particular universe unique. I do think that quantum cosmology and new galaxies elsewhere show us that this might not be so. That might go against traditionally accepted opinions, but our God-given intelligence to understand the natural world may lead us to discover we're not alone. If there is no designer, no creator God, how is it that our universe has a law-abiding system marked by beauty and simplicity? I wonder why our world is not in chaos. The only reasonable explanation for me is the God of the Bible. If it's only the reality of God's existence that explains the whole universe, then that must also be true of our lives. We are not here by accident, but creatures designed by a maker of limitless power and wisdom. The Bible opens with this magnificent statement: "In the beginning, God created the heaven and the earth." (Genesis1. v1). How simple those words are, and yet how fathomless!

In conclusion, writing on 'Belief Examined,' we are indeed free agents. Still, a basic morality that is possible is God-given and shaped by those aspects of human nature that are divine. If there truly is free will, the one most potent explanation for God is that He does not interfere - indeed, he cannot interfere. God's interference would effectively negate the freedom humans enjoy to do both great good and great harm to one another. I am alerted to the incredible events ahead in life.

Yes, there is violence globally; there is palpably so much evil that a coming global upheaval in human institutions is imminent. Well, how could it be otherwise if there truly is free will? Having set our universe in motion, God has to leave it to humankind to decide how to handle His existence; humanity is genuinely open to choose. Affirmative action is needed to benefit from the decline in human behaviour and avoid calamity. As believers, we know that having God in the universe runs better than a world without one, but the anxieties of life push us off course. The effect of having long-term goals in life is to make it happier, knowing that our life is taking functional disciplines from the moral agent that constructed us. My belief disciplines me, for I know that I would probably be far less responsible, far less ethical, and far less likely to seek the right path if I did not have a set of rules. These rules may often seem illogical or tedious, but they serve the purpose of discipline that the creator knows is necessary for all humans. Have a goal, ethical principles and a belief that must conform to morality, which is likely to be considered divine but changes as one grows and understands the natural world around them.

It seems morality is critical because, together with having a religion, it gives a framework to control those emotions that have arisen from the primitive beginnings of life, unlearned and inherited as instincts.

Finally, I would say that some intelligence must have created the universe. It's the only explanation for life's origin and complexity because of the most incredible mathematical simplicity and beauty that mark nature's laws.

God Please, God please, God please, please!
Written Wednesday 12th January 2005

The new year stretches before us, blank sheets waiting to be filled, and before I continue to bring you features in our lives, I will take stock of 2004 and use what I have learnt to guide me in this year, 2005. This year is a moment for new plans, new hopes, and an opportunity to put the usually bad luck and dreadful situations behind us, but I have woken up with a sense of anticipation of more gloom.

We are entering a worse year than the depressing year 2003 when I tried to take my own life. The present is pregnant with the future, but I am losing the dream I thought I'll like my life to be. My marriage is stable now, and this year, I hope to walk in a supernatural increase to be blessed in new dimensions. We have been at a 'not enough' level for many years, and I want to move into a miracle level to have enough. It will take a miracle to have enough to get by and have a basket full or a barn full, where we can invest and never worry about finances.

Our joint bank account has reached its overdraft limit of £1150. I borrowed £180.00 on my account overdraft for three months to help us through Christmas. Euphemia bought Christmas presents for our children only, and charity cards got sent to friends and relatives. Euphemia's bank account has also hit the overdraft limit when added expenses like the car needing a new silencer and exhaust pipe occurred over Christmas. I also used £190.00 of Georgina's student account to buy two new vehicle tyres and pay for a school trip deposit. I am not yet able to put the money back. My faith is to believe God can bring relief to our difficult financial situation. Soon, I'll be ready to step out of the boat and walk on water because we cannot manage our income, and it will worsen from 6/2005 when Living Allowance is £64.20 instead of £226.40 per month.

After reviewing our claim for benefits, the council told us that we were not entitled to council tax benefits and we must pay back all the money owed for the years 2003 to 2005. That was because we received tax credit which disqualifies us from having a rebate. For the year 2003-04, we owed £466.37, and for the year 2004-

05, £724.41, and we had to agree to pay £120.00 over ten months with Citizen Advice assisting us in working out our income and challenging the council. We pay £45.00 for 2003-4 and £75.00 for the year 2004-05. The fortnightly shopping falls on Euphemia's wage and £460.67 going towards the mortgage every month, and between £80.00 to £100.00 goes towards petrol per month. That leaves an insufficient amount for the food that we need. We have cut the portions of food we serve on our dinner plates, and we struggle when we run out of the essentials like bread and milk. I dipped into the spare change jar that contains 1, 2, 5 and 10 pence coins to make up the actual amount of money needed. £713.35 is the monthly bill of which only Sky Digital varies that amount by a few pounds. Euphemia's home pay is £740.00, and my benefits and all government benefits to the family amounts to £723.26. It does not take a mathematician to establish that we are at the <not enough> level. Outgoings exceed income, and it will get worse in June 2005 when another benefit is reduced.

'God please, God please, God please, please put more cash in our bank account to finally let us enjoy the kind of comfort and security we want. I cannot believe that God saved my life from suicide to remain in the situation of not having enough to pay bills, buy new clothes, do maintenance on our house or have a vacation. We are having trouble making ends meet and are fed up with the never-ending stream of debts and bills to pay. We want to ensure that our retirement is secure, but we do not have the means to do it. How far down do we have to be in our financial needs before God helps us? It only takes one lucky knock on our door instead of a knock on someone else's to have that lucky break. I want to seize the moment and act, and I am not walking on water yet because if a financial miracle is to happen, it takes faith to believe it will happen before June 2005, when our financial situation needs the kiss of life.

We are dying financially and only keep our heads above water by shuffling the little money we have around. We will be underwater by June 2005, and it is then that God will resurrect us and bring in some more money to our bank account. I am sowing seeds for God to release miracles in the material territory because today is not how I want to live for the rest of my life. Having to tighten our belts, watch every penny we spend, and feel like a weight is on our shoulders makes me think we are destined to be not so lucky. With more money to spend, we'll finally be free of all the problems that are holding us back now. An end to our financial worries and the beginning of our future happiness is insight.

Three tickets bought for the National Lottery won me £10.00 on Wednesday 22nd December 2004, and three tickets won me £10.00 on Saturday 1st January 2005. I believe that I may be on the threshold of an incredible chain of events bringing vast prosperity, possibly the kind of riches that may change my life in a way that seems almost impossible. I somehow subconsciously know to focus on the future to sense what lies ahead. I understand that the period between now and June 2005 may be deeply transformational, showing me significant potential prosperity. God is already in my tomorrow, and the fortune stemming from one or more financial event occurrences will rapidly materialise and result in a sudden and substantial breakthrough. If that does not happen, we are doomed.

I anticipate that I will get material luxury and personal bliss that will improve my lifestyle phenomenally. It will be bringing beautiful, worldly possessions and comfort that I have always desired. I applied to the Council Housing Department for a Housing Grant and Disabled Facilities Grant. The house is falling into disrepair, and the shower cubicle is too small. I asked for help to replace guttering, redecorate, install double glazing to replace a decayed window and improve the shower cubicle to make it easy for disabled use. The council could not offer me a housing grant because our property has not deteriorated enough, but assistance concerning bathing difficulties was referred to social care and health services. An occupational therapist accessed the shower room, and our request for a more oversized shower or to make the place a wet room was turned down. We are penniless and on a financial precipice because we struggle to pay the bills and eat properly. We live close to the edge, with nothing in reserve and plenty of bills to pay, and when an unexpected expense crops up, the dire nature of our financial situation is revealed even more. I am counting on attracting wealth through luck, and financial planning for debt is a time bomb. It is difficult to find the money for vital necessities, and we economise stringently to pay the bills.

On 08/01/2005, gale-force winds and heavy rain lashed and wholly removed a fencing panel at our house. God, please, please, please, please, we are so broke that paying the mortgage this month, the bills and food for our bellies is a task it seems we cannot meet, and now we have the fence to repair. I pray for our survival. I must have said this more than once, more than twice, but we often have no money. We will soon be feet under in a financial grave dug by our money problems, but I continue to pray for our survival and feel that something astounding is about to happen in my life to lift us out of this morbid gloom of financial disaster. Unfortunately, we cannot improve our income or get government benefits to increase our revenue. The benefits agency told me our income is £98.00 more than the qualifying amount for Income Support. I can only hope and pray that our luck will change so entirely out of the blue that I know God must be the guide.

I depend heavily on winning the lottery, but I can only buy one ticket a week now. The postal prize draws we have been chasing turned out to be a rotten scam; regrettably, I got hoodwinked by the advertisement's powerful, believable wording. I had even thought that God must be guiding this fortune to me, but after one year of not receiving more than a fiver and the letters were still dropping through the letterbox, the hope of winning a future in that way has completely faded. In addition, I was getting massive amounts of junk mail arriving through my mailbox, and I had to write to the Royal Mail to opt-out of receiving junk mail.

One part of my life feels out of control. I have no peace and happiness in this one area of my life because I struggle with finances. I am financially rutted and feel like I will be there forever; this is the only bleak area. I still hope to escape from this terrible financial circumstance of bills piling up and not making ends meet one day. My wife wants to do an extra job and her daily job, or do weekend working. I know she needs rest and does not want her to use the resting period for employment, but she said we need the income. I owe this woman, my dear darling, so much financially, and she deserves prosperity, and I aim to bring it to her one day. I have reached a dead-end in my career, and every day and night, prayer is causing me to slightly drifting into depression because, as yet, I can't see what God is doing, and there is nothing more I can do to bring more income into the home without His miracle.

Over two weeks into 2005, Saturday 15/01/05, I woke with the common cold and felt a little more depressed by my deteriorating circumstances. As I do not have thoughts of quitting but continue to believe that my faith in God can bring new birth to the financial situation, I am optimistic. Virtually everything I touch will be turned to gold because all of my dreams will start to come true; it's fantastic! The indisputable fact indicates that it's going to be a challenging year. Nowhere is that more the case than in our finances. There is no New Year cheer taken from the forecast, nor, it appears, is this a short-term blip in a month. The story has been the same for many years. The only exception was the few months after the road (accident) collision when it looked like we could manage with the generous help of the benefits system until it was taken away. I do wish us and all in peril a happy, healthy and prosperous New Year.

The Asian Tsunami
Written Wednesday 12th January 2005

On Boxing Day, the 26th December 2004, 17,000 people died after a massive underwater earthquake off Indonesia's coast triggered a tidal wave and devastated the entire coastline across southern Asia. Eighteen days on, and it's still difficult to comprehend the full scale of the tragedy that has taken place in southeast Asia, Somalia, India, the Maldives, Thailand, Sri Lanka, Indonesia and Malaysia.

I have been in mourning since and donated £15.00 to the Asian Tsunami Disaster and Emergency Committee. I am shocked by the vast scale of the catastrophe, which was almost of biblical proportions. It's a terrible human and economic loss to which western countries have pledged millions in aid. I have lived through four natural disasters of such magnitude in this modern history between 1970 and 2004. First, in Bangladesh in 1970, coupled with violent winds and heavy rain, flooding killed thousands and thousands. Second, in North Vietnam in 1971, heavy rain showers caused severe flooding, killing thousands of people. Third, in China in 1975, thousands of people died when the Yangtze River flooded. Finally, in 2004, monster waves, caused by an earthquake that measured nine on the Richter scale, killed many people in Asia.

Nature can be so destructive that the horror could swamp paradise islands in just seconds, killing thousands in its wake. Words alone are inadequate to describe what took place, and yet, amidst the grief and suffering, there is one element of hope in how the people of this country and countries worldwide have been desperate to do anything they can to help. The overwhelming majority of those killed, orphaned and made homeless are Muslim, and the Muslim Arab states did not seem to pull together like the Christian world in solidarity. When a calamity happens, my first inclination is how I can help and most often, I can only pray, for I cannot physically go to the scene of the disaster. My poverty does not usually allow me to give money, but this tsunami has called me to look beyond my own needs. Catastrophe seems to bring out the best in people and nations, and this tsunami has proven that humankind is ultimately good. The world has not turned its back on these millions affected by the terrible events on Boxing Day, 2004. Aid organisations, governments and individuals, including myself, have reacted with unprecedented generosity to assist the suffering. All of this gives me some cause to rejoice; it is too strong a word, given what has happened, but at the very least, it keeps me from despairing and looking at my struggle to put food on the table as a drop in the ocean compared to tsunami sufferers. They have lost everything.

A catastrophe of this magnitude reminds us that we are all still part of the human race, no matter the difficulties within countries. I felt pain when it happened, and it happened to other people, not me personally, but when I see pictures of orphaned children and the death of the innocent, it does not matter what colour the children are or from where they come. I feel grief because I care about the young and the vulnerable, wherever they might be.

Sometimes humanity is put to the test, and that test might have been personal faith in human nature. Despite dread and horror of what happened, society has passed, for the world has rallied together with countries vying with one another to see what we can do. Savage nature is a terrible reminder that despite those who died at the hands of other human beings, whether through war or terrorist horror on the scale of 9/11, there is always the danger that nature can and will strike many, many more of us down as casually as killing pest and inconsiderately as swatting flies. The thought comes that God is busy looking after the tsunami victims, and my problems get moved to the back burner. It seems that the deadly tidal waves were in keeping with an Old Testament God, who smites down his people with his terrible swords for their ignorant transgressions. There are many reasons for God to be angry these days because of wars, terrorism and suicide bombers, but I cannot square it in the random selection of places where loads of people died on Sunday, the day after Christmas, 2004. What kind of random act of God is that? I also cannot reconcile this incomprehensible tragedy with the Christian idea of a cuddly, New Testament God, as represented by Jesus Christ, a kind, righteous sort of person who Christians think gave up his life for the rest of us. Surely Jesus would not let this happen. The deity who created humanity and the universe, which is so enormously complex in design, is a vast, intelligent force called God. So, maybe there is a reason for this almost biblical tragedy in modern times. Maybe there are lessons to be learnt, and perhaps the first experience is that we should not slaughter each other, often in His name, with the casual carelessness of an earthquake.

In recent years, primarily since the atrocities of 9/11when, the dark spectrum of international terrorism held us in its influence. It has been all too easy to see the evil in humankind and not the good. It has been business as usual in our world of atrocities, and there has been violent death and destruction as this month's elections in Iraq loom. The savagery of the violence still happening in Iraq and the terrible suffering in Darfur, the horror of Madrid and Bali shocked the world, leading me to wonder if we shall ever see sunlight again.

A test awaits humanity as the world returns to normal, and the images of the Asian tsunami's hell on earth begin to fade; it would be all too easy to forget what has happened. The omens are helpful in the very act that aid agencies exist and people who work for them are a testament to decency; the human race might have its moments of wickedness but, underneath it all, there is good. So, I have no grounds to despair. The New Year has been ushered in sombrely globally. The little joy I have in my personal life, the tragedy has in packed it. The sad news made me ask if we should have celebrated the New Year. Nevertheless, there were still reasons to celebrate it.

The Children
Written Wednesday, March 2nd 2005

Katrina passed her driving theory test on Saturday, December 4th 2004 the practical driving test on Friday, March 8th, 2005. Unfortunately, the original driving school car that Katrina had lessons in was involved in an accident and was in the garage for repairs on the day before her driving test was due. Very well done on passing, Katrina. You have done exceptionally well to drive in an unfamiliar car that you had less than twenty-four hours to learn to manoeuvre and familiarize yourself with it.

On the Monday of December 6th 2004, Georgina passed the practical driving test on her second attempt. Georgina is in the university netball team, and she got picked to play in matches in Spain on March 19th 2005, for five days. Unfortunately, an accident on 02/03/05 happened during a netball game when a player trod on Georgina's Achilles tendon, which ruptured. She was admitted to Chase Farm Hospital in Infield, and she was put into a plaster cast from her left foot to the top of her thigh. Georgina expected to be in the plaster cast for two weeks, but the first change of the cast and adjustments to her foot is in 4 weeks. It could not have come at a worse time for Georgina. She planned to fly out to Spain in three weeks.

Jonathan had his left ear lobe pierced on Monday, December 20th 2004, and he told us in early November 2004 that he officially has a girlfriend called Jessica. As the children grew up, I promised them I would talk about relationships, sex and adulthood when they started to date in their teens. I had since reminded Jonathan that a fatherly discussion on manhood is to take place more urgently now that he has a girlfriend, before his 16th birthday in February 2005, when he reaches the age of consent.

Easter Saturday, March 26th 2005, the DLVA reinstated my license, and I am a named driver on the car insurance from today. It has been two years since I was behind the wheel. I now drive locally and make trips to Enfield. I act as a relief driver because the wife needs to make frequent trips to Enfield and chauffeur Georgina back and forth to the hospital. In stop-start traffic, my deformed foot aches with

559

having to use the clutch pedal frequently. What most concerns me is that reactions seem to be slower than they used to be. I am conscious that it takes me longer to make highway decisions; I feel tense when implementing them. However, the car's manual driving is done excellently without thinking; it's almost automatic - I have not forgotten how to drive. Therefore, I do not usually go solo, and the wife acts like a second pair of eyes and our daughter, a newly qualified driver, also looks out for my lapses of concentration. They tell me immediately to quicken my reactions when I am about to lose awareness.

Georgina returned from Spain on 23/03/05, and she had watched her team play. Unfortunately, her mobile phone was stolen from the hotel apartment where they stayed. Although the weather was disappointing, she had a fab time though it had rained heavily, almost like a storm.

SOS of Distress

Written Friday, April 1st 2005

I am a cash-strapped husband, and I rely on luck to supplement my cash flow, but gambling in that way for a mighty win could lead me into far worse money worries. I gamble irrationally in the belief that the lottery provides money for nothing - a mere pound a game, I tell myself. Tragically, so far, some weeks I have no money to bet with, but when I do, I buy a ticket and cross my fingers and steel my heart and worry that I may be a loser. Yet, astoundingly as it might seem, I expect to win, and that miracle to come will be the turning of a new leaf. I should be looking at gambling on the lottery as entertainment with prizes rather than making cash. I know this, but it was misrepresented as a way of making money, and as a long-term sick man on benefits, I treat gambling as a way of providing a living, but so far, it has not. The ironic thing is that after ten years of winning nothing more than the odd £10.00, I continue trying for the jackpot even though it is a challenge to find the money to pay for it. Wish me luck! Maybe the higher the suffering, the greater will be the anointed.

My weight is 16 stones, 4 pounds, and I have been advised to lose two stones. I had a GP referral to a gym to take up activity fitness exercises, typically costing £25 per month. It was reduced to £1.75 per session. Euphemia has become unhappy working at the nursery because of the changes they are implementing, and she is finding the stress unbearable. The writing up of the children's portfolios she finds very difficult. She has been working there for four years, and the details needed in the portfolio have become the most demanding. My voice is calling out an SOS of distress. HELP us.... I need money - I want to feel free from debts. Please help me turn my life around. God please, God please, God please, please! My astral heavenly voice talked over distance and time, through matter and the cosmic space. I imagined an incredible amount of money should be in store for me because the period of providential blessing was about to begin. When I close my eyes and pray, something always happens—a vision that glimpses into the future and a picture of pending events and revelationary images.

From Monday night, 28/03/05, my wife and I took turns reading chapters from the Bible in bed. I am being compelled to reach out and step out of the boat and walk on water. Thoughts are racing through my head. Incredible!!! I need to get everything down, for, in a sense, miracles are directly in my path. The enormous energy of the universe and all dimensions here, beyond, and the mysterious order of life are to ignite my life into a realm of indescribable reward and prosperity. The gloom of our situation of not meeting the demands on our money has made us unable to live well but solely trying to survive day by day. It's making me see visions. I see images. Pictures and frames of future events pour across my consciousness, vivid energies from other dimensions that tell me things will come right.

I have not buried my head in the sand because I know something needs to divert the shortages. How do I stop the scarcity of food and money for paying the bills? How? We are still going through hard times, but personal harmony and happiness come from all-around fulfilment concerning material comforts and personal enrichment. Be it luck or random fortune, the mere chance that is imminently forthcoming will suddenly break and bring significant prosperity and wealth. So, I continue to pray to God. I think what may happen very soon in a volley of extraordinary, magnificent events will be part of God's doing because this transformation looming directly ahead concerning prosperity and personal fortunes is a miracle of God. The impressions are flooding my senses. It speaks to a mirror of my most heartfelt desires. I cry out to Heaven, complaining about all the unhappiness I have to bear because we are short of money, but I never lost my dignity and endured day after day.

Even now, despite the enormous effort it requires, I am trying to deal with the difficult circumstances of our present life. I feel hemmed in on all sides and a kind of prisoner of destiny, not even my own. The more I fight to free ourselves, the tighter the hands close in, day after day. I have implored Heaven to help me simply because our situation has become so complicated. I called out for help, unconsciously called on the astral plane, and said prayers in my heart for some miracle.

I sometimes feel that I cannot take it anymore. I have enough problems and headaches, enough money worries, and never can do what I want. Enough petty arguments and stress are building up day after day. Every day that passes sees the same. I desperately need a change. I want a better life for us, one where I can stop worrying all the time and put an end to our financial problems once and for all. I am compelled to stay positive with every ounce of strength and believe that the possible breakthrough may quickly be fulfilled with indescribable, unbelievable riches and jubilation. I am anxiously expecting a radiant future.

I keep sensing the wind of change has already begun to clear away all the dark clouds in my life. Still, the reality is that it has not significantly materialised so that the visions I had can be lived out in a perfect reflection of my deepest desires. I am sensing a period of profound joy, peace, understanding, and blessed material comfort and financial security, helping straighten out our immediate problems. The signals that indicate the period of fantastic luck were due to start months ago. I expected to see a significant improvement in our material possessions, for I have been waiting for success for a very long time. I can only see the light at the end of the tunnel and a brighter patch of blue sky ahead in my vision of unique possibilities. Then, some dark cloud appears and obscures my future once again.

I want to take steps to turn our life around permanently, but I do not know what to do without seeking to find credit to get by. I believe a psychic message I received about winning the lottery is to come true. I have visions of a cheque worth millions of pounds meant for me as far as I can see. I have convinced myself that I am soon going to be rich. So far, my life has not changed one bit. I still struggle with all kinds of problems, but I think I have made the right choice by listening to my intuition. My intuition will be a faithful guide because the incredible vision I had an image of, which is sure to mark the beginning of my great good fortune, is a vision of wealth coming true. I understood that Heaven had given me a mission, and it's to make sure that this vision of happiness and wealth reinforces the positive vibrations that will guide me over the next few months.

April starts today, and it's so promising for me because I'll do everything possible to weigh the balance of luck in my favour to enjoy total success in everything I do and attain lasting happiness. This month is critical; I do not know how to get through it without the energy to strengthen the potential for great good fortune and success already inscribed in my future. The money will change my life entirely, and I have dreamed about this for a long time. I sometimes see our lives like a movie running through my mind, thinking about what I could do if only I had some real money of our own. But, for once, luck will be knocking on our door instead of somewhere else. So, I make sure to seize the moment and act, which means always having a pound to pay the lottery.

The days have moved on, and it's **Tuesday, April 26th 2005**. Only last week, Wednesday, April 20th, was our closest SOS call, yet we were barely able to save ourselves. Indeed, the financial situation is seeing more of those near misses until one day; God forbid, we have nothing to eat, nothing to pay bills with and no new clothes on our backs.

On 20/04/05, there was barely enough petrol in the car to get Euphemia to work and back home. The petrol gauge was almost on the red, and we could only pray that there'd be sufficient to carry her on her 16-mile return journey. Euphemia felt panicky, worried that she might get stranded by the roadside. Nevertheless, she braved the challenge and got to work and back home with the gauge now on the red. Benefit money will be in my bank account next week, 26/04/05, but no money existed anywhere, and by the end of the week, we will need everyday food items.

How did we get through the rest of the week until the Tuesday morning of April 26th? That is today. Cheques were used to make payments, knowing it takes 3-5 working days for the banks to take the money from my account. Thursday last week was the earliest I used a cheque to buy £29.99 worth of petrol, knowing that during the clearance days before the cheque cleared and the money was debited out of my account, benefit money should have been paid into the same account. At the weekend, I used cheques like instant cash payments to buy food, knowing full well that the funds were not in the account until today, 26/04/05. The pathway for that money expected today had already been worked out for bill payments. I played down the importance of having enough to pay them as if I was contented to leave them unpaid, but we have to eat; we had to buy food and pay for fuel. Contentment lies somewhere in the future; I am not content because I remain in the struggle to have enough to get by.

On April 26th, I learned that the benefit money (Tax Credit) had been adjusted to a new pay-out date, and payment will increase equivalent to inflation. So, instead of £134.26 arriving in my account today, £183.53 will reach the bills on Tuesday, May 3rd 2005, a week later. The cheque for £29.99 was debited today, making bank charges inevitable, and such charges use up the vital money we may have to live our lives. The fees for the bounced cheques are likely to be huge, and it gives the already greedy bank even bigger profits generated off its weakest, most unfortunate customers.

I am sick financially, and I need cheering up, which comes when I worship God. My spirit is lifted when I worship God. I have returned to worshipping God in my usual Church because it gives me a feel-good factor and refreshes my mood. I had stayed away from Church for months because of collecting money from the pews, and I had no money for the Church. I need the help the Church gives me spiritually, the down to earth preaching on life. That is a supernatural breakthrough because the time for turning has come. I saw that I had been placed there to praise, worship, and give the Church money if I had the money to provide. I had only withdrawn from

Church because I could not pay for spiritual service; any worldly events/services charge a fee and having no money kept me out of the pew. I feel I need what the Church offers and need to be in a place of worship and scrape up some cash. I used the last money in the house, including emptying the penny jar, and the total I found was 15 pence. I concealed it in a gift envelope and placed it on the offertory plate last April 24th. I am still saddened that I am unable to give a sensible amount of money to the Church. I collected loose coins that stood in a jar or lost miscellaneous coins in the house and raided the kids' piggy banks to have money to go to Church.

Knowing there is nothing monetary left to give the Church, this Sunday, I am preparing myself to put a note in the gift envelope that says, 'Sorry, no money, we are poor, pray for us." The bank account is empty, and there is no money in the house at all. But there will be a day of justice, for there is a turnaround, a supernatural turnaround. I came across a small handbook on Bible promises belonging to Euphemia, and she allowed me to share them. It gave vital scripture readings of the biblical commitment to provide help, hope and inspiration for the people of God. The combination of going back to Church and reading biblical promises in Ps112v1-4, Isa 43v1-2, Deut. 30v9-10 and Ps145v14 all seem like God has brought forth a miracle. Those verses are obtaining help, hope, and inspiration, especially Psalms 112v1-4. The Bible promises God will break forth an advantage, and I thank my lucky stars because luck will shine down on us.

I have gone back to worship God on a Sunday morning because, in the period of waiting for the promises, I need to praise God and dwell on His words, to provoke the blessing of God. So, my Sundays are spiritually filled, and I am relaxed by the religious atmosphere in the house that I allow Sundays to represent. It is peaceful. I saturate the evening with religious programming on the television or radio. We all have our own space on Sundays because I enjoy my programmes, but the family can also enjoy TV drama and soaps in the different house areas.

Today is Tuesday, May 24th 2005. Four weeks have passed, and there have been no changes in our SOS of distress. If anything, things have worsened. It's a crisis that devastates our lives built on hope, promises, faith and endurance. Five months ago, I had seen the inevitable if our circumstances were not altered within six months. Unfortunately, it's coming up to that six-month time limit, and I notice conditions that haven't changed. I have prayed, hoped and relied on biblical promises and luck, but the time, the portion of the past, present and future, exists only for a tiny bit longer before we run out of it altogether, and I have lost patience.

The feeling of expecting change when the change, in an awkward moment, cannot find us but stays somewhere else again gives me that hollow feeling instead of happiness. Lucky chance has not been able to find us because playing the games of chance, and the lottery has brought no substantial win. I am reasoning that I should discover employment again as circumstances rush me back to find work sooner than I would have liked to do. I tried to get Euphemia to look for new jobs, but that also looks fruitless. Does anything work to alter the course that is leading us to a kind of extinction? I have tried to help myself and looked for positive ways to beat this life threat against comfortable living, but neither God, science, nor nature has altered things yet. We will run out of essential food again by the end of the week ending 28/05/05. We have only water from the tap to drink. Bread, milk, eggs and meat are just the starters of a long shopping list of "Give us this day our daily bread" that we have no money to buy. Petrol for the car is going to be a problem too. Transport needs are essential because of commuting.

The following money for shopping is due on 03/06/05, and I do not know how we will get through the days until then. We are not meant to starve in a society with a welfare state, but the welfare money is also required to pay the bills. The quarterly energy bill was £617.65, which we had defaulted on the instalments of £90.00 per month. Anxiety is setting in on me because we still cannot make a payment. The council wants an immediate fee of £331.37 because we did not keep up with the payment arrangements, and recovery action will be taken unless the total amount is paid. The council will not enter into another agreement with me. I plead with them, but they have no compassion. Recovery action will be taken if I don't pay up.

Our son would like to go to the school-leaving ball with his girlfriend, and it requires dressing in an evening suit that can be hired for £50.00. I am in a dreamy state; all those things can get paid for within the next month. I must be dreaming. Otherwise, I must be jumping to conclusions. Could it be that faith, hope and the prospect of lucky chance are kicking in again in my desires, and as a human, I cannot live without those three things, or else I get into depression? All these financial pressures are making me feel thirsty to want to keep going to Church. Sunday and Thursday cannot come quickly enough to break the burden of daily life and allow me to chill out and relax in the pew, despite having no money for the plate. I put in the envelope a note, photocopied for continuous use, explaining that I am broke.

I continue to think that all the future changes I have been waiting for will come after a long time. Answers to prayers come to those who persist, and the full benefit is achieved when God wants to solve it. I pray that God will change the situation; I want to stop praying, but I must not give it up if I believe that the power of prayer can bring about such changes in our lives. I am not mindful of any changes yet, but I am sure that God will be doing something little by little, and it will begin to happen because the Bible says it guarantees to everyone who continues to ask, seek and knock. I think prayer is delayed to know God's way and grow in the spirit, and I will receive through a curious combination of circumstances. I am a spiritual person, the supernatural seems natural, and I honour God with all I am and have, and God will bless me with financial blessings, I steadfastly believe.

I am cheerful and optimistic again because a noticeable improvement in our lives should follow within months. I answered an advertisement for a Support Assistant for the Kettering Mind community; - The pay rate is £16,640.00 per annum. I have an interview for the job on 08/06/2005 and hope I'll be successful. Everything from then on will indicate whether I'll be able to keep my head above water. But unfortunately, some lousy past decisions have my confidence betrayed, leading to situations today that seems more difficult to tolerate. My thoughts have become currently negative in the majority because, to be frank, I am tired of waiting for a better life to come along. Most of all, I think I am in an extreme case of anxiety when it comes to money. Indeed, after the down, we are about to enter a favourable period, a decisive turning point for our future. I think my problem in life is not based entirely on a lack of luck, but rather a problem in choices and decision-making and proof of it is the current difficult situation I am in now. I am a hostage to my condition without any hope of getting out of it. So, I thought because, with every day that passes, it's another deception and frustration, I have to tolerate another day without any real hope of change. I have hope for change now because I have an interview for a job in 11 days.

Fortunately, every day from today, May 28th, will be the opportunity to rejoice since luck and God's grace finally smile on us. The uncomfortable situation I am in is the consequence of bad choices, mainly to do with finances. I must certainly not fall back into making the same mistakes. Destiny has granted us a lucky period; I must not waste it.

Before we could see the light at the end of the tunnel, we had a hellish difficult time as we noticed that God's deprivation and unmerited favour is not sufficient to keep. So I had asked Georgina, our student daughter, to pay housekeeping this once to get us through this challenging period where no money exists anywhere. She has a free overdraft on her student bank account, and the student loan pays for the Hall of Residence. Georgina has the overdraft to live off until the new loan for 2005-06 enters her account in September 2005. I asked her for £50.00, of which £17.50 went on petrol for the car and the rest went on shopping, which included using £7.50 from Tesco Club Card vouchers. I do not want it to be a trend to take housekeeping money from our daughter because she is not yet working; it's not earned cash, and it's not really to dip in it. It's not surplus money. However, Georgina uses her overdraft, and she still needs to get through the summer on it, spending sparingly to buy what she needs.

I've been writing that 'destiny' has granted us a lucky period because I successfully got a job interview. Still, morning tears moisten Euphemia's eyes and then flowed down her cheeks. Euphemia said that she feels depressed and lacks energy because our situation appears worse. Euphemia remained in her nightie and dressing gown all day, unable to do her usual tasks in the home or to accompany me to the supermarket. I went alone, and with each item placed in the shopping trolley, mental arithmetic was used to ensure I did not exceed the measly budget. It was all I had, but I retained £1.00 to buy a lottery ticket, estimated to be an £8million rollover. I tried to comfort my wife, but she had worried looks, and her face was without expression; bleakness has made her think of her mortality. She wanted to die, and she asked me to predict if she is going to Heaven or Hell. I do not believe a God of love would make a place as cruel as Hell for eternal punishment. Instead, I think the wicked will get zapped out of existence, and everyone else will go to their heavenly home. I told her, 'Things are beginning to improve.' I also told her, "Look, the council has accepted my proposal, and I have an appointment for a job interview. The Tax Credit overpayments for 2003-04 arose from an error on their part, and we will not be asked to pay anymore, and the money already paid will be refunded back to us. Keep the faith, my darling, keep believing for every day from today will be an opportunity to rejoice; we cannot look back now but look forward."

Today is Monday, June 13th 2005, and we are experiencing continued ups and downs in our lives. The Bible contains cosmic certainty. When are we going to stop living hand to mouth? Why so much uncertainty in our lives?! On Saturday 04/06/05, I won £10.00 on the lottery draw. I played two lines. Jonathan started part-time employment with All Sports retail store on 11/06/05, and I was interviewed on Wednesday, 08/06/05. I was unable to predict how it went. I was told I would find out in two days. It is the third day, June 11th, and it's the weekend. I have heard nothing by telephone or by letter. I assume that I was unsuccessful at the interview, and the job has gone to someone else.

We get good days and bad days, and it's always a challenge to know how to take a bad day and turn it around. But, unfortunately, the omens, the events that I regard as a prophetic sign, are no nearer destroying the menacing unfavourable issues in our lives. On the contrary, it seems as if trouble is imminent; as soon as one rises to have a good day, ominous is likely to be part of it.

On the same day as the interview, two domestic appliances broke down - the washing machine, which was temporarily fixed and the electric oven, which failed to work. So, we are making do with the grill to do the cooking and the microwave oven to prepare meals.

Today, 13/06/05, I have learnt that Georgina needs £588.13 to deposit advance rent from July 1st 2005, for a shared house, three student friends and herself. All students have to vacate the Halls of Residence ready for the new freshers. Georgina is to live at home for the duration of the summer. None of the students expected to live in the rented house before September, but they have to start paying rent from 01/07/05. The monthly rent for each student is £250.00.

Father's Day
Written Sunday, June 19th 2005

We are on the brink of ruin; only prompt action can prevent us from sliding further into the mire. I have run out of ideas, and it seems it's only by the grace of God that we will escape or get through these challenging months, still cheerful and smiling.

Alarm bells had been ringing for months, and we struggled to pay the mortgage, loans, buy food and pay monthly bills. Being disciplined with our finances was not a problem, but a financial meltdown is here. We have learnt to use money effectively, and there was no surplus to use as disposable income. I had jumped to the conclusion that I would be in employment, and the chance had come to turn our lives around. Instead, one hope after another was dashed. I cannot continue to hope, and there is not a positive outcome. My confidence keeps getting dashed. I did not get the job; I have not won the big money prize in the lottery, so it continues. I cannot deny that not getting the job has put me in a spin, and with the increased pressure since I'll be losing some government benefits, I feel hopeless. I have used the increase in Tax Credit and Living Allowance to pay all monthly bills to date, no arrears, but those bills' future payments cannot be met. I have only a few weeks left until things begin again to bite into us more severely.

There will be an unexpected shortfall of money in July 2005, and a significant part of our outgoings can never be guaranteed. I have lost confidence in hope because I am despondent, and trying to do things and make things happen to change our lives appears inadequate. Yet, when I think, I really cannot give up being hopeful because I'll be there when this hopefulness falls on barren ground. So, once again, I asked, 'God, please, God. Please, God, please, please help us to retain optimism and bring into our lives a financial blessing and lead us out of the mire of hopelessness.'

It is Father's Day today, 19/06/05, and the children have lifted my spirits. They have bought lovely cards, and Georgina made an exception and made her designer card. All the children used to design their cards for my birthday and Father's Day, but only Georgina has kept this trend going. So, I thanked them all and hugged and kissed them, and sent my fatherly love in a letter to Katrina.

I spent the afternoon at the local country park called Ichester Country Park. We had a picnic in the park. Katrina and Robert's absence did not stop me from creating a pleasant family atmosphere around the picnic table. I brought Katrina's cuddly big teddy bear to represent her, and the Bob the Builder soft toy stood in for Robert. I felt they were amongst us in spirit, but the reality was they were in Palma, Spain, on holiday until 23/06/05. My wife and I lay on the grass and watched the park's activities, admiring families with small children playing as our two big children went off to explore the beautiful scenery of the park. Euphemia and I reminisced as we lay in the shade of the 30-degree heat and groomed each other like primates do while they relax.

Four days after Father's Day, I picked up my pen again to let you know I won a prize in yesterday's lottery, Wednesday 22/06/05. I played two lines, won £10.00 and gave praise and thanks to God for this lucky period in my life. Thank God for this financial help and, Oh God, how we needed it, for straight away, the money was used to buy fuel for the car, which will last the rest of the week. Before the win, I thought that we were living in a state of deferred successes, hoping for better things. Otherwise, I would have given up entirely on hope. I believe keeping faith in 'deferred success' means accepting failure without feeling rejected. None of us can be a failure but just waiting for success to come along. I had talked of giving up hope earlier because my judgment saw a loser rather than a winner. Am I better motivated because I hunger for success or fear of failure? If there is no such thing as failure, say the traditionalists, there is no such thing as success. One does not mean anything without the other. Society's demand that some must fail; if everybody passes, what does that mean? I sense finality about it. Failure is too final, and it's not a practical or healthy concept to feed my conscience.

I talked of deferred success which embodies a great truth. Success lies in finding one's happiness, finding oneself, finding one's moment and finding one's place in the world, but who can say when that happens? It boils down to the fact that we all live in the hope of better times and better fortune. I cannot reasonably accept the idea that I am a failure. I am keeping faith in the notion of deferred successes. I am not ground down by my history of financial loss but animated by the hunger for 'deferred successes'. There will come a day when success is no longer deferred for my thoughts, and efforts are to make my ambitions come to pass. It feels essential for mental and spiritual health that I live in a state of hope. I think I have something that I want to do for myself and others and live in the country of 'deferred success' until I have achieved it. I am animated by the hope of success, not the fear of failure, and if by chance the deferred success seems too deferred to reach in this lifetime, I can always hope I shall find it in the world to come.

At the end of the month, I cannot believe that God has given us enough! I had prayed, "Give us this day our daily bread." (Matthew 6:11), but how much I expected God to supply fell short. There is a difference between genuine hunger and having a greedy appetite in every area of our lives. It's not that we want just a little more but that we want as much as we need. I want to believe - "God, you gave me just the right amount," but I struggle to feel that way about the sources entrusted to me.

Wealth is what I want, the kind of riches I thought faith would bring, but there is good and bad news about wealth. The good news is that God's Word does promise prosperity to the believer. The bad news is that it does not have anything to do with money. Yes, God's Word promises us great riches - treasures that we cannot even attempt to purchase with any amount of money. They are having all our needs met by God, the forgiveness of sin, mighty strength in our inner being through His spirit, Christ's hope of glory living in us and an understanding of God in whom have hidden all the treasures of wisdom and knowledge. We must seek, enjoy, and use these riches to glorify their source - our God almighty. The Bible is our instruction manual from God for navigating life's journey, but I do not merely own a copy. I studied parts of it and applied its teaching. I still have to pray and worry about how we are to meet each day-by-day requirement. We exist until this month's wife's wage cheque is cleared on Tuesday, July 5th 2005, or use the cheque book a few days earlier and have it coincide with the cheque clearance day.

I have been trying to pray instead of worrying, but they go hand in hand because prayer by faith is more profound than my physical senses. I sense the bottom is falling out of my world, so I worry as much as I pray. I want to believe that God can completely turn our circumstances around, but I am only sprinkled with the love of God and hold onto my working out of how to get through this challenging period on a budget that cannot sustain us. I am so torn again that I do not know what to do anymore. So I am leaving it up to God to give the wisdom to know how to destroy the environment and instead change to the situation I am so desperate for, allowing me to enjoy everyday life.

I cannot afford enough food, and I cannot provide enough fuel for the car; nor can I adequately have the basic needs of man, which are food, clothes and shelter. It's not easy to have enough money to pay the mortgage. I have not bought new clothes or shoes for the family in ages, and the table's food is rationed. It's because money is diverted to pay organizations for living in modern society, and as we own a house on a mortgage, it gets seen as a privilege. So such ordinary folk like us have to pay a high price to own property and care for ourselves adequately.

Today is Thursday, 23/06/05, and I went to St Michael and All Angels Church this morning. Tonight, I am bursting with enthusiasm to go to prayer and worship for the first time at the Kettering Christian Pentecostal, where my wife attends worship. I had thought that I would never go back to worship in a Pentecostal Church because it was there that my first mental illness manifested itself as being possessed. And the evangelical and the Pentecostal were not understanding what mental illness is and that I was not evil or possessed by devils.

In 2005, they did not adopt liberal thinking, and they are a backwards-looking community of people who need education. The real spirit of God's truth and the universe in this scientific age shows our minds, created by the creator, had positive and negative aspects that may work as opposed. It's nothing to do with demons or devils acting on it. The mind is the creator's handiwork, which we figured can malfunction and create bizarre experiences that put us in a different reality. Science is good for religion because it cleans up religion's hardcore and proves a creator; it tries to explain what God has done and how all this creation is for humankind's good and happiness. The church's form of worship is cosmetic, and the evangelical is emotionally rich in testifying the spirit, but they vow to false doctrines and hyped-up, excited emotion. I put this knowledge at the back of my mind; which church domination I went to, it does not matter merely being in a church and worshipping the one creator God with fellow believers enhances my happiness.

Some Church has excessive pouring out of emotions and speaks the Word as manifested in our physical scenes. The way they worship and pray releases stress that gets left at the church altar, which is fascinating. The Church's expression of faith made me even more convinced that my financial promise if I continued to hope and pray, is absolute because I am desperate.

I am short of essential food items we need, like eggs, milk, a tub of butter and a block of cheese. Georgina's overdraft again paid for them, but our son insisted that he wants to help with housekeeping with his first proper wage from his job. So, we had to get by for another two weeks on pittances squeezed out of the juggled bill payments and Georgina's overdraft paying for fuel for the car. So, I have stopped calculating and trust solely in God to bless.

I believed
Written Thursday, July 7th 2005

Without evidence, I believed that the mid-week lottery draw on 06/07/2005 had won me considerable money by God's far-sighted wisdom. I am writing about my sincere belief that God did not move through my predicament, but only by my faith, which seems like a chance to some people because they are blind and blinkered. My confidence was undermined by blindness in various ways, and God wills me to stay in the faith. I saw in that truth that God does all things, and nothing happens by chance but through the mercies of God. I am entirely conscious of the incredible luck that permits me to profit from the prediction of wealth that has come. It's like walking with my eyes closed and on the right path, which could become dangerous without warning. I want to change my way of life, but the blues' beat could plunge me into a bit of depression, and if I begin to lack confidence in believing I have won, then I run the risk of covering myself with alarming doubts. So I am following my instincts and don't listen to my thoughts as they could mislead me. Success is almost guaranteed, and everything I desire will be realized immediately; I examined the lottery tickets.

I will rest secure, for when I review the tickets in a few moments, I will be a new person with new perspectives and a whole new life. There can be no doubt that my instinct has a fantastic read because of its accuracy. I can confirm it, and I can reveal to you and not hesitate that the excellent news has no error. So, this is no false joy that I have won £10.00. Bravo! I am giddy, for I told myself, 'This is surely a sign from providence.' Ten pounds may not seem a lot to be frivolous happy about, but this is an extraordinary period, and an instinct again tells me big money is within my grasp. Luck is building up to produce real miracles. I am watching my life ready to turn towards the kind of unexpected happiness and greater joy that these few weeks of financial Godsend will bring in my life when I grasp the big money prize.

I am concerned; I am sure that the EuroMillions draw on Friday 08/07/05 is estimated to be 47million pounds, and Saturday's 09/07/05 Lotto super draw jackpot of 15 million pounds will introduce happiness and money that I can only imagine at present. I have to win a massive amount of money to stem the stringent cutbacks I will make to our already poor home economics. This month is triggering the most fantastic monetary gifts that I will probably ever experience in my life. Unforeseen and unexpected meetings may occur too with people who can help our situation. It appears that I deserve it more than anyone else because, however, I look at it, it seems that life has not been a picnic for us. I am in a panic today and every day to find ways to get by. A heaven-sent windfall capable of enriching my life far beyond anything that I could hope for would take away the panic. I beg Heaven to open up and place the lottery's main cash prize in my lap. I tell myself that things are already happening and that I will soon see a change that will probably shake up my emotional life and stop my worries forever. I do not have the slightest doubt that by the weekend, it will be decisive for me, either I have to cut the outgoings which are set up for our security or the opportunity that was written in my very near future will come to pass.

I risk losing the financial opportunity because I have no real money to buy the lottery tickets. I have taken money destined for direct debits out of the bank to play two lines on the EuroMillions, costing £1.50 per line, and two lines on the Lotto at a pound a line. I have to make money by 2/07/05 to revive my bank account, for there are not enough funds in the account to pay all the outgoing direct debits, and the game of chance might bring in the money needed.

My current way of life is not all that I would wish it to be, so I want to capture the infinite powers of chance, attract wealth in the millions and finally live a life of permanent financial ease. A series of opportunities to win big is within my reach, and my life will move out of the ordinary, and it will be the end of all difficulties. I imagine that, despite some doubts, I am positioned in one of the best circumstances for luck and wealth because energy is 'downloaded' on me to attract success and money. I HOVER MY PEN OVER EACH NUMBER when I mark the playing slip with six heavy horizontal pen marks. Then, I select the six boxes that give the most trembling vibes as I pray and imagine a force dropping my pen in the correct boxes that will tally with the lucky numbers. Sometimes I concentrate and randomly select what my mind sees, in a theoretical profoundly gifted insight, as to what may be the jackpot numbers. There is little chance I will sleep much at night. I am so anxious, and I get filled with unbelievable feelings of pending prosperity, riches, perhaps thousands of pounds in a sudden, dramatic financial breakthrough, pouring forth in a succession of episodes that is nothing short of miraculous. I stay awake praying or wake in the middle of the night and pray I will experience the blissful life in all its grandeur, the harmony that few people are ever able to realize.

Be damned, be damned, I won nothing on the lotteries on Friday and Saturday of the 8th and 9th of July 2005. My chosen numbers were mainly a digit different from those on the draw, and by not getting a cash prize, I now have to prepare to cancel direct debits, life policies, and cash plans to balance the books. £160.00 was wiped off our income when government payment for Living Allowance was slashed, and my continued use of the overdraft was a buffer. The wife and I sat down and thought hard about the cuts without affecting our essential modern requirements. Those occasions when having to pay for services necessary to run the home and protect the family. I will never give up hope on what I dream, for success is only 'deferred'.

On Friday, July 15th 2005, the EuroMillions jackpot was estimated to be 55 million pounds, and I had won only £8.00 from it. More than £88 million is up for grabs in the most prominent lottery weekend one week later. £18 million to be won on the Lotto - the 1,000th draw - and £66 million on offer for the EuroMillions draw. Plus, an estimated £4.4 million on Lotto Extra for which I do not buy tickets. I had gambled as much as I could, three lines on EuroMillions and two lines on Lotto. I could not get too carried away because the chances of winning are stacked against me. It was said that the odds of scooping the jackpot on Lotto is 1 in almost 14 million, while it is even more remote with EuroMillions at 1 in 76 million.

If I won the jackpot in any of the lotteries, the first thing I'd do is jump around the room screaming. After that, I would pray and spend the money on my family, friends and supporting my favourite charities, including churches and cash-starved causes and guarantee security in my old age.

Today is Sunday, July 24th 2005, and I have just looked at my lottery tickets this minute. Yes! You have guessed it, I have won nothing, nothing at all.

Events that put my problems on the back burner

Written Sunday, July 24th 2005

included 7/7 attacks.

Almost a month ago, on Tuesday, June 28th 2005, many warships, including lots of elegant tall ships and a flotilla of merchant's vessels, all swayed slightly amid the pull of the sea. In memory of England's most known battle of Trafalgar's and its famous casualty, Lord Nelson. They clustered off Portsmouth to celebrate the significant naval victory.

From July 6th to 8th, 2005, world leaders met at the G8 summit and 'Make Poverty History' was the cry from people worldwide to the world leaders and people campaigning for fair trade. Twenty years after Live Aid in the 80s, leading musicians took to the stage on Saturday, July 2nd 2005, in 10 city concerts worldwide in an antipoverty gig called Live 8, which kicked off in London's Hyde Park. It was an extravaganza with an estimated world audience of 5.5 billion people watching it. "The whole world has come together in solidarity with the poor," UN Secretary-General Kofi Annan said.

Live 8 was a massive success because it showed the possibility and potential of humanity. The weekend's momentum was not lost, nor was the message to the world's most potent leaders to make poverty lay in history. Still, anarchists launched a wave of brutal attacks against police in a bid to derail the G8 summit. Gangs of masked extremists from across Europe fought running battles in Edinburgh, where the G8 conference was held. The hate scenes were in total contrast to the joy and optimism of the worldwide Live eight concert.

Saturday, July 2nd 2005, also saw Venus Williams play in the Wimbledon lady's singles final. She staged a remarkable fightback against world number one Lindsay Davenport to claim her third Wimbledon crown. It was the longest final in history after two hours and 45 minutes of epic playing.

On Wednesday 6th July 2005, London beat favourite Paris to host the 2012 Olympic Games, there was a gigantic knees-up. This, jubilation and dancing in the street as ecstatic crowds in Trafalgar Square greeted the news of the capital winning the bid.

Central London came to a virtual standstill on Thursday, July 7th 2005, when four explosions hit the capital in a terrorist attack. The blasts brought carnage and grief to London's streets which, less than 24 hours earlier, had been gripped by Olympic euphoria. July 7th 2005, or 7/7, will be remembered as the day everything changed when London was paralyzed. Sixty people were dead, and hundreds more injured at the blast sites - tube stations and carnage from a bomb on a bus. The underground network was shut down, bus services were suspended, and many mainline train stations were closed. It was Britain's September 11th, almost four years after the attack on America; hundreds of Britons and I have lived in dread of a day like Thursday 7/7.

I dared to hope the British way of life was not under such an acute threat. Now I know different, for less than 24 hours after London's sensational victory to host the 2012 Olympics, the terrible events struck the capital and became known as the 7/7 bombings. Still, we must strike the right balance between expressing sympathy for the victims and displaying what I call 'Churchillian' determination to defeat terrorists, like Prime Minister Churchill during the Second World War. The battle must be waged against terrorists with sturdy steeliness and sensitivity to ensure the law-abiding Muslim community is not in danger of being alienated and stigmatized.

The attack on London, possibly a coordinated suicide bomber, which we have all feared for so long, has finally reached our shores. Mercifully, it was not as murderous as last year's assault upon Madrid's railway stations. Ever since September 11th 2001, the world has had warnings of terrorist sleepers living in our midst. Countless families will be struggling to come to terms with the loss or injury of a loved one, and my thoughts and prayers must be with them and with all those still fighting for their lives.

On Friday, July 8th, I woke to a new reality that war against terrorism had arrived on these shores and, with it, the horror that this implies. Britain is the fourth most prosperous nation globally, and what happened on 7/7 was barbarity without excuse or reason. Four British-born Muslims are the suicide bombers who massacred, to date, fifty-four people in London's tube and bus atrocities. Millions of people stood in silence for two minutes at noon on Thursday, July 14th 2005, to remember the victims of the London bombings.

On Sunday, July 10th 2005, the nation remembered its war heroes when patriotic cheers filled the air as the RAF's pride, a wartime Lancaster bomber, dropped its cargo of 1 million poppies over London. The flowers fluttered down over Buckingham Palace, and hundreds of hundreds of patriotic Britons stretched down The Mall and watched the blossoms float and sway in a beautiful mass until they settled on the people below and hands grasped at them. The city's celebration remembered the 60th anniversary of the end of World War II and those who fought and fell in it. The road to Buckingham Palace was filled with the excellent human tide, and the royal family gazed up with pride as poppies rained down on the balcony at Buckingham Palace. The commemoration was held halfway between VE day and VJ day.

On July 21st 2005, terrorists planted more bombs in London, but they failed to go off. Four men were responsible, and one of them was traced down in Italy.

Suicide bombers on Sunday, July 24th 2005, attacked Egypt's top resort, killing 88 people; some were British tourists.

After 36 years of bloodshed, violence and terrorism, the IRA finally declared it would lay down its arms and bring an end to 36 years of war. It is a crucial and defining point in the search for lasting peace with justice.

Some 1,000 people have been killed in India's worst monsoon on record as more than 3 feet of rain fell in 24 hours, almost twice as much as London receives in a year.

I am still waiting for it!
Written Friday, July 29th 2005

Today is Friday, July 29th 2005, and the energy company telephoned me and requested £270 by the end of August to bring the account up to date. Europe's biggest lottery prize goes up for grabs tonight; will that be an income source to pay for my energy usage and life's necessities? The EuroMillions jackpot now stands at £77 million after nine weeks of rollovers. I have bought four tickets using overdraft money; they could not be paid for in any other way. It could be me taking my place among the country's most prosperous if I win tonight's EuroMillions lottery jackpot. It will instantly catapult me to mega-rich status, even eclipsing football superstar David Beckham and Victoria, his wife. I am anxious to see if God will play a part and get His hand involved to make me a jackpot winner. With the odds of 76 million to 1, it's the Almighty that will probably release some supernatural power and include me in the top prize. Having a gamble and winning cannot be done alone. It cannot be that I am so lucky that I win, but it becomes possible with the help of the living God.

I have put the tickets in a safe place between the pages of my pocket-sized Bible at Psalm 112 and zipped it closed with the built-in zipper. I read Psalm 112, believing its words and praying that I shall receive the financial blessing because we live on insufficient funds.

Last Monday, July 25th, 2005, I had attended the United Reformed Church's monthly prayer meeting for the first time. The prayers were mainly silent, and individuals spoke out, in a moderate voice, the burden on their heart, one person at a time, and it sharpened my concentration. I could feel the depth of their feelings but found it hard to express my feelings and make my prayer request known to them. The session was a blessing, but nobody other than God knew why I need prayer because I did not open up. I think it will be different the next time I go. Attending my wife's church prayer meetings leaves me puzzled; is my silent prayer heard by God? Everyone prayed loudly all at once, and I was confused because I could not hear my thoughts through the loudness of their prayers. I cannot separate the noise of their prayers coming through my ears and that of the private prayer that I whispered. None had a focal point; it was a jumble of incoherent noisiness that led me later to have a hearing hallucination of a kind. I lacked concentration as the prayers were nothing but jungle noises, yelling and shouting.

The Church my wife always attends talks about how successful prayer has been for them, and I sensed that we need the faithful to pray for us to experience the incredible joy of answered prayer. So, I went to the Church for the first time on Sunday, July 31st today, with my whole family, and we had lunch with the congregation in the upstairs room. After lunch, my heart had burdened, and I wanted to talk to the Pastor. I asked the Pastor to pray for our household to see an improvement in our financial situation. I opened up to him and spoke to him about how hard it is living without enough to get by. I became emotional, and I could feel my eyes moisten.

In the Church, where activities had ceased, he prayed beautifully over me and said all the important things that gave me a feeling of peace and blessing. Tears just gradually eased through the ducts at the corner of my eyes as his prayer hit on the targets of our concerns and seemed to put pressure on God to empower us or take the situation in His hand and transform it. His prayer was so beautifully passionate and full of energy that I now have a new sense of hope.

However, I am experiencing more and more of a funny turn, a peculiar kind of confusion, a feeling caused by anxieties and stress. The first time it was extensively revealed to my wife after a car trip to Enfield, I was to pick her up from work in Wellingborough and then drive home to Kettering. I thought that I could not move any further when I reached Euphemia's place of work. I became pale and stared with little blinking of my eyes and movement; the familiar environment began to look unfamiliar and threatening. Everything seemed to resemble hostile faces, even inert objects like the different cars and lorries and looking at the sky. Buildings and ordinary people going about their business appeared threatening, and I shivered on a warm day. Everything seemed to move in slower motion. People, animals and things in their various settings were taking on a sinister look. I could not focus on people's faces or concentrate well on a conversation when spoken to face to face. It can happen in the home, but the difference was that I could not look at familiar faces and hold my attention on them without seeming shy and looked away from them, which they looked upon as being rude. My wife reacted in an ever so loving and caring fashion and sensed that change in me that started to show. She told me I was stressed, which made me lack concentration and likely led to panic and schizophrenia. I let her control the situation, like driving, for I was functioning as if my memory had lapsed. "I feel in distress at times or about to be distressed because I find myself concentrating harder and harder to complete the everyday monotonous tasks," I said to Euphemia. This condition had stopped me from driving and made me feel not part of the team when socialized in a group. I feel alone and unable to relate well when spoken to, and my speech came out a bit messy and cluttered because I forgot what they asked me. My eyes felt like they did not follow the movement they should, and they lifted under my top eyelid. It's a peculiar feeling, and I placed my hands over my face and closed my eyes to see nothing but darkness until it wore off. Sometimes it only takes a few minutes to wear off and depending on how much information from the environment my five senses pick up, it can bizarrely last for hours. It is mainly too much information coming into my eyes and ears from the background, creating overload and making me want to shut down and run away from the stimulants.

I react calmly but cannot easily relate to people and speak my mind. I get confused about the words to use to express myself. A hug settles it down a bit, but it is not resolved until I sit in a calm, quiet place and close my eyes and over time, the phenomenon disappears with the help of medication. The event usually shows itself around mid-afternoon to late evening. I have changed the time I take my medicine from 10 pm to an earlier time of 6 pm, and I succeeded in shortening the episodes, so they do not last as long.

I am still in contact with a psychiatrist who seemed more interested in my politics, love life, and explanation of God's nature than listening to me speaking about my anxiety and stresses. He mostly gets pleasure, I believe, out of our discussions on politics and the nature of God and my idea of Jesus's role in salvation and where the world affairs are leading societies. He takes a few notes on what I feel my life brings forth, hopeless situations under which to live. I talked to him about how I want to give up on believing in God because answered prayer is not happening. We discussed only things related to global happenings, the afterlife and my political view. He did not explore how they affect my inward emotions resulting in me weeping and my external behaviour to be anxious and restless. Even though he knows news stories distress me, I told him my faith remains because of only one reason; it's good to pray and believe prayer will get answered when God is good and ready. There is nothing better than to pray to what seems to be the truth about God and our existence.

My wife thinks the psychiatrist is unprofessional, and he is not helping my condition but gets me even more stressed. She comes with me to the psychiatrist appointments. She tells me to ask for a different consultant psychiatrist because he had missed that my mind was unwell when I attempted suicide. Now, he is stressing me on topics like religion, politics and world affairs. He did not look at my feelings or how my mind is getting worried and unable to cope.

A second appointment was made to see the psychiatrist within days of the previous visit, and he changed my medication to Abilify, aripiprazole 15 mg tablet. The tablet is working better than the ones previous, for it has eliminated the weird feelings I sometimes used to get and took in my stride, and I began to see them as part of the norm.

Today is Wednesday, August 10th; thanks to the new medication, my suffering from spells of functioning disability is over. On Saturday the 6th August, Katrina and Robert came down from Manchester and travelled to my cousin's daughter's wedding with us in a minibus. It was the first time the relatives met Robert, and I thought it was a lot of stress they went through with relatives inquiring and gossiping. Unfortunately, we had no money to contribute to the minibus cost or contribute to the wedding gift. It is not the choice I would have made if the situation was different, but we had to rely on the family's generosity with no spare money.

I had explored using some of the shopping money to buy Euphemia's outfit for the wedding and had hope that money would suddenly manifest itself when shopping in mid-August is required. That would not be wise, I told myself! Not only did I have to think about the wedding, but I had also to consider where the money could come from for the car service, MOT and breakdown cover. They are now all due, and the car is on the road illegally because the MOT has expired. Georgina had used some of her overdraft money to buy an outfit, and thanks to Jonathan's part-time job, he was able to buy a new shirt, tie and shoes. On the other hand, I wore my existing aged suit, which did not fit my body comfortably and managed to buy a brand-new shirt and tie to go with it. That was only possible because my sister Joan had given me £100 on July 31st towards the cost of preparing for the wedding, for which I was very grateful.

I want to provide for ourselves, but our income grows less and less, and I was forced to take money from those who appear privileged because they can go on holiday and eat out. So, I am grateful that Joan is one of those who offered to give; thank you, Joan!

In this new month of August, the media revealed an Irish woman had landed the biggest prize in European lottery history, a staggering 77million pounds. I dream of falling into that sort of fantastic jackpot won by Dolores McNamara in the EuroMillions lottery. It's always somebody else who wins! I had a couple of lucky numbers but not enough to give me a share of the small prize money. Economic distress is disrupting my belief system. Why does God allow his people to suffer or not have enough to live on, yet we still rejoice in the Lord? I had rationally worked out that there must be a God in the universe; see my writing called Belief Examined. I do not rely on my emotions to give me feelings of His existence and His workings. Habakkuk 3; 17 & 18 says, 'though the labouring for olives may fail and the fields yield no food, yet I will rejoice in the Lord.' I cannot find rejoicing in God joy when in economic distress. I celebrate moderately because spiritually, I need to worship, and in worship, I come to know and trust God and experience an absolute joy. I cannot worry about having good things that money can buy; it's not in my mind until after worship when I start to expect something from God. One gets a kind of complete bliss in prayer and worship, but the reality of hunger and low finances –do not strike the mind until afterwards, and I think God can deliver, and I must remain poised and waiting.

We can rarely clearly tell how God helps, but I must be prepared to rejoice in the Lord at all times. I wish my faith to increase because happiness depends on good happenings to celebrate at all times. I am practising it, but depression may creep in when nothing seems to be happening, and I cease prayer. I hope I will come to understand God more and trust God more. Even in my poverty, I should be able to rejoice in the Lord. When I shift my mind into neutral and just let it idle, I worry about money. Jesus thought that we are not to be full of care about it. We are not to worry about life's necessities because God, Himself, has assumed responsibility for our food and clothing and all our needs. Jesus instructed us to centre our entities on God's kingdom. Then clothing, food and life's necessities will be ours as well. What am I doing that His teachings can't be working? In Matthew 6; 26, he said, 'Look at the birds of the air.... Are you not of more value than them?'

I have focused my life on God and doing His will, but it's still challenging to have life's necessities. I do not think my concern for making money and keeping it over-shadows my respect for doing God's will because the poverty of purpose is far worse than the misery of my purse's poverty. I cannot possibly remember all of God's benefits to me in my life so far, but I am distressed that I cannot count, one by one, any of the blessings God gives each day. The first ray of sunlight from the eastern sky pushed open the morning door; God gives us life and his help to sustain it. Maybe God's goodness is as constant as the sun; I am afraid of forgetting what showers on us each day.

I am not conscious of being able to count his blessings in my life nowadays. I have often taken for granted the benefits, but I do not want them to be taken from me. I recognize how important even the most common gifts of God are, and every morning as I rise, I ask for financial blessings, and God's new mercies greet my eyes, but I am often unaware of them. I feel hopeless because I was unable to become rich in the month I expected it, July 2005, which reminds me that I am helpless without God, and if I want to be rich, I count all the things I have that money can't buy.

It never rains, but it pours
Written Wednesday, August 10th 2005

Things have moved on to be worse than ever, and from the human standpoint, it appears to be a tragic case of injustice, not a providential means of blessing. Later, I may learn that God permitted it for good. The biblical truth says there are no accidents in the lives of God's children, but I interpret these problematic experiences as seeming like a great calamity.

Things are going from bad to worse. It ought to be getting better, but the most worrying thing is the mortgage did not get paid in August. For the third Sunday now, I had concealed a note in an envelope with no money inside, and I placed it on the offertory plate. We are still treading the hardship road, and we have been looking to leave it quite soon, but we are bogged down, and in lifting ourselves out of it with our effort, we are making little or no progress. We have no one to turn to for a free financial gift that is substantial enough to make a difference.

Nevertheless, I am determined to make the right things happen and not be contented to wait and see what will happen. I lay no claim to sanctity, yet I felt the holy touch through my prayer and others praying for us for a moment. I had not sensed I would be more in-depth in the mire; I expected God to break in upon us at any moment and change the direction of our circumstances.

In prayer, I am primarily in wonder, awe and humility before God, ready to respond to my maker acting with me, but it seems like God does not get to a breakthrough. When He does, our circumstances will change for the better. People of prayer have been praying for us, and I feel deceived because God did not clarify that the travail and labour are needed even more as we wait for our prayers' results.

The transcendent reality Christians call God may have other ways of getting the financial blessings through to me in His wisdom and mercy. God revealed Himself to people of different religions, experiences, and cultures, and only the future can tell if this will continue to be so. Who believes with me that Christianity is only one of the many ways to come to know God? I seek the eternal mystery and transcendence to help me do something about our plight. My spiritual nature is continuously exploring the source of the creation of human society's purpose. The haves the have nots in this world and those not needing anything. The world leaves the poor with dreams and hopes to go on one day to be in the last place. I presuppose communication from both sides when in prayer because it's a relationship with the living God. I listen to words or hear unspoken thoughts, and God's initiative is not clear. God may be communicating with me through intuition, and my heart gets moved to respond in prayer or silent worship, but I want to be inspired and take action according to the Word of obedience. The exact relation in prayer is not when God hears what was prayed for, but when praying continues until I am the one who understands, who hears what God wills. I make demands in prayer, and the carrying out of the answer differs from the action dictated by reason or inclination. When it makes itself felt, an impulse and such an inspiration demands the impossibilities to seem possible.

Look how much poorer we have become; we sometimes relied on cooked left-over food from Euphemia's Christian Nursery workplace. The special meals for children are dished out for our evening supper, and the near-the-use-by dated food also provides feeding ourselves. The cupboard begins to look bare mid-month, and in August, there will be no meat on our plates. There will be no traditional meat dish, only a combination of limited mixed ingredients thrown together to make a meal without meat.

'It never rains, but it pours' - we are already having a hard time being cash-poor and time and time again, yet more demands are thrust upon the money. Utility demands, council tax and feeding ourselves are all squeezed out of the money, and nothing remains. Coping on a small income and living is so complex, and it gets worse when sudden demands on rainy-day money, of which we have none, makes it seem it's an existence we have to deal with; we are not living. There is no happiness in reduced spending purely on the necessities. Happy are the poor in heart, for they shall see God, according to the Beatitude. Every day, I beg my conscience to plan to increase our resources to have a main course meal and pudding like we used to. I have to use all the available income and bank credits to see us through to September 2005.

I could only pay the utility company £100.00, and it's not enough to clear the debt. They forced me to accept their demand to install pre-payment meters for our gas and electricity from September 14th 2005. Late payment was made to the mortgage company, and it is a blessing that our son works part-time because a proportion of his other wages, £25.00, helped with housekeeping and bought fuel for the car. Every bit of food from the cupboards, fridge and freezer was used to make daily suppers during the long month of August.

I searched the house for any carelessly discarded penny and miscellaneous misplaced cash to be able to buy a 35 pence newspaper to look at job ads. I have been to a job interview advertised in the local papers to be a Social Care Worker. The United Reformed Church prayer meeting for this month was on the night before my job interview, and I made an effort to go, which will be my second time at the monthly prayer meeting. This prayer time was another chance to put to God and tell the faithful we desire change in our circumstances. I need to share my prayer in the meeting because my praying is not changing anything fast. However, I can see a better future for us if I get the job, and I asked the Reverend to pray for my success in the interview, and with him, the people of faith were engaged in awesome praying for me. Could they shift the attention of God onto the plight of only one of his servants? Inevitably, indeed, as the force of the universe comes down upon me, I can persuade the interviewers that I am the right person for the job.

We are getting nowhere with one person working and the other on state benefits. I need this job or an excellent job to be able to move the family on. We do not want to stay as I previously described, but if I cannot get employment, the next stage in our struggle to live could be to beg publicly. But, oh God, let it not become that we have to beg or appeal to live a life of obedience.

I have just received a telephone call today, 26/08/2005, from Together, and my hopes for the future were nearly crushed because they offered me unpaid work, a voluntary position. The immediate prospect still looks like we will struggle for some time. They asked me to work as a volunteer, unpaid worker doing a few hours a week, and there is a possibility that it may lead to paid employment in the future with them. It's not what I was entirely expecting; it was a paid job I wanted. I am not disappointed because it's a positive step to see that my foot is in the door to paid employment in a brand-new career. I am getting close to earning a living in a job I am sure I would enjoy, which I will be doing as a volunteer. I will be in a profession I would willingly do for nothing because care work is a holy opportunity I will enjoy. It's a bonus if I could get a wage to do what I love. I need money, so I have to look eventually to make some earning from it.

'It never rains, but it pours,' and we are in the middle of the showers. We have no shelter to hide under nor an umbrella to put over our heads. We are getting soaked in this financial struggle, but we will escape pneumonia because if we can continue to hope, the rains will stop, and we will have a change of clothes. Our circumstances will get better beyond doubt because I believe it and am motivated to make it happen. We are trotting through the deep waters of trial and disappointment; everything seems to be going against us, but these apparent misfortunes are not accidents. God allows such things for a blessed purpose. I trust Him so patiently, but what looks like bad luck or an accident is God at work in us when viewed through human eyes. If I know God and have learnt to trust Him entirely someday, I will praise Him for it all. God transforms trials into triumphs, but at this time of hardship, His blessings are in disguise. In keeping with God's purpose, He might not answer my pleas for supernatural help that run through the pages of this book.

This year, 2005, I plead the most so far for God's intervention, yet in every circumstance, my plea should carry a stipulation, "But if not...." My attitude ought to mimic Christ; "O my God, if it is possible, let this cup pass from me; nevertheless, not as I will, but as you will." (Matthew 26v 39). I like to think I am willing to endure whatever will glorify God and work out His divine purposes, but faith says one thing and experiences show another. So, I asked myself, "Do I have the right kind of faith? My findings first gave me five statements on what religion is not; as I ponder them, do I have the right kind of faith? Then, it suddenly dawned on me that my hope is in the living God, believing in my heart that God has raised Jesus from the dead. I admit my sinfulness and desire to turn from them.

1. My faith is not in my ability to control my destiny.
2. My faith is not in my good name and right living.
3. My faith is not in my power to improve myself.
4. My faith is not in my ability to push all negative thoughts out of my head.
5. My faith is not in my sincerity.

It turned out that I reason primarily utilizing my heart and not my head. Therefore, I want to genuinely trust the author of our circumstances and rely on the Holy Spirit's power to work the miracles.

Do you know that nearly 80% of our household income is earmarked for essential bills and living costs before it even hits the bank account? I know it looks stupid to have yielded aggressive credit promotions and taken out personal loans and credit cards to protect or support a better lifestyle. They only help us maintain staying on edge and not falling off it and having to beg to get by. We carry substantial monthly commitments to support a decent living level which could be sustained if I had a paid job. Instead, I have to avoid a looming deepening debt crisis brought on by binge-borrowing and thanks to predatory credit promotions. We are scared to borrow on our house, although the loan may be cheaper and lower the APR. A slight downturn in the economy will put our home at risk as we struggle to meet mortgage and credit repayments.

America's worst natural disaster has intruded into my thoughts and wiped out the flow of ideas I had on personal challenges. Wednesday 31st August 2005, Hurricane Katrina devastated the city of New Orleans and across the Deep South. The death toll was expected to hit 10,000. Then, the second most destructive hurricane to hit the United States, Hurricane Rita, approached the Texas and Louisiana coastline. Rita calmed down and dwindled to barely hurricane status before arrival in Houston, Texas today, Saturday 24th September 2005. However, it brought driving rain that flooded low-lying regions, knocked out power to millions of homes and sparked fires across the region.

I have told you about the terrible storm that hit America, which took me briefly away from writing about the storm of life that no one is exempt from, to bring them to a more in-depth knowledge of God. While I do not understand why God allows trials to enter people's lives, I should not have to fear the storm of life around me because it proves my anchor's strength. The pre-paid meters for gas and electricity usage were to be installed on 14/09/05. I avoided having the meter fitted because I scramble together some money to pay off the arrears, and it was accepted. Through such a turbulent time, I had initially feared there was no way to pay this utility bill, upgrade the computer to Windows 2000, and pay off the arrears on all bills; it was the loan money I used, and there was nothing left for reserves.

Am I losing the race?

Written Wednesday 19th October 2005

I am losing a race against time as I try to find work and hope a miracle on the 'loaves and fishes' scale happens. But, to stave off grinding poverty in what may happen in a couple of years or definitely in old age, if I can't get to put some money away as disposable income, we wouldn't live comfortably in our old age either.

It's a grimmer picture than what's is being imagined because on Tuesday, 4th October 2005, I had to go to the A&E department of the local hospital, and they suspected I had a new fracture to my left foot. I had walked for four months without any walking aids, like sticks or crutches. Today, 19/10/05, there is a threatening financial catastrophe looming. I found out from the orthopaedic specialist that my foot has become increasingly arthritic and as the bones in the foot to the heel became twisted, the foot will become too painful, and movement of the foot will cease. When that happens, and the pain is also great, I will consider having the foot amputated below the knee and have a prosthesis (artificial foot) fitted. Meanwhile, I regularly take painkillers, restrict weight-bearing on that left foot, and use crutches. This bad news is a catastrophe in more than one way.

My first thought was that it meant gloom in our future because I may never be able to work. I am yet to grasp the seriousness of the diagnosis because I am still looking to find a job. Although not shortlisted for any recent applications, the Enhanced Disclosure for working as a volunteer has been successful. The organization, known as Together: working for well-being, asked me when I can start volunteering.

I am upset to look at how I expect to move forward, but instead, I got knocked back far beyond what I could have imagined. Things have gone beyond worse now after this sad news about the long-term outlook of my deformed foot. I may never be able to work again unless it's a desk job. God should supernaturally pay the bill now and keeps us going because we get bogged down more in-depth profoundly when the expectation was to get better. But unfortunately, they are not; we get kicked in the teeth by life's unexpected trials and unfairness.

It's devastating news that my foot will have to be amputated if God's healing does not stop the foot's degeneration. The medical profession has given up that my foot can be made stable with the joints being arthritic and taking pain relief in the long run. I am on the scrap heap of society, and only government benefits will allow me to live in a prejudiced society, for there is no employer out there who will employ me now with mental and physical disabilities. People may see and pity me, but remarkably, I do not feel finished in myself. I have a lot to give, and I am at my most productive in a sense because my mental health has stabilized since taking the new pills.

Twenty-eight years of my life have been lost in fighting the drugs that sedated me, slowed me and interfered with my regular, natural functions and behaviour in ways that made my personality shallow and introverted. I now feel lively and full of life with the will to experience life's sensations and mix with different people. I am to enquire if I can go back on total welfare and receive Living Allowance in full and remain claiming both benefits for all time into retirement.

There can be no progress if I have to rely on benefits continually in our lives. So I have asked the church leaders again and selected a group of people to pray for us, for things are getting worse and worse, and my prayers are not shifting the burdens. So many faithful believers were praying to God to lift our commitment, but to my surprise, they were no more successful in prayer than my solo prayer to God, and I know they now know our business.

I will not accept that my foot will have to be amputated in the future when the pain becomes unbearable. That causes me to cry out to God to heal me, but my faith does not incorporate Jesus as divine, and I may, after all, have had it wrong, and healing gets declined. I am searching for the truth about Christianity, and I have picked up several facts and many interpretations about Jesus. I asked the white Reverend from the URC to discuss Christianity with me and how believing in Jesus has taken the world's sins. How can Jesus bring me closer to God and his miracles by accepting Jesus as our saviour? Then, I can move God to engineer healing and prosperity in our life according to biblical promises.

I did not always believe that Jesus Christ is only a man; the assumption that Jesus is not divine grows because the Bible belongs mainly to a post-mythological way of thinking. Yet, it nonetheless retains many transitional characteristics. The most obvious is the pure myth of the story of Adam and Eve. What mattered was that they were made right and part of an ordered, structured universe in which God had a plan and purpose for humankind.

The Reverend believes that the devil has interfered in my belief and has caused unhealthy doubts cutting me off from God in Christ. He wants me to think again that the devil is real and can influence the faithful to backslide and probably lose faith altogether. The breakthrough may come late in your earthly years to have healing and prosperity, but think what's in store in eternity—bliss for the believers and hell for those who are not believers.

I began to wonder if I should convert back to believing that Jesus is the physical offspring of God and accept the virgin birth story. The incarnation meant that God and man were joined together in Jesus; God becomes a man. The minister and my wife believe it's the devil working to stop the original Christian belief from accepting again, and they are all praying for my wholeness. I have come far in my approach to what Christians believe, that Jesus was literally God's son and divine.

I have called myself non-Christian because I could not accept what is false about Christianity. I have grown and know the absolute truth about Christianity and now call myself a Christian reformed. I am not any Christian but a Christian reformed. The distorted perspective in Christianity was removed as I think for myself and begin thinking again, not ending it. The cosmological experience in which the only adequate explanation for all the causal processes in the world and the entire cosmos must lie in that which is itself uncaused, the source of all that is God. Suffering, anger and doubts have turned my thinking explicitly conceptual, but still a highly abstract form of thought that made me see the Jesus of history better. I could not understand Jesus or Mary as living human lives in the Bible's text until I saw the abstract form of writing like poetry and its symbolic meaning.

I realise my new facts and new interpretation can be traumatic for the conventional religious believer, but truth has to be lived, reimagined, rethought, and seen as progress. I have come to think that Christianity is not the story of God and Son, but part of God at work supremely in human life, that of Jesus. Learning the truth about the phrase 'son of' can mean somebody's actual son, but it can also symbolically be used. To be called a 'son of God' means that they are very holy and God-like. 'Son of God' is a metaphor for a faithful, devout servant of God, full of God, suggesting that the person was very close to God. Self-education has revealed that 'son of God' and 'God, the son' are originally different. 'God, the son' means the God who filled the man. As a Christian reformed, the story of the crucifixion of Jesus still stands with resurrection. Even the development of the cross gets understood in various ways, but it's not confusing. There is no one way of seeing it, but I can say that God was doing something in Jesus on the cross.

Modernist Christian reformists

Written Wednesday 19th October 2005

For me, atonement sacrifice, paying the price of human sins by Jesus's death and shedding his blood to purify the whole human race is not the essential message of the Cross. Some of the Christian church fathers were the people who formed and founded the modern church, which has its base on the father of orthodoxy, Athanasius. The Cross shows God is involved in everyday life struggles and stands alongside people who suffer and gives them courage. God has entered all the world's darkness and come out the other side, showing that darkest times can be transformed and that good is more potent than evil in the end. Jesus did something to save people on the Cross, for God came close to human life and entered its darkness to transform it into glorious light in the resurrection. So, Christians accept that the burden of guilt rolls away when confronted with the forgiving Godly minded Jesus on the Cross. Life in this world can threaten the soul's wellbeing, and to get through it safely, one needs to avoid occasions of sin and discipline the body and the passions.

I had to widen my horizons, not narrow them for the questions that rose when I saw the problems of Christology. Christology's beginnings were to define the relation of the divine, the narrow sense of the word, and the human in Christ. I am in the dark regarding Christological development about word flesh, God-man Jesus Christ's redemption through Christ. It has always been the motive force of Christian faith, with later penitential discipline. As we have received it, Christianity is handicapped by errors and reconstructing Christianity is a revolution in thought. Still, I have to be careful with mental health problems, and I so easily be led up the wrong garden path with the ideas coming out of my head.

Escape Christianity's errors; I needed to start from the historical Jesus and his message about God's kingdom on this earth. Faiths seemed to be creating a modern version of Jesus's kingdom, a religion full of belief and entirely focused upon two things simultaneously. First, it's the here and now and the beautiful imaginary sacred world glimpsed in worship and entered permanently after death. Second, there is a mistaken interpretation of Jesus as the co-equally divine son of God incarnate. Still, the belief that a controlling supernatural parallel world beyond this world is a regulative, real spiritual place. I more than half know the truth about human life in my heart, and I no longer have any excuse for lying to myself or living in ignorance. However, there is no scientific proof of life after death, but that does not mean that people cannot live spiritually in some new form in another world or on another level of reality.

I believed the disappearance of Jesus's body is a one-off, and the same God who did not let Jesus's flesh rot promised we could survive death. But, Instead, in a different way, God has prepared a remedy through which He will restore human beings to their original harmony and perfection.

Jesus's teaching about love, peace, forgiveness, and repentance has made us acceptable for the heavenly session. God's kingdom's spiritual realisation on earth can be achieved if sin is eliminated from society's person and the structure of sinful systems falls. These structural sins that encouraged racism and unfair trading systems are examples of those that stop forming God's kingdom on earth. I had followed the implications of contemporary cultural belief. I assumed there were no errors in developing the opinion, but I was appalled when I gained a clear perspective on what is taught as truth in Christianity.

Many Christian people think the devil has influenced me to turn from contemporary Christianity. It's not the devil but the intellect that has declared that the traditional philosophical underpinnings have broken down. The confluence of physics, biology and psychology made an indelible mark on my understanding. The learnt reality that emerges from historical development from biblical times and discoveries made in my daily living recognised the inadequacy of maintaining a belief based purely on religiousness in Christianity. I have grown up and don't need to be lied to about the Christian faith any longer. Christianity's modernity will blow off the ecclesiastical roof and challenge us to discover whether the kingdom's treasure is right in front of us, not permanently postponed in deferring our lives for some big pension plan in the sky. For far too long, the church has been making excuses for Jesus by continuing to justify its operation and muffling the words of the historical Jesus. The church has suspended Jesus in the heavens and kept Christians on their knees. Christians know a home is out there, but we cannot get there quickly because either death has to come first or a breakthrough in high technology to detect the supernatural realm.

Why do Christians concentrate on death before this extraordinary life is lived? Death is not an event we live to experience, for life has no end like how our visual field has no limits. Eternal life belongs to those who live in the present as well as those who have gone before us. Life, through a conscious twist, became a sacred continuum. Evolution had taken a critical turn through and by us. In the very midst of contingency, finitude and transience, our life becomes endless, outside limits, as we give ourselves to life's imminent inter-connections. Here and now is the time and place to come alive, and we should not get misled into deferring our life for the ancient human hopes. Instead, faith-filled people should start to rebuild the long-awaited kingdom of Christ's teachings in this material world.

What the Reverend said about Jesus, the devil and Hell, was basically what traditionalist Christians believe and, given time, it has lost general intelligibility. It sounds more like the internal jargon of a cult. The new breeds of Christians have lost some confidence in the objective truth of the central Christian beliefs. As a Christian leader, the Reverend honestly believed that a reasonable and plausible rational case could be made public for the authenticity of Christian doctrines. Today, as Western churches are emptying, I know it cannot, and contemporary full-scale Christian metaphysics is needed. Traditional philosophical faith arguments for God's existence and attributes and the reality, moral freedom, and immortality of the human soul have been broken down. The world view of natural science has replaced the ancient Christian natural philosophy. The underlying assumptions of traditional religion, such as dividing the world of human experience into two vast realms of the sacred and the profane, have disappeared.

Western society is no longer tradition-directed in the old way; we no longer assume that our life must always be framed by a fixed body of revealed truth taught by the church and the Bible. In a pluralist democratic society, people are suspicious of ideologies that make totalizing claims, and Christianity offers a proper form of life not absolutely proven. Still, because we gave up that idea, it rings true to my sense of me. It rings true to the way things currently are and true to our life as we now live it, and by our faith, it's really about eternity.

Rationalizing Christianity's reformation is needed for today's people, but giving up dogma gives up the idea of revealed truth and acknowledging that all versions of Christianity, from the oldest to the newest, are simply what the historians know them to be, namely human cultural formations. I am a Christian reformist, not out to form another sect in the Christian religion but develop a new form of religious life that will be genuinely truthful, liveable and productive. However, I still have a personal feeling for the old brand of religion though it is based upon an almost outrageously wrong, lousy misinterpretation of the original meaning and message of Jesus. Therefore, I cling no longer to Christianity's old brand name that traditional Christians have misread Jesus.

It's time to give the Jewish teacher an intelligible and attractive account of a Christian form of the religious life, for it may now be too late to restore the church and the credibility of Christian doctrine. The man whose teachings sparked off the development of Christianity, Jesus of Nazareth, preached in the here and now the possibility of immediate coming, which he called the kingdom of God. Unfortunately, he died without seeing the domain become established. After his death, the kingdom still seems to have been delayed to this day. We were lead to believe He believed he was raised, and some claimed others had already risen with him; therefore, the domain began. As the risen Lord was visible only to believers, there was difficulty only to the eye of faith. The world seemed to be going on just as before. Thus, the primitive church began to look up to and worship an ascended Lord Jesus Christ, calling upon him to come back soon, and it expresses eschatological hope. Doctrinal beliefs, which had begun as excuses for the temporary absence of Jesus and his new kingdom world, are now our passports to heaven. You are not preparing for Him to come to you but are preparing yourself to go to him. Life is spent readying oneself for death. Everyone's first concern in life must be for their eternal salvation, to which the church holds the only key. The church over-reached itself and began to provoke dissent among mystics, Protestants and rebellious theologians.

To see why it is now time to abandon church theology and push the Christian movement forward into the next and long-promised stage of its historical development, one must see a new ethic and a new way of relating oneself to life in the gospel. It is post-ecclesiastical and post-dogmatic.

I have been praying for God's forgiveness over the years if I have got the message about Jesus wrong. So many Christian cultures' writing about Jesus is that there is just one image of Jesus, namely that of a divine saviour of ecclesiastical faith. I want people to feel free to depict sacred subjects in a way that enables them to picture either Mary or Jesus as having lived ordinary human lives. So much is known about him, probably much more about him since he walked the Galilean hills. There is plenty of evidence now that brings this elusive founder of Christianity out of the shadows and adds unique fresh insights about his life and times. There is compelling historical evidence that a man called Jesus formulated a series of ideas developed by his followers and still resonated worldwide. The question that gets asked - 'Is Jesus really the son of God?'- well, that is not something that can be proved in a way. One either believes it or doesn't, and I do not, but I continue to live a fully acknowledged truth of life and know the supreme religious joy that I will be full of faith and in a state of grace when I die.

I did all that was required of me and learnt the truth, but I still seriously doubt that I believe it all. My belief is an immediate kind of religious faith that I have always thought possible and hoped for, if not in this life, then at least after death. The Messianic age, variously called Millennium, the New Jerusalem, or the Kingdom of Christ, is coming. The living and the dead will experience the Messianic age. The dead remain entirely out of existence because their soul has completely gone on the day the nation of Christ comes.

Seeing with the eyes of the heart
Written Tuesday 1st November 2005

As I face the harsh reality that I will lose my foot, global conditions and natural disasters remind me of the importance of hope and dreams.

Last month, on Saturday 8th October 2005, an earthquake-ravaged Pakistan, Kashmir, Afghanistan and India, killing more than 90,000 people, virtually wiping them off the face of the earth. Thousands of children died in the earthquake, and a town ceased to exist because the deadly quake had wiped out a generation. With hope amid the devastation of the quake, rescuers pulled live children out four days later.

'There is no such thing as a hopeless case,' I tell myself. The Asian earthquake rescuers hoped to find survivors; hope and dreams are complimentary messages of darkness in our individual lives. My word of the night is that my foot will be amputated one day to stop the suffering and transform it into joy and redemption. I had been in what I thought was a hopeless situation in the past and attempted suicide. I had lost all hope and experienced sadness and came to despair at that time. Suffering in my life and the world, will it ever end? Our God does not forget those who are suffering and oppressed, so they tell me. It's on hope and dreams that a better future will get built when faith in God is not lost or given up. My own experiences of hope and dreams are liberating experiences where darkness gradually changes to light.

My foot may never need amputation if I hope for the best, but other dark times are ahead, and I am vulnerable to it if hope goes. It seems to be part and parcel of the human condition that our individual and global suffering is not optional suffering and can either embitter or exalt us. The pain has become a spiritual transformation when understood as having a role in God's design for the world and ourselves. The universe we inhabit will always be suffering until God's dream comes true, which Jesus teaches. My relation to God is no longer dominated by the need to be assured of my sins or restrained by a disciplinary system of religious laws taught and enforced by a large class of spiritual professionals. Instead, it's become easy and spontaneous to be natural in life to fulfil my part of God's dream. Jesus preached the kingdom, a new nation of ethical obedient people to the highest principal laws, but the church was what we got. Over a dozen or so centuries, it developed into the most spectacular, highly differentiated and cruelly persecuting system that there has ever been.

The vast apparatus of religion is the church; the Bible, the creeds, the sacraments, the ministry, canon law and the rest are all the substance of Christianity. It is indeed officially 'necessary to salvation, and ordinary believers do not see the great myth of orthodoxy. Nevertheless, it is something transitional and very imperfect that we should be longing to be delivered. Orthodox doctrine is not scriptural, and it gets Jesus badly wrong. We have to relearn what religion is and how it works to liberate us and help us build our world in the model of Jesus's teachings.

I called modernist Christianity before, and the Christian religion was a state waiting and readying itself for a promised, better world. It is highly reflective and creedal. It is a matter of having faith, believing 'the faith', and adhering to the creed. Only God could bring in a better world. The creed/ philosophy was a supernatural story about how God had initially created the world and was presently working, redeeming it. Christian doctrine has a nasty, lousy smell morally now because living by it is harmful to people's mental health. Take the two great Christian dogmas, that of the incarnation and the Trinity; they are wrong. Neither is thoroughly scriptural. For the sake of everyone's mental health and its ministers' long-term well-being, we ought not to go on any longer believing in the unbelievable and defending the indefensible. Doctrinal revision is urgently necessary just on critical biblical grounds. Essential theology generally has achieved nothing. It has not been conveyed to the broader public and has made no difference to the churches because, most probably, vicars/ministers learnt it. Still, none are brave enough to preach it from the pulpits to empower the congregation.

In this new and increasingly globalised western culture, secular fulfilment of Christian hope should be recognized. Suppose we can show this contemporary culture, history, and religious significance. In that case, we can pioneer new ethical values and lifestyles that express the generosity and compassion of God. Then we will indeed gradually build Thy kingdom come on earth. It will be a full realisation of religious hope as there can be. So, the Christian pessimist amongst us, the religious conservatives who hate the contemporary culture and see it as the product of a great rebellion against God, has it wrong.

The gospel of Jesus Christ brings release from something spiritual or something material, or is that a wrong kind of division? Jesus promised a blessing upon those who are both materially poor and spiritually reliant on God. For God has concern for our material conditions as to true wholeness of existence. Is our living on the bare minimum and our purely selfish life implanted by God to draw ourselves to him and his purposes for us? I do not know the reason why discontent still exists. The new form of Christianity has shifted the discontentment and the ancient Christian belief that God stepped into his creation, rather like a novelist writing himself into his own story and came to us as Jesus.

A new world faith began from the life and teaching of the humble, spirit-filled man from Nazareth. The title 'Son of God' is poetic. I have since learnt it's a metaphor, and it should not be taken word for word. The 'Son of God' means that Jesus is the holiest person ever to have lived. To the early Christian, he was a man, full of God, and though the title came to mean much more, later on, Jesus was a man full of God, through whom salvation was going to go to the world. It was only then that the title suggested that Jesus was divine and more than an ordinary human. It must have been the belief in the resurrection that started the church thinking that Jesus was uniquely one with God. When they thought of Jesus, they thought of God and man together. The two were inseparable. Powerful metaphors have lost their original force and meaning. That is true of 'Salvation' and 'Redemption', which, if they mean anything today, are the idea of going to church or getting to heaven. Christians believed that Jesus was God, and the man was joined together somehow; God became man. Jesus was a real human being with his feelings and his mind. Yet, he was linked, uniquely, to the nature of God.

I am a new breed of Christian believers who believe in its symbolic language, meaning that God's presence was focused on the life of Jesus more than anywhere else on earth. The manner and nature of God's joining with the man in Jesus were seen as a mystery that ultimately defies words. Science tries to sum the universe up by way of mathematics, forces and chemicals. Human beings are on earth to reproduce the species. These things are all true, but we need personal values and explanations of the universe too, and this is where my belief in God comes in, and Jesus taught us these values. We are people who cannot just be reduced to these mechanical forces. God contains the entire universe within himself and is beyond human understanding and a mystery. God is to be found deep within people, as the source of our life and everything. God is rooted in the centre of all things, flowing through everything.

In a previous chapter called 'Belief Examined,' I wanted to prove God's existence and verify that there must be a God in all theories. But who would ever have thought that Jesus, a carpenter's son, would come to be regarded by millions as the human being most like God? So, like God, he came to be identified with God Himself as the Son of God. The attempt to prove there must be a God is a matter of faith and trust, but the language about the Trinity stretches my imagination, my understanding to the end. The Father is the creator, the Son is the Redeemer, and the Spirit is the life-giver or sanctifier who makes holy. One God working in three ways and is threefold in Himself. He can relate to himself and act outwardly into the world. Yet, it's beyond my understanding of three in one person or one in three persons.

Christian marriage is one of the more attractive and durable creations of ecclesiastical religion. I believe in it though it seeks to moralize nature in a long-term and disciplinary way. Its reciprocal life vow has something unconditional and fixed in the temporal world. I believe in Christian marriage principles, but its suspicious exclusive and penal character marks it belonging to the church's historical age. People are learning to use sex as being merely the best and most precious form of interpersonal exchange, and it's more than that. Free love is not suitable for the kingdom unless its free love decides to win the same partner each day. The nation on earth must continue long-term relationships with disciplinary rules, forget suspicious marriage characters, and live coupled to 'one love' until death.

Discovering the truth about Jesus has inspired my heart and reaffirms my faith. That is inevitable since, while my thinking has evolved, my core beliefs have remained the same.

Mencap has shortlisted me for the position of a support worker. The selection process is in two stages, a visit to the home to meet the staff and the people living there. The informal visit is tomorrow evening, Wednesday 2nd November - and the interview with two home managers is on Thursday 10th November and is expected to last approximately one hour. I think I can persuade Mencap that I am the right person for the job. That is a hope that has come to me at a time most needed. It may be wishful thinking or groundless belief, but the job description feels right for me to work with people with learning disabilities. Mencap is specific about their requirement to employ disabled people and give a candid interview.

My wife has a chance to escape the dull environment of her present nursery job to work in a new nursery 25 hours a week. It's only in hope as I helped her fill out the application form to be a Nursery Assistant. The hope has become closer to expectation because Euphemia was invited to an interview on 15th December

2005 at the new nursery called Caring Kindergartens. My deep conviction is that our lives will turn, and we will not suffer another blow, a kick in the teeth. This most improbable situation is transferrable. It can be turned into a structured system to eat correctly, pay the bills, and live fully. And with the possibility of employment restrictions lifting from our lives, we are in the grips of a transformation. My view of our future is optimistic. I see we are moving on and not walking in the shadow, yet it's behind us. The darkness in our lives is behind us, but optimism relies on appearances. It appears to me I will get the job, and my wife will get the new job that offers reduced hours. I pray to God if presence changes into pessimism because the reality is that the job is not mine, do not let me despair, make me a realist and show me a vision of hope again.

Hope Under Attack Again
Written Monday 28th November 2005

With all the devastation seen on the television news, it is fair to say that hope is under attack. Whether these disasters are natural, man-inspired or in my personal life, the level of confidence carried is under attack. I hope for myself and also for all those I care for while believing in a God-inspired future. But hope has to be reduced to the powerless level of fate like buying a lottery ticket.

On 22nd November, I received a Mencap letter offering me a relief support worker's job. I accepted the position, which was offered subject to a satisfactory criminal record check. The next day, my pulse raced, and sweating started because sudden severe pain developed in my deformed foot and on the following day, the 24th, I could not bear weight on that foot. I had to use a pair of crutches to get about or hop on one foot. I talked to my GP about it, and he thought it might settle down, and I was to take stronger painkilling tablets.

Today is Monday 28th November 2005; there has been no improvement in the limb, and it's excruciating to try to stand. I have written to Mencap today to inform them that I have changed my mind because I am no longer physically fit to carry out the duties. An internal battle began between sadness and anger, and it got painful, so I gave up in anger with my face resembling a red traffic light. I had looked forward with confidence that I had secured a promising career, but again, I dealt with disappointment that affected my inner person. It's a hopeless condition that my soul becomes unanchored throughout, consistently losing the fight to better ourselves. I talked to myself, and my God-conscious insisted on muscling in on my conversation, and amazingly I find we are meant not to live without hope, no matter the circumstances.

As I told her, my wife said it's another significant setback for us and devastating news, as Christmas is only four weeks away. "Karl, you cannot walk, praise the Lord, we have no money for our bills or to buy enough food, praise the Lord. Praise God, Karl, fixed on the God of hope, for I believe things will get better because Jesus told me. So, do not get worried. Allow God to deal with things." I almost wanted to laugh in disbelief; ", Giving praise to God no matter what the circumstances is tough to do," I said.

Our hopes had been dashed when they were expected to be fulfilled. Our future looks bleak again, and hope is deferred again, making my heart sick, so I must have the longing fulfilled. It cannot be now that I will never work to see the family financially better off. There is a regression as we move further down the road from hope to hopelessness. My dreams are not realized, and a sense of unrelenting disappointment brings me close to despair. Day after day, hour after hour, I feel frustration that the hope has eroded from me because, at the last moment, I had to decline to work.

However, this personal challenge and those I can foresee have shown me, God, in a new way that I will eventually be able to move from hopelessness to faith, from disappointment to confidence and from despair to hope again. However, these moments are when reckless choices can be made, as I am at a point of desperation. Although I had resigned myself to believing that things will never change and that a breakthrough is a fantasy, life can take us from hope to disappointment; The God of hope can help, no matter what the circumstances look like, seemingly impossible situations. Based on this revelation and the word, they will be transformed, and dreams will come true. Therefore, I tell myself I will yet praise him, my God, and though I felt discouraged, I refuse to dwell on my circumstances. Indeed, as my wife also said to me, "Karl, turn your attention to God, speak the word to your soul, and you will be strengthened and encouraged by God." My wife asks me to take my eyes off the problems and look to the God of hope. Despite the negativity and hopelessness that are surrounding us, she says, "Karl, hold on firmly to hope in God, and the Lord will restore. You will be able to walk again, and we will have enough to live on and be filled with faith and hope, so when you pray, believe that you will receive it."

It takes a humble heart and a keen ear to catch the still, small voice of God. It's another day, Tuesday 29th November. Yesterday, the 28th, was a fate-filled day because I was shaken by God's working anonymously in the things my wife said to me. I needed the ability to hold onto dreams and make one of the small steps, not leaps, for there is no such thing in the Bible as a leap of faith. Instead, it's a book about people who took small steps that led to a selection of giant leaps for the kingdom of God.

The gulf's acute awareness of current reality and future desire can bring a sense of powerlessness and paralysis. God promises prosperity, and we step into famine or something like it. I need sheer trust, not in any dream but purely in the one from whose ideas come.

Once again, we are at the darkest point before dawn, and we keep making tracks and establishing the momentum to believe the sky's the limit; then it's time for a step of faith again. I am still building up my life to retake steps in the middle of this storm of life that is ruining or moving forward and challenging me to adapt to restricted mobility. I feel we live on less than God intended for us, and we are not at a comfort level where God can challenge us to give beyond at some point. I believe everything indeed belongs to God, so if God controls the comings and goings of our money, this is why we have relied on God's promise to meet our needs. I trust Him in our finances and want to experience the incredible joy of participating in His purpose on the earth to give generously, not limited by fear and not only having to trust our earning ability and live with anxiety. I am dealing with an opponent trying to stop my spirit of goodness, having the highest sense of significance and security. I'm engaged in a fight. I am not struggling; I'm wrestling because I am in a battle. The Bible has many accounts of wrestling, but none more vivid than that in Job's life. People often want to run from their trials and cocoon themselves in material and physical comforts to stay protected from all danger and harm in this sophisticated Western culture. I desire a life without risk and have tried to defend myself against it at every point by having insurance where I can. Still, some guarantees are not affordable, and we are left with insecurities. I do not approach risk heavy-handedly but assess every risk because if we are not careful, we can suffer at the expense of adventure.

I have personal struggles, but I am engaged in the cosmic wrestling that God calls me to in his kingdom. Perhaps the wrestling's purpose is not the victory but the process, where abandonment throws us into the arms of the loving God, wherein, amid our battles, we encounter his power and grace. The Bible teaches that we develop through our trials when we wrestle with the things that test our faith. We do not fight on our own like a poorly equipped soldier, but instead, I go to battle with prayer, praise and authority that will bring submission over my enemy. Job's world tried to prove that people may only follow God for what they receive from him. Take all that stuff away, and they either turn on God or turn their backs on Him. As the story unfolds, we see that Job not only suffers a dramatic personal loss but that he is also taunted by those close to him. He's in a real battle, wrestling in his mind, spirit and emotions. Yet Job stays faithful to God throughout his trials! What a man.

Kingdom life is about transformation, and I keep asking that the God of our Lord Jesus Christ gives me the spirit of wisdom and revelation so that I may know him better and be as steadfast as Job. I have a sense of 'calling' and optimism that these are the days of the Lord's favour and sensing that God's plans are about to be turned loose in my life, for I hope and have expectations again. It follows that I do not fuss about what's on the table at mealtimes. Whether the clothes in the closet are in fashion, I am trying to relax, not be so preoccupied with getting, so I can respond to God's giving. I am trying not to worry about missing out because our everyday human concerns will contact me if I give my full attention to what God is doing right now and do not get worked up about what may or may not happen tomorrow. God will help us deal with whatever hard things come up when the time comes.

Crisis at Christmas time
Written Monday 12th December 2005

Hard things have come up, and I am finding prayer difficult, but at its most passionate, it's the response to the situations which seem not merely tricky but insoluble.

I am just an ordinary guy in the hands of an extraordinary God, but I have yet to discover that prayer works in the difficult situation we face. Over many years, our cry has been to the Almighty, 'Help us live in prosperity and good health.' Today's prayers are repeated prayers that have been said many times, and the result is still not in yet. Prosper us, dear God, as we continue to live on not enough. Last month and this month, I had to deposit £50.00 into Georgina's account because she is short of living expenses. The second phase of her student loan is not due until January 2006. Living in the capital city needs product planning and strict budgeting. Georgina did that, but three weeks before she expected to come home for Christmas, Georgina has run out of money.

Georgina works one evening at Tottenham Football Club in the common room as a waitress and gets paid monthly. We cannot make outgoing calls on the telephone or watch Sky channels on the television; they have been suspended until we pay the bill. Further services will be lost because I can't pay the bills. I also have not paid the council tax so that I can have some spending money for Christmas. I am one month in arrears with the other bills and am cutting corners to try and have money to buy our son and daughters Christmas presents. Some relatives and friends may not notice that we are broke and cannot afford the simplest gifts and might gossip in disbelief that not even a Christmas card will be sent to them. Our financial situation is so dire that I always worry about bills because income is insufficient to pay all the tabs and live a comfortable life, which means further cuts. I had made more stringent economics, spent less on food and stopped buying clothes. (My wife needs a new coat).

The crisis has driven me to gamble every few lost pound coins found in the house. I played the lottery for a big win; the bet will make me a fortune. I shall win.

Soaring energy bills have plunged us into 'fuel poverty', and it's a constant struggle to pay for heating and lighting our home. Our plight could get even worse because I have no money to pay this month's energy bill, and we are in arrears of £498.48. Forecasters predict the country will be hit by a severe winter, and our suppliers may be cut off or installing gas and electric pre-paid meters may again be advised.

I am in extreme anguish for sinking under a mountain of bills, and the money problems are over our heads, and sadly we will face Christmas being deeply in debt. We plan to spend Christmas at our daughter's home in Manchester and help her with the cost of providing Christmas dinner and a celebration party. It has been some time since the electric oven stopped working and it's still not repaired. The Christmas roast will, therefore, be cooked at Katrina's house. There are no festive decorations in the family home this Christmas, not even a Christmas tree. We hope to create a fun, family, homely environment at Katrina's flat so that we can enjoy the festive season. One of the wife's church sisters, a single homeowner, named Phoebe, took Euphemia to the supermarket at the beginning of the month, bought good quality household products and food, and paid the total cost for the shopping. Phoebe also gave Euphemia £20.00 in a sealed envelope as she continued to express what she feels is God's call on her to help us. Phoebe's giving was exceptional; we praised God for her generosity and kindness and thanked her. People were praying so intently for us, but the result gave us a further period when we still have to endure drought and dryness. It appears it will be a season of difficulties even though God's people prayed for us in unity as one loud voice, so it seems prayer is no magic formula to change situations. God has not yet dispatched an angel to free us entirely supernaturally.

You and I live in the real world. I had a compelling vision and direction straight from the heart of God, so I thought to have growth and move out of not having enough, but we are not automatically exempt from problems and difficulties. If I could only break our poverty cycle; I can feel overwhelmed, but I cannot change the world; I can just change someone else's world and break their cycle of hardship when I learn how to break mine. I rely on getting the total Living Allowance backdated to August 2005 to clear the bills and ease our poverty. Every Christmas, the church reads the dreams God gave to Joseph and the wise men, but I harbour my thoughts or harness them to turn them into reality. Hanging on to my ideas can be hazardous for my health because the gulf between what is and what will one day be can lead to mini-paralysis. The gap is so vast that any effort to bridge it is often seen as pointless. I am impatient with the dream because every step towards it looks like a backwards step, yet everyone might step closer to a breakthrough. I feel in my heart that success will come because I would have reached and changed life's circumstances, so successfully navigating each step would make me happy.

Today is Tuesday 20th December 2005, and mental stress is pursuing me like a predator. The burden of preparing for Christmas on top of the weight of managing day-to-day makes me unable to sleep soundly at night. It has come to a head, for I had had no sleep at all for the last two nights. I am about to go to bed this evening at 7:30 pm, and I took a sleeping pill to prevent my worried mind from sliding into illness because I lack sleep.

Good morning! It's another day, the 21st of December. It's a morning in which I made a shopping list of the bare minimum of food and drinks to buy for Christmas. I have deleted items from the list that seem essential to making Christmas special. That is because we must not overspend; we cannot pay it back. I have pinched money from council tax payments, energy payments and Euphemia's monthly wage; taking into account the 1st January 2006 mortgage payment is the only way to have some cash for Christmas. I did ask the bank to increase my overdraft for Christmas. My account was increased by £40.00 to its maximum limit of £70.00. According to the bank clerk, the overdraft on the joint account is reduced from £1150 to £900 because less money goes through the account report; therefore, further overdraft was not granted. I manipulated some of the money meant for bills, and it has gone towards meeting Christmas expenses. My brother Lascille and my parents gave us cash handouts. £90.00 was given and shared with our children to buy presents that they acknowledged as Mum and Dad giving them money. The children have no idea that it's their uncle and grandparent's gift of money for us so that they can have a present said to have come from us. My parents gave the children money to share equally between themselves, and my brother has wrapped gifts for them to open on Christmas Day.

Just lately, our misfortunes seemed like they have begun to turn a little, but it was just a blip that never developed into anything. I dared to hope for a modest U-turn when I saw I could walk without crutches and found a job. The wife had interviews to work in a nursery with better pay and reduced or full-time hours, but the kind of nursery work may be unsuitable because she was to look after babies of 0-2 years of age on floor mats. So, I am ending the year as I spent most of it, as a weakened figure with a debt burden. 2005 seems to have been the year for natural and personal disasters, earthquakes, floods, droughts, hurricanes and us plummeting faster into decline. There have also been human-made catastrophes with terrorist incidents, wars, and famines, while there is growing evidence that human activity is changing the makeup of the world's climate.

There is no doubt that we live in challenging times, but I cannot take much more of this downturn in our economy. I feel beaten for the second time, but I will not do anything stupid or risk my life again to transform our lives. God can see that the burden will become heavier and heavier in the new year when Tax Credit payments get reduced because it was reviewed, and adjustments will be made from a four-weekly amount of £165 to £128 in January 2006. I have been stressed in prayer for the past week because God felt fit to test us still like this, and I pray to him, wishing and hoping that Christmas and the New Year do not turn out to be old magic and remain unchanged.

After last night's restful, unremembered dreamy night's sleep, I am energized and open my life to good fortune by reflecting this morning on wishes that I would like to see come true. I salvaged £5.00 from the Christmas spending and bought lottery tickets for tonight's draw, Wednesday, 21/12/05. The card has energized me to win the top prize because I have worked out a formula using the letters C. H. R. I. S. T formulated into numbers. I predict that finally, later tonight, I shall obtain the luck and happiness I so sorely need. I could win as much as three million pounds with this ticket, and it won't be just plain luck. If I did not win tonight's, I should try to find the money to play the same numbers for Saturday's draw prize of 15 million pounds. My life has been beset with all kinds of late problems, and I fight with difficulty, especially in our financial situation. Nevertheless, I try my best to remain courageous and hopeful and continue the struggle against adversity, against what appears to be a series of injustices.

I have reached my limit. I feel like throwing in the towel once and for all because I have come to believe that turning my life around is impossible. On the other hand, I am unsure because my calculations have convinced me that I am on the verge of great success. My desperate situation is to be transformed from one day to the next. I will soon witness the incredible transformation of my life. I shall see a modest immediate future change that is long-lived, and my family situation will evolve as I embark on the perfect road to success. Thanks to the digital strategy I developed with the game of chance, it will help me benefit financially. I will experience the happiest Christmas of my adult life because urgent money problems, paying our bills, getting out of debt, not having enough to feed ourselves on and so on will all be resolved. I am forced to survive on less and less each month, which are tough financial straits. However, that will be broken tonight with tonight's predicted giant lottery win. I shall wait until next morning to learn the truth of my sure belief that I shall begin a new and perfect life, blessed with all the money I will ever need. I believe my prediction is accurate;

I cling to that hope, and seeing my past gone, I well up as my present and future begin to change. More specifically, I can see why I was unlucky with money. I saw the solutions to the problems as I risked this gambling spurt on the lottery tonight and probably again on Saturday's draw. I cannot stop myself from saying tonight's lottery jackpot is intended for me. It's a fool-proof guarantee because I prayed about it, and I feel the strangest things to make the dream a reality. Transformation vibrations are running through me, the waves of luck, pleasure and money. And I know it is foolish nonsense, but I have nothing to lose but a fortune to win in that way.

As you know, Christmas is a beautiful time to celebrate the good things life can bring, and it's a particular time for family and friends to get together. First and foremost, Christmas is a Christian festival, celebrating the birth of Jesus and all the hope his life on earth has brought to humankind. Second, it brings the promise of peace and prosperity for all. I think this Christmas brings us personal peace, happiness and well-being. I am looking forward to using our wealth to help to eradicate poverty. If Christmas 2005 is not a prosperous one, the coming of the New Year and Christmas again (2006) is fresh hope for the future and new optimism for life's opportunities. I sincerely hope that we will enter 2006 prosperously or that the year shall bring us prosperity because I fear more government cuts are on the way and breaking even looks further away. I have stepped up looking for a financial recovery plan that does not rely on gambling alone, but high-profile measures must be included to break even in 2006. One such action is using energy more efficiently, turning lights off and lowering the heating setting.

I am looking forward to an eventful 2006 and hope it will be a better year than 2005.

Not So Happy New Year
Written Wednesday 18th January 2006

A familiar greeting at the beginning of 2006 was Happy New Year, and people seemed to say it with sincerity. I began the New Year full of good intentions. Yet, the resolutions so earnestly made have proven difficult to keep. I very much hoped that our lives would be different; Christmas would have been turned on its head to come to terms with ending 2005 as multimillionaires with no money worries.

I woke up from having a nap on the sofa and checked the lottery ticket on Teletext and could not believe it; it was a disappointing result because not a single line had any winning combination of numbers. I did not win any prize money. I managed to fund Christmas spending and did a slight overspend, which would not break the bank for most people, but spending that little more during the festivities was the last straw for us, who are already financially overstretched. I have already made bad decisions in this New Year that plunged us into the previous financial situation. We are choosing between eating and paying the January bills, and nothing has changed there. The oven was fixed, and it cost £65.00, which added to our financial hangover for another year.

The wife has changed her mind and handed in her notice and quit the Christian Centre Nursery job. Euphemia accepted the new nursery position at Caring Kindergartens nursery in Wellingborough, and she has a starting date on Monday 6th February 2006. Work forms such a huge part of Euphemia's life; it's essential that what she does gives her far more than just money. Hopefully, being employed in a separate nursery setting will bring back the sense of self-worth, fulfilment and enjoyment that has disappeared from the Christian Centre Nursery.

I have just learnt that my dad's diagnosis of Parkinson's was incorrect because, after a CT scan, the doctors found Dad has a rare brain disease called Progressive Supranuclear Palsy. Its symptoms mimic those of Parkinson's disease.

Today is Wednesday 18th January, and we will run out of food by the weekend of 21st January. We have only the last few tin stocks and frozen vegetables left to eat. Between us, there is only £40.00 in the bank to last us until 1st February when money will enter our account. We'll have to manage for two weeks on £40.00, which may mean not having a hot one-course meal. Shopping worth £35.00 was bought this weekend, and God only knows if we will ever be able to live other than merely existing. We had bought mainly supermarket's brand value foodstuff. I still hope this year before us will be happy and well for all of us. Of course, harsh reality has, all too often, not offered a new beginning. I need strength beyond mere willpower if I ever know the peace of mind and remain motivated to reach that lifestyle I so crave. God's spirit living in my life provides strength beyond myself and what better time than the first month of the year to reflect and plan.

I have inhibitions, and my behaviour cannot act out eroticism, but a big chunk of my mental furniture has shifted. Hence, I tolerate explicit material that I would not have accepted in 1971, age fifteen, at the height of the Mary Whitehouse campaign against pornography. I had a solid, firm conservative affiliation to it up to a year ago. For many years, I had internet access connected to our home computer, but only this month took delight in watching clips of pornographic images from the World Wide Web.

There is no more significant issue needing consideration than living within our means, and a pleasant new year stretches before us if the unforeseen twists and turns of life do not discourage me from trusting God. I enter the new year by submitting all of my plans to God again and depending on Him to help me accomplish all that He wants me to do. That's because I recognize the unpredictability of life, like that of the National Lottery draw, although I included God at the centre of my planning. In the previous twelve months, I had a mix of experiences that brought great joy or deep grief and sadness. Last year, we had a day of celebration when we celebrated my dad's 80th birthday with a party and mourned my aunt's husband's passing away. Laughter and tears, success and failures, pleasure and pain are all part of life day by day and year by year. As I stand on the threshold of a new year, my prayer of faith and anticipation gives only assurance that God is with us and that He is in charge but does not assure me that the financial security I yearn for will occur this year 2006. I venture into the unknown with him, and if the Lord so will, I shall see a financial peace today or tomorrow. I cannot see an ending to living on not enough day after day without a victory over poverty, and I am willing to entrust our future more to the Lord God to see an end to it.

As I move along on my earthly pilgrimage, I sometimes stumble in the darkness of disbelief. When prayers appear not to be answered, my head tells me to accept the

God-denying theory part of evolution. Darwinists are continually making a form of the realization that there is no life after death. There is no ultimate foundation for ethics, no ultimate meaning for our existence, no free will for being here - and now, is filled with the experience of purpose and hope if we have faith in God. The indwelling Holy Spirit in my open heart and mind has only assured me of a blessed eternity and that life on earth for us humans is a social obligation. People live in a problem-filled world and should be standing in line to grab the offer of a future free of difficulties, sorrow and pain. Instead, we are promised a life of fellowship with God in a place the Bible calls home with no issues; heaven is an area with no more tears. A future full of suffering, regret and anguish won't disappear in this world, but a home can be reserved in heaven, the place of eternal joy and peace with God. I act in what I think is the 'call' of God and step out in faith, but when I approach a list of difficulties of a personal nature day by day, they swamp the day that the Lord has made, and it's hard to rejoice and be glad in it like the psalmist Says. Psalm 118, v24.

I thought that I had immunity from the effect of troubles because in God, I trust, and I look to experience measureless blessings. Why is it so hard for me to be filled with celebrations of God's goodness and mercy during trouble and pain when the psalmist had no problem rejoicing? I often wait for God to display a great answer to my prayer before I feel like singing His praises, but God does not owe us any miracles. He does not need to do anything to prove His greatness. God has already given us an incredible display of His power in His creation. He has conducted the most miraculous transaction known to humankind, bringing us from spiritual death to spiritual life. When I look at the calendar, our circumstances allow me to mark off 'bad days'; although I try to receive each day with joy, some days end in disappointments. My trust in God sometimes gets blocked by my fear that I cannot see that God's deliverance will come as we try to live our life. Our obstacles appear huge when I look back and reassure myself by recalling what God has already done on our behalf, especially saving my life from a road accident. That backward look gives me more confidence that God will deliver. I have come to learn that instead of dwelling on all the unpleasant possibilities that lie ahead or happen day-to-day, I should thank God for the day and enjoy what we can now and entrust the future to Him. Whatever God permits, He will provide and won't let us be tested without giving us all the grace we need, the Bible says. Life has continuously been hard for us, but it's much harder for some than for others. Putting my trust in God does little to change that. Nothing in the Bible promises us a free pass merely because we are believers. Some of our wounds may not heal, and some of our deficiencies may not be corrected during our lifetime. They may even get worse, as I have seen in respect of finances.

Anticipating what God has in store for me can put a smile in my heart. Hope gives me poise and lets me live with inner strength because I know that I will be dramatically different from now. I walk with my eyes to the ground and take heart in what God has in store for me to lift me from feeling defeated. I'll live today with the courage God gives me and make what I can of my afflictions. I'll try to rejoice because all that degrades and limits me is only temporary. It will be gone –some of it sooner rather than later. I have a living hope in the risen Christ which suggests that God's glorious best for me lies ahead. A film director, Woody Allan, has been quoted as saying, 'If only God would give me some clear sign, like making a large deposit in my name at a Swiss bank!' One of the reasons I found for not believing God often boils down to wanting God to do something to prove Himself. Sadly, I miss seeing the countless things He has already done in making a to-do list for God.

On A Knife's Edge
Written Friday 17th March 2006

We are on a knife's edge following the regular convention of struggling to manage day by day. We are severely overstretched, and it has become an emergency because money has run out, and it's two weeks before the end of the month when payment will enter our bank account again. Before that, we have to live on nothing. I say to heaven, "Why do you do this to me? I do not understand. Oh God, how are we to live for the next two weeks without money and food? We have got by to this day, 17th March and surely the policy of 'Give us this day our daily bread' should not rely on getting by from one day to the next on hope alone."

We had a shortage before, where cash and food had been absent, and we used cheques to tide us over, but it was only a gap of a week then we received government benefits money and Euphemia's wage. This time, it's two weeks before we see money through the bank account, and cheques cannot be used because funds would not be available; the cheques would bounce. What are we to do? There is no housekeeping, and for the second time, I have been denied the Living Allowance benefit without reports from the expert who knows about my disabilities. I am still fighting the decision without going through the appeal process because we live on a shoestring. I had only one plan to help us get by: defeat the government's rejection of my claim through no expert opinion regarding my disabilities. I suspected the verdict to come when the pressure to live day-to-day is at a peak, and the money would ease the pressure-cooker conditions under which we operate. Things are boiling, and not having the extra government money means there is no release of pressure or the flames' quenching fuelled by not enough. It was a culpable lack of foresight that I did not plan a strategy in the event of losing the claim for Living Allowance. There is a reliance on faith and hope even though we are patently very close to an outright emergency on everything that's to do with the need to make payments or knowing from where our next meal is to come. Despite prayer, hope, and belief, many years of promises to beat this condition of struggling day in and day out are still unbeaten.

It's destroying us, and I can guarantee nothing, for even with the strength of prayer, the condition has not eased. I feel better for praying, but so far, it has not changed the situation around. It registers upon my consciousness that I am failing because I have made myself completely unemployable. The responsibility for feeding and keeping a roof over our heads is mine, not the State's. Instead of claiming handouts, I would like society to offer me a hand up, becoming employed again. I lack the courage to believe that everything can be different one day, yet I should never think about giving up hope.

I feel imprisoned in a grey cloud that is becoming harder and harder to struggle through, and I am challenging my fate and thought I could get out of this and succeed. Instead, I think of the future and cannot relax. I wake each morning experiencing some uneasiness, restlessness and dissatisfaction with the world. I hope that the series of adverse events, which brought more than our share of bad luck, is at an end by the time we pass through this challenging calendar month of March 2006. I am desperate to figure out how to get through these days to experience moments I feel spiritually gifted, God willing. I think I am here to do great things with my life and consciousness. In those euphoric moments, I become free of failure and failings. I feel that something astounding is about to happen because I possess extraordinary and rare traits. Am I dreaming? I have visions of two weeks of being impoverished, yet some thoughts come to the fore that appear to be light at the end of the tunnel. A fantastic reward from heaven will put a lot of money into our bank account. I continuously expect this money to come to break the gloom because I certainly know deep inside that wealth would be a pleasure I could relish one day.

You will soon learn if I did the right thing by listening to my intuition to have a flutter on the lottery instead of buying a loaf of bread and a litre carton of milk with the last of the money. The realizations of a wish I have about the upcoming jackpot made me gasp at the magnitude and enormity of what, in a sense, cannot be described. My life and future may soon be illuminated beyond imagination because spontaneously spilling forth in a brilliant rush is a random sequence of miraculous blessings. My sincerest wishes are rapidly emerging, delivering into my vast world wealth, material riches that defy belief.

I speak endlessly, wanting to get the privilege of power over money as if it was raining down on me, but the stroke of luck of my life, which is the kingdom of the privileged, is again delayed. The lottery jackpot was not mine, but I did win a minimum prize of £10.00, making it possible to buy a few more things than a loaf and a litre of milk. The essential requirement regarding our dietary intake will probably be missing, and there will be no surprise that the family loses weight. Our plight drove me to tearful despair because I am suffering from the anguish that does not allow one to see the planned future. I feel more durable than ever to carry the 'can' because I rely on God to keep us in good health and have the kind of humane system that can keep fighting the intruders that prevent good health. I feel I am in a dream state, watching someone else's life at the moment because I had done the right things and expected problems and worries to move away and finally to forget about them, and growth should no longer be led by unattainable desire. Although we have plummeted to an all-time low financially, I am waiting for tomorrow, and when tomorrow comes, I will wait for the next day and see what comes. I get faithfully caught up in a pre-ordained natural consequence of the world's close systems, making things happen because of things that have happened before. I did not prove to myself or anyone that I had sorted out my affairs because I am carried along in some predetermined faith bubble. The self seated in my brain looks out through my eyes, wondering about free will because I cannot seem to do anything that will set us free from this circumstance. My conscious self inside me made decisions on governing, like a political person, but being faith-a-list-tic justifies the idea that nothing I can do will make a difference since my faith relies on a religious belief system. Not just the next two weeks, but the course of my immediate future should directly be transformed due to the transformation of the way my destiny unfolds. I expect a new and much more beautiful life because the problem of having to live on the breadline has been tormenting me for so long, and it can be resolved. I continue by the grace of God to be forever hopeful and work to see my life ignite with marvellous achievements and tremendous rewards. There is the most fabulous period ahead that my life has ever known. I am filled with unbelievable pending prosperity and financial breakthroughs that are nothing short of miraculous. For the first time in ages, I can see things beyond where life changes completely. I know that things will work out in my favour and an astonishing manner because I have never stopped fighting courageously the streak of persistent and tenacious lousy luck, which has been following me around for much too long. I see through the darkness of the next two weeks, just like watching a film in a cinema. My visions are transparent and, surprisingly, should turn out accurate. I shall write again and explain how we got through on a knife's edge.

Today is Monday 3rd April 2006. We have made it through two weeks of food drought, but it's not over yet. There are more periods of the exact prediction because we cannot spend the necessary money to buy enough food when there are plenty of demands on the month's wage. It makes me want to yell, "For God's sake, stop this ever-increasing pressure of food drought on our cash-strapped family. Give us the ability to pay what we owe and meet our needs to live on enough!"

I borrowed money from our son, who gets a weekly wage since the retail store take-over by J.D Sports. I also used his EMA money. Those funds made it possible to have some food in the house until we completely ran out on Tuesday 28th March, when it was hard to find the day-to-day ingredients to prepare meals. All the food stocked in the house was entirely gone by Tuesday 28th March; both the fridge and freezer were empty except for half a litre of milk and a few slices of bread. There was nothing left in the cupboard except a half bag of flour, cooking oil, salt, a quarter box of cereal, some tea bags, drinking chocolate and less than a quarter bag of sugar. Our last meal came out of the barren kitchen on Monday 27th March - sausages, potatoes, gravy and sweet corn.

I wait for the forces in the cosmos that God has put around his creation to begin to act in my circumstances, and I ask the help of heavens such as the likes of angels, saints, Jesus and God himself to respond soon. The next day, we were unsure where our next meal would come from unless we chanced using the cheque book as ready cash.

From the date of our son Jonathan's 17th birthday, on 21/02/06, I funded four of his driving lessons with a driving school costing £19.50, and after that, Jonathan used part of his weekly wage to have instruction with the driving school. On Tuesday, 28th March, Jonathan had his first lesson in the family car with me. There was no additional cost for car insurance. Only an excess of £400 applies if he causes an accident. As soon as the banks closed, I used the chequebook at the supermarket. I spent £127.30 on shopping and £31.50 on car fuel. Euphemia's wages are paid directly to her bank account on the last working day of the month; no more waiting for her work cheques to clear as in her previous job. Something is seeing us through, and it will be credited to my belief system, which will transform my misfortunes. I pray, and it's like I have put in an order for the deliverance. I ask when it will be delivered. There is no answer, but I am sure that the message has reached the supplier.

Hooray! £840.40 was deposited into Euphemia's account on 31/03/06 from her new job at Caring Kindergartens nursery. £195 pay the latest loan and cheques that were debited from the joint statement. However, the need for the money has risen; not only does it need to give Euphemia spending power on things that are for vanity, such as make–up and hairdressers. They make her feel good, but the money is also required to replace worn-out or too small garments and so on, and buy a further month of food and petrol. Catering for life's sudden demands is stretching the money far too much. However, Euphemia's closest uncle died, and the money will have to reach to buy a wreath and pay for travel. The funeral is to take place on Friday 7th April 2006, and she is to attend the church service and the ceremonial burial in London where he had lived. It's a sad time; it's always hard to know just what to say, but my loving thoughts and deepest sympathy were expressed to Euphemia to help her through the grief.

Dark clouds still linger, and the misery of just getting by has spread into another month, April. I glimpsed in my imagination; it will suddenly come to an end. The latest victim of the financial crisis that has been hitting us is Georgina. Katrina and Robert are scraping by too and are looking to marry in late 2007. They hope for a financial turnaround by 2007 to ease their cash-strapped situation. They all know what it's like to have nothing, and I always want to mollycoddle Georgina because she is a single girl, alone in London's capital city and having to budget for three months on a student loan not be easy. Her last payment for term 2005-6 is due on Monday, 24/06/06, and as of 29th March, I sent Georgina money to buy shopping and pay off the minimum from her credit card bill. Georgina's used car has made it extra tricky to budget, and thank goodness it is roadworthy. Georgina has no money left in the account that pays her student accommodation house rent on the 1st of April, and I cannot help. When the action is taken to recover the rent, it will mean paying it for her, not her, because the working spouse is the guarantor.

All utility gas, electricity and water prices have rocketed, included council tax. The mortgage payments are not affordable, and we struggle with that. Euphemia is working long hours from 7:30 am; she can arrive no later than 7:50 am and finishes work at 5:30 pm. When the rota is operational, it's an alternating week where she works from 8:30 am to 6 pm. Our monthly bills stop us from investing any money or doing any travelling other than commuting. Euphemia's new job is going well, but I still worry about her job security. I would like her to cut her hours, but it's not an option because we need the money, and even early retirement may not be possible. The government rose the retiring age to sixty-eight years old; it was previously sixty-five years. Euphemia has stopped contributing to her pension fund to use the money for today's living. Home loan payments, feeding ourselves, other bills and debts to pay are making work-life balance a real issue. Euphemia has no actual downtime with work hours being so long, and she has social commitments most evenings in the week. Four out of five evenings, Euphemia's time is spent learning at the college or a hobby. Fitting them into a typical day makes it one long day. Euphemia gets up at 6:15 am and does not get to relax at home until 9:15 pm most weeknights.

I have made some most ill-judged decisions in my life, and it's because I am so busy focusing on how we are to get by that I burn the midnight oil working out a strategy for the next day's shuffle of needs, which has always been hugely financial. As a result, I become tired during the daytime. On top of all the other worries that can affect our health, the most worrying thing is spending less time keeping fit and eating less healthy than we would like to. I have a 24-hour monitor on my arm to check my blood pressure. I have reported to MHRA on the yellow card scheme about the medical side effects of my taking anti-psychotic medication. I was experiencing prolonged, painful erections, and my sexual desire has increased. I first recognized I was frustrated when Euphemia was not co-noodling with me at the beginning of 2006. I spent New Year's Eve night alone out on the town.

Going out to pubs and clubs by myself felt strange. It was an alien world compared to the cocooned world of being with my partner; I love relaxing at home with the family. I did not like the environment of noisy pubs and clubs, and I would have instead taken sanctuary in a church and do churchly things. To see the world of raw, bare indecent exposure in skimpy garments is too revealing to a man of Godly decency and principles in public unless it's in the privacy in a private place. I explained to Euphemia that I spent a dull time out and was not feeling like going out without her by my side. We went to a quiet pub a few days later. Euphemia revealed she felt trapped by episodes of abuse that had happened in her life, and it was her fault. She feels she has a low libido and only feels loved by God. She said she is ashamed of her body except for her face and people never really loved her; they just wanted her for what they could get. I understood better not to pressure her for a physical relationship as her story moved me, and my moist eyelashes dipped in the fluid built up around my eyes. I encouraged her to talk to a professional counsellor, and I learnt Euphemia has the number of a counsellor given to her by her doctor going back to 2004. After the sad talk, Euphemia promised she would open up to a counsellor to get her life back to moving forward because none of it was her fault.

Debt Merry - Go - Round
Written Tuesday 9th May 2006

We are forced to trust God totally, and some days the best we can do is just hang on by the skin of our teeth. We are just hanging on and not letting go of the rope. He's the God who raised the dead, and we look to Him to pull us through when we do not have the answers to manage diminishing resources. I cannot see how to move forward; all I can do is look up and trust God to pull us through.

I am in a tight spot today, Tuesday 9th May, and I hang on by a thread and shuffle debts and paying bills to give us enough for providing food. We are on our final warning before the Council takes us to court if another payment gets missed. The same goes for utilities. We will be forced to have pre-paid meters, or our suppliers may cut off supply. I make excuses for God to myself for not transforming this difficult time. There is a massive gap between our ultimate destination and having sufficient to live. The excuses pile up like dirty dishes in a sink; it feels like it takes God too long to make provisions, and I make excuses for Him. The Psalmist wrote, 'No good thing will He withhold from them that walk uprightly.' (Psalm 84:11 KJV) These days are complicated, and days will continue to pass as we pursue our goals.

The days passed have added up to months, and months became years, and it's tempting to think the amount of time God is taking to do his part is too long. I have taken the first small step to the ultimate big goals by surfing debt merry-go-round, looking for open doors to lift us off the bottom. I continue to seek out material resources to get by. One financial slip has spelt disaster as we are over-committed as I look for freedom from commercial pressures. The debt-to-income ratio is too high, and we have to choose between paying the bills and eating. Each month, I cry, "The resources are not there to see us through week by week." We live day-to-day on borrowed money from our son's weekly wage to get by. The struggle is immense; we have no idea if tomorrow we'll be able to eat once the mortgage gets paid, I shuffle bill payments to prioritise orders, fill the car tank with fuel, and the cheque for £130.35 for this month's shopping is deducted. What's left? Nothing's left because the rest of the income is retained for direct debits. The bank charges can often exceed £100 per month for going over the overdraft limit, including costs for returning unpaid direct debits.

The human body needs food, and I have a massive shortfall to buy the required shopping essentials to feed the body. There is no money in the bank account; we are in the harshest period so far. It's the most extended drought season we have had since I relied on a willingness to accept whatever comes, knowing that we'll win and come out stronger by God's grace. Somebody needs to address the other side of believing in God for no other reason than to uphold reality. I have put a lot of biblical input into the difficulties and pressures we are enduring. However, no amount of biblical information exempts one from struggles. God promises no bubble of protection. If I could ask guys like Job, Joseph, Daniel and Paul, I would become acquainted with ancient tough times forging authentic characters. Instead, my flimsy theology gets exchanged for a set of convictions that enable me to accept whatever comes as the bottom falls out, and life tries to pound me into a corner of doubts and disbelief. We continue to be in a storm, and I begged to be taken out of it because I am physically and emotionally exhausted. Day after day, life gets tougher; we keep our eyes on deliverance or to be able to outlast the season of the storms and grow stronger. Each day, we only draw strength from God within, which restores hope by putting the problem into perspective and making the day-to-day struggle bearable.

Today is Sunday 2nd July 2006, and the struggles are becoming more and more robust. The battles are following us through the calendar months, and they are not confined to spring. The difficulties have entered the summer month of July 2006 too. I continue to write more of the same struggles in our lives, which do not allow us to taste the pleasures of life yet, like a holiday. I find it hard to believe someone like me - well-brought-up - has a reasonable intelligence level and is sensible, yet it has been so stupid to get caught up in poverty. I work hard, but my stupidity was my attempt to end my life, and its consequences have led to tough struggles. The odd flutter on the National Lottery is causing an addiction. I need to win big, but I love the high thrill of even a measly winning, even if it is only £10.00. So I played again and lost some of that precious win. However, the promise of a big success around the corner and repurchase a ticket is a bit of excitement in my life. It seems a simple way to pass a dull time that occupies my conscience when circumstances are unchanged.

In the previous two months, May to June 2006, we have seen my parents move into sheltered accommodation. I began to work as a volunteer at Together, the mental aftercare service for people recovering from mental illness. Jonathan has passed his driving theory test. Greater and greater hardship is sparking emergency measures, and it's all to do with not having sufficient income or money in reserve. The family tax credit has failed to enter our bank account for June 2006, and the bank will hit us hard with bank charges because of failed direct debits and interest charges. No payment schedule was on the computer system for June. Nobody in the government department could tell me why this was so, but they began investigating the problem from the inquiry made about the missing payment.

Georgina has moved to a new student house to live with four female students. The rent is £281.00 per month. £607.79 is required for the deposit and guarantor credit search before she can take up the tenancy. The new rent for the house is needed on 1st August, and Georgina is broke. No money exists anywhere, but somehow, we need to help Georgina through the summer months until her student loan arrives in the autumn. Katrina has returned to university to study part-time for a primary teaching degree, and she is a student at Hope University Liverpool.

Unimaginable hardship has been upon us for months, and the strains are higher than before. All the time, I pray for the burden to ease, but time and time again, it's an increase of the load, and it's the direct result of our prayers. It's in the hands of God for the trauma of not having enough to live on to ease, though I do not pray so sincerely anymore because it triggers depression. I live my days mindful of God and his purposes and exercise the right things to do according to my conscience, knowledge and grace. I shall do all in my power to try and create the good life that money can bring, but I know any further commitments on the same income and the strain will be too high. The entire future of our finance probably rests on some certainty that it is to materialize in the next few weeks, or I must continue hoping and relying on luck and moderately praying for the items of my dreams. I am persistent in asking God's help in private silent prayers and believing those things of the heavens, like angels, saints, Jesus and the forces in the cosmos, that God has explored uniformly all around his creation to help. We are again going through a very challenging time in our lives, and it's essential to look for the positive and faith in a more prominent being and placing an order for deliverance from the God who knows everything. I will credit my belief system for suddenly transforming my fortunes. I will still be somewhat surprised because I had waited so long and lost my heart sometimes. I think prayers are being answered at a time when I least expect it. The universe came into existence from God's big bang, and the key to making circumstances alter for my benefit is not merely by wishing but to think positively and order hope to arrive. I believe this new approach always remains positive in the face of hopelessness and call it to transform back to hopefulness. I have ordered hope, luck, and faith to arrive like a mail-order hamper into my situation, and in this way, I will expect it to arrive. In some respects, placing requests in prayer is like putting it to myself because it involves directly acknowledging what I want, which spurs me on to achieve it in God's name, being that the working of the grace is within me. There is undoubtedly a supernatural or mystical element involved to activate the prayer.

I accept that everything is one in the cosmos and that I can connect with the entirety's power by prayer. By maintaining faith, hope and love in some amount, the energy from these three things regenerate a positive attitude. My soul, which is like inner loving motivation, is making me do everything in my power to bring about a fantastic comeback or have a life of abundance which will be seen through this new approach. I have adopted a new, positive thinking approach to turning my life around, and philosophies and ideas help make things go my way because I visualise my goal, which helps make it come true. In the randomness of stuff in the cosmos, the ethos is to have a definite sense of direction. I am doing what is needed to get through difficult times - pray, positive thinking, belief, hope - and focusing on one's goal and visualizing it helps it come true, and it certainly seems it will work for me, thank God.

A glimmer of hope has come. The banks increased our overdraft by another £150 to £1300. Standard Life Insurers' endowment is being floated on the stock exchange and makes cash or shares pay-out of around £900 to its members. I have signed the papers to have the cash payout, and Euphemia will hold on to her shares to see the value grow. At the moment, the actual amount the shares are worth is unknown until 17th July. The Welfare Rights Office has advised me to continue with the struggle to restore Living Allowance. I have a hearing due at the appeal tribunal on Tuesday 15th August 2006, and if successful, our finances can be stable rather than in continual turmoil.

I look physically more able-bodied today but more emotional as it feels it's a typically lower mood than when I claimed in October 2005. I understand that the tribunal will be looking at how I submitted the new claim in October 2005 and not how I am now. I do not know if you can visualize when my writing tells of our literal condition of not having enough to live okay. We are near breaking point where fresh air is the only thing we can take without occurring costs. Be sure of one thing; I am not exaggerating what's happening to us. It's nothing short of miraculous that we can hold out.

Days become weeks, weeks turn to months, and we are still on edge, and the scale has tipped to hit the ground hard, but so far, this chancy living is soon to be balanced out on the level. For the past few months, there were times when we had absolutely nothing to live on, and chance stepped in with a temporary break in the circumstances and changed it for a moment, and the scale tipped the other way gradually. Sometimes, something suddenly brings temporary relief like fantastic foodstuff and petrol money from my mother, and we were able to eat, and soon the scale was back to a steep tilt on the edge of life, which is unbalancing us. I have almost unconsciously created my life due to the upset, and my inner expectations remain strong because prayer is beginning to help. Problems solved? Hardly. It's not long before next month when it comes to a complication increasing the crisis deeper.

So it had been, but beyond the next few days, our lives will change completely, and it's due to having a permanent change for good because something extraordinary happened late last night, 1st July 2006. I can't explain why, but last night I was attracted by an irresistible force and sat down at the edge of the bed. Despite the lateness of the hour, I then went downstairs and made a firm decision to find a peaceful solution to this serious problem that is tormenting me almost day and night at the moment. I spent long hours downstairs concentrating and working on what I could do, but I had trouble connecting with creative thoughts. I was about to stop when I suddenly had a psychic flash due to fatigue. A tremendous financial windfall chance is imminent, probably it's the Standard Life pay-out, and signs of renewal in the whole of our lives are taking place. I have adopted a new positive thinking approach that adapts to turn my life around, and philosophies and ideas help make things go my way. We've struggled all our lives, but soon we can taste the pleasure of life.

Today is Saturday 8th July 2006, and things are very tough on us, but soon, when I put down the pen and stop recalling events, the good life that money can bring will form my re-call to take up the pen again.

Getting the life I want
Written Wednesday 18th October 2006

Three months ago, I was pretty far short of having the power within myself to change my life for the better and fulfil my potential. The power of positive visualization has created strong confidence and stops me from blaming the world and other people for everything wrong in my life. The sad truth is that it's probably easier to handle myself as a victim than take control and change my life for the better and fulfil my potential. Neither time nor people standstill, and I wanted something to change, and I accept that I have to change something. I continually keep our relationship renewed and always search for a job because we are financially stretched. My head's internal voice strangely gives me all sorts of messages; I became aware of it when I was critical and negative. Reassuring tones in the voice create a more favourable result because my aim in my mind is to do something every day, however small, towards achieving my goals. I am listening to intuitions and taking a few minutes to track my action towards my goals. I regularly imagine what it would be like to live the life of my dreams. I base my approach on getting what I need according to the best Christian-Jewish ethics and doing what I enjoy and won't harm anybody else.

Bill payments have outstripped our income, and we relied on my father-in-law's allotment produce and my mother's cash hand out of £30 a week to feed ourselves. The past months have been hard, and we pulled through to today financially because Standard Life's pay-out of £900 was a moderate help. My parents sold their house in September and now live in a modern sheltered accommodation. Mother and Dad gave each of us, their five offspring, £3000. Even with this money, we aren't out of the woods, and I still cannot live modestly.

I failed to win the appeal to restore my Living Allowance. DWP says that I was not virtually unable to walk, which was the criteria to secure the benefit. I approached two banks to take out credit to have some joy in life by spending on my desires and not living to pay bills. I asked the Abbey Bank and Yorkshire Bank to consider me for a credit card even though I am unemployed. I told them of my unpaid volunteering job. I have joined the 'now' culture that is not used to saving for things like my parents and grandparents were. Credit cards were the way to get the money as they were freely available if you were working. I assumed I'd be treated as a particular case because I may get a job soon and because I have been banking with both banks for many years. Abby Bank offered me a credit card with a limit of £1900, and Yorkshire Bank offered a credit card subject to seeing current wage slips. I took out credit, believing God's universe would not beat us further into the ground, for it's time to be lifted out of the miry clay of just getting by. I am using credit to make living comfortable; I have been fighting to live without borrowing on credit, but spending a lifetime in the red is expected to be the norm. It's just the way things are these days to have any reasonable standard of living. There is never any money to save, and we budget like mad with most of the money going towards paying bills. We cannot enjoy a comfortable existence without extra borrowing. It is perilous to have taken out credit and not be sure we can always meet the minimum repayments, but this will give us a modest living. I have attracted the resource I need to change, and a wish-fulfilment message to God was the backbone to good luck.

The Together organization's volunteering job has offered me an interview to get on the payroll as a Social Care Worker.

I was successful at the interview, and today, 19th October 2006, a letter arrived confirming the provisional offer subject to satisfactory references. I will be contacted to agree on a starting date with the customary six months' probationary period.

Autobiography Resumed
Written 10th March 2010

I paused for almost three and a half years from writing my autobiography. Then, once employed as a Social Care Worker supporting adults with mental health needs, within that period, in 2007, my dad passed away.

From November 2006 to August 2009, I had a very successful career with Together's charity organisation: working for well-being. However, my ambition to earn a more significant wage and carry more responsibility to feel even greater fulfilment in my work led me to actively look for a new job from September 2008 to August 2009.

The initial impetus was to have substantially higher take-home pay. Although I was employed, modest living was not achieved without borrowing. Having employment, credit was easy to obtain, even though I realized it's not affordable on my current income.

Euphemia trusts me, and she warned me and said, "We must try to save up; it's not a good idea to borrow so heavily against our wages". I cannot sustain the repayment and adequately provide for housekeeping and bills. I wanted to make home improvements and pay for our daughter's wedding, and I went against my wife's best advice because the whole nation seems to be borrowing instead of saving to get what they want instantly. I sensed something would have to give in the economy, and the government will have to give out help to us who legitimately can show what the money was used for, like home improvements and essential projects. I borrowed from seven creditors, including my mortgage provider, which increased our debt from £20,000 to £60,000.

In 2007-2009, Britain's debt crisis deepened and caused a Credit Crunch and an economic recession which is still being felt today 10/03/2010, although it is being said that there was growth in the economy. The country is beginning to come out of recession. For us, it meant we were in no position to repay the jumbo loans. I had over-stretched ourselves, and it was irresponsible lending by the banks to have been too flexible.

I started my new job on 24/08/2009 in Kettering after months of interviews throughout Northamptonshire, Bedfordshire, Buckinghamshire, and even in the London borough of Enfield. The employer, a brand-new social housing service supporting the mentally ill, employed me as a senior community support coordinator.

After losing this challenging and rewarding job following my first months' probation review, my mental health deteriorated swiftly. All the evidence points to genetic makeup and the stresses of the past years multiplied to give an explosive reaction to schizophrenia. The country's economic winds may be changing, but we still have to batten down the hatches because the things that affect us are still blowing in the wind. Our whole household income comes from government subsidies because we both have health problems and cannot go back to work at the moment.

Euphemia was diagnosed with clinical depression and is on medication. She has been off work since June 2009 and is no longer in receipt of Statuary Sick Pay. She claims Employment Support Allowance like me, and on top of that benefit, I get Disability Living Allowance and Council Tax exemptions. The years had been bitterly stressful, and I blame myself for seeing Euphemia fall into depression because I did not follow her advice on our economic recovery. As well as having problems with her employment workload, my selfish, self-centred expression of my feelings of our relationship in these books has shown torn threads. We argued and found it very difficult to move forward when we dipped back into the books and read the stories directed at Euphemia, which described her as apathetic. Her voice was seldom heard, challenging what I wrote. Her feelings were hurt, she read the writing out of context, dramatizing deliberately to inflate the situation out of proportion, which is entirely wrong, and I avoid doing that.

Writing about my love life was meant for my partner to acknowledge my needs and desires. The key to my book is total honesty, as seen through my eyes, which may seem harsh. "I make apologies for hurting your feelings, darling, and I am sorry that I did not listen to you more and take on board your life experiences to make us live more compatible lives." Though she forgives, I cannot forget how I have hurt her and myself. We continue to live in pain when we recall painful memories. We are in the twenty-eighth year of our marriage, and each time compatibility is raised, I know that I have to find a way forward, and when I can't see a future for us, I know that I have to find a way on because it's not the correct sequence of events. I love her; Euphemia has put up with me and my harsh criticisms, and in today's reality, she is a gem, a gem of a wife and mother, and I couldn't bear to lose her. However, there comes the point when we have to stop this repetitive thing that attempts to wreck our marriage.

So far, we have relied on the foundation of our love to remain keen to turn things around. It's like a deep raw wound that just goes on weeping and weeping, and we have both come to the point of giving up on our marriage. It's emotionally draining, and we were again concerned about our compatibility and money worries. It seems when a good patch of stability is formed in our relationship, and our finances are looking positive, opposing forces force their way in again, acting upon the situation and knocking us back. Almost as soon as stability comes, it is followed by a strain that is pulling at it. When it snaps, we have a knockback.

We are happy today in our relationship, and Euphemia tells me to stop worrying about a lack of money. One main thing that continues to cause havoc in the money worries and affects our relationship is a repetitive thought that I can't control. "Karl, you were not wealthy when we got married, and it did not matter then, and it still does not matter now, as long as we are together." I want to make up for not going away on a honeymoon. She deserves much more than I have given, and my worst nightmare is Euphemia will leave me. She is a perfect woman, and her perseverance is admired; she could have left me. "Darling, words cannot express my gratitude for the un-measurable love and caring you have shown to me. I have been foolish to quarrel to such an extent that we sometimes feel like giving up. I want you to know that I share wholeheartedly the vision that binds us together." To quote the vows, 'For better, for worse, in sickness, in health, till death do us part, according to God's holy law."

In 2009, caused by marital discontent, I committed adultery. The problems of today are not related to our relationship. One has to change the mortgage to interest-only payments and the government paying part to our mortgage provider directly. We have not the choice to decide to keep the mortgage on part-repayment.

The scheme is not in place yet, and we owe £2,008.00 arrears on the mortgage, which we have to pay our lender in agreed instalments. We have no vehicle/ investments to pay the capital of £82,000 at the end of the mortgage term, which only has eleven years left to run. We continue to struggle to meet our daily living costs, including bill payments, and give our lender some money for the arrears taken from our government benefit payments. The maintenance issues of the property are a cause for concern. We have already spent a lot of money on home improvements in 2007-2008. Still, there is a significant structure fault in the lintel on the upper floor. I am discussing with the house insurance company to accept a valid claim under the policy's accidental damage to the property.

Regarding Payment protection on the mortgage, the application was declined. I complained about the length of time it took the insurers to inform me of the six-month decision, and I argued I had mis-sold the policy. The Financial Ombudsman may have to be involved because the insurance company has not responded to my letter yet.

Psychotic Episode 2009
Written 10th February 2010

I have had chronic paranoid schizophrenia and multiple hospitalisations for psychiatric issues throughout the decades and successfully emerged from them. I had a lengthy stable period on a drug called Aripiprazole, and when taken in conjunction with an antidepressant called Duloxetine, I respond favourably quite quickly to it when psychotic.

Before the psychotic episode, which had me sectioned under the Mental Health Act on 13th October 2009, I knew that the stress level I was under was high. I felt I could cope; it was not uncommon for people who take on challenges that stretch their capability. I needed to succeed in the new job with a supervisory role because I was up for the challenge, and it raised our income considerably and brought overwhelming job satisfaction. I thought the length of stabilization of the disease made me immune to relapses because the medication works well, and I had never stopped taking it. But when I began to have disproportionate stress levels to everyday events, I had no control over them, and the things I should have been able to deal with seemed out of my control. I began to lose my ability to interpret reality, became quite suspicious, and saw people discrediting me. I was a service user in the Mental Health Care service, and it seems it was involved in a conspiracy that had stressed me. I was not coping adequately in my new job linked to the mental health service as their clients were users of the services too. My employment then appeared like a set-up experiment to test my competency as a known schizophrenic working with people with mental health problems even though I showed no symptoms of this illness myself. I had successfully worked in that field previously for three years. My employer was a qualified psychologist working in psychoanalysis and a psychiatric nurse and social worker. A psychiatrist would come to visit clients, but I believed that I was being observed too. I tried to challenge my notions, but it seemed I was collecting more evidence through reasonable, natural suspicions, which then grew to be paranoid. I became strained when all my work appeared like an analytic exercise, and I was being employed to be studied. I began to lose effective communication over the phone and mixed my private and home life with work. My pronunciations of names over the phone to a good personal friend I have romantic involvement. I muddled her name on an evening off when I misdialed her number to my employer's work mobile. I thought I said, 'Hello Marie,' but it may have sounded to them as, 'Hello Mary,' an employee with the company. The employer did not mention anything to me about it the following day; I was instantly dismissed and escorted off the premises based on poor communication skills, as discussed two days before on my first months' probation review report.

I was devastated and did not deserve to be treated like I had committed a criminal offence and be kicked off the premises. The stress signs of psychosis appeared; I lost the ability to relax or concentrate, was forgetful, lacked sleep, and had unusual perceptions. I talked in ways that were difficult to understand in part because I stammered excessively. I could not compose myself to fight or argue that it was an unfair dismissal. My main concern became signing on to receive the highest government benefit I was entitled to have. I was told I needed a sick note from my GP to get Employment Support Allowance, or else I would only qualify for Job Seeker's Allowance, which gets paid at a lower rate. The GP gave me a sick note to excuse me from seeking work for four weeks due to acute stress-related illness.

Within a week of losing my job, my wife noticed a profound change in me, which at first did not seem to fit the recent paranoid schizophrenic relapse, and one more week later, I was hospitalised. Euphemia saw puzzling behaviours within me. There were calls to organize me and the paper trail of all the letters and documents that came in the post, which I kept filed away going back to the year 2000, and a voice in schizophrenia insisted I de-clutter the house. As soon as they came into my head, I took on tasks and swiftly threw out the items to prevent chaos in my life and the cosmos. As a member of the universe, I needed to do my part to get organized. I started tidying my wardrobe and the housekeeping files and presented myself neatly in appearance to look more respectful than 'cool'. Our home being clean was a way to prevent a collapse of order. I sensed a tragedy in our world and the spiritual round.

Euphemia went to Clarendon House (Community Mental Health Headquarters in Kettering) to arrange for a psychiatrist to come out to assess me. Although she stressed I was not well, she was told to encourage me to come to the clinic on Monday morning because the weekend is upon us, and they closed at the weekend. My wife asked for my psychiatrist to see me but was notified he was on holiday, but then noticed him passing in the corridor of Clarendon House, which perplexed her.

So, she turned to her GP, and he responded and saw me. He confirmed I was not well, but there was not much he could do at this stage because they wanted me to say I needed help and be admitted voluntarily to the hospital. I was motionless, sitting on a stool, and expression-free; there was no eye contact, and when he spoke to me, I could not communicate with a response. I was almost like a mute and got up and walked away. I understood his inquiries. I had clear awareness, and my intellectual capacity was maintained. Still, I was experiencing thought disorders, thought broadcasting, assuming he had read my thoughts, thought insertion, my thinking had split, giving another running commentary and ideas that were supposed to be kept secret. My ability to distinguish between reality, myths and fantasies of my imagination was almost wholly lost. The science-fiction world and virtual reality in a world of artificial intelligence, the spiritual world and space, the make-believe and the dark recess side of the mind create imaginary creatures manifested through vivid dreams. Television, radio, magazines and newspapers became real entities that I could have touched, tasted, smelled and been part of what seems to be live photophobia. This fictitious world I am seeing and have unusual beliefs did not leave me without a mixed emotional fight with my conflicting feelings.

I cannot remember the first week of my hospital admission, but I can recall seeking ways to get back to my natural and rational self, and the entire weird experience struck me like dreams of a kind. However, my mind's eye never drifted off into unconsciousness. My schizophrenic breakdown tilted me on the edge of human evolution because I sensed I was on the brink of insanity. The early man acted on primitive instincts and had beastly aggressions. I was on the edge of modern man's existence. It may have been an overactive imagination and vivid dreams that leapt me back into evolutionary history to the days of Adam and Eve and catapulted me through today into the tomorrow to glimpse my future. My ego, I, and soul, the immortal element of self, the voice that is my psyche or spirit was obeying automatically like a twitch or reflex response. I could not make decisions because of conflicting feelings and was given an automatic shove by the creator, God. I increasingly recognized emotional stress and difficulties in life experiences mixed with the genetic makeup that induced schizophrenia in me continuously despite medication. The lessons are never the same as before. I psycho-educate myself when the illness is in remission and wrote about it to reduce public ignorance, discrimination, and prejudice about the disorder.

Have you any idea what was going on in my head?

The correct answer is no. Having a conversation with me during a psychotic episode, you would soon learn that my whole personality was affected from the outset. My wife's support and love/devotion were immeasurable. I speak daily secretly in my heart, thanking God for her and His continued blessings upon her and the children. I prayed that we would heal from our afflictions, and He would continue to guide us through the up and downs of life and safeguard us through this life and help us be happy and contented. I continue to uphold her with courage and help her fight her depression to be restored to good health and strength in this time of trauma. The following are some sayings, phrases and descriptions of a pattern of behaviours that I had exhibited; Now, explore with me what was in my head:

"Please don't put on the TV; they can see us." The TV and radio had made a slap-stick comedy about me and not taking my mission serious. **The people on that program are laughing at me and making fun of me.** *They think I am a coward and a wimp because I preached no violence in my telepathic broadcast and walk about as a pacifist. They are teasing me to fight and drink alcohol like a real man.* **Black people are not getting the same broadcast coming into their homes like the rest of the population, and** *they know who we are and are talking down to us because we think differently.* **They did not make us but have used technology to block our telepathic transmission to each other.** *I can read their mind, and they understand mine, but it's draining when I prevent my mind's energy and thoughts from leaving my head to stop the intruders. The mind control traffic signals; as I approach, I trigger the control box to change—no need to look behind. I know who is coming up behind me.* **Their language is the same as Black people's, but they can change it to suit themselves in any circumstance by playing with words to fool us and laughing about it.** *They use the exact words with a different meaning we have not learnt yet, to fool us. We have to learn the language from them because it's not our own. Black people did not evolve the English language whites grasp quickly in what context Black people use it. Still, we struggle to understand white people as individuals speak and, even more so, in group discussions.* **They communicate telepathically to one another, and when they meet with us, they use secret signs. They have almost unnoticeable gestures to stop us from getting to know their body signalling code.** *I can recognize the Androids and people with artificial intelligence.* **I know which human has a chip in their brain and is getting control.** *There are intellect robots amongst us that can reproduce copies of themselves, and the single mechanical robots are working in the engine room of this spaceship.* **The known world and terrestrial beings know of me, and they want**

me dead because they are irritated by my message of peace and freedom for the captives. *I broadcast that I cannot be killed; my creator God has made real humans immortal and will protect me.*

I receive a message that a battle will occur through the television and radio, and sitting in front of the TV or standing near the radio will mean certain death or capture. I prepare myself by posting one of my prayers slips at every exit point in the house, including fixed glass window ledges. *I transmitted electrical energy from my mind to break off outside communication, and the telephone stopped working temporarily. The kettle sparked out, tripping out the mains electric supply and the RCD switch.* My wife and son struggle to get the RCD switch to stay on to restore power. She uses her mobile to contact the electric company, and they give instructions on tests to circuits, and the power comes back on. Each **night, all the lights are left on fully bright. It could be controlled from the dimmer switch. I pace up and down throughout the house to keep watch, then settle in front of the TV where the science fiction films were zapping at me, and they battled into an invisible field, falling just short of dropping through the TV screen.** I went to church and continuously cried in the Pentecost Church, asking that the people be enlightened and bring the gospel into this modern world setting. **Technology is to change their way of worship.** Women should be taking central positions in the church, and their theology needs to be reformed. They are too blind to notice they have been fooled by untruth in the religion, and the practice of superstitions is stifling intellectual inquiries about faith. **I had an Identity crisis with confusion over sexual orientation.**

Puzzled by the races being identified by skin colour, either black or white, I wanted to have no part in this distinction and obsessively demonstrated by showing my skin's dark and light shade. With an endless repetition, I insisted that it should not matter what shade of surface we are. We are all the same underneath. My head's angry voice tells me that God is white, and you and your people will suffer if you do not accept that God is white and controls black people; they have no free will. Underneath, you are pale; inside your body is pale flesh, and underneath, we are all the same. God is neither black nor white, but He has to be one or the other. So I argued with the voice until I was exhausted. Floods of tears streamed from my eyes as my soul cried with sorrow, a plea that black people would be freed from the white people's puppet play. My conscience reacted to the intense suffering as I sobbed, "Karl, you are not The Saviour," then a little low-pitched softened voice said, "Why are you doing this to yourself?"

Momentarily, I had the chance to think clearly and, in my inner silence, explained. I have never thought I, Karl, was a Saviour, just a nice guy with a big heart with altruistic, philanthropic interests. The purpose of my altruism is to serve to help people and be willing to risk my life for my wife and family, but it was channelled wrongly. I am a good, generous and kind-hearted man. I cannot understand why I am so troubled over the things I can do nothing about them. My sexuality was re-clarified by the dormant self as being bi-sexual and continues to bug me, suggesting I was chosen like the gradual change from night-to-day—the self saw reality in the same way as the majority of ordinary people in the population.

It has been sheer hell hearing my brain turning over, but only sometimes it made entertaining listening when all those critical voices, the gloomy, dim memories and fears were shut out. I had experienced stuff of science-fiction, illusion, thoughts and sensations fed into my brain. My senses were unreliable, and my dreams created confusion. My eyes were open, and I talked, but what was happening? I was never sure if I was hallucinating or dreaming or that my memory was not playing tricks. The experience of dreaming was indistinguishable from my conscious understanding. I could never be confident, sure that something I thought to be the case was, in fact, the case. I had to try to discard any belief susceptible to the slightest degree of doubt because perception from the senses' data drove a wedge between me and the external world. The biological and dreamed simulated mind were indistinguishable. The real world of the hospital, home and the environment around me was based on perceptions gained via my senses, usually mediated by my use of reason. But the visible world was playing tricks. There were entities 'out there,' physical, spiritual things that played a significant role in getting to know the world because I had a widespread doubt over my senses as a reliable pathway to knowing the truth.

These psychotic experiences exist independently of my knowing ethical facts or mathematical properties, where everything is imperfect and constantly changing in the world. I believe all my ideas come from God, and since God is good, He will not deceive me. My power of observation and reason from God will lead me to exist mentally in other worlds, leading me to the truth, not falsehood, then enlightenment, knowledge and wisdom.

The World is my Oyster
Written Thursday 11th March 2010

The one thing that's not orbiting around my planet is enough money to change my lifestyle. I did not have a penny, scrimped and scrimped, hoping and planning for this to end.

I have always worked hard to provide for us, and I will appreciate having money. However, I am gambling with my future by hoping for a lottery win or an inheritance to fund our mortgage capital repayment and retirement. I scrimped to put £2.00 towards a lottery ticket and £2.00 for church collection. I would love to put money into a pension or savings account instead of relying on a lottery win or an inheritance windfall.

I believe I am on a mission of greatness, not in the world definition of importance in terms of power, possessions, prestige and position, but to act like a servant. It is fueled by my genuine religious beliefs, which I fostered as a boy, aged eleven when I entered secondary school. I declared I wanted to grow up to be a man of faith and believe in the promises of God. Teaching trust, honesty, belief, hope and love are fundamental to my psyche, and I shunned my divine calling. God wants his people to prosper, and I believe my prosperity will come to help others to faith one day. Everything in life - good or bad - happens for a reason, and in every situation is an opportunity for God to reveal himself, but it seems He is far away. Still, we have been grateful to see God using us in my purpose-driven life to provide comfort and direction to people who think God's belief is not working for the good and the positive, although it makes no difference if one believes or not. My story is a self-help manual so far, as it was written to say I have found strength and encouragement in these pages due to my ordeals of searching for the truth and having faith in God to work through ordinary or miraculous means. Also, people can use my stories as examples that confidence in the creator works. As I sometimes struggle with this straightforward instruction to have faith, I swallow this digestible message and burp because it does not seem to sit comfortably when things in my life are not working out. I learnt that God is in charge of everything, and I recognize a wave of God's spirit in worship, through prayer, in other people. I try to follow the example of Christ by being loving, forgiving and overcoming temptations, but due to the mix of my belief and my personality, there is a feeling of guilt.

I have firm convictions forged by an early involvement with Christianity that drives and inspires me. This belief makes me feel God is holding something back until I can ride the waves of life like an experienced surfer. I have been grieving and searching for answers to the possibility of losing our home soon and whether it is God's will that we lose our house.

I was led back to contact an all-black African religious organization, the Elemental Evangelical born-again Christian Fundamentalist Church sect. Again, I received an incredible blessing. I feel I have plenty there, but the reality of the world is that I exist on a few. I get lovely benefits from two other forms of Christian worship, the United Reformed Church and the Church of England, not forgetting the third, the Pentecostal Church, KCC. The variety of the spiritual mix in worship is soul-fulfilling. I feel incredibly blessed. I thirst if I do not attend the churches to feed the addiction to worship and be inspired by the word of God. The teaching of faith and its practice. I am addicted to them. My faith endeared me to practise church unity spiced with diversity in worshipping the same, one and only Almighty God. It's an exceptional phenomenon; so intense are my worships that each week my whole life is led to reach that moment again of the beginning of the weekday. I try to live in the moment day by day, but I cannot help feeling the weekdays are rushed, and in no time, it seems, the weekend comes around. It may seem astonishing; I do not place great emphasis on Bible study and prayer to approach God as a Best Friend. Instead, I see 'religious' loudmouthed people, fully experienced in prayer and reading their Bible, harassing and causing an affray to God.

The prayer said from others in silence or low-toned feeble words, as mine often is, seems to be inadequate to reach the ears of God because it is not articulated in a stream of confidence, nor does it sound richly fluent in the mother tongue. I am in contact with God as a living being, going about my purpose-filled life, guided by his grace and mindful I am shaped for serving Him and walk humbly and share the faith messages. I pray consciously and unconsciously about my everyday business with a lot of energy and passion at the time. There is no advantage in this kind of prayer; they are answered in the same way as other said prayers. New to exaltation, people may share my testimony because they do not distinguish the invocation into categories like mine. The peace and love of God be with you! Amen.

Pray for It.
Written Friday 12th March 2010

I sub-headed this section of writing Pray for It because dreams come true with wishful prayer, and asking others to pray for us is cosmic and boosts the ordering in prayer and worship. God responds in possibilities and opportunities which enter our lives in earthly time before our human flesh dies. There is strength and power in the faithful praying together because it is reinforced and convinces you that prayer is reliable. Nothing is as successful as success itself in answered prayer, be it a yes, no, or wait. It nurtures the believer that God has dealt or is dealing with the prayer request. But God does not deal with the things we could deal with ourselves with his given grace. I believe that good things come to those who wait, but why it takes so long for suitable items to arrive, and why does the wait have to go hand in hand with all these obstacles of hard and testing times?

All I have right now is my dreams, so I will close my eyes and pray and dream and wait for that precious tomorrow when I can wake up to my dream coming true - a mighty win. Instead of doubting that prayer works, it won't be successful if I do not believe it has been delivered successfully to the creator. One must say trustfully, He grants us full blessings sometimes, in ways never thought possible. I will wait as long as it takes and stay healthy, for my intuition sometimes guides me in a gentle way where I will find the God-given answer. Still, I have to remain alert in my thinking and attentive once the prayer gets sent to receive all the necessary information and deal with the answer positively. It appears not to be the answer I was looking to obtain. I had to remind myself that all things work together for good for those who believe in God. I must prepare myself with the hopeful expectation that prayer will change our circumstances profoundly. By God's grace, I think I will have a lottery win and create the condition by having a lottery ticket to practically draw the event into our life. I claim the victory by saying, "I am rich," - expressed in the present tense rather than the future tense, - "I will be rich," because the right vibrations are in the moment, the here and now, and the cosmic energy created by God brings good luck.

"I thank you, God, that you heard me." The day will come when the lottery ticket, no matter how dismal our present situation may be, shows I have won. God's name is at stake in my destiny as I am a witness. Amen.

My Infidelity
Written on Wednesday 24th March 2010
(adult theme)

On 24/10/1981, I gave a solemn vow to God and a public declaration of my love for Euphemia by entering into the institution of marriage.

God ordained me to have a lifelong interpersonal relationship, intimate and sexual, in matrimony. I violated the terms of marriage by my unfaithfulness on 15th February 2009. The act of marriage created legal oblations between the two of us and spiritual and religious ones too. Legal and ethical reasons and falling in love established us with a nuclear family unit and faithful to my partner. Still, because romantic love and pure affection were missing in this voluntary contract, in which, by agreement, we chose to become husband and wife. I committed a sexual sin/ crime when I had sexual relations with a beautiful divorced, mature sixty-year-old mother of four with grandchildren.

I felt rejected by Euphemia, and I desired an affair to have variety and combat the feeling of ageing. Euphemia told me to go and be free because she cannot give me what I want. "I want you to be happy, and you cannot be since you are not getting it off me; go and find it out there," she said. Marriage was supposed to produce the most intimate, wholesome and mutually fulfilment, and Euphemia was right. We could not feel the right atmosphere to engage in sexual relationships, but I begged her, "Please, I want you, only you, and things will come right."

"It's been twenty-six years, and we aren't compatible; go and find that woman who will do everything you want, and we can remain friends." It did not sit well in my heart, but I had already committed some kinds of sexual sin because I do not pretend that I do not thirst for water and watched sexually explicit films on late-night TV and the internet.

After months of rejection and Euphemia's push, I thought to have an affair to seek sexual gratification and help my self-esteem. But first, I experimented on her to gauge her feeling if I had natural sexual desires for another woman. Then, I assessed her attention on me when we walked down the street, and I gazed at an attractive woman. Euphemia did not attempt to distract me from focusing my attention back on her. I could no longer deny my sexuality, and it is natural for men to desire women and women to prefer men. My belief was in getting married to direct sexual desire properly, a passion for closeness, friendliness, safety and love. Love that is God-given to satisfy partners and to lose one's virginity in marriage. But I lust after something forbidden, to covet when my belief system was modified to suit worldly expectations. No longer do I comfortably accept that sex is reserved for marriage and sex outside of marriage is a crime/sin of adultery or fornication. It first came to light that I began not sticking to my belief system when my children became sexually active outside marriage and were in love; I did not condone it because they were old enough to decide to act the way their conscience led them.

There were sequences of events that led to unfaithfulness. I became accustomed to even bored Euphemia's low sex drive. Romantic activity is seen as a sex chore when the practice has been previously scheduled in my head to engage and enjoy making love with her. After the lapse of several weeks, usually, the call of nature urges Euphemia to procreate, it's pleasurable, unique and memorable, and I wait until nature retakes its course. It became hard for us to make love to pleasure each other for gratification's sake, other than a committed act; our belief system tells us to stick at it, and it will get better. Having a low awareness of sex drives, I thought Euphemia's love for me was pending, still to be decided.

She asked that we have time apart, go our separate ways for a while to sort ourselves out and for her to feel wanted and not be a sex object to my desires. I was shocked to learn that my marriage partner felt unloved, and the loving bits were missing. Euphemia seemed to suggest that I cannot get another woman in bed and is fed up with me feebly trying it on, knowing she is not interested. The well-known notion that people with schizophrenia find it hard to form relationships drove my desire to cheat and laid down the idea as a myth. Nevertheless, I desired the 'bone of my bones' and looked upon another woman whom Euphemia could see that I did not want to take her place. But, possibly the other woman could become my mistress.

In front of God, separately, in our relationship with Him, we prayed for our relationship to be stitched and have a bond that His resources and strength are available to give us. Even before our marriage, we included God in our lives and had ups and downs, and now in our marriage difficulties, we hoped to look to God for help and guidance. There was so much other stress in our lives from the combination of this, Euphemia's work issues, my search for a new job, insurance claim problems, housing issues and when the bailiff from the Council wrongly wanted to process items from our home or demand money. It simply showed our continued difficulty in financial and social requirements that our income cannot cover. We wanted a holiday together to refresh ourselves and have 'me time' and could not see a way to get it. Combined with our relationship difficulties, I believe that caused Euphemia to become clinically depressed in November 2008. She is on prescription drugs and a therapy program that challenges her negative thinking and builds on the positive side of her personality and situations. I blame myself for her depression because, for years, due to my insecurities, I have pressured her to love me in the ways I can interpret love.

Euphemia had returned to work but had to leave again after a few months. She has not worked yet since 1st June 2009 but, her job with the employer remains open for her to resume after she is fully recovered. Euphemia does not get sick pay any more from her employer and has to claim Employment Support Allowance. I have been foolish and blind; Euphemia has gracefully stood by me, knowing my criticisms that were not always constructive and made her feel harshly hurt. I want to quench the pain in her heart with beta-blockers. I cannot go back on what I said, but I asked her to pardon me because words can hurt like I had thrown a punch, and I am sorry.

It was early September 2008, on a working holiday to Blackpool with three male service users for a charity I worked for called Together: working for wellbeing. The beginning was from a glance on a coach journey where I gave flirty attention to a mature woman who was a support worker to a young female service user. It came to be more than just by coincidence, like fate had played a part in it. We became much more than just good friends when the holiday was over. The seating arrangement on the coach was pre-selected by the tour operator. Our party of people was picked up in Wellingborough and another party in Northampton. She was in the party of people picked up in Northampton and was seated just one seat in front of me on the other side of the aisle. We both had taken outer seats and could have held hands across space in the aisle. Though I found this lady attractive, I unashamedly rested my left hand over my right hand to clearly show my wedding ring on my finger during the journey. I telephoned Euphemia and spoke to her in the romantic format I always take when talking to her.

I was not discreet in my conversation on the mobile phone because I wanted people to eavesdrop on the exchange. When I said, "Darling, love you lots," and 'lovely' in the conversation with my darling wife, heads were turning. It came as a surprise that her twin-bedded room in the hotel was next door to my twin-bedroom suite. We casually chatted about our work in public places when we bumped into one another as we chaperoned. I felt an extraordinary friendship because I sensed a deep attraction from her telling me that she fancied me. Her eyes seemed intensely bright when she saw me and greeted me with a marvel of smiles, and I followed suit and smiled from ear to ear because she was attractive and flirting seemed an exciting thing to do. I had already assumed that she was very near the pension age for women. Sixty was a mother and grandmother, her husband had died, or she was divorced. I lightly touched her shoulder and hand when in conversation and laughed and smiled during our small chats. It felt comfortable and heart-pounding when I saw her present herself for the evening meal at the hotel. In the lounge, we glanced into each other's eyes in a sexy way, smiled and looked away, and before too long, we turned again, and our eyes met. We laughed almost uncontrollably but, it had to be discreet, so I hid some of the smiles by quickly taking out my handkerchief and pretending to blow my nose. I was flattered and took the opportunity to show I was interested in her in the form of avoidance; I left the scene with a charming wave to her, and I smiled. The following days and after dinner, I toured the Blackpool beach and the local amenities with the service users, and when late evening came, she asked how I had spent the day and which places I had seen? It turned out that sometimes we visited the exact locations and just missed seeing each other by fractions because of her time tallying with mine. Yet, some days we did not bump into each other.

At last, at dusk before the morning departure from Blackpool, she suggested she have an early night, and it would be nice if we could keep in touch. I immediately reached for a pen and paper to write down her details and to give her mine. I had a pen but no paper, so I told her I would slip my details under her bedroom door and said, "It was my pleasure to have known you." On my way to bed that night, I wrote my full name, address and landline telephone number concealed on the inside page of a tourist directional leaflet that I picked up in the hotel lounge and pushed it under her bedroom door. In the morning, she slipped her details to me and said, "Thanks; do give me a call some time."

During the homeward journey, she revealed a lot about herself in a moderate tone of voice. The coach travelled through some lengthy traffic jams that induced fatigue onto most of the already sleepy passengers. She told the history of her marriage to a black man and why she had to divorce. She had to take early retirement because she had breast cancer and had to have a mastectomy. I openly shared that I am happily married, and my work sent me with these guys who have mental health problems to support them on their holiday, and I also suffered from a mental health problem. She asked for the name of the illness. I was reluctant to say, "Hum, schizophrenia." However, it turned out that she has a family member who continues to suffer from the condition, which fueled another conversation line. We parted company with our first hug at the intersection point, then the final leg of the journey was in a mini-bus. I gave brief feedback about the trip to the manager and staff, and my shift was over.

I told Euphemia that on holiday, I had met a lovely lady named Marie who lives in Northampton, and we said we would keep in touch; "I'd like to phone her now to tell her I reached home safely."

"It's nice you have women friends, but just a friend?" I broadly smiled as I lowered my head from Euphemia's eyes and replied, "Just a friend; I'll call her now." I picked up the phone and dialled her home number. Euphemia watched TV and looked at me out of the corner of her eye as I had a brief conversation with Marie. I phoned Marie a few times a week at first, and most times, Euphemia would be in the same room. Finally, Marie asked, "It must be uncomfortable for your wife to hear you speaking to another woman." "We have a sort of open relationship, and she trusts me," I reassured her.

From then on, I began to stay up late and make secretive personal phone calls on the home phone and gave her my mobile number, but she said she could not afford the cost of ringing mobiles but that she uses a pay as you go mobile phone sometimes. Then, during Sunday dinner with the family, I answered a phone call from Marie. "Daddy has a girlfriend," Euphemia said to our adult children, and I laughed, "She is just a friend," I insisted, but I could not stop the grins and the puffed-up cheekbone exposure.

By Christmas 2008, three months on, Marie and I had come to need each other physically. It stemmed from sexy messages we texted each other, sexy late-night chats, and we arranged to meet up on two occasions, and I began to fall in love. We met in Abington Park, the first meeting since the end of the holiday, and we strolled in the park holding hands. Very nervous that known passers-by may see us, our hands trembled when we could see people walking in our direction at a distance. Would it be someone who recognized us? We were both on edge until we sat down on a bench and spent the rest of the time chatting. I met her again at her home, a one-bedroom ground floor flat on a council estate in the town centre, and she was babysitting her granddaughter. She managed to throw on me a craving, passionate kiss, my first experience of a French kiss with tongues, while the child played in the middle of the floor with her toys without any attention to our quick adult play in an obscure corner. I sipped cups of coffee afterwards, chatted and listened to her selections of CDs and came away two hours later, imagining I had been swinging from the chandelier.

I began to send Marie love letters, expressing that I had fallen in love with her because she reached and pressed the button to my soul, so I was in love. I found it incredible to have fallen in love with another woman when I love my wife. I love two women intimately. Marie impregnated my soul with her warmth, beautiful spirit, and smile. Our emotional conversion of needing togetherness had shown we were connected on so many other levels that the relationship did not appear wrong.

At the same time, I was aware Euphemia was falling ill. I tried to persuade her to go to the doctors', but she refused to go. My concern grew further as Euphemia found her job extremely stressful and rejected every advance I made to comfort her, and only depressive sentences came from her lips; "I should not be here. I feel useless and want to die. I feel like walking in front of a bus or taking lots of pills and not waking up." I dropped off Euphemia at work, and I watched her masking her feelings by trying to put on a brave face with a single smile because of work ethos - 'Do not bring or discuss problems in the workplace; be happy.' If it is the workplace that is causing some of the problems, what does one do? I drove back to our house; it was one of my weekdays off work, and I pondered what to do. I rang the doctors' surgery and asked could an urgent message be sent to Euphemia's doctor to speak to me today about concerns I have about my wife. I had asked her to go and make an appointment to see him, but she said no. I was told that the doctor would call me soon after morning surgery, and he did. I explained to him the observations I had made and what Euphemia had said to me that made me think she was in crisis. "Try to persuade her to come with you to see me when she finishes work; surgery will already have closed; just ring the bell, and you will be let in."

Euphemia gave me a quick flash of a simple smile when I asked, "How was work today, darling?" And her reply was unconvincing, 'Alright.' Euphemia looked astonished when I told her I was not driving her home but straight to see the doctor first. The doctor immediately signed Euphemia off sick from work because of depression and got a prescription for Fluoxetine.

I spoke to Marie, telling her what started as flirting had got so severe that I found it hard to dash our desire to make love in the forthcoming new year but that we should let the busy period of Christmas pass first. "I am sorry, but I love my wife who is suffering from depression, and we had built up this hope and dream which wants us to be with each other but, I could never leave my wife, I care for her deeply, though lying in bed at night, I find myself thinking of you. The time we have shared will always be special memories, but I must say goodbye, Marie." She said she understood because I am a good man and recognizes my marriage is important to me, but we have desires. She called me her toy boy and said she had never been out with a married man. She thinks she knows how my wife may be feeling because her divorce was because her husband was cheating on her. She wanted me to call her by a pet name, saying she rather liked 'Babes' as romantic recognition of the love that must end. I texted final goodbyes and added in 'bye, Babes', and it lifted the romance off the back burner, and it flourished again in earnest. I felt euphoria to reply to her text messages, lost my inhibitions, and ignored the consequences because I lust for this woman.

On Valentine's Day, I arranged to see Marie at her home at 7:30 pm and told Euphemia I was going around to see Marie at 7:30 pm, having started to get ready and I would not be too long. I just came out of the shower room, sexually charged, when I received a text message saying her son and grandchild had come around unexpectedly, so she would see me another time. We met the next day and made passionate love in the afternoon. After several hours of adult play, we hooked up sensitively, channelled the craving, raging urges, and then relaxed. She slaughtered me in her need to take me. The pleasuring was equally shared; she was orgasmic, and I enjoyed our hooking-up immensely without evidence of a climax. Suddenly, while making love, a realization came forth as the intimacy caused our bodies to produce natural fluids and erotic scents. 'OH MY GOD' came to mind because I could not believe I was performing the act of physical love to another woman; it's a dream! Did I sleepwalk into her bed? I was confused for a split second to explain it to myself as a conscious choice. But, again, it's not a dream; this was my present reality; I made love to another woman. As I basin-washed and got dressed, I couldn't believe my betrayal of my marriage vows and yet I couldn't feel guilt. I wanted to feel guilty, but I sensed that I came out of it all shining as I sincerely loved her because fate put us through this.

Marie and I plotted to hook up again; being away from me is killing her because she wants to give me every ounce of her love. Shots of guilty feeling riddled my mind suggesting it would be harmful to my marriage, and I could imagine the dreadful hurt it would cause Euphemia. Marie's life moved on without me. She came to accept her soul's cry to let me rekindle my marriage with my wife and be a good friend to the most sensitive, caring, tender, considerate, loving man who had touched her life. Marie and I believed in the afterlife when we wake up in the precious tomorrow. My wife has always been my lifetime soul mate, and she will rejoice to have had, as lover and friend, a good man of faith.

One can give without loving, but I cannot love without giving, and Marie comes back in my mind from time to time like a favourite song. I feel like a spark of life has been rekindled inside me as my marriage seems to gain something positive out of my relationship with Marie. It was only the one time I had physical relations with Marie. My life in love with Euphemia has grown into a beautiful, wholesome relationship with some passionate lovemaking. I can promise you, my darling, that I will give you every ounce of my love that my heart possesses to the very last breath of my being. I never realized that the stars sparkled so brightly or that the sunset held so much beauty; only now, I notice all that when I am waiting for your love. I know, Euphemia is simply amazing; I have a great marriage and sharing everyday problems and joy without having to leave one another's side is a wake up too!! I will always love you; it hasn't changed in years and won't, not even in a lifetime. It is you and me, Darling, forever.

Listening deeply to myself and my wavering Belief

Monday 26th September 2011

I have worked conscientiously, determined to take great strides forward throughout the one and a half years of being absent from writing. But, for years, the significant issues that have paralysed us are eating more into our souls' fabric, and we may lose our house.

In April 2011, the mortgage provider said they would not accept interest-only payments after February 2012. Proceedings will start towards repossessing the house if we cannot begin to repay capital and interest. So, things are tight, both of us being unemployed and hoping that employers may see our talents in volunteering for an organisation. Euphemia has been volunteering at 'Sure Start' children's centre since March 2011 and me at 'Together: working for mental wellbeing' since 2010. We receive state benefits, ESA £216 fortnightly, DLA £275 4-weekly, and Carer's Allowance £220 4-weekly. However, £81.90 per month we have to contribute to the mortgage, and the state makes up the difference that covers the interest only on the mortgage payment of £290. Euphemia is entitled to JSA, but she must sign on at the Job Centre every two weeks to keep up to date credits on her national insurance.

On Sunday, 21st August 2011, I wrote this prayer to keep our house from repossession:

'Almighty God, as you know, we are behind in our house payment and only pay towards the interest on the mortgage, but soon the lender wants interest and capital payment to prevent a repossession order being served on the house. Please show us mercy and favour, so we do not lose our house. Please help us resolve our financial hardships. I know I have made mistakes in life. Please forgive me and help me to do better. I am so thankful for everything you have given my family and me. You have helped me through so many bad times in my life. I am so grateful to have this house and your blessings and care. I am sincerely grateful for our house. I ask for your help to let us keep it. I give this house over to you, for it belongs to you no matter what. I ask that I pay the mortgage

again, and we thank you for this or something better. I have looked for a natural solution, and it has failed, and now we need the supernatural help of thee, our Lord. We know the thoughts that you have for us! Thoughts of good and not evil! Lord, open up the storehouse for us and guide us in every way. Give us our daily bread. Lord, we pray that you will intervene and save this house and thank you in advance for working it out to stop the repossession. God, our help in ages past, our hope for years to come, I turn to you. With complete faith and trust, and hope! You alone have all the answers, Lord; I trust in you, Heavenly Father/ Mother, God almighty, to help us. We have nowhere to go. May the grace of God allow us to keep our house, and we ask for your wisdom, your will and plan for this house, and we commit this house to you for your glory and honour in Jesus's name. We thank you, heavenly Father/Mother, for hearing and honouring the prayer. Amen.'

On 6th September 2011, we instructed an estate agent to market our house at £174,995, although they thought today's market price should be between £160,000 and £165,000. To me, £160,000 - £165,000 is only the actual value of bricks and mortar; we need to recoup the cost for the modern kitchen and shower room and other refurbishments not taken with us on house sales. I paid about £40,000 to modernise the home, and it's a debt we are still paying. The estate agent informed us that a prospective buyer would like to view the property on Thursday 29th.

The house was put on the market for sale and viewed on the internet from 13/09/2011 and marketed in local newspapers with no sale board outside the home to show the locals we were moving. I want to keep in reserve the option to stay. To continue our life in the street, with the locals oblivious to our business. I do not want us to feel humiliated if we do not sell because the will to save it is stronger than the intention to go. The interest generated so far means two visitors coming on Thursday.

I have woken from a light 5-hour sleep and reached for paper and pen; it is 3:30 AM Tuesday 27/09/11, and the house sale weighs on my mind. I weigh up the balance between selling and not selling. Consciously or subconsciously, the power of the universe is coming to my aid to give me a lottery win tonight or in the coming weeks so that we can lose debts and pay for our house to continue to live in it. Sometimes I have to choose between buying a loaf of bread costing £1.00 and buying a £1.00 lottery ticket. We squeezed, and the church donations come from leftover one penny and two pence bits left at the end of the week. Sometimes, I do not even have 45 pence a day to buy a newspaper.

I have this thought/mental image that I will have a win on the Euro lottery tonight. I am confident about my capacity to achieve, solve problems and think for myself. I have imagined heading towards goals with courage, determination, and action. It has a direct effect on my emotions as I am approaching it in the right spirit. As I listen in on my self-talk, I also observe and ask myself, why am I thinking these thoughts? Where is it taking me? It seems to be helping me feel confident, but I have an inner critic in that wicked little voice inside my head that finds faults, complains and condemns. It is the voice that sews doubts; 'yes, but supposing...?' If going unchallenged, this inner critic has given me the power to destroy my confidence and lower my self-esteem. I render the negative thoughts entering my mind about my predicament as powerless because I change the ideas to something positive as soon as they pop into my head. I silently interrupt the unwanted thought, but my mind is not a vacuum; I can not stop thinking. I try to dispense with negative thoughts immediately as not the truth, just realising them for their only negative thoughts. My subconscious wants to hang on to existing habits, and it feels like I am lying to myself. I have to affirm that negative thoughts are false ideas, false concepts, with nothing to sustain them, and they vanish from my consciousness into a pile of dust in the centre of my head. These specks of dust of doubts, anxiety and self-expressed disapproval get swept and bagged up and given no room in my conscious as I allow myself a warm inner smile.

We have had our names put down on the council waiting list since June 2011 and were accepted for housing under band C because I have difficulty using the stairs, and they feel a bungalow or a ground floor flat will be more suitable. However, if we are evicted from our house, the council will band us in category A for urgent housing. God has a reason for allowing things to happen. We may never understand His wisdom, but we simply have to trust His will. If God answers my prayer, he's increasing my faith, but if He delays, He's expanding our patience. If He does not answer, He knows we can handle it. It takes time to permanently change my thinking from a somewhat pessimistic view of our life to great optimism and confidence about getting back on my feet. I am more self-aware, set goals and think more confidently, but, occasionally, I have felt myself slipping back a little from time to time. However, the overall trend is beginning to go upwards, and I see the setbacks, so keep calm and keep making an effort despite it.

I promised myself that from now on, I'd sow only 'seeds' of positive thoughts, fantasies and mental images, words and actions that will boost my confidence, improve my relationships and make me feel good about myself. I am planting the seeds of faith in my consciousness through intentions, thoughts, attitudes, and beliefs, nourishing confidence. No matter what actions and words have gone on in past events or now, circumstances have a unique way of making sense of it. My genetic inheritance and hormones program me to have generosity and kindness, a selfless love. An acorn in good soil, I cannot help it grow into a mighty oak; it is genetically programmed that way. I am committed to doing whatever it takes to see us prosper because my motives are sound, and I expect prosperity to flow towards me. I realized I am not going to wake up full of happy thoughts naturally, but if I could change the way I feel, just through my thought processes, I would smirk at the disempowering ideas because they are nonsense.

I have found part-time work as a Community Support Worker in social care, which started on 07/09/11. It is only 5 hours a week, but it will lead to full-time employment in due course. There's nothing more important than finding a purpose that inspires, motivates and gives life meaning and direction. I enjoy doing the job, and I put my heart and soul into it, and everything seems to change from a humdrum life. Lying dormant somewhere in my consciousness, waiting to be revealed, is my prayer life. I have this notion that I do not need to pray as my life is destined in a certain way, and God knows my destiny. It feels it has already been mapped out because I have an overall sense of purpose that benefits others as well as myself, and sometimes, I pray simply the Lord's Prayer and just add, "Good night or good morning God, Jesus, the angels and all the saints" at the end of it. Sometimes, I do not pray at all. Then, all of a sudden, it erupts out of my soul in a crisis. I sometimes forget to do it daily, but I still feel prayer; I sense it's a blessing and believes in it most time.

I have a 'Life Mission Statement' to spread peace, love, and happiness to encourage people to live life to the full and help others do the same. I will give my whole body to medical science at the point of organic death to advance humankind's knowledge to know the mind of God. Play with my body and brain to practically identify soul/spirit and God's existence in humankind's skull to discover the whys of our individual unique human life over other species on earth and probably the universe.

Today, Wednesday 28th September 2011. Do you remember the mental image I had that I would win on the lottery? Well, hip, hip hooray, I have won, but it's only £4.80. I played two lines, £2.00 per line online, and received an email to view my online account this morning. The belief of a win was accepted as accurate, and it has built up my confidence. Most of my expectations have their origins in childhood conditioning and my cultural background. They were absorbed mainly without effort until I reached maturity and acquired all the beliefs I hold now as I learned to interpret the world for myself. I sometimes dispute the old conclusions, re-evaluate, and update my belief system because incoming evidence supports a new way of thinking. The hive of my mental activity, the subconscious that lies below the threshold of momentary awareness, has just floated up, thinking that I must check that my monthly benefit will be paid into the bank as calculated. Oops, I have made a blunder; things are going a certain way, and it seems there is nothing I can do about it to stop it. If I do not cancel the direct debits and standing orders, the bank will clobber me with hefty bank charges. I would need to bring the outgoings back within the overdraft limit of £250.00; however, there is a catch 22 in that the companies I do not pay will add charges for failed payments, and my credit rating history may be affected again.

Monday 03/10/2011 - I have spoken to the personal banking manager, who advised me to move the standing orders dates and cancel the direct debits to stay within the overdraft limit. He says the bank cannot permit lending more to an overstretched customer. They have to abide by the financial service guidelines. The bank computer system rejected a temporary increase in overdraft. I cancelled the car insurance and the breakdown cover. Still, I knew it was a considerable risk, and I am trying to distract my attention from the thought of having to drive without motor insurance until Thursday. That day, the car is for the commute to work and chauffeur mother to medical appointment check-up. In the next few days, I get referred continuously to my stored thoughts and memories for information and guidance, setting up a cycle where I repeatedly think about what an experience it would be to drive without insurance. I cannot silence the inner critic with realistic self–talk. There must be an alternative so that I do not break the motoring law. I am focusing my mind on finding solutions and asking myself, 'What can I do to solve this problem? I have made a mistake when Euphemia's Carer's Allowance gets paid into the bank, and I want to chastise myself, but it is better that I learn from it for the future and look for a better way to calculate the four weeks when the benefit is due.

Tough it Out and Trust God's Timing
Thursday 06th October 2011

I wondered what Job's secret was to toughing it out and trusting God's timing. He had lost everything, including his children, vast land holdings, servants and incredible wealth and his health, and he endured without becoming bitter. Job did not sin nor blame God. So, what was Job's secret? I need some of that! To recognize God's right to control events in my life and when the dust settled, to understand that anything God permits is ultimately for the best and seeing God in it all.

The estate agent has asked me to lower the house price to the marketing valuation of £165,000, which should see buyers coming through the door and making offers. I bickered, arguing for 20 minutes with the agent. Finally, I compromised and reduced the price from £174,995 to £169,995, and their advertising included the words 'offers over'.

I complain from time to time and wish my circumstances were different, but I have the gift of life; there are people in the graveyard that would gladly change places with me. I mourn because I tend to gravitate towards what is damaging rather than what is positive. I have made terrible mistakes, stumbled and fallen. It may lead to our house being repossessed. Thank God I am fighting to retain it by getting up again; many do not make it, but, although I have advertised the house for sale, I wrote the prayer called Keep our House from Repossession to rush through His purpose or wait trust God's timing. Until 1st February 2012, we have to pay interest and capital to prevent our mortgage provider from applying to the courts to repossess the house. I had debt advice from the government Consumer Credit Counselling Service back in 2009. They made arrangements to offer minimum payments on the credit cards and loans to my creditors remaining in place. From time to time, every six months for some and others every year, we re-negotiate a new acceptable low payment with interest remaining frozen. I had sought advice from Accommodation Concern, a housing advice charity. Not paying the interest and capital for over two years showed the lender had given adequate time of grace to make provision since we 'defaulted' on the mortgage payments; the lender is within their right to stop accepting interest only and seek outstanding balance.

Every way I turn to advisers, friends, family, and hearing from professionals who have my best interests at heart, They all say it's a big lottery win you need. So many years had passed, and the critical problem of debts and making our way through life comfortable is still to be realised. Time is moving even faster as I creep past 55 years on the 14th of September, and not knowing exactly how or when things will come right, it calls for me to shut up and get on with it, make it happen. It is like a sharp knock on my funny bone; it hurts, but the pain passes, and one continues doing what one has to do. Deep within, I know it will become right because I have a deep dependency on God, who planted a dream in my heart, and He has just started preparing me for its fulfilment. He strengthens my character and confidence, but I grow frustrated and rush things because I do not understand His timing. Weeks, months and some years had passed from when the issues turned into a hanging crisis. There is nothing any mortal can do but to shift money into our hands. I carry a seed that cannot be harvested yet, and it feels like a faith thing. The money will stop the nightmare that sees us having nowhere to live, and the deep dependency on God is because I am being led into steps of faith that stretch me beyond my present comfort level. But I must trust God's timing, remembering that there is no instance where He was ever late in the scriptures. I am preparing my heart to sprout, and ultimately God's purposes will be released and displayed because every seed I sow will multiply back to me many times over. Like a jingle on a radio station that repeatedly reminds the listeners of a critical message that the broadcaster wants to imbed in the listener's mind, I must be steadfast, or in contemporary terms, Tough it out! Tough it out and Trust God's Timing.

On Sunday 9th October 2011, Euphemia attended the harvest festival with me at the Anglican Church. We raided the larder for foodstuff to make up a shoebox parcel, knowing we would not have enough food left to carry us through the week.

Deep inside lies a centre of absolute stillness and peace at my very core, which brings a profound sense of well-being. However, the evidence is that we are broke; the essentials like milk and bread, a snack bar, are beyond our means because the last few pence (80 pence) went towards collection in the second church service we attended. By Tuesday 11th, all the essential foodstuff would have been finished, and I should be frustrated, but peace is in my heart because, in my daily life, my human experience of not enough is sufficient, for God will supply our daily bread (what we need each day to survive). State benefit will arrive, and that is the correct perspective in an imperfect world. God, the universal intelligence, works tirelessly for our service, guiding and supporting us, nourishing my mind and body and taking care of us. I imagine I could live securely in the knowledge that everything that happens is for my ultimate benefit. Even the most ordinary moment is a precious gift, and the future has a habit of taking care of itself because the only moment over which I have any control is now.

On reflection, we are more than a collection of bones held together by muscle and soft tissue that needs nourishing by food and more than a collection of thoughts and emotions; it's because I think and what I am thinking is profoundly spiritual. Spiritual awareness and knowledge allow me to deal with life's difficulties because I wish the world were different at the root of my anxiety—no wars, famine, etc. I want plenty for all. I tell myself precisely everything is as it should be and always works out for the best. I had practised as a young man to give up being dishonest and don't allow untruth to pass my lips, and when I fail, I just start again (God forgive me, I say to myself) and have not given up to this day because I gain confidence from it and peace of mind. I have found simultaneous healthy selfishness, high self-respect and a disinclination to make sacrifices without good reason. In my relationships, it is a fusion of the ability to love and, at the same time, have respect for others and respect for myself.

In the same way, I love people. I am kind, and honestly, it happens automatically without giving it a thought. Natural actions are there in my nature, and I am unapologetic for the substance that triggers good and virtuous behaviours.

Similarly, a strong man is strong without being, a rose emits a perfume scent, and a child is childish. I realise that I love for others' being; that is to say, all aspects of my loving needs little motivation. There seems to be a shortness of trying, striving, or straining in others' loving.

My daily life desires are a means to an end rather than ends in themselves. I want money to pay off debts, including the mortgage, and it has caused symptoms that pass through my consciousness daily. I have a compulsive desire to win the lottery, and the symptoms are a never-ending, constant motivational drive with a psychic feeling of guidance. I need to eventually know the big win to give me satisfaction in a relative one-stop along the path of things that seem to get arranged in graded order, like the fundamental need for food, love and shelter. Feeding ourselves adequately and maintaining a roof over our heads and love are primary goals that need satisfying. They motivate my behaviour because at 55 years old, I should have reached or nearly reached these fundamental goals.

Making a Will with a wavering belief
Monday 31st October 2011

I do not relish the idea of thinking about my death, and yet it is vital to give it some consideration because if I die without a will, it can make life even more difficult for the loved ones I leave behind. I do not like the thought of having to plan for when I may not be around to support my wife and family. Given that a will is a legal document, I think it worth paying a professional to write it because my circumstances are not straightforward; a DIY one will not do.

The death of someone close is painful beyond words, so having a will goes a long way to make a difficult time more manageable. One of the points I would like to have written in the Will is my choice for my dead body donated to medical science for teaching and research purposes, dispose of the remains by fire, and scatter the ashes to have organic intentions.

I remembered at the memorial on 6th October for my dad, who died a few years ago (2007), and he was continuously remembered. So, some access to my computer some details about Dad is required.

For some time now, I have come to know that Georgina's boyfriend, Rob, was not brought up as a Christian, and he says he has no faith and is an atheist, but I think he is spiritual. He has proper behaviour at our Christian rituals in our home and our ways as Christian believers. What gives meaning and purpose in life can be religious faith, but I can see that anything or anyone who derives sense, hope, and self-acceptance is a belief. He shows personal respect and understanding. He has said around the dinner table that his upbringing and adult life are without a religious belief, regardless of a sense of connection, hope, and purpose. I think there can be terminology confusion when talking about religion, spirituality, belief or faith. A person's sense of their place in the universe and how they relate to it can be, but not always, regarding an idea of a 'higher power', God, that falls under a religious faith, but they may identify themselves as spiritual. Although Rob has not got a label that neatly falls under a religious faith, it's a deliberate choice he made knowing he is an adult. Still, spirituality encompasses religion and belief and can be broader than this. Rob has not yet found a religious system that perfectly fits his quest for understanding and meaning around the big questions of life and death.

Like ourselves, most people have the organized form of spirituality characterized by a faith leader, holy scripture, a traditional concept of a higher power/God and its set moral codes and ethics. That is how people with religion organize their way of relating to what they hold to be sacred and transcendent. Their spirituality is more secular and independent of ideas of values, identity and humanity. I am pleased, though; Rob concealed the transcendent. He has developed a healthy relationship with our daughter (Georgina). He stands in the right relationship with himself, others, and the world around him, part of English culture. England is becoming increasingly diverse, and people will move between faiths or from belief to unbelief and then back to trust. I hope that Rob can shift; although he has not affiliated with religious institutions, their lives' spiritual dimension is essential. When he goes to invited church services with our Christian daughter, happiness and welfare can be sought.

The ideas or concepts have dominated Christianity as to how individual happiness and welfare should be sought. One of the views or myths held up a specific type of man as ideal, the spiritual man, Jesus. And it is generally assumed that if only this idea is followed, individuals and their welfare would be sure to result. It works well for most people, but this idea has failed me, and it belongs to the Middle Ages, not in the 21st century's psychologically healthy thinking person. I am disturbed or frustrated because life is not fair and looking to Jesus, year on year, without the desired results, frustrates me. My inner nature dictates that I learn to reject conceptions that have been determined as unreliable evidence but retain a sense of hope, purpose, and connection to God. Relationship with others, the cosmos, and the environment is a reasonable option.

My belief is wavering because we are so, so in a rut. My sisters and brother are suffering from diseases. The worst is with my sister Joan, who has breast cancer and has already had two mastectomies undergoing chemotherapy. I rather say I believe in God than the spiritual man Jesus who looks to God too for deliverance. I am so frustrated because the 24/10/2011 was our pearl, thirtieth wedding anniversary; It came and went without a celebration. Our house is still under threat, and we have to sell up, against my better judgment, although we would rather stay in the place we love and made our home. Nothing so far has changed to see this house remain in our hands, and it feels like we are running out of time, but will prayer turn things around? It just seems to be getting worse. One bad thing leads to another worse something happening. Now the boiler has broken down, and the water stopcock has snapped off. I have to find a way to pay for these things. Why am I not seeing improvements? I am praying hard enough for them and putting in practical efforts. I am just coping because I have the determination to solve the problems or deal with them. I have not met our basic needs yet; we still struggle to buy food, clothes, heating and secure a roof over our heads, which induces frustration in my attempt to change our circumstances through part-time paid work, the lottery wishes and, volunteering. The national mental health service user's-led charity called National Survivors Users Network (NSUN) elected me as one of its Trustees at the AGM on 01/11/2011. I get a break from my worries by attending the meetings.

Our environment seems planned and hostile to change, and characteristically, success is more or less hard to achieve. So, instead, I try to make things happen rather than letting things just happen. Of course, I wish the basics were not evil or sinful, and there is nothing necessarily wrong with wanting food, safety, a sense of belonging and love, social approval and self-approval. These are desirable and praiseworthy wishes, I believe.

So far, the boiler engineer has attempted to diagnose the problem with the boiler three times, and he is coming back again today, Thursday, 24th November. A boiler protection plan now takes care of breakdowns—the current bill for £285.00 is to pay in instalments of £23.75 per month. We had to pay a plumber £135.00, including costs as he altered the water mains to isolate the cold water and fixed a rusty leaking gas valve. Our car was vandalised between 5:45 pm on 22nd, and 10:25 am on 23rd November. The vehicle parked two cars short of our front door had the driver's side wing mirror smashed and hanging off, and the high-level brake display lights crashed too, costing us £129.75 to replace the mirror, and the high-level breaking light had adhesive tape to hold it. That vandalism added to the misery and increasing debt.

Grandchildren
In the year 2012 – 13

These continual stories are from 2011 onwards, and writings began four years later on Sunday, 01st February 2015.

There have been many times when I wondered if I would ever get to write about positive experiences. With spring approaching, I will look at past accomplishments, which had helped us grow and be more in touch with myself and my family.

A brief self-evaluation showed that I had clear goals in the past three years, but they are yet to be accomplished, something different from the status quo. I look at my mortality edging closer to the grave and marvel at the life cycle. I have experienced immense happiness attached to the continued struggle to get by. I am passionate about turning negative experiences, mainly mental distress, stigma, and discrimination, into quantifiable positive actions. I have not changed the 'desired' goal based on difficulties. It has been an immense journey for us in these years past. An incredible number of years has been an enormous privilege and fit the set of circumstances at that particular time and gave happiness and growth.

Becoming grandparents was something we anticipated for a long time. We expected our married daughter to be the first to give us a grandchild. So, it came as a shock that our youngest adult child, Jonathan and his partner, had a baby and were married in the same year of the child's birth in 2012.

On Monday, the 30th of January 2012, our first angel grandchild, Iziah Lorenz, was born. An honour, unlike almost every other reward in life. I am a grandparent and did not have to work for it, and he carries my middle name Lorenz; Thank God for the luckiness of miracles and an almighty life change, which confers us a new status and role in our family. We are seen as one of the older generations, and I am happy with the title granddad. Euphemia was glad for the title granny, unlike parenthood, not a job description but rather a state of being. As far as we are concerned, life has nothing sweeter to offer than the care of grandchildren, and our married daughter, Katrina, was expecting her first child in 2013, so we will have the titles, grandma and grandpa.

2013 was a privileged year for us. Our pregnant daughter and her husband Robert came to England in July 2013, and we got a glimpse of the pregnant bump and shared in her joy as Katrina told the relatives of her happiness to be pregnant despite the cravings.

In the same month (July 2013), we celebrated Georgina's graduation from the University of East Anglia in Norwich. She gained her Masters in Physiotherapy and went on to work in Kings Lynn Hospital.

Our second little angel grandchild was born on Tuesday 10th of September 2013, and was named Isaac James. Having grandchildren is like being in love. I see the child's beauty, which hits me anew each time and to have the privilege of sharing in its pristine innocence is fantastic. The gift of grandchildren brought an unexpected glow to the winter and autumn blues when they were born. I feel very close to all my offspring because it is an extra reward for parents to be united by a universal love for a child and share concerns.

We are now grandparents to three boys. Jonathan's wife, Zoe, had another child on Wednesday, 26th February 2014, and the little angel was named Kyven Denzel. We show grey hair on our heads, so we are the family's old heads because we age quickly in the child's universe. Our age brings traditional attributes of respect and wisdom, but the child will grow up, I will die. I know our time with them is brief, and the very brevity of the relationship aids to its passion and preciousness of every moment. For me, being a grandparent has a very particular poignancy, never more so than now that my dad died in 2007, and my mother died on Sunday 24th August 2014. Now, it is my turn to play the role of grandad/grandpa to a new generation, and I am always aware of the echoes and repetitions of my parents watching me play their part with approval. Life goes on; bless their souls. Nothing has given me such a sense of ultimate realization of my aims and hopes as the existence of our children and our children's children. It's the most fulfilling time of my life. I am reasonably sure every parent says at one time or another, 'I can't believe how fast the time has gone,' but it's unbelievably true.

Nothing is unbelievably more authentic than our twenty-three-year-old son, Jonathan, giving us our first grandson. They had Iziah christened and got married in the same year, 2012. His marriage took place in a Church of England parish in West Worthing on Friday 26th October 2012, and he bought a house on a mortgage in Goring-by-Sea. The happy couple's marriage has overwhelmed us with emotion. His mum's cheeks flowed with tears of joy, and my attention was drawn to Jonathan walking down the aisle in an expensive pair of white trainers. He set the footwear fashion trend for his era, and only time will tell if it caught on and stood the test of time.

Holiday in Singapore from Tuesday 10th December 2013 – Thursday 2nd January 2014

Written Tuesday 3rd February 2015

Our second grandson's expected arrival triggered an urgency to go to Singapore as our eldest daughter, Katrina, and her husband Robert settled and made it their home for the foreseeable future.

It had been on our minds to go out there one day before they returned to England to live, but we never thought it could happen at will, 'Where there's a will, there's a way,' without years of planning and disruption to finances. The holiday would be our first proper spell of sunshine abroad in more than thirty years of marriage. We had never had a holiday other than a one-week break in Europe many years ago, and we have yet to have a honeymoon.

Euphemia and I were earning, but the wages were only sufficient to pay living costs, including a monthly mortgage of £986. There was no disposable income or savings we could have accumulated and put toward the desperately needed holiday. My work gradually increased from five hours to sixteen hours and then to twenty-four hours a week, and I qualified for working tax credit, a government benefit. We began to add a saving component to our monthly budgeting and accumulated just over half of the £1136.00 fare for two to Singapore.

At the beginning of 2013, Katrina and I searched the internet for the cheapest flights to Singapore, and even the work's manager got involved and found us an agent. My manager often flies to Australia and changes plane, usually in Singapore, and put me in touch with a travel agency. The holiday was booked with extra funds donated to us by Katrina. We had six months to save up the vacation spending money, and the saving pool grew to £500.00 by December 2013.

Euphemia and I were producing extra adrenaline through our veins when our second grandson was born on the 10th of September 2013, and the holiday neared.

We skyped, video-linked to Singapore in real-time three times a week to keep in touch and noticed the connection was so good that the picture and audio seemed to present them as their physical presence is in our house.

As autumn turned to winter, it almost felt like time had sprinted forward to December, and the holiday was only days away.

On 10th December, our flight departed from Heathrow to Zurich, then a night flight at 22:45 to Singapore. I have albums of photographs of our pleasant, joyful stay in Singapore and an organized trip to Banton Island for a one-night visit that showed us a different place in the Far East. Pictures say much more than words, so I encourage you to see the photos; I have over 200 snaps. Spending quality time with our loved ones overseas is the greatest gift we can have, and capturing moments on camera can tell the memorable holiday's moving story. The holiday was an excellent opportunity for all of us to take a break from work schedules and spend some quality time together. I unhooked from work, fully present and mindful of taking in those special moments when we hugged and moments of outrageous laughter. As we slowed down enough to take in the beauty of the new country and its culture, the unique gift of the season there, with long daily periods of sunshine and warmth of over thirty degrees centigrade, it took away any winter blues we had brought with it. There were some quick showers of rain as the day cooled on some days of the holiday; An umbrella may be needed some time but never a need for a coat or mackintosh; one quickly dries out in the heat of the sun.

We would like to mention a quick note of thanks to Katrina and Robert for the enjoyable holiday. We had a fabulous time, and thank you all for making it such a memorable experience. On our return to England, I received a text message from my work manager to come into work the next day, 3rd January 2014, as arranged. Heading back to work and my daily home life routine immediately switched my thoughts from holiday mode to go out there to do what it takes to put in some serious sweat, blood and tears to achieve goals and bring down obstacles. I confessed to working colleagues, my manager, family and friends that I had a great break, and I was marvellously refreshed. I increased my well-being and happiness by being thankful for an enjoyable holiday with the children and grandchildren and the sense of achievement of mastery in my work.

The wind-down of the year 2013 to begin 2014 (December 2013 to January 2014)

Written Tuesday 3rd February 2015

I had moved powerfully into the new year with a year-end review of 2013, and I'll yearn for certain aspects of my life to change in 2014. Nevertheless, three main goals continue to be carried forward year by year:

1. It is trying to affording the roof over our head.
2. Money in the bank.
3. Enough food in the home.

Too many times, past mistakes were made, and failure was experienced. But I feel some gratitude for all I have, good health, a loving family I hug tight and appreciate. The winding down of one year and the revving up of the next was a time of reflection, gratitude and hope. I had reviewed 2013 using categories based on:

- **Financial** achieved a holiday even though it was tough on the purse.
- **Health** achieved continued stable physical and mental health.
- **Spiritual** attended church when desired, paying my minimum in the collection of £3 to £5 weekly. I have always refused to attend church when I cannot squeeze out the minimum theological fee. I believe excellent church services deserve it.
- **Relationships** achieved excellent communication with spouse, family and friends.
- **Career** very pleasing appraisal 'continue the good work; a valuable member of the workforce' (Manager).

2013 was a good year for us, and I had approached 2014 with writing on the slate where I needed to bridge the gap between where we are and where we want to be. Having had a good honest look at what is getting in the way and re-evaluating what it will take to get what we want eventually, money topped the ladder, and as my career appears to have prospects for promotion, I'm not worried. I had my annual appraisal (2013), and I had regular supervision with the manager. The manager was pleased with my work, and the clients adore my professional approach.

The satisfaction for my work also emerged in my annual appraisal report in January 2014. New possibilities appeared to open up, and I set my sights higher. I looked to be promoted to senior support worker by the following annual review in 2015.

Between January 2014 and June 2014, just six months, things weren't working how planned because stress and anxiety were much too commonly experienced. As the working hours increased, the workload challenged my ability to deliver good quality care at a high standard. I had easily neglected the need to prioritize rest in my life. Communication with co-workers and the manager became counterproductive because issues and incidents did not get dealt with productively. The co-worker and supervisor exchanged conversations with the manager complaining that I challenge their authority as senior team players for the client's best interest. My co-worker targeted my core values and beliefs as he let out his frustration.

An incident broke out between the co-worker and me on 29th March 2014. The manager pinned up a note about affray, and more ground rules were introduced, the known ones were tightened up, and there were stricter working practices with tick lists to the job description. The paper trail was already large to comply with regulations, and there became more writing to show for each worker's daily jobs. It was hard to work with my colleagues because I did not know how to take them. Were they sarcastic or making fun of me? I sensed that some protocol and training advice was not followed, and my strict principle to stick to an ethical code of practice was being laughed at and ridiculed. I got lost in self-criticisms and negative thinking and could not shift my focus. I got tunnel vision on the problems that the work pressure and colleagues' attitude had on my psyche. My threshold for handling stress was reached when I whistle-blew, and the management came down heavily on me because I put my allegation in writing before speaking to the manager about my concerns. The paper trail can lead to the CQC, Care Quality Commission, picking it up, and the company's reputation may be taken to the cleaners as there will be a thorough investigation. The manager believed a good talking to the accused was all it would have taken.

The company's internal investigation began on the accused's side, and on the day of the first hearing on 21st May 2014, I was made to feel that what I saw was inaccurate. They say it could have developed from my imagination based on another trivial incident where the facts were the manager's word against mine. We witnessed variations in the view of the truth on the same matter. My ability to cope and think was overwhelmed, I responded in writing on 24th May in response to the verbal attack in the hearing, and I believe that was the last time of clear observable thinking.

I think I worked for another week, not feeling quite like myself. Clients were asking me if I was all right. A second hearing was planned for the day manager returned from a trip. Suddenly, overnight, I lapsed on the morning of Friday 30th May, showing psychotic symptoms of schizophrenia. (*This date above may not be accurate, but it acts as a guide in fingering out the period I was psychotic at home and did not turn up for work.) I was detained in hospital under the Mental Health Act for 28 days from Thursday 5th June 2014 till Wednesday 2nd July 2014, and I responded well to increased medication. However, I lost about two weeks, 12 to 14 days of memory. I have no memory of my first two weeks as an inpatient.

The trip into psychosis again, as previously in 2009, was an incredible journey in which I operated in a kind of cocoon or bubble where my steps avoided entering personal space so there would be no personal contact with people. I walked on the planet with no sensory experience of my feet being firmly on the ground. Things mechanical in everyday use such as vehicles, the boiler, fridge and washing machine had their obedience and thought artificially designed to run the programme. If the mechanical devices ran smoothly to the end, I would whisper, 'Thank you, thank you,' but if the device was labouring, I whispered, 'Sorry, sorry, sorry,' as I touched it to calm the heavy vibrations. I was hypersensitive to objects that people of good strength and hearing would not find noisy or unable to contact/pick up and discard. I could not decide what to throw away into the black bin, going to a landfill or incinerated. I cowardly put everything that human hands had made into the blue recycled container for reincarnation. Things that mimic nature, such as soft toys and people's photos, took on a physical change. When I looked at them and touched them, a state of artificial life emerged that I could not bring myself to destroy or recycle; every damn thing condemned for the trash heap was alive in my fairy-induced conscious imagination.

I was going around saying sorry, sorry, and sorry to inert objects, minerals and vegetables. Even the waste of toileting, bathing and the wastewater from washing-up dishes are seen as merely moving organisms through the planet and forced out and scattered into the vast darkness of space by the earth's spinning. Of course, it is boloney - nonsense, but when in a state of psychosis, one does not feel part of ordinary existence. It's an alien world in every sense of the word.

Psychotic Episode in 2014, June to July 2014

Written Thursday 05 February 2015

I experienced many positive symptoms in the psychotic state, the behaviours not seen in healthy people. Hallucinations, delusions and some persecution and thought disorders are the positive symptoms that cause me to lose touch with our everyday reality. They remained severe until I received a higher dose of medication in the hospital. The primary disorder is the hallucination of 'voices' talking to me about habits and behaviour, ordering me to do things, and rushing me with the commands. Also, smelling odours that no one else detects and feeling an inert something. For example, feeling tiny things piercing my skin has invisibly heavy air-born germs pressing down on me and sensed they are getting through invading my body and spreading uncomfortable feelings. The feeling of turning around without being touched and having foul tastes was another type of powerful hallucination that the medication controlled. I was fearful when I believed white human males were broadcasting thoughts to leave women alone because it was known I could smell ovulating females without invading their personal space. The voice sounded utterly honest and seemed to be coming from outside me, but other people couldn't hear it.

On another occasion, I had to do what the voice told me, even when I knew I should not because my self-talk or inner speech said no. The sound coming from outside me was intense, troublesome and understandably irritating. My thoughts were passive and surrendered. The following are other brief personal stories of how the disorder of schizophrenia affected how I think, feel and behave during the period before detention in the Welland Centre, St. Mary's Hospital. It would be the second time I had been detained at this hospital.

Vehicles have artificial intelligence and travel above the surface of the road at night. So, road safety became an issue. I felt threatened by some bearded men and frightened by their grins and the territorial power they exhibit when women are around. I saw films on TV, and the stories fit into my circumstances, and comedy actors like the recently deceased star Robin Williams, who played wimp roles, acted like me in real-time. Everything on television seemed to be real-time, people on it could see me, and I was influencing the outcome even if the film or programme gets repeated. But again, it was portrayed by a leading actor playing the fool, or on the radio, saying things that especially connected to me, and I sensed a coding in what they said and, in the music they played, they mocked me.

The exception was classical music, which inspires my mind to feel calm and peaceful, relaxed normality in the turbulence of believing things utterly different from everyone else. Then, a voice compelled me to drink a full tumbler of my warm urine to experiment with self-efficiency and recycle the nutrients from my body to prevent illness. In the interest of science, the voice commanded me to note in my head taste, scent and sensation and lots of sugar were stirred into the remaining half-full glass, and it frothed up and overflowed the rim of the glass. I quickly held the sticky glass, closed my eyes and swiftly gulped its content down my throat, swallowed in gulps and burped.

I would spend hours in the garden and parks observing insects and the movement of the clouds; the sounds of birds chirping seemed to have something to do with me. I gently touched foliage and whispered to the plants and insects. I prevented causing their death by not brushing them away as pests or stepping on them. In my mind, there was a robust external voice tempting me to drink from an old barrel of water with green algae floating on the surface. There were noticeable moving microbes in the water. I felt a sense of having my head pushed downwards to get my mouth closer to the water when there was nobody else there. I was assertive in my thought by repeating the same critical word over and over again, no, no, no, and walked away from the scene. I believed I was broadcasting my thoughts to the world and into the universe and became convinced that others (people of colour, mainly) were plotting to harm me. I was told by the voice to invent something that has never been done before and, if I could not, go back to basic engineering to start the ideas. In my bedroom, ideas came, but they drifted from idea to plan; the thoughts wandered. After a minute or two, when there was a clear connection between them, I ran downstairs to gather material I wanted to use to make the part, but I couldn't remember the original idea. I would go up and down the stairs several times until one thought was a fixed belief; to make a device with homemade materials to keep the rubbish bin in the kitchen permanently open. However, concentration was weak, and again, thoughts were disconnected, and it was hard for Euphemia to understand what I was doing and why. She found I had propped the bin lid open using one brand new chopstick that we brought back from our holiday in Singapore. Each time Euphemia would remove the chopstick, I would replace it with another one. Never a growl or quarrel between us, I took to going back to bed and slept.

I feel uncomfortable with people, except for my wife, children and close relatives. The domesticated animals seemed curious; then, they do what they always do, like all pets.

Two Sunday morning church services started at 9 am-10 am, and the other from 10:30 am-11:30 am in two various locations, and I swear to God I can hear the service and sermon as I stayed in bed cuddled up under the duvet. One service was at the Anglican Church a few metres from the house, and the other was at the URC church about one mile away.

I recall only one inpatient episode of delusion, which can be explained as part of my culture, background and religion. I was petrified going to bed at night because I feared the black African males, who must have been in dreams, were plotting to kill me. I have no idea what had happened from admission to waking up two weeks later on a bed in a secure room and being scared of African men. They told me I was not in a coma, but I have no laid down memory to call upon; I can only go on what my family said to me about what they can remember about my first two weeks as an inpatient. It had to be a dream seen as from an evolutionary (long) sleep. When I woke, I remembered coming out of the proverbial soup and growing to be a man on the wild plains of Africa. I did not believe in superstitions, witchcraft, angry spirits, and the devils like the people there. I did not remember being born from a woman, a birth mother; I just saw myself "here." I was intrigued by the sun's movement and all of creation, and I had a deep sense of being mortal and having a soul, a part of me that is not subject to death. I tried to sermonize my belief to the natives that we are moral agents to the earth and believe only in the creator God to whom worshipping would be appropriate. I was captured and bound, and rituals of a sacrificial nature were performed over my body. I struggled to release myself, unaware I was wriggling myself free from under the tight sheet and blankets covering the hospital bed. I battled with this same dream, and it seems for a long time. I was frightened to sleep because the night staffs were mainly African men and women who sometimes sang or hummed redemption songs at about six o'clock in the morning.

The objective reality was different because I had observed faulty vivid perceptions and delusions out of my mind, unable to identify actual events. Nevertheless, I was suspicious of them and sensed a connection besides our very dark skin.

They were talking to each other in their native African language. There's a plot to have me killed. As I got better, I realised I was safe and was in a hospital setting. I tried to participate in OT (occupation therapy), but I could not complete the simplest tasks. Understanding instructions and following the instructions was nearly impossible. I had settled better in sleep, and the absurd ideas disappeared, but I could not perform folding or cutting paper to make things like origami, do collages or paint the Union Jack flag on a piece of paper and cut out its shape. Full recovery took a long time; although the positive symptoms had disappeared before leaving the hospital, intellectual disability and negative symptoms persisted and were troublesome. I had to remind myself that I would be okay, and I could get through. Don't give up. My family, the wife, Euphemia, my children, my mother, Merle, and Joan, were just some people who kept me grounded to gain the bigger picture. They were unmeasurably supportive and helpful as I bounced back, and life got tricky as I again came face to face with worry, fear and uncertainty.

Worry Fears and uncertainty
July to December 2014
Written on Sunday 8th February 2015

I was facing many different barriers to a healthy, productive life after another lived experience with schizophrenia. I tended to worry about things such as the negative symptoms which manifest themselves, such as laziness. It stopped me from feeling motivated and having the energy to get up and go to fit back smoothly into regular day-to-day living and society and return to my job when the period of sick leave was over. Other barriers, such as preventing cash flow and growth of the relationship with my spouse, worried me because I may worsen again and go back into the hospital again or need lengthy intensive support at home for the rest of my life. I feared that our mortgage and utility bills would not get paid, and it was the worst worrying predicament I could face.

During my incapacity, my mother's generosity made her give Euphemia £2500 in cash, which paid for the inevitable outgoing payments that would have been missed. There was considerable uncertainty in my mind about my ability to carry out any work that counts as earning a living because schizophrenia had this time damaged some of my cognitive functions. Memory, understanding conversation and verbal communication were showing impairments. There was a tendency to worry more than helpful when I had a meeting on 29th October 2014 in my home. My manager and deputy talked about reasonable adjustments if I returned to work when the medical certificate expired. The unfortunate truth is that I will never be able to stop worrying because a government benefit will cease (DLA) and be replaced with Personal Independent Payment (PIP), which re-engages me with worrying thoughts. PIP requires answering a questionnaire on a form before being called for a face-to-face assessment. Euphemia felt it out of her depth to fill out the form and gave it to my current psychiatrist, responsible for my overall care for the past two years, to complete it by the extended deadline. I was in the hospital at that time.

The changes from getting sickness benefits and decreased working tax credits since declaring myself sick and giving medical certificates to my employer gave us cash flow problems. I began to receive £72.40 a week paid into the bank fortnightly from National Insurance Contribution-based Employment and Support Allowance six months later, 15th November 2014. The DWP may need me to attend a Work Capability Interview with a personal advisor if I'm not in the support group, which is determined from the questionnaire sent to me. I need a plan to actively prepare for a future situation that deals with the problems that cause me to worry repeatedly.

The DWP decided that I was not entitled to PIP because I don't meet the criteria. However, they realized I have a disability or health condition and told me that the monthly £305 Disability Living Allowance would end on 2nd December 2014. I turned gravely to my faith and asked a friend, URC member Barbara Thomas, who gave £50 and my sister, Joan, who often gave cash to help us with anything from £20 to £100. A most welcome organic food parcel by my in-laws (Mr and Mrs Simon) nourished us, and the last in-coming money for December 2014 came in Euphemia's usual wages of £701 a month. My brother-in-law gave Euphemia £300 for the work we had done to organise his house and move to a flat.

There are high levels of uncertainty in our lives, and my hands seem tied, or it's out of our hands to do anything. We can only wait for the results of fate or luck. I acknowledge that chance is not a rational way of actually helping to control events. Still, even by people of faith, we are perceived to be susceptible to influence from outside forces. Therefore, I cannot turn to superstitions or charm as a method of goal achievement and confidence-building. Unfortunately, though, it felt like no matter how hard I try, things don't work the way I planned. Life just seems to be full of one failure after another. It's been exhausting, and I get worrisome thoughts that I may lapse again under the stresses of life's stepping stones to success.

My GP and psychiatrist are working together to drug me with short-term use of another antipsychotic medication called Haloperidol. In addition, diazepam was prescribed for short-term use, along with my regular antipsychotic medication Aripiprazole because we all know too well that schizophrenia can make dealing with everyday life events an excessive stressful challenge.

If there is one thing that faith can add to my life, it is a sense of hope and optimism. I am not going back to work. I sent a resignation letter to the manager, and the consequences of that decision are long-term stress because I do not have enough money to meet my basic needs. So much of everyday life includes doing things called 'work'- but I can't handle it, so I quit and believe in fate to bring money to meet our basic needs. My core belief gives me the way to live my life with values, the right attitude and not relying on work to sustain my happiness. A job should have brought in enough money to live comfortably and possibly increase our joy. It didn't, because I think the most meaningful things in life are family, friends, community and helping others, and rewarding work are not about the money. Part of my core belief is connecting to a higher power. Whatever name or label people give to this spiritual source is irrelevant, in my opinion. The important thing is the sense that there is something higher than us and that I don't have to carry the entire burden alone. Faith enhanced my ability to deal with life's ups and downs and bounce back from those difficulties.

One such difficulty that needs us to stay hopeful is balancing income and expenditure again. The only profit we had from December 2014 was the two-weekly £144.80 Employment Support Allowance payments and Euphemia's wages of £701.00. If you do the maths, the income was not enough to pay priority bills when the mortgage was £986.07, decreasing life insurance and home insurance was £93, dual fuel bill £190, ad discounted water bill £28.00. The reduced council tax was £41.00. So far, the arithmetic doesn't include household services like telephone, TV licence, broadband internet or motoring expenses, road tax, car insurance cost, or breakdown cover. Likewise, the equation doesn't add up our food and housekeeping things like toiletries, cleaning products, and money for clothes and hairdressers. Nevertheless, three main goals continue to be carried forward year by year, and my faith strengthens my outlook for them to be better one day before reaching the grave. A year on, again, and we are no closer to accomplishing:

1. Trying to affording the roof over our head.
2. Having no money in the bank.
3. Having not enough food in the home.

My confidence took a hit at this point, Christmas, December 2014, because it showed I had failed in my ambition and goals. I could not see any accomplishment and had a mood change; although I knew so much of life was out of my control, I had aimed to follow my bliss and gain a personal prize. Money was tight, and I gave up my job rather than giving consent for my manager to get a medical report from my doctor on which she would base her decision to take me back or end my zero-hours working contract. I experienced an unexpected challenge to bounce back as self-trust has dwindled, and I don't feel empowered about our life. I lost a grip on my self-control and made choices that are not intentional, and my integrity was urged out, leaving me feeling regret and guilt. I didn't feel great about myself, but I simply had self-talk, and that inner voice began telling things that tore me down and lifted me at the same time. I was yet to reach a stable point where positive statements would suddenly make my problems disappear or feel like I was dealing with things. I couldn't –let go of the emotional baggage I carried and get my head around these life events that brought temporary unhappiness.

On Sunday, 24th August 2014, my mother's sudden death at age eighty-five was a painful loss and trauma that brought sadness, lasting weeks and running into months. All in all, life events with their uncertainty impacted my happiness, but being value-driven has given me the sense that our lives have meaning and are meant to fulfil some larger purpose. In addition, I derived satisfaction from within the face of incredible hardship with my religious/ spiritual faith practice, preventing me from being too focused on what others are getting where the grass often looks greener.

Celebration and tragedy in 2014
Written on Sunday 8th February 2015

Much is unknown about the future, which leaves it mainly up to the imagination and natural disposition to play a considerable role in thinking about the future.

I had known for some time, before poor mental health, that Katrina and family were to visit England for eight weeks and in between the trip to a friend's wedding in Australia, our grandson was to stay with us for a week in the period. On Sunday the 20th July 2014, soon after their return, Isaac would be christened. A few days (5?) after I got discharged home, the thrilling sight of our grandson turned life's lemons into lemonade rather than viewing our lives as shadowed by a dark cloud. I paid attention to 'family', and it improved my mood and future outlook.

Is my glass half empty or half full? It was not always easy to look on the bright side when from July to December 2014, I didn't believe that I had control over good things happening. I felt better equipped to handle adverse life events because I prepared for the worst and hoped for the best. During that period, life threw curveballs, and I was not as cheery as I could have been. The best possible circumstances for the year came when my frail mother, Joan (sister), and all of us (my family and the in-laws and friends) attended Isaac's christening at the same church where Katrina and Robert were married, Manchester. Afterwards, we had a celebration lunch and mother was not feeling well and Joan, who lived with our mother, started the long journey home when mother had a bit to eat and had seen the christening cake cut.

Five weeks later, we suffered a loss. On Sunday, 24th August 2014, my mother suffered a stroke when she had an afternoon rest and catnap in bed. I felt overwhelming sadness, and I found myself faking smiles as I tried to find solace in our grief. There was emptiness, a sense of solitude. The enormity of the moment meant I was fragile in my recovery; hence, the clinicians introduced short-term medication. After about three weeks, I momentarily suspended my heart-heavy burden. I was to go on holiday with Jonathan's family and the in-laws, but I changed my mind because I felt such an immense loss, so Euphemia went with them on the 13th of September. Three days before was mother's funeral on 10th September 2014. Tears fell from my eyes cathartically at the graveside, and I was emotionally enabled, and I allowed others to comfort me. Getting through the grief was tough; it was the most challenging thing in the year because it involved my heart. They say that when we love deeply, we hurt deeply. I was aching at losing my mother so suddenly, and healing began to happen when memories popped up about my mother, making me smile. As a family, we talked of mother verbally and did not bottle up all that we were feeling, and Euphemia, too, was involved in the decisive moments of healing. She was with me when I didn't wish to talk, I only spoke in my heart, and self-talk and Euphemia shared in silent restoration. We felt better by crying out the natural by-product of our sadness, our tears.

My mother's Eulogy
Written Sunday 31st August 2014

Mother died Sunday 24th August 2014, funeral Wednesday 10th September 2014.

Nearly everyone claims to have the best mother ever, but I won that lottery because of the love and compassion shown to us. We reflect on our dear mother's life, and we share thoughts and memories about her at this time. Mother was brought up with traditional values and learnt the skills that a woman of her era should, like cooking, sewing and crochet. Mother has always been my support, strength and comfort when times were tough. I don't know how I will cope without my mother—it leaves a massive hole in my life, but I draw strength from the things she taught me and God's words.

Mother was a very compassionate person, and she loved her family and friends very deeply. We were taught solid values and family importance, good manners, respect, faith, hard work, kindness, tolerance, generosity, forgiveness, and love. These values have made us who we are, and we thank her so very, very much. Mother knew she had to let go and allow us to make our own mistakes and choices in life, and she remained prayerful and hopeful when times were tough for us.

Mother's faith was rooted in hope, the hope that good will always triumph over evil, the belief that peace defeats war, the hope that life defies the grave. Mother is an outstanding example of true Christianity of the soul in heaven.

She did not go from life to death, but she's merely asleep until God awakens her. Mother's trust was grounded in unconditional love. She loved nature, enjoyed tending her garden, and saw that others' day-to-day judgment and action shaped what often happened in an unfair world.

She watched the television news prayerfully because she wanted the awful things in the world to stop. However, when fictional dramas and soaps were on television, our mother couldn't easily be distracted from Coronation Street, EastEnders, and Emmerdale. Of course, she enjoyed these programmes for their entertainment value, but she felt empathy for the characters.

Mother's most exceptional quality was encouraging us to make the best of everything and face problems head-on. She was a proud woman who believed that obstacles could be overcome if we communicate with God.

In closing, I'd like us to celebrate and praise God for the life she lived. Unfortunately, we have lost many family members and friends over the years, including Dad, but we are comforted that Mother and Dad are in heaven and we all will meet again in the eternal home.

I know that my mother is in Christ, so that I can say **to God be the Glory**. We love you, our mother.

10/09/2014
Table Grace

It was an honour to stand in the church and share my precious memories of our dear mother. Of course, all will miss her, but her mind will live on in all of our hearts forever.

I would like to thank all of you here on behalf of my sisters, brother and myself, and the rest of my family for your efforts, great and small, to help us mark our mother's passing.

As we are now about to partake of this food and drinks, let us digest some words of the grace of thanksgiving.

Lord God, we thank you for all the good things of your providing.
We pray for the time when people everywhere shall have the abundant life of your will.
What we eat, we give thanks for it in Christ and ask, let it be blessed.
Spread your mercy from the tables, we pray. And thanks for all the benefits which thou have given us through Jesus Christ our Lord.
Amen.

10/09/2014
Message from Katrina, Georgina & Jonathan on wreath card. They are written in bold.

In Loving Memory.
Our beloved Granny,
Forever in our thoughts.
You'll be dearly missed.

With love and affection
Goodnight and God bless.
Granny, granny, we love you
Granny, we will miss you
Granny, we will treasure you in our hearts
You were as powerful as the sun, which shone so bright
You were as cute as a bunny and smelled like flowers
Granny, we love you
Granny, we will miss you
Granny, we will treasure you in our hearts.
Written by Jahmia, Sianne and Theo Shakespeare 7.9.2014 and read by them in the church service.

10/09/2014
Toast read by Georgina

Housekeeping announcements,
We are not expecting a fire drill today, so please leave the building in an orderly fashion if the fire bell rings.
There are two fire exits on my left, and the main entrance door at the back is also a means of escape, and we gather in the car park.
The toilets are situated as you entered the building on the right-hand side.

Ladies and gentlemen, as we are now to partake of the food and drinks, I'd like to say a few words on behalf of my dad, aunts and uncle to thank you all for being here today to say goodbye to our dear grandmother and mother.
She will be significantly missed, but I know her memory will live in our hearts forever.
Let us take a moment to say a few words of the prayer in thanksgiving:
Let us pray: O Lord our God, we humbly come before you to thank you for the many blessings you have provided.
Though our hearts are filled with sadness for those who have lost loved ones, we pray for the Holy Spirit to comfort them.
Please continue to strengthen and sustain us, bless what we're about to receive, and ask these things in Christ Jesus. Amen.
I think facing our first Christmas without my mother's presence was one of the most challenging things I will ever endure. We spent Christmas with Jonathan's family, the in-laws, their relatives and friends.

Review of 2014 using categories based on:

- **Financial** very poor, in deep debt because much less than the usual average monthly money was coming in.
- **Health** poor, I relapsed.
- **Spiritual** I could not attend church because my minimum contribution to the collection plate of £3 to £5 weekly couldn't be met—I suffered spiritual withdrawal symptoms.
- **Relationships** reminded me what's essential, sharing activities, interests and living together. More time needs to be devoted to the relationship with the spouse.
- **Career** Terminated.

I had contemplated about the year 2014, and my thinking had a negative self-punishing quality about it because I often thought, 'I'm a failure.' It just popped into my head at any moment, and my thoughts collected evidence for why it is true. I managed to stop entertaining the idea in the rough and hectic time of the year and focus on what I can learn from life's significant setbacks.

A letter to my psychiatrist
(Inserted in the book February 2015)

Dated: 17th November 2014

Howdy do Doctor
Re: Employment.

Throughout my employment history, I have had relapse after relapse. There was no discrimination between the types of work I did, some were low stress and had few responsibilities, and still, relapse occurred. I have been involved in precision engineering, basic engineering, shelf-packing, sewing plastic bags, social care work, and assisting clients' care. All this work has seen my condition worsen. The stress of work aggravates my schizophrenia, and the stimulation of daily challenges with co-workers and the manager seems to cause a decline in my cognitive functioning.

For many years, my symptoms were well controlled. It did not hinder my career efforts until people stressed me and uncomfortable situations with social interactions became too challenging to deal with. I don't know why I cannot understand sarcasm or sarcastic remarks and why I am sensitive to criticism and specific humour. I have this hypersensitivity, and I rehearsed or replayed the situation over and over in my head. I find doing role-plays unbelievably challenging because I can only be true to myself. However, I excelled at work until poor symptom management had affected my skillset and ability to function in the work environment. I have identified why it's hard for me to hold down a job in mainstream society leading to retirement age. Work provides me with a sense of purpose, dignity and social inclusion. I achieve functional re-mission for a time, but the nature of my disorder is such that my ability to sustain my rational processes is damaged. Understanding and using the information to make the right decisions and using information immediately after learning it is inadequate. It causes me emotional distress, and it's hard to lead a healthy, fulfilled, successful life at work. My inner voice, the voice I hear in my head when reading, my internal monologue somehow becomes faulty too. My rational connections with the world do not function well, fooling my belief system into believing what I was thinking or what I believe is true and correct, but others can tell my thinking processes were unsound. It was difficult to accept that what I was thinking was crazy. It's a 'catch 22' because understanding that I have had psychosis says I am remembering correctly and therefore not crazy/insane, and I could only have been psychotic if I believe that I was not.

I will be more alert to emerging symptoms or worsening cognitive functions and take prompt action. Still, I am frightened to go back into the work environment because mental symptoms are challenging to recognize.

The Journey into psychosis always seems like a mystical experience because the phenomenon puts me in a parallel reality with cosmic forces acting and putting me in touch with infinity and the eternal, giving me the feeling of being immortal, invincible.

The rigid control of rationality no longer restricts one. I began to be in this mystical journey of mathematical theories and metaphors, dictating this reality's truth. I feel I have unique insights and special powers, and the feelings were disabled when helped by artificial support like medicines. Just like deaf, blind or physically disabled people have guide dogs and wheelchairs or crutches, it is reasonable to say that my 'crutches' are chemicals that act on biochemical imbalances in my brain. I can say for sure that I would not function as I do without having such medication. Let the truth be told that taking medication has side effects that can be problematic, even disabling. When stress and pressure cause me to break and malfunction, the medicine gives relief and hope of functioning reasonably; I am rational again. I tend to overreact to stress with my emotions and with cognition. My coping mechanisms are to do with my mental processes trying to defend against the stress and strain. My mind races, and I become vigilant, more suspicious as it craves a healthy person's perspective with sound logical, rational reasoning.

I had lost my ability to remain rational and began to go crazy. My mind reverted to an evolutionarily earlier way of functioning. Eating as much as I could, stealing or hoarding food, and tending not to look at the people I talked to or who wants to speak to me. Smells, fear and love, were enhanced, and suffering in vigorous activity moved me to tears. Jokes are perceived as threats, and I misinterpret communication by co-workers and employers as hurtful insults or hostile criticism. Going back to work will compel me to avoid the persons, places, and things where I am likely to encounter expressed emotion, but preventing such circumstances will not always be possible. It seemed to be part of my schizophrenia that shows up my vulnerability in employment. I haven't yet found a proper mechanism to deal with this faultiness when facing unfair criticism, which causes frequent breakdowns. The nature of my disorder is such that my ability to sustain my rational processes is damaged. The activities that do not tax my logical skills, like music, poetic-type endeavours, dance, writing and art, are much easier to handle and engage with them. Since my latest relapse, I linked my high self-stigma levels to low motivation to work because I feel I can never do it again. I am not able to return to work, even after symptoms stabilised. There will be problems with task performance as I will find it hard to fulfil the full job description. That is because of some physical disabilities that I have and having trouble thinking clearly. I had struggled with everyday emotions and workload, which had led to conflicts with co-workers. I have trouble prioritizing, making the right decisions, and remembering things, and I lack cohesion in parts of speech and coherence.

Doctor, this letter was written to show that the route back into full employment is not realistic for me, but I still need to earn and not live off welfare. I found the whole business of returning to work very frighteningly, and I don't know how I can ever do it again.

Yours sincerely,
Karl Willett.

The struggle of Making a Living with Schizophrenia
Written Monday 16th February 2015

I'd like this year to be different and forgive myself when I screw up. I had often beaten myself up for mistakes and felt stuck, then made poor choices. Ignoring myself may lead to making better, healthier choices and being more skilful in decision-making. Then, when I fall off the wagon, I wouldn't be too upset because I will try and figure out what went wrong and then let it go, and getting myself back on track would be my hope.

January 2015 was hard for us because we were in fuel poverty, made payment plan arrangements to pay the £312.87 fuel bill, and had not paid January's mortgage payments totally; we had arrears of £486.00. We arranged with the mortgage company to pay £550 for the next two months from a mortgage of £986.18 monthly, and they will look at things again after three months. I had filled in an MI12 claim form for the government to pay a percentage of the mortgage interest. The decreasing life insurance premium from Legal & General I cancelled, as I cannot afford the £50.86 a month, and the council tax was reduced to £41.00 per month.

Euphemia and I have looked at having a lodger in our home, but I am uncomfortable with the idea, even though we had drawn up a lodger's agreement to let out a bedroom. There is so much red tape letting a room as a claimant of council tax benefit and ESA that we'll be more disadvantaged and see no genuine interest in letting out a place. Our hope lies in me meeting the ESA Support Group's eligibility criteria, which will increase my payments to £108.15 a week. I had asked PIP to reconsider their decision in October 2014 that I don't meet the criteria. My most profound, heart-wrenching prayer is that they change their minds, and over £444.00 will become part of our income. Those two benefits would bring in £877.40 monthly, plus my wife's wages of £701.00 per month, making a total income of £1,578.40. We would be able to make our way in life, although it will still be a struggle. The alternative to losing one of those benefits might wind up with us having no place to live and increasing our debt burden.

On 16th January 2015, I received a letter from the ESA saying I was placed in the Support Group. Hip, hip, hooray, and thank God! But the challenges are not yet over. In a perfect world, I would be able to focus on my recovery, first and foremost, without having to worry about having a roof over our heads and food on the table, but that's just not our reality. No sooner have I seen an obstacle (the obstacle of ESA) removed than another has taken its place in the form of the Council Tax Award Support problems. An error was made when we were assessed in July 2014. Therefore, the Council Tax Support did not cover the total amount of Council Tax payable, and we will have to pay the difference, which is £504.75 due by the 1st March 2015. I have learned that I have to rely on myself to get what I want out of life, although I gave up work because I can't hack it in so many different ways. (See letter to doctor re, Employment) Through the eye of faith and in some cases, I can see factual evidence that our economic state of depression will lift forever.

The month of **February 2015** has come swiftly, and the arrears on the mortgage have amounted to £923. I have nine things on my prayer list to benefit us, of which four are faith-based, and the other five are related to gaining proof that we will live comfortably, praise be to God.

1. Mother's inheritance/friend donation. *(Answered prayer)*
2. PIP to see I am eligible for the benefit. *(Answered prayer but not as expected)*
3. MI12 form about the government paying a percentage of mortgage interest. *(Not answered yet)*
4. Giant lottery wins with moderate gambling. *(Not answered yet)*
5. Leave room for the unexpected and miracles to happen. *(i.e., PPI answered prayer)*
6. Support Group for ESA. *(Answered prayer)*
7. Suitable lodger (not responded yet)
8. Get involved in clinical trials. (not *answered yet)*
9. *Euphemia's employer has reorganised and restructured the program that engages families with babies and young children. Euphemia found that her line manager is less supportive since the change, and the workplace has a less friendly atmosphere. As a result, she is unhappy about working there. (I pray for her to be happy in her work and the people she works with to show consideration.)*

On 7th February, I received a cheque for £1600. The children were given £967.00 from their mother's cash inheritance. Surprise surprise, surprise, on the 9th of February, an unexpected letter arrived resulting from a reassessment of a Payment Protection Insurance (PPI) loan policy. The revised decision had summarised a total payment to us of £3,992.50. I banked the cheque today, Thursday 19th February 2015. What does the supreme force in the universe have in mind for us? I am worried that it is not a long-term solution to the mortgage payments and keeping a roof over our heads even after the money is in the kitty.

A letter came today (19/02/15), giving the reconsidered decision on (PIP) Personal Independent Payment. Unfortunately, the decision was upheld that I don't meet the criteria. What a blow! A disappointment; we must continue to hunt for a long-term solution to our everyday living problems.

I give myself some thinking time, about two hours, during the day to effectively worry about the problems and then switch off and do something else. I do feel gratitude for all that we have, thankful for the little things reminding us of the meaning of life. I had placed a lot of importance on work and family and had very high confidence in those, but now that I have no job, I feel less capable. The frequent psychotic episodes shatter my plan every time I am anything worthy.

I have explored how I can serve and contribute to others, and the world around me since working for a living set off my schizophrenia. I have emailed research study centres and put my name forward to be part of clinical trials for schizophrenia, but I have yet to speak to my psychiatrist about it. I am passionate about involvement in clinical trials because it's about giving and sharing for me. My soul enjoys giving to others and helping them feel happy, and being involved as a guinea pig in trials creates something that improves people's lives. Doing so feels like a need in my life, like the basic universal need for water, shelter, food and clothing. It's part of my happiness and fulfilment.

I am relying on irrational hope!

Written Monday 30th March 2015

I have no contingency plan at the moment to lower life's stress levels, except praying and keeping irrational hope alive. I am determined to go on and let things work themselves out for good. But, unfortunately, I have not bounced back from the relapse, and it's probably because of my age. I am no spring chicken at this time of my life.

Euphemia and I visited our son and family and spent a weekend with them. On the Sunday 8th March, which was the third Sunday in Lent, we attended church at Parish of St Richard in Goring, our first church service for 2015. Due to financial and social reasons, my church attendance has declined dramatically. Since the breakdown, I am more socially withdrawn, but the cash offering prevents me from regular worship, fellowship, and prayer in church. I don't want to fall into the trap of only attending church on life-changing events and the church's biggest calendar festivals. I delight in the range of opinions on doctrine and practices offered in a religious institution, but my pride stops me from stepping into the building because I am broke.

I have restricted myself from church until I can pay my way with priority or disposable income set aside for religious activities. The PPI money has given us a breathing space to maintain monthly payments for a few more months. It's the only money in reserve for the monthly deficit of £726.00. We cannot generate any more income due to our financial circumstances being unlikely to improve in the foreseeable future. It allows us to pay the mortgage, bills and other outgoing expenses by budgeting this vital resource sensibly. With continued budgeting of the PPI money carefully, it is due to see us through to the beginning of June 2015.

Euphemia has been taking our neighbour's child to nursery before she goes to work and baby-sitting when required in their home. This arrangement started in June 2014, and it has been a valuable way to earn petty cash that could be used solely for her, but as you may gather, sometimes, when desperately short of necessities, it was used for that. Hope keeps us going because it focuses on the future, and being in the now is somewhat denied because it is encountering gloom, cynicism and passivity. I am not suggesting hope cannot be found in the living moment of 'now' as in yearning for a brighter tomorrow in which I envision a future in which I want to participate. The future is not yet determined, life is open-ended, and hope is the source of courage for counteracting gloom, cynicism and passivity. I feel I am suffering deeply financially, and faith is not aware or reasonable enough to penetrate financial darkness; it is fundamentally an illusion. It perpetuates misery if it is a lingering hope. A good wish is authentic, realistic and clings, which requires courage, wisdom, insight and sustaining abilities in the face of suffering, and it needs faith to work. Hope is not the same as blind optimism, and it was not based on impossible dreams or magic wands but distinguished by mere wishing.

I have wished for financial wealth through the lottery. It has not worked. A big lottery win is unrealistic because of the mathematical odds, but I had included reasonable expectations. It came about that £20.00 was won on the health lottery on 25th March 2015, which seemed appropriate knowing the odds of winning. I have changed my mindset and stopped wishing on a star that takes no effort, but I hope effectively, which requires enormous effort and will shape our lives. The most active faith component is in the hidden ingredient with a placebo effect, transcending emotion. Hope has become a moral virtue, and though often despair operates alongside it, hope is not easy to sustain. The desired hope to win big on the lottery has eluded me. It has frustrated me because this week, the same person won the big jackpot for the second time, and one person won £53 million on the EuroMillions Lottery. I felt I had been let down.

My last week (Tues 31/03/ to Wed 08/04/2015) of what I called moderate gambling. It could be seen as heavy gambling on the game because I spent £25.00 in one month. I am returning to having a flutter at will because it is not sustainable to gamble frequently. Vital necessities are being squeezed out of the weekly budget since I increased the rate and the amount I play on the lotteries. I am now putting a lot of effort into concentrating on getting my nine creditors to write off the debts by asking them in writing.

Overall, the creditors have ceased collection activity, and I am no longer obliged to make any token repayments, so I rejoice over that. However, some creditors ask for further information from my psychiatrist, and others have not responded yet.

The month of **March 2015** has come swiftly to an end, and by the grace of God, we go into April. I continue to maintain prayer lists which are kind of selfish. I check in to evaluate my progress of what faith with works has done and is doing. I have seeded the ground and covered the soil with my aspirations, simple mental ideas or applied physical effort to things which faith and hope act upon. Praise be to God for the fruit they will bring forth.

- I seek eligibility for the PIP benefit again *because the condition has worsened. I have received a new application form.*
- MI12 form about the government paying a percentage of mortgage interest is ongoing.
- Giant lottery wins with moderate gambling resulted in an only minimal gain. So, I am going back to the odd flutter only.
- Leave room for the unexpected and miracles to happen. (*Unexpected payment for £313.57 arrived into our account from a Standard Life investment*)
- I am paying, in instalments, the council tax's overpayment that the council claim we should have noticed. Citizen's Advice helped us reclaim the money because they claimed some liability for processing the application wrongly. It's ongoing.
- Looking for a suitable lodger is on hold.
- Get involved in clinical trials. I am yet to speak with my psychiatrist.
- *Euphemia's employer has reorganised and restructured the program that engages families with babies and young children. Euphemia found that her line manager is less supportive since the change, and the workplace has a less friendly atmosphere; she is unhappy working there. (I pray for her to be happy in her work and the people she works with to show consideration.) Ongoing, Euphemia still feels unsupported, but the work itself is alright.*

I have asked creditors to write off the debts and am waiting for some more creditors to respond.

- I was expecting to hear something about mis-sold PPI on my credit card taken out in 1998 following the investigation that PPI was mis-sold on a loan I took out with the Bank of Scotland, and I was refunded that money.
- I was awarded Employment Support Allowance, income-related and not contribution-based, which allowed me to apply for a boiler grant to replace my ten-year-old boiler with an "A"-rated version.

I am Stuck in Limbo
Written on Saturday 06th June 2015

It seems that I have difficulty choosing the right course of action to achieve my goals. I feel stuck in limbo, wanting a healthy life but unable to take the necessary steps to make it. For example, my claim for interest payments for our housing costs on the M112 form was turned down because the income received exceeds the amount ESA can pay me by £33.15.

I had a small win on the lottery amounting to £4.00 in April 2015. The Citizen's Advice has told us about the overpayment of the council tax. Euphemia will have to declare her dyslexia and that our disability played a good part in not noticing the error. We decided to accept the Council's decision to pay £130.00 per month, including this year's Council Tax, to clear the debt. We gave up the fight with the council and did not pursue on the ground of both of us having poor mental health and not having the capacity to recognise the council's error as the Citizen's Advice suggested.

From April 2015 till now, Saturday 06th June 2015, Euphemia's working week has been four days. I agreed with her to turn down full-time work; We will not see any financial benefit, and she would lose the core pleasure of having a day off in the week to catch up on essentials that make life meaningful other than work activities.

We were delighted to see Katrina and our grandson in England for the Easter holiday from Friday 20th March to 10th April 2015. They plan to return to the UK at Christmas time this year, with her husband as well.

In April 2015, I had a PPI credit card refund of £1,293.34, and with that money, I bought a dining table and six chairs, a garden shed and a front gate from reputable internet sites. Npower carried out a home energy assessment, and British Gas surveyed intending to replace our floor-standing boiler. Both companies suggested replacing the boiler with a wall-mounted type. Npower proposed relocating a new boiler into the back bedroom with no cost under the government boiler replacement scheme. British Gas would transfer the boiler onto a wall in cupboard space in the kitchen for £250.00 under the same government boiler replacement scheme. We had chosen to mount the boiler in the back bedroom to save us from redecorate, but after time elapsed and careful consideration, we changed our minds and wanted it mounted in the kitchen. We await a recent British Gas survey to determine whether the specifications and location remain as previously seen.

There were two no-shows on the PIP home visit, and I cancelled an inconvenient visiting time to be rescheduled. The stress had me talking to the duty mental health worker and visiting the GP for anxiety tablets, 2mg of Diazepam, and 7.5 mg of Zopiclone sleeping tablets. I needed to show how my mental illness affects my daily living, and Euphemia and I thought that the PIP assessor visit went well, and we felt confident that it would result in an award. I had seen the newly appointed psychiatrist with Euphemia in May 2015, and he says he made a mental note of my request to take part in clinical trials. The psychiatrist filled in debt and mental health evidence forms to send to my creditors, and our discussion covered my wellbeing. He seemed to think that I am symptom-free on a high dose of 30mg of Aripiprazole. The positive symptoms of antipsychotic drug therapy are an essential aspect of schizophrenia being under control. Managing positive and negative control was not discussed with a psychiatrist. I acknowledged my need for the medication for the rest of my life. I knew the risk of relapse and the worst awful quality of life if not taken. I want to be on a moderate dose of the medication to reduce the negative symptoms. I am looking for better tolerability of my negative traits. I aim to be on the recommended daily dose of 15 mg of Aripipozole as I see the stresses in my life diminish.

I have difficulty with moving and joint pains, muscle pains with pain in my legs and stiffness. I am continually feeling exhausted with weakness in the body, and although the same symptoms show up in tapering off the high dose, there is a feeling it will not last. I am concerned about mortality being on such a high amount of the drug, given the long-term implications on my health. Negative symptoms that are also troublesome are weight gain and headaches. I had gained one stone and went from 14 stone with my clothes on to 15 stones. I lack motivation, though it's not because I lack goals or do not enjoy pleasure and rewards. Motivation gets stifled because decision-making and good choices are in limbo, and the medication gives no relief from this. The Kettering Mental Health team is to look after my care, and I am assigned to a psychiatrist, but it is all to change, and I will have to contact my GP when I have psychiatric problems. Without monitoring, I'll leave on the high dose without reviews.

On Tuesday, 2nd June 2015, I reduced 30mg of Aripiprazole by a quarter and took approximate 20mg using a pill cutter to slice the pill and take the three-quarter piece in a daily dose. I researched the internet site's findings and will declare my action to my psychiatrist when I see him in five months before the changes to the service are implemented.

Activities bring me a momentary sense of joy and relaxation, but it leads directly to stress when trying self-motivation tactics. I have spent seventy-five per cent of my time trying to find a lasting solution to fund the mortgage repayments and twenty-five per cent of my time focusing on the problem. I received a little financial support from Joan and Merle when they visited me. The most recent financial gift was £40.00. In addition, my in-laws give food from time to time, and when we see them, Sunday lunch is served to us.

We have fallen behind with the mortgage by £700.00 for the 1st of June 2015 payment. An arrangement was made with the mortgage provider to pay £286.18 for three months, June to August 2015. They request that I fill out their income and expenditure form and provide them with all the details required to assess our present financial position. I am relying on qualifying for the PIP award to move forward, and it is a testing time.

Today, 06/06/15, I received a letter from PIP about my claim. I was too nervous about opening it, so I asked Euphemia. It says they are sorry it has taken longer than expected to give me a decision, but they will contact me as soon as they have made the decision. I am worried, which is highly uncomfortable, and stopping would be a welcome relief, and until I know PIP's resolution, I am on edge. It's hard to get grounded in the present because the worries are happening in the present. The concern over mortgage debt is my present worry, and the solution to it is mainly PIP's decision being in our favour. I visualize success and feel it and listen to classical music. Music grounds me when my mind gets cluttered with disturbing thoughts, and it calms me. I imagine a positive outcome, and it melts my worry; this visualization holds off anxiety.

The scale remains tipped

Written Friday 16th October 2015

This summer, 2015, has seen apathy and hostility towards refugees in Europe, despite many drowning in the Mediterranean Sea while trying to reach the continent. Europe experienced an unprecedented influx of economic migrants and refugees, touching the Western nation's rawest nerves. In September, it took the image of a dead child to end apathy towards mass refugee deaths on European shores. The shocking photos of a three-year-old Syrian boy refugee drowned and washed up on the Turkish beach will go down in history as the moment Europe's 'immigrant crisis' getting recognised as a human migration tragedy.

I had yearned to fast forward time to know the decision of my PIP claim because my eggs were all in one basket. Our financial well-being depended on it, and I did not have to wait long for the decision. Finally, on the 9th June 2015, the decision was made, and I curled up almost in a ball in the adjustable computer chair with my muscles tense and shallowly breathing when I read it. PIP is made up of two components, the Daily Living component and the Mobility component. Each part comprises two rates, Standard, the lowest price and Enhanced, being the highest rate. I was awarded only the standard rate Mobility of £21.55 a week until 14th May 2019, and the descriptors scored zeros for Daily Living with schizophrenia. It was unacceptable that we will further fall behind with mortgage repayments, and daily living will continue as a struggle.

This storyline continues to slip into painful thoughts and rev up my feelings because they have been in the face of adversity for a long time. They present a set of circumstances that demand skills, and I cannot understand the continuous setback. To understand it would minimize its power to overwhelm me, I have not learnt how to respond to this problem with life facing me. For years, it's been a constant repetition of the same problems, difficulties with living costs and paying the housing cost. I saw time fast-forwarded; it's like a magic button was pressed; please have it be another day, another week and another month already. It came too quickly when another month arrived because expected economic changes had not happened through the months, and life moved on swiftly. I had months with miraculous days in them, experiencing joy, excitement, calm and connection with my loved ones. My wife and I met Georgina's new boyfriend, Adam, on Saturday 25th July, and they have been dating for five months. My sister-in-law gave birth to a baby boy in August, and our niece gave birth to her second boy child in September. I challenged myself not to worry, and I learnt something interesting and surprising about myself. I can stop worrying in a desperate time and instead re-assess our needs, dreams, brainstorm, look at the bigger picture and even make a few big changes by shifting my mindset. Today is Friday, 16/10/15, and basic home economics have not changed due to further setbacks. Things happened that have seemed inevitable without a shift in luck. I can identify stories in this month that continued to emerge as the most persistent. No matter how hard I try, it is always challenging to stay in the moment and refocus on looking for hidden opportunities rather than ruminating about it or fretting about the future because both trigger painful feelings. I have a vibrant inner life; my thoughts, environment, and memories create strong inner responses to life events. Am I normal? I am troubled by inner voices (not schizophrenia-related, which will make the voices outside of one's head) and small obsessions. I think I am different; I have weak powers of concentration and sometimes poor self-control, but I have only the vaguest hope of knowing without direct access to other people's thoughts. We all only pick up a small fraction of signals going on globally, those for which we have developed specialised sensors. There are many other signals out there like x-ray and gamma-ray, among others. We are completely blind to them. No matter how hard we try, we'll never see that part of the spectrum naturally. I have returned to my local church, St Michael's, on Thursday mornings from 10th September and the URC from Sunday 4th October 2015. I had not sat in the pew for over nine months. It's not the objective truth because my personal feelings and opinions influence my interpretation, but the dates and figures are accurate. I found it difficult thinking optimistically to shift the way I feel and respond to having mortgage arrears of £1839.28 and a regular mortgage payment of £934.92 down from £986.18 from 1st September 2015. My wife's working hours have increased from 21 hours to 28 hours, affecting my ESA claim because the permitted hours were up to 24 hours. ESA was re-catalogued from income-based to contribution-based, which exempts us from free health care. We are a month behind with our council tax, with arrears of £117.00. I have underpaid tax during the period 5th April 2015 by £318.80, and the total tax credit overpaid is £1078.89. Our daily living costs are met with help from a family giving us foodstuff and small change. Once a week, we have cereal for our main evening meal, and sandwiches also replace a hot evening meal on a weekday. Georgina gave us money to buy fuel for the car, and we are thinking seriously of visiting the soup kitchen set up by churches to feed the poor. Next week, Thursday 22 October, all foodstuff will have been used up; there is no money in our bank accounts. The soup kitchen is run only on Thursdays. The wife says she would go, but can I lose my pride and go or wait for the next day for the ESA payment. A food shortage marks this autumn, and the lone tragedy may energize sympathy and compassion. I Presenting an unsettling picture of the current situation to you, the reader, and it may suddenly change your mood, but people like you could have predicted it. The catalyst was money shortage, and you were sensitive to the large–scale problem, and I imagined you are willing to donate to my cause but have worries about the financial and emotional cost of trying to help me. The capacity to feel sympathy for my needs was limited, leading to compassion fatigue, apathy and inaction. Is there a collapse of compassion? My suffering seemed to represent itself as a choice, although the situation is a constraint beyond my control. I appeal to you, the reader, to respond with a financial donation later and not suppress your moral emotions. The scale remained tipped as my life's good and bad qualities are unbalanced and can be seen as life's paradox.

Balancing the Scale
Written on Wednesday 3rd February 2016

All my endeavours are now in positive motion.

An unexpected payment of £20.40 from Standard Life's yearly dividend entered the bank account on Tuesday 20th October 2015, and we could buy some food. We have continued to have breakfast cereals or porridge for our tea time meals once a week, and our health cost is met by the NHS scheme for people on low pay until October 2016. The mortgage is paid in two instalments a month. All our credit cards and loan repayments have been suspended, except Euphemia's sole credit to her creditor, who accepted a payment of £2.00 per month toward clearing that debt. The council reduced the council tax to £5.00 per week, reviewed again in three months.

My mind is continually impressed by how we manage to get through day by day, month after month, on virtually fresh air. Every last penny gets used just to get by. The most significant burden is our mortgage; the mortgage company has threatened court action. If we do not pay sufficient mortgage repayments, our house may get repossessed as the arrears continue to mount up. We are faced with unique challenges to balance the scale, and 'self-talk' inevitably has a toxic impact on emotional and psychological health if I focus negatively on the obstacles.

I am relatively optimistic, and I hope that 2016 brings out my best so that I can stay comfortable in my skin, no matter my challenges! The chatter in my head that directly reflects my conscious perceptions and reaction to events impacted my mood, outlook, and emotions. It potentially had negatively influenced my understanding of events and my interaction in October 2015. I was dragged down by evaluating my set of circumstances in black and white, and there were no grey areas in my perceptions. Rather than judging events on their own merits, I saw them as proof of a broader pattern that the worst does happen, but does it spell doom? There are cognitive distortions to my 'self-talk' because my mind automatically defaults to the negative, but in time, I'll carve new channels along which my thoughts can run. Instead of seeing gloom and hopelessness, I am channelling out a better and realistic assessment of my situation.

I hope to no longer be using energy to dwell on all that's wrong in our lives, and I'll be using it to make things right. As I move forward, listening to 'self-talk', I am more aware of this internal dialogue and persistently challenge any faulty or unhelpful thoughts that arise. All my needs will be met as answers are revealed and tremendous results are achieved.

I am attempting to closure this chapter because this memoir is to be taken to a publisher. This autobiographical book is mostly prose, outlining personal reflections on my life, exploring many emotions, and coping strategies. I was to learn and what you, the reader, would have also read is how it felt to pass through ordinary life stages through a lens of living with schizophrenia.

One of the key themes in my writing is a religious devotion to fueling my mental illness. I do not know if the written word of the Bible enters my brain, and I interpret sacred text and doctrines differently from people without schizophrenia. Can you tell me? It might be the springboard to help me distinguish between hearing an actual voice versus feeling God's spirit within. One's been concreted, and the other one's abstract. I was 'hyper' religious because I was confused, lost in life and needed some type of hope. I turned to God for answers and understanding because my schizophrenic episodes fuelled an obsession with a higher power.

I had the experience of hearing a voice that was an audio hallucination and spiritually having God connect with me. There are plenty of people who have a strong belief and connection with God. I was so hyper-religious that I was willing to die for my faith in God. I would have the willingness to die for God's sake because I have the right kind of motive. 'Greater love has no man than this than to lay down his life for his friend.' (John 15:13) Perfect love fills me with thoughts of harmonious joy overflowing goodness, fulfilment and satisfaction in every area. I commune with my indwelling spirit where I am immersed in peace and love, and I am grateful that I can hear the still small voice of truth showing me clearly with its wisdom. My mind is continually impressed with images of right action. The thought or feeling in opposition to the proper steps divinely guiding my life was released in an inpatient psychological hospital setting because these are symptoms of acute schizophrenia.

The all-knowing intelligence that is within me directs all of my actions into constructive channels of self-expression. Everything in my life is controlled by love, harmony, compassion, empathy and wisdom; I don't take anything for granted.

Some people say my illness nearly kill me in attempted suicide. I may have had akathisia symptoms over and above the environmental, emotional, and social pressures. I continue to tell people that I think the near tragedy was my own rational choice. I feel lucky to be alive. I feel like every day is a gift that I almost did not get to experience. This knowledge makes being grateful for things practically second nature.

Life has its ups and downs, disappointments and tragedies, and I'm better at dealing with schizophrenia and the tough stuff that comes up in life. For those of us with mental illness and those without, life can knock us out and knock us down, but we must not be defeated and keep getting up and putting up a good fight again and again.

My life's stories will continue to open up in an autobiographical literary fashion, but I say goodbye now.

May the blessing of God rest on this imperfect effort in this book and go with us all.

Follow me online to find out more:
http://www.karllorenzwillett.co.uk

Frequently Asked Questions

What is Schizophrenia?

Schizophrenia is a severe, chronic, and debilitating neuropsychiatric disorder that involves a profound psychopathology disruption of cognition. Defects in thought processes, emotional responsiveness, perception, and altered sense of self and alterations in reasons affect the patient. It is an illness that compromises the effective functioning of the individual in social, occupational and daily life.

What is psychosis?

Psychosis is where you see or hear things that are not there (hallucinations) or believe things that are not true (delusions).

The main symptoms of psychosis are hallucinations, delusions and disorganized thinking, speech and behaviour effects. They may come on gradually and build up over time, or they may come on rapidly. People experiencing psychosis may not be aware that the experiences they are having are not ordinary. To them, what is happening in their minds is very real.

Psychosis can be dangerous, frightening, isolating, and disabling because the patient believes that people are reading their minds or plotting against them, or others are secretly monitoring and threatening them or controlling others people's thoughts.

Can antipsychotic agents help symptoms of psychosis?

Antipsychotic medications can reduce or relieve symptoms of psychosis and help to calm and clear confusion in a person with acute psychosis. However, these medications do not cure the underlying condition. *Combining antipsychotic medication with other therapy and support can help people manage symptoms and improve quality of life.*

What do Antipsychotic Medications do?

Psychosis is believed to be caused, at least in part, by the overactivity of a brain chemical called dopamine, and antipsychotics are thought to work by blocking this dopamine effect. This blocking helps by correcting imbalances in brain chemicals that help brain cells communicate with one another to make the symptoms of psychosis—such as voices and delusions—less commanding and preoccupying. Still, it does not always make them go away completely. For example, people may still hear voices and have delusions/ fantasies, but they can recognize what isn't real and focus on other things, such as work, school or family.

Side effects of Antipsychotic Medications

Antipsychotic medication can cause unpleasant side effects, especially when severe symptoms and a higher dose of medicine is used. However, side effects should become mild or at least tolerable when the amount is reduced and as your body adjusts to the presence of the drug.

Most side effects will go away when you stop taking the drug. However, there is a risk of a condition that causes people to make involuntary movements, known as tardive dyskinesia, which can be permanent.

Some people accept the side effects as a trade-off for the relief these drugs can bring. Others find the side effects distressing and may choose not to take the medication. If you are troubled by any adverse effects, it is best to continue to take your medication as prescribed and let your doctor know as soon as possible.

What famous person has schizophrenia?
Celebrities with Schizophrenia

- Edward Einstein. The youngest child of Albert Einstein.
- Lionel Aldridge.
- Zelda Fitzgerald.
- Peter Green.
- Darrell Hammond.
- John Nash.
- Skip Spence.
- Jim Gorden
- Syd Barrett
- Vincent Van Gogh

How to use the yellow card scheme

If you think you have a side-effect or suspected adverse drug reaction to any therapeutic agent. You can report this on the Yellow Card Scheme. You can do this online at www.mhra.gov.uk/yellowcard

The Yellow Card scheme can also report medical device incidents, reactions to vaccines, herbal and fake medicines.

Lightning Source UK Ltd.
Milton Keynes UK
UKHW010007261021
392837UK00010B/568/J

9 781802 272031